EDMUND RANDOLPH

EDMUND RANDOLPH
A BIOGRAPHY

John J. Reardon

MACMILLAN PUBLISHING CO., INC.
NEW YORK
COLLIER MACMILLAN PUBLISHERS
LONDON

Library of Congress Cataloging in Publication Data
Reardon, John J
  Edmund Randolph; a biography.
  Bibliography: p.
  1. Randolph, Edmund, 1753–1813.
KF363.R35R42   973.4'1'0924   74-18458
ISBN 0-02-601200-6

Macmillan Publishing Co., Inc.
866 Third Avenue, New York, N.Y. 10022
Collier-Macmillan Canada Ltd.

First Printing 1975

Printed in the United States of America

To Joan

Acknowledgments

Undertaking to write the life of an individual whose private correspondence can only be found in the collections of his contemporaries is to incur a tremendous debt, not only to the libraries involved, but more particularly to the individuals who gave or deposited their ancestor's papers in these libraries. Fortunately, Virginians have a historical conscience which makes them keenly aware of the importance of placing the papers of their distinguished forebears in public depositories for the use of scholars. As a non-Virginian I must commend them for their foresight, and as the biographer of one of their statesmen I must thank them for making so much valuable material so readily available to scholars.

Then there are the obligations one incurs toward the professional men and women who maintain these collections and place them at the disposal of the scholar. I could fill several pages with the names of librarians, archivists and the directors of manuscript divisions who have assisted me in this long search for material on Edmund Randolph. But having done so I would have slighted, in a sense, another group of individuals—the associates and assistants of these directors and the countless staff members who assisted me on a day-by-day basis. The person who worked overtime so I could finish examining a particular collection before leaving the city. The person who could decipher any handwriting—even James Monroe's. The person who spent hours in hot and musty stacks looking for a misplaced folder of manuscripts while I worked comfortably in the "main reading room" on other material. These are the people I cannot forget, for it is this group that contributed significantly to this biography.

Finally, every author has to have a base, the place he returns to—to put it all together. Here his needs are different. He needs the ready association with people who are confronted with the same problems as he is; he needs a good library with all the printed source material that he will inevitably have to consult as he is organizing and writing his book; and, of course, he needs an academic association that is both

[vii]

pleasant and understanding. In my case that base was the city of Chicago.

At the University of Chicago were the editorial offices of the James Madison project, the individuals who were collecting and editing *The Papers of James Madison*. I virtually lived with them for several years. They were my associates, along with their co-workers in Virginia, during the formative years of this study.

As I traveled around the country paging through one manuscript collection after another, I virtually ignored the published holdings of the libraries I visited. I did so because I was confident that virtually everything I needed, even the most obscure study in local history, was available at Newberry Library in Chicago. It was in this hot, then cold, then remodeled, then climatized fortress of scholarship that this work was put together. It is to the director and staff of this library that I owe my greatest debt.

I also owe a debt of gratitude to Loyola University of Chicago. A score of close friends from both the administration and faculty have waited patiently for this book to appear. I thank them for their patience, support, and—most important of all—understanding and encouragement.

There is one final and very specific note of thanks that must be made. Tazewell Hall, the Randolph family home in Williamsburg, was rebuilt and refurbished by Mr. and Mrs. Lewis A. McMurran, Jr., in Newport News, Virginia. With unbelievable generosity, Mr. and Mrs. McMurran allowed me to send a photographer into their home so that I might include pictures of the restored Tazewell Hall in this biography. They are to be commended not only for preserving a historic home of considerable architectural value, but also for their willingness to share it with others.

The one aspect of this study that cannot be assigned to others is the instances of error that inevitably find their way into a work of this size. For that I can only offer a personal apology.

We watch while these in equilibrium keep
The giddy line midway

ROBERT BROWNING
"BISHOP BLOUGRAM'S APOLOGY"

CONTENTS

[xi]

CONTENTS

III

THE CABINET YEARS

IV

LAST YEARS

ILLUSTRATIONS

(FOLLOWING PAGE 272)

Edmund Randolph
William Randolph
Mary Isham Randolph
Sir John Randolph
Lady Susanna Beverly Randolph
Peyton Randolph
Elizabeth Harrison Randolph

There are no known portraits of Edmund Randolph's parents, who left the country in 1775 to reside permanently in England.

VIRGINIA'S REVOLUTIONARY LEADERS

Meriwether Smith
Richard Henry Lee
Thomas Nelson, Jr.
George Mason
Edmund Pendleton
Patrick Henry
Benjamin Harrison, Jr.
Henry Lee
James Monroe
James Madison
Charles Lee

RANDOLPH'S CONTEMPORARIES IN THE LEGAL PROFESSION

John Marshall
St. George Tucker
John Wickham

Preface

The present biography, undertaken at the suggestion of the late Douglas Southall Freeman, carries with it several presuppositions. The first is that key secondary figures are as worthy of biographical study as the primary men and women who shaped the course of history. Secondly, it is the author's contention that the formative years of American history have been ill-served by the preoccupation of biographers with the more obvious figures of the period to the neglect of those who worked with them. And lastly, it is at least a working hypothesis that the lives of secondary figures are frequently more accurate barometers of the triumphs and frustrations of an era than are the lives of their more prominent colleagues.

Quite apart from my own talents as a biographer, the life of Edmund Randolph provides a unique focus for the study of the formative years of our nation's history. A public person who was almost always at center-stage, he remains sufficiently detached from the momentous events of the period to keep them in proper perspective. Reading the scattered remnants of his considerable public correspondence, one is struck by the ease with which he isolates the partisan motives of his colleagues and casually separates issues from their political trappings. He is, above all else, the experienced public statesman who unwittingly serves as the dispassionate commentator on his own age. His life can be the historian's most reliable barometer of the political climate of America in the last quarter of the eighteenth century.

As a private person, Randolph is a more obscure subject. His personal correspondence was lost sometime during the nineteenth century, and as a result we know very little about his personal and family life. Rather than substitute fiction for fact, it seemed more appropriate to develop what is known about his private life within the context of his public career, for he was above all else a public person.

Like most secondary figures in history, Randolph fits into the age in which he lived. He did not shape his era; he responded to it. It seemed

[xv]

more essential to develop the role he played in this nation's history than to artfully recast the era to fit the man.

There is a personal note that should be made before the reader ventures further into this text. I have been both humbled and inspired by the distinguished historians and biographers who have worked in this period of American history before me. I have, however, felt obliged to find my own Randolph in the contemporary record of the times. These investigations have sometimes led me to a different interpretation of the man or the times. I have chosen not to dwell on these differences because I feel that disputatious scholarship is dubious scholarship.

Lastly, a note on the person to whom this book is dedicated. Authors frequently acknowledge the research assistance, moral support, stylistic wisdom, etc. of their wives. Let the record show I had all this and more.

SEAWARD
COTUIT, MASSACHUSETTS
JUNE 16, 1974

PART I
FORMATIVE YEARS

Edmund Randolph was born at a time when Virginia was at the zenith of its colonial development: proud, urbane, self-confident and eminently successful as a colony. Presiding over this prize English possession was an obviously self-reliant colonial aristocracy of "gentlemen freeholders" whose life-style determined the very character of the colony. The Randolphs of Williamsburg were a part of that aristocracy and Edmund Randolph, like so many young boys similarly circumstanced, was raised in accordance with its precepts.

As a Randolph he also inherited very particular family traditions: a commitment to the law as a profession and a distinguished record of public service in Virginia's colonial government. He would dutifully serve these traditions, but outside forces, in the form of growing colonial resistance to the policies of the mother country, would give a very different orientation to the manner in which he would satisfy them. In time, he found that both traditions made him a part of the momentous events that unfolded during his lifetime.

1

Youth, 1750–1769

It was the spring of 1750 and the eager young man was preparing to return home to Virginia to embark upon a legal career. The young colonial was John Randolph, the youngest son of the late Sir John Randolph, the former attorney general of the colony, and the grandson of the now almost legendary William Randolph of "Turkey Island," the patriarch of the Randolph family in Virginia.[1] John Randolph was only twenty-one when he left England, yet he had spent several years reading law at the Inns of Court as a student of Middle Temple. Having been called to the bar the previous February, he was now returning to Virginia to establish himself in a profession that had come to be identified with his family.[2]

John Randolph easily readjusted to life in Virginia. His family name assured him a prominent place in Williamsburg's rather active social life and his older brother Peyton, successor to his father as attorney general of the colony, lost no time in introducing him to the leading lawyers in the community as well as the judges of Virginia's prestigious General Court, which met in Williamsburg.[3] In a short time he was arguing cases before this court, pitting his considerable abilities against some of the most talented lawyers in the colony. Clients were plentiful and a promising law practice was realized in a matter of months.

It seems he was equally successful at winning the attention of the young ladies of Williamsburg and not above using his reputed virtuosity as a violinist to expand his acquaintances among the more attractive female members of this colonial society. It was not surprising therefore when, a short time after his return to Virginia, he began to court the winsome Arianna Jennings, the only daughter of Edmund and Arianna Vanderheyden Jennings. Edmund Jennings was attorney general of Maryland and a distinguished member of that colony's legal profession.[4] One suspects that John Randolph met Jennings' daughter in the course of his ever-expanding law practice. Whatever the circumstances, it was not very long before a serious courtship developed. John Blair's *Diary*

[4]

records the happy ending of this courtship—as well as the real or imagined cause of the bridegroom's paroxysms: "hot day . . . Mr. J.R. got an ague [*sic*] since married. Speaker signed license." The entry was for July 1, 1751.[5]

Several months after his marriage John Randolph was elected to his first public office when he was chosen for a seat on the Common Council of the city of Williamsburg.[6] Although a comparatively minor office, it marked the beginning of his public career. Three months later, when Virginia's House of Burgesses assembled in Williamsburg for its spring session, he was named as its clerk.[7] It was an office that had been held by his father and grandfather before him and that assured him of a close association with the more prominent and powerful members of the Virginia legislature.

The monetary rewards of this office, though nominal, were put to good use as his family gradually began to increase in size. During the summer of 1752 his wife gave birth to their first child, a girl, who was named Arianna, after her mother. In the following year, on August 10, 1753, a son was born, who was named Edmund after his maternal grandfather.[8] John Randolph, who was just beginning to establish himself in Virginia society, now had the added obligation of preparing his son to follow in his footsteps. It was an obligation he did not take lightly.

If one word could adequately describe Edmund Randolph's childhood, undoubtedly it would be "carefree." Unlike most of the children of Virginia's more prominent families, he was not raised in the isolation of a family plantation but in Williamsburg, the seat of government for colonial Virginia. One suspects he found this small colonial village a rather exciting place in which to grow up. Young Edmund knew most of the young people in the village, whereas the sons and daughters of plantation owners had only the companionship of the children of slaves and indentured servants. He had the varied experience of neighbors who would scold him one day for running through their carefully tended gardens and then befriend him the next with some freshly baked pastry. Numbered among his acquaintances were most of the storekeepers along the Duke of Gloucester Street and the gregarious blacksmith on Prince George Street on the other side of town. He even knew something of the mysteries of the local taverns and ordinaries filled with travelers from other parts of the colony. In contrast to those Virginians who viewed Williamsburg as the colony's genteel capital, for Edmund Williamsburg was home.[9]

The busy convivial atmosphere of the community also influenced the daily routine of his family. Since his parents' home at the south end of England Street was only a few blocks from the center of town, it always seemed to be the scene of much activity.[10] During the day townspeople dropped by to discuss some legal or business matter with his father or to visit with his mother. Having guests for dinner in the evening was taken for granted. On special occasions the Randolphs gave elaborate parties attended by the governor, his lady and virtually all the prominent people in Williamsburg. Edmund probably found all this very exciting, and if he was not plying his mother and father with endless questions, he was interrogating the household servants. At his worst he was a persistent boy who insisted on testing the patience of everyone who tried to curb his inquisitive spirit.

Edmund had certain misgivings about the other members of the Randolph household—his two sisters Arianna and Susan. Arianna was the most troublesome, particularly when she took advantage of her position as the eldest of the three children. Susan—Edmund called her "Sukey" —on the other hand, seldom interfered with his daily life and apparently was his ally in the youthful skirmishes that inevitably erupted among three children. Edmund, it seems, would have preferred two brothers, but it was not long before he learned how to devise means of overcoming the strong feminine influence within his family.[11]

When his sisters became absolutely impossible he took refuge in the home of his aunt and uncle on Nicholson Street, just a few blocks away.[12] Since Peyton and Elizabeth Randolph had no children of their own, they delighted in the frequent visits of their nephew. Peyton Randolph was interested in his nephew's future and shared John Randolph's concern for the boy's education and training. Edmund, in turn, idolized his uncle, whose dignified bearing and seemingly inexhaustible wisdom stood in sharp contrast to the plain habits and uneducated manners of the townspeople with whom he chatted daily. If his uncle was his idol, then his Aunt Elizabeth was his understanding mentor, curbing his boyish exuberances and patiently listening to his youthful tales of triumph and sorrow. It was, one suspects, a rather idyllic background: a young boy growing up with his sisters in a pleasant colonial village, secure in the love of his parents and the indulgent affection of his aunt and uncle.

In contrast to the carefree character of his childhood, his education must be viewed as a reminder of the status of the Randolph family in Virginia and as a direct preparation for Edmund's role in the colony's future. Probably he was allowed to attend the local elementary school with the other children of the village, but at the age of ten his parents no doubt enrolled him in the grammar school that Virginia's own College of William and Mary maintained for the children of the leading families in the colony and for the more promising students in the community. It was here, under the watchful eye of the master of the school, the Reverend Josiah Johnson, that Edmund began his formal education in the classics. Classes began at seven in the morning and continued until six in the evening, with only a short break at midday. While Edmund probably found these long hours of study very trying, he accepted them as an inevitable part of growing up.[13]

Other skills to be mastered during these years were stressed by his parents and taught by the appropriate instructors. There were dancing lessons and, in all likelihood, even some modest efforts to introduce him to a musical instrument, since his father had considerable talent as a violinist. Much more interesting to Edmund, however, were the games of trap ball or pall-mall organized among the boys in the grammar school, or the wild foot races down the center of the Duke of Gloucester Street at the end of the school day when the pent-up energies of the young people exploded on the village. All in all, these were happy times spent in the company of his boyhood companions and presided over by demanding but generally very understanding parents.[14]

As Edmund grew older he came to understand more about his family and the colonial village in which they lived. He discovered that twice each year Williamsburg was filled with rather important individuals from all parts of the colony who gathered for the meeting of the House of Burgesses, the lower branch of the colonial legislature. During such meetings the inns and rooming houses in town were filled to capacity as all manner of colonials journeyed to Williamsburg to seek favor from the legislature or to conduct some important business. It was not long before Edmund, like his father, was referring to those gatherings as "publick times." For him, they were fun-filled weeks when many young friends came to Williamsburg with their parents. There were parties to attend, and generally an elegant reception for the legislators and the more influential residents of Williamsburg at the residence of the governor of the colony on the other side of town. This was when the theatre offered the finest plays in its repertoire and when the racetrack at the edge of town was busiest. Edmund Randolph was absolutely certain that Williamsburg was the most interesting place to live in all Virginia.[15]

Much of what transpired in Williamsburg during these weeks was beyond his grasp, but he could not help but note that his father and uncle and their associates were much more interested in the legislation being considered by the Assembly than most of the townspeople. There was, it seemed, a certain group of Virginians who assumed a kind of personal responsibility for the general well-being of the colony and its people. The more important members of this group sat in the House of Burgesses, for it was this branch of the legislature that attracted the greatest attention. For Edmund, Williamsburg was rapidly becoming more than a friendly little colonial village; it was the capital of Virginia, the seat of government for England's largest colony in the New World. And the men who came to town twice each year were not just planters—they were, with some exceptions, the more powerful members of the Virginia gentry, the "gentlemen freeholders," as they were called, who ruled the colony with the quiet authority of an established aristocracy. And young Edmund, without even beginning to know why, came to understand that his father and uncle belonged to this group and that they, like their father and grandfather before them, had a kind of family obligation to take an active part in the affairs of the colony.[16]

Edmund Randolph's carefree and almost paradoxically protected youth coincided with the years of growing tension between England and her American colonies as the various colonial assemblies, jealous of their rights in matters of taxation, resisted the efforts of the mother country to secure additional revenue in the colonies. He saw at first hand, but only gradually realized, the public implications of his father's and uncle's private convictions.

The first crisis arose in 1764 when Chancellor of the Exchequer George Grenville presented a comprehensive program for raising additional revenues in America to help defray the cost of England's military establishment in the New World. One of Grenville's proposals, a stamp tax on various types of printed material, aroused intense hostility in several American colonies, including Virginia. The Virginia House of Burgesses filed formal petitions of protest with the Crown and the two houses of Parliament, and instructed its agent in England to work against the passage of the act. The several protests of the colonies failed to deter Grenville or dissuade Parliament and the Stamp Act became law on March 22, 1765.[17]

Like most members of the Virginia gentry, the Randolphs questioned Parliament's right to enact such a law. In November, 1764, Peyton Randolph, as a burgess from Williamsburg, served as chairman of the committee that drafted the original petition of protest against the proposed Stamp Act.[18] A year later, after the act had been passed by Parliament, he took an active part in the heated debate that surrounded Patrick Henry's famous Virginia Resolutions.[19] In both instances he was one of the most outspoken advocates of a moderate position, anxious to preserve colonial rights without creating a serious and irreconcilable division between the colony and the mother country. In all likelihood John Randolph, the now rather influential clerk of the House of Burgesses, shared these sentiments.

Since the House of Burgesses had adjourned before Massachusetts invited the colonies to send delegates to a Stamp Act Congress in New York City on October 7, 1765, Virginia could be little more than a sympathetic spectator to the proceedings of this group. The colony remained fixed in its opposition to the act, however, and, like most of the other American colonies, refused to sanction the use of the stamps.

Nonimportation agreements among colonial merchants brought prompt results when English merchants, fearing financial ruin from the decline of colonial trade, pressured their government to repeal the act. Parliament's reluctant compliance with their demands resulted in an immediate return to orderly government in all the colonies.[20] In Virginia the successful resolution of the issue served to reaffirm the policies of those colonial leaders who insisted that the colony be firm but responsible in its dealings with the mother country.[21]

Shortly after the news of the repeal of the Stamp Act reached Virginia the colony lost one of its most powerful political figures. On May 11, 1766, John Robinson, the speaker of the House of Burgesses and treasurer of the colony, died unexpectedly. Since succeeding the late Sir John Randolph as speaker in 1738, Robinson had held virtually absolute control over the public careers of all who served in the Burgesses, arranging key committee assignments for some, granting special favors to others and ignoring those who failed to meet his exacting loyalty test. Robinson's death and the subsequent discovery that as treasurer he had loaned some of the colony's redeemed—and supposedly destroyed— paper currency to his friends caused the Virginia aristocracy to reassess its hierarchical structure. To avoid any future criticism it was deemed appropriate to split the two powerful offices that had been held by Robinson between two men. Peyton Randolph was named speaker of the House of Burgesses and Robert Carter Nicholas was named treasurer of the colony. Robinson's closest friend and most promising political lieutenant, Edmund Pendleton, was given the almost impossible task of settling the Robinson estate and satisfying its principal creditor—the Virginia treasury. Following his election to the office of speaker, Peyton Randolph was obliged to resign as attorney general of the colony. To the surprise of no one, Lieutenant Governor Francis Fauquier named John Randolph to the office. Quietly and unobtrusively the mantle of political power began to be transferred to a new generation of gentlemen freeholders—talented, resourceful and, most important of all, exemplary members of Virginia's very self-conscious gentry.[22]

In the meantime the English ministry was still struggling with the problem of raising sufficient revenue to meet the cost of its colonial establishment in America. In 1767 Parliament was obliged to reduce the British land tax to satisfy the demands of Englishmen for some form of tax relief. This meant a loss of £500,000 in home revenues and made new colonial taxes inevitable. The resulting legislation, drafted by the current Chancellor of the Exchequer, Charles Townshend, not only provided for the more efficient collection of existing duties but also imposed new duties on glass, lead, paint, paper and tea, the additional revenues to be used to maintain English troops in the colonies as well as to help defray the cost of supporting civil government in America. The so-called Townshend Acts met with strong opposition in the colonies. Town meetings passed new nonimportation agreements in an effort to force Parliament to repeal the legislation and the Massachusetts House of Representatives denounced the acts and drafted a circular letter in an effort to gain the support of other colonial assemblies. The ministry's unqualified condemnation of these actions only served to promote new and more stringent nonimportation agreements.[23]

The initial response of the Virginia Assembly to the Townshend Acts was more temperate than that of the Massachusetts legislature. The Burgesses, in consultation with the Council, or upper house of the legislature, petitioned the King and the two houses of Parliament to repeal the new duties. In a separate resolution they endorsed the actions of the Massachusetts legislature and invited other colonies to join with them in a "firm but decent opposition to every measure which may affect the rights and liberties of the British colonies in America."[24]

As the various colonial petitions against the acts reached their respective audiences of King, Lords and Commons, the nonimportation agreements slowly began to take their toll on English trade. But this time Parliament was adamant; the legislation would stand and appropriate action would be taken against those who defied the laws.[25]

When the Virginia legislature convened in May of 1769 the Burgesses were visibly annoyed by the failure of Parliament to repeal the Townshend duties and openly critical of the British ministry for having condemned the Massachusetts legislature for its circular letter. A conciliatory address by Virginia's newly appointed governor, Baron de Botetourt, failed to improve the disposition of the gentlemen freeholders, and on May 16 the House of Burgesses, after having again elected Peyton Randolph as speaker, unanimously approved a set of resolutions that reiterated the rights of the colonial legislature in matters of taxation and condemned a recent proposal of Parliament that Americans who resisted the enforcement of the Townshend Acts be brought to England for trial. Governor Botetourt's response to this display of "independency" was to summon both houses of the legislature to the Council Chamber and dissolve the Assembly.[26]

Undaunted, the burgesses promptly reassembled as private citizens at Williamsburg's Raleigh Tavern, elected their speaker, Peyton Randolph, as "moderator" of their meetings and resumed their discussions on an appropriate response to the obvious hostility of England toward the legitimate protests of the colonists against these laws. On May 18 they established the Virginia Association, a formal agreement not to purchase English goods, as well as a long list of European luxury items, until the Townshend duties were repealed. One by one the former burgesses affixed their signatures to this extraordinary document. The first to sign was their "moderator," Peyton Randolph; the second was Treasurer Robert Carter Nicholas; the seventh the rather austere George Washington; the forty-fifth the very colorful Patrick Henry; the fiftieth the young and handsome Thomas Jefferson—it was a veritable roster of Virginia's gentlemen freeholders.[27] Of those who failed to sign none was more obvious by his absence than the colony's attorney general. John Randolph, who was serving in the Burgesses for the first time as an elected representative of Lunenburg County, was not prepared to endorse the actions of this rump session of the Burgesses, however serious the occasion or valid the complaint.[28]

The very different responses of the two Randolphs toward the formal dissolution of the Assembly and subsequent meeting in Raleigh Tavern suggests the dilemma that would soon confront the colonists as evidence mounted that England was fully determined to assert its authority in America. For John Randolph, the answer was a reluctant acquiescence to these ill-conceived efforts of the mother country to tax the colonies; for Peyton Randolph, the answer was a firm but temperate insistence on colonial rights backed by economic sanctions, proclaimed, if necessary, by an extralegal association of former burgesses. The influence and prestige of both Randolphs was sufficient to make the position of each highly significant.

Fifteen-year-old Edmund must have experienced some of the drama that surrounded the dissolution of the Assembly and this meeting in Raleigh Tavern. He certainly knew that his father was deeply troubled by the meeting and did not sign the Association. He also knew that his uncle had been elected "moderator" of the group and that his views carried great weight in its deliberations. What he could not understand was why his father felt obliged to accept the authority of Parliament while his uncle seemed prepared to question it. By the time he was old enough to comprehend why the two men thought as they did, he was old enough to realize the disastrous implications of their respective positions.

2

Commitment, 1770–1775

As the decade of the seventies opened, Edmund Randolph was six-teen, intelligent, probably rather studious and naturally curious about the political world that surrounded him. Given his family's preoc-cupation with public affairs, it would have been difficult for him to be otherwise. As a Randolph, his future was virtually predetermined. He would attend college and then prepare for a legal career and some type of public service in the Virginia colonial government. This was what his father and grandfather before him had done, and it was simply assumed that Edmund Randolph would follow in their footsteps.

If there were any doubts, they arose because of the uncertain times in which he lived. The apparent hostility of Parliament toward the various colonial demands for the repeal of the Townshend Acts had eroded the ties that bound the colonies to the mother country, and the recent reports of an open clash between British regulars and the residents of Boston suggested these ties could be severed rather easily. There would have to be an abundant display of good will on both sides if relations be-tween England and her colonies were to be improved, and, at least as far as Virginia was concerned, England was going to have to make the first move. No one dared predict how the crisis would be resolved, least of all a boy of sixteen.

Such was the situation as Edmund prepared himself for the next phase of his education—gaining admission to William and Mary College's School of Philosophy. Qualified applicants of the grammar school had to sustain an oral examination before the president and faculty of the college prior to being admitted to the School of Philosophy or, in the case of those planning to enter the ministry, the School of Divinity.[1] On June 23, 1770, the president and masters of William and Mary College resolved that "Messrs. Edmund Randolph, William Leigh, Thomas Hughes and Dolphin Drew be removed to the Philosophy Schools [sic]."[2]

Admission to the School of Philosophy did not bring with it any drastic changes in Edmund's daily routine. He apparently continued to live at home, preferring the rather flexible supervision of his parents to the more rigid regulations of the college.[3] As contrasted with the grammar school, the subjects taught in the School of Philosophy were probably more interesting to him simply because of their greater variety and practicality, and the limited but impressive collection of books in the college's library broadened his intellectual horizons.[4] As might be expected, he performed well. Six months after entering the School of Philosophy he was elected to one of the "two first studentships" in the college. The resolution of the president and masters of the college, dated July 9, 1770, passed unanimously.[5] The appointment was for one year and carried a stipend of £30, plus free board and tuition. Although far from impoverished, the Randolphs were not indifferent to the financial benefits associated with this award, and Edmund promptly used a portion of his stipend to purchase the academic cap and gown required of all first-year students in the college.[6]

Stimulated by the varied academic offerings of the School of Philosophy, he continued to excel in his courses and was awarded the studentship again in 1771.[7] That same year he was asked to deliver one of the orations at the college's Founder's Day ceremonies. Each year the college set aside one day to honor King William and Queen Mary, the reigning monarchs when the college was founded. Randolph's oration was a florid testimonial to the benefits of knowledge and truth and a glowing tribute to the wisdom and foresight of William and Mary in providing for the establishment of the college. Toward the end of his oration he added a brief eulogy to Baron de Botetourt, the late governor of the colony who had died in Williamsburg the previous October. He closed with an exhortation to his fellow students:

> Arise, renounce the errors of your age, and approve [sic] yourselves worthy of royal patronage. If past hours have escaped unimproved, quit not the present opportunity, but, like holy Plutarch, clasp the parting angel to thy bosom, until he blesses thee. Let future statesmen, future lawyers, future divines here spring up, but such statesmen, such lawyers, such divines, as shall strive to do honour to their family, their country, and this, their *Alma Mater*.[8]

The oration, reported the *Virginia Gazette*, was delivered with "such spirit and propriety as to obtain the just applause of a numerous and attentive audience," and, the *Gazette* continued, when the "academical exhibitions" were finished, the remainder of the day was spent in "a decent festivity, suitable to the occasion."[9]

In late October or early November Randolph resigned his studentship. The action does not appear to have been a precipitous one because

William Leigh, another recipient of the studentship, also resigned at this time.[10] Then Randolph also abandoned his studies in the School of Philosophy. His failure to complete the remaining two or three months of study necessary to satisfy the two-year program of the college must have been disappointing to his parents.[11]

The interruption in his education was only temporary, however, and within a matter of a few months he was training for a career in the law. It was not uncommon for younger members of the Virginia gentry to study law without ever committing themselves to it as a profession. It was always considered useful, particularly to those who expected to enter public office. Most young Virginians obtained their legal training by serving as apprentices to a practicing lawyer—preferably a highly successful one. An apprentice would involve himself in the daily affairs of his legal mentor, gradually assuming many of the more routine duties of an attorney's practice, such as preparing simple writs or deeds or collecting unpaid debts for a client. After he had mastered the more obvious aspects of the profession, he began to accompany his mentor on his rounds of the various county courts, observing lawyers and judges in action and acquiring familiarity with the processes of adjudication. Between court sessions the aspiring apprentice sat and listened to the lawyers talk about their cases. Thus, he would learn from their experiences as well as from his own personal observation. It was an educational process that emphasized the practical aspects of the law. For the more industrious apprentice, there was a body of literature to be mastered— the standard treatises on English common law, the most recent compilation of Virginia's colonial statutes, plus whatever fragmentary records existed of the decisions of the colony's General Court.[12]

In Edmund Randolph's case the mentor was his own father, the attorney general of the colony and one of the most accomplished members of the Virginia bar. If variety and experience and an extensive practice made for a good mentor, Edmund Randolph had one of the best in Virginia. John Randolph apparently brought Edmund along gradually, measuring his enthusiasm for the law before deciding whether he would keep him on as an apprentice or send him to London to read law at one of the Inns of Court. He probably had serious reservations about the Inns since his own training there had proved to be of little actual value in his own practice. When it became evident that Edmund had no burning enthusiasm for the law, the idea of an Inn's training was abandoned.[13]

While it was not uncommon in Virginia for a young man to seek "certification" in the law after the briefest apprenticeship, it is highly unlikely that John Randolph permitted his son to do so. One suspects that Edmund was more knowledgeable in the law than many a practicing lawyer when he appeared before a "person or persons learned in the law" to seek formal certification. Then, if he followed the pattern of most young lawyers, he next sought "qualification" in several of the county courts in the colony. He undoubtedly qualified before Williamsburg's Hustings Court, the judicial arm of government within the city, as well as before the court for James City County, the county in which Williamsburg was situated. It was in these courts, and in the courts of adjacent counties, that he gained his first experience as a practicing lawyer. Most of the cases in these courts were fairly routine actions in debt or trespass, and one assumes that he handled them with ease, gaining confidence with each case.[14] It was not long before Edmund began to attract clients in his own right, particularly from the area around Williamsburg. He sought and was granted membership in the Williamsburg lodge of the Ancient Order of York Masons in March, 1774, further expanding his social, and presumably his professional, contacts. In October of that same year he was asked to revise the bylaws of the lodge and promptly accepted, flattered by the members' apparent confidence in his legal ability.[15]

Edmund Randolph entered the ranks of the elite of the profession when he qualified to practice before the Virginia General Court, the colony's highest court. His admission came some time before August, 1774, for it was at this time that Thomas Jefferson transferred his pending cases in that court to Randolph.[16] Jefferson had been elected as a delegate to the Virginia Convention that was due to meet in Williamsburg in August, 1774, and while in the colonial capital he intended to represent several clients at the fall session of the General Court. Illness prevented him from attending the convention and the General Court, and necessitated the transfer of his clients to Randolph.[17] Edmund had a very businesslike circular printed to inform those affected by the transfer of his determination to conscientiously fulfill the responsibilities entrusted to him. It was a rather unorthodox approach—unless, of course, the circular was intended for a wider audience. Interestingly enough the circular carried an additional suggestion:

> However, should you now think me worthy and capable of the charge, I flatter myself that you will have no cause at any future day to forfeit such an opinion of me, and hope that you will not repent in having me engaged for you on any other occasion.[18]

Randolph seemingly assumed that Jefferson was no longer interested in these clients and had permanently transferred them to him. Unfortunately one can only speculate as to Jefferson's reaction when he learned of the circular.

Edmund Randolph was a student at William and Mary's School of Philosophy when the North ministry came to power on February 10, 1770, setting the stage for a relaxation of the tension between the colonies and the mother country. North succeeded in getting Parliament to agree to a partial repeal of the Townshend duties, retaining only the duty on tea as a symbol of the government's authority to impose such taxes. This action, plus the failure of the ministry to press for a renewal of the despised Quartering Act of 1765, led to a general abandonment of the various nonimportation agreements that had been established in response to the Townshend Acts.[19]

The policies of the North ministry served to defuse the crisis created by the Townshend Acts and some colonial leaders even began to explore the possibility of a reconciliation between the colonies and the mother country. Unfortunately the relaxed atmosphere was rather short-lived; the burning of the schooner *Gaspee* off the coast of Rhode Island in June, 1772, set the stage for a new crisis. The subsequent decision of a Commission of Inquiry to send those accused of perpetrating the offense to England for trial rekindled all the old animosities. In the succeeding months several of the colonies, among them Virginia, established Committees of Correspondence to coordinate the colonial response to this latest evidence of the Crown's apparent distrust of its American subjects.[20]

Then, with supreme insensitivity to the mood of the colonies, the English government passed the Tea Act, granting the British East India Company a virtual monopoly on all tea sold in the American colonies. The act, approved on May 10, 1773, served as a focus for American discontent as no previous piece of legislation had done, and in each of the cities scheduled to receive consignments of tea a concerted effort was made to prevent the British East India Company from delivering the product to their agents in America. Boston responded with a self-styled "tea party," the more radical element in Massachusetts serving notice on Parliament that the colonies were no longer willing to subordinate colonial interests to the needs of the mother country. This time Lord North and Parliament refused to back down. They interpreted the wanton destruction of property as arrogant lawlessness and retaliated with punitive legislation against both the colony and the city of Boston.

Virginia was not indifferent to these developments. Several weeks after the Virginia Assembly convened for its usual spring session it learned that Parliament had passed a bill closing the port of Boston and that further punitive legislation would follow. The House of Burgesses, never inclined to shrink from responsibility when the rights of a colony were being challenged, promptly passed a resolution establishing a day of prayer and fasting out of sympathy for Massachusetts. Anticipating even more radical measures in support of Massachusetts, the newly appointed governor of Virginia, John Murray, the Earl of Dunmore, promptly dissolved the Assembly. Unhesitantly the burgesses shifted their meeting to Raleigh Tavern and as private citizens once again converted themselves into a quasi-official assembly in order that they might "advise" the people of Virginia as to the best means of securing their rights and liberties. On May 27, 1774, a new Association was established and Virginia's Committee of Correspondence and Inquiry was instructed to communicate with the other colonies and urge each of them to immediately appoint delegates to a general or continental congress.[21]

There was a fundamental difference in the response of John and Peyton Randolph to this latest crisis. Peyton Randolph was still speaker of the House of Burgesses, and after its dissolution he was elected "moderator" of the meeting at Raleigh Tavern. Having been chairman of the Virginia Committee of Correspondence and Inquiry since its formation in March of 1773, he had the latest intelligence from Massachusetts as well as the necessary experience to play a significant role in formulating the policy that established Virginia's leadership in rallying the other colonies to support Massachusetts.[22] By contrast, John Randolph, who had reentered the House of Burgesses as a representative of William and Mary College, replacing John Page, declined to take part in the meeting at Raleigh Tavern and refused to sign the new Virginia Association. Save for the governor, he seems to have been the highest-ranking official in the colony to withhold his signature.[23]

No one, least of all Edmund Randolph, could ignore the implications of the different positions taken by John and Peyton Randolph. Unhappily he found himself more in sympathy with the views of his uncle than with those of his father. One suspects that Edmund desperately hoped this latest crisis could be resolved to the mutual satisfaction of both his father and his uncle and the positions they represented. Any other solution was simply incomprehensible to him—in May, 1774.[24]

Virginia's efforts to promote a meeting of delegates from all the colonies quickly gathered support, and on June 17 the Massachusetts House of Representatives issued a call for an intercolonial congress to meet in Philadelphia the following September. One by one the colonies began naming their delegates to this congress. Almost without exception they selected their most powerful and experienced leaders. A Virginia Convention meeting in August, 1774, named seven of the most influential members of the House of Burgesses as its representatives. Peyton Randolph headed the delegation, his political influence being second to none in Virginia.[25]

When the First Continental Congress assembled in Philadelphia on September 5, the more moderate element succeeded in electing Peyton Randolph president. After several weeks of intense debate between the more radical and the more moderate factions in the Congress, the delegates approved a forthright declaration of colonial "rights and grievances." Furthermore, using the Virginia Association of May, 1774, as their model, the delegates established a general Association for all the colonies. The Association stated that as of December 1, 1774, all imports from Great Britain were to be halted. A committee was to be elected in every town, city and county throughout the colonies to enforce the Association, and any colony that failed to honor the Association was to be boycotted. Before adjourning on October 26 the delegates agreed to meet again on May 10, 1775, if American grievances had not been redressed.[26]

The actions of Congress removed all doubts about the determination of the colonies to present a united front, while at the same time forcing all but the most indifferent to choose sides. No colony was more aware of this than Virginia, and in March, 1775, a second Virginia Convention met in Richmond to name delegates to the Second Continental Congress and to formally authorize the arming of the militia for the defense of the colony. Peyton Randolph, who had been elected president of this convention without opposition, knew, as did most of the Virginia gentry, that armed conflict was now almost inevitable.[27] For John Randolph this outcome was totally unacceptable, and he could only hope that Parliament and its ministers might be magnanimous rather than vindictive in dealing with the colonies. As for Edmund, he accepted the unpleasant fact that it was no longer possible to amicably resolve the differences between England and her colonies. There remained only the very difficult personal decision of whether he would, like his uncle, join with those who were preparing to take up arms in defense of colonial rights or, like his father, remain a loyal subject of the King.

The time for decision came much sooner than even he had expected. On April 20, 1775, Governor Dunmore openly invited colonial resistance by removing the gunpowder from the public magazine in Williamsburg; on the 29th word of the battles of Lexington and Concord reached the Virginia capital; and on May 2 Captain Patrick Henry, commanding the Hanover County "volunteers," marched on Williamsburg intent on forcing the governor to return the colony's gunpowder to the public magazine.[28] When the Second Continental Congress convened on May 10, it virtually institutionalized the rebellion by assuming responsibility for military operations throughout the colonies.[29]

The Virginia House of Burgesses assembled as scheduled on June 1, 1775, but almost everyone knew that it was acting out the final scene of a drama that had suddenly become irrelevant. Peyton Randolph, representing Williamsburg, was again named speaker, while his brother once again served as the representative of William and Mary College.[30] Six days after the session began, Governor Dunmore rendered its deliberations superfluous by virtually abdicating his office and retreating with his family to the safety of the H.M.S. *Fowery* anchored off Yorktown.[31] Dunmore's abrupt departure from Williamsburg caused John Randolph to become a self-appointed intermediary between the governor and the House of Burgesses. Tirelessly he traveled back and forth from Yorktown to Williamsburg, carrying messages, explaining the position of the burgesses and probably pleading with the governor to return with his family to the colonial capital. When the burgesses were investigating Dunmore's role in the removal of the gunpowder from the public magazine, it was John Randolph who offered the most temperate account of the governor's action.[32] Never had he taken such an active part in the proceedings of the House of Burgesses and never had he worked so diligently to resolve the differences between the governor and the legislature. It was a frantic and almost pitiful effort to gain time, the only remaining ally of those who still hoped to effect a peaceful solution of the dispute. But John Randolph's efforts were in vain. Before this final session of the Burgesses had adjourned, word had reached Williamsburg that the Continental forces around Boston had engaged a superior force of British regulars on Breed's Hill and given an excellent account of themselves. The events in Boston, plus the threat posed by the British naval forces being assembled by Dunmore, caused Virginia's colonial leaders to call for a third Virginia Convention to meet in Richmond in July. By the time it assembled, Virginia was, for all practical purposes, without a government.

As the delegates journeyed toward Richmond for this convention, Edmund Randolph was preparing for a journey of his own. After weeks, perhaps months, of reflection he had decided on his own course of action. He would cast his lot with those who were in arms against the mother country by joining the Continental Army organizing under George Washington's command outside of Boston. It was a most difficult decision, but one that could no longer be avoided however much he might have wished to do so. Parting from his family with a heavy heart, he left home in mid-July. He recognized that his father strongly disapproved of his decision, and he knew that his mother and sisters, though more understanding, were deeply troubled by his choice. As he journeyed northward he was very much alone. His hopes for the future would never dim his memories of the past.[33]

His first stop was Philadelphia to secure supporting letters from the Virginia delegates to Congress. He already knew most of them because of their political associations with either his father or his uncle: Benjamin Harrison, second only to his uncle in his advocacy of restrained opposition to the Crown; Richard Henry Lee, the Virginian whose statesmanlike ability even the cantankerous John Adams came to respect; the distinguished Edmund Pendleton, the most conservative member of the delegation; and the more familiar faces of Patrick Henry and Thomas Jefferson.[34]

Edmund was quite candid about his objectives. He wished to serve on Washington's staff and needed the assistance of the delegation to gain such an appointment. Benjamin Harrison knew that young Randolph had more on his mind than a comparatively safe assignment in the Continental Army. "[H]e fears his father's conduct may tend to lessen him in the esteem of his countrymen," he wrote to Washington. He regretted, he continued, bothering Washington with applications of this sort and promised to avoid them as much as possible in the future, "but I could not refuse it on this occasion, well knowing that a most valuable young man, and one that I love, without some step of this sort, may, from the misconduct of his parent, be lost to his country." He even urged Washington to write a few lines to Randolph to assure him that his services would be welcome.[35] Several days later Richard Henry Lee provided a second letter. Noting Randolph's eagerness to serve, he reminded Washington that it was important that "our young gentry" gain experience in the military. Henry and Jefferson added their signatures to this letter and, since the mails were no longer safe, it was decided that Randolph should carry it with him to Cambridge where Washington had established his headquarters.[36]

Randolph left Philadelphia during the first week of August and reached Cambridge shortly before the 15th of the month.[37] Washington had been in Cambridge since July 2 attempting to organize the ill-trained and poorly equipped forces that had faced the British regulars in Boston. Fate, it seems, had made this charming college community on the north bank of the Charles River the focal point of the colonies' defiant challenge to the authority of the mother country. Washington's headquarters and residence were in the home of John Vassal, a Tory who had taken refuge in Boston. The house was located just east of the college campus on the road to Watertown.[38]

Randolph's arrival probably elicited nothing more than the usual courtesies from the headquarters staff, already plagued by a constant stream of visitors and favor-seekers. He probably did not see Washington until evening when the general, as was his custom, joined his staff for dinner. This was not their first meeting, for Randolph must have at least made his acquaintance when Washington was serving in the House of Burgesses, although the marked difference in their ages would make it highly unlikely that either had formed any fixed impression of the other.[39] There was much talk about—the activities of Governor Dunmore in Virginia and how the colony was responding to the threat, the latest information on the actions of Congress, and perhaps Randolph brought some verbal communication from the members of the Virginia delegation. If the conversation happened to touch on the subject of his father's sympathies, it can be assumed that Washington, knowing Randolph's concern lest his own loyalty be suspect, quickly reassured him that the letters of Harrison and Lee were all the proof he needed to secure him a place on his staff. It was decided that he would be appointed aide-de-camp, replacing Thomas Mifflin, who was about to be named quartermaster general of the "Army of the United Colonies."[40] In General Orders issued on August 15 it was stated that "Edmund Randolph and George Baylor Esqrs. are appointed Aids-de-Camp to the Commander in Chief. . . ."[41] The appointment was to take effect immediately.

Working under the watchful eye of Joseph Reed, who supervised Washington's headquarters staff, Randolph was immediately put to work copying Washington's official correspondence, preparing duplicates of important letters for transmission either to Congress or to some subordinate officer in Washington's command.[42] As soon as it was discovered that he had some ability in the art of composition he was entrusted with the task of drafting letters from Washington's notes and scribbled memoranda.[43] His skill in handling this assignment must have come to Washington's attention almost immediately, for in less than two weeks he was writing letters for Washington over his own signature. This was obviously more than a clerical chore, for misconstruing the intentions of the Commander-in-Chief could cause no end of difficulty and some of his letters touched on fairly sensitive matters. Quite properly he began each letter with the words: "I have it in command from his Excellency. . . ." What followed was frequently expressed in rather brusque language, but aside from his youthful bluntness he was an intelligent and accomplished correspondent totally dedicated to the cause and the man he was serving.[44]

Like everyone else who served on Washington's headquarters staff, he was usually overworked. He did find time, however, to write to his friend Jefferson and to Richard Henry Lee to complain of the "supineness" of Virginia for allowing Dunmore to roam and pillage the colony at will. From both men he demanded an explanation and the latest news of the colony. His letters burned with the enthusiasm of a young rebel, impatient with even the slightest evidence of procrastination among Virginians.[45]

It was September 9 before the *Virginia Gazette* reported on Randolph's appointment as aide-de-camp. There were no details, just the simple announcement.[46] On the same page there was another announcement. It read: "Yesterday morning John Randolph, Esq. his Majesty's Attorney General for this colony, with his lady and daughters, set out from this city, for Norfolk, to embark for Great Britain."[47] The matter-of-fact style of the *Gazette* concealed the very deep personal anguish that lay behind this decision. In late August John Randolph conveyed all his property to his friends John Blair and James Cooke and to his brother Peyton. They were instructed to sell everything, pay his debts from the revenue collected and forward the remainder to him in England.[48] As a loyal subject of the Crown he could not join the rebellion, and as a Virginian he could not bring himself to take up arms against his own people. To remain quietly in the colony as a private citizen, resigned to whatever political settlement emerged from the conflict, was an unworthy course for a person so closely identified with Virginia's colonial government. He felt he really had no choice; he must take his family to England until the conflict ended and the dispute was resolved.[49]

Undoubtedly Edmund learned of his family's departure a few weeks later, for ultimately all news reached Washington's headquarters. It was not, of course, unexpected, but this did not make it any less difficult to accept. Fortunately he was distracted by his work and the camaraderie of Washington's headquarters staff. He was more grateful than ever to Washington for the appointment as aide-de-camp.

Then, a little over a month later, he was stunned by the news that his Uncle Peyton had died unexpectedly in Philadelphia of an apoplectic stroke.[50] For Edmund, his uncle's passing was a deep personal tragedy, made doubly so by the recent departure of his own parents. He was forced to ask for permission to leave Washington's staff, at least until he could put family matters in order.[51] He left immediately for Philadelphia to accompany his aunt on the long and lonely trip back to Williamsburg. He knew he would be expected to advise her in the complex legal matters associated with the settlement of the estate and, of course, he would now have to confer with the two remaining agents handling the sale of his father's properties.[52]

Returning to Williamsburg one day after a new Virginia Convention had assembled in the capital, Edmund had ample opportunity to converse with the delegates about the mood of Congress, and to provide them with the latest intelligence from Washington's headquarters.[53] Their main interest was, of course, Governor Dunmore and the threat posed by his forces in the Norfolk area. Edmund was taken into their confidence without question, his service with Washington having removed all doubt about his support of the rebellion. He had proudly established his credentials as a patriot, thus assuring himself of a part, albeit a small one, in the drama that would soon be known as the American Revolution.

PART II

THE VIRGINIA
YEARS

Soon after Edmund Randolph returned to Virginia he found himself being drawn into the mainstream of its political life. Selected as the state's first attorney general six months after his return, he discovered that the office permitted him to observe first-hand the operations of the new state government and gave him considerable personal political influence.

His service with the Virginia delegation in the Continental Congress signaled his emergence as a leading public figure in Virginia. But after eight months in Congress he was forced to return to Virginia to attend to the increasing responsibilities of the attorney general's office and the demands of an expanding private practice.

Congressional service and an intimate political alliance with James Madison had made him a confirmed nationalist bent on strengthening the Confederation. But once he was back in Virginia he discovered that his colleagues in state government, far from being paralyzed by the problems facing the new nation, were perfectly willing to meet the challenge of the eighties. It gave a somewhat different orientation to his congressionally nurtured nationalism as he discovered that a well-ordered state government could effect a large measure of its own recovery.

Yet his continued interest in strengthening the national government and his growing personal political influence virtually assured him a prominent role in the Annapolis and Philadelphia conventions. It was in connection with this latter convention that he dramatically displayed his fierce political independence. He became a self-styled "recusant" in the bitter debate over the new federal Constitution. In the end his national sympathies caused him to support the Constitution but the experience had a profound effect on his future political style. Henceforth he would be the arch critic of all forms of political polarization and the tireless advocate of the "middle position" in the resolution of national problems.

Behind this very prominent public image was a private person, a *rather obscure figure who somehow seems to have found the time to manage his properties, placate his own as well as his father's and his uncle's creditors, build an impressive law practice and, above all, be an attentive husband and an indulgent father.*

3

Political Appointments in Virginia
January 1776–June 1781

On returning to Williamsburg Randolph discovered that Virginia was involved in a somewhat different type of military conflict from what he was familiar with in Cambridge. Although the forces at Lord Dunmore's disposal represented but a fraction of the strength of the British in Boston, they had virtually closed Virginia's ports and were threatening the entire tidewater region south of the York River. Randolph was amazed at Virginia's helplessness and impatient with her leaders because they could not drive Dunmore's forces from the colony. Virginia's Committee of Safety, composed of some of the colony's most experienced and respected leaders, seemed in Randolph's eyes wholly unequal to the challenge that confronted it—British sympathizers went unpunished, arms and ammunition were in very short supply, the colony was desperately in need of salt and not so much as a single vessel was being armed to protect ships carrying supplies to Virginia. Some even said that Dunmore could take Williamsburg if he chose to move against the city. The situation was probably somewhat less catastrophic than the impatient young aide-de-camp suspected, for Virginia was far from paralyzed by this threat. But it was a different Virginia from the one he had left six months earlier. No longer were Virginians thinking in terms of a short dramatic conflict; it was now quite evident that this was going to be a long, hard struggle, and Virginians were going to pay dearly for their cherished colonial rights.[1]

In the meantime the Virginia Convention, which was gathering in Williamsburg when Randolph reached the city on December 5, was trying to bring some semblance of order to the colony's military efforts and, at the same time, provide a kind of *ad hoc* government for the colony. Under the experienced leadership of its president, Edmund Pendleton, the convention's first order of business was to provide for the establishment of such regiments of militia as seemed necessary to protect Virginia's coastal regions from attack by Dunmore. It also reviewed the work of the Committee of Safety and provided for its continued existence until more permanent administrative machinery could be established to handle the day-to-day problems of the colony.[2] By January 9 the convention was prepared to move against those colonials who supported Dunmore, and to this end appointed a committee to draft an ordinance for punishing the "enemies of America" in the colony. The resulting document, one of the most significant passed by this convention, was to provide Randolph with his first assignment since returning to Virginia. He was named one of three judges to a Court of Admiralty established to ensure the strict compliance of Virginia to the provisions of the Continental Association.[3] The nominal financial remuneration that came with the post was less significant to Randolph than the appointment itself, which indicated that the convention acknowledged his credentials as a patriot.

Since he still considered himself a member of Washington's headquarters staff, he deemed it appropriate to keep the general informed of all that transpired in Virginia. He provided useful commentary on Dunmore's activities, as well as some information on the deliberations of the convention. He told Washington of the establishment of a Court of Admiralty but did not mention that he had been appointed one of its judges. One suspects that he withheld this information because he feared that Washington might interpret the appointment as an indication that he had abandoned whatever plans he had to return to the general's staff. When the convention adjourned on January 20, he asked the printer, Alexander Purdie, for copies of the *Journal* and the *Ordinances* so that he might forward them to Washington.[4]

All the while he was occupied with family matters. His aunt was now alone in the big house on Nicholson Street and her needs had to be attended to. Now that she was home in Williamsburg her many friends were more than willing to help her, but there were certain things that only Edmund could handle—the practical decisions associated with the management of Peyton Randolph's land and slaves in York and Charlotte counties, estate problems and the inevitable personal family matters. In addition, he was obliged to consult with those who were responsible for the sale of his father's properties and the payment of his debts. Not being a direct heir to his uncle's estate and not sharing in any of his father's assets, which seemingly were to be converted into British currency and forwarded to him in England, Edmund probably lived with his aunt—at least until he acquired an income in his own right. He might even have tried to resume a modest law practice, accepting such clients as sought his services.[5]

Early in April he was elected as a delegate from Williamsburg to the new Virginia Convention scheduled to meet in the colonial capital in May.[6] As an alternate to the respected George Wythe,[7] who was serving with the Virginia delegation in Congress, he found himself thrust into a far more important assignment than he had ever expected when he returned to Williamsburg in December. He took his election to the convention very seriously, knowing, no doubt, that many expected this convention to formally proclaim the colony's independence and determine its new government. A subsequent invitation from Congress to serve as muster master for the district of Virginia had to be declined because a local ordinance prevented elected representatives of the people from holding military posts. ". . . I cannot desert them, without the highest violation of gratitude," he informed the President of the Committee of Safety.[8]

As the delegates to the convention converged on Williamsburg, a feeling of excitement and tension gripped the old colonial capital. Once again it was "publick times," but now the stakes were much higher. This was not a colonial legislature resolving colonial grievances; rather it was a revolutionary convention seeking to determine the ultimate fate of Virginia as a colony. As Randolph nervously took his seat in the chamber that had been used by the House of Burgesses, he found himself surrounded by some of the colony's most powerful and respected leaders. Many of them, such as Edmund Pendleton, Robert Carter Nicholas and John Blair, were contemporaries of his father and uncle with equally long and distinguished records of service to the Crown and the colony. He very respectfully acknowledged their nods of greeting, sensitive to the fact that in the confusion of this opening session they even took notice of him. Glancing around the hall as it filled, he was relieved to find that some of the delegates in the room looked every bit as young and inexperienced as he was: a rather shy and unassuming young man from Orange County by the name of James Madison, a Henry Tazewell representing Brunswick County on the Virginia–North Carolina border, a Mann Page from Spotsylvania and a Henry Lee from Prince William County who looked even younger than Randolph.[9] Patrick Henry was, of course, very obviously in attendance but Thomas Jefferson was not, the continuous sessions of the Continental Congress keeping him in Philadelphia, along with Richard Henry Lee and George Wythe, in whose place Randolph himself was serving.

The convention organized itself almost casually, naming Edmund Pendleton as its president and then, in imitation of the administrative structure of the House of Burgesses, appointing committees of Privileges and Elections, Propositions and Grievances, and "Publick Claims." Randolph found himself routinely appointed to each of these standing committees because Pendleton chose to put at least one delegate from each of the colony's constituencies on every standing committee.[10]

The first business of the convention was to deal with some of the more practical problems facing the colony and review the decisions that had been made by the colony's Committee of Safety since the close of the last convention. It was not until the 15th of the month that the convention officially turned its attention to the awesome question of independence. When the delegates met that day and resolved themselves into a Committee of the Whole on the state of the colony, Pendleton drafted a resolution which, he hoped, would remove whatever apprehension the delegates still had about making a unilateral declaration of Virginia's independence. Rather than calling for outright independence, Pendleton's resolution merely instructed Virginia's delegates in Congress to urge that body to declare the "United Colonies" free and independent, thereby promoting a joint statement of independence by all the colonies. A second resolution, also drafted by Pendleton, provided for the appointment of a committee to prepare a declaration of rights and a plan of government for Virginia.[11] Both resolutions were reported out of the committee and approved unanimously by the convention.[12] A Grand Committee was immediately appointed to implement this second resolution. Its chairman was Archibald Cary, a delegate from Chesterfield County with a long record of service in the House of Burgesses. Like Peyton Randolph, he was generally considered rather conservative in his sympathies and at this time was, at best, a cautious advocate of American independence.[13] Twenty-eight delegates were appointed to this committee, the secretary of the convention recording their names in the order in which they were appointed. The eighth delegate to be appointed was Mr. Edmund Randolph of Williamsburg; it was an honor far exceeding his influence or his experience in public office.[14] Randolph, it seems, had been accepted by his peers. His commitment to the American cause was now totally beyond question and he was, in a sense, being told that he could take his place in the ranks of Virginia's Revolutionary leaders, that he was now a member—albeit a junior member—of Virginia's ruling gentry.

While the convention turned its attention once again to practical problems, the Grand Committee was engaged in preparing the declaration of rights and plan of government for the colony. At first the committee made little progress; the multiple views of its many members seemed to defy reconciliation. The addition of George Mason to the committee on May 18 served to instill a new sense of urgency into its efforts and he quickly gained an ascendency over the committee's deliberation.[15] It was Randolph's first contact with this respected and learned Virginia planter, and he quickly came to appreciate his brilliant and perceptive intellect. The committee completed a draft of the Declaration of Rights on May 26 and on the following day presented it to the full convention. It was decided that the delegates should be given at least two days to study the statement, and May 29 was set aside for its consideration. On June 12, after several days of close debate, an amended Declaration of Rights was approved by the convention.[16]

In the meantime the Grand Committee had turned its attention to a plan of government for the colony, maintaining an exhausting schedule in an effort to put the document into final form before the convention lost its momentum. It completed its work on June 24, and two days later the convention took the document under consideration, sitting once again as a Committee of the Whole. Somewhat surprisingly, the convention gave only three full days to a discussion of the document. The delegates, noting that the plan of government made the lower house of the legislature the ultimate source of all authority, accepted it with only a minimal number of amendments. With its acceptance on June 29 the state of Virginia became a reality.[17]

For Randolph, however, there were other committee assignments. Some, at least, seem to have been made in recognition of his previous acquaintance with the issue under consideration. Such would appear to be the explanation for his appointment to a committee to amend the ordinance for punishing the "Enemies of America in This Colony."[18] As one of the judges of the Court of Admiralty under the original ordinance, he was apparently considered a natural choice to serve on the committee to amend it. In addition, he was appointed to a committee to draft several bills relative to naval affairs.[19] He was even named the chairman of a committee to determine the proper salary of the individuals who had been employed to "fill up" the treasury notes issued by the colony.[20] In several instances Randolph appears to have been primarily responsible for the ordinance that the committee drafted.

One might also conclude that the convention was not above exploiting his youthful zeal, for who else would have willingly served on a committee that counted and measured the width of the windows of the jail in Williamsburg? The more venerable members of the Virginia gentry certainly could not have been asked to perform this task, nor would they be willing to inspect the interior of the jail that, according to the committee report, had "an offensive smell which . . . would be injurious to the most robust health."[21] While all of these appointments were relatively minor, several occurred during the time the Grand Committee was engaged in critical discussions on a plan of government. The month of June was particularly hectic. Randolph probably dashed from one committee meeting to another with all the seriousness and urgency of a Pendleton or a Mason.

Though Edmund Randolph had no illusions as to his personal influence in the convention, he also had no illusions about the ultimate significance of its actions. Virginia now had made the fateful decision for independence and the rebellion had become a revolution. The colony had been moving in this direction for several months, as the short-sighted policies of Lord Dunmore turned more and more Virginians against the mother country. The winter of 1775–1776 was a critical period for Virginia. By the time the convention met in May, 1776, turning back was virtually out of the question—nothing remained but to give formal witness to an accomplished fact.

Randolph had openly cast his lot with the patriots when he elected to join Washington at Cambridge. In the months that followed he came to view the separation of the American colonies from Great Britain as inevitable. After his return to Virginia his assessment of the mood of the colony always pivoted on the question of independence. To Washington he wrote: "This looks like business, but I cannot swear we are uniformly decisive."[22] For him, the May Convention was important as an explicit repudiation of Virginia's colonial status, but in his enthusiasm for the American cause he would have preferred to see Virginia defiantly proclaim its independence from the mother country, courageously setting a course that Congress and the other states would follow.

The convention had one last chore before adjournment—the selection of the various state officials under the new constitution. The delegates named the popular and volatile Patrick Henry to the governorship in a close contest with the more conservative Thomas Nelson, Jr., the former president of the Executive Council of colonial Virginia. Henry was obviously Virginia's most notable revolutionary, his famous Stamp Act resolves having made him a legend in his own time. His selection as the state's first governor seemed to symbolize Virginia's determination to make its break with England irrevocable.[23]

To the office of attorney general the delegates named Edmund Randolph, ironically giving the young Virginia patriot the same office that his father had held under a Crown appointment.[24] In reality the appointment was little more than a symbolic gesture, however, for the office had few responsibilities at this time. The new state constitution, while providing for the creation of an elaborate hierarchy of superior courts for the state, offered no timetable for their establishment. The new courts were to come into being through a series of establishing acts to be drafted by the state legislature. There was to be a Supreme Court of Appeals, a court of final appeal, a new General Court, somewhat more restricted than the General Court of the colonial period, a Chancery Court to handle equity proceedings and, as was befitting a sovereign state, a Court of Admiralty.[25] As attorney general Randolph would, of course, be expected to represent the state in each of these courts once they came into being. Unfortunately the legislature would take several years to implement this court system, and even after it did pass the necessary legislation, the war discouraged most litigation. Thus for the next few years the state's first attorney general would have very few duties, except perhaps to keep himself available in case the governor or some other officer of government should seek his advice on some legal question. He was, of course, free to pursue a private practice so long as it did not involve him in a conflict of interest with his public office.[26] But clients were few and far between, and like most lawyers, Randolph had very little to do. In short, he had ample free time to further his own future and solidify his place in the mainstream of Virginia's political life.

The May Convention also brought about a change in Randolph's personal life. One of the delegates to this convention was Robert Carter Nicholas, the former treasurer of the colony and a close friend of Edmund's father and uncle. At the outbreak of hostilities in 1775 Nicholas moved his family out of Williamsburg to the safety of his plantation in Hanover County. He returned to Williamsburg for the convention, having been elected as a delegate from James City County. His return was of particular importance to young Edmund Randolph for it reunited him with Elizabeth Nicholas, the treasurer's youngest daughter. Edmund and "Betsy" had grown up together in Williamsburg; they had played together as children and had been educated in the same elementary school. They had, in Edmund's words, "an early partiality" toward each other. The events of 1775 had separated them: Elizabeth went with her parents to the family estate in Hanover County and Edmund joined Washington's headquarters staff in Cambridge. Reunited by the convention, Edmund and Betsy spent every available moment together. As the convention drew to a close, Betsy's father apparently suggested that the family move back to Hanover County. The young couple, rather than risk another painful separation, decided to get married. They were wed on August 29 in Bruton Parish church in a simple Anglican ceremony.[27]

Elizabeth Nicholas Randolph was twenty-three when she married, exactly one day younger than her husband. Doted upon and undoubtedly indulged by loving parents as a child, she became in her late teens a very proper young lady with a taste for fine clothes and the more elegant things of life. Edmund, it seems, was totally devoted to Betsy, and in times of crisis she became his most important source of support and encouragement. Their marriage was almost predestined; its beginnings, quite literally, went back to the cradle.[28]

The happy young couple had been married only a few months when Edmund, in response to an urgent plea from his Aunt Elizabeth, agreed to return to Philadelphia to arrange for the transfer of his uncle's body to Virginia. When Peyton Randolph had died in October, 1775, his wife had arranged for his temporary interment in Philadelphia because the unsettled condition of the country had made it all but impossible to bring his body back to Williamsburg. Now that the military situation had become somewhat more stabilized, Elizabeth Randolph was determined that her husband's body be brought home. Edmund, responsive to her wishes, set out immediately for Philadelphia. The sad assignment was accomplished without incident, and he was back in Williamsburg by November 26. As he approached the city he was met by state and town officials, who formally escorted his uncle's body to the family vault in the chapel of the college. It was Virginia's final act of homage to one of its most distinguished colonial leaders.[29]

Shortly after his return Randolph began to assume a wider range of public offices. Although comparatively minor in character, they did serve to keep him in the public eye and establish his reputation as a conscientious public servant. On November 30 he was elected mayor of the city of Williamsburg. It was an office that involved him in the monthly sessions of the town's Hustings Court and the rather frequent meetings of the city's corporate officers in the Williamsburg "Common Hall."[30] In addition, he had been named to one of several committees engaged in compiling an inventory of Lord Dunmore's personal property. John Blair, one of the leading lawyers in Williamsburg, and Randolph were assigned the task of compiling the inventory of Dunmore's personal property in Williamsburg. Although appointed by the convention that met in May of 1776, they were unable to file a report before that convention adjourned. When the newly elected state legislature assembled for its first session in October, 1776, the two men had completed their work and prepared a formal memorial summarizing the manner in which they had executed their commission. The memorial plus the accompanying account books and papers were referred to the Committee on Public Claims for review. This committee reported that those responsible for the inventory and disposition of Dunmore's property had "rendered a full and faithful account of their transactions."[31]

When the Virginia Assembly convened again in May, 1777, it renewed Randolph's appointment as attorney general. It was now, for all practical purposes, a permanent appointment and, at this time, carried a salary of £200 per year.[32] Shortly before this he had been elected to the board of governors of William and Mary College and had been named rector of the college, a title given annually to whomever was elected to preside over the board during the ensuing year. The Revolution had so disrupted the educational functions of the college that the board of governors had relatively few responsibilities. Randolph, however, did preside over the board during an investigation of charges reflecting on the conduct of three faculty members, one for alleged Tory sympathies. The investigation was terminated after only one meeting when it was learned that the charges against them had probably been fabricated.[33]

In May of 1778 Randolph acquired still another office when the powerful House of Delegates named him as their clerk. His father, of course, had held the equivalent office in the House of Burgesses for several years, and the appointment was a sign of the growing influence of another Randolph. The duties of the office were about the same, but it is unlikely that Edmund Randolph had the same personal power as his father, who had held the office under somewhat different circumstances. As for the monetary rewards, no doubt Edmund put the salary of £300 per year to good use.[34]

Randolph occupied himself with his limited law practice and these several minor offices until June, 1779, when he received his first significant appointment from the Virginia Assembly. He was named a delegate to the Continental Congress. Normally the Assembly elected the state's delegates to Congress in May or June of each year, and the delegates began their term of service the following November. In the present instance, however, the Virginia delegation had been cut sharply by the resignation of four of its members. The legislature attempted to remedy this situation by holding two elections, one to fill the unexpired term of those who had resigned and a second to select the full delegation for the twelve-month period beginning in November. Randolph was elected to one of the current vacancies and also to a full term.[35] This meant an immediate departure for Philadelphia. He was forced to resign as clerk of the House of Delegates but he chose to retain the office of attorney general.[36] Since that office carried few responsibilities at this time because the Revolution had disrupted Virginia's judicial system, he felt he could discharge them by periodically returning to Williamsburg.

He left Williamsburg during the second week of July after securing the services of John Beckley to attend to the needs of his clients in private practice.[37] Although he didn't like the idea, it was agreed that Betsy should remain in Williamsburg until he determined if he could serve in Congress and perform the duties of the office of attorney general at the same time. The trip northward was uneventful and he was in Philadelphia by July 21, probably securing accommodations at a public inn near the rather modest State House where Congress was meeting. He presented his credentials to the president of Congress the next day and immediately took his seat with the Virginia delegation, currently composed of the controversial and eccentric Meriwether Smith, Cyrus Griffin, a young man only slightly more experienced than Randolph himself, and William Fleming, a lawyer whom Randolph knew slightly from the Virginia Convention of May, 1776.[38]

Within a short time Randolph discovered that Congress was struggling vainly to cope with an unbelievable variety of military and financial problems and its effectiveness was being seriously compromised by deep personal and regional quarrels and a dangerously high rate of absenteeism among the delegates. He soon sensed the frustration and frightening indecisiveness of Congress as it laboriously and indiscriminately grappled with all manner of business, postponing major problems to bicker over minor issues. The Virginia House of Delegates probably seemed most efficient by comparison. He could not have helped but wonder whether Congress really needed the services of another part-time delegate like himself.[39]

For several months prior to his arrival Congress had been fairly regularly engaged in defining the American position in preparation for the future peace negotiations with Great Britain. Randolph arrived in time to witness a tedious review of the language to be employed in defining our fishing rights off the banks of Newfoundland. The subject had such a long and involved history that Randolph could not even begin to grasp the significance of most of the seemingly minor word changes being proposed. He participated in most of the roll calls, but he could do little more than follow the lead of the other members of the Virginia delegation. He did sense a "southern position" in these matters, but failed to see how it could be served by a hair-splitting debate over the wording of the congressional statement.[40] Congress was quick to put its new delegates to work and soon after his arrival Randolph was given several committee assignments. Most of them were relatively unimportant, but he willingly assumed them.[41]

He had been in Philadelphia less than a month when he decided it had been a mistake for him to have accepted the appointment to Congress. The way Congress and its committees conducted business required the continuous presence of a delegate in Philadelphia, and as the attorney general of his state Randolph felt that he could not remain away from Virginia indefinitely. From the very beginning he had suspected as much and these few weeks of congressional service served to confirm his suspicion. He decided upon an immediate return to Virginia so that the legislature might have an opportunity to choose a successor during its fall session. The day after the Assembly convened, he submitted his resignation to Benjamin Harrison, the speaker of the House of Delegates:

> I repaired to Congress, in obedience to the commands of the General Assembly at their last session, and in conformity to my own opinion that no citizen ought to decline a service, to which he might be called by the voice of his country without good cause. To such of my friends, as urged me to accept

the appointment, I repeatedly represented my situation in life, and the dependence of my family on the fruits of my profession. They thought, that I might discharge both public and private duties by returning from Philadelphia to the different courts. With this idea I yielded to their application. But after having made the experiment I find, that to be in Virginia at those seasons when the office of the Attorney General may require my presence, will leave a small portion of time indeed for my attendance at Congress. . . . I therefore intreat the General Assembly, whose frequent instances of favour towards me would render any defection from the service of my country unpardonable; to consider my embarrassments, and to believe, that nothing, but my obligation to those, who look up to me for support, would induce me to resign a seat, so honourable in itself, and demonstrative of public approbation.[42]

Randolph's resignation was accepted and on December 14 a successor was named to fill the vacancy.

This had not been an easy decision, for he obviously would have preferred to remain in Congress. For all its indecisiveness Congress was the political instrumentality of the new nation, and to participate in its decisions was to play a vital role in the American struggle for independence.

Randolph was to regret this decision in the months ahead as a series of military reverses shattered the complacency of the state and its officials. Just weeks before he was appointed a delegate to the Continental Congress a British naval force seized and burnt Norfolk and Portsmouth. The incident revived the state's deep concern over Williamsburg's vulnerable position and caused the Assembly to precipitously transfer the capital to Richmond.[43] Since the transfer was to be effected in 1780, Randolph's first order of business following his return to Virginia in August, 1779, was to acquire a home for his family in the state's new capital. This was no small task because Richmond, a small and relatively insignificant county seat, was not ready to accommodate the state government, much less house the legislators who would crowd into the city each May and October for the semiannual sessions of the Assembly.[44] Apparently Randolph succeeded in finding something, for in January, 1780, he published a notice in the *Virginia Gazette* of his forthcoming departure from Williamsburg and announced that henceforth he intended to confine his practice to the state's Court of Appeals, High Court of Chancery and Admiralty Court. He would, however, be willing "to attend the trial of any particular cause in the County Courts, should the parties concerned choose to employ me."[45] It was a rather pompous bit of professionalism given the limited activities of most Virginia courts during these years.

Not long after Randolph moved to Richmond the mood of the state changed perceptibly. The war seemed once again to be drawing closer to Virginia as the British began to renew military operations in the southern colonies. In December, 1779, General Clinton began to move some eight thousand British regulars from New York to South Carolina in a determined effort to capture Charleston. On May 12, 1780, the city fell. A considerable number of American troops, including Virginians, were captured in the engagement. A few weeks later a British force under Lieutenant Colonel Banastre Tarleton destroyed an entire Virginia regiment at Waxhaw Creek on the border between North and South Carolina. And from the north came even more alarming intelligence—a report that the militia under Washington had mutinied at their Morristown encampment.[46]

The summer passed uneventfully save for the Battle of Camden in South Carolina. But in October a British force under General Alexander Leslie landed at Portsmouth. Before a force of Virginia militia could be gathered to challenge him, he had reembarked to join the British forces in South Carolina. Then, on December 30, a British invasion fleet under Brigadier General Benedict Arnold appeared off the Virginia coast. With complete contempt for Virginia's hastily assembled militia, Arnold, on his first assignment as an officer in the British Army, sailed up the James River, landed his forces at Westover and moved directly against Richmond. He burnt the city and then quickly withdrew to an encampment at Portsmouth, reclaiming the fortifications that had been left by Leslie.[47]

For Randolph, Arnold's bold stab at Richmond must have been a thoroughly unnerving experience for it forced him to move Betsy to safety at a time when she was well advanced in her first pregnancy. The evacuation was accomplished without incident, and when Arnold withdrew to Portsmouth two days later the young couple, much relieved, returned to their home. In February Betsy, none the worse for her experience, gave birth to a boy who was promptly named Peyton after Edmund's illustrious uncle.[48]

All the while the main British army in the South, now under the command of General Charles Cornwallis, was moving northward through the Carolinas, and the American forces under Major General Nathaniel Green had not as yet been able to stop them. The objective of these British forces was clearly Virginia, since its capture would be a serious blow to the American cause. When Arnold was reinforced in March by a sizable British force under Major General Phillips, Randolph undoubtedly took the precaution of moving his wife and infant son some distance outside of Richmond to a site that was not likely to attract British troops. He himself probably returned to the city and remained until the Assembly met on May 7. It was learned then that Cornwallis was rapidly approaching the Virginia–North Carolina border, and there was no force in the field that could even hope to stop him. The entire state government abandoned Richmond and retreated to Charlottesville, where the legislature resumed its session on the 28th of the month. In the two weeks that followed, Cornwallis' forces roamed the countryside at will, even sending a raiding party into Charlottesville, a venture that almost succeeded in capturing the Assembly.[49]

When the legislature retreated further westward to Staunton in Augusta County, it was a severely chastened group of state leaders that met to conduct the state's business. The Virginia forces under the command of the colorful Marquis de Lafayette were reduced to waging a shameful game of hide-and-seek with the enemy, knowing full well that to do more was to invite defeat. And they had learned that little tangible aid could be expected from Congress or General Washington, who stubbornly insisted that Virginia could be most effectively relieved by mounting a full-scale attack on the British forces that remained stationed in New York. The steadily deteriorating military situation was the central concern of the legislature, and all manner of emergency measures had to be taken in an effort to contain Cornwallis and his destructive cavalry.[50] But the legislators were also responsible for electing state officials for the coming year, an obligation they were not prepared to slight even in the present crisis. On June 13 they elected the state's delegates to Congress for the coming year and among those chosen was Edmund Randolph. The following day the legislature filled the vacancies in its present congressional delegation, and Randolph was elected as a replacement for Benjamin Harrison.[51] Recent events and the rather obvious expectation of the state legislature shattered whatever doubts he might have had about returning to Congress. Yet the request to serve as Harrison's replacement was not to his liking, for it meant leaving Betsy and his infant son behind in Virginia at a time when much of the state was being harassed by a British cavalry that seemingly defied capture. He vowed to bring them both to Philadelphia just as soon as they were strong enough to undertake the long journey northward.

4

Delegate in Congress
July 1781–March 1782

Randolph left Virginia on July 6. To avoid capture he traveled north to "Frederick-town" in Maryland and then east to Baltimore, where he picked up the main road northward. He arrived in Philadelphia on Monday, July 16, which was reasonably good time considering the circuitous route he had taken.[1] The city itself was quite familiar to him since he had spent several weeks here in the summer of 1779 during his first congressional appointment. He probably stayed in one of the public inns until a room was available in the boardinghouse that was run by Mrs. Mary House and her daughter Mrs. Elizabeth Trist, the most popular stopping place for Virginians serving in Congress. The House–Trist residence, as it came to be called, was not only convenient to the Pennsylvania State House where Congress met, but also quite superior to many of the other boardinghouses in the city.[2]

The atmosphere of Philadelphia was much different from the way he remembered it. The city seemed to be in a state of perpetual turmoil, its citizens at odds with the pacifist and pro-English sympathies of its Quaker residents and resentful of the high prices and perpetual shortages that had plagued the city since the British withdrawal in 1778.[3] Randolph was shocked to discover that it would take $20 per month in specie (over $900 in Continental currency) to cover his room and board, and that he frequently had to pay Mrs. House in advance so that she could meet her weekly food bill. To board his horse cost him an additional $24 per month in specie, and he was told that his laundry bill would run as high as $6 or $7 per month.[4] Virginia would, of course, compensate him for these expenses, but he began to wonder if he could afford to bring Betsy and his son to the city to live.

Randolph had not been in Philadelphia very long before he became aware of the rather obvious decline that had taken place in the quality of the delegates serving in Congress. With a few noteworthy exceptions, Congress was composed of sincere but rather undistinguished delegates who had neither the prestige nor the influence to command the type of respect that body so desperately needed.[5] In terms of age and experience the Virginia delegation actually seemed quite strong by comparison with the others. Two of the men, Joseph Jones and Meriwether Smith, were as old as Randolph's father, while Theodorick Bland, Jr., appeared to be about ten years older than Randolph himself. Each of them had an extended period of congressional service to his credit.[6] Only the shy and unassuming James Madison, who had entered Congress in March, 1780, seemed to be Randolph's contemporary. Unimpressed with the quality of the other state delegations and younger than Jones, Smith and Bland, Randolph instinctively gravitated toward Madison for advice and companionship.

Randolph had first met Madison at the Virginia Convention of May, 1776, but apparently had little or no personal contact with him while that convention was in session. In the intervening years while Randolph was serving as attorney general of Virginia Madison was elected to the House of Delegates and then to the State Council, which allowed for at least a casual acquaintanceship to develop.[7] In Philadelphia this quickly grew into a valuable political alliance and friendship. For Randolph, it was a happy alliance, making his congressional assignment the most rewarding of any he had held thus far in his public career.

For the first few days Randolph was busier than most of the delegates as he tried to familiarize himself with the more important items on the congressional agenda. Yet he could not help but worry about Betsy and his infant son. He wondered how they were getting along, worried about the possibility of their being captured and fretted over their health. He simply could not rest until he had them with him in Philadelphia. He would, he decided, bring them both to the city just as soon as the baby was strong enough to make the trip.

Given his recent experiences in Virginia, Randolph took up his congressional responsibilities with few illusions about the prowess of the Continental forces currently challenging the British in the southern states. If, as was reported, the military situation had become less precarious in the North, it certainly had not improved in the South. Virginia, for all its wealth and influence, could not muster sufficient forces to challenge—much less defeat—Cornwallis' army, and the other southern states seemed to be even more helpless. The future seemed grim, and no one, least of all Edmund Randolph, dared predict how much longer it would take to clear the southern states of British troops. No one, of course, suspected that Yorktown, the decisive battle of the war, was a mere two months away. Such good fortune was simply beyond the imagination of even the most optimistic Virginian in July, 1781.

In the gloomy atmosphere of the Continental Congress a decisive military victory was not even a dream. When Randolph arrived, Congress was scrutinizing the language of the recently ratified Articles of Confederation in a desperate search for additional authority so that it might at least begin to deal with some of its more serious problems. All the while it was engaged in this search it kept trying to resolve the country's mounting financial problems, solve the sensitive question of how the western lands ceded to Congress by Virginia, New York and Connecticut were to be disposed of, and last, but certainly not least, formulate a viable foreign policy for the nation.[8] Within a matter of weeks after entering Congress Randolph was assigned to committees that directly involved him in each of these problems. Undaunted by the awesome work load thrust upon him, he plunged into his committee assignments with enthusiasm, determined, above all else, to be a credit to the state he represented.

The first of Randolph's major committee assignments came on July 18 when he was added to a committee to prepare an ordinance establishing a Court of Appeals for admiralty cases. The committee's task was but a part of Congress' search for additional authority under the Articles of Confederation. James Madison had been the first to recognize the importance of establishing the judicial authority of Congress under the Articles, and in April of 1781 had suggested that Congress establish a Court of Appeals for admiralty cases.[9] Although a relatively modest proposal, it proved sufficiently controversial to precipitate a congressional debate that was carried on intermittently for several months.

Randolph's involvement in the matter seems to have occurred almost by accident. Madison's motion of April, 1781, was referred to a committee which brought in the suggested ordinance a month later. After being read twice it was recommitted to the same committee, which proceeded to bring in a new ordinance on June 4, 1781. Like the first ordinance, it survived two readings, only to be postponed for later consideration. It was not until July 18 that this second ordinance was revived. Several sections were approved by Congress, but the bill was recommitted for a third time.[10] By this time Randolph had entered Congress. Since he had served as one of the judges of the temporary admiralty courts Virginia had established in 1775, he had at least some direct experience in maritime law. Apparently this limited association with a state admiralty court was brought to the attention of Congress because when the bill was recommitted for the third time Randolph was added to the committee. More significantly, the committee's instructions were enlarged and they were now asked to bring in an ordinance for "regulating the proceedings of the admiralty courts of the several states in cases of capture . . . and to call upon the several [state] legislatures to aid by necessary provisions, the powers reserved to Congress by the Articles of Confederation on the subject of captures from the enemy."[11]

The committee turned to its task with remarkable vigor and presented its report to Congress by August 14. Randolph's presence seems to have influenced the work of the committee, for its report contained the draft of a revised ordinance on the Court of Appeals and a new ordinance to ascertain "what captures on water shall be legal." The latter ordinance, drafted initially by Randolph, was presented in response to the broadened powers granted to the committee.[12]

Because Congress showed considerable interest in this new ordinance, further consideration of the ordinance establishing the Court of Appeals was dropped for the time being. The new ordinance was read and considered at length; some sections were agreed upon, others were removed or altered and several were recommitted to the committee. In due time the committee reported back to Congress, and on August 28 Congress once again resumed active consideration of the ordinance. For the next three months it remained under study; in fact, hardly a week passed in which Congress did not devote at least some time to the subject. Paragraphs were removed, only to be subsequently replaced; the most meticulous attention was given to the wording of each sentence. Madison suggested some twenty amendments and, in time, most of them were incorporated into the final text. James Lovell of Massachusetts presented some "remarks," and they, too, were considered by Congress. Finally, on December 4, 1781, Randolph saw the product of his first important committee assignment emerge from its third reading and secure congressional approval. The resulting ordinance retained the character of the original measure as drafted by Randolph. The changes, reflecting a congressional concern for detail that even the legal mind of Randolph must have found somewhat excessive, were technical.[13]

Shortly after Randolph was named to the committee on the Court of Appeals for admiralty cases a second committee assignment was given to him. Like the preceding one, it was related to the efforts of Congress to increase its authority under the Articles. On March 6, 1781, Congress had established a committee to "prepare a plan to invest . . . Congress . . . with full and explicit powers for effectually carrying into execution in the several states all acts or resolutions passed agreeably [sic] to the Articles of Confederation."[14] Hoping to make the most of the present opportunity to interpret the Articles as broadly as possible, the committee turned to its task with enthusiasm. Madison, who had been named to the committee, told Jefferson their object was to give Congress "coercive powers" competent to "compel obedience." He also referred to an "implied right of coercion."[15]

The report of this committee was laid before Congress in May. It took cognizance of certain deficiencies in the Articles and suggested an amendment that would give Congress the authority "to employ the force of the United States . . . to compel [the states] to fulfill their federal engagements" if they should refuse to abide by an ordinance of Congress. Congressional *authority*, the report noted, was clearly established by Article 13. All that remained was to vest Congress with the requisite *power* to ensure the preservation of that authority. The delegates were not prepared to go this far; they prevented further consideration of the subject by referring the matter to a Grand Committee.[16] For those who hoped for the rapid solidification of congressional power under the Articles, the referral to the Grand Committee was a bitter pill to swallow. "Quidnunc politicians," said John Mathews of South Carolina, "who . . . tremble at the very idea of doing anything that is not strictly enjoined them by their *father's will*."[17] The Grand Committee reported back to Congress on July 20 and, as was expected, its report was much more restrained than that of its predecessor. It recommended only that the states pass laws granting Congress the authority to impose limited embargoes in time of war, and also that the requisition quotas that Congress assigned to each state be met through a specific appropriation by the respective state legislatures and paid directly to the collectors appointed by Congress. The delegates seemingly were unimpressed by these recommendations for the Grand Committee was dissolved and its report was referred to a new committee consisting of Oliver Ellsworth of Connecticut, James Varnum of Rhode Island and Edmund Randolph.[18] This committee went to work almost immediately, only to find itself deprived of Ellsworth's full services by ill health.[19] This placed considerably more responsibility on Randolph and Varnum, the latter of whom had been an outspoken advocate of increased power for Congress. The committee delivered its report on August 22.

The report opened with a blanket request that the committee be discharged from its responsibility for preparing a formal exposition of each of the powers of the Confederation lest the omission of any power be later construed as an argument against its existence. Then, too, the report noted it was better to wait until an issue arises that brings the power of the Confederation into question than to create one by crystallizing opposition to the Articles before they had been given an opportunity to stand the test of time. Within its recognized area of jurisdiction there were, however, many things that Congress should do—the committee listed twenty-one. The report then turned to the sensitive issue of extending the powers of Congress. The committee suggested that it would be appropriate for Congress to ask the states to extend its authority in seven areas in order to give it the power to: levy an embargo in time of war without limitation; prescribe rules for impressing property into the service of the United States; appoint the collectors of taxes and direct the mode of accounting for taxes imposed through the requisition system; provide for the admission of new states into the Union; stipulate in treaties with foreign nations for the establishment of consular power without reference to the state; seize the property of a state delinquent in meeting requisitions; and lastly, liberalize the voting rules under which Congress functioned. It recommended further that a committee be appointed to prepare a representation to the states setting forth the necessity of these supplemental powers.[20]

The report, in the hand of Varnum, was considerably milder than the views he had expressed a few months earlier. One can only surmise that the report's more limited assessment of congressional power under the Articles was due, in part at least, to the presence of Randolph on the committee. Congress failed to act on the report; scheduled to be the order of the day on August 23, it simply disappeared from the *Journals.*[21]

All that was salvaged from these months of earnest effort to strengthen the authority of Congress under the Articles was a resolution recommending that separate taxes be imposed by the states for the payment of their requisition quotas, and that the moneys so collected be paid directly to the authorized representative of the Superintendent of Finance. This resolution was presented to Congress on November 2, 1781, as a part of the report apportioning the quotas of each state for an $8 million requisition that had been authorized by Congress. Edmund Randolph wrote the resolution.[22]

Randolph also had some contact with the western land cessions that were pending before Congress at this time. Maryland had ratified the Articles of Confederation only after Virginia, New York and Connecticut had agreed to cede certain of their western lands to Congress. The intended transfer of these lands to Congress embroiled that body in a long-standing dispute between these states and several western land companies with sizable holdings in these areas. Since their claims had never been recognized by the states, the companies quite naturally turned to Congress for verification of their titles.[23]

Randolph's introduction to the subject came when the memorial of William Trent on behalf of one of these land companies was routinely referred to the committee the week when Randolph was the chairman. The committee report, advising Congress as to the proper disposition of the memorial, was written by Randolph. It recommended that Congress refuse to consider the memorial until certain offensive passages had been removed. Congress, in turn, found the language of Randolph's committee report so belligerent that it ordered the report stricken from the record and, as frequently happened, simply did nothing about the memorial.[24]

It was October, 1781, before Congress resumed consideration of the western land cessions. At Madison's urging, Congress agreed to review a committee report that had been submitted to it the previous June.[25] To Madison's chagrin, Congress referred the whole matter to a new committee which, in accordance with its instructions, proceeded to undertake a complete review of the titles of New York, Connecticut and Virginia as well as the claims of the various land companies that had memorialized Congress. The committee invited each of these states to testify before it.[26] Madison, Jones and Randolph were representing Virginia in Congress at this time, and they, arguing that Virginia's title was above question and under no circumstances subject to congressional review, unequivocally refused to appear before the committee.[27]

This committee reported to Congress on November 3, and recommended, among other things, that Virginia's cession be rejected and that Congress urge Virginia to pass a new act of cession giving the national legislature unconditional title to Virginia's western lands.[28] It would be several months before Congress would see fit to act on these recommendations. In the meantime the Virginia delegation thought it prudent to remind Governor Nelson that an intemperate response on the part of the Virginia legislature to this report might create even greater problems than the one they were trying to solve. Their letter, written by Randolph, quite properly placed the issue in the larger context of the struggle for independence:

> But let a greater point be consulted. The late capture of the British army opens the avenue of peace. It will be instantaneously shut up, if Great–Britain should have a single glance of a fracture in the American chain. The great ally too, whom we already have, and the two other powers whose friendship we solicit may be shocked by such a procedure. But let the event of the present report be what it will, I hope that no legislative act may be done beyond a protest against the authority now exercised by Congress and a repeal of our cession.[29]

This proved to be Randolph's last observation on the subject while he was serving in Congress, but the question of Virginia's western land cession would remain a matter of some concern to him in the years ahead.[30]

Randolph was two months into his congressional service before Betsy felt their infant son was finally strong enough to undertake the long and difficult journey to Philadelphia. They arrived in the latter part of

September, only a few weeks before the cold damp days of autumn descended on the city.[31] Randolph was absolutely delighted to have his little family with him, and one can imagine him proudly showing off his firstborn to a less than enthusiastic Madison, a bachelor with an instinctive preference for the less volatile members of the human race. After Randolph had his wife and baby reasonably well settled, he turned his attention once again to his congressional duties, relieved, at last, of the worry for his family's safety.

On October 24, a few weeks after Betsy's arrival, Washington's terse announcement of Cornwallis' surrender at Yorktown was joyously communicated to Congress. Randolph immediately asked for the floor and moved that Congress:

> . . . at two o'clock this day, go in procession to the Dutch Lutheran Church and return thanks to Almighty God, for crowning the allied arms of the United States and France, with success, by the surrender of the whole British army under the command of the Earl of Cornwallis.[32]

The dispatch with its enclosed articles of capitulation was referred to a committee of intelligence of which Randolph was a member. No committee was ever given a more pleasant assignment. They were "to report . . . the most proper mode of communicating the thanks of the United States in Congress assembled to General Washington, Count de Rochambeau, and Count de Grasse."[33] The committee performed its task with enthusiasm and drafted resolutions giving recognition to Washington's "vigor, attention, and military skill," Rochambeau's "cordiality, zeal, judgment, and fortitude," and Grasse's "zeal and alacrity." The committee requested that the articles of capitulation be kept secret for the present.[34] In the first week of November Randolph addressed his first long letter to Governor Nelson since the surrender:

> The capitulation of York will create leisure to our country to weigh the crisis of her situation. I give her present circumstances the appelation of a crisis, because upon the measures which she may now adopt depends her rank in the political world.[35]

Yorktown may well have marked the end of a long and bitter struggle, but for Edmund Randolph it was really just the beginning. In a new nation the future is always more important than the past.

Late in November Washington arrived in Philadelphia to receive a proper welcome from Congress. Somewhat hesitantly it asked him to remain in the city for a short time in order to consult with the committee that had recently been appointed to arrange for the military needs of the nation for the coming year. Washington was only too willing to comply and immediately entered into consultations with the committee. Their report, presented on December 10, warned that the victory at Yorktown would not relieve the nation of its heavy financial burdens because an effective military establishment would have to be maintained during the coming year. British troops still controlled important areas of the country, and there was no guarantee that this one decisive victory would bring about a satisfactory peace. Randolph, who was a member of this committee, was in full agreement with its recommendations.[36]

A few days after the committee report was presented, Randolph was called upon to prepare the initial draft of a circular letter to the states urging their compliance with the recent request of Congress for men and money. Since he had served on the committee on quotas and on the committee on military needs for the ensuing year, he was the logical person for the assignment.[37]

Randolph had entered Congress several months after that body had transferred responsibility for the financial affairs of the Confederation to Robert Morris in the newly created office of Superintendent of Finance. Morris took office in May of 1781, just as Cornwallis was moving into Virginia, and for the next few months the Superintendent necessarily had to devote virtually all of his energies to marshalling supplies for the army. Thus it was not until after the British surrender at Yorktown that Morris could turn his attention to the more basic issue of financial reform.[38]

The broad powers granted Morris at the time of his appointment did not absolve him from the responsibility of securing congressional approval for at least the more important features of his program. It was in this context that Randolph first came to appreciate the extent of Morris' control over the financial affairs of the Confederation. In May, 1781, shortly after taking office, Morris had recommended that Congress establish a national bank. Congress readily complied by authorizing Morris to issue securities, and even allowing him to arrange for the election of a board of directors for the bank.[39] Matters did not progress as smoothly as Morris had expected, however, and it was not until December that the Bank of North America formally applied for its charter of incorporation.[40] To the Superintendent's chagrin, Congress, insisting it had no authority under the Articles to issue the charter, rejected the bank's application. Randolph was named to a committee to acquaint Morris with the constitutional limitations under which Congress was forced to operate. Morris, who had committed his own reputation as well as public funds to this project, had no intention of seeing his work undermined by the constitutional scruples of Congress. He bluntly reminded the committee that Congress had already bound itself to granting the charter by its resolution authorizing the establishment of the bank. To deny the charter at this time, he insisted, was to injure the operations of his public office and to leave the stockholders free to withdraw their subscriptions. Faced with these unpleasant alternatives, the committee drafted an ordinance of incorporation and presented it to Congress on December 29. Its report reiterated Morris' arguments on the necessity of immediate action on the ordinance. Both the committee report and the ordinance of incorporation were the work of Randolph. On December 31 Congress, bowing to the insistent demands of the Superintendent of Finance, passed the ordinance.[41]

Several days later, when a post was available to carry a letter to Virginia, Randolph drafted the delegation's regular letter to Governor Benjamin Harrison in which he reported on recent congressional activities. While scrupulously avoiding any reference to his own role in the events, he carefully categorized the various opinions expressed in Congress on this ordinance of incorporation and closed with the remark, "we hope [the ordinance will] be complied with by the several legislatures."[42] The evidence seems to indicate that Randolph was one of those who, while accepting the bank as a necessity, doubted the constitutional authority of Congress to grant such a charter. His preamble to the ordinance of incorporation, which Congress refused to accept, indirectly admitted that congressional authority in this area was questionable.[43]

Like most of his colleagues in Congress, Randolph was as much a witness as a participant in the formation of financial policy during this period. The decision to transfer much of the responsibility for Confederation finances to Morris had been made before Randolph entered Congress, and the process was well underway by July, 1781, when Randolph arrived in Philadelphia. During the eight months he sat in Congress he saw Morris systematically expand both the power and the prestige of his office. The episode of the ordinance of incorporation dramatically revealed the extent of congressional dependence on his services. The Congress he left in March, 1782, was no longer the master of its own financial house, for Morris was doing what Congress could not do—achieving financial stability by harnessing private credit to the benefit of the Confederation.

In many respects the temporary character of congressional service precluded a normal family life for Edmund and Betsy and their child. They lived in rented accommodations, knew comparatively few people in Philadelphia, and because of the spiraling prices had to live modestly to keep from going into debt. They did have the companionship of Edmund's colleagues in Congress, and presumably many of them, particularly Madison, were frequently dinner guests at their home. Now that his wife was with him, Edmund took a more active part in the social life of Philadelphia—at least to the extent of attending official functions and the occasional dinner party Philadelphians gave for members of Congress. It can be assumed that Betsy would have insisted upon attending the lavish official receptions of the Chevalier de la Luzerne, the affluent French minister to the United States. The city offered concerts and an occasional theatrical production, although financial considerations may have restricted the Randolphs' attendance at these functions. Altogether theirs was not a pleasant or comfortable existence, but it was far superior to the emptiness and worry that came with family separation.[44]

Randolph's association with the diplomatic activities of Congress provided him with a thorough introduction to the several diplomatic problems of the Confederation. Shortly before he arrived in Philadelphia Congress had established a five-member peace commission and had redefined our "ultimata" for peace. The immediate effect of this action was to lessen, for a time at least, the likelihood of a major debate on foreign affairs. Save for the efforts of the French to get the United States to consider a Russian offer of mediation, little of consequence took place during the summer of 1781. It was not until after the British had been defeated at Yorktown that diplomatic matters once again came under congressional review.[45]

On January 9, 1782, a congressional committee under Randolph's chairmanship recommended that the American minister in Paris be authorized to sign a consular treaty with France. This recommendation was the outgrowth of a memorial in July of 1781 from Luzerne which Congress referred to a committee under Randolph's chairmanship. The committee began a long and tedious study of the proposal; however, its progress was necessarily affected by the frequent changes in its membership. The report of January 9, which Randolph wrote, contained a draft treaty and extended comments on Luzerne's memorial. Congress sent the treaty to Luzerne, who suggested certain changes, and a slightly amended version was approved by Congress on January 25. It proved to be the basis for a formal consular treaty with France.[46]

This was but the first of several committee assignments that gave Randolph some insight into the workings of America's expanding diplomatic organization. He also served on a committee on salaries and, a short time later, on a committee that sought to define the functions of the Department of Foreign Affairs. The report of the latter committee laid down the proposition that was ultimately to serve as the formal justification for the establishment of our diplomatic service: "[T]he governing power in the United States should [no longer] . . . remain ignorant of the views and designs of foreign nations."[47]

Randolph's most impressive contribution to the diplomatic activities of Congress did not become public until several months after he had left Philadelphia. On November 17, 1781, the Massachusetts delegation laid before Congress a resolution passed by their state legislature urging Congress to instruct our peace commissioners to insist on firm guarantees for American fishing rights on the banks and coast of Newfoundland in the forthcoming peace negotiations. The issue, which had agitated the New England states for some time, was referred to a committee that reported back to Congress on January 8, 1782. The committee took it upon itself to prepare a formal directive to our peace commissioners instructing them to make France, to whom we had entrusted our cause, "fully sensible of the extent and foundation" of our "desires and expectations." The commissioners were to impress upon the King the great importance we attached to the multiple boundary questions, the preservation of our fishing rights on the Newfoundland banks, the question of confiscated property and the return of Loyalists to America, and the right to enter into any commercial arrangements with foreign powers we might find conducive to our interests. The report was viewed by some as an attempt to enlarge our "ultimata" prior to the opening of formal negotiations. It seemed to be a return to the rigid policy of 1779 when almost every one of these issues was considered by one or the other section of the country as a *sine qua non* to a satisfactory treaty.[48]

On January 22 the report was referred to a new committee composed of Edmund Randolph, Daniel Carroll of Maryland and Joseph Montgomery of Pennsylvania. They were instructed to collect such facts and observations as would support the claims set forth by the original committee. Randolph seems to have assumed much of the responsibility for collecting the requisite information, which involved a careful examination of colonial charters, treaties, a variety of British statutes and the acts of the several colonial assemblies. It was a monumental task which, when combined with his other committee assignments, must have placed heavy demands on his time and energies. The "Randolph 'Facts and Observations'" consisted of a report of some forty folio pages plus a small encyclopedia of supporting documents.[49] Randolph finished his draft of the ponderous report shortly before he left Congress in March, 1782. Before departing, he turned it over to Carroll, who added certain "sundry remarks and observations." Carroll left Congress in May, but passed the report on to Montgomery, the only remaining member of the original committee still in Philadelphia. Montgomery presented it to Congress without alteration on August 16, 1782.[50] The reaction of the delegates varied. Theodorick Bland, Jr., and Arthur Lee of Virginia argued that certain passages in the report cast doubt on Virginia's title to her western lands, while Madison and John Witherspoon of New

Jersey sought to preserve the report in its original form. Madison and Witherspoon recognized by now that to accept the removal of a single "offensive passage" would be to invite an endless list of changes that would ultimately make the report worthless. Bland and Lee, however, would not be silenced, and the debate grew more and more intemperate. A motion to send the material to the Secretary of Foreign Affairs for transmission to our peace commissioners was laid aside, and in its place was substituted a less controversial one—to commit the report to a new committee. Congress seized upon this suggestion as a means of escaping from an unpleasant controversy and the "Facts and Observations" went into the congressional graveyard of unfinished business. The new committee never reported back to Congress.[51]

Randolph, it seems, had decided to return to Virginia as soon as he finished this report. Several factors undoubtedly influenced his decision. First and foremost, Congress would have little to do in the months ahead. The financial problems of the country had been turned over to Morris, and the peace negotiations were, of necessity, in the hands of our diplomatic representatives in Paris. So he would take advantage of the probable lull in congressional business to return to Virginia and attend to the responsibilities of the attorney general's office and his own neglected practice. Friday, March 15, was his last day in Congress. He spent Saturday and Sunday preparing for the long journey home and making a few farewell visits to colleagues. On Monday morning he started for Virginia with his wife and son. The journey to Baltimore was difficult, but the remainder of their trip was comparatively easy. By mid-April, he informed Madison, they had settled in a "humble cottage . . . which forms a contrast with Philadelphia, that nothing can reconcile me to [but?] the presence of my domestic triumvirate, and the pleasures of my library."[52] The ultimate decision as to when or if he would resume his congressional duties was still several months away.

The eight months of congressional service had given the twenty-nine-year-old Randolph a valuable introduction to a rather diverse range of domestic and foreign problems. It was this kind of experience that made him one of Virginia's more knowledgeable young public servants. And, like so many who served in Congress, he returned to Virginia with a decidedly national outlook. However, he soon discovered that the needs of Congress did not always deserve the highest priority, and that in some cases a state must first solve its own problems before helping Congress.

5

National Focus in a Virginia Setting
April–December 1782

O nce back in Virginia Randolph found himself being pulled in two different directions. After eight months of congressional service his sympathies were decidedly national, and he was convinced that representing his state in Congress was the highest form of public service. Yet he discovered that Virginia was anything but a political wasteland. As he found himself being drawn into its problems, he discovered how difficult it was going to be to sort out his priorities. There was, he discovered, important work to be done in both places.[1]

The Virginia to which Randolph returned was different from the one he left in July of 1781. Arnold's raiders were now but a memory; gone, too, was the frightful strain of Cornwallis' invasion when a marauding English cavalry forced the state legislature to take flight; and no longer did a British fleet move with impunity along Virginia's coast. The strain of battle had passed. But Virginia had paid a terrible price for its decisive military victory over the British invader. The prolonged drain on the resources of the state had left it prostrate, and everywhere there was evidence of dangerous economic strain. Virginians knew full well that the future strength and influence of their state could not be secured by basking in the glow of the Yorktown victory. If the state was to pay its war debts, establish its economic solvency and retain its dominant influence in national affairs, it must put its own house in order by accepting the unpopular burdens of heavy taxes and a sound money policy and introducing rigid economies into the operations of its own government. Some hard and perhaps unpleasant decisions faced the leaders of the state during the months ahead.[2]

As Virginia was bracing itself for stringent economies, Congress, equally hard pressed for funds, pleaded with the states to meet their tax quotas under the requisition system.[3] Virginia, not indifferent to this plea and quite cognizant of the many hardships that plagued the central government, insisted nonetheless that it could only offer limited assistance, at least for the present. It was, after all, Virginia, not Congress, that had borne the brunt of the conflict during the final months of the war, and thus the state had to give priority to its own needs over the needs of Congress.

Not surprisingly Randolph began to sense this new emphasis shortly after his return to Virginia. He was quick to discover that with peace the center of political life seemed to be shifting back to Virginia. Virginians were looking to their own legislature rather than to Congress for leadership and seemed more interested in resolving local issues than in immersing themselves in national problems. It was an outlook Randolph was reluctant to endorse, but, good or bad, it seemed destined to breathe new vigor into the political life of Virginia.[4]

Randolph was not alone in his assessment of the current political mood of the state, for two of his congressional colleagues, Arthur Lee and Joseph Jones, were hastening back to Virginia to take their seats in the forthcoming session of the legislature. In time even Madison would abandon his seat in Congress and reenter Virginia politics.[5]

The Assembly became the truest barometer of the mood of the state, for it reflected, as no other branch of government could, the priorities of the electorate. Given the apparent shift in priorities, the present legislature was expected to be composed of men interested in resolving the most pressing problems of the state. How much this attitude might cause them to ignore the needs of Congress remained to be seen. When the first session of the Assembly opened in May, it was discovered that some of the most influential public figures in the state had been elected to sit in its chambers. Randolph informed Madison that among those elected to the House of Delegates were: Arthur and Richard Henry Lee, who were already in Richmond; Patrick Henry who, Randolph learned, would make his appearance somewhat later in the session; and Thomas Jefferson, who had been elected by the citizens of Albemarle to fill one of the two seats of that county.[6] He could also have noted the presence of Dr. Thomas Walker, Meriwether Smith and John Page, as well as the younger faces of James Monroe and Henry Tazewell in the House. In the Senate sat such experienced public servants as Joseph Jones, Archibald Cary, Henry Lee, Joseph Cabell and William Fitzhugh.[7] All had a long and distinguished career in Virginia politics, and their presence was certain to be felt in the forthcoming deliberations of the legislature. Randolph said that the people, "impressed by the embarrassment of the times, have elected the most able men, altho' they did not offer themselves."[8]

Initially Randolph viewed this session with alarm. His greatest fear

was that popularity-seeking delegates would attempt to solve the growing currency shortage by authorizing the issuance of paper money. He
admitted that the presence of Richard Henry Lee would provide some
insurance against such shortsightedness, but his fears were not easily
calmed.[9] In all probability the refusal of Congress to accept the conditions laid down by Virginia for the cession of her western lands would
bring this issue before the legislature once again. The conduct of Congress in this matter (and Randolph was familiar with every last detail of
it) might well cause the Assembly to withdraw its offer to cede these
lands to the central government. The other alternative, and the one
preferred by Randolph, was for Virginia to gather such evidence of its
title as to establish beyond question its right to set forth conditions in its
act of cession.[10]

While the legislature was in session Randolph carefully followed its
deliberations. He even attended some of the sessions and was constantly
weighing the strength of the contending factions. As a member of the
congressional delegation he felt obliged to make himself available to
report on the activities of Congress, yet he recognized that with his
congressional colleague Arthur Lee in the House of Delegates he was not
really needed. If, he informed Speaker John Tyler, the House should
like to be advised of anything that happened in Congress before the
arrival of Mr. Lee in Philadelphia, "I shall be in readiness for their
summons."[11]

When this first session ended, the Assembly had compiled an impressive and, in Randolph's view, a responsible record. It did not adopt a
paper money policy. It did pass legislation which it hoped would provide sufficient revenue to meet at least partially the state's financial
commitments to Congress, as well as to those who had served in the
Continental line, and the wages and salaries of state officials.[12] More
significantly, it did not over-react to the refusal of Congress to accept the
conditions of Virginia's act of cession of her western lands. Instead, in a
remarkable display of patience, it appointed a committee to establish
Virginia's title to these lands so that Congress would understand that
the state had a right to insist on the prohibition of the titles of the land
speculators as a condition of her act of cession.[13] And toward the end of
the session it passed a joint resolution instructing Governor Harrison to
"correspond with the state of Maryland upon the propriety and benefit
to both states of harmonizing as much as possible in the Duties, Imports
or Customs that are or may be laid on Commerce."[14] The resolution
came in response to an invitation from Maryland to join the maritime
forces of the two states in defense of commerce in the Chesapeake. This
was not the last the Virginia Assembly would hear of this project. It

"breathes so much harmony," Randolph informed Madison, "that something of the virulence respecting western territory ought to be abated on this account."[15]

In short, the state's apparent preoccupation with its own affairs was not accompanied by any evidence of indifference to the needs of the country as a whole, and Randolph was quite pleased. It was the kind of atmosphere in which he could work and at the same time feel he was helping sustain the Confederation.

The summer passed quietly, so quietly in fact that Randolph found himself apologizing to Madison for the "barrenness" of his letters. He pleaded lack of news because of the calm that descended on Virginia between the spring and fall sessions of the legislature.[16]

The October session of the legislature, its priorities noticeably altered by the failure of many delegates to attend, was more parochial in its outlook and, to Randolph, a disaster.[17] Generally it confined itself to fairly routine administrative and local legislation that was, at worst, innocuous.[18] The one exception was a bill passed late in the session repealing a law passed by the Assembly in June of 1781 granting Congress the authority to levy a 5 percent duty on imports.[19] This sudden and unexpected repudiation of an earlier legislative commitment to Congress, coming at the very moment a congressional mission was journeying to Rhode Island to literally plead with the recalcitrant leaders of that state to allow Congress to levy a duty on imports, was a bitter pill to swallow. "I begged the gentlemen," Randolph explained to Madison, ". . . to reflect on the present if not perpetual impracticability of executing the scheme of assessment therein prescribed [i.e., the requisition system in the Articles]. . . ." Congress must, he urged, have an independent stable fund. He also noted that European loans could not be expected to serve perpetually as a source of revenue for the payment of our creditors in Europe. But to these and other "reflections" he received the same answer—the act of the Assembly the previous year had been passed without thought and amidst the alarm of war. He was, he reported, powerless to turn the tide. He told Madison that he would probably bear the brunt of the ridicule in Congress and that the comments of the Rhode Island delegates would be merciless.[20]

Was this the policy that resulted from the new political outlook he had detected shortly after his return to Virginia and which he was cautiously beginning to support? To put one's own house in order was one thing; to adhere to a policy which, in Randolph's view, would paralyze the central government was something else again. Randolph unequivocally condemned this repeal of the impost. He knew only too well that the indifference of Rhode Island had already brought the Confederation dangerously close to collapse. He found little evidence of statesmanship in a legislature that was willing to risk everything merely to satisfy what it suspected was the current political mood of Virginia.

With the war over, Randolph found that more than the political mood of Virginia had changed. The conflict, particularly the final months of the struggle, had embittered the populace toward England and those who had helped its cause. In counties that had suffered from British occupation the bitterness of the people toward those who had supplied or sheltered British troops knew no limits. Property was confiscated, homes destroyed, cattle and slaves seized. County authorities, fearing that the animosity of the people would be turned on them if they intervened, dared not halt the attacks on those considered British sympathizers. People were accused indiscriminately and, were it not for the fact that the law restrained the lower courts from hearing cases of treason, scores could have been tried. Fortunately individuals so charged were usually tried by the General Court, which only met in Richmond. Since few complainants were willing or financially able to journey to the state capital to testify, only a small number of persons were actually brought to trial.[21] Those who were formally charged usually fared better than those who were not because Governor Harrison and the Executive Council were generous—some said too generous—in the use of the executive pardon.[22] For the majority, however, there was no assurance that a court of law would clear their names or order the return of property that had been seized or destroyed. Only the cooling of tempers and the warning of the more responsible citizens of the community checked the wave of indignation that swept through parts of the state.[23]

Randolph as a lawyer and as the state's attorney general had little sympathy with those who took the law into their own hands. The practical obstacles to an endless series of treason trials before the Virginia General Court were, for him, welcome barriers to an epidemic of legal witch hunting. His own involvement appears to have been limited to advising the governor as to certain legal technicalities associated with the use of the executive pardon and the handling of several treason cases in the General Court.[24]

While the average person displayed hostility toward those who had cooperated with the British during the last months of the war, many state officials, not wishing to appear lenient in matters involving "the enemy," were concerned about British vessels entering Virginia's ports under flags of truce granted by Congress for the purpose of transporting Virginia tobacco to New York. In May the House of Delegates went so far as to consult Attorney General Randolph on the specific question of whether Congress had the authority to grant a flag of truce under the Articles. Randolph believed it did and so informed the legislature. In fact, the previous year Governor Nelson had specifically instructed Virginia's congressional delegation to secure a passport from Congress to permit Virginia to purchase salt in Bermuda. Was Virginia to recognize congressional authority when it served the interest of the state and deny this authority when it did not? The House, unmoved by Randolph's logic, passed a resolution against this action of Congress. The resolution met with strong opposition in the Senate and was amended "so as to destroy its force." The House ultimately yielded to the Senate position —a shift in attitude that Randolph described as "revolutionary."[25]

No sooner had the Assembly adjourned when a dispute erupted between state officials and one of the ships that had been granted a flag of truce by Congress. Randolph hastened to Williamsburg to investigate the circumstances surrounding the incident. It seems the ship in question had violated the provisions of its flag of truce by bringing British goods into Virginia when, in fact, it only had permission to carry tobacco out of the state. State authorities, sensitive of their rights where Great Britain was concerned, had promptly seized the vessel. After first ascertaining the circumstances surrounding the case, Randolph secured the ship's release. He admitted to Madison that she had brought a considerable quantity of British merchandise into the state, adding:

> . . . if it had not been for my aversion to interrupt the schemes of Mr. [Robert] Morris in the management of finance, and my apprehension lest the enemy should be clamorous and troublesome, if she were condemned without the most direct and pointed evidence—I was so well satisfied with my suspicion that I would have laboured strenuously for confiscating her.

Randolph's patience soon did wear thin. When a second ship violated the provisions of its flag of truce a week later, he libeled her without hesitation.[26]

The return of peace also meant the beginnings of a number of civil cases to recover real or personal property that had been lost or abandoned during the Revolution. Most of these cases involved matters which, of necessity, were under the jurisdiction of the General Court or, if appealed, were argued before the state's highest court, the Court of Appeals. Randolph seems to have had some of these cases, all of them rather routine in nature.[27] Since both of these courts met twice each year in Richmond, their terms running consecutively, all of Randolph's court work was concentrated in April and May and in October and November.[28] Cases involving the recovery of property were certain to multiply in the years ahead and Randolph could not help but recognize that by their very numbers they would provide a rather substantial source of income. The prospect of earning a comfortable living from an extensive private practice could not be overlooked in deciding on his future public career, particularly when it did not preclude a seat in the legislature as well as a continuance in the office of attorney general.

Interestingly enough, it was this latter office that made him one of the principals in one of the most significant cases ever to come before the Virginia Court of Appeals. The case of *Commonwealth vs. Caton et al.* involved the validity of a pardon granted by the House of Delegates to three men found guilty of treason by the General Court. What made the case so significant was that this pardon was perfectly valid if judged by the language of the state's constitution, but insufficient if judged by the language of the state's law against treason passed in October, 1776. It was the first instance where a law of the state was in obvious conflict with the Virginia constitution.[29]

The constitutional impasse created by this conflict between the language of the law and the language of the constitution was succinctly stated by Randolph in July, 1782, shortly after the matter was brought to his attention. It was important to him because as the principal legal officer of the state he knew he would be obliged to represent the commonwealth in court. As he put it in a letter to Madison:

> A late incident will probably try the fortitude of our judiciary, by calling upon them to say, whether a law, contrary to the Constitution, is obligatory. The power of pardoning is delegated to the governor by the act of government [i.e. the Constitution] under two exceptions only: the one, where the prosecution may have been carried on by the House of Delegates, the other, where the law shall otherwise particularly direct. In either of these instances the *House of Delegates* is declared capable of pardoning. The law against treason, passed at a session subsequent to the one which formed the Constitution, strips the governor of all authority to pardon in cases of treason and vests that in the *General Assembly*, and thus interchanges with the Senate the peculiar rights of the other branch of the legislature.[30]

At the opening of the General Court Randolph, representing the commonwealth, moved that the prisoners might be brought up and a new rule made for their execution. Counsel for the prisoners presented the resolution of pardon passed by the House and asked that the prisoners be discharged. Randolph argued that the resolution was invalid and could not operate as a pardon. The court, after first taking the matter under advisement, ordered that it be "adjourned" to the Court of Appeals because of its "novelty and difficulty."[31] On October 29, 1782, the Court of Appeals convened to hear the case of *Commonwealth vs. Caton et al.* Appearing on behalf of the commonwealth was its attorney general, and on behalf of the prisoners Andrew Ronald and Samuel Hardy.[32]

Randolph opened the case, arguing that the pardon was void "as the Senate had not concurred." The clause in the Virginia constitution, Randolph continued, might be read two different ways:

> One was to throw the words, "or the law shall otherwise particularly direct," into a parenthesis, which would confine the separate power of the lower house to cases of impeachment only, and would leave those where the Assembly had taken it from the Executive to the direction of the laws made for the purpose. The other was to take the whole sentence as it stands, and then the construction will, according to the obvious meaning of the Constitution, be that, although the House of Delegates must originate the resolution, the Senate must in all cases concur, or it will have no effect. For it would be absurd to suppose, that the same instrument which required the whole legislature to make a law, should authorize one branch to repeal it.

In either case, Randolph insisted, the result would be the same, the pardon of the House of Delegates would be ineffectual.[33] Edmund Pendleton, the president of the court, saw fit to observe that the cause of the state was argued "fully and learnedly."[34]

Counsel for the prisoners argued that:

> . . . the language of the Constitution embraced both sets of cases, as well as those of impeachment, as those where the Assembly should take the power of pardoning from the Executive: and, in both, that the direction was express that the power of pardoning belonged to the House of Delegates. That the words of the Constitution, and not conjectures drawn from the supposed meaning of the framers of it, should give the rule. That the act of the Assembly was contrary to the plain declaration of the Constitution, and therefore void.

The defense closed with a plea that mercy should incline the court to a construction in favor of preserving life.[35]

Randolph, in reply, insisted that compassion had no place in the case, that the act in question preserved the spirit of the constitution and, whether it did or not, the court had *no authority* to declare it (i.e. the law) void.[36] After the "volunteers at large" had spoken, the court recessed until November 2, 1782, at which time it delivered its opinion.[37]

The court decided that the pardon granted by the House of Delegates was void. The vote was six to two. Justices George Wythe, John Blair, Paul Carrington, Peter Lyons and Richard Cary voted with President Pendleton in the majority. Only Bartholomew Dandridge and James Mercer voted in the negative.[38]

As to the all-important constitutional question, it was decided that the treason law was not in conflict with the constitution. Only Cary,

Wythe, Pendleton and Mercer specifically passed on this question in their opinions. Of these, Mercer's was the most significant. He stated unequivocally that the court *must* declare the constitution superior to this act of the legislature, "that by the former [the] power of pardon was, in all cases, in which the Executive was restrained, reserved to the House of delegates *alone.* . . ."[39] Both Pendleton and Wythe in extended opinions maintained the court had authority to do this, but insisted, with considerable difficulty, that in the present instance the law and the constitution were not in conflict.[40]

Randolph, in reporting the decision to Madison said: "The judges . . . avoided a determination, whether a law, opposing the Constitution, may be declared void. . . ." Then, reflecting on this, he continued: "There surely was prudence in the path which they took. But I doubt not that to any but lawyers the construction *by which the two were reconciled,* would appear intelligible."[41] Randolph had seen the basic incompatibility between the constitution and the law during the preceding summer, and this unflattering assessment of the court's opinion suggests he felt the court should have ruled against the commonwealth. As attorney general and as a self-conscious patriot he probably felt he had a duty to protect the convictions, which he knew were perfectly valid in themselves. As a lawyer he didn't expect to win, believing that the constitution should prevail in instances where the constitution and the law were in conflict.[42]

Randolph's very obvious concern with the direction of Virginia's policy during this period, and his preoccupation with his growing law practice and the increased responsibilities of the attorney general's office, were matched by several less obvious family problems that would ultimately exercise some influence on his future plans. First and foremost was the well-being of his wife Betsy who was expecting another child. Betsy's health was always a source of some worry to Edmund; her various indispositions, whether real or fanciful, seemed to be frequent enough to cause Randolph to be somewhat solicitous about her health. Now that she was carrying another child he was overly apprehensive, particularly as the expected date of birth drew near. Then there was the very obvious decline in the health of his aunt in Williamsburg. "I fear," he wrote to Madison, ". . . that I shall be soon deprived of a second mother and a relation having equal affection and partiality for me as if she had been connected with me by the nearest ties of blood." There were frequent trips to Williamsburg to visit his aunt, followed by hasty returns to his home outside of Richmond as he attempted to watch over both his aunt and his wife.[43] Betsy's "indisposition" ended in October when she gave birth to a daughter whom they named Susan. Edmund was relieved, and delighted at the prospect of raising a daughter. During the next few weeks the proud father never seemed to be able to get much farther from his home than the center of Richmond as he kept a paternal watch over his first daughter. He told his bachelor friend Madison—with some truth—that he was absorbed in the business of the General Court.[44] His aunt's illness was, of course, beyond cure, and he could do little but try and satisfy her simple needs during these final weeks or months of her life.

Apart from his family responsibilities there was also little doubt that Randolph preferred Virginia to Philadelphia as a place to live. The pace was slower and more pleasant, and he and Betsy felt they were among friends rather than acquaintances. Their home outside of Richmond was more than satisfactory; it was a "humble cottage" that permitted him to be "agreeably" surrounded by his family and his library. While there were still shortages in the state, he noted, "we wish for much less than we did whilst surrounded by the luxuries of Philadelphia. . . ."[45] Ambition and national inclinations aside, he was simply happier in Virginia than in Philadelphia. It was home.

As the end of the fall session of the legislature of 1782 drew nearer, Randolph knew that he could no longer postpone his decision on whether to retain or surrender his seat in Congress. As a public person he had an obvious preference for service in Congress, but he also knew that Virginia politics were becoming increasingly important. Then there was his law practice and the increase in the work load of the office of attorney general. Neither was overwhelming at the moment, but both showed signs of becoming more demanding in the future. On another level there was the question of his family responsibilities. The birth of a daughter, the illness of his aunt and the resultant increase of his responsibilities for the management of his uncle's estate, all pointed to an extended residence in Virginia.[46] And last, but not least, there was a significant legislative assignment that remained to be completed.

When the House of Delegates took up the question of Virginia's western land cession at its spring session it had appointed a special committee to collect the necessary evidence to establish Virginia's title to these lands. Named to this committee in the order of their appointments were George Mason, Thomas Jefferson, Arthur Lee, Edmund Randolph and Dr. Thomas Walker.[47] Randolph assumed that Mason, as the first named, would take responsibility for organizing the committee. When first Mason and then Jefferson failed to act, Randolph, who felt the legislature had shown great restraint toward Congress in this matter, took things into his own hands.[48] He asked Arthur Lee to secure copies of certain documents for him in the archives of Congress and offered to serve as an intermediary between the various members of the committee if they would assume some of the burden of preparing the report.[49] Nothing was done during the summer and, with the exception of Lee and Dr. Thomas Walker, no one seemed the least bit concerned about the report. In August Randolph informed Lee that he could not even consider resuming his congressional duties until the pamphlet was "in greater forwardness."[50] By December he had voluntarily assumed complete responsibility for the report and had actually begun drafting it himself.[51] The "vindication,"[52] as he called it, was so important that he felt he should remain in Virginia until it was completed, approved by the other members of the committee and seen through the printers.

On December 10 he so informed the House, asking it to nominate a successor to fill his seat in Congress. To do otherwise was not only unfair to Virginia but also a disservice to a Congress which had a perpetual problem with absenteeism.[53] To Madison he wrote: "It was with *much difficulty* that I prevailed upon myself to take the measure of resignation. . . ."[54] He sincerely meant it.

6

Lawyer and Attorney General
January 1783–August 1786

Not yet thirty years old, Randolph may have hoped that within a year or two he would once again be able to reclaim his seat in the national legislature. He assumed that the report on Virginia's western lands, which he had cited as a reason for resigning his seat in Congress, would be out of the way in a matter of months. The critical question, however, was how long it would take him to achieve the degree of financial independence he needed to reenter Congress. He was moving into a position of preeminence in the legal profession which, with the attorney general's office, would satisfy his financial needs and at the same time sustain his claim to a public career just as soon as circumstances permitted.

Except for a few cases that virtually demanded his undivided attention Randolph usually handled the responsibilities of the attorney general's office in conjunction with his private practice. During the spring of 1783 he did have a case that would have placed extraordinary demands on his time were it not for the fact that he was thoroughly acquainted with the issues under dispute. The *Case of the Loyal and Greenbriar Companies* involved claims to lands within the charter-based boundaries of Virginia which these two land companies were attempting to validate. The case came before the Virginia Court of Appeals in May of 1783. Randolph, representing the state of Virginia, argued that since the conditions set forth in the original grants to these companies had not been fully complied with, and the reasons given for nonfulfillment were insufficient, the request to validate these claims ought to be denied. If, Randolph further insisted, "the claimants had delayed performance of the acts necessary to the fulfillment of the conditions, they must abide by the consequences." The counsel for the land companies responded that there was a difference between a condition upon which a right was to accrue and a condition to defeat a right. The conditions set forth in the grants to these companies were of the latter type and, in equity, required only substantial performance. In the present case, it was insisted, substantial performance had been demonstrated and what remained to be done could be accomplished without any loss to Virginia. The court decided in favor of the companies and ruled their grants ought to be confirmed.[1]

Randolph apparently was disturbed by the decision and felt the court's ruling might make it more difficult for Virginia to settle its differences with Congress on the exclusion of the claims of other land companies in the territory it had offered to cede to the Confederation. As the most active member of the committee that had been appointed to establish Virginia's title to its western lands he felt he should draft a preliminary report on the progress of the committee as a means of reminding the legislature that a defense of Virginia's title to its western lands was being prepared. For some reason, probably his preoccupation with a complex dispute between the state of Virginia and Simon Nathan, his report was not completed until November, 1783.[2] By the time he had transmitted it to the House of Delegates, Congress had restated the terms under which Virginia's cession would be accepted, which caused Virginia to adjust the conditions of its own act of cession.[3] The effect of these concessions was to render Randolph's preliminary report largely superfluous and it was immediately tabled.[4] Virginia ultimately agreed to the cession of its western lands without further consultation with Randolph or the other members of the committee. Some months later, in May, 1784, Randolph informed Jefferson that he was preparing a copy of the "manuscript defence of our claims to western territory" for his approval. He asked Jefferson to correct the "defects of documents" from the sources available to him in Europe.[5] Apparently he was planning to complete and publish the report in strict compliance with the original assignment from the Assembly.

During the summer of 1783, when Randolph should have been working on the report on Virginia's western lands, he found that much of his time was taken up with the "Nathan Case."[6] The case had its origins in an agreement between Simon Nathan and General George Rogers Clark, commander of Virginia's military forces in Illinois country. Nathan had accepted bills of exchange issued by Clark and others under his command in return for furnishing much needed military supplies for Clark's forces. The state unwisely accepted these bills of exchange before obtaining any information from Clark on the scale of depreciation prevailing in Illinois country at the time of the transaction. When this information was received, it was discovered that Virginia had agreed to accept the bills at more than Clark had actually intended. Virginia then attempted to force Nathan to accept payment at a lower rate, but he insisted the state was bound by its original agreement. After a series of moves and countermoves by each side, the dispute was finally referred to a two-man board of arbitration which decided in favor of Nathan. In the spring of 1783 Governor Harrison forwarded the award of the arbiters to the Assembly with a full account of the proceedings up to that time. After reviewing the matter a committee of the House of Delegates recommended that the balance which the arbiters said was due Nathan ought to be paid with interest at 6 percent from June 8, 1780. The House rejected its committee's report and called for further arbitration, naming Attorney General Randolph as Virginia's representative at these hearings.[7]

Randolph approached the assignment with considerable reluctance.[8] Virginia's refusal to abide by the decision of the first board of arbitration did not reflect favorably on the state. It will, said Madison, "require all your eloquence I fear to shield the honor of the state from its effects."[9] Randolph began to collect the necessary documents in July and set off for Baltimore, the seat of the hearings, in early August. He was back in Richmond by the 20th of the month without, he informed Governor Harrison, having been able to settle the claim.[10] Soon after his arrival in Baltimore he had been forced to agree to the nomination of Thomas Jennings as arbiter in place of Daniel Dulany, the original choice of Virginia. This obstacle having been overcome, he found the arbiters unwilling to proceed to a decision until certain additional information had been provided. It was therefore agreed that the parties involved and the two arbiters would meet again on the third Thursday of December at Alexandria.[11]

At the appointed time Randolph went to Alexandria only to discover that Jennings had failed to appear. At Randolph's suggestion, "Mr. Ridgler," the other arbiter (and Nathan's choice at the meeting in Baltimore) was prevailed upon to serve as Nathan's counsel in an effort to resolve the dispute without further delay. "It was then proposed," Randolph later reported to Governor Harrison, "that we should state a case to be submitted to the final decision of Mr. Thomas Jennings, our former arbitrator, and Mr. John Hall, both of Maryland and eminent in the law, and the latter lately elected into Congress. Should they disagree, it was also proposed, that their umpire should decide. I assented to this proposal on condition of the confirmation by the executive, my powers not reaching so far." "This step," he noted, "will throw the business into a proper train, it being stipulated that no counsel shall attend on either side, and that the award shall be in the most solemn form."[12] But the business was not "thrown into a proper train," and in May, 1784, Randolph was still seeking a decision from the governor on whether the Assembly would permit him to abide by the procedures agreed upon at Alexandria.[13] In June the House of Delegates gave its approval.[14] Two years later John Marshall and Cyrus Griffin, who had been subsequently appointed to hear the controversy, decided in favor of Nathan. For some reason their decision also failed to close the case, and the ultimate outcome of the dispute remains shrouded in mystery.[15]

Less than a month after Randolph's trip to Alexandria to resolve the "Nathan Case," Governor Harrison sought his advice on still another complex matter. At issue was the question of whether Virginia was obliged to surrender one of its citizens accused of committing a crime in another state. George Hancock of Virginia had allegedly assaulted a certain Jonas Beard, a justice of the peace and a member of the legislature of the state of South Carolina. The governor of South Carolina, Benjamin Guerard, had demanded that Governor Harrison surrender Hancock to the authorities of South Carolina in order that he might be brought to trial. To support the claim, affidavits were presented as proof of the assault. What made the case particularly sensitive was that the Fourth Article of the Articles of Confederation was made the basis for the demand.[16]

Randolph was quick to recognize that the request placed Virginia in a difficult position. To refuse, he pointed out in his opinion to the governor, would weaken the power of the Fourth Article, while to submit would leave the executive open to the charge of having compromised Virginia's sovereignty and exposed one of its citizens to prosecution on the mere demand of the governor of another state. Randolph believed the state should move cautiously. The governor should take note of the fact that the validity of the charge against Hancock could not be determined from the information presented in the affidavits. He should therefore challenge the demand of South Carolina because of its inadequacy and imprecision. Randolph further advised that he distinguish between the extradition of a fugitive who had fled from his own state after committing a crime and the extradition of a fugitive who had fled into his own state after having committed a crime in a neighboring state. The wording of the article, he insisted, was not meant to deprive a state of the right to protect its own citizens from arrest without preparatory inquiry. The Fourth Article, said Randolph, "operates no further than to procure respect [between states,] not supremacy or infallibility to public acts." A fourth obstacle, he continued, was the significance of the term "high misdemeanor." Was the assault a high misdemeanor, as alleged in Guerard's letter? Not only was Virginia uncertain as to the circumstances of the case, but Governor Harrison had received no information as to whether the alleged act was in fact a high misdemeanor under the laws of South Carolina. Randolph recommended that Hancock not be surrendered to South Carolina authorities.[17]

Either pleased or uncertain of his arguments, he sent a copy of his legal opinion to Madison and a summary of the opinion to Jefferson.[18] Madison replied that he had perused his "observations" with "pleasure and edification." He then proceeded to develop his own views and, although never expressing disagreement, indicated he had little or no sympathy for Randolph's opinion. ". . . the respect due to the chief magistracy of a confederate state, enforced as it is by the articles of Union, requires an admission of the fact as it has been represented." If the explanation is ambiguous or incomplete, then would not mutual confidence call for clarification rather than suspicious and specious refusal? Madison thought so.[19] Randolph did not renew the discussion. The Executive Council accepted his views and advised Governor Harrison not to comply with the request of Governor Guerard.[20] Several months later Randolph informed Jefferson that the demand of South Carolina had been under discussion by the legislature of that state and that the latest accounts indicated that Governor Guerard's conduct had been "abandoned, if not reprehended . . . as the effect of indelicacy and vehemence of temper."[21]

The duties of his private practice were usually far less interesting to Randolph than these state issues. Much of his time was spent in routine matters, such as preparing wills and deeds or advising clients on business or contractual matters. He represented creditors trying to collect debts and debtors trying to prevent foreclosure on their property. He defended criminals and petty thieves, vagrants and members of the gentry, anyone and everyone who sought his services. If fees were important to him, they never seemed to be a barrier to accepting a client. The spring and fall terms of the General Court and Court of Appeals were the busiest weeks of the year for Randolph. During some terms his case load was so heavy he was obliged to be in daily, almost hourly, attendance in these courts. His practice was said to be the largest in Virginia, and his income second only to that of his colleague Henry Tazewell, one of the most distinguished members of the Virginia bar at this time.[22]

This almost obsessive absorption in the law left Randolph physically exhausted for weeks on end and susceptible to all types of respiratory infections. In January, 1784, he was complaining about a "troublesome cold," and in April he wrote to Jefferson: "I have been forbidden by an unusual sensation in my head for some time past, to write a line, which the duties of my profession did not exhort from me."[23] Some time during the year he had the good fortune to acquire an assistant, probably a young man preparing himself for the law.[24] While this aid relieved him of the more routine aspects of his practice, it did not lighten his work load. He now could leave Richmond for weeks without feeling he was neglecting his public office or his established practice in that city, for his assistant could advise him immediately if something of importance arose in Richmond. Thus instead of using his assistant to lighten his work load, Randolph used his services to expand his practice outside of Richmond. The results were predictable. For several months in 1786 he was again plagued by a series of "colds" so severe as to virtually immobilize him for several weeks. In May Joseph Jones wrote:

> The Attorney was indeed in bad health before the [Chancery] Court broke up, being scarcely able to speak loud enough to be heard and was compelled for want of voice, which a severe cold deprived him of, to relinquish the business in Williamsburg. Before it was finished and since his return he has been very ill. He is now better, took the air in his chariot yesterday but in such a state of health as to require much caution to [steer?] clear of danger— he had several [blisters?] on him and at this time can speak only in whispers. I think this attack will make him more cautious in [the] future and not so freely venture [his] health for the sake of money.[25]

From a legal point of view Randolph's most important case during this period stemmed from his private practice rather than his public office. In May of 1786 he appeared before the Virginia Court of Appeals representing Isaac Hite and John Green in one of Virginia's most significant western land cases.[26] The case of *Hite et al. vs. Fairfax et al.* had its origins in the tangled title to the lands of the Northern Neck,[27] the area of Virginia that lay between the Potomac and Rappahannock Rivers and stretched from the Chesapeake back to the quiet reaches of the Shenandoah Valley. In 1735 Virginia's lieutenant governor, William Gooch, issued patents for some fifty-four thousand acres of this land to Jost Hite and Robert McKay in defiance of the earlier proprietary rights of Lord Thomas Fairfax to the whole of this area. Caveats were entered against the issuance of the patents by Lord Fairfax, and under orders of the Privy Council a commission was appointed to establish the true boundaries of the proprietorship.[28] The commission found the lands surveyed by Hite and his associates came within the boundaries of the Fairfax proprietorship.[29] To avoid further confusion—and also to keep Hite and his associates from leaving the lands on which, of course, they would now be obliged to pay quitrents—Fairfax promptly agreed to issue patents to Hite and his associates for the lands in question. When Hite's claims were presented to Lord Fairfax, he refused to issue the patents as promised until new surveys had been made. Fairfax insisted that Hite's surveys of his original claims included only fertile bottom lands and left the less valuable adjacent upland areas isolated and inaccessible. Hite and his associates filed a bill in chancery in the General Court in October of 1749 claiming that Lord Fairfax had refused to issue the patents in conformance with his promise and, moreover, had conveyed a portion of Hite's lands to other persons. In 1769, after the death of both Jost Hite and Robert McKay, an interlocutory decree was entered in favor of the plaintiffs declaring that they were entitled to such lands as they had actually surveyed prior to Christmas, 1735. The decree was confirmed on October 15, 1771, and the court then ordered Lord Fairfax, in accord with his promise, to execute the deeds to the plaintiffs for such lands within the fifty-four thousand acres included in their surveys as were not possessed by any other person prior to 1735.[30]

The Hite interests were not satisfied, however, and after the Revolution Isaac Hite and John Green took the case to the Virginia Court of Appeals. Hite and his associates were appealing such parts of the decree of the General Court of October, 1771, as confirmed the grants made by Fairfax to other parties before the commencement of the suit in 1735.[31] The case was heard in May of 1786. Representing the Hite interests were Randolph and the brilliant John Taylor "of Caroline"; representing the Fairfax interests—including, of course, all those who held disputed land under a grant from Fairfax—were John Marshall, the future Chief Justice, and Jerman Baker. Collectively they spent a total of six days in oral arguments before the court.[32]

Randolph was the first to speak. Working from elaborate notes, he stressed the equity rights of his clients rather than attempting to establish their claims through the stricter rules of real property law. He very deliberately appealed to the conscience of the court in an effort to undermine the more technical arguments likely to be advanced by the Fairfax attorneys. He made much of the fact that the Hite interests had actually brought fifty-four families into the area and that the effect of Lord Fairfax's promise was to persuade Hite to continue his settlement efforts. There would, he insisted, be an obvious unfairness under the judicial interpretation of the scope of the original promise to leave his clients with anything less than the full title to the fifty-four thousand acres in question.

Even in outline form, it is possible to sense his impressive style and subtle coloring as he warmed up to his cause. There were references to Charles II "mimicking majesty," and passing observations to the effect that this was a dispute between "poor farmers" and "rich lords." It was, in fact, a masterful display of his talents as an advocate.[33]

Baker, representing the Fairfax interests, spoke next and argued that the plaintiffs were trespassers since their claims were based on the unauthorized acts of the colonial government, i.e. the patents issued by

Lieutenant Governor Gooch in 1735. Taylor, in the final statement for the plaintiffs, questioned the legitimacy of the Fairfax grant in the first instance, arguing that it was made and confirmed by Charles II and James II, respectively, at times when neither of them was on the throne. He also argued that those who held land under a grant from Lord Fairfax could not plead ignorance of the grant to the Hite interests or Lord Fairfax's subsequent promise to issue new patents to Hite and his associates, for both events were a matter of record. Marshall spoke last and, like Randolph, he relied more on his persuasive rhetoric than on a careful legal argument. After a "bare perusal of the papers," he found it difficult to understand why it was even necessary to defend Lord Fairfax's title. There were references to the "pretensions" of the appellants, while Lord Fairfax's conduct was characterized as above criticism and entirely consistent with his proprietorship. It was a magnificent performance on both sides, for these were experienced and resourceful lawyers and they enjoyed the professional rivalry that such a case inspired.[34]

With the future of virtually the whole northern section of the Shenandoah Valley at stake, the Court of Appeals decided for the plaintiffs. The court ruled that those holding lands from the late Lord Fairfax within the area of the original surveys of Hite and McKay were obliged to surrender the same to the plaintiffs.[35] The decision ended a controversy that had agitated Virginia's western settlements for over fifty years.

One of Randolph's biggest problems as a lawyer was his susceptibility to the requests of friends for free legal advice. He deeply resented their claims on his time and professional talents and, on occasion, he flatly refused to assist them. There was one, however, who was never turned down and whose smallest request became a command. George Washington could lay claim to Randolph's services for as long as the general might need him. Randolph established their relationship soon after Washington returned to Virginia. Replying to a letter from the general, he said:

> I received your favor of the 10th of July by the last post. You will excuse me, I hope, from accepting fees for any business which I may execute for you in the line of my profession. It is indeed a poor mode of acknowledging the repeated acts of friendship, which I have experienced from your hands; but I beg to be gratified in this, the usual way in which lawyers give some small testimony of their attachment.[36]

In the months to follow there were numerous requests from Washington for assistance in unraveling the legal aspects of his complicated and sorely neglected business affairs. There were disputed land titles, the recovery of moneys from the estates of deceased friends who had, in years past, turned to Washington for a loan, and business ventures that required his legal counsel. Randolph always responded without hesitation, more than willing to assist the man whose conduct toward him in 1775 had removed all doubts as to his loyalty to the American cause.[37]

In one of Washington's speculative business ventures Randolph took a particular interest, and even became financially involved himself. Washington, like several other farsighted Virginians of the time, was quick to see the great potential in the development of the James and Potomac rivers as avenues of trade. If properly developed, they could link tidewater Virginia to the Ohio and Mississippi rivers. It was a challenging idea, and several eastern states with navigable rivers were earnestly exploring the possibilities for establishing their own link with the great inland water system. Washington wanted Virginia to be first, and he was particularly anxious that the state work jointly with Maryland on the project. To this end he used his influence to secure the Assembly's support for the development of these two rivers. Randolph, sharing his enthusiasm, seems to have been one of those instrumental in the establishment of the James River and the Potomac River companies. He and Washington exchanged frequent correspondence on the activities of the two companies. Washington served as Randolph's principal informant on the activities of the Potomac River Company, and Randolph performed the same service for Washington insofar as the James River Company was concerned. Randolph approached Washington on becoming president of the latter company, and when he refused, acted as his spokesman at the first meeting of the company's stockholders. At this meeting Randolph was himself elected one of the directors.[38]

The attorney general's private life offered him some relief from the drudgery of his law practice, although even here there were problems and personal sorrow. Randolph never hid the fact that family responsibilities, including certain unexpected financial pressures, influenced his decision to remain in Virginia. The death of his aunt during the winter of 1782–1783 sadly, but irrevocably, solved one of his problems by ending weeks of suspenseful waiting as well as innumerable trips to Williamsburg to see that everything was being done to make her comfortable.[39] Her death, although expected, was a great loss, for Elizabeth Randolph and her late husband had been like second parents to Edmund since his mother and father went to England in 1775. Her passing inevitably left him with a host of legal problems to resolve. Under the provisions of Peyton Randolph's will his estate was to pass to his wife, and on her death to his brother John Randolph, and then to Edmund.[40] No sooner was his aunt laid to rest than certain of his father's creditors began to demand payment of his debts from the estate, and insisted that Peyton Randolph's considerable properties be sold to satisfy these debts. Edmund arranged several meetings with these creditors to see if they would permit the debts to be paid from the income from the estate rather than the estate itself. When they rejected his proposal, he decided to let them take their claims into court, where he felt he might have a better chance of protecting the estate that would ultimately pass into his hands. Anticipating an extended period of litigation with his father's creditors, he concluded there might be certain practical advantages in retaining the office of attorney general while these cases were before the courts.[41]

It was in the midst of his quarrels with his father's creditors—and perhaps because of the demands of these creditors—that he decided to sell his farm outside of Richmond and move into the city. He purchased a home on Shockoe Hill not far from the capitol. The farm, containing some 470 acres, was placed on the market in September, 1783. The advertisement carried an assurance of immediate occupancy. The move to Richmond not only gave him some additional revenue with which to satisfy some of his father's creditors, but it also eliminated the daily six-mile journey into the city.[42]

In May of 1784, some seventeen months after the death of Elizabeth Randolph, Edmund learned that his father had died in England the previous January.[43] As was true in the case of his aunt, the news was not totally unexpected for his father's health had not been good in recent months. He wrote immediately to his mother. Expressing his sorrow and his increased concern for her well-being, he urged her to return to Virginia where she could be assured of his constant attention to her personal and financial needs. If she did choose to remain in England, he promised her that ample funds would be placed at her disposal so that she would not want for anything that money could provide.[44] Consistent with John Randolph's own wish, his body was returned to his native Virginia to be interred in the chapel at William and Mary. Edmund completed all the necessary arrangements, and then journeyed with his family to Williamsburg in December, 1784, to pay his final respects to his father.[45]

The year 1785 found Edmund and Betsy happily awaiting the birth of their third child. When John Jennings Randolph was born in October there was not a prouder family in Richmond.[46] John was a strong and healthy baby, and he brought a new happiness into the Randolph household.[47] Plans were made to have the baby baptized in November, and Madison, who was in Richmond attending the fall session of the House of Delegates, was asked to stand as his godfather.[48] With the birth of their son, Edmund and Betsy began looking forward to the future

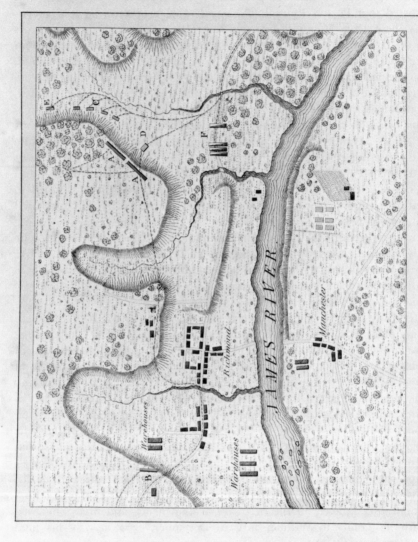

Skirmish at RICHMOND Jan. 5th 1781.

A. Rebel Infantry. B Rebel Cavalry. C. Queen's Rangers. D. Queen's Rangers Cavalry. E. Yager's. F. British Army.

with a little more optimism than they had been able to muster in recent years.

Randolph had become one of the more public-spirited citizens of Richmond. In 1785 he was named deputy grand master of the Virginia Lodge of Masons. Because James Mercer, the grand master, was in poor health many of the responsibilities of his office were thrust upon Randolph. Including among these was helping to oversee the construction of a new Masonic Hall in Richmond, of which the cornerstone was laid in October, 1785. Motivated not only by a sense of responsibility but also, apparently, by a natural curiosity about every last detail in the construction process, Randolph took great interest in the project.[49]

In addition Randolph was also actively interested in plans for the construction of a new capitol in Richmond. Jefferson, then in Paris, had been asked to secure an architect to design the building. By the time this request reached Paris and had been complied with, the state had already started constructing the building. When Jefferson learned of the impetuousness of the state's officials, he immediately asked Randolph to intercede, urging him to use his influence to halt construction until the architect had completed his work. The resulting design, Jefferson assured him, would be well worth the delay. Randolph was not wholly successful. A "strong party" in the Assembly, he reported, was trying to halt the construction completely, and the directors, despairing of ever receiving the plans from Jefferson's architect, had adopted the strategy of beginning construction immediately lest the whole project be scuttled. Months later, when the plans finally did arrive from Europe, it was decided to adapt them to the construction already completed. "To pull up all that had been done, would have been to strengthen the opposition," Randolph informed Jefferson. He would, however, direct Mr. Dobie, the superintendent of the project, to furnish him with a narrative of the proceedings "in technical language," which he would immediately forward to Jefferson.[50]

The Randolphs also had a more active social life now that they lived in the city. Since he was attorney general and one of Richmond's most prominent citizens, Randolph and his wife entertained frequently. This was not only expensive—for Betsy was inclined toward very formal and elegant dinners—but also, according to St. George Tucker at least, a bit stuffy. Writing to his wife on April 3, 1786, he observed:

> I had the honor yesterday of dining with Mr. Attorney. When I entered the room the whole court and bar were seated in [*sic*] their tables—not another person in the room—I told the Attorney that I thought at first I had mistaken his invitation and had gone to a funeral. I thought he did not much relish

the joke. Baker, Warner, Lewis and myself (who went together) were the only guests in colours.[51]

The spring of 1786 was particularly busy for Randolph. The Hite case was before the Court of Appeals—visible evidence of his extensive private practice. His case load was far too heavy for one person to handle and the lack of proper rest and probably of adequate meals ultimately caught up with him and he was in and out of bed with a series of violent colds. He never had the leisure to recover from one before being laid up by another.[52] At Betsy's insistence, plans were made for an extended vacation just as soon as the Court of Appeals closed. The family was happily preparing for their trip while Edmund handled his remaining cases on the court's calendar. Everyone looked forward to several weeks of rest and relaxation away from the oppressive heat of Richmond. And then came the most crushing tragedy of all—the unexpected and unexplainable death of their baby.[53]

Edmund and Betsy were paralyzed with grief. When their eldest son Peyton was born, they had several anxious months worrying over his obviously frail health, but Susan and John were such healthy babies at birth that they never even considered the possibility that anything might happen to either of them. John's death was the most shattering experience in their ten years of married life; it was a void they felt could never be filled.

7

Catalyst of the Annapolis Convention
September 1786

For weeks Randolph, unwilling to do anything except console and comfort his grief-stricken wife, was enveloped by a mood of depression. He failed to fulfill the minimal duties of the attorney general's office, he ignored his law practice and he lost absolutely all interest in public affairs. Letters went unacknowledged and probably unread. It was a dangerous and an unhealthy frame of mind, and the deliberate inactivity only served to prolong and deepen his depression. It was most fortunate, therefore, that a matter in which he had always had great interest was about to be made the subject of an important interstate conference. Early in September delegates from several states were scheduled to meet in Annapolis, Maryland, for the purpose of devising a uniform system of commercial regulations for the states, and Randolph had been nominated to head the Virginia delegation. When the time arrived, he had no choice but to attend.

The scheduled conference grew out of the efforts of Virginia and Maryland to promote the joint development of their common waterways. As early as 1782 the Virginia Assembly had made provisions for regular discussions with Maryland regarding the defense of the Chesapeake. With the formation of the Potomac River Company a few years later, cooperation became a virtual necessity. It was impossible for the dream of connecting the Potomac with the Ohio to become a reality without close cooperation between the two states.[1] In June, 1784, the Virginia legislature passed a resolution appointing commissioners to meet with commissioners from Maryland, "to frame such liberal and equitable regulations concerning the . . . [Potomac] River as may be mutually advantageous to the two states." The resolution went on to name Edmund Randolph, James Madison, George Mason and Alexander Henderson as Virginia's commissioners.[2] During the fall session of the Assembly the subject was again considered, and, at the initiative of the lower house, new resolutions were passed to enlarge the authority of the commissioners. They were now instructed to communicate with Pennsylvania to seek its cooperation in this common venture.[3]

To these more recent moves of the legislature Randolph was a complete stranger, although he normally displayed an unusual concern for legislative matters. More serious was the fact that Governor Patrick Henry, who had been elected in November, 1784, to succeed Benjamin Harrison, had failed to act on the resolutions, with the result that the four commissioners were never notified of their appointments nor of the subsequent resolutions empowering them to communicate with Pennsylvania. In Maryland, by contrast, as soon as the legislature appointed its commissioners, Governor William Paca wrote to Governor Henry suggesting that the commissioners of the two states meet in March, 1785, at Alexandria, Virginia. Receiving no reply from Henry, Governor Paca mistakenly assumed that Virginia was satisfied with this arrangement and would have its commissioners in Alexandria at the appointed time. When the time for the meeting arrived, only Mason and Henderson were present and both men had learned of their appointment by accident.[4]

Assembled by chance, the two Virginians waited several days for Randolph and Madison to appear, Mason stubbornly refusing to proceed without them. Realizing, however, that the Maryland delegation would be "much disgusted" if something wasn't done, the two Virginians finally agreed to open discussions and, at the invitation of Washington, they adjourned to Mount Vernon for their meetings. There, in an amicable atmosphere, the foundations were laid for an annual conference between the two states.[5] It was the most that could have been hoped for, given the circumstances.

Randolph learned of all this later, and in July he wrote to Madison:

> Our apparent disobedience to the appointment of the assembly must be ascribed [to] the forgetfulness of our friend Henry. Genl. Washington having inquired from me the reason for our non-attendance at the time and place marked for the conference by the government of Maryland, I immediately applied to the govr. for information, whether he had communicated the resolve of that state to the deputies. He could not recollect; but seemed anxious to avail himself of the probability of having inclosed it to you with several other public papers. Even Mason and Henderson knew nothing of the meeting; and would have been absent but for the activity and urging of the general.[6]

When the Assembly met in October, 1785, Mason and Henderson filed a written report with the speaker of the House which summarized their conversations with the Maryland delegation. They also transmitted a copy of the compact they had agreed to and the letter that had been sent to Pennsylvania.[7] Mason, who had intended to explain the conduct of the Virginia commissioners, was obliged to forego the trip to Richmond because of poor health. He asked Madison if he would assume responsibility for informing the House of the chain of circumstances that had kept the commissioners in virtual ignorance of their assignment.[8] The Assembly was quick to recognize that inefficiency rather than indifference accounted for Virginia's limited role in the conference and that what had been accomplished was indeed commendable given the circumstances under which the conference met. By January 4, 1786, both houses of the Assembly had approved the compact and recommendations of the conference.[9]

But events were soon moving toward an even more ambitious scheme —a conference of delegates from several states to seek solutions to their common problems. The Maryland legislature not only ratified the report of its commissioners but also proposed that Delaware as well as Pennsylvania be invited to participate in the future meetings the Mount Vernon Conference had recommended be established on an annual basis.[10] Although deeply embroiled in debate on several other issues of vital importance to the state,[11] the Virginia House of Delegates was quick to seize upon the idea and to propose a still more ambitious venture. On January 21, 1786, it passed a resolution extending an invitation to all states to meet:

> . . . to take into consideration the trade of the United States; . . . to consider how far a uniform system in their commercial regulations may be necessary to their common interest and their permanent harmony; and to report to the several states such an act relative to this great object, as, when unanimously ratified by them, will enable the United States in Congress effectually to provide for the same.[12]

Engineered by Madison, this resolution gave an entirely new meaning to the modest proposal for annual meetings.[13] For this new venture the legislature named Randolph, Madison, Walter Jones, St. George Tucker and Meriwether Smith.[14] Randolph, by virtue of being named first in the resolution, was considered to hold seniority over his colleagues. Not one to ignore an opportunity to implement a project of which he approved, he promptly dispatched a memorandum to Governor Henry requesting an authentication of the resolution of the legislature in order that a correspondence might be immediately opened with the governors of the other states.[15] On March 1 he wrote Madison:

> . . . Annapolis is the place, and the first Monday in Sep. the time for our convention. That city was preferred as being most central and farther re-

moved from the suspicion, which Phila. or N. York might have excited, of congressional or mercantile influence.[16]

Randolph spent the next few months energetically organizing the Virginia delegation. He even employed the services of former Governor Benjamin Harrison in an effort to arrange a meeting of the Virginia delegates prior to the Annapolis meeting.[17] His efforts were frustrated by the hopeless inefficiency of the mails and, more seriously, by the apparent indifference of some of the state's appointees to the goals of the meeting. By the end of May he was certain only of Madison's and St. George Tucker's attendance. Equally disturbing were the reports that were circulating regarding the indifferent response in several of the other states.[18] Randolph was not overly optimistic, but he had done all he could. Fortunately he had fulfilled this aspect of his assignment before the unexpected death of his infant son, for the weeks that followed were enveloped in sorrow and silence. It was not until he actually arrived in Annapolis that he again showed any interest in the purposes of the conference. Actually the meeting proved to be a blessing in disguise, rekindling his ambition and reviving his interest in public life, particularly in efforts directed toward strengthening the central government.

Virginia watched with only mild curiosity as the delegates from the various states began to converge on Annapolis, a quiet and peaceful community on the banks of the Severn River. The delegates took their lodging and meals at George Mann's City Tavern, the most comfortable accommodations in town. They held their meetings in the Senate chamber of the State House, which Maryland had placed at their disposal.

In response to Virginia's invitation, New Hampshire, Massachusetts, Rhode Island, New York, New Jersey, Pennsylvania, Delaware and North Carolina had appointed delegates to the convention; but Connecticut, South Carolina, Georgia and, most surprisingly, Maryland itself, had failed to do so.[19] While most state leaders could generally sympathize with the purposes of the convention, there were many who were less than enthusiastic over the prospect of holding a convention at this time. Some of them feared it would only serve to undermine the Confederation and the current move to vest Congress with authority to regulate trade for fifteen years. Others suggested that the Virginia resolution was too ambitious in its intent and would be thwarted by the absence of so many states.[20]

Little did these prophets of failure realize how close their expectations came to being realized. When the first session opened on Monday, September 11, only twelve delegates from five states were present. It was a sad commentary, indeed, on the degree of cooperation that could be elicited from the states and on the extent of the delegates' commitment to the objectives of the convention. Virginia was represented by Randolph, Madison and Tucker; from New York came Alexander Hamilton and Egbert Benson; from New Jersey, Abraham Clark, William C. Houston and James Schurman; from Pennsylvania, Tenche Coxe; from Delaware, George Read, John Dickinson and Richard Basset.[21] Randolph had made the acquaintance of several of these men during the months he had served in Congress, but the others were complete strangers to him.

It became evident almost immediately that the commercial objects of the meeting could not be fulfilled. Only three states—Virginia, Delaware and New Jersey—had enough members present to fulfill the minimum delegation requirements established by their respective legislatures.[22] After John Dickinson of Delaware had been selected chairman and the credentials of the delegates had been reviewed, a committee consisting of Egbert Benson, chairman, and Coxe, Clark, Read and Randolph was appointed "to consider of and report the measures proper to be adopted by this Convention."[23]

When the committee met, Randolph was asked to try his hand at preparing a first or preliminary draft of the kind of recommendations the committee might submit to the full convention.[24] The "Randolph Draft Report" opened with a simple factual account of the states that had and had not sent delegates. This was followed by the observation, later deleted, that Maryland had omitted to appoint commissioners for some unknown reason though it was "certain however that this state, as well as those [remaining?] whose proceedings no notice has been [received?], are strong in their support of federal government."[25]

Next came a series of brief paragraphs quoting the exact language of the formal resolutions defining the nature of the authority granted to each state delegation. Each state had given its delegates authority to enter into some form of an agreement to establish a uniform system of commercial regulations among the states. But the New Jersey delegation was also given the authority to consider "other important matters [as] may be necessary to their common interest and permanent harmony."[26]

The "Randolph Draft Report" then went on to suggest a course of action the convention might follow:

> Resolved, therefore, that it is the opinion of your committee, that the commissioners, now assembled, have no authority to execute the business, expressed in the several resolutions ~~which appointed them~~. of appointment. [*sic*]

Resolved that it is the opinion of your committee that [— — — ?] commissioners ought to meet in the city of Phila., on the 10th day of May next, for the purposes expressed in the several resolutions of appointment.

Resolved, that it is the opinion of your committee, that a committee be appointed to prepare and report an address to the several states, stating the particulars of the foregoing report—urging the necessity of a meeting to be held in Phila. on the 10th day of May next for the ~~purpose above mentioned~~, and submitting to them, how far it may be expedient to ~~authorize~~ vest their future commissioners with *powers, coextensive with those now given by New Jersey.* [*sic*][27]

The reaction of the Benson Committee to the "Randolph Draft Report" can only be inferred from the final report of the committee. The absence of so many states, the Benson report observed, made it "inexpedient" for the convention to proceed to the business committed to them; "nevertheless the object of the present meeting appears to the Committee of too much importance . . . not to be pursued, and under this impression the Committee think it will be proper to recommend, in strong terms, a further meeting of commissioners of all the states." Since, the report continued, "the matter intended for the consideration of this Convention would essentially affect the whole system of federal government, and the exigencies of the United States, in other respects, are of such a nature as to render it advisable that the commissioners, who may be appointed for the proposed meeting, should be authorized to deliberate on *all such measures* as may appear to them necessary to cement the union of the states. . . ." In the light of these facts the committee submitted the following resolution:

That a Committee be appointed to prepare an address to the several states stating the reasons which have prevented the commissioners now assembled from proceeding, at this time, in the business entrusted to them, recommending a future meeting of commissioners at   on the   day of   next, to be vested with power, and submitting to the state the propriety of extending the powers to be given to the future commissioners *to every other matter* respecting the Confederation, and that the commissioners of such future meeting be instructed to report to the United States in Congress assembled, agreeable to the 13th article of the Confederation.[28]

After the report of this committee had been accepted by the full convention, then a second committee, apparently under the chairmanship of Alexander Hamilton, was appointed to prepare the "address to the several states." On September 13 the delegates assembled to hear the "address," which became the only formal pronouncement to emerge from the convention.[29]

Analyzing the authority granted to the respective state delegations by their legislatures, the "address" noted that the New York, Pennsylvania and Virginia resolutions were essentially similar, while those of Delaware and New Jersey had significant differences. Delaware's resolution contained the explicit provision that any act framed by the convention must be reported to Congress, accepted by it and then confirmed by every state legislature before taking effect. Far more significant was the New Jersey resolution since that state gave its delegates substantially greater authority by empowering them "to consider how far a uniform system of commercial regulations *and other important matters* might be necessary to the common interest and permanent harmony of the several states." This, the "address" continued, "was an improvement on the original plan and will deserve to be incorporated into that of a future convention." Since the defects "in the system of Federal Government" are more numerous than those implied by the resolutions from most of the states, "your commissioners are of opinion that a convention of deputies from the different states, for the special and sole purpose of entering into this investigation and digesting a plan for supplying such defects as may be discovered to exist" should be preferentially considered by the respective states. Therefore:

> . . . your commissioners . . . beg leave to suggest their unanimous conviction, that it may essentially tend to advance the interests of the union, if the States . . . [would concur] in the appointment of commissioners to meet at Philadelphia on the second Monday in May next, to take into consideration the situation of the United States, *to devise such further provisions as shall appear to them necessary to render the constitution of the Federal Government adequate to the exigencies of the Union. . . .*[30]

It would appear that the "Randolph Draft Report," written, one must conclude, soon after the Benson Committee was appointed, had set forth rather clearly the basic points that ultimately came to be identified with this convention. The group as assembled could do nothing about the matters entrusted to it; therefore it should recommend that the states send delegates to another convention, and the delegates appointed to this future convention should be given the same broad powers that were granted to New Jersey's delegation at this convention. With some slight variations the Benson Committee reiterated each of these points in its report, and the committee that prepared the "address to the states" then gave formal expression to these ideas. It would be imprudent to suggest that Randolph was the architect of the proposals that emerged from the Annapolis Convention, but it would be folly to state that he had little or nothing to do with the ideas found in the famous "address to the states." The essential points of that address were determined by the convention before being committed to a drafting committee, and all of them can be found in the first rough document to be prepared at that convention—the "Randolph Draft Report."[31]

the delegates dispersed. Each one was publicly committed to work for a

When the "address" was given final approval by the full convention, new convention. Hamilton and Madison journeyed northward together, Hamilton to New York and Madison to Philadelphia for a short stay.[32] Randolph returned to Richmond. But first he stopped at Mount Vernon to give Washington a full account of the proceedings. It can be assumed that Washington was pleased with the recommendations of the Annapolis Convention, especially in the light of its limited attendance. Randolph undoubtedly would have preferred to linger several more days at Mount Vernon, for the congenial atmosphere and hospitality of Washington's pleasant home on the Potomac were always difficult to resist. Regrettably the duties of his profession necessitated an immediate return to Richmond where the General Court was about to open. Although heavy rains slowed his progress, he was back in the capital by the third week of September.[33]

8

Governor of Virginia: A New Challenge
October 1786–April 1787

October brought Richmond back to life after an unusually warm summer which had forced many of its more prominent citizens to leave the city. As usual, the opening of the fall session of the legislature signaled the revival of political life in the city. As the delegates began arriving at the inns and boardinghouses, Randolph sought out his many friends in the legislature in an effort to secure support for the recommendations of the Annapolis Convention. He didn't anticipate problems, but he hoped the legislature would be unequivocal in its endorsement. These conversations with his friends proved to be more significant than he had expected. He discovered that many of the delegates considered him the most logical candidate to succeed Patrick Henry as the state's next governor.[1] If the sentiments of his friends reflected the views of a majority in the House and Senate, he would be forced to make some significant adjustments in his life. The Senate's inability to conduct business because it lacked a quorum delayed the decision for a few weeks, but on November 7 the two houses, by joint ballot, elected Edmund Randolph Esq. governor of the state of Virginia.[2]

One of the first to write to him after his election was Washington. His note of congratulation was anything but optimistic because of his doubts about the future:

> Our affairs seem to be drawing to an awful crisis: it is necessary therefore that the abilities of every man should be drawn into action in a public line, to rescue them if possible from impending ruin. As no one seems more fully impressed with the necessity of adopting such measures than yourself, so none is better qualified to be entrusted with the reins of Government.[3]

In his reply Randolph admitted that he had many misgivings about accepting the office:

> I am sensibly affected by your friendly congratulations. You will readily, I hope, believe, that I class them among the auspicious events of my life.

But in truth more difficulties are in prospect, than prudence ought to have prompted me to encounter. The nerves of government seem unstrung, both in energy and money: and the fashion of the day is to calumniate the best services, if unsuccessful. What then am *I* to expect? Not much of approbation I fear; I must be content to ward off censure. However, I shall offer myself to these risques without shrinking, and make the motives atone for the miscarriages in the execution.

He added:

The part, which I purposed to take in your affair with the Hites, would have been perfectly consistent with my duty to them. But my new arrangement has rendered it unnecessary to enter now into the detail, as my lips are closed as to a profession, which from the earliest moment of my life I abominated, and from which I was determined to escape, as soon as I was possessed of a competence.[4]

He could not help but believe that the governorship of the state of Virginia offered a greater challenge than the dull routine of the legal profession, and the year ahead seemed likely to be an eventful one. He resigned as attorney general and with absolutely no regrets turned over his considerable private practice to John Marshall.[5] He took the oath of office on December 1, 1786.[6]

Randolph knew that the office he was assuming had very limited powers. The Virginia constitution of 1776, like most of the state constitutions written during the early years of the republic, had systematically stripped the office of governor of much of the power it had possessed during the colonial period. The language of the constitution was quite explicit:

. . . he [i.e., the governor] shall, with the advice of a Council of State, exercise the executive powers of government according to the laws of this commonwealth; and shall not, under any pretence, exercise any power or prerogative by virtue of any law, statute, or custom of England. . . .[7]

Beyond this essentially negative definition of the authority of the office, the only specific power held by the governor under the constitution was that of granting pardons, and even that was circumscribed by certain restrictions.[8] The salary was £800 per year, four times what Randolph had received as attorney general.[9] It was less than he needed, but, judging from his reference to the subject in his letter to Washington, he apparently considered it adequate for at least a year or two.[10]

Fortunately the Council of State, with which he shared his executive powers, was composed of men he had known for many years. Joseph

Jones had served with him in Congress and was a close confidant of both Randolph and Madison. Carter Braxton, probably the most conservative member of the Council, was a contemporary and close friend of his late father and uncle. In point of years of service the senior member of the Council was Bowling Stark, the former state auditor who had been serving on the Council since 1778. Dr. James McClurg, a physician by profession, was also an old family friend. He had grown up in Williamsburg and, like Randolph, had moved to Richmond after it became the seat of government. The president of the Council and the lieutenant governor of the state was Beverley Randolph. He was a year younger than Edmund, and again, a friend of many years. Completing the Council were Sampson Mathews, Miles Seldon and James Wood. Of the three, Wood, having served with distinction in the Virginia militia as well as the legislature, was the most experienced and probably the most influential. As president of the Society of the Cincinnati in Virginia, he was a man of considerable power within the state.[11] Aside from the Council of State, the immediate staff of the executive consisted of three clerks: a drawing clerk to draft the official documents emanating from the office of the executive, a copying clerk and a clerk of foreign correspondence. It was a more than adequate staff given the authority of the executive, but it was something less than satisfactory for the many assignments Randolph found for it.[12]

The governor's house was a "wooden structure" on Shockoe Hill that was considered only a temporary residence.[13] Randolph's predecessor did not hesitate to criticize the accommodations, and after he moved, the Council of State authorized such repairs as the state's contingency funds would warrant.[14] Since the Randolphs already had a comfortable home on Shockoe Hill, it might be safe to conclude that they did not move into the governor's residence immediately.[15] If so, their home life would have been little disturbed by Edmund's new office. Obviously they had to do a certain amount of official entertaining and perhaps there was an increase in the number of house guests, but their style of life did not radically change. Randolph was, after all, a prominent member of the community, and the governorship added little to the social standing of his family.[16]

Randolph took his seat on the Council of State with few illusions about the office to which he had been elected. He knew enough about government procedure to realize that efficiency, initiative, persuasion and sound administration were all legitimate instruments of power. He would use each of them to expand the influence of his office. His approach is revealingly illustrated by a memorandum book he kept while governor. Begun on November 30, the day before he took the oath of office, its daily entries indicate not only the volume and variety of the business that crossed his desk but also the procedures he followed in handling the duties of the executive. Daily, each letter, memorandum or petition that he received was noted in his book on pages that had been divided into six columns labeled "Time," "Subject," "Advice," "To be Done," "Done" and "For Assembly or Congress." Notations under the fourth, fifth and sixth of these headings provided him with a rather simple yet useful method for keeping track of everything that came across his desk. Days, weeks or even months might pass before the broad-penned "X" appeared in the "Done" column, ending all further consideration of that particular entry. Matters that had to be brought to the attention of the Virginia Assembly or Congress carried an entry in the last column, and these usually took much longer to resolve. Randolph's "memorandum book" did not necessarily make the cumbersome machinery of government function more smoothly, but it did bring some efficiency into its operations as department heads began to receive gentle reminders that an earlier request had not as yet been complied with.[17]

The first step in this move toward greater efficiency came within days of his election to the Executive Council. Orders, in fact meticulous instructions, were sent to the heads of the various departments on the procedures they were to observe in filing reports and maintaining the records of their departments.[18] A circular letter was sent to the appropriate county official demanding a full report on the status of the militia in that county. The importance of the subject, Randolph very pointedly observed, will "operate with you, as an irresistible reason, why the information now desired should not be delayed for a moment."[19]

Next came a formal tour of Virginia's naval installations. With unheard of zeal he spent several weeks inspecting the naval facilities at York, Hampton and Norfolk. He took careful and elaborate notes and submitted detailed recommendations to the Executive Council upon his return. The Council spent several days reviewing his findings and, in conformance with a law passed at the previous session of the legislature, drafted very detailed instructions on the manner in which the naval officers should report to the executive.[20] Within a matter of weeks virtually every state official was made acutely aware that Randolph was embarked on a determined assault on the complacency and inefficiency in the various departments of state government.

Of the many problems Randolph inherited from his predecessor one of the most vexing was the unstable condition of the Virginia frontier. Shortly after he assumed office he was confronted with a serious political crisis arising from the military exploits of General George Rogers Clark. Governor Henry had authorized Clark, then a resident of the Kentucky district, to organize a force of Kentucky militia and undertake an expedition against the aggressive Shawnee and Wabash tribes living along the Great Miami and Wabash rivers. Clark, who had earlier sought the support of Congress for this expedition, began to organize the militia in September, 1786, using Clarksville as his base. When adequate forces had been assembled, he dispatched Colonel Benjamin Logan along the Great Miami while he took the remainder of the militia up the Wabash. Logan successfully executed his assignment, but Clark suffered a serious setback. As he was moving northward up the Wabash, his forces mutinied and deserted him in large numbers. He was forced to retreat to the relative safety of Vincennes without ever having engaged the Indians. Here, with the remnants of his forces, Clark attempted to cover his disgrace by negotiating for the pacification of the area. When the Indians rejected his offer, he decided to hold the post for the winter and reopen negotiations with them in the spring. While wintering at Vincennes, he found it necessary to enlist men and commandeer supplies, including items reputedly owned by Spanish subjects trading in the area.[21]

Clark's action led several leading citizens in the Kentucky district to file a formal protest with the governor, a move inspired in some measure by political opposition to Clark. The memorial was sent from Danville on December 22, 1786, and carried sixteen signatures, including those of James Wilkinson, Thomas Marshall and Harry Innes, three of the most powerful political figures in the area. The memorialists suggested that the property in question had been seized for private use, that Clark was unfit to retain his command because of his excessive drinking habits and that the assembled militia were to be used against the Spanish at Natchez instead of the Indians.[22] The memorial reached Randolph in February and placed him in an extremely embarrassing situation. Since January he had been trying to get Congress to assume the cost of this expedition and had instructed the Virginia delegates to work toward this end. He had even gone so far as to transmit a personal letter to the president of Congress on the subject.[23] Now the memorial of protest, substantiated by other letters, clearly indicated Clark had exceeded his authority, particularly in the seizure of Spanish property.[24]

The Council of State labeled Clark's actions "an offence against the law of nations," and ordered that all information as to his activities be immediately transmitted to Congress. The Virginia delegates were instructed to urge Congress to arrange for the signing of a treaty with the tribes in question, and the Council recommended that General James Wilkinson, Colonel Richard Anderson and Colonel Isaac Shelby, all residents of the Kentucky district, be immediately appointed commissioners to undertake this assignment. In addition, the Council notified Clark of their disavowal of his acts and ordered James Innes, the attorney general, to take legal action against those charged with seizing Spanish property. A formal proclamation was issued by the Council so that the state's actions might be publicized as widely as possible.[25] Randolph assumed personal responsibility for executing the directives of the Council, and the following October he gave the Assembly a full account of what had transpired.[26]

Randolph and the Council had, unknowingly, worked a profound change in the political leadership of Virginia's frontier settlements. Although the charges against Clark were never pressed, he did lose most of the influence he had had in the Kentucky district. By contrast, General Wilkinson's prestige was enhanced considerably by the incident. It was a change that would affect not only the future of Kentucky but also the relations between the United States and Spain in the years to come.

The governor's principal concern during the winter of 1786–1787 was how the country would respond to the Annapolis "address."[27] From all corners of the land came word of growing unrest: of Daniel Shay's leading a group of angry farmers in Massachusetts, of courts and legislatures being threatened by mobs in Vermont and New Hampshire, and of new and more determined efforts to introduce a paper money policy in several states that had been able to avoid it up to this time. No state appeared to be immune from the disturbances, and the situation in Rhode Island bordered on anarchy. Therefore, like everyone else who believed that the Confederation was perilously close to collapse, Randolph watched approvingly as the various state legislatures endorsed the Annapolis "address" and named their delegates. He was as concerned as Madison over the apparently deliberate refusal of the New York and Massachusetts legislatures to take any action. Madison kept him remarkably well informed of events in Congress and fed his crisis-ridden image of the times by viewing with alarm virtually everything that ran contrary to the avowed objects of the proposed convention.[28]

Randolph, of course, was no Madison; he could do little to influence state leaders outside of Virginia. But he could help to circularize the November 23 decision of the Virginia legislature which unanimously endorsed the call for a new convention and, more particularly, he could implement the December 4 resolution which named the members of the Virginia delegation.[29]

The legislature elected an impressive delegation: Washington, Henry, Randolph, John Blair from the Court of Appeals, James Madison, George Mason, the author of the Virginia constitution of 1776, and the distinguished jurist George Wythe. If all of these men could be persuaded to serve, Virginia would have a most influential representation for the proposed convention.[30]

Two days after the legislature named the members of the Virginia delegation Randolph wrote to each of them informing him of his selection.[31] The letters, drafted hurriedly by an executive who was bent on making his office a model of efficiency, were generally rather brief and formal. But to one letter Randolph gave particular attention. General Washington could not be merely informed of his appointment; he had to be treated with great deference and, more important, encouraged to accept. Randolph knew that if Washington agreed to lead the Virginia delegation it would serve notice on all the other states that Virginia was unequivocal in its support of the proposed convention. He was well aware that Washington had a passion for retirement and, what was worse, a sense of honor that would incline him to abide by his announced decision never again to accept a public office. The younger Virginian and former aide-de-camp had to convince rather than cajole: "The inefficiency of Congress you have often felt in your official character; the increasing langour of our associated republics you hourly see; and a dissolution would I know be a source of the deepest mortification."[32] The letter was a masterly blend of deferential language, subtle persuasion and quiet diplomacy; but Washington was immovable. His letter was courteous but frightfully blunt, the assignment was "incompatible with other measures which I had previously adopted."[33] Randolph laid the letter before the Council recommending that they not nominate a replacement, as they were empowered to do, in the hope that Washington might be persuaded to reconsider his decision. They readily agreed and Randolph promptly notified Washington and expressed the hope that he would not remain fixed in his determination to refuse the appointment.[34]

In February Randolph received a letter from Henry declining the appointment. Couched in the most polite language, it did not give the slightest hint of Henry's true feelings.[35] Writing to Madison several days later, Randolph reported: "I have assayed every means to prevail on him to go thither. But he is peremptory in refusing, as being distressed in his private circumstances."[36]

The Council did not delay in naming a successor in this instance. Thomas Nelson, Jr., was named, and Randolph promptly notified him of his appointment.[37] Much to Randolph's discouragement, he, too, declined the appointment. The Council next turned to Richard Henry Lee, a name both feared and respected in Virginia's political circles.[38] Burdened by ill health, Lee was reported to be in virtual retirement at Chantilly, his country home. Randolph had learned of his presence at a public gathering at the Northumberland Court House and concluded he had not yet "quitted the field of politicks."[39] A staunch opponent of all schemes to enlarge congressional authority under the Articles, his presence on the Virginia delegation became particularly important after Henry's firm refusal. Lee, too, declined to serve, citing his poor health as an excuse.[40] Some months later Lee stated, with greater candor, that he would not sit in Philadelphia in judgment of a body, i.e. the Continental Congress, on which he had loyally served as a Virginia delegate in New York.[41] For the time being Randolph abandoned all hope of filling this vacancy. Fortunately all the other delegates except Mason and Washington had since signified their intention to attend the convention.

Mason was apparently beyond the reach of Randolph's letters for they continually miscarried. Randolph was still trying to notify Mason of his appointment in April, and his views on the mail service in Virginia had become almost unprintable. He dared not speculate on how long it would take to secure a reply.[42]

Securing Washington's acceptance remained to be done, and it would have to be promoted with the greatest delicacy. Madison was informed of Washington's earlier refusal and encouraged to try his hand at persuading the general to change his mind. This Madison had been doing since early November.[43] His letters, reportorial in content, were deliberately designed to impress Washington with the seriousness of the times. The theme was always the same: only the approaching convention, composed of responsible leaders from each of the states, could save the country from its present crisis. Randolph tried once again himself:

> I must call upon your friendship to excuse me for again mentioning the convention at Philadelphia. Your determination having been fixed on a thorough review of the situation, I feel, like an intruder, when I again hint a wish, that you would join the delegation. But every day brings forth some new crisis, and the confederation is, I fear, the last anchor of our hope. Congress have taken up the subject, and appointed the second Monday in May next, as the day of the meeting. Indeed from my private correspondence I doubt whether the existence of that body even [thro?] [sic] this year may not be questioned under our present circumstances.[44]

The letter was dispatched on March 11, and Randolph knew that time was growing short. The vacancy would have to be filled if Washington again declined. Weeks passed and Mount Vernon seemed as remote as Boston. Finally, early in April, came the long-awaited reply. Randolph's letter, Washington began, had not reached him until the 24th, and then an indisposition had prevented him from acknowledging the receipt of it. Then came a long rehearsal of the reasons for his earlier rejection and, finally, the words Randolph was searching for: "However, as my friends, with a degree of solicitude which is unusual, seem to wish for my attendance on this occasion, I have come to a resolution to go. . . ."[45]

This was all Randolph wanted to know. Virginia would now have its most distinguished citizen at the head of its delegation. A short time later Randolph also received a letter from Mason accepting his appointment.[46] With only one vacancy to be filled, the Council at the last minute named one of its own, Dr. James McClurg, to complete the Virginia delegation.[47] Nothing remained but to prepare for the trip northward.

Most of the delegates, governed by their respective public or private responsibilities, had indicated that they would proceed independently to Philadelphia. As early as March 8 Randolph had asked the Council to authorize the use of the state vessel *Liberty* to carry Judge Blair and Judge Wythe to the "head of the bay."[48] He had no intention of letting the "badness of their cavalry" interfere with their attendance at the convention.[49] Washington, in accepting the appointment in April, stated he would meet Randolph in Philadelphia, a promise certain to be kept with meticulous punctuality. And Mason, who hoped to travel to Philadelphia by way of Annapolis, "in order to have a little conversation with some of the Maryland deputies on the subject of the convention," suggested that Randolph stop at Gunston Hall on his way northward.[50]

But the young governor decided to remain in Richmond until the last possible moment. He had no pressing public responsibilities, but he did have an important private one. On April 17 Betsy gave birth to another daughter whom they proudly named Edmonia.[51] Until mother and child were clearly out of danger had had no desire to leave them. In the meantime Madison, still a carefree bachelor, was blandly encouraging him to arrive in Philadelphia early since, he insisted, there was much to be discussed before the meetings began.[52] But Madison would have to wait; Edmund would not leave home until Betsy was up and around again and Edmonia was several weeks older. Finally on May 5 he bade goodbye to his family and headed toward Philadelphia.[53] The challenge laid down by the Annapolis "address" had, in fact, been accepted. What lay ahead, in Randolph's view, was an opportunity to construct a new government that would secure the respect and support of all.

9

The Framer Who Stood Apart
May–September 1787

The road to Philadelphia was by this time a familiar one to Randolph. Like other Virginians who had served in Congress, he knew most of the better inns and eating establishments along the route. Although his task was a serious one and Madison had been unrelenting in his plea for an early arrival, he chose instead to travel at a leisurely pace in order to collect his thoughts on the matters that lay ahead. The countryside, bursting with the new life of spring and noisy with all manner of busy sounds from field and forest, was pleasantly green and fresh-smelling. It almost made him forget the swollen streams that had to be forded and the mud and ruts of the roadway, inconveniences that were a part of travel in the spring. But whatever the difficulties, he enjoyed the solitude of the journey and the forced disengagement from the cares of public office.

He arrived in Philadelphia on Tuesday, May 15,[1] and went directly to the familiar boarding establishment owned by Mrs. Mary House, the accepted lodgings for Virginians in Philadelphia on official business.[2] There he found Madison, who had been waiting impatiently for almost two weeks for his fellow delegates: Washington, whose arrival the previous Sunday had generated much excitement, Judges Wythe and Blair, and Doctor McClurg.[3] Only Mason was missing, and he was expected in a few days.[4] Thus the full Virginia delegation assembled before most of the other states had a fraction of their representatives in Philadelphia. It was no small achievement, and Randolph, as the organizer and nominal head, could claim some share of the credit.

Without delay, and undoubtedly at Madison's urging, the Virginia delegates began conferring each day for several hours in the morning on a draft of the "plan of government" they hoped to present to the Convention.[5] Then at three o'clock in the afternoon all of the delegates would gather at the State House to check on new arrivals and determine if they had as yet achieved a quorum. On Sunday, May 20, the Virginia delegation, Washington excepted, attended Mass at a Catholic Church in the city, a venture undertaken, said Mason, "more out of compliment than religion and more out of curiosity than compliment."[6]

Throughout this first week and much of the next the pace was rather relaxed, the atmosphere congenial and marked by a warm and friendly exchange of views between the delegates. Mason, who could hardly qualify as an inveterate optimist, perceived great unanimity among the delegates and found less opposition to the great principles "of our mission" than he had expected. It seemed that most of those who. had journeyed to Philadelphia were prepared to accept some rather significant alterations in the Articles, if not out of conviction at least out of necessity. How long this attitude would prevail remained to be seen.[7]

Unlike many of the other delegates, Randolph was unusually busy during this first week and a half in Philadelphia. Besides attending the morning "consultations" of the Virginia delegation and the gatherings of the delegates at the State House at three in the afternoon, he had other matters to attend to. The Society of the Cincinnati, an association of Revolutionary War officers, was meeting in Philadelphia at the time and Randolph was anxious to renew some of the acquaintances he had made while serving on Washington's staff. His motives were not purely fraternal for he was anxious to know how they assessed the approaching convention so that he might have some insight into the current mood of the country.[8]

In addition to his official and quasi-official activities Randolph was also trying to find living accommodations for his family, whom he had rather impulsively decided to bring to Philadelphia. He now realized that the Convention would probably be in session considerably longer than he had originally anticipated, and he had no desire to endure a long separation from Betsy and the children. On May 25 he found several fairly spacious rooms in a home near Mrs. House's residence that he felt would permit the family to live in reasonable comfort. He moved the next day and a few days later sent word to Betsy that she and the children should join him as soon as the baby was strong enough to travel. He was now ready for the work that lay ahead.[9]

The move came none too soon, for on Friday the 25th a sufficient number of delegates had gathered in Philadelphia for the Convention to have a quorum. Washington was unanimously elected president and the Convention was officially in session. Only the delegations from Massachusetts, Connecticut, Georgia and New Hampshire remained to be completed, and all save the last expected their full delegations to be present by Monday or Tuesday of the coming week. The state of Rhode Island had refused to appoint delegates, but its absence was viewed with regret rather than alarm. A day or two more was spent in resolving a variety of preliminary matters, but by Tuesday the 29th the delegates were ready to begin their work in earnest.[10] When the Convention assembled at ten that morning, the chair recognized the governor of Virginia. Randolph's speech initiated the formal consideration of the question of revising the "federal system," the avowed purpose of the Convention.[11]

He began by expressing regret that it should fall on him rather than someone with "longer standing in life and political experience" to initiate the discussion, but as the Convention had been originated by Virginia and some propositions were probably expected from his state, this task had been imposed on him by his colleagues. The Convention, he continued, must prevent the "fulfillment of the prophesies of the American downfall." Any revision of the "federal system" must involve an investigation: "1. into the properties which such a government ought to possess, 2. the defects of the Confederation, 3. the danger of our situation, and 4. the remedy."

Speaking to the first point, he called for a government that would promote security against foreign invasion and prevent dissension between the states and sedition within them. It should, he continued, provide those benefits that would be lost to the states if they acted separately, and be strong enough to defend itself against encroachment. Lastly, it should be "paramount to the state constitutions."

Turning to the second point, he stated that he had the greatest respect for those who had drafted the Articles of Confederation. Yet if one considered the obvious inability of these men to foresee the problems that were now confronting the country, then defects and deficiencies in the system were inevitable. This was not meant as faint praise, for he understood only too well the problems involved. Point by point he enumerated the defects of the national government for the assembled delegates. It could not: repel invasion, check rebellion, protect commerce, promote agriculture or manufacturing, improve navigation or defend itself against encroachment from the states. In its authority it was even inferior to the state constitutions. For Randolph, as for most of the delegates assembled in the State House that morning, this litany of defects could only lead to one conclusion—the country was now in grave danger.

Taking up his third point, he very bluntly identified that danger:

> . . . let us not be afraid to view with a steady eye the perils with which we are surrounded. Look at the public countenance from New Hampshire to Georgia. Are we not on the eve of war, which is only prevented by the hopes from this convention[?]

Our chief danger arises from the democratic parts of our [state] constitutions. It is a maxim which I hold incontrovertible, that the powers of government exercised by the people swallow up the other branches. None of the [state] constitutions have provided sufficient checks against the democracy.[12]

If all could not nod their heads in agreement, each at least knew the danger that was uppermost in Randolph's mind. These were not uncommon sentiments in the months following Shays' Rebellion.

Having defined the problem, Randolph proceeded to the most important part of his address—the remedies. Fifteen in number, they were the blueprint for a central government that would be republican in form but conceived along radically different lines from that of its predecessor.

The first resolution was the most important and set the stage for what was to follow: "Resolved, that the articles of Confederation ought to be so corrected and enlarged as to accomplish the objects proposed by their institution; namely, 'common defence, security of liberty, and general welfare.' "

The remaining resolutions spelled out the "corrections" and "enlargements" that the Virginia delegation or, more accurately, Madison had in mind. They called for a government with executive, legislative and judicial branches. The legislature was to consist of two houses, each of which would be proportioned "to the quotas of contribution or to the number of free inhabitants, as the one or the other rule may seem best in different cases." The lower house would be elected by the people and the upper house by the lower house from a "proper number of persons nominated by the individual legislatures." As a check upon the legislative authority, a council of revision was to be created with a veto power over acts of the national and state legislatures. The resolutions also recommended that provisions ought to be made for: the admission of new states into the Union, guarantees of a republican form of government and the right of amendment. Lastly, it was suggested that whatever "amendments" to the Articles might be provided for by this Convention should be ratified by assemblies expressly chosen for this purpose by the people. In closing, Randolph exhorted his fellow delegates "not to suffer the present opportunity of establishing general peace, harmony, happiness and liberty in the United States to pass away unimproved."[13]

The Virginia Plan, as it was ultimately called, was revolutionary in its implications. It envisioned a government of vastly expanded authority, independent of and superior to the state governments. Its hallmark was its nationalism; its link with the past was its republican principles. If implemented by the Convention, the present government of and by the states would be replaced by a government that derived its authority directly from the people, but which, however, would have the necessary safeguards against the "excesses of democracy." These proposals did not shock the assembled delegates because, in Mason's words, "the most prevalent idea I think at present is a total change of the federal system."[14] If Madison's ideas fell on fertile ground, Randolph did a convincing job of sowing them in his opening speech. Only time would reveal how bountiful would be the harvest.

At ten the next morning the delegates again reassembled in the "long room" of the State House, and the Convention resolved itself into a Committee of the Whole House to consider the fifteen resolutions that had been presented the previous day.[15] Randolph was the first to speak; he asked that the first of the resolutions he had offered the previous day be postponed and that he be permitted to substitute three new "propositions" in its place. Collectively they were more pointed in their meaning:

1. that a Union of the States merely federal will not accomplish the objects proposed by the Articles of Confederation, namely common defence, security of liberty and general welfare.

2. that no treaty or treaties among the whole or part of the States, as individual sovereignties would be sufficient.

3. that a *national* Government ought to be established consisting of a *supreme* Legislative, Executive, and Judiciary.[16]

Immediately several delegates questioned the intent of these new propositions. Did these new proposals envision the complete abolition of state governments? The last one certainly seemed to imply as much. Randolph responded that they meant no such thing. They were, he insisted, merely general propositions intended as an introduction to the resolutions that followed. It was these resolutions, he said, that established the broad outlines of the system he had in view. For the moment at least, this explanation was accepted.[17]

The committee then shifted its attention to the second resolution in the Virginia Plan: "2. Resd. therefore that the rights of suffrage in the National Legislature ought to be proportioned to the Quotas of contribution, or to the number of free inhabitants, as the one or the other rule may seem best in different cases."[18] Again, the language of the resolution troubled some of the delegates. Madison and Randolph tried to substitute a less controversial wording of the resolution, but their efforts failed and ultimately the committee simply passed a motion postponing it completely.[19] Their action only served to leave unresolved a problem that would plague the Convention to the very end.

The first full day of formal debate had ended. As the delegates drifted slowly into the busy street in front of the State House, they must have reflected on how difficult the task that confronted them was going to be. As Mason had suggested earlier, they might all agree that the Articles were inadequate but, if this day was any indication of their sentiments, they seemed to be less than unanimous about the remedies that should be applied to correct these inadequacies.[20]

Each day thereafter the delegates assembled at the appointed hour, resolved themselves into a Committee of the Whole House, and then, point by point, worked their way through the resolutions of the Virginia Plan. During these first few weeks Randolph played a relatively minor role in the discussions. If asked a specific question, he would answer it. Generally he preferred to leave the defense and explanation of the plan to Madison.[21] There were occasions, however, when he found it necessary to reassure one or another of the delegates that the Virginia Plan did not, in fact, seek to destroy the power of the states. The more frequent the complaint, the more dogmatic became the denial. He ultimately came to resent any remark that construed his initial statement in this light. At one point he strongly implied that he considered the preservation of the legitimate power of the states more important than the Union itself, an observation that must have sent a shiver down Madison's spine.[22] On June 8 he was provided with an opportunity to vote on a motion that pointedly touched on this issue. Charles Pinckney of South Carolina moved that the national legislature be given the authority to veto any state laws it judged to be improper. Randolph, along with Mason, voted in the negative, while the other members of the Virginia delegation, Washington excepted, voted in favor of the proposal. The motion failed by a vote of three states to seven, with one state losing its vote because it had an equally divided delegation.[23]

It soon became evident, however, that Randolph was also opposed to the reverse arrangement, namely the states infringing upon the rights of the central government. When Elbridge Gerry of Massachusetts proposed that the national executive be elected by the governors of the states, Randolph promptly challenged the suggestion. He recited a long list of arguments against it. A national executive appointed in this manner, he insisted, would be in a rather poor position to defend with vigilance the authority of the central government against state encroachment. Gerry's novel motion had little support and was overwhelmingly defeated.[24]

It was while the Virginia Plan was still before the Committee of the Whole House that Randolph first began to question the manner in which certain features of the plan were being implemented. He became the outspoken advocate and leader, if Madison is to be believed, of those who were working for the establishment of a plural executive.[25] The issue arose in connection with a discussion of the seventh resolution of the Virginia Plan, which provided that the executive be chosen by the legislature, be ineligible for a second term and enjoy such "executive rights" as were then vested in the Congress of the Confederation.[26] On June 1 James Wilson of Pennsylvania moved that the executive should consist of a single person, a proposal that promptly set off a heated debate on the relative merits of a single versus a plural executive. At first Randolph merely listened, seemingly prepared to let others carry the burden of the debate during most of this day's session. Then late in the afternoon, as the meeting was drawing to a close, he abruptly broke his silence. He very bluntly stated that he was irrevocably opposed to Wilson's motion. He regarded it, he said, "as the foetus of monarchy." We had no cause, he continued acidly, to make the British government our prototype. He could see no reason why the "great requisites" of the executive department could not be lodged in three persons as well as one.[27] The subject was postponed without a vote that day, only to be revived again on the next by John Rutledge and Charles Pinckney of South Carolina. Again Randolph was on his feet, insisting that he could not do justice to the "country" that sent him to the Convention if he silently accepted the "establishment of a unity in the executive department." He felt an opposition to it, he said, which would last as long as he lived. It was, he again insisted, susceptible of being converted into a monarchy. He would prefer a three-member executive with each person drawn from a different section of the country.[28] There was no mistaking his mood. He was incensed by the stubbornness of most of the delegates in refusing to recognize the dangers he felt were so obviously inherent in a single executive. When the vote on Wilson's motion was finally taken on June 4, Randolph found himself in the minority both in the Virginia delegation and in the final tally of the states.[29] It was the first significant decision of the Committee of the Whole House with which he was in total disagreement.

Another matter was also causing Randolph some concern at this time. He began to be concerned that the government envisioned by the Virginia Plan might not be secured against the "excesses of democracy." He had alluded to this danger in his speech on May 29 when presenting the Virginia Plan. He referred to it again on May 31 and June 12 during the committee's consideration of the term of office for those in the upper house of the legislature. On each occasion during the debate he let it be known that he considered the upper house the bulwark against "democratic licentiousness." "If it be not a firm body, the other branch being more numerous, and coming immediately from the people, will overwhelm it." At another point he spoke of the "demagogues of the popular branch."[30] Most of the delegates probably shared his convictions as well as his concern, but his attitude toward the people was probably too hostile for most of them. It was on occasions such as these that they were grateful they had had the foresight to impose a rule of secrecy on the proceedings of the Convention, for such language could hardly endear them or their work to the people.

On June 13 Nathaniel Gorham of Massachusetts, the chairman of the Committee of the Whole House, reported to the Convention that the committee, having completed its review of the Virginia Plan, was prepared to submit the resolutions that it had agreed upon.[31] In spite of some notable changes the nineteen resolutions reported out of committee that day retained most of the essential features of the Virginia Plan.[32] The Virginia delegation, and Madison in particular, must have been pleased by the report. It was certainly a far more comprehensive endorsement of their views than any of them would have expected two or three weeks earlier. Once the resolutions had been read into the record, the Convention adjourned for the day.[33] When it reassembled the following morning William Paterson of New Jersey sought the floor to ask if the Convention might be immediately adjourned for one day in order to give several of the delegates an opportunity to prepare an alternate plan to the one approved by the committee. Out of courtesy the governor of Virginia seconded his motion, and it was promptly passed by a unanimous vote.[34]

On June 15 the Convention met pursuant to its adjournment the previous day and the chair promptly recognized Paterson. He proposed, he said, to lay before the Convention a plan which "several of the deputations wished to substitute in place of that proposed by Mr. Randolph." He offered nine resolutions that were designed to enlarge and clarify the authority of the Confederation in those areas where it had proven most deficient. By common consent it was agreed that both plans should be referred back to the Committee of the Whole House "in order to place the two plans in due comparison."[35]

The following day the committee began considering the first resolution of the so-called New Jersey Plan. Like the first resolution of the Virginia Plan, it embodied the central idea around which the remaining resolutions had been constructed: "Resd. that the Articles of Confederation ought to be so revised, corrected and enlarged, as to render the federal Constitution adequate to the exigencies of Government, and the preservation of the Union."[36] John Lansing of New York was the first to speak. The choice facing the Convention, he said, was a simple one. The plan that had been proposed by Mr. Randolph was beyond the power of the Convention and therefore had slight chance of securing adoption, while that of Mr. Patterson, "by sustaining the sovereignty of the states," faced no such impediments. "New York," he continued, "would never have concurred in sending deputies to the Convention if she had supposed the deliberations were to turn on a consolidation of the states, and a national government."[37] Patterson spoke next, giving a long and closely reasoned justification for the New Jersey Plan. To attempt more than what had been proposed in this plan, he insisted, would be to pass beyond the authority granted to the Convention by the states. The people, he said, were not opposed to the Confederation, merely to its lack of power. What was required of this convention was nothing more than to fulfill that need.[38] After he had finished, James Wilson of Pennsylvania rose to defend the Virginia Plan as agreed to by the Committee of the Whole House and, more particularly, the principle of national government. He began by contrasting the two plans and then discussing at length the specific points that seemed to disturb the delegates opposed to the Virginia Plan. He had no fear, he said, that "the people would not follow us into a national government"; they would, in fact, be more favorably disposed toward the Virginia Plan because, unlike the New Jersey Plan, it would have to be submitted to them rather than to the state legislatures for ratification.[39] The fundamental issue was now clearly before the Convention. Was the central government to be national or federal in structure? This was the crucial question, the one that had remained unanswered up to this time.

As yet no one had spoken from the Virginia delegation, and one can imagine the furtive glances toward that section of the hall where Madison was sitting. It was Randolph, however, who took the floor first. He was not, he said, "scrupulous to the point of power. [But] when the salvation of the republic was at stake, it would be treason to our trust, not to propose what we found necessary." "The true question," he noted, "is whether we shall adhere to the federal plan, or introduce the national plan. The insufficiency of the former has been fully displayed by the trial already made." Powers cannot be given to a body "inadequate . . . in the point of representation, elected in the mode in which they are, and possessing no more confidence than they do. . . ."[40] "I am certain," he continued, "that a national government must be established, and this is the only moment when it can be done—And let me conclude by observing, that the best exercise of power is to exert it for the public good."[41]

His language was strong, his tone, again, dogmatic. He had, said Madison, "painted in strong colours, the imbecility of the existing confederacy and the danger of delaying a substantial reform."[42] As far as Randolph was concerned, the New Jersey Plan was fundamentally unsound in that it presumed that the government of the Confederation could be salvaged. He was convinced that it could not and felt that further procrastination would be the height of folly.

The debate continued two more days; attention and undoubtedly attendance were at an all-time high. On June 18 the delegates heard Alexander Hamilton deliver a long and brilliant speech in favor of a government more powerful than anything envisioned by either of the plans under consideration.[43] The next day Madison gave his long-awaited critique of the New Jersey Plan. Point by point he discussed the issues, calmly and judiciously, without a trace of rancor or contempt.[44] Even those who had little sympathy with his position could not help but respect his undramatic, closely reasoned presentation. When he had finished, the fateful vote was taken. It was decided seven states to three, with one divided, that "Mr. Randolph's plan" should be re-reported to the Convention without further alterations.[45]

With this vote behind it the Convention began its formal consideration of the Virginia Plan as amended by the Committee of the Whole House. Sitting now in full session rather than in committee, it took up each of the resolutions, debating and amending them further or merely giving final approval to what had already been debated at length in the Committee of the Whole House. Randolph contributed very little to these deliberations save for an occasional comment or suggestion.[46] Undoubtedly the recent arrival of his wife and children made it somewhat difficult for him to give his full attention to the Convention, particularly while they were still getting settled.[47] The departure of Judge Wythe for Virginia because of the illness of his wife also constituted a minor distraction. It left a vacancy on the Virginia delegation which Randolph chose not to fill, at least not for the present.[48] As the sessions continued, the ability, seriousness and integrity of the delegates became more and more evident. Mason had been right when he observed early in the Convention: "America has certainly, upon this occasion, drawn forth her first characters; there are upon this convention many gentlemen of the most respectable abilities; and, as far as I can yet discover, of the purest intentions."[49]

Progress, however, was slow and by the first week in July the patience of the delegates was beginning to wear thin. It was Dr. Franklin who first sensed the tension and suggested that it might be appropriate to ask a member of the clergy to open each day's session with a prayer asking for divine guidance. The suggestion placed the Convention in a rather awkward position. What would the people think if such an innovation were introduced so late in the Convention? Might they not become apprehensive that the Convention was torn with dissension? The governor of Virginia had an answer. Invite a member of the local clergy to deliver a sermon to the Convention on July 4 to commemorate the nation's independence and then simply retain his services for the purpose of delivering a prayer at the opening of all subsequent sessions. This would give a "favorable aspect" to the measure.[50] Randolph's practical approach to arranging for prayers for the Convention does not appear to have been accompanied by any theological doubts as to the efficacy of the maneuver.

On July 6 Randolph found himself appointed to a committee of five to determine the ratio of representatives to population in the lower house of the legislature.[51] This committee was created after a Grand Committee of one delegate from each state under the able chairmanship of Elbridge Gerry of Massachusetts had suggested on July 5 that representation in the lower house be determined proportionately according to the population of the states and representation in the upper house be equal for each state.[52] These proposals had been advanced by the Grand Committee as a compromise to resolve a very dangerous impasse over the method of determining representation in each branch of the legislature.[53] Since the delegates were in serious disagreement on how certain features of the compromise were to be implemented, these proposals promptly met with considerable opposition. Their greatest source of concern was what would constitute the most satisfactory ratio of representatives to population in the lower house.[54] It was to resolve this issue, and hopefully to salvage the compromise, that the Convention appointed the Committee of Five.

This committee, under the chairmanship of Gouverneur Morris of Pennsylvania, reported back to the Convention three days later. In its report the committee arbitrarily assigned a fixed number of representatives for each state for the first meeting of the lower house and recommended that henceforth the lower house be authorized to "augment" the number of representatives in its own house whenever increases in the wealth and population of the country might require it.[55] Randolph was unhappy with the report and said so during the course of the debate. If the future enlargement of the house were left to the decision of legislators, it would seldom be enlarged, for the legislators would be reluctant to dilute their own power, or so it seemed to Randolph.[56] The Convention was also displeased with this report and referred the section assigning each state a fixed number of representatives for the first meeting of the legislature to another Grand Committee under the chairmanship of Rufus King of Massachusetts.[57]

King's committee had their report ready the following day, and it was accepted with only minor alterations.[58] As soon as it had been approved, Randolph moved that the initial report of the Committee of

Five on which he had served be amended so as to provide for a periodic census, "in order to ascertain the alterations in the population and wealth of the several states" for the purpose of reapportioning representation in the lower house.[59] Before Randolph's motion could be brought to a vote, it became hopelessly entangled in the slavery issue. Hugh Williamson of North Carolina moved the postponement of Randolph's motion and the substitution of one of his own which contained a provision for taking a census of "the free white inhabitants and 3/5th[s] of those of other description . . . and that the Representatives be regulated accordingly."[60] Randolph, while readily consenting to the substitution of Williamson's motion, refrained from any comment on the three-fifths proposal. He confined his remarks to the question of establishing a permanent and equitable method of determining the proper distribution of representation in the lower house.[61] When Randolph finished, Pierce Butler and Charles Cotesworth Pinckney of South Carolina demanded that "blacks be included in the rule of representation equally with the whites." A heated debate ensued with Williamson's motion being defeated just prior to adjournment.[62]

The following day the Convention resumed its discussion of the manner in which representation should be apportioned in the lower house of the legislature. Its first order of business was an amendment offered by Gouverneur Morris. It provided that, since representation was to be determined "according to the principles of wealth and number of inhabitants," direct taxation ought to be proportioned according to representation.[63] Randolph remained silent until Oliver Ellsworth of Connecticut introduced an amendment to the Morris motion to the effect that "the rule of contribution by direct taxation for the support of the government . . . shall be the number of white inhabitants, and three-fifths of every other description in the several states."[64] Randolph was dissatisfied with Ellsworth's motion, for it failed to meet the danger that had initially prompted him to propose a periodic census for reapportioning representation in the lower house. The legislature, he insisted, might still evade or pervert the rule so as to "perpetuate the power where it shall be lodged in the first instance." He proposed in lieu of Mr. Ellsworth's motion of amendment "that in order to ascertain the alterations in representation that may be required from time to time by changes in the relative circumstances of the States, a census shall be taken . . . of all the inhabitants in the manner and according to the ratio recommended by Congress in their resolution of the 18th day of April, 1783 [i.e. calculating the Negro at three-fifths of their number], and that the legislature of the United States shall arrange the representation accordingly." It was regrettable, he said, that slavery as a species of property existed, but so long as it did the holders would require this security.[65] Ellsworth withdrew his motion and seconded that which had been offered by Randolph.[66] Randolph's motion was promptly amended by James Wilson so as to provide that representation would be proportional according to direct taxation and the amount of direct taxation would be altered on the basis of a periodic census in which Negroes would be calculated at three-fifths of their actual number.[67] It passed in this form at the end of the day's session.[68]

By the end of June it was becoming increasingly apparent that Randolph participated in the debates only when he was dissatisfied with the manner in which the Convention was proceeding. He was also becoming noticeably annoyed by the attitude of the delegates from the small states. On June 30 Gunning Bedford, Jr., of Delaware denounced the Virginia Plan in a long and bitter speech in which he stated unequivocally that he did not trust the large states.[69] Then, during the first two weeks of July, Randolph found the delegates from the small states pressing for what he felt was an unjustified advantage in the debate over representation in the national legislature.[70] Their aggressiveness irritated him and made him apprehensive as to the Convention's chances of success. He realized that their legitimate fears had to be respected, but as the governor of a proud and powerful state, he was not going to allow them to intimidate the Convention by projecting an image of helplessness and attributing sinister motives to virtually every proposal advanced by a large state.

Early in July he began to formulate a set of proposals that he hoped would accommodate the demands of the small states without surrendering completely to their wishes. On July 10 he showed Madison a draft of his proposals.[71] They consisted of five resolutions. The first suggested that when certain matters of particular interest to the small states were being considered—he listed thirteen—each state would have only one vote in the lower house of the legislature. In all other matters the right of suffrage in this second branch was to be "proportioned according to an equitable rule of representation." He also proposed that on certain "important questions," which he did not itemize, a greater number of votes than a mere majority be required for the passage of a bill in the upper house. In addition, the people of each state were to have the right to adopt any form of "republican government" or adopt any laws they thought best, provided they were not contrary to the "articles of Union." If the national government should veto a state law because it was considered in violation of the "articles of Union," that state might appeal to the national judiciary. Or if an individual should consider himself injured or oppressed by a law passed by the state, he, too, might appeal to the national judiciary, which should be given the authority to declare the law void.[72] Randolph hoped that these resolutions, when coupled with some type of proportional representation in the legislature, would conciliate the small states without weakening the power of the large states in either house of the legislature.

On July 16 the Convention formally accepted a slightly amended version of the Grand Committee's compromise of July 5, thereby resolving the impasse over the method of representation in the two houses of the legislature[73] and rendering Randolph's proposals superfluous. Since this compromise provided for equal representation of each state in the upper house, it gave the small states considerably more strength in the legislature than Randolph had envisioned. Madison summarizes Randolph's response:

> The vote [accepting the report of the grand committee] of this morning [July 16] had embarrassed the business extremely. All the powers given in the Report from the Committee of the whole were founded on the supposition that a Proportional representation was to prevail in both branches of the Legislature—When he [Randolph] came here this morning his purpose was to have offered some propositions that might if possible have united a great majority of votes, and particularly might provide against the danger suspected on the part of the smaller States, by enumerating the cases in which it might lie, and allowing an equality of votes in such cases. But finding from the preceding vote that they persist in demanding an equal vote in all cases, that they have succeeded in obtaining it, . . . he could not but think we were unprepared to discuss this subject further. It will probably be in vain to come to any final decision with a bare majority of either side. For these reasons he wished the Convention might adjourn, that the large States might consider the steps proper to be taken in the present solemn crisis of the business, and that the small States might also deliberate on the means of conciliation.[74]

Obviously Randolph was troubled by the turn of events, and his motion for adjournment was accorded the same respect as had been given a similar motion by the small states several weeks earlier.[75]

On the morning of the 17th there was a meeting of a number of delegates from the large states to decide what should be done. They discovered they could not reach agreement on the rule of representation for the upper house which would both meet their needs and be acceptable to the small states. "It is probable," Madison observed, "that the result of this consultation satisfied the smaller States that they had nothing to apprehend from a Union of the larger, in any plan whatever against the equality of votes in the 2nd. branch."[76] When the delegates reassembled in the State House later that day, Gouverneur Morris moved to reconsider the resolution that had been agreed to the previous day concerning the "constitution of the two branches of the legislature."

His motion was not even seconded.[77] The Grand Committee's compromise of July 5 remained intact. For the small states it was a major victory, but a victory that had antagonized many delegates from the large states, including Edmund Randolph of Virginia.

As the Convention moved on to consider other sections of the Virginia Plan, a guarded sense of optimism began to manifest itself among the delegates. A major obstacle had been surmounted and, for the moment at least, the apportionment issue was closed. Randolph, who was still annoyed by the compromise, followed the proceedings of the next few days with care, commenting from time to time, but refraining from any extended remarks on the matters under discussion.[78]

On July 19 the Convention turned its attention to the ninth resolution of the Virginia Plan as reported out of the Committee of the Whole House. Since the resolution dealt with the executive branch, Randolph once again took an active part in the debate. He spoke out against the dangers of a single executive but did not renew his earlier suggestion for a plural executive. He advocated instead a provision that would limit the executive to a single term. He pointed out that it would afford the country some protection against the holder of that office developing "monarchical tendencies." Equally important was the effect this would have on the relationship between the executive branch and the legislative branch of government. If the executive was made ineligible for a second term, Randolph noted, there was little likelihood that he would court the friendship of the legislature, and thereby a separation of these two branches of government would be guaranteed.[79] This point was particularly important to him since he assumed the Convention would adhere to the procedure set forth in the seventh resolution of the Virginia Plan, which provided that the executive be chosen by the national legislature.[80] Randolph had hardly finished speaking on the subject when, to his utter chagrin, the Convention decided that the executive should be chosen by electors specifically appointed for this purpose by the respective state legislatures.[81] Thus before this day's session had ended, his remarks had been rendered superfluous without even partially satisfying him on the subject of an overly powerful executive. And, once again, his involvement in the debate can be explained by his dislike for the manner in which the principles of the Virginia Plan were being implemented.

By July 23 the delegates had virtually completed their task and were ready to turn matters over to a drafting committee in order that a formal document might be prepared from the debates and resolutions of the Convention up to this time.[82] The assignment was entrusted to a Committee of Detail, which was chosen by ballot on July 24. It was composed of John Rutledge of South Carolina, chairman; Edmund Randolph; Nathaniel Gorham of Massachusetts; Oliver Ellsworth of Connecticut; and James Wilson of Pennsylvania.[83]

Given the expectations of the Convention for an early report, the committee members went to work immediately for they knew that their task was a formidable one. With the exception of James Wilson, none of the delegates was particularly well qualified for the assignment. Randolph had little to recommend him unless it was his considerable legal experience and the fact that he had formally introduced the Virginia Plan, which may have caused some of the delegates to assume he was one of its principal authors. Either he was assigned or else voluntarily assumed the task of drafting the preliminary sketch of the Constitution for the committee.[84] The result of his efforts was a series of notes on what constituted the appropriate format for a constitution as well as sketches or outlines of each of the major sections that would appear in the document. Laying down his prescription for a good constitution, he rather presumptuously advised his colleagues on the committee:

1. To insert essential principles only, lest the operations of government should be clogged by rendering those provisions permanent and unalterable, which ought to be accommodated to times and events, and

2. To use simple and precise language, and general propositions, according to the example of the (several) constitutions of the several states.[85]

He went on to stress the importance of a preamble as a means of calling attention to the fact that the Articles of Confederation were inadequate to the needs of the country and that it was this inadequacy that gave birth to the Federal Convention and the ideas that emerged from it.[86] His sketch of the Constitution adhered closely to the resolutions that had been passed by the Convention between June 19 and July 23.[87] In some cases the sketch consisted of little more than the resolution of the Convention in outline form. Being a Virginian, he instinctively referred to the lower house as the "house of delegates" but such slips did not alter the essential meaning of the Convention's resolutions.

In sketching the provisions relating to the upper house, here referred to as the Senate, he introduced an elaborate procedure for determining the wages of Senators which, in effect, took the matter completely out of their hands.[88] Having previously voiced his concern over the extent of authority that was being lodged in this branch, it was not surprising to find him advancing specific proposals to prevent the Senators from determining their own salaries. It stands in sharp contrast to his section relating to the lower house of the legislature, which contained nothing on this subject.[89] The provisions were never included in the draft constitution reported out of this committee.[90]

Of greater interest was his provision requiring the vote of two-thirds of both houses of the legislature for the passage of navigation acts.[91] This matter had never been discussed by the Convention; it was introduced here for the first time. Although the provision reflected Randolph's strong feelings on the subject as well as the long-standing opposition of many people in the country toward legislation of this type, it seemed incongruous within the context of this document. It was included in the draft constitution as reported by the Committee of Detail, only to be subsequently removed by the Convention.[92] Before the Convention was over, Randolph let it be known that he strongly disapproved of the decision to exclude this provision from the Constitution.

In the section relating to the office of the executive Randolph included a provision making the occupant subject to removal on impeachment by the lower house.[93] It represented a significant improvement in the resolution of the Convention, which merely provided for executive impeachment without specifying how or by whom this was to be accomplished.[94] Randolph's proposal was incorporated into the committee's draft constitution, only to be rejected by the full Convention in favor of a provision that gave the Senate the power of removal through impeachment.[95] Thus the Convention further enlarged the authority of the legislative house Randolph already viewed as the bastion of small state power.

Randolph's preliminary sketch closed with an outline of an address to the people which would establish the propriety of the proposed reform. The implication was that the people were more or less entitled to such an explanation.[96]

In general it can be said that the preliminary draft adhered closely to the resolutions of the Convention. Where the resolutions offered no guidance, Randolph apparently followed his own personal convictions. His preliminary draft was read and revised by Rutledge.[97] Several subsequent drafts were prepared by James Wilson.[98] He used Randolph's preliminary sketch as the basis for these various drafts, and, as has been noted, a number of Randolph's ideas found their way into the draft constitution that became the report of this committee.[99]

The Committee of Detail reported back to the Convention on August 6 and, as might be expected, the pace of the meetings now quickened.[100] The controversial subjects that had slowed the Convention during the early weeks of the session had been thoroughly aired by this time. In effect, prolonged debate was not only unnecessary but repetitious. There were, however, some exceptions. When the Convention reached Article IV on August 7 objections arose from every quarter of the room. Since the article defined the composition and authority of the House of Representatives, it naturally embodied some of the provisions of the Grand Committee's compromise of July 5. Several of the objections were minor in nature and were quickly resolved, but others, touching on the basic problem of representation, only reopened old wounds. Randolph sat silent throughout the whole of this day's session.[101] On Wednesday, August 8, the Convention voted seven states to four to remove the all-important Section 5 from this article. Section 5 provided that all bills for raising and appropriating money should originate in the House of Representatives, and that these bills could not be subsequently altered or amended by the Senate.[102] The next morning, as soon as the other delegates had taken their seats, Randolph rose in his place and announced that he was giving notice of his intention to move for a reconsideration of the vote of the previous day on Article IV, Section 5.[103] Two days later, on August 11, Randolph was allowed to introduce his motion for reconsideration. In cold and measured language he stated his objections against striking this section from the Constitution. He had not wished for this privilege while a "proportional representation in the Senate was in contemplation, but since an equality has been fixed in the house, the larger states would require this compensation at least." He reminded the small states that the large states had consented to an equality in the Senate because it was coupled with this provision; it was, in effect, an integral part of the compromise offered on July 5.[104] Randolph's motion for reconsideration carried and the following Monday was assigned for reopening debate on Section 5.[105] On the appointed day the whole issue was fully debated once again, with Mason, Wilson and John Dickinson of Delaware speaking in support of Randolph's motion. Gerry of Massachusetts spoke against the motion, and Madison without actually taking sides offered a suggestion for further altering the wording of the section.[106] Randolph, who had stated earlier that he would not repeat his reasons for asking for a reconsideration, found it necessary to take the floor once again. He regarded, Madison reported:

> . . . this point as of such consequence, that as he valued the peace of this country, he would press the adoption of it. We had numerous and monstrous difficulties to combat. Surely we ought not to increase them. When the people behold in the Senate, the countenance of an aristocracy; and in the president, the form at least of a little monarch, will not their alarms be sufficiently raised without taking from their immediate representatives, a right which has been so long appropriated to them.[107]

He did not repeat his earlier reference to the section being an integral part of the compromise on representation, but confined himself to the observation that he wished to prevent popular objections to the plan and thereby ensure its adoption. After Randolph finished, the Convention voted on Section 5 sentence by sentence. In each instance it upheld the vote of August 8 by striking it from the draft constitution.[108] A month later, on September 8, the section was reinstated in the Constitution in a somewhat modified form; but by then Randolph's attitude toward the whole proceedings had undergone a marked change.[109]

On August 22 Randolph made what proved to be his last major effort to alter the draft constitution as it had been reported out of the Committee of Detail. It involved one of the more warmly contested matters in the Convention—the issue of slavery, a subject on which Randolph had remained silent since mid-July.[110] The occasion was a debate over Article VII, Section 4, which deprived Congress of the authority to impose a tax or duty on the importation of "such persons as the several states shall think proper to admit; nor shall such migration or importation be prohibited."[111] It was proposed by Charles Cotesworth Pinckney that this section and several others in the same article that were still under consideration be committed to a Grand Committee with the hope that the differences among the delegates might be resolved by a compromise.[112] In speaking to this motion Randolph let it be known that he could never agree to Section 4 of this article as it presently stood in the draft constitution; he would sooner risk the Constitution itself. The Convention, he said, was confronted by a dilemma. By agreeing to the clause, it would "revolt" the Quakers, Methodists and others who owned no slaves. And yet, by rejecting it, the Convention might make it impossible for two states to remain in the Union. "Let us then . . . try the chance of a commitment [to a Grand Committee]."[113] The motion carried.[114] The committee's solution, as reported to the Convention, was to word the section so as to allow the national government to levy a duty on slaves imported into the country, while guaranteeing the states that no restriction would be imposed on that trade before the year 1800.[115] Although the provisions of the section were subsequently amended, at least the foundation was laid for another compromise which apparently was more acceptable to Randolph than the original version in the draft constitution.[116]

As the Convention moved toward the day of its final adjournment, each delegate knew that he would soon have to decide whether to endorse or reject the instrument of government that was being drafted. No one was completely satisfied with the document, yet all knew that it was made up of numerous compromises that had to be accepted if their common goal was to be achieved. In the last analysis each delegate had to decide whether this or any subsequent convention could devise a better constitution.

For Randolph this decision was to be painfully difficult. In mid-June, during the first weeks of the Convention, when the delegates were debating the relative merits of the Virginia and New Jersey plans, he was an attentive and constructive participant in the debates, for he believed a free and open discussion of the two plans was desirable. Moreover, he obviously felt that the delegates made a wise choice when they decided to take the Virginia Plan as the blueprint of the new government. This was not merely pride in the plan because it emanated from Virginia but a total commitment to the idea of a national government that was neither dependent on nor destructive of the authority of state governments. But gradually, in late June or early July, Randolph began to grow more cautious and revealed his increasing concern over the manner in which the Virginia Plan was being implemented. He was convinced the small states, taking advantage of their voting strength in the Convention, were determined to protect their own interests while being almost contemptuous of the needs of the large states. The concessions made by the large states on the critical issue of representation in the legislature were most distasteful to him. Throughout the month of July and during much of August he began to take exception to certain featured of the document as it took form, and not infrequently he was challenging the persistent efforts of the small states to gain a greater influence. While his language was frequently harsh, his comments were always in the context of one who was committed without reserve to the document that was being drafted. If he defined differences in terms of large-state versus small-state interests, he never implied these differences were beyond resolution by the Convention. Most significantly, he was never outside the spirit of compromise that kept the Convention in motion.

By mid-August, however, he began to manifest a more hostile attitude. His efforts, between August 11 and 13, to reinstate Section 5 of Article IV were more than an attempt to hold the Grand Committee's compromise intact. As far as Randolph was concerned, the small states were repudiating their half of the compromise when they voted to drop this provision from the draft constitution. He was not prepared to let their actions go unchallenged. Much to his chagrin, his move to reinstate Section 5 failed completely.[117] It was not, however, until the 29th of August that the depth of Randolph's dissatisfaction was fully revealed. The occasion was a motion by Charles Pinckney of South Carolina requiring a two-thirds vote of both houses for the passage of all laws regulating commerce.[118] It provoked a heated debate that lasted the better part of the day.[119] Randolph was the next to last person to speak to the motion. His views proved to be less significant than the tone of his remarks. "Mr. Randolph said," Madison reported:

> . . . that there were features so odious in the Constitution as it now stands that he doubted whether he should be able to agree to it. A rejection of the motion [Pinckney's] would complete the deformity of the system. . . . What he had in view was merely to pave the way for a declaration which he might be hereafter obliged to make if an accumulation of obnoxious ingredients should take place, that he could not give his assent to the plan.[120]

Two days later, as the Convention was considering the article relating to the method of ratification, Randolph stated that, in case he could not accept the final document, he hoped that the Convention would make some provision whereby the state ratifying conventions might propose amendments to the Constitution which, in turn, could be submitted to another general convention, "which may reject or incorporate them as shall be judged proper."[121] The suggestion, aside from being rather presumptive, was a new one for Randolph and a sharp departure from the position he had held thus far. He had always attached considerable importance to the method of ratification, but up to this time presumably he was in agreement with the procedures set forth in the Virginia Plan. He said no more at the time, and apparently no one felt obliged to question him.

During the first week of September he once again began to take some part in the daily proceedings of the Convention, but now he was openly hostile. Delivering curt notices of his dissatisfaction with whatever happened to be under discussion, he became a mere critic. He rejected one suggestion because it strengthened his "general objections against the plan";[122] to another he announced his "inflexible" opposition.[123] On September 5 he observed that some suggested changes in the plan "made a bold stroke for Monarchy."[124] When not delivering these dogmatisms, he remained a silent and, one suspects, a sullen observer. It was not something that had happened this particular week or the preceding one; rather his grievances were cumulative, a reflection of his growing dissatisfaction with the instrument of government that was being drafted.

On the following Monday, September 10, the weeks of growing discontent erupted. The occasion was a motion to reconsider Articles XXI and XXII of the draft constitution. They both dealt with the method of ratification.[125] In the course of the debate Randolph demanded that the ratification procedure outlined in the draft constitution be completely revised. His speech, as reported by Madison, was a virtual ultimatum:

. . . if no change should be made in this part of the plan, he should be obliged to dissent from the whole of it. He had from the beginning he said been convinced that radical changes in the system of Union were necessary. Under this conviction he had brought forward a set of republican propositions as the basis and outline of a reform. These Republican propositions had, however, much to his regret been widely, and in his opinion, irreconcileably [*sic*] departed from—In this state of things it was his idea and he accordingly meant to propose, that the State Conventions should be at liberty to offer amendments to the plan,—and that these should be submitted to a second General Convention, with full power to settle the Constitution finally—He did not expect to succeed in this proposition, but the discharge of his duty in making the attempt, would give quiet to his own mind.[126]

After several other delegates had spoken, a vote was taken on the motion to reconsider. It carried by a vote of seven states to three.[127]

The Convention immediately began the formal discussion of Article XXI. After an attempt by Hamilton to amend it had failed, it was approved in its original form.[128] The Convention then turned to Article XXII. Since Randolph had previously served notice that he intended to offer an amendment to this article, he was promptly recognized by the chair. Madison reported his remarks at length:

[He] . . . took this opportunity to state his objections to the System. They turned on the Senate's being made the Court of Impeachment for trying the Executive—on the necessity of ¾ instead of ⅔ of each house to overrule the negative of the President—on the smallness of the number of the Representative branch—on the want of limitation to a standing army—on the general clause concerning necessary and proper laws—on the want of some particular restraint on Navigation acts—on the power to lay duties on exports—on the Authority of the general Legislature to interpose on the application of the *Executives* of the States—on the want of a more definite boundary between the General and State Legislature—and between the General and State Judiciaries—on the unqualified power of the President to pardon treasons—on the want of some limit to the power of the Legislature in regulating their own compensations. With these difficulties in his mind, what course he asked was he to pursue? Was he to promote the establishment of a plan which he verily believed would end in Tyranny? He was unwilling he said to impede the wishes and Judgment of the Convention—but he must keep himself free, in case he should be honored with a Seat in the Convention of his State, to act according to the dictates of his judgment. The only mode in which his embarrassment could be removed, was that of submitting the plan to Congress to go from them to the State Legislatures, and from these to State Conventions having power to adopt, reject or amend; the process to close with another general Convention with full power to adopt or reject the alterations proposed by the State Conventions, and to establish finally the Government—He accordingly proposed a Resolution to this effect.[129]

The delegates sat in stunned silence. This was the most detailed criticism of the draft constitution yet made by a member of the Convention. It was Dr. Franklin who broke the silence. An experienced and unflustered parliamentarian, he entered a routine second to Randolph's motion to amend Article XXII. Mason then suggested that perhaps the motion should lie on table "for a day or two to see what steps might be taken with regard to parts of the system objected to by Mr. Randolph."[130] Since the Convention had appointed a Committee of Style and referred the revised draft constitution to it two days earlier on September 8, there was little the Convention could do to meet the objections Randolph had raised until this committee had completed its work.[131]

The Committee of Style reported back to the Convention on September 12, and on the following day the delegates began their final review of the redrafted constitution. Randolph did suggest certain word changes, but for the most part he was a silent witness to these last-minute alterations.[132] By September 15 the work was virtually complete; the Constitution was in final form.[133] Once again Randolph took the floor. It pained him, he said, to differ with his colleagues and he anxiously wished for "some accommodating expedient" that would save him from the embarrassment of not signing the Constitution. Again he introduced his motion for changing the method of ratification. "Should this proposition be disregarded, it would . . . be impossible for him to put his name to the instrument."[134] Mason spoke next, and Madison faithfully recorded his remarks:

> It was improper to say to the people, take this or nothing. As the Constitution now stands, he could neither give it his support or vote in Virginia; and he could not sign here what he could not support there. With the expedient of another Convention as proposed [by Randolph], he could sign.[135]

This was powerful support for Randolph since Mason was one of the most revered members of the Convention and the delegates knew and respected his democratic sympathies. Charles Pinckney of South Carolina was the next to take the floor: "These declarations from members so respectable at the close of this important scene, give a peculiar solemnity to the present moment." Like Randolph and Mason, he did not approve of everything in the Constitution. "But," he continued, "apprehending the danger of a general confusion and an ultimate decision by the sword," he should give the plan his support.[136] Gerry of Massachusetts spoke next. He outlined his objections to the Constitution in much the same manner as Randolph had done several days previously. "Under such a view of the constitution, the best that could be done . . . was to provide for a second general convention."[137] Madison's "Notes" tell the rest of the story.

> On the question on the proposition of Mr. Randolph. All states answered—no.
> On the question to agree to the constitution as amended. All states ay.
> The constitution was then ordered to be engrossed.
> And the House adjourned.[138]

On Monday, September 17, the engrossed Constitution was read. After extended remarks by Franklin and a brief discussion of a further change in the clause defining the ratio of representatives to population, the question to agree to the enrolled Constitution was taken. All states answered "ay."[139] Randolph then rose to address the Convention. Again Madison reported his remarks:

> Mr. Randolph . . . apologized for his refusing to sign the Constitution, not-withstanding the vast majority and venerable names that would give sanction to its wisdom and its worth. He said however that he did not mean by this refusal to decide that he should oppose the Constitution without doors. He meant only to keep himself free to be governed by his duty as it should be prescribed by his future judgment—He refused to sign, because he thought the object of the Convention would be frustrated by the alternative which it presented to the people. Nine States will fail to ratify the plan and confusion must ensue. With such a view of the subject he ought not, he could not, by pledging himself to support the plan, restrain himself from taking such steps as might appear to him most consistent with the public good.[140]

Randolph's position may have been consistent with his convictions, but it carried little weight with his fellow delegates who could, in the light of this final statement, suspect the sincerity of his actions. Was Randolph being honest or clever? Was he anxious to save the country from the chaos he believed was certain to accompany the inevitable rejection of the Constitution, or was he merely covering all his options so that he could support the position that seemed most popular once the document had been made public? The delegates, one suspects, leaned toward the harsher judgment.

The day after the Convention adjourned, Randolph sent an official copy of the Constitution to Beverley Randolph, the lieutenant governor of Virginia. In an accompanying letter he took note of Mason's and his own refusal to sign, adding: "[I]t is not, therefore, to be concluded that we are opposed to its adoption." The circumstances surrounding their decision would be explained after they had returned to Virginia. A postscript noted that he would necessarily have to delay his departure from Philadelphia for several days because Betsy was not in the best of health.[141]

The Randolphs left the city the following Saturday, September 22, although Betsy had not fully recovered from her "indisposition." By the 29th they had reached Bowling Green, some thirty-odd miles north of Richmond, with Betsy's health actually improving as they drew closer to home.[142] As Randolph made his way southward he was constantly inquiring into the reactions of the people to the new Constitution in the communities through which he passed. His findings were admittedly fragmentary, but he reported them to Madison in language that reflected both surprise and relief. Baltimore "resounds with friendship," Bladensburg "approved," while in Alexandria the inhabitants were "enthusiastic" and taking steps to "force my dissenting colleague [Mason] to assent to a convention."[143] Had the governor of Virginia misjudged the mood of the people? Perhaps the country might accept the Constitution in spite of its faults.

10

Recusant
October 1787–1788

Before Randolph had reached Richmond, the Constitution he had refused to sign had survived its first test. An indolent Congress,
plagued by perpetual absenteeism, had been assembled at the urging of
its president, Arthur St. Clair, to act on the new Constitution. The document was delivered to Congress on September 20, and Wednesday, September 26, was assigned for its consideration. Apparently no one in
Congress was bold enough to suggest that it not be forwarded to the states
for ratification, but some were prepared to transmit it under a resolution
noting that the Convention had exceeded its authority. A motion suggesting as much was offered by Richard Henry Lee of Virginia and Melancton
Smith of New York, only to be postponed by Congress in favor of a motion by Abraham Clark of New Jersey and Nathaniel Mitchell of Delaware which was noncommittal but implicitly sympathetic. But the
Clark-Mitchell motion was similarly postponed by the supporters of the
Constitution in favor of a third motion that would openly recommend
ratification. Introduced by Edward Carrington of Virginia and seconded
by William Bingham of Pennsylvania, it "recommended to the legislatures
of the several states to cause conventions to be held as speedily as may be
to the end that the same may be adopted, ratified and confirmed." Carrington's motion and the two that preceded it were stricken from the
record and a fourth resolution by Nathan Dane of Massachusetts was
inserted into the *Journal*. Like the first resolution of Richard Henry Lee,
Dane's resolution would transmit the Constitution to the states with an
insinuation that the Convention had exceeded its legitimate authority.
Mysteriously, every one of these resolutions was abandoned and on Friday, September 28, Congress unanimously approved an obviously noncommittal resolution that simply transmitted the document to the states.[1]
It reflected, but did not reveal, the extent of congressional opposition to
the new instrument of government.

Randolph learned of the details from Madison as he was trying to
resolve the question of how he would transmit the Constitution to the

[121]

Virginia Assembly.[2] He knew, for instance, that the language he used might influence the Assembly's procedures. He had thought about this on his journey home from Philadelphia and had hit upon a plan he felt would be wholly consistent with his conduct in Philadelphia. He would, he told Madison, urge the Assembly to make the necessary provisions for a state ratifying convention:

> . . . but if they should wish amendments let them be stated and forwarded to the states: before the meeting of the convention [in Virginia] an answer may be obtained: if the proposed amendments be rejected, let the constitution immediately operate: if approved, by nine states, let the assent of our convention be given under the exception of the points amended.

He then noted, by way of justification, that: "This will, I believe, blunt the opposition, which will be formidable, if they must take altogether or reject."[3] His justification seemed more obvious than his rather impractical procedures, at least as they had been outlined to Madison. And Madison, for all his experience with Randolph's prose, must have been baffled by his confusing sentence structure and strange punctuation and probably wondered just how effective he would be in explaining all of this to the legislature.

While waiting for Madison's reaction, Randolph had no choice but to turn his attention to the many other matters that would have to be brought before the legislature.[4] His preoccupation with the proceedings in Philadelphia and his extended absence from the state as a delegate to that Convention left him singularly unprepared for this legislative session. With the help of Lieutenant Governor Beverley Randolph and the Executive Council he reviewed the principal problems confronting the state, deciding what would and would not be brought to the attention of the Assembly. Reviewing back correspondence and reports, conscientiously piecing together the details of what had transpired over the past four months, he was at his desk all day. Beverley Randolph had been efficient in handling the executive responsibilities and nothing had been neglected, but Edmund Randolph, it seems, wanted to become thoroughly acquainted with everything before deciding what should be referred to the legislature.[5]

In addition, he was preparing a special message for the General Assembly concerning his own conduct at the Philadelphia Convention. He began to put some ideas on paper within days of his return to Richmond and hoped to have his statement ready when the Assembly convened on the 15th. He worked on it every opportunity he had by squeezing in an hour here and an hour there and working late in the evening when there were fewer interruptions. It was made doubly difficult by the realization that his refusal to sign was becoming a subject of considerable political importance in Virginia. He resented the endless speculation concerning his motives and was determined to prepare a statement that would remove all doubts about his attitude toward the Constitution. The task proved to be even more difficult than he had expected. As people began to take sides for and against the Constitution, more and more significance was attached to his decision to withhold his signature. Every new rumor as to his real motives served to impose new burdens on him and complicate the drafting of his statement.[6]

By the time he finished the letter, it had become, for all practical purposes, a major political testament. It sought to answer all those people who were anxious to construe his conduct as evidence of unqualified opposition to the Constitution. The "letter," dated October 10, began by analyzing the past and present inadequacies of the Confederation. This was followed by a comparatively short summary of the powers which he felt the government of the United States ought to enjoy and the reasons why he felt these powers could not be "interwoven" into the present Confederation. He concluded: "My inference from these facts and principles is, that the new powers must be deposited in a new body, growing out of a consolidation of the union, as far as the circumstances of the State will allow." But, he continued, some might consider a total dissolution of the union or even partial confederacies as more desirable. Addressing himself to each of these possible solutions, he painted a picture of intolerable hardships if either was attempted:

> I come, therefore, to the last and perhaps only refuge in our difficulties, a consolidation of the union, as far as circumstances will permit. To fulfil this desirable object, the constitution was framed by the federal convention. A quorum of eleven states, and the only member from a twelfth have subscribed [to] it; Mr. Mason of Virginia, Mr. Gerry of Massachusetts, and myself having refused to subscribe.
>
> Why I refused, will, I hope, be solved to the satisfaction of those who know me by saying, that a sense of duty commanded me thus to act.

To subscribe, he continued, would bring immediate gratification and place him in the company of America's most distinguished and respected statesmen and earn for him the "first applause" of a grateful nation.

> . . . I suspected, too, that there was something in the human breast which, for a time would be apt to construe a temperateness in politics, into an enmity to the union. Nay, I plainly foresaw, that in the dissensions of parties, a middle line would probably be interpreted into a want of enterprise and decision. But these considerations, how seducing soever [sic] were feeble opponents to the suggestions of my conscience. I was sent to exercise

my judgement, and to exercise it was my fixed determination . . . [knowing] that self-approbation is the only true reward which a political career can bestow, and that popularity would have been but another name for perfidy, if to secure it, I had given up the freedom of thinking for myself.

He would have preferred to have ascertained the "temper and genius" of the people in Virginia as to a radical change in government before the Philadelphia Convention but this was impossible. With the Confederation "tottering" from its own weakness and the Convention serving as a "signal" of its total inefficiency, "I was therefore ready to assent to a scheme of government, which was proposed, and which went beyond the limits of the confederation, believing, that without being too extensive it would have preserved our tranquility, until that temper and that genius should be collected."

To achieve this end he tried to alter the method of ratification advanced in the Convention so that the people might have an opportunity to propose amendments to the Constitution before it went into effect. When his motion was defeated, he expressed his unwillingness to sign the document. "If . . . I had signed, I should have felt myself bound to be silent as to amendments, and . . . [bound] to support the constitution without the correction of a letter."

Indicating his unwillingness to do either, he meticulously analyzed all the possible implications of his signing. This was followed by an explanation of why the amending process provided for in the Constitution was inadequate in his opinion. Imperfections and changes, he insisted, could be made more safely if the means was provided for amending prior to ratification.

> I confess, that it is no easy task to devise a scheme which shall be suitable to the views of all. Many expedients have occurred to me, but none of them appear less exceptionable than this; that if our convention should choose to amend, another federal convention be recommended; that in that federal convention the amendments proposed by this or any other State be discussed; and if incorporated in the constitution or rejected, or if a proper number of the other States should be unwilling to accede to a second convention, the constitution be again laid before the same State conventions, which shall again assemble on the summons of the executives, and it shall be either wholly adopted, or wholly rejected, without a further power of amendment. I count such a delay as nothing in comparison with so grand an object; especially too as the privilege of amending must terminate after the use of it once.

Having insisted on the necessity of amending the document before ratification, he concluded his "letter" by "setting forth the particulars, which I conceive to require correction." He listed the equal representation of each state in the Senate, and the absence of any provision in the Constitution requiring something more than a mere majority for the passage of laws regulating commerce as his main objections. He added eight others, each of them points he had raised in the course of the Convention.

He closed with an apology for having been so tedious in this explanation of his conduct.[7]

Once written, the document was laid aside. It would be sent to the speaker of the House of Delegates when the Assembly convened and thereby become a part of the public record.

While Randolph labored over his political testament, the members of the legislature began gathering in Richmond. And while it might have been just his imagination, it seemed there was a much larger number of "politically influential" Virginians sitting in the House of Delegates than usual. There were three former governors: Patrick Henry, Benjamin Harrison and Thomas Nelson, Jr.; a surprising number of former delegates to the Continental Congress, including Archibald Stuart, Meriwether Smith, Theodorick Bland and Joseph Jones; plus, of course, the very influential George Mason. In addition, there was his brother-in-law, George Nicholas from Albemarle County, who was a warm advocate of the Constitution; the very engaging and ambitious John Marshall from Henrico County, who had deliberately sought a seat in this Assembly to promote the constitutional cause; and the overly cautious and generally unpredictable James Monroe from Spotsylvania.[8] Two men whose views on the Constitution would weigh heavily with the delegates would not be present; George Washington and Richard Henry Lee did not seek seats in the House, although neither would have been opposed in their respective constituencies if they had chosen to run. Their influence, however, would still be felt—Washington, the unswerving supporter, quietly promoted the Constitution, and Lee was its most perceptive and harshest critic.

Almost as soon as the delegates arrived in the Virginia capital they began collecting rumors and counting heads on the constitutional question. In taverns and inns, in private homes and public buildings, anywhere they met, they exchanged information. Every legislator had carefully assessed the attitude of the people in his own county and, with a little encouragement, would venture an opinion on the attitude of people elsewhere. Rumors flourished and died like the heat of the autumn sun; it was virtually impossible to separate fact from fiction. It was still too early to discern the strength of contending factions within the legislature but not to sense the dominant mood of its members. By the time the session opened, it was a foregone conclusion that the vast majority of the legislators, responding to the apparent sympathies of their constituents, were at least prepared to implement the ratification procedures set forth in the Constitution itself.[9] Still unresolved was the question of whether the critics of the Constitution would try to use this session to promote amendments and a second federal convention.

The impetus for such a course of action seemed to rest with Virginia's governor, and as the legislators assembled in the capital on the morning of October 15, an atmosphere of anticipation surrounded their opening session. The governor's traditional opening message to the speaker of the House of Delegates would surely carry some reference to the Constitution. Virtually everyone knew that he disapproved of the method of ratification set forth in the Constitution and that he wanted to give the people, through their elected representatives, an opportunity to propose amendments to a second federal convention. But how? Would he suggest that the Virginia legislature or a state convention be the architect of these amendments? Then there was the question of who was to call this second federal convention now that Congress had indicated its unwillingness to challenge the ratification procedures devised by the delegates in the Philadelphia Convention. His message left them thoroughly confused. It was nothing more than a dull matter-of-fact statement of the subjects the legislature should try to consider during this session. Nineteen separate documents accompanied his message as enclosures, and one of these was the Constitution. The governor said: "The Constitution, proposed by the late Federal Convention has been transmitted to me officially from Congress. I beg leave therefore now to enclose it. No. 14."[10]

That was all; not another word on the Constitution. Surely there was a reason. Edmund Randolph was too accomplished a politician to allow such an opportunity to go unexploited. Before very long they had an explanation for this astonishingly routine method of transmitting the Constitution. Friends of the governor were saying that he was completing a special message on the Constitution for the legislature. It wasn't quite ready yet, but it would be in a few days or perhaps a week. They reported, too, that the governor was concerned about the rumors that were circulating regarding his motives for not signing and that his message would carry a full explanation of his conduct in Philadelphia and his views on ratification.[11] So the Assembly would have to wait a little longer. But while waiting, the House of Delegates automatically referred the document to a Committee of the Whole House and assigned Wednesday, October 17, for its consideration. Eight days later, without the benefit of Randolph's message, the House of Delegates unanimously approved a resolution recommending the submission of the Constitution to a "Convention of the people, for their full and free investigation and discussion."[12] The Senate's concurrence was taken for granted and came a few weeks later. Still there was no message from the governor.[13]

Although it didn't help the legislature, Randolph's account of all this to Madison carried a special significance:

> The first raptures in favor of the Constitution were excessive. Every town resounded with applause. The conjectures of my reasons for refusing to sign were extraordinary, and so far malicious, as to suppose, that I was chagrined at not carrying every point in my own way or that I sought for popularity. These were the effluvia until the Assembly met.
>
> A diversity of opinion appeared immediately on the convening of that body. . . . Among the heroes of opposition were: Mr. Henry, Mr. Wm. Cabell, Colo. Bland and Mr. French Strother. A great ferment was kept up until Thursday last, when, contrary to my expectations the debate for calling the convention was conducted with temper, and a vote passed unanimously for that purpose, *freely to discuss and deliberate on the constitution*. This is a happy and politick resolution; for I am thoroughly persuaded, that, if it had been propounded by the legislature to the people, as *we* [i.e., the Philadelphia Convention] propounded it, the constitution would have been rejected and the spirit of union extinguished.

And with regard to his special message to the speaker of the House:

> I have thought proper to postpone any explanation of myself, except in private, until everything is determined, which may relate to the constitution. I have prepared a letter [i.e., to the Speaker] and shall send you a copy in a few days.[14]

Many in the legislature might have construed Randolph's official silence as evidence of deliberate procrastination until the true temper of the state was known, but Madison knew better. Randolph was not an acquiescent politician who merely followed popular opinion, but a man who knew precisely what he wanted. What he wanted was this Constitution, provided certain features in it were altered.[15] His problem, and Madison recognized it almost immediately, was that he had not found a way of expressing his dissent without playing into the hands of those who appeared anxious to have the Constitution drastically amended or defeated. He and Patrick Henry had held several meetings during the preceding weeks, and the results, Randolph candidly admitted to Madison, were anything but satisfactory: "He and I have had several animated discourses; but he recedes so far from me, that we must diverge after a progress of half a degree farther."[16] He was unwilling to do anything that might serve Henry's cause lest he destroy the very thing he had helped to write. And the alternative, to advocate the ratification of the Constitution as written, involved him in a contradiction. Randolph's categorization of the various groups in Virginia gave him away: on the one side were the "warm friends," on the other was the "party *positively* against" and in the middle were the *"recusants"*—Mason, for the present at least, and himself.[17] It was not an enviable position. Randolph knew it and so did Madison.

The Assembly's resolution authorizing a state convention to consider the Constitution did not lessen legislative interest in the subject. The newspapers were filled with articles for and against, and every Virginian who came to Richmond was expected to provide the latest information on the mood of the people along his route. Legislative matters having no direct connection with the Constitution were being considered as political barometers of shifting attitudes, and each vote a certain indication that the temper of the Assembly had turned decisively this way or that. Randolph was convinced, for example, that a bill repealing all previous laws against the recovery of British debts would be defeated because the opponents of the Constitution disapproved of any measure that might eventually make Virginians answerable to the obviously more powerful judicial system of the proposed new government.[18] Legislative procrastination delayed final passage until December; however, by then a more sensitive barometer of legislative sympathies was available.[19]

On November 30 a Committee of the Whole House reported a series of resolutions that urged that the necessary funds be appropriated to defray the expenses of delegates to the forthcoming Virginia convention and also, "in case the said Convention should judge it expedient to propose amendments," that funds be provided to send deputies to a second federal convention.[20] The resolutions were extremely important for they implied that the legislators wanted the delegates to the Virginia Convention to propose amendments and further expected them to recommend that these amendments be considered by a second federal convention. The supporters of the Constitution challenged the proposal, but the resolutions carried with sixteen votes to spare.[21] In the days that followed, some considerable pressure must have been placed on those who supported these resolutions, for the final bill, as passed on December 13, carried not a single reference to a second federal convention. It did provide funds for communicating with Virginia's "sister states or the conventions thereof" and "collecting the sentiments of the union respecting the proposed federal constitution," but, unlike the committee's resolutions, it did not presume to dictate to the state convention.[22] A subsequent resolution that a circular letter be sent to the states suggesting the possibility that Virginia would propose amendments was defeated in favor of a motion instructing the governor to transmit copies of the above law to the executives of the other states. It placed the Virginia Assembly on record as favoring "communication" and no more.[23] Randolph noted these legislative efforts with apprehension and cited them as evidence that "the current sets violently against the Constitution."[24] It is quite likely that he found the proposals perfectly sound but was suspicious of the motives of those who pressed for their adoption.

As week after week went by without any public disclosure of Randolph's own views on the Constitution, some members of the legislature began to grow restless. Those who resented his official silence knew he had had a "letter" ready for more than a month. Early in December they decided to force the issue. A statement signed by Meriwether Smith, Charles M. Thurston, John H. Briggs and Mann Page, Jr., invited him to make known his views. Since none of the four had much enthusiasm for the Constitution, their statement was a masterpiece of political rhetoric:

> It has been reported in various parts of the state that the reasons which governed you in the disapprobation of the proposed Federal Constitution, no longer exist; and many of the people of this Commonwealth have wished to know what objections could induce you to refuse your signature to a measure so flattering to many principal characters in America, and which is generally supposed to contain the seeds of prosperity and happiness to the United States.
>
> We are satisfied, sir, that the time is passed when you might with propriety have been requested to communicate your sentiments to the General Assembly on this subject; but, as you have been pleased to favor us with your observations in private, and we conceive they would not only afford satisfaction to the public, but also be useful by the information and instruction they will convey, we hope, you can have no objection to enable us to make them public through the medium of the Press.[25]

Randolph replied:

> Your favor of the second instant, requesting permission to publish my letter on the new Constitution gives me an opportunity of making known my sentiments which perhaps I should not decline. It has been written ever since its date, and was intended for the General Assembly. But I have hitherto been restrained from sending it to them by motives of delicacy arising from two questions depending before that body, the one respecting the Constitution, the other myself. At this day too I feel an unwillingness to bring it before the Legislature, lest in the diversity of opinion I should excite [a] contest unfavorable to that harmony with which I trust the great subject will be discussed. I therefore submit the publication of the letter to your pleasure.
>
> I beg leave however, to remind you, that I have only mentioned my objections to the constitution in general terms, thinking it improper and too voluminous, to explain them at full length. But it is my purpose to go at large into the Constitution when a fit occasion shall present itself.[26]

The "letter," apparently still dated October 10, was enclosed. If Randolph expected these gentlemen to rush his letter into print, he was mistaken. For some reason—perhaps it was not as valuable to them as they had expected—they held the "letter" until the end of the month before placing it in the hands of Augustine Davis, the publisher of Richmond's *Virginia Independent Chronicle*.[27] By the time it appeared in print, the opponents of the Constitution had virtually abandoned their efforts to make the Assembly a forum for their views.[28]

In the meantime Randolph sent copies of the "letter" to his friends. Madison, who had been promised a copy in October, found it enclosed in a letter dated December 27, and there was not a line of explanation as to why Randolph had waited two months before sending it. He pretended total indifference as to how it was being received—"what the general opinion is, I would not undertake to vouch because I stay much at home, and I find daily reason to distrust reports which always receive a tincture from the wishes of the narrator." A few lines further he observed, somewhat more candidly:

> I need not assure you, that it would give me no pleasure to see my conduct in refusing to sign, sanctified, if it was to produce a hazard to the union; and if I know myself, I have no extreme ardor to acquire converts to my opinion. But I verily believe, that the only expedient which can save the federal government in any shape in Virginia, will be the adoption of some such plan as mine. However the high-toned friends of the Constitution are very sanguine, that the whole will be run through with ease.[29]

He still believed his objections were valid and the remedy he proposed worthy of support, but he was becoming increasingly concerned lest this position "produce a hazard to the union." The supporters and opponents of the Constitution were generally unwilling to countenance a middle position, and Randolph was now more afraid than ever that his "letter" might play into the hands of Henry and his supporters.

The reaction to his letter was somewhat less impassioned than he probably expected, for he disappointed everyone. Supporters of the Constitution were content, since they considered it moderately sympathetic, or, as Madison put it, "the arguments contained in it in favor of the Constitution are much stronger than the objections which prevented his assent."[30] Those who opposed the Constitution viewed it more as an explanation of his own conduct than a criticism of theirs, and they probably assumed it would have little influence outside of Virginia. Only one Virginian, Spencer Roane, thought his letter worthy of a public rebuttal, and he found the effort rather unrewarding. He shared many of Randolph's objections to the Constitution and probably understood the difficulties under which the governor was laboring. His brief essay, "A Plain Dealer," noted the inconsistency between Randolph's itemized objections to the Constitution and his apparent willingness to accept it even if the effort at amending failed.[31] But Roane knew better than to press his point too forcefully, for he recognized that Randolph was trying to sustain his specific objections to the Constitution as well as his lack of sympathy for the position of Henry and his followers. To the extent that these twin objectives reflected the concerns of many thoughtful Virginians, Spencer Roane was on dangerous ground.

By the time Randolph's "letter" was made public, the ratification procedures recommended by the Philadelphia Convention had been sanctified by three states. State conventions in Delaware, Pennsylvania and New Jersey had ratified in December, their actions seemingly indicative of a general willingness to accept the document as written. It was admittedly dangerous to presume that other states would be governed by a similar outlook, but supporters of the Constitution grew more optimistic. Some of the initial enthusiasm for the Constitution had waned, yet the evidence was that, of the people who were interested in such matters, a majority were prepared to give it their support.[32] Georgia and Connecticut ratified during January, and all eyes turned toward Massachusetts where opponents were said to outnumber supporters. As the delegates gathered in Boston, virtually everyone suspected the document was about to face its severest test.[33] If it was rejected by the state that had rallied all the others to the American cause in 1775, it might well be rejected by several of the other states still to be heard from. At the opening of the Massachusetts Convention the opponents of the Constitution held the majority but their potential leaders, John Hancock, the governor, and Samuel Adams, the firebrand of the Revolution, seemed unwilling to serve as their spokesmen. For a time it appeared that the supporters of the Constitution might be able to swing the convention into their favor, but the longer they debated, the more uncertain they became of their strength. Opponents ridiculed the pretentiousness and undemocratic sympathies of those who urged ratification, and insisted Massachusetts would become a pawn of southern slaveholding planters who would control the new government. The advocates of the Constitution, suspecting they were outnumbered, proposed that the state recommend a series of amendments "subjoined to their ratification." Governor Hancock was urged to suggest this solution to the convention and agreed after being rather pointedly reminded that where public office was concerned, he might have more to gain by supporting the Constitution than by opposing it. The maneuver worked and on February 7 the convention ratified the Constitution by a vote of 186 to 168, and recommended that nine amendments be "introduced into the said Constitution."[34]

Word of Massachusetts' ratification quickly reached Virginia, and Randolph sent his reactions to Madison in New York several days later. His candor with Madison was remarkable considering their differing attitudes toward the Constitution:

> The decision of Massts. had it been adverse to the constitution would have damned it here. But as it is, it fixes the event, if New York, New Hampshire and Maryland should follow the example. This must be understood with this restriction; that altho. 9 states will force Virginia by their assent to come in, there is reason to believe that no intelligence of that sort can reach us before our convention meets. . . .
>
> But to return to Massachusetts—what a paltry snare? Some of the amendments are inadmissible, others point against the negro [sic] states, and the others milk and water. The first is among the rocks on which the old confederation has split; the 2nd. is aimed against the southern states—the 3rd. provides [against] no real danger; the first part of the 4th. is as the 3rd. and moreover destroys an essential idea of a national government, the 5th., tho' a new and juster [sic] theory now prevails, ought to be left to the occasional wisdom of congress; the 6th sounds an unnecessary alarm; the 7th strikes not at all the most exceptionable points of the jurisdiction; the 8th I conceive is not true in supposing even at common law a trial of fact to be best *on all occasions* by a jury; and the 9th. can have been designed only to make out a number of amts. equal to the no. of states, who may give birth to the government.[35] In short, H[ancoc]k proposes them not in the form of objections, but *to remove fears*. And I do not conceive that Massachusetts may be yet said to be fairly enlisted; altho. to me it is satisfactory, since the men of talent and property are in its favor [against] the Shayites [sic], and the gentlemen of bad fame with whom we recusants have been classed.[36]

Randolph was unhappy with this first attempt of a state convention to suggest amendments. The amendments were designed to "remove fears" rather than correct errors; they were a maneuver rather than an honest effort to reform the Constitution. The ultimate decision of the Massachusetts Convention was "satisfactory" to the extent that "men of talent" were supporting it, while only "Shaysites" and "gentlemen of bad fame" were opposing it. He obviously resented being "classed" with the latter group. Madison must have found his language most interesting. He would have expected as much from any of the "friends" of the Constitution, but not from a self-styled "recusant."

It was becoming more and more uncomfortable to be in the middle and Randolph didn't like it. As Madison had astutely observed to Edmund Pendleton: "[T]he question on which the proposed Constitution must turn is the simple one whether the Union shall or shall not be continued. There is in my opinion no middle ground to be taken."

Those who were in opposition, he insisted, "are as heterogeneous as can be imagined" and either work for or have a "real tendency" toward disunion.[37] Randolph would not have agreed with this assessment and would have probably insisted a middle position did not necessarily carry with it a "tendency" toward disunion, but he would have had to admit that most of the evidence seemed to support Madison's assessment. It was no longer a question of giving comfort to the enemy; it was the ignominy of being classified as one of them. He didn't think he had said or written anything that might be used by those who opposed the Constitution. But how could he avoid being classified as an advocate of disunion?[38] The answer was obvious—he would throw his support to those who advocated ratification.

As the time for electing delegates to Virginia's convention approached, the political climate was once again subjected to careful analysis. A letter that did not devote a substantial amount of space to assessing the mood of the state was considered worthless and its author indifferent to public issues. Not only was one expected to provide the latest information on the views of friends and acquaintances with political influence, but also to report on the current attitude of groups within the state known to be somewhat hostile to the Constitution.

Edward Carrington, reporting to Madison early in February, found that Henry's "politics" had been so industriously propagated in Cumberland, Pohatan and Chesterfield counties that the people "are much disposed to be his blind followers." He still lacked "satisfactory information" about the disposition of the "southern counties," but he was fairly certain that the "doctrine of amendments" had taken such a "strong ground" within the state that the direct adoption of the Constitution could not be expected unless nine states approved before Virginia's convention met.[39] Several weeks later Randolph reported that Henry had written him to the effect that he would oppose the Constitution "even if only ½ a state should oppose." And, Randolph continued:

> The baptist [sic] interest and the counties on the south side of [the] James River, from Isle of Wright [county] upwards, are highly incensed [i.e pleased] by H—y's opinions, and public speeches, whensoever occasion has presented. As to the temper on the north side, I cannot clearly discern it. But upon a review made by Mr. [John] Marshall of their comparative strength, he seems to think, that the question will be very nice.[40]

And beyond the Alleghenys was the Kentucky district, concerned that the legislature of the new government, safely under the control of northern states, would give away the country's navigation rights on the Mississippi in return for a paltry trade treaty with Spain or some other foreign power. Henry had these votes unless the fears of Kentucky's delegates were neutralized.[41]

The election was held on the first Monday in March. When it was over, the political prognosticators were still uncertain of the relative strength of the contending forces in the forthcoming convention. Most of the better known critics and advocates of the Constitution had been elected to the convention. Henry won easily from Prince Edward County, where he had recently settled; while Mason, facing possible defeat in Fairfax County, where he lived, accepted an invitation to run from Stafford County, where he won handily.[42] Orange County elected Madison, and Caroline County almost instinctively turned to Edmund Pendleton as its representative. But apparently neither faction had captured a clear majority of the delegates, and many counties had unhesitatingly elected men who were on record as undecided and, furthermore, gave every indication of remaining so until the document had been fully debated in convention. And then there was Edmund Randolph, almost in a category by himself and yet too experienced a politician to be a party of one. The voters of Henrico County had selected him as one of their delegates, along with John Marshall who, by contrast, supported the Constitution unequivocally.[43] And the more Virginians debated the relative merits of amendments "prior to ratification" versus amendments "subsequent to ratification," as Massachusetts had done, the more confused the picture became. It made things terribly complicated for those who insisted on predicting what the convention would do.

Early in April Randolph's brother-in-law, Colonel George Nicholas, was insisting that a majority of the delegates were for the Constitution, but Randolph thought differently. He told Madison:

> . . . a comparison of the intelligence which centers here [i.e. in Richmond] from the various parts of Virginia, persuades me, that he [i.e. Nicholas] at least mistakes the degree of the majority, and leads me to suspect, that it lies adverse to the Constitution so far as *previous* amendments go.[44]

If, as Randolph suggested, there was no certain majority for the Constitution and there was considerable evidence that a majority of the delegates would also reject the idea of "previous amendments," the only other alternative was to do as Massachusetts had done—ratify first and then recommend that certain amendments be considered by the new government. Randolph had never had much faith in the so-called Massachusetts formula and now he even began to have serious doubts about pressing for "previous amendments" in Virginia. He explained them to Madison:

Two objections have always struck me, as deserving [of] consideration on the subject of previous amendments; one, that under their cover, a higher game might be played, the other, that the hope of obtaining them might be frustrated by the assent of too many states. The former I fear more and more, daily, not knowing how far the schemes of those who *externally* patronize them, may internally *extend*, believing that personal irritation has roused some to enlarge their original views of opposition, and having myself no disposition to enjoy the credit of establishing my opinion at the expense of public safety. I mention these things in confidence; especially as my final determination will not be taken, until I hear something from Maryland at least.[45]

James Madison must have read these lines with great satisfaction, for his good friend and political ally had finally seen the light of day. Randolph had not "always" believed that there were serious weaknesses in this approach, although it was true that he had "always" assumed that Henry was prepared to play a "higher game." But it seemed that Madison's frequent letters on the questionable motives of those who opposed the Constitution had finally caused Randolph to abandon—or almost abandon—his cherished formula for ratification. Madison, confident of Randolph's attachment to the Union and undisguised contempt for Henry, had been predicting as much for several months.[46] Now he knew that Randolph was with him. The only question that remained unresolved was the role Randolph would play in the convention and that, in all likelihood, would not be decided until the delegates had assembled in Richmond.

In the meantime the country was drawing closer to a final decision. While the Massachusetts method of ratification was still the principal topic of conversation, Rhode Island rejected the document in a popular referendum. The outcome was more or less expected because those who supported the Constitution were boycotting the referendum and pronouncing it as an illegal method of ratification. Rhode Island seemed to be determined to live up to her reputation as "the colony of the otherwise-minded." But then Maryland ratified during the last week in April, and South Carolina approved it on May 23. In each state the advocates of the Constitution had seen the document ratified by a comfortable margin, which made the prospects for the future "promising." Eight states had now ratified, and the New Hampshire Convention, which had adjourned on February 13, was due to reconvene on June 18. If New Hampshire acted favorably, the Constitution would have the requisite nine-state approval to go into effect. But the two states that were being watched with greatest interest were Virginia and New York. Both states had scheduled their conventions for June. If Virginia or New York rejected the Constitution, those who led the opposition would be in a position to force amendments on the new government for no one saw much chance of its surviving very long if either of these very influential states remained outside the Union.[47]

The month of May found the "friends" of the Constitution in each state laying their strategy with care. Their best calculations indicated that they would not have a safe majority in either convention. In New York they didn't even come close. In Virginia Patrick Henry, George Mason and, indirectly, Richard Henry Lee would lead the opposition to the Constitution, while in New York the opposition would be led by Governor George Clinton, ably assisted by DeWitt Clinton, Abraham Yates and Melancton Smith. Clinton was a master politician and had an immense personal following in his state, while in Virginia, Henry's talent in debate and statewide popularity were admitted to be second to none. Madison would manage the defense in Virginia, and the brilliant and shrewdly practical Alexander Hamilton would do the same in New York. Since Virginia's chances of ratifying were infinitely better than New York's, it was understood that Hamilton would try to delay the vote of the New York Convention until Virginia had acted. If Virginia ratified, then New York would be under considerable pressure to "come in," for it would be inevitable that the new government would be given a fair trial and nothing would be served by obstinate rejection. If Virginia failed to ratify, then New York's rejection would be a foregone conclusion.[48]

As the delegates began to converge on Richmond for the convention, Randolph tried to clear his desk of a backlog of unfinished state business. He knew from experience that conventions tended to be exhausting affairs, and he felt he had both a personal and a public obligation to be in daily attendance. He still had not offered a wholly satisfactory explanation for his own conduct at the Philadelphia Convention. Now he felt he had the added responsibility of publicly dissociating himself from Henry. In fact, if he wanted to save the Constitution in Virginia, he probably would have to do much more. If Henry held true to form—and everyone expected he would—he would try to win over the uncommitted delegates at the convention with his persuasive oratory. The only person of comparable political stature who could weave a spell over the convention with almost as much effectiveness was Virginia's very popular governor. If Randolph, a self-proclaimed "recusant," were to openly and dramatically cast his lot with the "friends" of the Constitution, Henry might be foiled.

11

Advocate, June 1788

Sunday, June 1, dawned clear and warm as the last of the delegates arrived in Richmond. And, in the familiar spirit of legislative openings, the taverns and rooming houses were filled with delegates exchanging greetings and catching up on the latest news. Nor was the Constitution the only subject of conversation among these men. An unusual spring drought was beginning to affect their crops, particularly in the tidewater region. Facing a possible loss in revenue from a small harvest, they talked about this problem almost as much as they did about the Constitution.[1]

The principals in the great constitutional debate, Madison, Henry, Mason and Randolph, were all present and were busily and very obviously assessing the sympathies of the delegates. Their would-be associates, somewhat less conspicuous in the confusion surrounding the opening of this extraordinary gathering, were also beginning to circulate among the delegates.

Lending their support to Madison were two of Randolph's brothers-in-law, George and Wilson Cary Nicholas, both representing Albemarle County. They were actively soliciting support for the Constitution during these final hours before the convention convened. Equally zealous, though probably less effective in winning over the undecided delegates, was Henry Lee from Westmoreland. A perceptive analyst of Virginia's political currents, he had been one of Madison's most useful correspondents these past few months. Representing Williamsburg was James Innes, one of the most talented lawyers practicing in Virginia and a very persuasive speaker. It was expected that the advocates of the Constitution would put his considerable skill to good use on the floor of the convention.

Supporting Henry and Mason on the other side of the constitutional question were Benjamin Harrison from Charles City County and William Grayson from Prince Edward County, plus two or three younger, and therefore somewhat less influential, delegates. Like many of Virginia's senior statesmen with a public career that extended back into the colonial and Revolutionary periods, Harrison had very considerable experience and an eminent respectability that could not be easily ignored. His critical attitude toward the Constitution was well known and, even more significant, was recognized as being wholly free of personal political ambition. Grayson, who was considerably more fixed in his opposition to the new instrument of government than Harrison, was expected to play an active role in the convention's proceedings. He was convinced that government under the Articles offered southern interests far greater protection than would the national government established by this Constitution. He distrusted the commercial interests in New York and New England and suspected they would willingly abandon our navigation rights on the Mississippi for a self-serving trade treaty. He was therefore an invaluable ally to Henry and Mason.[2]

The convention opened in the temporary capitol building at Cary and Fourteenth streets. The first few days were spent in choosing the officers and standing committees and determining the rules of procedure that would govern debate.[3] The delegates also decided to move their meetings to the more spacious accommodations of New Academy Hall situated on Broad Street between Eleventh and Twelfth streets.[4] The supporters of the Constitution secured their first victory in the selection of Edmund Pendleton as president of the convention, although his prestige would hardly have permitted the choice of any other.[5] It was Wednesday afternoon, the 4th, before the convention, sitting as a Committee of the Whole Convention with George Wythe presiding as committee chairman, could give its full attention to the Constitution.[6]

Unwittingly George Mason had placed a powerful weapon in the hands of the supporters of the Constitution when he moved that the document be considered clause by clause.[7] The advocates of the Constitution were perfectly willing to defend the document in this manner if that would ensure its ratification.[8] Thus formal consideration of the document began after the convention secretary, John Beckley, had read only the preamble and first two sections of Article I.[9] It was the second section of Article I, which contained the controversial paragraph providing for proportional representation in the lower house of the legislature, that initiated the debate.

George Nicholas was the first to secure the floor. Masterfully defending the principle of proportional representation, he spoke at length in support of these two sections.[10] When he had finished, Henry sought recognition, and Wythe nodded in his direction. Henry called upon Virginia's delegates to the Federal Convention to give an accounting of their conduct or, to put it in Henry's language: "You must, therefore, forgive the solicitation of one unworthy member to know what danger could have arisen from the present Confederation, and what are the causes of this proposal to change our government."[11]

Henry took his seat and Wythe now acknowledged the raised hand of the governor. Tall, yet rather portly for thirty-five, Randolph had a commanding appearance, an image that was considerably enhanced by the uncertainty that surrounded the role he would play in this convention.[12] The chamber fell silent, for everyone realized that Randolph might well be the person who would decide the fate of the Constitution in this convention. Indeed, Henry had provided him with a perfect excuse for speaking so early. Here was the first of Virginia's delegates to the Federal Convention to explain his conduct before this convention. He started off slowly, engaging in rhetorical flourishes that might have impressed a different audience. But this particular audience was not interested, for they knew that Henry would put on a better performance before this convention closed. Then Randolph got down to cases:

> Before I press into the body of the argument, I must take the liberty of mentioning the part I have already borne in this great question; but let me not here be misunderstood. I come not to apologize to any individual within these walls, to the Convention as a body, or even to my fellow citizens at large. . . . I come hither, regardless of allurements, to continue, as I have begun; to repeat my earnest endeavors for a firm energetic government; to enforce my objections to the Constitution, and to concur in any practical scheme of amendments, but I never will assent to any scheme that will operate [toward] a dissolution of the Union, or any measure which may lead to it.

This much, at least, was clear: he was for the Constitution with amendments, and he was, above all, interested in preserving the Union. But still he had not publicly committed himself on the all-important question of whether he would work for amendments prior to ratification or accept the method now immortalized by the Massachusetts Convention. The delegates and the numerous spectators crowding the back of the chamber did not have long to wait:

> As with me the only question has ever been between previous and subsequent amendments, so will I express my apprehensions, that the postponement of this convention to so late a day has extinguished the probability of the former without inevitable ruin to the Union, and the Union is the anchor of our political salvation; and I will assent to the lopping of this limb (meaning his arm), before I assent to the dissolution of the Union.[13]

That night, when Madison wrote to Washington, he reduced Randolph's oratory to its bare essentials: "The Governor has declared the day of previous amendments passed and thrown himself fully into the federal scale."[14] Madison had suspected as much for weeks. What was most gratifying to him was that Randolph had decided to commit himself so early.

The debate the following day set the tone of the convention for the next week. With Article I, Sections 1 and 2, still under consideration, the advocates of the Constitution launched their offensive. Pendleton spoke first and he was followed by Henry Lee of Westmoreland.[15] Pendleton lent a respectability to the cause which only Washington, were he present, could have enhanced. Lee, a brilliant young military leader during the Revolution, spoke the sentiments of those Virginians whose public life, like Randolph's, did not extend into the colonial period. Both men directed their speeches toward the sections of the Constitution under consideration, but both also seized the occasion to attack Henry. Henry had said very little so far and had done nothing to warrant such attention. It almost seemed as if they were trying to overwhelm the controversial delegate from Prince Edward County before he could cast his spell over the convention.

If such were the plan, it was to no avail, for Henry was next to take the floor. Graciously he acknowledged the complimentary references to him in Lee's speech. His tone was calm; his cadence measured. Point by point he referred to the arguments of those who had spoken before him, shifting from Lee's speech to Pendleton's, and then back again. Turning to his own attitude toward the Constitution, he very candidly stated his opposition: "It is said eight states have adopted this plan, I declare that if twelve states and a half had adopted it, I would, with manly firmness, and in spite of an erring world, reject it." On and on he went, tactfully turning the arguments of his opponents against them. Attempted by another, the speech would have been pure demagoguery; coming from Henry's lips, it was a masterful demonstration of his persuasive style of oratory. The people who crowded into the back of the chamber listened in respectful silence. For fully three hours he held the audience's attention and not once did interest lag or his voice falter. When he sat down, everyone knew that Patrick Henry had mounted his expected offensive against the Constitution.[16] It was evident, too, that he was not going to adhere to Mason's resolution that the Constitution be discussed section by section. He had delivered a broadside, and the supporters of the Constitution would have to counter with a complete defense or see their precious handiwork buried under an avalanche of words.

In all probability Madison and his supporters held a virtual council of war that evening. A plan of action had to be agreed upon to counter Henry's skillful oratory. It was now obvious that he was trying to win over the uncommitted members of the convention before the Constitution had been debated in full. To resort to a closely reasoned and scholarly analysis of the document would only supply him with new material for his broadsides while convincing few of the delegates. Then, too, only Madison possessed the kind of detailed knowledge necessary to engage in such an analysis, and he could not begin to match Henry as an orator. The solution was obvious; someone must be assigned the task of meeting Henry on his own ground. Only Randolph and James Innes of Williamsburg could even hope to match him in debate and, of the two, Innes was reputed to be the more skilled. Unfortunately Innes lacked the prestige and political influence of the governor and did not have the kind of understanding of the document that came from having attended the Federal Convention. More importantly, Randolph was a late convert to ratification. If he had seen fit to cast his lot with the supporters of the Constitution, possibly he could persuade others to do the same. The idea was at least worth trying. Randolph would take the floor the first thing the next morning. According to the plan, he was to hold the floor as long as he could and then surrender to Madison. Madison, in turn, would hold the floor until he tired and then surrender to George Nicholas who, it was hoped, would be able to talk until the hour of adjournment. Then at least Henry would be denied the opportunity of intoxicating the audience two days in a row.[17]

When the convention assembled the next morning, the 6th, Randolph was on his feet the moment the delegates resolved themselves into a Committee of the Whole. Addressing the committee chairman, George Wythe, a man who had been a colleague of his father and uncle during the late colonial period when Randolph was but a young boy growing up in Williamsburg, he said: "Mr. Chairman, I am a child of the Revolution. My country very early indeed, took me under its protection, at a time when I most wanted it, and, by a succession of favors and honors, gratified even my most ardent wishes." Wythe and others understood what he meant. Shifting away from his own past, he began to construct a broad-based defense of the Constitution: drawing examples from English history, citing instances where states had been delinquent or indifferent to their responsibilities under the Articles, and expounding on the many problems Virginia would face if she remained aloof from the new government. It was such a remarkable array of facts and quotations that his audience suspected he must have spent the entire night collecting the necessary material for this speech. He was, in effect, serving notice on the delegates that he intended to take an active role in promoting the ratification of the Constitution.[18]

Saturday provided more of the same. Francis Corbin of Middlesex County, Randolph and Madison spoke in the morning.[19] Then in the afternoon the apparently inexhaustible Patrick Henry took the floor. Henry took very deliberate aim and launched into an attack on Randolph; he chided him for his inconsistencies and demanded to know why he now advocated ratification. Randolph, sensitive to such charges, became irritated with Henry's sarcasm and interrupted his speech to accuse him of misconstruing his remarks. Henry compounded the injury by pointedly refusing to take cognizance of Randolph's complaint.[20] Fortunately for all concerned, Sunday was a day of rest. But on Monday morning Henry was once again ready to do battle. His stamina as a speaker was a constant source of amazement to his opponents.[21] When he took his seat, Henry Lee of Westmoreland took up the thankless task of attempting to answer him.[22]

Randolph waited patiently for Lee to finish and then rose in his place:

> Having consumed heretofore so much of your time [i.e. the delegates to the Convention], I did not intend to trouble you again so soon. But now I call on this committee [of the Whole Convention], by way of right, to permit me to answer some severe charges against the friends of the new Constitution. It is a right I am entitled to, and shall have. I have spoken twice in this committee. I have shown the principles which actuated the general Convention; and attempted to prove that, after the ratification of the proposed system by so many states, the preservation of the Union depended on its adoption by us. I find myself attacked in the most illiberal manner by the honorable gentleman (Mr. Henry). I disdain his aspersions and his insinuations. His asperity is warranted by no principle of parliamentary decency, nor compatible with the least shadow of friendship; and if our friendship must, *let it fall, like Lucifer, never to rise again.*

His angry voice, barely under control, creased the packed and silent chamber as the eyes of every delegate shifted from Randolph to Henry and back again. He continued:

> Let him remember that it is not to answer him, but to satisfy this respectable audience that I now get up. He has accused me of inconsistency in this very respectable assembly. Sir, if I do not stand on the bottom of integrity, and pure love for Virginia, as much as those who can be most clamorous, I wish to resign my existence. . . . When I had the honor of being deputed to the federal Convention, to revise the existing system, I was impressed with the necessity of a more energetic government, and thoroughly persuaded that the salvation of the people of America depended on an intimate and firm union. The honorable gentlemen there can say, that, when I went thither, no man was a stronger friend to such an union than myself. I informed you why I refused to sign.

He then paused and picked up his now well-known "letter" of October 10 and proceeded to read the concluding section to the delegates. After he had finished, he began to explain the consistency of his present position with his earlier conduct.

Henry interrupted him in mid-sentence and announced that he had not intended to offend anyone and that he was sorry if he had offended Randolph without intending it. Randolph, refusing to accept the apology, turned toward Henry and coolly observed that he was relieved at what the honorable gentleman had said, "that were it not for the concession of the gentleman, he would have made some men's hair stand on end, by the disclosure of certain facts." Henry, his eyes flashing with anger, was again on his feet. He demanded that Randolph explain himself or retract his last statement. The governor ignored him and without so much as a pause resumed the defense of his own conduct.

He was, he continued, no more or less attached to the Union now than he had ever been and he could prove it by the public letter he held in his hand. He had, he said, fully informed the freeholders of Henrico County of his views and stated that he did not wish to be elected to this convention. He had never created the impression, however, that he was going to do anything but support the Constitution if they elected him as one of their delegates. He then marched up to the desk of John Beckley, the convention secretary, and defiantly threw a copy of his "letter" on the desk, and announced that he was making it available for the *"curious and malicious."* Returning to his place, he resumed his attack on Henry by belittling his views and citing the inconsistencies in his earlier remarks.[23]

By the time Monday's session had reached the hour of adjournment both men were apparently prepared to meet on a field of honor to settle their differences. Fortunately cooler heads must have prevailed, and the meeting never materialized.[24]

On Tuesday the atmosphere grew more relaxed as other delegates gradually began to enter into the debate.[25] For Randolph, it was a welcome relief because it lessened considerably his own duties on the convention floor. Having assumed prime responsibility for answering Henry, he had no choice but to be present every day from the opening of the session at eleven in the morning until adjournment late in the afternoon. Such a schedule left him with little time or energy for the day-to-day responsibilities of the governorship which, it seems, were simply ignored. The Executive Council did not meet, letters went unanswered and absolutely nothing was done to prepare for the forthcoming special session of the legislature.[26] As the burden of the debate shifted to others, Randolph began to think about giving some time to these other responsibilities. He probably decided that if the debate lagged or the delegates began to argue about technical points, which only Madison could really handle, he would slip away early and attend to some of the matters that were once again beginning to collect on his desk.

As for his family life, it was virtually nonexistent. Being both a permanent resident of Richmond and the governor of the state meant he probably had to entertain delegates in his home rather frequently and with some degree of elegance. But these affairs were anything but relaxed social gatherings. Instead they served only to disrupt normal family life and strain the budget. His wife and children saw him as much as ever, but seldom, it seemed, as husband and father. He was home a great deal, perhaps even more than usual, but always as a public man engaged in public business. It is possible that the rest of the family just decided to wait until July when all this was supposed to end and when, they hoped, they could all vacation together in the mountains away from the heat of Richmond and the burdens of public office.

When the session opened on Friday morning, the 13th, George Nicholas tried to bring the delegates back to a clause-by-clause discussion of the Constitution, as had been the original plan.[27] Henry was quick to voice his opposition and asserted that the document should continue to be discussed at large. He then went on to express the wish that the transactions of Congress relative to the navigation of the Mississippi be communicated to this convention by those who had sat in Congress at the time.[28] It was, as Madison was quick to recognize, a brilliant move.[29] Henry knew the issue had been a sensitive one in the Kentucky district since August, 1786, when Congress authorized John Jay, as Secretary of Foreign Affairs, to "forbear" from insisting on our navigation rights on the Mississippi in return for a favorable commercial treaty with Spain. Everyone suspected that the delegates from Kentucky were judging the new Constitution solely on whether the government created by it was likely to protect their navigation rights on the Mississippi or would bargain them away in return for a favorable trade treaty with a foreign power. It was not merely a matter of the delegates explaining their conduct or voting record in Congress; they had the added burden of trying to convince the delegates from Kentucky that their rights on the river would be more secure under the Constitution than they had been under the Articles. At stake were thirteen crucial votes from the seven Kentucky counties, plus the vote of those delegates from Virginia's other western counties who might follow their lead.[30]

To all this Randolph should have been nothing more than an interested spectator for he had not sat in Congress during these critical debates. But at the end of a day devoted to comments by those delegates who had been members of Virginia's congressional delegation at the time, Randolph rose to throw one further charge at Henry in connection with this particular subject. Henry, he said, was deliberately attempting to use this issue to seek votes against the Constitution rather than debate the document on its merits. He was, as everyone realized, absolutely right, for this was precisely what Henry was attempting to do. Having leveled this charge against Henry, he then proceeded to do the same thing himself by offering his own views on the Mississippi question. When the debate ended inconclusively late in the afternoon in the midst of a violent—though very welcome—thunderstorm, Kentucky's delegates were still suspicious of the new Constitution and reluctant to give it their support.[31]

It was after this debate ended that the tone of the sessions suddenly changed for the better. All the next week the convention moved through the Constitution, article by article, section by section. Madison and Mason carried much of the burden of arguing their respective positions. The delegates must have listened in sheer admiration as two acknowledged constitutionalists quietly and dispassionately discussed the merits and deficiencies of the new instrument of government with only an occasional rhetorical flourish. Two generations of Virginians, made partners by the Revolution, locked in brilliant debate. It stood in sharp contrast to the verbal histrionics of Randolph and Henry.[32]

Circumstances did, however, provide Randolph with certain responsibilities during this stage of the convention. Mason and Randolph had, of course, held very similar views on the Constitution during the final weeks of the convention in Philadelphia. It was only natural, therefore, that Mason would occasionally seize the opportunity to publicly chide Randolph for his inconsistencies by noting the differences between his past and present views of the Constitution. Randolph was quick to take up the challenge. He admitted his earlier opposition and stated that nothing had occurred to alter his views. He was still plagued by the same fears that caused him to speak out at the Federal Convention, but, he insisted, Mason should not therefore conclude that he was bound to reject the Constitution or, in the context of the current debate in this convention, to insist on amendments prior to ratification:

> I repeat it again, though I do not reverence the Constitution, that its adoption is necessary to avoid the storm which is hanging over America, and that no greater curse can befall her than the dissolution of the political connection between the states. Whether we shall propose previous or subsequent amendments is now the only dispute. It is supererogation to repeat again the arguments in support of each; but I ask, gentlemen, whether, as eight states have adopted it, it be not safer to adopt it, and rely on the probability of

obtaining amendments, than, by a rejection, to hazard a breach of the Union?[33]

He was readily admitting that he still held to most of his original objections, but, given the alternatives open to Virginia—this Constitution or the dissolution of the Union—he now felt that he had no choice but to support ratification and then hope for subsequent amendments.

The weekend of June 21–22 brought a brief reprieve from the heat of debate if not the heat of summer, but Monday found the tiring delegates again uncomfortably assembled in the overcrowded New Academy Hall. It was believed and hoped that this would be the final week of the convention. By Monday afternoon each section of the Constitution had been read and debated.[34] What remained to be decided was whether Virginia was going to insist on amendments prior to ratification or, as the supporters of the Constitution were urging, ratify and then suggest amendments. The debate reverted to the rambling style that characterized the first week of the convention.

Again Henry moved into the forefront, although now he seemed to assume that the supporters of the Constitution had gained the upper hand. His defensive attitude was most evident in his speech on Tuesday morning, the 24th, which, while not as spellbinding as some of his earlier efforts, was his most balanced and dispassionate speech to date. It was at this time that he made his first formal presentation of the changes he sought in the document. They consisted in a set of resolutions that amounted to a declaration of rights and a series of amendments that were designed to correct what he felt were the more objectionable features of the Constitution. He made a long and moving plea for prior amendments and coupled it with a threat to withdraw from the convention if this procedure was rejected.[35]

Randolph secured the chairman's attention and rose to reply. Henry's amendments could not, of course, go into the record without some comment on them, but more serious in Randolph's view was his threat to withdraw from the convention. If he carried out his threat, and if others seized upon such a method to avoid voting on the Constitution, the convention would disintegrate. This proposition had to be refuted before it gained additional supporters:

I beg to make a few remarks on the subject of secession. If there be in this house members who have in contemplation to secede from the majority, let me conjure them, by all the ties of honor and duty, to consider what they are about to do. Some of them have more property than I have, and all of them are equal to me in personal rights. Such an idea of refusing to submit to the decision of the majority is destructive of every republican principle. It will kindle a civil war, and reduce everything to anarchy and confusion. To avoid a calamity so lamentable, I would submit to it, if it contained greater evil than it does.

As for the amendments, Randolph took them up one by one. He attempted to show that some of them granted rights that were already guaranteed by the Constitution, while several of the others would only weaken the authority of the central government under the new Constitution. It was a speech directed not at Henry but at the delegates whose votes still remained in doubt. It was more of a plea for ratification and subsequent amendments than a total and unqualified rejection of Henry's amendments:

> Reflect on the facility of obtaining amendments if you adopt, and weigh the danger if you do not. Recollect that many other states have adopted it, who wish for many amendments. I ask you if it be not better to adopt, and run the chance of amending it hereafter, than run the risk of endangering the Union. The Confederation is gone; it has no authority. If, in this situation, we reject the Constitution, the Union will be dissolved, the dogs of war will break loose, and anarchy and discord will complete the ruin of this country. Previous adoption will prevent these deplorable mischiefs. The union of sentiments with us in the adopting states will render subsequent amendments easy. I therefore rest my happiness with perfect confidence on this subject.[36]

Rhetorical language aside, Randolph believed what he was saying. The survival of the Union was now the only thing that really mattered, and all other issues were subservient to it. Randolph's own "conversion" lent sincerity to his arguments.

The convention had reached its final phase. As the crucial moment of voting drew near, one delegate after another took the floor to express his views. Each one spoke candidly, more for the record than with any thought of swaying the convention.[37] Henry was among them. He assured the delegates and the public audience that was now packed into the back of the convention hall that should his proposals be defeated, he would work "peaceably" to remove the defects of the Constitution.[38] Randolph was the final speaker before the Committee of the Whole Convention adjourned for the last time:

> Lest . . . some future analyst should, in the spirit of party vengeance deign to mention my name, let him recite these truths—*that I went to the federal Convention* with the strongest affection for the Union, that I acted there in full conformity with this affection; *that I refused to subscribe because I had, and I still have, objections to the Constitution,* and wished a free inquiry into its merits; and that the accession of eight states reduced our *deliberations* to the single question of *Union or no Union.*[39]

The committee then reported out a preamble and two resolutions. The first resolution simply expressed the opinion of the committee that the Constitution should be ratified. The second recommended that whatever amendments were "deemed necessary" should be referred to the consideration of the first Congress that should assemble under the new Constitution, "to be acted on according to the mode prescribed in the 5th Article thereof."[40]

The convention then took up the first resolution. When it was read for the second time, a motion was made to amend it and substitute the following:

> Resolved, That *previous to the ratification of the new Constitution* of government recommended by the late federal Convention, a declaration of rights, asserting, and securing from encroachment, the great principles of civil and religious liberty, and the unalienable rights of the people, together with amendments to the most exceptionable parts of the said Constitution of government, *ought to be referred by this Convention to the other states of the American confederacy for their consideration.*[41]

A vote on the motion to amend was taken—ays 80, nos 88.[42] The motion was defeated, marking the last effort of Henry, Mason and their supporters to secure amendments prior to ratification. The resolution, as reported out of committee, was then voted on and, as expected, the supporters of the Constitution carried the resolution. The vote was 89 to 79.[43] The second resolution, as reported out of committee, was then agreed to with only minor changes.[44]

Those who had taken an active part in the proceedings of the convention divided as expected. Among the rank and file the vote was less predictable. Ten of Kentucky's thirteen delegates voted against the Constitution, while the delegates from the tidewater region and from Virginia's northern counties generally supported it. Delegates representing the counties between the Shenandoah Valley and the Ohio River, who theoretically should have voted with the Kentucky delegates, cast their lot with the supporters of the Constitution.[45] But it was very close and a shift of five delegates would have meant the passage of the substitute resolution calling for amendments prior to ratification.

With these crucial votes out of the way, the convention appointed two committees; one to prepare a form of ratification and the second to "prepare and report such amendments as by them shall be deemed necessary. . . ."[46] Randolph was made chairman of the first committee and a member of the second.[47] The question of the form of ratification, having been the subject of general discussion before the Committee of the Whole Convention, was quickly resolved. The form that was adopted was the one originally suggested by Randolph.[48] Thus, on

June 26, the engrossed Constitution was signed by Edmund Pendleton on behalf of the convention in a brief formal session.[49]

On the following day the committee appointed to prepare amendments was ready to deliver its report. George Wythe, its chairman, introduced some forty amendments.[50] The first twenty were identified as a bill of rights, corresponding rather closely to Virginia's Bill of Rights, which had been drafted some twenty years before by Mason. They were accepted without debate.[51] The remaining amendments, presumably authored by Henry, were designed to promote the changes advocated by those who had worked against unconditional ratification. When the convention turned to this second act of amendments, a motion was made to strike the third. It read as follows:

> When the Congress shall lay direct taxes or excises, they shall immediately inform the executive power of each state of the quota of such state, according to the census herein directed, which is proposed to be thereby raised; and if the legislature of any state shall pass a law which shall be effectual for raising such quota at the time required by Congress, the taxes and excises laid by Congress shall not be collected in such state.[52]

Its intent was all too clear to the supporters of the Constitution, and they would have no part of it. To their surprise the motion to strike the amendment failed by a vote of 65 to 80.[53] Apparently the "friends" of the Constitution were not going to have things completely their own way. There were obviously a number of delegates who felt that Henry and his supporters had the right to strive for this amendment in Congress and so voted even though they were not in sympathy with it themselves. But Edmund Randolph was not one of them; he voted with the supporters of the Constitution to strike the amendment. His disdain for the amendment itself—traceable no doubt to his own congressional service—accounted for his opposition. All the amendments that had been introduced by Wythe's committee were then approved.[54] The struggle for ratification in Virginia was over; the Massachusetts formula had found useful application.

As news of Virginia's ratification spread northward, news of New Hampshire's ratification was being carried south. The newest state in the infant nation had the distinction of being the ninth state to ratify, the requisite number for the Constitution to go into effect. Virginia came next, and then all eyes turned toward New York where the opposing factions were engaged in a bitter and closely contested struggle and where Virginia's favorable vote was considered highly important. The New York vote came on July 26—30 to 27 in favor of the Constitution. Hamilton and his followers, outnumbered from the beginning, had engineered an amazing political victory. The Constitution now had a practical as well as a legal foundation, and the forces of nationalism were clearly in command.[55] The states remaining out of the Union would, in time, give their assent also, for now they really had no choice.

For Randolph, the whole experience was, in a sense, very depressing. He always felt that his honest efforts were continually being frustrated by the momentum with which the whole constitutional question was moving toward a climax. He believed that his objections to the Constitution were never given a fair hearing because there never seemed to be an opportunity to implement a practical procedure for considering them. He knew they had been introduced too late in the Federal Convention to be considered by that body, but he hoped he would at least have the requisite support to gain a last-minute revision of the ratification procedures so that they might be considered by another convention. He did not secure this support, and from this point on the whole process seemed to work against a second convention. The decision of the Continental Congress to forward the document to the states without any recommendations and the prompt ratification by several states, followed, in turn, by Massachusetts' ratification and subsequent amendments, made another convention impossible and seemingly unnecessary. By the time the Virginia Convention met, the issue had become further complicated by the fear that Henry's insistence on prior amendments might ultimately promote not an improvement in the Constitution but a dissolution of the Union. It seemed that once again practical political considerations prevented Randolph from openly advocating a plan for revising the document before it went into effect. Ultimately he found himself forced into a position where he had to accept the idea of subsequent amendments or risk everything, even the Union itself.

These fourteen months of constitutional debate had still another message for Randolph which he found very distressing. For the first time in his public life he discovered how futile and unpopular it was to advocate what he called a "middle position." The Constitution polarized public opinion as he had never seen it polarized before. The result was a hardening of factional lines to the point where being the advocate of a "middle position" was considered reprehensible. He didn't like the kinds of remarks that were being made about him; he didn't like being denied the right to advocate the Constitution on his own terms and, most important, he didn't like the "either-or" atmosphere that was beginning to surround the discussions of public issues. The ultimate acceptance of the Constitution and the prospects of a new and more effective government quickly cooled the political climate, but Randolph seemed to suspect that the character of American political life was undergoing a change, the implications of which he resented.

12

The Governor Focuses on State Problems October 1787–November 1788

During the fourteen months of his intense involvement—first rejection, then hesitation, finally assent—with the constitutional issue, Randolph could not ignore his duties as governor. Between his return from the Philadelphia Convention and his resignation as governor in November, 1788, he was deeply involved in a number of fairly serious state problems. The most significant of these, at least from his point of view, was the growing demand among the debtor groups for an expansion of the state's currency through the issuance of "paper money." While fully aware of the financial strain under which these people were living, Randolph had little faith in their "paper money" remedy. In March, 1787, he noted the apparent resurgence of a paper money faction in the state and sarcastically remarked to Madison that if its advocates were successful at the polls, "who can say, that an asylum will not be opened in the temple dedicated to fraud?"[1]

After Randolph left for Philadelphia in May, 1787, isolated instances of protest against the shortage of money were reported in several counties south of the James River, but for some reason he was never informed of them.[2] Then in late August, at the very time the Philadelphia Convention was putting the Constitution into final form, he received an alarming report of an insurrection in Greenbriar County, one of the state's more important frontier counties on the western slopes of the Appalachians. The first information came from the county lieutenant, George Clendenin, the ranking law officer in the county. He was anything but reassuring.[3] Randolph promptly referred the matter to Lieutenant Governor Beverley Randolph in Richmond and asked that it be immediately brought to the attention of the Executive Council.[4] As reports reached him of "commotions . . . rising in some other important counties," he became very concerned and wrote once again to the lieutenant governor and inquired why he had received no information on the Greenbriar disturbance: "I must therefore repeat my entreaty to you for a particular detail on this subject, as I shall not consider myself as

[151]

authorized to remain here longer than I can prepare for my return, if the confusions be truly stated."[5] A few days later he learned that the commotions in Greenbriar County had subsided.[6] He remained apprehensive about the situation but, for the time being at least, he abandoned all plans for an immediate return to Richmond.

When he returned to Virginia a few weeks later he was given a full report on the Greenbriar incident as well as the other disturbances that had occurred during his absence from the state. It was decided that a full transcript of all correspondence on the Greenbriar insurrection should be forwarded to the House of Delegates so that they might know how the Executive Council had responded to the crisis.[7]

As the delegates gathered in Richmond for the opening of the Assembly on October 15 everyone was, of course, discussing Randolph's refusal to sign the Constitution and terribly interested in how he would explain himself in his formal letter to the speaker of the House of Delegates. In that letter Randolph was noncommittal on the Constitution, but reminded the legislature that the state was confronted with a host of other problems, including a grave monetary crisis that demanded its immediate attention.[8]

Wholly confident of its ability to cope with each and every problem mentioned in the governor's letter, the House of Delegates accepted its assignment with equanimity. In rapid sequence it authorized the calling of a state convention to consider the Constitution (without waiting for Randolph to declare himself), routinely reelected Randolph to a second term as governor and selected Virginia's delegates to the Continental Congress for the coming year. Only then did it matter-of-factly turn its attention toward the smoldering antagonism of those who felt the state should relieve the grave money shortage by authorizing the issuance of paper money.[9] The first move of the House was ruthlessly decisive: "Resolved, . . . That the making [of] paper currency, or anything but gold or silver coin, a tender in discharge of debts contracted in money, is contrary to every principle of sound policy as well as justice."[10] The resolution passed unanimously.[11] Then, after considering and rejecting a proposal that would have permitted the payment of private debts through installments, the House initiated a thorough review of the state's existing tax laws with the intention of providing some form of tax relief for people with limited financial resources.[12] It was a difficult problem to solve, for the tax revenues of the state had to be maintained at a level sufficient to provide for the normal needs of the state, the annual requisitions of Congress and the very considerable interest payments due on the Revolutionary debts.

The result of these efforts was a general revenue bill that abolished the highly unpopular certificate tax, increased the duties on a long list of foreign imports, decreed that arrearages in back taxes should, when collected, be applied to the discharge of all warrants issued by the state, authorized the use of certain state warrants to discharge unpaid taxes and allocated moneys collected from the land tax and slave tax to meet a portion of the balance due on the requisition payments owed to Congress.[13] A separate bill designed to offer "great relief and ease to the Citizens of this Commonwealth" authorized the payment of certain taxes for the current year in "tobacco notes" rather than currency.[14] Some further easing of public concern was obtained when the legislature, in passing a bill that authorized the recovery of debts by British creditors, inserted a suspending clause into the act that made fulfillment of certain provisions of the peace treaty by Britain a prior condition to the implementation of this act.[15]

Randolph was probably very pleased with this legislative record. It was essentially quite conservative, particularly in its approach to monetary problems, and he took comfort in this for he had little or no faith in paper money. Yet it was a record that was responsive to the needs of the people and involved substantive rather than token remedies at a time when many people were under great economic strain.

The first significant step in providing for the gradual reduction of the state's public debt was also taken during this session of the legislature, and Randolph must be given some of the credit for advocating the passage of a bill to set up the machinery for accomplishing this task. In May, 1787, Arthur Lee, a member of the Confederation's Board of Treasury, alerted Randolph to the fact that many states were establishing special funds for the express purpose of purchasing on the open market the depreciated public securities of their own state and of the United States. Pointing out that the public securities of the United States simply had to increase in value once the Constitution was ratified, and any state that had the foresight to purchase them now would certainly realize a sizable profit after the federal government was established, he urged Randolph to do the same in Virginia.[16] Randolph received Lee's letter while he was in Philadelphia and promptly forwarded it to Richmond for presentation to the Executive Council. He frankly admitted that, absorbed as he was in other matters, he could not decide whether the advice should be accepted or rejected.[17]

After Randolph returned to Richmond it was decided that the matter should be brought to the attention of the legislature, with the result that it, too, was included in his official letter to the speaker of the House of Delegates.[18] The Assembly promptly recognized its significance, and on December 14 a law was passed providing for the establishment of a sinking fund to be used to purchase state and Continental securities at current market prices.[19] This meant that the state, if it could find the necessary funds, would be able to retire a portion of its own public debt at less than face value. It also opened up the possibility of the state's being able to realize a profit on the public securities of the United States by purchasing them at less than face value and then holding them until redeemed by the new federal government, presumably at a higher value. Although the funds to activate the sinking fund were never available during the remaining months of Randolph's tenure as governor, the essential legislation had been passed during his administration.[20]

As with many other states, Virginia's economic solvency seemed ultimately to be linked to the question of whether its considerable claims for Revolutionary expenses would be absorbed by the Confederation. For Virginia, this involved the heavy expenditures directly associated with the Revolution plus the added cost of financing military operations in the northwest territory, land that was subsequently ceded to the Confederation. Both of these matters reached a critical stage of negotiations during Randolph's second term, and he found he had to give them the highest priority.

The matter of securing compensation for the defense of the northwest territory came under his scrutiny first. When Virginia ceded her western lands to the Confederation, it was agreed that Congress would absorb all expenses associated with the defense of that area during the Revolution.[21] In accordance with the provisions of the instrument of cession, the amount of compensation was to be determined by a three-man commission. Congress and the state of Virginia were each to appoint one commissioner and they, in turn, would select the third. This three-man board would then examine the records of the state and jointly determine the sum that was owed to Virginia for the defense of this territory.[22] After some delay Virginia named William Heth as its commissioner and Congress appointed Edward Fox. Their choice as the third commissioner was David Henley.[23] A few weeks after Randolph became governor, he learned that the commissioners could not carry out their assignment because the Virginia accounts for this military operation were so disorganized and incomplete as to defy any assessment of the state's expenses.[24] Responding to the commissioners' request, Randolph asked Leighton Wood, Jr., of the solicitor's office to try and put the accounts in order. This was done, and by March 10, 1787, the accounts, such as they were, were ready to be examined.[25] A few weeks later Edward Fox, the commissioner appointed by Congress, resigned, thereby causing further delay.[26] This was the status of the problem when Randolph left for the Philadelphia Convention.

In April Congress appointed John Pierce to the vacancy created by Fox's resignation, and shortly thereafter the commissioners resumed their deliberations. Pierce, who also held the office of Commissioner of Army Accounts, had a reputation for being meticulous and scrupulously honest.[27] In August Heth and Henley found themselves at odds with Pierce, who categorically refused to accept several major accounts in Virginia's claim. When Pierce discovered he could not persuade Heth and Henley to his point of view, he became disgusted with the proceedings and returned to New York.[28]

Virginia's Executive Council was delighted with this turn of events for it gave them additional time to substantiate the state's claims.[29] Colonel Benjamin Logan, lieutenant for Lincoln County, was asked to supply supporting records for several of the accounts and, equally important, to contact William Clark, the brother and former secretary to General George Rogers Clark, in order to urge him to leave immediately for Richmond to assist in verifying the accounts.[30]

Several weeks after Randolph returned from Philadelphia he received a letter from General Clark himself in reply to this request of the Executive Council. Clark indicated that the type of records being sought simply did not exist, and what did exist was already on file in the auditor's office in Richmond. He suggested that it might be more practical to work from existing records and accept the results rather than try and verify each of these accounts, a task that could only be accomplished by returning all the accounts to him in Kentucky.[31]

Clark's letter left the issue totally confused and forced the Executive Council to refer the whole matter to the Assembly.[32] The House of Delegates responded to the crisis by appointing a special committee to consult with the commissioners and see what could be done to resolve the problem. Much to the chagrin of this committee, Pierce absolutely refused to consult with it and insisted that it was improper to communicate information to one party, Virginia, without the knowledge and consent of the other party, the United States. Resenting Pierce's apparent hostility toward Virginia, the House passed resolutions calling for the suspension of all further proceedings by the commission and directing Virginia's delegates in Congress to ". . . urge Congress to take measures for doing justice to this state . . . by reimbursing the sums which Virginia hath actually passed in acquiring, maintaining and defending the territory ceded to the United States."[33]

At Randolph's suggestion Heth was asked by the Executive Council to leave immediately for New York so that he might be present when the matter came up in Congress.[34] He agreed and was on the scene when Madison raised the issue in Congress. Typically, Congress appointed a special committee to consider the subject, and Heth soon learned that the committee's chairman, Jeremiah Wadsworth of Connecticut, was anxious to see the matter settled amicably outside of Congress rather than open the door to a full congressional debate. Heth asked Randolph to vest him with the authority to act as a negotiating agent for the state. For some reason neither Randolph nor the Executive Council saw fit to act on this suggestion, with the result that no action was taken by either party in the dispute.[35]

Finally, in April of 1788, Virginia's delegates in Congress, despairing of ever getting the claim settled, urged Heth to resume negotiations with the other commissioners to "effect a close at the highest sum you can procure by compromise or any other mode of negotiation which to you shall seem most practical."[36] In conformance with these instructions Heth and Henley resumed discussions, and on May 15 they transmitted a letter to the President of Congress awarding Virginia $500,000 in specie "as a full compensation for all expenses paid by said Commonwealth and incurred as necessary and reasonable in subduing British posts and maintaining forts and garrisons within and . . . in acquiring any part of the territory ceded and relinquished to the United States. . . ."[37] Pierce, who had fallen ill, did not participate in this decision.[38] On May 26 Congress rejected a motion that the report be transmitted to the Board of Treasury, thereby leaving the issue unresolved until the formation of the new federal government.[39] It was ultimately disposed of by Secretary of the Treasury Alexander Hamilton's plan for the general assumption of all state debts associated with the Revolution.

The matter of determining the extent of Virginia's expenditures in direct support of the Revolution was time-consuming for Randolph and taxed his patience almost to the breaking point. The basis for any state's entering a claim against the Confederation was a provision in the Articles of Confederation that stated: "All charges of war and all other expenses that shall be incurred for the common defense or general welfare, and allowed by the United States . . . shall be defrayed out of a common treasury."[40] When Congress turned its attention to this subject after the war, it discovered it had a monumental problem on its hands. Depreciated currency, unauthorized expenditures, fragmentary or lost records, and total disagreement over what was meant by the clause "expenses . . . for the common defense or general welfare" foreclosed any easy solution to the settlement of these accounts. The states with larger claims, like Virginia, used the delay to their advantage by pushing through Congress several very important ordinances relaxing the restrictions on the type of expenditures that could be included under the "general welfare" clause of Article 8.[41]

It was May of 1787 before Congress set up the necessary machinery for receiving and processing these claims. Under the provisions of this May ordinance the country was divided into five districts, each with its own congressionally appointed commissioner. Each state was expected to present its claims, properly documented, to the commissioner assigned to its district. The ordinance also stipulated that each state would have six months after the arrival of the district commissioner to file its claims.[42]

Though it had taken Congress five years to pass this ordinance, Virginia was totally unprepared to meet the deadline. On January 11, 1787, not quite four months before the ordinance was passed, the legislature named Andrew Dunscomb as the commissioner of state accounts and charged him with the responsibility of preparing the state's records.[43] Dunscomb, the former state commissioner of military claims, assumed his new duties promptly.[44] Unfortunately he had barely begun to get the state accounts in order when word reached Richmond that Congress had passed the all-important May ordinance establishing the necessary machinery for processing these claims.[45]

Randolph, who had had only limited contact with the problem prior to his departure for Philadelphia, obviously wished to see Virginia fully compensated for its Revolutionary expenditures. He knew Dunscomb was working diligently at his task, but he had no idea how he was progressing. Then on December 21, 1787, a little over two and a half months after he returned from Philadelphia, Randolph was formally notified by William Winder, the newly appointed United States district commissioner for Virginia and North Carolina, that he was in Richmond ready to receive and review the Virginia accounts.[46] The same day Randolph also received an almost hysterical letter from Dunscomb stating he was virtually paralyzed in his work because the accounts of the state were completely disorganized and hopelessly incomplete. He asked Randolph if he might make a formal report to the Executive Council so that "they may take the same under consideration and give such relief as may appear proper."[47] Randolph had no choice but to acquiesce to his request and on February 2, 1788, he filed a full report with the Council on Dunscomb's behalf.[48]

The Council agreed to assist Dunscomb in any manner it could, but very pointedly reminded him that it could neither arrange and verify the state accounts for him nor provide answers to the technical questions raised in his report. It asked to be informed immediately if he felt he could not have the accounts ready by June 20, 1788, the day that Commissioner Winder's six-month period of official residence in Virginia expired.[49] When Dunscomb admitted that he could not meet that deadline, Randolph and the Executive Council had a major crisis on their hands.[50] They had to decide whether to ask Congress for an extension of time in which to file their claims or allow Dunscomb to present the accounts in whatever form he happened to have them at the time Winder's period of residence expired.

Since the Council was beginning to have serious reservations about Dunscomb's ability to handle his office, it was decided that it would be wiser to ask Congress for an extension of time. Randolph immediately instructed the Virginia delegation to request an extension from Congress.[51] The Virginia delegation introduced a motion to this effect and it was promptly referred to the Board of Treasury, under whose jurisdiction the settlement of all state accounts had been placed.[52] On May 7, 1788, the board filed its report with Congress and recommended that Virginia's request be denied. It did agree, however, to the filing of claims in the form in which they had been maintained by Virginia rather than forcing the state to convert its accounts to the preestablished "headings" which the board had determined would be the basis for all state claims.[53] Congress unhesitantly endorsed this decision, and the unhappy news was sent to Randolph. The Virginia delegates, knowing the sentiment of Congress, recommended that Dunscomb be instructed to either surrender the accounts in their original form or provide Randolph with a detailed report as to why he could not surrender them, which, in turn, should be immediately transmitted to them so that they might lay it before Congress.[54]

Since mid-November, 1787, Randolph had been subjected to a constant stream of communications from Dunscomb itemizing his difficulties and asking for guidance on virtually every problem he encountered in the process of collecting evidence in support of Virginia's claim. Randolph had long since decided that Dunscomb was more adept at complaining than at getting the accounts in order, and was now more convinced than ever that Virginia needed additional time to put her accounts in order.[55]

When Randolph learned that Virginia's request had been denied, he seized on the suggestion that he submit a detailed report to Congress on why the state could not surrender its accounts.[56] Dunscomb was ordered to prepare such a statement. The document, being but a systematic presentation of his many letters of complaint to Randolph, was completed in less than forty-eight hours and then hurriedly forwarded to the Virginia delegation in New York.[57] In his covering letter, dated May 25, Randolph stated categorically that the problem was not one of filing claims under a different set of "headings" from those in which the Virginia accounts had been kept; the problem was that Virginia lacked the necessary proofs to support her claims.[58]

The Virginia delegates, knowing the state's six-month deadline would expire on Friday, June 20, acted immediately on Randolph's request. On June 6 they introduced a motion in Congress to secure additional time for all states to file their claims—a move designed to gain the support of other states having difficulty meeting their deadlines. Once again their motion was referred to the Board of Treasury.[59] This meant, of course, that Congress would not act before June 20. The Virginia delegates urged Randolph to have Dunscomb file the claims on schedule, "in whatever arrangement they may be," and then make adjustments in the light of subsequent events.[60] This was done.

As might be expected, Dunscomb very deliberately notified Randolph of his compliance with the deadline. He also thought it advisable to explain to Randolph that he had placed the vouchers for certain accounts in bags, which he then tied and labeled "not arranged." Randolph was also relieved to learn that the ledgers containing the extracts copied from the Receipt Books in the treasurer's office carried the signed oaths of the clerks who had copied them, swearing to the fact that they had indeed copied the extracts from the Receipt Books in the Treasury.[61] With all of Virginia's claims on the point of being disavowed because of their disorganization, Randolph found this pedantry almost beyond belief.

On June 24, four days after Virginia's deadline for filing, Congress granted all states a three-month extension to complete the preparation of their accounts.[62] The extension had been recommended by the Board of Treasury in response to the Virginia motion of June 6.[63] When Edward Carrington, writing on behalf of the Virginia delegation, notified Randolph of this decision he added:

> I hope the time now given will be fully adequate to the object. . . . This, however, depends greatly upon the commissioner on the part of the state. A man of capacity and an accommodating disposition may remove difficulties which to one of another disposition may stand as insufferable obstacles.[64]

Randolph knew, of course, that Carrington was absolutely right, but finding such a person was easier said than done.

About the time he received Carrington's letter he had a fairly severe bilious attack which confined him to his bed for the better part of two weeks and left him quite weak for some time thereafter.[65] It was August 19, therefore, before he got around to asking William Davies, a former member of the state's Board of War, to serve as "counsel" to Dunscomb in the ordering of state accounts. Davies was a man of considerable experience and ability and Randolph suspected he would not be very enthusiastic about working with Dunscomb. He urged Davies to "ride over" to Richmond so that he might explain the "particulars" to him.[66] Davies apparently accepted the governor's invitation and came to Richmond to discuss the appointment. Randolph even permitted him to take some of the records home with him for more careful scrutiny before making up his mind on whether he would accept the assignment.[67]

In the meantime Randolph made a personal investigation of Duns-comb's office so that he might know first hand of the progress Dunscomb was making in organizing the accounts and collecting the necessary proofs to substantiate them. He was forced to admit, albeit reluctantly, that Dunscomb was not magnifying the difficulties—the state's records appeared to be every bit as disorganized as he claimed. Randolph did feel, however, that the state could supply adequate proofs for all but 8 of the 130 categories of Revolutionary expenses authorized by Congress. Several of those that could not be substantiated involved sizable claims, but the picture was not as bleak as Randolph had originally sus-pected.[68] And since the Confederation would soon be replaced by the new federal government, there was obviously less concern about honor-ing the three-month extension granted by Congress.

During the first week in October Randolph received a letter from William Davies accepting the position as "counsel" to the commissioner of Virginia accounts.[69] Randolph was pleased since this seemed to be the only possible way of ending Dunscomb's constant complaints. A few weeks later he was certain he had the right man when he learned that Davies had very shrewdly provoked a quarrel with Commissioner Winder as a means of halting all further negotiations. Annoyed and disgusted, Winder decided to return to New York without taking the accounts with him. Davies promptly reclaimed them and ordered that they be retained by the state until properly organized.[70]

Randolph was mercifully relieved of all further responsibility in the matter when he left the governorship, and the state's claims remained unsettled until 1790 when they became a part of Hamilton's ambitious program to have the federal government absorb all state debts associated with the Revolution.

Davies ultimately moved to New York where he became, along with the ever-present James Madison, an astonishingly effective advocate of Virginia's interests. In the final statement of state accounts Virginia emerged with a credit of $9,085,981, the highest of any state in the Union.[71]

It seems safe to conclude that Randolph's administrative energies greatly influenced the preparation of both the northwest territory ac-counts and the Revolutionary War accounts. He may not have had the satisfaction of seeing these matters resolved during his governorship, but he certainly could take much of the credit for having prevented a pre-cipitous settlement of Virginia's claims that would have deprived the state of sorely needed funds. This was no small accomplishment if one considers the limited authority of the office in which he was serving. And, for all his national sympathies, Randolph proved to be a rather aggressive advocate of Virginia's interests, particularly where state revenues were involved.

While Randolph was trying to manage the successful presentation of these various Virginia claims, most of his fellow citizens were preoccupied with the forthcoming convention to consider the Constitution. That convention could not have come at a less opportune time for Randolph insofar as the responsibilities of the governorship were concerned. It was very difficult to sustain the momentum of that office and play a crucial role in the convention. At the same time, he was placed in an awkward position because of a dispute between the judicial and legislative branches of government.

In an effort to restructure the Virginia court system the Assembly in its last session had passed a bill creating a new district court system for the state. These District Courts were intended to relieve the General Court of its more routine cases and thereby eliminate the impossible delays being experienced by those with cases pending before this higher court. Unfortunately the Assembly failed to provide for a separate group of judges to preside over these courts. Instead it simply increased the number of General Court judges by four and then assigned the duties of these District Courts to this expanded roster of General Court judges.[72] Since these same judges also had to sit twice each year on the Court of Appeals, they found themselves saddled with an impossibly demanding court schedule. The law met immediate opposition when the Court of Appeals convened in May, 1788. The judges insisted quite correctly that the legislation was infringing on the independence of the judiciary by assigning additional duties to the judges of the state's highest court without any corresponding financial compensation. Even more important, the act could serve as a precedent by which some future Assembly might intimidate the judiciary by arbitrarily multiplying the assignments of the judges. A Remonstrance, signed by all the judges of the Court of Appeals, was forwarded to the governor with the request that it be laid before the Assembly at its next session.[73] Randolph considered the matter serious enough to bring it to the attention of the Executive Council where it was decided that the Assembly should immediately be called into special session.[74] Monday, June 23, was set as the date for convening the special session, and a proclamation was issued accordingly.[75]

When the Assembly met on the 23rd it lacked a quorum because the convention considering the Constitution was still in session and individuals holding seats in both bodies refused to attend the special session until the Constitution had been voted on.[76] That vote came on June 25, and the next day the special session of the Assembly had its quorum.[77] When the legislators assembled, they found that their ever-efficient governor had already transmitted his official letter to the speaker of the House of Delegates. In it he called their attention to the Remonstrance of the judges of the Court of Appeals as well as to several other items of lesser import.[78] Most of the legislators, who had now been in Richmond for the better part of four weeks as convention delegates, were not particularly anxious to extend their stay several more weeks merely to correct an oversight in a previous piece of legislation. Tired of their cramped living accommodations and tavern meals and concerned about the condition of their summer crops, they made quick work of the Remonstrance. They simply suspended the operation of the law that had prompted it.[79] It was easier to postpone the establishment of these District Courts until the next legislative session than it was to correct the existing law.

Thus the special session lasted less than a week and should have had little or no significance for Randolph. But it did. For a few days he was somewhat apprehensive about how the legislature might handle one of the enclosures he had transmitted to them. The item in question was a letter from Governor George Clinton of New York to Randolph in his capacity as governor of Virginia. The subject of the letter was the Constitution.

The story behind this letter is almost as intriguing as the contents. In December of 1787 the Virginia legislature, in a bill to defray the expenses of delegates to the state's convention to consider the Constitution, had gone on record as favoring friendly communications between the states regarding the Constitution.[80] This statement was included as a means of forestalling those who would use this bill to appropriate funds for sending delegates to a second federal convention.[81] After it was passed with this less controversial provision, a subsequent resolution of the Assembly instructed the governor to transmit copies of this law to the executives of the other states in the Union and to request them to communicate the same to their legislatures. Randolph did this and dated each of his brief letters of transmittal December 27, 1787.[82] For some reason the letter that had been sent to Governor Clinton did not reach him until March 7, 1788, only a few days before the end of the New York state legislative session and *after* that body had authorized the calling of a state convention to consider the Constitution.[83] As requested, Clinton promptly transmitted the act of the Virginia Assembly to the legislature, but it failed to act on it.[84]

On May 8 Clinton informed Randolph of this fact and noted his own complete agreement with the objectives the act sought to promote:

I cannot refrain expressing regret that a similar conduct has not been observed by the states who have already had the proposed system under consideration. Friendly communications on the subject and temperate discussions would, it is to be presumed, have had a most happy tendency in accommodating it much more to the sentiments and wishes of the people of America than is likely to be the case in the form it is offered by the general convention and acceded to by some of the states.[85]

When Randolph received this letter he laid it before the Executive Council, which judged it to be a public rather than a private letter and advised him to transmit it to the forthcoming special session of the legislature.[86]

Much to Randolph's astonishment, his handling of Clinton's letter outraged George Mason, his former ally in Philadelphia, who was convinced Randolph had managed the whole affair in such a way as to serve the interests of those supporting the Constitution. Mason, although not a member of the legislature, drafted a resolution stating Randolph should have immediately laid the letter before the state's constitutional convention when it assembled early in June rather than holding it until the Assembly convened in special session. A second resolution called for the appointment of a legislative committee to wait on the governor and inquire why he had not laid Clinton's letter before the convention and had delayed making it public until after the Constitution was ratified. The resolution would also have the committee inquire into the reasons why Randolph's letter of December 27, 1787, failed to reach Clinton until March of 1788.[87] The language of the resolutions reflected Mason's anger and suggested that he was trying to promote a full-scale investigation of Randolph's conduct in this matter. His efforts apparently failed, for the *Journals* of the Senate and House contain not a single reference to a legislative inquiry into Randolph's conduct in the handling of this matter.

It is safe to assume that Randolph did in fact transmit the act of the legislature to Clinton on December 27, since the entries in both the Executive Letterbook and Randolph's own personal Memorandum Book suggest all these letters were routinely sent at the same time. And the New York governor candidly states in his reply that the letter was "committed to the post office at Richmond," thus ruling out a negligent personal messenger and placing full responsibility for the delay on the post office.[88]

Clinton's letter of May 8 was sent to the House of Delegates rather than to the convention because the Executive Council had decided its contents dictated such a course of action. Mason was quite correct in stating that the letter was not made public until June 26, the day after the Constitution had been ratified, but this was because the House of Delegates lacked a quorum and did not conduct any formal business until that day.[89] Randolph had dutifully transmitted the letter to the speaker on June 23, the date the special session was scheduled to convene and two days before the Constitution was ratified by the convention.[90] It was the fault of the legislature that it was not made public until the 26th. Mason, who was unhappy over Randolph's changed attitude toward the Constitution, may have written these resolutions before familiarizing himself with the details of the governor's conduct. When he learned that Randolph had acted at the direction of the Executive Council, he may have had second thoughts about trying to promote a legislative investigation of his conduct.

Like most of his predecessors in the governorship, Randolph had his share of Indian problems because of the relentless westward advancement of the frontiersman. He was fortunate enough to escape a major crisis during his first one-year term in office, but in his second term he was confronted with a fairly serious situation involving the Overhill and Middle Cherokee tribes on Virginia's southwestern frontier.[91] Fortunately Randolph had acquired the confidence of these tribes by befriending a Cherokee chief who was passing through Philadelphia when he was attending the Federal Convention. Randolph had used the occasion to assure the chief that Virginians wished to live peacefully with the Cherokee nation. He gave him several gifts and prepared a "talk" which he asked the chief to read to all the Cherokee tribes on his return.[92] Although Randolph did not know it at the time, the good will engendered by this meeting proved to be an invaluable asset to him in the months to come.[93]

In May, 1788, Randolph received word from Colonel Joseph Martin, Virginia's former Indian agent to the Cherokee nation, that there had been repeated clashes between white settlers and Indians along Virginia's southwestern frontier. The immediate cause of the unrest was the continuous movement of white settlers from Virginia and North Carolina into the lands of the Overhill and Middle Cherokee tribes in open violation of the recently signed Treaty of Hopewell.[94] Randolph responded to the crisis by promptly ordering the Virginia delegates to use Martin's letter to initiate a congressional inquiry into the disturbances.[95] Since Martin had suggested it was imperative that the United States government appoint a special Indian agent to the Cherokee nation, Randolph was anxious to have the full text of his letter laid before Congress. Congress referred the letter to Secretary of War Henry Knox, and he responded by issuing a report that sharply criticized white settlers for occupying lands belonging to the Cherokee nation. He recommended the appointment of an Indian agent to work with the Cherokee tribes and to handle violations of the Treaty of Hopewell.[96] Congress implemented this recommendation, and Colonel Joseph Martin was appointed to the post.[97]

In June Randolph received an even more alarming report from Martin indicating that the entire Virginia–North Carolina frontier was on the verge of open warfare.[98] Randolph once again referred Martin's letter to the Virginia delegates with instructions to bring it to the immediate attention of Congress, and sent Andrew Moore, a member of the Executive Council, as his personal emissary to the Cherokee nation to reassure them of his desire for peace. Moore carried a "talk" from Randolph which declared that Virginia would respect their lands and disclaimed any responsibility for the acts of violence carried out by frontiersmen from Virginia and North Carolina. Randolph's "talk" was favorably received by the chiefs of the Cherokee nation and contributed somewhat toward easing tension.[99]

In the meantime Congress was implementing Knox's suggestion that the government take decisive steps to see that white settlers honored the boundaries set up by the Treaty of Hopewell. A "talk" was prepared and Knox was authorized to use federal militia to clear white settlers from Cherokee lands.[100] While these actions reflected at least a temporary awareness of the plight of the Cherokee, they failed to protect their lands and in time the Treaty of Hopewell was "adjusted" to accommodate the white settlers.[101]

Generally Randolph tried to pursue a course of action that suggested that Virginia was not indifferent to the interests of the Cherokee, while at the same time trying to nudge Congress into taking steps to implement its treaty obligations with these tribes. It was a policy of which many white settlers in the area disapproved, but this did not seem to trouble Randolph half as much as irresponsible frontier warfare.

One last problem relating to Virginia's frontier confronted Randolph before he left office. Under the provisions of Virginia's cession of its western lands in 1784, the land bounties issued to Virginia troops of the Continental line could be redeemed for land between the Scioto and Miami rivers on the north side of the Ohio River if good land on Virginia's military reserve south of that River proved to be insufficient.[102] On July 17, 1788, Congress passed a resolution declaring all land surveys made for Virginia troops of the Continental line north of the Ohio to be invalid until the deficiencies in land on the south side of the Ohio "shall be ascertained and stated to Congress."[103] The resolution seemed to question Virginia's right to occupy the lands north of the Ohio until the state had proved to the satisfaction of Congress that all good lands south of that river had been taken up by bounties. Randolph resented this congressional presumptuousness and he dispatched a strong letter of protest to the President of Congress.[104] His protest brought prompt congressional action, and on September 1 a resolution was passed stating that "the act of Congress of the 17th of July last was not meant, nor is so to be interpreted, as to infringe any stipulation in the cession made by Virginia to the United States."[105] When the General Assembly met in October, 1788, the House of Delegates passed a resolution commending Randolph for the way he handled the affair.[106]

As Randolph's second term of office was entering its final months a move to promote a second federal convention to consider amendments to the Constitution began to gather momentum in several states. The proposal emanated from the New York ratifying convention, which had unanimously agreed to the drafting of a circular letter to all the states recommending a second general convention.[107] It represented a last desperate effort to take the question of amendments out of the hands of the new Congress and place it before a presumably more pliable convention of all the states. The circular letter, dated July 28 and signed by George Clinton, the president of the New York Convention, reached Randolph during the first week of August.[108]

Randolph, who had always resented the all-or-nothing ratifying process that had been built into the Constitution, found the proposal particularly attractive. He had, of course, been one of the first persons to advocate a second convention to consider amendments and had abandoned the idea only after Madison had convinced him that Henry and his followers were using the proposal to promote the dissolution of the Union. But that danger, if it ever existed, had passed; the Constitution had been ratified and a new federal government would soon be in operation, a visible symbol of the nation's unity. A second convention, sensitive to the wishes of those who had serious doubts about certain features of the Constitution, could not help but effect changes that would improve the document. Almost instinctively he began to give serious thought to resigning the governorship before his term expired so that he might run for a seat in the legislature and thereby influence the legislative response to this proposal.

True to form, he bared his political soul to Madison:

Governor Clinton's letter to me for the calling of a convention is this day [August 13] published by my order. It will give contentment to many who are now dissatisfied. The problem of a new convention has many difficulties in its solution. But upon the whole I believe the Assembly of Virginia *perhaps* ought, and probably will concur in urging it. . . . I do indeed fear, that the Constitution may be enervated; if some states should prevail in all [of] their amendments; but if such be the will of America, who can withstand it? For my own part, I fear that direct taxation may be too much weakened. But I can only endeavour to avert that particular evil, and cannot persuade myself to thwart a second convention merely from the apprehension of that evil. This letter [from Clinton] will probably carry me sooner into the Assembly, than I intended. I will prepare a draught upon this subject and forward a copy to you as soon as I can. My object will be (if possible) to prevent instructions from being conclusive, if any should be offered, and to leave the conventioners perfectly free.[109]

Madison must have been thoroughly discouraged as he read these lines. Randolph, it seemed, had a proclivity for striking out on his own in support of dubious causes. After months of close attention to the progress of the Constitution through the various state conventions, Virginia's supposedly very knowledgeable governor still did not seem to realize that there was a concerted, nationwide effort by opponents of a strong central government to significantly change the document. Madison had no choice but to conclude that Randolph actually believed that a second convention was in some way going to reflect the "will of America." Why, Madison must have asked himself, was Randolph not able to understand that virtually everyone who supported the Constitution had some objections to it, yet, in their desire to see it succeed, would not endorse any effort to amend it outside of the form prescribed by the document itself. For all his practical experience Randolph was still functioning as a political loner, stubbornly refusing to recognize the hazards in a second convention.

Madison, quite prudently, waited a few days before replying, and then, as was his custom, sent a very friendly letter to Randolph systematically identifying the dangers that might arise if a second convention took place. He did not make a single derogatory comment about Randolph's position but hit heavily on the prospect of amendments being obtained by "management" and "extorted by menaces."[110] Randolph was unimpressed and candidly reminded Madison that the advocates of the Constitution were anything but virtuous statesmen:

> I confess to you without reservation, that I feel great distrust of some of those who will certainly be influential agents in the government, and whom I suspect to be capable of making a wicked use of its defects. Do not charge me with undue suspicion; but indeed the management of some stages of the Convention created disgustful apprehension of the views of some particular characters. I reverence Hamilton because he was honest and open in his views.[111]

Madison thought otherwise, but knew better than to pursue the matter with Randolph. He had absolutely no desire to lose a close friend and valuable political ally in the present situation, particularly if Randolph decided to enter the legislature.

By September, 1788, Virginia's political climate was supercharged with excitement in anticipation of the approaching legislative session. It was this session of the Assembly that would elect Virginia's two United States senators, determine the state's congressional districts for the election of representatives of the new House of Representatives and, of course, respond to this latest request for a second convention to amend the Constitution. Randolph decided to remain on as governor until after the Assembly convened so that he could prepare the official letter to the speaker of the House of Delegates and thereby influence the agenda of the session. It was, as might be expected, a very long letter. Among other things, it took note of the state's differences with Congress over Virginia's military reserve north of the Ohio and of the current status of negotiations in the settlement of the state's various claims against the Confederation for expenses associated with the Revolution and the defense of the northwest territory. There was a report on the state's sinking fund, the steps that had been taken to bring the grievances of the Cherokee tribes to the attention of Congress, plus numerous other documents and papers that had been forwarded to the governor for transmittal to the Assembly, including, of course, the very important letter from the New York Convention suggesting a second federal convention.[112]

Once this message had been delivered, Randolph began making the necessary arrangements to enter the legislature. His friend Samuel Griffin, the elected delegate from the city of Williamsburg since 1786, agreed to resign so that Randolph might offer himself as a candidate for his seat.[113] On November 10 Randolph wrote to Madison: "On Friday I shall be a member [of the House of Delegates]. I could not get in sooner, as a vacancy could not be sooner created than today."[114] On November 11 the House of Delegates issued a writ for a special election to fill the vacancy caused by Griffin's resignation. The following day Randolph's letter of resignation as governor was laid before the Assembly.[115] The election was held immediately and Randolph took his seat in the House of Delegates on November 15.[116] Apparently such things could still be "managed" among the Virginia gentry with little fear of reprisal or recrimination.

But to his utter chagrin Randolph found himself entering the legislature one day after the House had approved a resolution in support of the New York Convention's proposal for a second federal convention.[117] Henry, as might be expected, led the fight in support of the second convention, while Francis Corbin, with the assistance of John Page and Edward Carrington, authored the resolutions in opposition to such a convention. The overwhelming defeat suffered by the "friends" of the Constitution—the vote was 85 to 39 against Corbin's resolutions—would seem to suggest that Randolph's presence in the legislature would not have made the slightest difference in the outcome of the voting.[118] At best he might have been able to temper the language of Henry's resolutions, but this is doubtful. The irony is that every important decision associated with the establishment of the new federal government had been made *before* he took his seat in the legislature.[119]

It was all very frustrating, but frustration was probably what Randolph felt about his entire experience in the governor's office. He chafed at the inefficiency and ineptness of state officials like Dunscomb, at congressional procrastination over matters of vital interest to Virginia and, most particularly, at the tendency certain elected officials had of postponing or ignoring matters that did not lend themselves to easy solution. By contrast he was almost too tenacious, too bent on devising different ways of achieving the goals he sought. The most obvious example was, of course, his efforts to amend the Constitution. Only a very stubborn person with fiercely independent convictions would have been willing to go to such extremes as resigning the governorship to promote a convention that probably never really had a chance of meeting, much less fulfilling its purpose. But this was Randolph's way of doing things. When he believed in something, he stuck with it until every conceivable approach had been tried. He paid dearly for his convictions by losing some of his friends and gaining many enemies. His only satisfaction, and he was very conscious of it, was that he was marching to the beat of his own drum.

13

A Man and a State in Transition
November 1788–December 1789

From the start of the legislative session in October Randolph had carefully followed the proceedings of the Assembly and counted the days until he could take his seat in the House of Delegates. Everyone knew he wanted to have a direct voice in the handling of the proposal for a second federal convention as well as several other measures associated with the organization of the new government. And he made no secret of the fact that he was promoting the candidacy of Madison for a seat in the United States Senate.[1] If he entered the House too late to share in these decisions, it didn't dampen his enthusiasm as a delegate. In obvious recognition of his political influence he was promptly named to the three most important standing committees of the House. Within a week he was busily drafting amendments to several of the bills pending before these committees.[2] He was a major political force in the state, as concerned with the success of the new federal government as he was with the effort to revise its Constitution at a second convention.

Aside from matters touching on the formation of the new national government, Randolph took greatest interest in the legislative efforts to reestablish the District Courts and generally reorganize the state's court system. Since the original District Court bill of January, 1788, had been suspended by the special session of the legislature in June, 1788, as a result of the Remonstrance of the judges of the Court of Appeals, reorganization of the court system was considered an unavoidable responsibility of this legislative session. Five days after Randolph took his seat as a delegate a Committee of the Whole House reported out a series of resolutions defining the manner in which the courts should be restructured.[3] A Committee of Sixteen was then appointed to draft the necessary bills pursuant to these resolutions; not unexpectedly, Randolph was named to this committee.[4]

Randolph appears to have been the principal architect of several of the bills prepared by this committee. He played a significant role in drafting the bill reestablishing the District Courts and prepared the initial draft of the bill restructuring the High Court of Chancery. He also drafted the legislation that completely separated the Court of Appeals from the other courts in the state, the judges of this court being, very properly, relieved of their assignments in the various other superior courts.[5]

This is not to say that Randolph was responsible for the reorganization since he, like the other members of the Committee of Sixteen, was expected to bring in bills consistent with the guidelines established by the Committee of the Whole House. It was the resolutions of this committee that actually defined the essential features of the reorganization. His authorship or coauthorship of the original drafts of several of the bills associated with this reorganization are more properly a reflection of his wholehearted approval of what was being done.

The net effect of this legislation was to bring the court system into line with the adjudicative needs of the state. The District Courts gave Virginia an intermediate system of superior courts that would be able to handle most of the cases that previously had been carried on appeal from the county courts to the General Court. This lightened the case load of the General Court and provided the average litigant with a regional appellate system that would prove to be both more efficient and less expensive than the previous arrangement. In the restructuring the General Court became, in effect, a higher appellate court, since most of the cases reaching this court would come by way of an appeal from a judgment of one of the District Courts. The Court of Appeals, now composed of five instead of eleven judges, acquired an independence consistent with its preeminent position in the state court system. The decision to abolish the state's admiralty court in this restructuring process was, of course, nothing more than a recognition of the new federal government's paramount authority in maritime matters. Collectively the legislation passed during this session gave Virginia one of the most efficient and eminently usable court systems in the Union.[6]

When the last of these court reorganization bills had been voted on, Randolph asked the House for permission to absent himself from the last few days of the session since nothing of importance remained to be considered.[7]

In less than a week's time Randolph was preparing to move his wife and children back to Williamsburg, a task he wanted to accomplish before formally resuming his private practice. Sentimental reasons would seem to account for his decision to resettle his family in the old colonial capital of Virginia.[8] Its richly shaded streets and old but elegant homes, its peaceful atmosphere and its stately public buildings, symbols of an era that had passed, reminded Edmund and his wife of their happy, carefree youth, For them Williamsburg was home; the quiet serenity of the town provided a welcome relief from the more hurried life of Richmond. This was particularly important since the Randolphs were expecting another child and Edmund was most anxious to have the family securely settled in Williamsburg well before the baby's birth.

Once settled, Randolph turned his attention to the all-important matter of rebuilding his law practice. Clients were not hard to find and cases in Williamsburg were virtually his for the asking. He would have accepted most of them without a moment's hesitation were it not for a law restricting the practice of attorneys that had been passed at the last session of the legislature. Designed to keep the less competent lawyers out of Virginia's higher courts, the law stated that an attorney could not represent a client in an appeal before one of the state's superior courts if he had already appeared on behalf of this client in one of the state's lower courts.[9] Thus a litigant wishing to carry a case on appeal to a higher court had to retain a different lawyer from the one who represented him originally. The principal beneficiaries of this law would be the attorneys who confined their practice to Virginia's higher courts, which always met in Richmond. The net effect of the law was to make the capital the mecca of a professional elite and virtually the only place where an attorney could be assured of a prestigious and lucrative practice. The law forced Randolph to refuse to represent clients in the lower courts so that he could orient his practice as much as possible toward these higher courts. He reconciled himself to frequent trips to Richmond and perhaps even a temporary residence in the city if during consecutive court terms he would have to argue cases before more than one court.[10]

And so he began what he came to describe as "my vagrant life between this place [Williamsburg] and Richmond."[11] It would have been a burdensome routine for any man, but for one who had no great enthusiasm for practice it was probably a nightmare. But he threw himself into his practice, always knowing that one day he would return to public life. Anything was tolerable for a time and if the law provided him with an income sufficient to meet his current financial needs, it would be well worth the effort.[12]

In the meantime the Randolphs were anxiously awaiting the birth of their fifth child. The household was put in readiness, the children were kept quiet and out of the way, and everything possible was done to ensure Betsy's comfort. The baby, a girl, arrived on schedule and Edmund happily resigned himself to the prospect of presiding over a home overrun by little girls.[13] This latest addition to the family was named

Lucy. It was a joyous occasion and both parents, remembering the sudden and unexpected death of their son three years previously, were silently grateful that Lucy was a strong and healthy baby.

The other children probably accepted their new sister with reluctance as they found themselves fighting a losing battle with her for the attention of their mother and father. Peyton, who had just turned nine, was probably displeased at having to put up with a third baby sister, while six-year-old Susan felt she had acquired new responsibilities with this latest addition to the family. As for Edmonia, at two she was thoroughly baffled by all the excitement and unable to understand why she was no longer the center of attention when friends dropped in to visit with her mother. Within a short time, however, little Lucy was accepted for what she was—a baby sister who generally made a nuisance of herself.

This rather idyllic, yet typical, domestic scene suddenly faded when Betsy began to complain about "sores" in her mouth that refused to heal. The symptoms were unmistakable. She appeared to have a cancerous condition that gave every evidence of very rapid development. Randolph, who had absolutely no confidence in the quality of medical services in Virginia—"nay, even that species of aid which can merely flatter is unattainable"—decided that he would have to take her to Philadelphia or perhaps even Europe to gain the kind of medical attention needed to arrest the disease. To Madison he wrote:

> I have resolved, if the alarm should prove decidedly true, to carry her to Europe or Philadelphia. The former holds out the best source of hope; but I see not a chance of converting property into sterling money. The latter would be visited with more ease. But as I should be obliged almost to become a resident there, should I go upon such an errand, pecuniary difficulties would be equally great. An effort, however, must be made, even at the risque of my whole fortune. Indeed I have sometimes seriously thought of attempting something professional, should I be compelled to visit Philadelphia without being able to raise money from my estate. In that case a new revolution will take place with me. For if I found I could live there, I should emancipate my slaves and thus ending my days, without undergoing any anxiety about the injustice of holding them.[14]

Madison read these lines with great concern and wrote Randolph immediately to express the hope that these ulcers were not in fact evidence of a cancer.[15] In the succeeding weeks Betsy's condition apparently stabilized sufficiently to cast some doubt on their original diagnosis but not to remove their apprehensiveness. It would be several months before she improved to the point where she ceased to be a major concern to her husband.[16]

By June of 1789 all eyes were on New York where the new government was taking shape. Washington's inauguration on April 30 may have been the symbolic beginning for most people, but the more experienced political leaders in the country knew that the government would face its first real test in the months ahead.[17] The new Congress seemed to be extremely slow about passing the highly publicized tariff bill that would provide the government with a temporary source of operating revenue, and Washington was allowing petty office seekers to distract him from the task of selecting the heads of the major executive departments. It might, as Arthur Lee had suggested some months earlier, "be wise . . . to learn to walk, before we attempted to run," but many began to wonder if the new government was capable of anything better than a crawl.[18] Those who knew Washington were not alarmed because they expected him to move ahead cautiously and collect advice and information from people he trusted before making decisions. The indecisiveness of the new Congress was more difficult to explain since virtually everyone expected it to be a marvel of efficiency compared to its predecessor. Virginians naturally made unfavorable comparisons with their own state legislature, which in recent years had proved capable of handling an unbelievable number of difficult problems in a single session.

In July the new government seemed to come alive. The Tariff Act was signed into law on July 4, and a tonnage act taxing vessels using our ports went into effect on July 20. The establishment of a Department of Foreign Affairs and the designation of John Jay as its acting head indicated the executive departments were at last beginning to be organized. In the succeeding weeks the departments of War and Treasury were established, and the office of Postmaster General was created. Henry Knox, who had served as Secretary of War during the Confederation, was asked to remain as head of the same department under the new government. The difficult task of heading the Treasury went to the young and energetic Alexander Hamilton of New York, and Samuel Osgood was named Postmaster General. Washington hoped that Thomas Jefferson, currently serving as the American minister to France, would accept his offer to head the Department of Foreign Affairs.[19]

Randolph followed these developments with great interest and once again Madison became his principal informant. Though Madison's letters were less frequent than they had been when he was reporting on the activities of the Continental Congress, they were no less perceptive.[20] Randolph was not always pleased with what he read in these letters, but as the months passed, even he had to admit that the new government was working rather well. Where others saw evidence of slow progress, Randolph, with several years of practical experience behind him, saw caution. He knew a new government could not be created overnight and he respected Washington's measured response to the administrative problems that confronted him. What pleased him most was the complete collapse of all organized opposition to the Constitution. Its severest critics seemed prepared to work within the system rather than undermine its operations. He still believed that some people might try to scuttle the new government if it showed signs of faltering. However, the apparent ease with which it was winning the confidence of the people caused him to discount their chances of success. All in all the future looked fairly promising—at least as long as Washington remained at the helm and Madison sat in Congress.[21]

In mid-June Madison, anticipating a House debate on the Senate-sponsored bill establishing the federal judiciary, casually asked Randolph to look over a copy of the bill and observed that "such remarks as your leisure will permit, will be acceptable and useful."[22] A similar request went to Edmund Pendleton.[23] Preoccupied with his wife's illness, Randolph had let several previous letters from Madison go unacknowledged, but this one received his immediate attention. His comments were fairly brief and were directed toward specific features of the bill. He observed that it might be given a more accurate title and suggested that the number of judges on the Supreme Court might be increased to nine or eleven so that the Court might be able to hold its own "against eleven state judiciaries." He further suggested that it was also important that the Court have an odd rather than an even number of judges, given the intended composition of the bench in the lower federal courts. He was more concerned, however, with the way the bill defined the jurisdiction of the federal courts and characterized it as inartful, untechnical and confusingly worded. It would, he noted, have been better to simply let the language of the Constitution prevail. He also questioned the wisdom of using one law to establish the entire federal judicial system: "I cannot discover what disadvantage the system would have sustained by dividing the courts into separate laws." His trained eye also caught the meaninglessness of a clause that said no man could be sued except in his own district, "or where the writ shall be served." Rhetorically, he asked: "What limitation is this?" His major objection, however, seems to have been the amount of "minute detail" incorporated into the bill:

Every attempt towards it must be imperfect, and being so may become a topic of ridicule to technical men. I wish this idea had been thought worthy of attention; thus the bill would have been less criticized. I wish even now, that the judges of the supreme court were first to be called upon before a definitive step shall be taken. A temporary provision, until their report can be had, surely is not impossible.[24]

Randolph's comments reached Madison several days before the House received the judiciary bill from the Senate. But by this time the House was considering amendments to the Constitution, and all other matters, including the judiciary bill, were laid aside. The bill was not brought up in the House until mid-September, and by that time Madison's attention had been diverted by the debate over the site of the permanent seat of government. Madison took little or no part in the debate, and Randolph's and Pendleton's comments were apparently ignored.[25] In a subsequent letter to Pendleton, Madison observed, rather apologetically, that "The attachment of the Eastern members, the difficulty of substituting another plan, with the consent of those who agree in disliking the bill, the defect of time, etc., will however prevent any radical alteration."[26]

While Randolph was waiting for Madison to acknowledge his comments on the judiciary bill and, more importantly, to report on the House's handling of the constitutional amendments, he received a very interesting letter from Colonel Cyrus Griffin. Griffin, a former member of Virginia's delegation to the Continental Congress and the last President of that Congress, was not one of Randolph's regular correspondents, and his letter came as something of a surprise.[27] Griffin had written at the request of President Washington, who, as Griffin explained it, was anxious to know whether several individuals associated with the judiciary in Virginia were interested in serving in the judicial branch of the federal government. Griffin said he had had a long conversation with Washington regarding appointments to the judiciary and to the customs service. In connection with the former, Washington had mentioned the names of Pendleton, Wythe, Lyons, Blair and Randolph, inquiring specifically if Randolph "had ever intimated a wish to serve in that [the judiciary] or any other line under the Federal government." Washington had apparently asked Griffin to initiate informal inquiries to each of these individuals and to this end Griffin wrote to Randolph. He also asked Randolph to assume responsibility for asking Wythe and Blair if they were interested in serving in the federal judiciary.[28]

Randolph was flattered that Washington was considering him for a federal post but totally at a loss as to how to respond. He was obviously interested, but not right now. He had returned to private practice because it was the only way he could acquire the additional income he needed to meet his many financial obligations. A federal appointment or even offering himself for a seat in Congress was a possibility, but not for several years—not until he had extricated himself from his precarious financial situation.

Once again he turned to Madison. When he withdrew from private practice to accept the governorship of Virginia, he confided to Madison, he had only one important personal debt to pay. This debt, resulting from a recent land purchase, was to have been met by selling certain of his other land holdings. Unfortunately when he attempted to sell these lands, he discovered they would bring him far less revenue than he had expected and would involve him in a substantial loss of money. Thus the debt arising from his land purchase remained unpaid, and this fact partially accounted for his recent return to private practice.[29] In addition, he had to recognize that his medical expenses might increase sharply if the ulcer Betsy complained of did in fact prove cancerous. And lastly, he had just learned that an additional debt of about £800 was chargeable against his uncle's estate, placing even further demands on his income. If certain of his properties could be sold, some of these debts could be met, but at present these lands, he predicted, would bring only a fourth of their real worth. In short, public office outside of Virginia involved him in the type of personal sacrifice he was not at present prepared to make.

But Randolph was not finished:

> Colo. G's letter has, however, caused me to reflect upon a different destination. It would bring with it many conveniences in reference to the complaint of my wife, if a northern journey should be deemed necessary for her. But these would be counterbalanced by the load of calumny which should be poured upon me. . . . For it has been insinuated (and in defiance of truth) that my espousal of the Constitution had alienated even its friends from me, who would not elect me to the House of Representatives. The insinuation has been carried so far as to apply it to the disposal of offices under government. My sincere desire then would be to have it in my power to *refuse,* and actually *refuse* an office. But as the tender of a post could not be made on such ground, I commit myself to you, and leave you to represent this business to Colo. Griffin as you please, if you think that there is no impropriety in my enlisting under Federal banners. And yet I ought to add that nothing definitive can be said until I learn the changes which the [judiciary] bill has undergone.[30]

Madison, by now an expert interpreter of Randolph's sometimes tortured reasoning processes, must have winced as he read these lines. Having offered irrefutable evidence that he could not accept any public office that would require him to curtail his law practice or leave Virginia for any length of time, he then reversed himself and expressed an interest in a federal appointment. Not only would it permit him to live in a city where adequate medical facilities were available for Betsy if she needed them, but it would also demonstrate to his political enemies that the friends of the Constitution, far from rejecting him, actually valued his services. The suggestion that he be offered a federal post so that he might reject it was incomprehensible. Did he really mean what he said?

Finally, the sanctimonious observation that he could not commit himself until he learned more about the changes in the judiciary bill was the height of arrogance. Madison must have heaved a sigh of resignation and made up his mind then and there that Randolph's more indiscreet statements had better be conveniently forgotten when the matter was explained to Griffin. The House's decision to postpone consideration of the judiciary bill until the question of amendments had been resolved lessened the need for any immediate decision on the appointments to that branch of the government.

Having left the matter in Madison's hands, Randolph turned his attention to other things. He remained in Williamsburg during the last two weeks of July, but the first part of August found him traveling first to Leesburg in Loudoun County "to argue a cause against Mr. P. Henry," and then to Fredericksburg, and from there to the Green Mountains where he remained "for some time." From here he went to his plantation in Charlotte County and intended to return to Williamsburg about the middle of September.[31] Madison was kept informed of his whereabouts and was instructed to contact Betsy in Williamsburg "should any communication from your quarter be necessary to be answered by me."[32] But Madison had nothing to communicate, at least nothing relating to Randolph.

Randolph returned to Williamsburg during the second week of September, physically exhausted from his travels and ill with a quartan fever. During the first few days he was home he was so ill that he could not even attend to his neglected business correspondence and an urgent request from Madison that he expand on his previously prepared "introductory discourse" on the Federal Convention was allowed to go unacknowledged for the better part of two weeks.[33] By the end of the month he thought he had recovered sufficiently to attend to some of his professional responsibilities, but then the fever returned and once again he was forced to curtail his activities.

During this second convalescence he received the communication he had been waiting for and which he was beginning to believe would never come. It came not from Griffin or Madison but from President Washington himself. It informed him, unofficially, that he intended to appoint him Attorney General of the United States and expressed the hope that he would accept the office. The letter went on to observe:

> Notwithstanding the prevailing disposition to frugality, the salary of this office appears to have been fixed, at what it is, from a belief that the station would confer pre-eminence on its possessor, and produce for him a decided preference of professional employment.[34]

The remark indicated Washington had been fully apprised of Randolph's considerable financial difficulties and was trying to reassure him that a lucrative private practice could be anticipated if he accepted the appointment. It appeared Washington was most anxious to have him become a part of the executive branch.

Randolph was flattered by the promise of appointment and obviously anxious to accept, but he felt obliged to give Washington a full account of his many financial problems.[35] He also informed the President that he would like to remain in the Virginia Assembly until the end of the ensuing session because he was engaged in preparing a revision of the laws of Virginia and was anxious to complete this "indispensable business" before leaving the legislature. This task, plus the need to put his plantations on a "proper footing," arrange his "private affairs" and "carry his family to New York," would render it impossible for him to assume the duties of the Attorney General's office before next March. "In the meantime," he remarked, "if any professional aid should be demanded by government, I hope that there would be no impropriety in soliciting the aid of some gentleman of the law on the spot, to render it in my behalf." Thus, assuming the Judiciary Act contained nothing "which I cannot get over," and further assuming Washington was agreeable to this delay of five months, he would accept the appointment.[36] It seems Randolph expected the President, like Madison, to have unlimited patience in dealing with him, particularly when he was trying to reconcile the conflict between his financial needs and the challenge of a new public office. His letter was dated October 8, 1789.

The letter reached New York while Washington was on a tour of the northeastern states, thereby ruling out a prompt reply.[37] When the newspapers reported that the President had returned to New York on November 13, Randolph, who was now busy with legislative duties, assumed he would soon receive an acknowledgment of his letter and an indication of whether the President had any objection to the proposed delay in assuming the duties of the office. Randolph waited until November 22 and not a line from the President. Could Washington be seeking the services of another—someone willing to enter immediately upon the duties of the office? He wrote again to the President:

Dear Sir:

Immediately upon the receipt of your private communication of my appointment, I wrote to you with a head very much disordered by a fever. As soon as I recovered, I should have written to you again, had I not heard of your tour to the East. By this time I presume you have returned, and therefore beg leave to inform you that I shall leave Virginia on the 15th of

January for New York. The reason why I do not make an official reply to
your official favor is stated in my former letter. Should you wish to see me
earlier than the day which I have fixed above, I will endeavour to obey your
summons.

The rest of the letter carried routine news about the activities of the
Virginia Assembly as if Randolph were one of Washington's most faithful correspondents.[38]

It was an ingenious letter, designed to claim the Attorney General's
office before Washington could withdraw his offer of it, as he had every
right to do given the less than enthusiastic language of Randolph's
earlier letter of acceptance. Perhaps it occurred to Randolph that this
was Washington, not Madison, at the other end of his correspondence,
and that the man who occupied the presidency might not have the time
or patience to wait for Randolph to sort out his personal and professional priorities and resolve his scruples about each and every clause in
the Judiciary Act.

But Randolph's fears were unfounded. As this letter traveled northward, Washington was acknowledging the letter of October 8 and in
more generous terms than even Randolph expected:

> Your letter of the 8th of October gave me pleasure as I not only entertain
> hopes, but shall fully expect from the contents of it to see you in the office
> of Attorney General when the purposes mentioned by you for the delay are
> answered.[39]

The matter was resolved, the appointment was Randolph's and nothing
remained to be done except to place his personal affairs in order so that
he might assume the office as soon as possible.

On October 19, less than two weeks after Randolph mailed his first
letter of acceptance to the President, he was obliged to once again take
up the duties of an elected delegate to the Virginia Assembly. He arrived in Richmond several days before the Assembly convened and,
although still a little weak from his recent illness, managed to put in an
appearance at the various social gatherings that usually preceded a legislative session. As might be expected, he was the center of many strategy
sessions and privy to every rumor about the expected political composition of the legislature. Aside from Patrick Henry, he was probably the
most powerful political figure in the House.

When the House appointed its standing committees for this session he
was named chairman of Propositions and Grievances and named third
to each of the other standing committees of the House.[40] This was no

small accomplishment since the House of Delegates, like the House of Burgesses before it, usually demanded some years of legislative service before appointing a person to a ranking position on any of these standing committees.

The first significant business of the legislature was the subject Randolph had previously cited as his main reason for returning to the House for this session—a complete review and consolidation of the laws of Virginia. On October 24 a Committee of the Whole House recommended the appointment of a special committee to examine the laws of the state to determine which of them were still in force. This committee reported back to the House on November 2, and the report became the basis for appointing a special committee of lawyers to prepare a definitive edition of the laws of the state.[41] The House named Randolph to the first committee. When this committee reported back to the House, Randolph assumed responsibility for drafting the bill that authorized the establishment of the special committee to prepare the revision.[42] He was subsequently named to this second committee when his bill was approved by the House. This special committee was given until the next session of the General Assembly to prepare a definitive edition of the laws of the state.[43]

When the committee members met, they discovered that much of their work had already been done for them by Randolph. It seems that he had been concerned about the absence of an authoritative compilation of Virginia laws for some time, and was furthermore convinced that the only realistic solution was to have the legislature authorize a new edition that would supersede all earlier editions.[44] To this end he had begun collecting the laws himself and apparently had much of the basic work done before the Assembly convened on October 19. It was not a matter of presenting the committee with a *fait accompli*; rather it was an illustration of Randolph's industry and his general impatience with the perpetual disorganization of Virginia's laws and court records.[45]

There was, however, another matter on the agenda of this session of the Assembly that was far more important than the effort to prepare a definitive edition of the laws of the state. This was the amendments to the federal Constitution that had been forwarded to the Assembly by Congress at the close of its first session. Congress, in obedience to the wishes of several state ratifying conventions, had reviewed the various and sometimes duplicate amendments proposed by these conventions and referred twelve to the state legislatures for possible adoption. It was October before most Virginians learned which amendments had been approved by Congress and many delegates did not see the text of these amendments until they came to Richmond for the opening of the legislature. Thus the initial reaction was predictably cautious, with those most critical anxious to have the subject referred to the next session of the legislature.[46] Their position was well taken since it was probably much too soon to judge the temper of the state on the points covered by these amendments.

When the amendments came up for consideration before the Committee of the Whole House in November, Patrick Henry tried to get the necessary support for a motion to have the matter referred to the next session of the Assembly. His effort failed and the amendments were voted on by a Committee of the Whole House article by article. The first ten were readily approved but, to the surprise of many, Randolph mounted a strong attack against the last two.[47] These amendments sought to establish two analogous propositions: first, that rights not specifically enumerated by the Constitution were retained by the people; and second, that powers not specifically delegated to the federal government by the Constitution were retained by the states or the people.[48] Randolph's objection to both of these articles was largely theoretical in that he argued it was dangerous to try and protect "rights" and "powers" by stating they were "retained" or "reserved." He insisted that it would be much safer to have amendments that explicitly prevented Congress from extending the power of the federal government.[49] His opposition was sufficient to persuade a majority to vote against the last two amendments in the Committee of the Whole House, although a few days later, when the formal House vote was taken, all twelve amendments were approved and sent to the Senate.[50]

Here they encountered considerable opposition and the Senate decided that the Third, Eighth, Eleventh and Twelfth amendments should be "postponed [un]til the next session of the Assembly, for the consideration of the people."[51] The House of Delegates refused to agree and the Senate refused to alter its position, so each branch of the legislature appointed a Committee of Managers in an effort to reconcile the two positions. Randolph served as chairman of the House committee. To the utter astonishment of most Virginians neither branch of the legislature would retreat from its respective positions, thereby deadlocking the legislature and foreclosing any decision on the amendments during the current session.[52]

As the two houses were trying to reconcile their differences on the amendments, Randolph, in a classic display of independence, laid before his fellow delegates a detailed criticism of the Virginia constitution and called upon the House to pass a resolution recommending to the "good people of this Commonwealth" that, taking these weaknesses and omissions into consideration, they instruct "the next or some future session" of the Assembly to take whatever steps were necessary to convene a constitutional convention for the purpose of writing a new state constitution.[53] His proposal hit them like a bombshell. Not that a constitutional convention was wholly beyond contemplation—few would have been so rigid in their attitude—but the unrestrained critique of the present constitution probably caused them to sit transfixed in their chairs.

He began by observing that the convention that had drafted the original constitution did all that "patriotism, firmness and zeal could accomplish," but having lived "in a dependency on the English monarchy, they were destitute of those lights which the exercise of self-government have since produced." They wrongfully supposed, he continued, that the executive branch of government posed the greatest danger to civil liberties and that these liberties would be most secure if "unbounded" power was vested in the legislature. Laboring under this misapprehension, they drafted a constitution that, time had revealed, had many errors, "great in number and fatal in their influence." He then proceeded to itemize them one by one, without the slightest concern for the sensibilities of his audience. He dismissed accepted political procedures as absurdities, mocked many of the restrictions and restraints that were built into the existing constitution and predicted that the power presently vested in the legislature would terminate in legislative corruption. His choicest phrases were reserved for the manner in which the executive had been constituted: "their pay is in proportion to the smiles or frowns of [the legislature]" and "the office may be so much impoverished as may be unworthy of acceptance to all but those who can consign themselves to the humor of the legislators."[54] On and on he went; the delegates sat in disbelief as they listened to his devastating indictment of a constitution many of them believed was second to none in America.

The delegates had no trouble getting his message—the House of Delegates had far too much power and the other branches of government had too little. He was absolutely right, of course, but never had this been said with such cutting sarcasm, with such contempt. They responded with undisguised anger. It was moved to amend Randolph's motion by striking out everything after the word "Resolved" and "inserting in lieu thereof the following words: "That the foregoing statement contains principles repugnant to Republican Government and dangerous to the freedom of this country, and therefore ought not to meet with the approbation of this House, or be recommended to the consideration of the people."[55] To prevent matters from getting completely out of hand it was moved that Randolph's original motion and this amendment be postponed until March 31, 1790, a meaningless date well beyond the time the Assembly was normally in session.[56] John Dawson assessed the incident perfectly when he observed: "I fear that by this impolitic step it will be difficult to procure a Convention for the purpose of amending our state Constitution for many years."[57]

Even Randolph's closest friends had to admit it was an "impolitic step," given the generally benign attitude of most Virginians toward their constitution and the men who had drafted it. Randolph must have known this because he had in his own way contributed to the fiction that Virginia's government was second to none in the nation. Could it be that he had found from practical experience that the office of governor was so abysmally ineffective that the whole apparatus of state government should be overhauled? Or was it just a case of having had his constitutional instincts sharpened and refined by his experiences in Philadelphia? His critique of the state constitution carried several references to the federal Constitution and the delegates must have noticed that the Virginia constitution was always compared unfavorably with the national document. One can only conclude that both experiences influenced Randolph's thinking and, regrettably, also contributed to his strong rhetoric.

By the time the session adjourned on December 19 Randolph was exhausted. It had been a particularly demanding session, and he had made it his business to be on the floor of the legislature during every critical debate. If a passing observation of the experienced Joseph Jones is to be believed, his very presence determined the pace of public business: "The Assembly are as usual moving slowly in the public business slower than I think they would have done but for Mr. E. Randolph's indisposition the last week which disabled him from attending the house for some days."[58] He seemed to be interested in almost everything that came before the legislature and his presence was reflected in virtually all the major issues considered during this session.[59] It was in fact a rather impressive performance for one who was about to quit the field of Virginia politics for a federal position.

As soon as the Assembly adjourned, Randolph began making preparations for his journey to New York. Since Betsy was pregnant once again, it was decided that the family would remain in Williamsburg until the baby was born and mother and child were strong enough to undertake the arduous journey to New York. This meant that Randolph would go to New York alone, take the oath of office, and then attend to any legal matters Washington might be holding for his consideration.[60] If he could be spared, he would return to Williamsburg some time in May in order to be with Betsy when the baby was born. If public duties prevented him from leaving New York in the spring, he would simply wait until after Congress recessed for the summer when, of necessity, the wheels of government would turn more slowly. Whatever he did, he expected to lead a rather solitary life in the months to come.

Anticipating a return to Williamsburg in a matter of two, possibly three, months, he decided against any formal abandonment of his private practice. Undoubtedly cases scheduled to be argued at forthcoming sessions of the superior courts had to be entrusted to the care of others, but the remainder of his clients were apparently left in the dark about his future plans. For all he knew he might be spending four or five months of each year in Virginia if the duties of the office of Attorney General were not too demanding, and if this should be the case, he wanted to retain as much of his practice as possible. Everything, in short, was left in abeyance until he could familiarize himself with the new government and the way it functioned.[61]

The transition then from Virginia lawyer and legislator to principal legal officer in the new government was gradual and hesitant and, like many of Randolph's decisions, filled with doubts and misgivings. He was instinctively a Virginian and his public life thus far had been little more than the fulfillment of a family tradition of public service. But now he was about to embark upon a new career, a career that demanded new loyalties and a different set of priorities. It had not been an easy decision for him to make. Within days of his acceptance of the attorney generalship he candidly admitted as much to Madison: "There are many causes, however, which besides the curse of expatriation (you see I am not yet a strict American) must detain me here some time. . . ."[62] It was a very telling remark and Madison, who thought he knew Randolph so well, must have realized how terribly foolhardy it was to try and categorize this man. If emotional and private considerations caused Randolph to reflect again on his decision to leave Virginia, the realities of a viable national government dictated that he hasten to New York. In the final analysis he knew the future of America was to be fashioned in this temporary capital of the new national government, or, indeed, it would have no future. Randolph was enough of an American and too good a Virginian to ignore this challenge.

PART III
THE CABINET
YEARS

The acceptance of the office of Attorney General of the United States initiated the most important period of Randolph's public life. Although initially he was little more than a legal adviser to the President and his Secretaries, he soon found himself being thrust into a far more important role. As the political rivalry between Hamilton and Jefferson intensified, Washington began to rely more and more on his Attorney General for political advice. By the spring of 1793 Randolph's uncanny talent for identifying the "middle position" had made him indispensable to the President.

The resignation of Jefferson from the Cabinet in December of 1793 led to Randolph's appointment as Secretary of State and, paradoxically, to his diminishing influence among the President's advisers. As long as Jefferson and Hamilton were both serving in the Cabinet, the two opposing political creeds of Federalism and Republicanism had brilliant expositors. Once Jefferson left, this polarizing process came to an end. In the ensuing months Randolph found it increasingly difficult to chart a "middle position" for Washington. The result was a lessening of his influence over Administration policy. The process was hastened by the resignation of Hamilton on January 31, 1795, which further diminished the ideological style of the Cabinet.

The Jay Treaty of 1795 was not to Randolph's liking. He discovered he was in the unenviable position of seeing others determine American foreign policy while he, as Secretary of State, could do little more than influence the manner in which it was being implemented. In the debate over the treaty he found himself classified as an opponent and, in the eyes of some, an obstacle to ratification. Randolph's influence in the Administration came to an end when a dispatch from Jean Fauchet (the French minister to the United States) suggesting Randolph had solicited funds from him was intercepted by the British and sent to their minister in Philadelphia. The subsequent transmittal of this dispatch to Washington, his confronting Randolph with it and Randolph's prompt res-

[189]

ignation marked the end of Randolph's Cabinet career. Randolph's desperate efforts to clear his name were to no avail, as the heated political climate of the times precluded a fair assessment of his conduct.

Being a member of neither political party, he was a person no one bothered to defend or denounce now that he had lost the confidence of the President. His power had been grounded in Washington's trust, and when that trust was terminated, he had no further influence in national politics.

14

Casual Legal Adviser in
a New Government
January 1790–September 1791

The journey northward in the middle of winter was predictably unpleasant; Randolph's heaviest winter clothing offered little protection against the damp cold and bitter winds of January. More than once he was thankful he had not attempted to move Betsy and the children in such weather. Arriving in New York by February 2, he was actually surprised that he had completed the trip without succumbing to a cold or worse.[1] His first responsibility was, of course, to notify the President of his arrival. Observing the usual courtesies, he probably left a note with one of Washington's secretaries—at the pleasure of the President he would return to pay his respects and receive whatever instructions Washington might have for him.

While awaiting word on when the President would be able to see him, he sought out his fellow Virginian and sometime political mentor, James Madison. The acknowledged leader of the House of Representatives and a confidant of the President, Madison was eminently qualified to brief the new Attorney General on the activities of Secretary of War Knox and Secretary of the Treasury Hamilton, currently Randolph's only colleagues in the executive branch. The most interesting development, and probably the only one Madison wanted to talk about, was Hamilton's Report on Public Credit. Submitted within the last two weeks, while Randolph was en route to New York, it offered a plan for funding the nation's foreign and domestic debt including all unpaid state debts contracted during the Revolution.[2] Madison was only beginning to sense the full implications of the report himself, but his developing concern over some of its more significant features instinctively led Randolph to reflect on the broad political implications of the report.[3]

Of more immediate concern to the Attorney General was the forthcoming session of the Supreme Court which, in compliance with the provisions of the Judiciary Act of 1789, was to convene on the first Monday in February.[4] Four of the six Justices, Chief Justice John Jay and Associate Justices William Cushing, James Wilson and John Blair,

and Randolph were on hand to present their commissions and be "qualified according to law." The first term of the Court lasted only one day
and, of necessity, was devoted to organizational matters. Among its several directives was a ruling that all attorneys intending to practice before the Court must take an oath to support the Constitution and
uphold the laws of the United States. Being the only attorney present at
this first session of the Court, Edmund Randolph undoubtedly became
the first attorney to be admitted to its bar.[5] That evening the members
of the federal bench and the Attorney General were the guests of honor
at a "very elegant entertainment" at Fraunce's Tavern on Courtland
Street.[6]

Randolph's responsibilities as Attorney General were quite explicitly
defined by the Judiciary Act of 1789. He was to prosecute all suits in the
Supreme Court in which the interest of the United States was involved,
and he was to provide legal advice to the President and the heads of the
various departments whenever they requested it.[7] Since there were no
cases before the Supreme Court and Washington seemingly had no need
for his services, there was virtually nothing for him to do. Rather than
remain idle in New York, Randolph asked Washington for permission
to return to Virginia. The President allowed eight days to pass before
acknowledging Randolph's note. The abruptness of his reply suggests
considerable and well-justified annoyance with Randolph's seemingly
casual attitude toward his office. Randolph was free to leave New York
but, he added, "[I hope] . . . that your absence from the seat of government will not exceed the time mentioned in your letter to me of the 5th
instant."[8] Subsequently Randolph received three requests for opinions
on relatively minor legal matters which caused him to postpone his
departure until the end of the month.[9]

He arrived in Williamsburg on the first Sunday in March to find the
household alarmed over Betsy's health. She was, he promptly reported to
Madison, "incumbered with a dead foetus of more than seven months
old." "I am," he continued, "endeavoring to ward off by medical aid the
consequences of the event." Although concerned, he seemed optimistic
about her eventual recovery: "She is now in good spirits and therefore, I
trust, the mischief will not be fatal."[10] But his optimism was short-lived:
"It is now a fortnight since she was confined to her room," he reported
on March 15, "and every appearance grows more and more critical."
Since his immediate return to New York was now wholly out of the
question, he asked Madison to explain his delay to the President. "If my
absence would not precipitate her death I shall [sic] leave home without
hesitation. . . ."[11] Subsequent letters gave evidence of some gradual
improvement of her condition, but she became despondent at the mere
suggestion of his leaving:

. . . I should quite her without hesitation. But she is impressed with a belief she cannot escape death, and altho' tolerably lively now, would sink, I suspect, into despair, were I to leave her. What am I to do? I see no other alternative, than this; that I must surrender the office, if my absence cannot be dispensed with.[12]

While awaiting word on the President's reaction to his continued absence from the seat of government, he tried to settle some of the matters he had left unresolved when he left Virginia in January. He made a brief report to Governor Beverley Randolph on the progress of the committee engaged in preparing the definitive edition of the laws of the state.[13] He arranged with his brother-in-law, Wilson Cary Nicholas, for the sale of a portion of his property in Charlotte and, if Betsy's condition permitted, he intended to go to Richmond for the "discharge of the coming taxes."[14] And lastly, there was the familiar problem of trying to satisfy another of his uncle's creditors without disposing of any of his uncle's lands.[15] Then, toward the end of April, he began to make arrangements for an extended absence from the state in the event of Betsy's complete recovery. Wilson Cary Nicholas, Nathaniel Burwell and Benjamin Powell were granted power of attorney over his property. Nicholas was to manage his two plantations in Albemarle and the one in Charlotte, Burwell his property in James City County and Powell his holdings in and adjoining Williamsburg. Matthew Pearson, another friend, was granted power of attorney for the settlement of his accounts.[16]

The premature birth of a dead fetus on May 19 ended the crisis in the Randolph household and, as Randolph reported it to Madison:

> The gloom of our house is conver[t]ed into general satisfaction, at the escape of our friend from the most critical danger. I have this moment informed the President that I shall accompany my family by sea, or the head of the bay, and that we shall have no delay, but what may be necessary for Mrs. R[andolph] to recover from her temporary weakness.[17]

Betsy began to regain her strength, but her recovery was nowhere near as rapid as Randolph had expected. He remained in Williamsburg for several more weeks, and ultimately he was forced to leave without her. It was decided that Betsy and the children would join him later after she had completely regained her strength.[18]

Randolph returned to New York early in July to find the wheels of government turning in a most unusual manner. Jefferson, who had assumed the duties of Secretary of State in March, and Hamilton and their associates were in the process of negotiating a settlement of two issues that had almost paralyzed Congress for the better part of these last four months. The two issues were: Hamilton's Funding bill, the legislation embodying his plan for the gradual liquidation of the public debt; and the bill establishing the permanent seat of the federal government, a matter of vital interest to Jefferson and most southern senators and representatives. The settlement that was arranged gave Hamilton the necessary support to secure the passage of the Funding bill with its controversial provision for the assumption of state debts through the House of Representatives, in return for like support for Jefferson's efforts to have the permanent seat of the federal government located in the South, specifically on the banks of the Potomac River. It was also agreed that Philadelphia would be the seat of government for the next ten years. While many considered this settlement a rather crude example of political horse trading, Randolph was probably prepared to accept it for what it was—a very resourceful solution of two issues that had virtually paralyzed the machinery of government.[19]

As for his own office, he still had very little to do. The Supreme Court was due to convene again on the first Monday of August for its second term, but there were no cases for it to consider.[20] Hamilton, Jefferson and Knox had asked Randolph to consider several rather routine matters, but the President seemed to be almost unaware of his existence.[21] When a New York newspaper questioned the constitutionality of a bill authorizing Congress to convene its next session in Philadelphia, the temporary capital, the President asked the Secretary of State rather than the Attorney General if it was proper for him to sign the bill effecting the transfer.[22] The only substantive assignment Randolph had had to date came from the House of Representatives, which instructed him to report to its next session on the judicial system of the federal government. He was flattered by the assignment because it would provide him with an opportunity to undertake a systematic analysis of the Judiciary Act of 1789 which, he felt, had many faults.[23]

In late July or early August Betsy and the children joined him in New York. Since the seat of government would soon be transferred to Philadelphia, he decided that rather than have his family spend the next couple of months in New York in temporary accommodations, he would try to settle them immediately in the Quaker City.[24] Knowing that Congress was at the point of adjournment and that the President was about to depart on a short visit to Rhode Island, he casually asked Washington for permission to spend several days in Philadelphia settling his family.[25] The President promptly acknowledged his request, stating that he had no objection to the trip if there were "no obstructions of an official nature." He did advise the Attorney General to inquire of Jefferson and Knox if his services might be needed to draft a proclamation for the President in connection with the recently concluded treaty with the Creek Indians. If a proclamation was not contemplated by either of them, he was free to go to Philadelphia.[26]

Edmund, Betsy and the children arrived in Philadelphia on August 19 and, in the words of William Knox, brother of the Secretary of War, "[are] in possession of every spare corner of" the Trist boardinghouse. The next day, benefiting from preliminary inquiries as to the availability of homes in the city, he took possession of a house at the corner of Twelfth and High streets, somewhat to the west of the center of town.[27] Several more days were given over to getting the family settled, with Randolph hoping to get back to New York soon after the President returned from his tour of Rhode Island. Once again his timetable had to be abandoned when he found himself asking for permission to remain away from the seat of government because Betsy was ill. Washington, with unbelievable patience, granted Randolph's request and observed that he would be leaving for Mount Vernon himself within the next few days.[28]

As the seat of government was in the process of being transferred to Philadelphia, Randolph knew he would be completely free of public responsibilities for the next few months. He could attend to the needs of his family, initiate a modest law practice and, for the first time in eight months, lead a tranquil life. Before Betsy's health was fully restored, she was further immobilized by a sprained ankle. While far from serious, it did serve to confine her once again to her room, a confinement she suspected was becoming almost as inevitable as the seasons.[29] Equally inevitable, it seems, were the not infrequent requests from Randolph's creditors for some compensation on overdue notes. Amounts are difficult to determine, but apparently he was constantly juggling funds or notes to meet these demands. He did not confine himself to borrowing from his friends in Virginia; soon even his acquaintances in Philadelphia were made intimately aware of his constant financial embarrassment. He did his best to meet the note holders' demands and impatiently inquired of his brother-in-law Wilson Cary Nicholas whether the sale of his land in Charlotte had been accomplished as requested. "I shall," he wrote, "be put to straits without such a sale and with that aid I could swim clear."[30]

The private practice on which he had depended to supplement his regular income proved less rewarding than he had expected, and by October he told his friend Henry Tazewell that he still had no assurance that he would be employed in anything more than "capital causes." His family, he insisted, was practicing strict economies; apparently they were living more or less within the $1,500 salary of his office.[31]

It is possible that he received some compensation for representing his native state in a rather unfortunate dispute with Pennsylvania over the verification of certain land patents. Virginia had ceded certain of its lands to Pennsylvania with the understanding that Pennsylvania would honor all previously issued land patents in the ceded territory. When the Virginia patent holders presented their claims, however, Pennsylvania refused to honor them until she had been presented with an official set of Virginia's land laws. Randolph offered his services to Virginia to protect the interest of those whose title might be jeopardized by this ruling. Governor Beverley Randolph and the state's Executive Council willingly accepted Randolph's assistance and asked that he inform them as to the actions he had already taken to protect the interests of Virginia citizens. The governor and Council also asked if he would provide them with more precise information on the laws or parts of laws that Pennsylvania insisted be authenticated. An amicable solution must have been worked out because it ceased to be a matter of concern to the officials of the two states and to Randolph.[32]

When the Third Session of the First Congress convened in Philadelphia on December 8, 1790, Randolph was nearly finished with his Report on the Federal Judiciary. Several more weeks were apparently needed to put it into proper form, but by the end of the month it was ready. The report as presented consisted of an enumeration of what he conceived to be the "principal defects" of the Judiciary Act of 1789, followed by a draft of a new judiciary bill incorporating the changes he suggested as well as such parts of the original bill that seemed worthy of retention. Although the report was filled with rather obvious disavowals of any attempt to question the wisdom of Congress in its approval of the original Judiciary Act of 1789, it did in fact challenge many of the act's essential features. Of prime concern to Randolph was the confusion that would reign if the area of state and federal jurisdiction in judicial matters were not more clearly delineated. He carefully defined the sphere of interest of each judicial system by noting the areas of concurrent power and, more importantly, the nature of the judicial power that had been granted to the federal government under the Constitution. Secondly, there was the question of the manner in which an appeal might be taken to the federal courts. Randolph suggested two possible methods: (1) convert the Supreme Court into an appellate tribunal over the supreme courts of the several states; or (2) permit removal by *certiorari* before trial. Of the two, he thought the latter more feasible. Thirdly, Randolph suggested that the practice of allowing judges of the Supreme Court to serve on the Circuit Courts be halted and cited several practical legal dangers that might arise under such a procedure. Lastly, he raised the issue as to the forms of law that should be observed in equity, admiralty and maritime jurisdictions, specifically "whether they are to be according to mere civil law, unqualified by the usages of any modern nation, or under limitation." He believed that limitations were essential to alleviate the severity of the civil law in certain areas and that until Congress could provide such limitations through legislation we ought to rely on those found in British law. Minor matters he merely incorporated into the draft bill; he felt a detailed explanation was unnecessary.[33]

Postponing for the time being any consideration of the report, the House referred Randolph's proposals to a Committee of the Whole House.[34] Randolph had no trouble finding an explanation for their inaction. His report was being totally ignored as the legislators took sides on two new reports that had just been submitted by the indefatigable Secretary of the Treasury. In the first of these reports Hamilton offered a series of proposals for new excise taxes; in the second he outlined his plan for the establishment of a "national" bank.[35] Once again the Secretary's supporters and critics braced themselves for an extended debate on his proposals to the exclusion of almost every other subject, including the Attorney General's Report on the Judiciary.

The debate over the bank bill, which was particularly heated, did not escape the attentive ear of the President, particularly when Madison began to question the constitutionality of the measure.[36] Confronted by a bill that was being challenged on both constitutional and political grounds, Washington activated his all but dutyless Attorney General and asked him to submit a formal written opinion on the bank bill. Randolph, uncertain as to how the bill was to be examined, decided to confine his opinion to the constitutional aspects of the measure. Appended to his formal opinion was a summary of the arguments for and against the bank as found in the public press. "I am," he confessed, "uncertain whether its expediency [also] constitutes a part of your inquiry from me. If it should be your pleasure, that I should enter into *this* branch of the question, I can accomplish it on the notice of a few hours."[37]

In his analysis he acknowledged that the issue of constitutionality turned primarily on the right of the federal government to incorporate a bank. The rights granted to the bank as a corporate entity would be clearly authorized if the right to form a corporation was itself comprehended within the wording of the Constitution. It was obvious, Randolph noted, that the power of creating a corporation was not expressly given to Congress in the Constitution. If, therefore, it had this power, it must be "because the nature of the Federal government implies it or . . . because it is involved in some of the specified powers of legislation or . . . because it is necessary and proper to carry into execution some of the specified powers." Methodically, Randolph analyzed each possibility and found each wanting. To accept any of these propositions would be to stretch the meaning and intent of the Constitution far beyond its intended boundaries and render meaningless the limitations placed on the authority of the central government. "In every respect, therefore, under which the Attorney General can view the act, so far as it incorporated the bank, he is bound to declare his opinion against its constitutionality."[38]

The President, unconvinced by Randolph's reasoning, decided to consult his other advisers. He turned first to Jefferson and asked him to examine the bill and submit his views as to its constitutionality. Jefferson's response, though brief and skeletonized in form, was prompt, dogmatic and, as it happened, completely in accord with the views of Randolph. It was obvious that Jefferson was irrevocably against this bill. While his reply examined the measure under several different headings, his principal argument was against its constitutionality under the still-unratified Tenth Amendment to the Constitution:

> I consider the foundation of the Constitution as laid on this ground, that "all powers not delegated to the United States, by the Constitution, not prohibited by it to the states, are reserved to the states or to the people." To take a single step beyond the boundaries thus specially drawn around the powers of Congress is to take possession of a boundless field of power, no longer susceptible of any definition.

Save for the last paragraph of his opinion where he recognized Washington's ultimate responsibility in the matter his tone was firm and unequivocal. The opinion may have been written in haste, but the basic ideas, typically Jeffersonian, reflected an abiding fear of unlimited power in the central government.[39]

The next day Washington turned to Hamilton. He asked the Secretary of the Treasury not only to consider the validity and propriety of the act, but invited him to answer the objections raised by Randolph and Jefferson in their opinions. Although no deadline was mentioned, he did ask Hamilton to provide him with a written opinion "as soon as is convenient."[40] As it was being written, Washington requested Madison to draft an appropriate statement in the event he decided to veto the measure.[41] On February 23 Hamilton laid a long and masterful opinion before the President.

The Secretary of the Treasury lost no time in enunciating the principle that, in his mind, established the constitutional legitimacy of the bank:

. . . that every power vested in a Government is in its nature *sovereign*, and includes by *force* of the *term*, a right to employ all the *means* requisite, and fairly *applicable* to the attainment of the *ends* of such power; and which are not precluded by restrictions & exceptions specified in the constitution. . . .

Having set forth his basic premise, he went on to consider the objections that had been raised by the Secretary of State and Attorney General. Item by item he challenged his colleagues. He refused to concede a single point, and was content with nothing short of total refutation.[42] On February 25, two days after receiving Hamilton's opinion, the President signed the bank bill.[43]

Innocently, almost accidentally, the debate over the bank bill had given rise to a fundamental reanalysis of the meaning and intent of the three-year-old Constitution. Jefferson's and Hamilton's "cabinet" opinions, written within the framework of an immediate and practical problem and having obvious political overtones, were destined to have far-reaching implications. Encompassed in their opinions were two essentially different interpretations of the Constitution which, in turn, laid the foundation for the emergence of two diverse political creeds.

Of the three opinions presented to Washington, Randolph's was quite obviously the least impressive. He said the substance of the dispute, "as far as [he] . . . was able to discover," was constitutional and for this reason he confined himself to a discussion of the subject under this heading. But uncertain of how the President expected him to handle the question, he felt compelled to supplement his analysis with a summary of the arguments pro and con as found in the "public prints and other sources of communication," and even offered to examine the expediency of the measure if the President so desired.[44] The resulting opinion, marred by this uncertainty, was a rather routine lawyer's brief, proper, methodical and obvious, but not a particularly brilliant assessment of the bill's constitutionality.

From a purely administrative point of view, this request for an opinion on a measure of questionable constitutionality suggests the President was beginning to use his Attorney General as one of his advisers on legal matters. The office still did not have the influence of the other departments but at least it was beginning to acquire an identity. The administrative precedent set by Washington in this instance could not henceforth be routinely discarded without inviting criticism. And once the President began to consult the Attorney General, his department heads lost the option to bypass that office however inconvenient this practice might be to them. The weight that would be attached to the opinions emanating from that office would, of course, be determined by the degree of

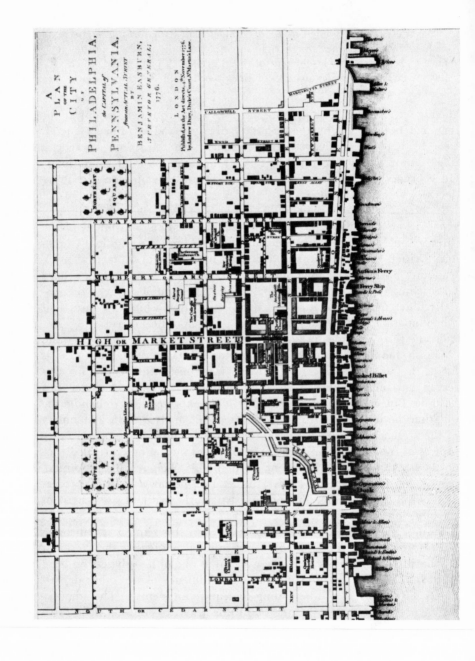

respect Washington and his department heads had for the man who occupied it. In Randolph's case it was still too early to pass judgment for, with the possible exception of this bank bill, he had had little or no opportunity to display his legal expertise.

The adjournment of Congress on March 3 and the departure of the President about two weeks later for an extended tour of the southern states and a brief visit to Mount Vernon once again signaled the curtailment of most governmental activity. For Randolph, it meant a comparatively quiet summer in Philadelphia with his family. Betsy, for a change, was in good health and the family found themselves enjoying Philadelphia—a "stupendous city" Randolph called it.[45] During Washington's absence he took it upon himself to attend to the various personal interests of the President in much the same fashion as he had in Virginia during the 1780s. When he discovered the recently passed Pennsylvania manumission law would permit the slaves in Washington's domestic household, as well as his own, to gain their freedom if they remained in Pennsylvania for six months, he advised Mrs. Washington to break their period of residence by taking them out of the state.[46] Although no advocate of slavery,[47] he recognized that Washington could ill afford the financial loss if his slaves were freed, and as for the slaves themselves, he believed they were likely to experience far greater hardship as freedmen in Philadelphia than they would at the hands of their benevolent master. But Randolph served as more than a legal adviser. During the President's absence he and Betsy saw to it that Mrs. Washington had their companionship by dining with her on occasion as old friends.[48] Such attention, though appreciated, probably was quite unnecessary for Washington had left the overly protective Tobias Lear and his wife Polly to attend to the needs of Martha and the household.

Of an official nature, and far more significant, was Randolph's handling of a sensitive controversy that had developed over the arrest of two men who had fled to Virginia to escape criminal prosecution in Pennsylvania. Governor Thomas Mifflin of Pennsylvania sought to maneuver Washington into making the federal government the instrument for compelling Virginia to return the men.[49] Randolph would have no part of it and so advised Washington. Whatever the merits of Pennsylvania's position—and Randolph recognized that Mifflin was on much stronger legal ground than his antagonist, the attorney general of Virginia—he felt interference by the national government was unnecessary. "But now to interfere would establish a precedent for assuming the agency in every embryo-dispute between states. . . ."[50] Randolph set forth for Mifflin's guidance the procedures he should follow to meet the objections raised by Virginia and advised the President to transmit them to the Pennsylvania governor. Washington accepted his suggestion, and Mifflin, in turn, accepted Randolph's advice.[51]

The only issue to stir the cauldrons of political rivalry during these months arose as a result of Jefferson's indiscreet and unintended endorsement of Thomas Paine's *The Rights of Man*, the latest tract to appear from the pen of America's most famous Revolutionary pamphleteer and political agitator. Jefferson had been lent a copy of Paine's book with instructions to pass it on to one Jonathan B. Smith, whose brother was going to reprint it for distribution in the United States. Jefferson not only complied but also attached a brief note casually expressing his approval of the work. Much to his surprise, the enterprising publisher reprinted Jefferson's remarks on the front of the American edition, implying that he was sponsoring a man who, in the eyes of many, had become a self-appointed missionary of world revolution. By the end of May most newspapers in the country had reprinted his remarks and Jefferson, who detested controversy, now found himself swirling in the center of it. What made matters even more painful, his remarks were construed as a public attack on his old friend John Adams' *Discourses on Davila*.[52] Randolph was quick to learn of Jefferson's accidental endorsement, and after being challenged by Britain's Major George Beckwith concerning its implications, he sought out Jefferson for an explanation.[53] Jefferson was already well aware of the damage that would probably be done, and Beckwith's efforts to read an official endorsement into Jefferson's published letter only increased his embarrassment. Jefferson wrote Washington a letter of explanation and then embarked on a month-long tour of New York and New England with his friend Madison.[54] Randolph, who remained in Philadelphia, probably spent many an hour explaining the circumstance of Jefferson's famous endorsement. It was a matter of no small consequence, for political differences were becoming more pronounced with each passing week during this spring and summer. By the time Jefferson returned to Philadelphia on June 19, the Paine issue had become a *cause célèbre*. Early in June there began to appear in a Boston paper a series of letters signed "Publicola" which bitterly attacked Paine's *The Rights of Man* and, by implication, its supposed advocate. Initially Jefferson, Madison and Randolph assumed the author was John Adams, but before long it was learned that it was not the Vice President but his brilliant young son, John Quincy Adams, who had penned these letters.[55]

Jefferson's fingers may have been burned but still he was not prepared to abandon Paine. The fiery essayist was not only a friend but a political symbol as well. July found Jefferson and Randolph assiduously cultivating Paine's name as the successor to Samuel Osgood in the office of

Postmaster General. It was Randolph who formally recommended him to Washington.[56] To Madison he revealed their motives:

> Mr. J. and myself have attempted to bring Paine forward as a successor to Osgood. It seemed to be a fair opportunity for a declaration of certain sentiments. But all, that I have heard, has been, that it would be too pointed to keep a vacancy unfilled until his return from the other side of the water.[57]

The Jefferson-Randolph alliance did not, as Randolph had correctly predicted, succeed in getting Paine appointed to the vacancy. The post went instead to Timothy Pickering, an uncompromising foe of Jefferson. In August Jefferson was writing to Madison: "Try to arrive here on Tuesday, time enough (say 4 o'clock) to come and dine with E. Randolph [David] Ross & c., half a dozen in all *en petite comité.*"[58] If, as Randolph himself described it, "the *standard* of republicanism has been erected," then the Attorney General appeared to be identifying himself with its cause during these spring and summer months.[59]

Randolph's conduct raised some interesting questions as to his future role in the Washington Administration. His initial response to his appointment had been, at best, casual; then it shifted to a gradual involvement in the affairs of the Administration, and finally, in recent months, to a rather close identification with the man who was erecting the "standard of republicanism." Having resolved his family worries and seen his office finally emerge from virtual obscurity, he had still to find his place in the Administration. He could remain as a sort of friend and legal adviser to Washington or he could enlist under the "standard of republicanism." The former was obviously not enough for him and the latter, he would soon realize, cramped his political independence. It would be several more months before he discovered that he could be much more useful to Washington as a political adviser than he could as a mere Attorney General. And, as had happened in the past, he found external events irrevocably fashioning the role he was to play in the circle of presidential advisers.

15

Spectator to a Growing Political Rivalry
October 1791–February 1793

The opening of Congress on October 26 signaled the revitalization of the machinery of government following several months of comparative quiet. Randolph, who had had little to do in recent months, found his chores increasing as the President and his department heads returned to their desks. The increase in the routine activities of the Attorney General's office—significant assignments were still rather infrequent—resulted largely from the fact that Randolph had abandoned the casualness that marked his first year in office and was giving the position his undivided attention.

The only substantive assignment from the President during the winter of 1791–1792 was a request that he examine the "laws of the general government which have relation to Indian affairs" noting such defects as might require supplementary legislation. It was essential, Washington observed, that the country live in peace with the Indians by prohibiting land companies from arbitrarily selling lands that the United States had promised to respect.[1] Beyond this, his chores were largely administrative, such as collecting documents and preparing an executive pardon for one Samuel Dodge or transmitting a presidential commission to one of the newly named federal district attorneys or marshals.[2]

Somewhat more significant were the requests for legal opinions from the President's Secretaries. Between December, 1791, and August, 1792, there were several instances when Randolph was called upon to render an opinion on a potentially sensitive legal issue. On December 5 the Secretary of State sent Randolph a memorial from George Hammond, the British minister, which challenged a ruling rendered by the Supreme Court of Massachusetts against one Thomas Pagan, a British citizen.[3] In a suit for damages initiated by Thomas Hooker against Pagan the Massachusetts Supreme Court had decided against Pagan and further ruled that Pagan's request for an appeal to the United States Supreme Court be denied. It was this ruling that caused Hammond to request the intervention of the Secretary of State.[4] Randolph, in reply to Hammond's memorial, expressed the opinion that Pagan had not exhausted the legal remedies available to him under the law and suggested that he apply directly to the United States Supreme Court for a writ of error which, if granted, would permit the Supreme Court to review the decision of the Massachusetts court regardless of that court's earlier ruling: "[T]he usage of Sovereigns," he noted, "is not to interfere in the administration of justice, until the foreign subject who complains has gone with his case to the dernier resort. . . ."[5] Several months later, in June of 1792, Jefferson forwarded to Randolph the formal complaint of F. P. Van Berckel, the Netherlands minister to the United States. The complaint alleged that a process had been forcefully served on one of Van Berckel's servants at the minister's own home in violation of his right to diplomatic immunity under the law of nations. Once again Randolph insisted that the proper course of action was to appeal the decision to a higher court. He outlined the various legal remedies available to the servant and the probable consequences of the alternatives suggested. But until all appeals within the state and federal judicial systems had been exhausted, he refused to intervene in the case.[6]

In addition, there were two inquiries dealing with the internal administration of the Treasury and State departments. In June, 1792, Hamilton sought a ruling on the propriety of a Treasury Department officer disposing of his holdings in public securities for profit. Randolph ruled that if the officer in question had agreed to sell his public securities prior to the passage of the law that prohibited such transaction, the agreement to sell could well be construed as actual disposal. On the other hand, if the agreement to sell came after the law in question went into effect, the law acted as an absolute barrier to the sale of such securities by any Treasury Department officer.[7] In July, 1792, Jefferson queried Randolph on whether he could ask the President to appoint a chief coiner under the Mint Act at a time when the Senate was not in session. Randolph informed Jefferson that the President had the constitutional right to fill vacancies that occurred whenever the Senate was not in session, but the vacancy in question had come into existence when the Mint Act was passed, during which time the Senate was, of course, in session. Since Jefferson had failed to act on the appointment then, he must now wait until Congress reconvenes: "The spirit of the Constitution favors the participation of the Senate in all appointments." The right of the President to make appointments during the recess of the Senate "is to be considered as an exception to the general participation of the Senate. It ought to be interpreted strictly."[8]

Quite apart from these legal opinions Randolph clearly signaled his total involvement in the office of Attorney General when he sought to acquire some degree of administrative authority over the federal district attorneys in the thirteen districts set up under the Judiciary Act of 1789. On December 26, 1791, he informed Washington that his office, "in the course of its execution," revealed certain defects which he hoped "will not be deemed unworthy of remedy." The Attorney General, he noted, is frequently requested by the heads of the various departments to initiate and prosecute suits in the lower courts. "It has been always my inclination to conform to their wishes, but a want of a fixed relation between the attorneys of the districts and the Attorney General, has rendered it impossible for me to take charge of matters on which I was not authorized to give instructions." Also, the federal government was frequently affected adversely by cases in the lower courts, and the Attorney General, being totally unaware of the litigation, was unable to offer any assistance to the federal district attorney representing the government's interest. In both instances the absence of a defined relationship between the district attorneys and the Attorney General prevented the latter from fulfilling his responsibilities:

> For this purpose the attorneys of the districts ought, I conceive, to be under an obligation to transmit to him a state of every case in which the harmony of the two judiciaries may be hazarded, and to communicate to him those topics on which the subjects of foreign nations may complain in the administration of justice.[9]

His objections were well taken for the Attorney General was, in fact, virtually isolated from the subordinate federal attorneys and wholly dependent on their personal good will for the coordination of the activities of the legal representatives of the federal government.

Washington, who always insisted that the recommendations of his advisers stand on their own merit, transmitted Randolph's letter to Congress without comment.[10] The Senate tabled it without debate, while the House referred the matter to a committee, which communicated its recommendations to the House on January 18, 1792. The House, in turn, passed a resolution that met each of the difficulties of which Randolph complained. A bill was ordered and subsequently reported pursuant to this resolution, but for some reason no further action was taken on the matter.[11] Randolph seems to have left no record of his reaction to this second instance of legislative indifference to his proposals to reform the judiciary.

Randolph's silence may be traceable to the fact that he was beginning to acquire a new role in the circle of presidential advisers, which shifted his attention to more pressing matters. This new role, literally imposed on him by external forces, was that of political adviser to the President.

Two factors, developing at about the same time, contributed to Randolph's growing influence. The first was the President's decision to employ a more systematic means of collecting the views of the department heads on major issues. The gradual development of the Cabinet—although Washington never used the term—inevitably brought Randolph into the formal circle of presidential advisers.[12] The second, and even more important, factor was Washington's growing concern over the political rivalry that was developing between the Hamiltonian Federalists and the Jeffersonian Republicans. During the winter of 1791–1792 differences of opinion between these two major department heads were converted into fixed political creeds that elicited the religious support of their followers. The more heated the political atmosphere became, the more uncomfortable the President became with the conduct of Jefferson and Hamilton. He needed now what he had never needed before, an adviser loyal to him rather than to his Secretary of State of his Secretary of the Treasury, someone who could help him keep the presidency above politics. Washington gradually came to believe that Edmund Randolph was such a person.

In January of 1792 Washington asked Randolph if it would be appropriate for the President to recommend a digest of federal laws to Congress. Randolph counseled against making such a recommendation. It was a matter of no political consequence and Randolph's answer was very matter of fact. What made it so interesting was his reason for counseling such a course of action. The political climate, he observed, was not conducive to such an abstract inquiry:

> In the midst of the agitations which have been or will be produced by deliverations [*sic*] on the war, the excise, the fisheries, manufactures, the trade with Great Britain, the regulations of a mint, the militia, and many other topics of an *animating cast*, it will probably be asked, what peculiar and immediate urgency has the President remarked, for inviting Congress to this abstract inquiry?[13]

Washington readily accepted his advice and probably made a mental note of his Attorney General's perceptiveness when it came to measuring the mood of Congress.

Although Randolph never mentioned it, one of the items of an "animating cast" agitating Congress at this time was a representation bill reapportioning the seats in the House of Representatives to conform to the population figures established by the census of 1790, the country's first census.[14] When the bill emerged from Congress on March 26, it contained an apportionment formula of doubtful constitutionality.[15] Washington, instead of asking Randolph for a formal opinion on the bill's constitutionality, asked him to assume responsibility for collecting the written opinions of each of the department heads, as well as preparing one himself. Randolph had all four opinions on the President's desk the following day.[16]

In his own opinion Randolph explained in great detail how the bill employed two radically different principles in apportioning the House seats. It fixed the total number of Representatives in the House on the basis of the population of the United States as a whole, and then turned around and apportioned the number of Representatives for each state on the basis of the population in each state. The state, Randolph insisted, was an indissolvable political unit, and under the Constitution both the total number of seats in the House and their distribution could only be determined by the population of the states themselves, each state being accorded one Representative for every thirty thousand inhabitants. The use of two radically different principles in the bill was, for Randolph, evidence of the bill's unconstitutionality: "Here lies the radical objection, and the violation of the constitution."[17]

Of the four opinions Jefferson's was the most detailed since he carefully weighed the merits of the several different methods of apportionment and concluded, as Randolph had, that the bill was unconstitutional. Unfortunately the impact of his detailed analysis was compromised by the inclusion of a suggestion of doubtful relevancy in support of his recommendation for vetoing the bill.[18] Hamilton seems to have been the least familiar with the subject and drafted his opinion without even seeing a copy of the bill. In his opening paragraph the Secretary of the Treasury, writing—as he frequently did—in the third person, expressed the opinion that "from the account he had had of it, he takes it for granted that he cannot have misconceived its contents so as to cause any material error in the process of his reasoning."[19] Washington was not prepared to view the subject with such casualness. Knox, emphasizing his unfamiliarity with the subject and his inability to pass judgment on the constitutional question involved, urged Washington not to veto the bill. The Secretary of War apparently was of the opinion that the President should exercise the veto power only when there was overwhelming evidence that a bill was unconstitutional.[20]

On April 5, the day after the department heads and the Attorney General had submitted their views, Washington visited with Jefferson. The opinions that he had received, he told Jefferson, were divided along sectional lines. If he were to side with Jefferson and Randolph as he was inclined to do, would he not then be accused of showing a sectional bias in his veto? Clearly the bill did not apportion representation in the manner intended by the Philadelphia Convention, but, he asked, was the method unacceptable within the language of the Constitution? Jefferson expressed the opinion that it was. Returning home, the President sent a messenger for Randolph. When the Attorney General arrived, he was instructed to find Madison and go with him to Jefferson's residence. There, the three Virginians were to reassess the constitutionality of the bill and, if united in their views, to draft a veto message for the President. Randolph left immediately, conscious no doubt that the President, still uncertain, now had but one day in which to reach a decision on whether or not to veto the bill. In a short time Randolph returned with a brief veto message upon which, he informed Washington, all three men agreed. Washington read the statement without comment but still was not fully convinced. As the Attorney General was leaving, the President walked with him to the door:

"And you say you approve of this yourself!"

"Yes Sir," said Randolph, "I do upon my honor."[21]

Washington said no more. After Randolph left, the veto message was transcribed without change and forwarded to the House of Representatives.[22] Washington had vetoed his first bill. After a futile attempt to pass the measure over his veto,[23] an appropriately revised bill was introduced that provided for a House of 103 members apportioned by state on the basis of one Representative for every thirty-three thousand inhabitants. It passed the Senate and House in two days and on April 14 Washington affixed his signature to the bill.[24]

By the time the revised apportionment bill had the President's signature, summerlike heat had begun to make living in Philadelphia somewhat uncomfortable. Washington, tired and deeply troubled by the partisan political climate that his two principal Secretaries seemed to inspire, waited impatiently for an opportunity to return again to his beloved Mount Vernon and be freed, at least for a couple of months, from the turmoil of public office.[25] By the time he left the city on July 11 John Fenno's *Gazette of the United States*, the newspaper supporting Hamilton's policies, and the *National Gazette*, the intemperate journal of Jeffersonianism edited by Philip Freneau, were engaged in a relentless and bitter debate over public policy.[26] Washington, disturbed by the harsh language of the two papers, left the city convinced that he had an obligation to see if he could reconcile the differences between his two Secretaries. He would use these summer months, when Congress was not in session, to try and persuade them to abandon their partisan activities. A letter to Hamilton in July, itemizing the complaints against his financial policies, sought to measure the extent of the differences between the two men. The complaints, although attributed to individuals "less friendly . . . to government," were in fact drawn from a letter from Jefferson of May 23. Would Hamilton furnish him with his ideas "upon the discontents have enumerated"?[27] Perhaps if each man set forth his ideas honestly a basis might be found for resolving the differences between them.

Before receiving Hamilton's reply Washington received two letters from his Attorney General. The first, hurriedly written, contained bits of news from Philadelphia.[28] The second, the product of several days' labor and much reflection, urged Washington to reconsider his previously announced wish to retire from public office at the end of his first term.[29] The arguments advanced by Randolph were well known to the President, for Madison in his conversations with Washington had already exhausted most of the reasons for remaining in office.[30] What attracted Washington's attention was Randolph's rather distinctive analysis of the current political mood of the country:

> It cannot have escaped you, that divisions are formed in our politics, as systematic as those, which prevail in Great Britain. Such as opposed the constitution from a hatred to the Union, can never be conciliated by any overture or atonement. By others it is mediated to push the construction of federal powers to every tenable extreme. A third class, republicans in principle, and thus far, in my judgment, happy in their discernment of our welfare, have notwithstanding, mingled with their doctrines a fatal error, that the state assemblies are to be resorted to, as the engines of correction to the federal administration. The honors, belonging to the chief-magistracy are objects of no common solicitude to a few, who compose a fourth denomination.[31]

It was clear to Washington as he read these lines that here was a man who belonged to the republican "denomination," but not uncritically; he could find a "fatal error" in Republicanism. But more important to Washington was Randolph's ability to see a division in politics that was "systematic." To this Washington could subscribe unquestionably, for it was the very heart of the problem. To the extent that political views of men had become "systematic" the political atmosphere had lost the open-mindedness that prevailed during the early years of Washington's presidency. Political differences and even political factions were inevitable, but fixed political creeds were corrosive.

Before the end of August, Washington had Hamilton's reply to his letter of July 29[32] and probably a neat pile of Philadelphia newspapers containing the most serious charges and countercharges yet to appear in the press.[33] The influence, if not the actual hand, of Hamilton was evident in some of these pieces, and the articles in Freneau's paper were clearly written with the assistance of individuals close to the Secretary of State. Hamilton's answer to the twenty-one objections communicated in Washington's letter of the 29th was uncompromising and the tone self-righteous: "I feel I merit them [the objections] *in no degree*, and expressions of indignation sometimes escape me, in spite of every effort to suppress them."[34] Before receiving this reply Washington had dispatched an almost pathetic appeal to Jefferson for political moderation. Calling for "mutual forebearance" on both sides, he pointed out that internal dissensions were "tearing our vitals" and the survival of the Union was at stake.[35] An almost identical letter was sent to Hamilton three days later.[36] Both men responded during the second week of September, each claiming he was the injured party and placing the blame on the other.[37] Washington's two Cabinet officers seemed to be intransigent in their views. With the opening of Congress fast approaching, the President decided to wait until he returned to Philadelphia before making any further efforts to reconcile the differences between them. In the meantime he refrained from making a final decision on his own retirement. The future held many uncertainties, not the least of which was the effect the political partisanship of his two principal Secretaries would have on the credibility of his own Administration.

In the weeks immediately preceding the President's return Randolph concerned himself with the growing unrest against Hamilton's financial program, particularly the opposition to the excise tax. While the President was still at Mount Vernon he provided him with a personal assessment of the situation in Virginia and Pennsylvania, the areas of greatest concern among those who were apprehensive about the growing hostility to Hamilton's financial program. Opposition in Virginia, Randolph reported, was directed primarily at the Bank, although the disfranchisement of the excise officers was also "said to be mediated at the next session of the Virginia Assembly." In Pennsylvania several persons had been convicted for assaulting an excise officer. These convictions, Randolph maintained, would strengthen the hand of the government while having an adverse effect on the "ticket" of the party that stood in opposition to Hamilton's program within the state. The prospects for the "friends of stable government" were, in effect, more promising than earlier reports reaching Philadelphia had indicated.[38]

At the same time, and on an official level, Randolph, in conjunction with Knox and Hamilton, was engaged in the preparation of a proclamation against the growing hostility to the excise tax in the counties of western Pennsylvania. The proclamation, as drafted by Hamilton, was designed to intimidate those who were attempting to prevent the collection of the excise.[39] Randolph, as the government's principal legal officer, felt that the language of the proclamation was far too strong, and he argued that it should say no more than was actually intended. Since it would ultimately appear over the signature of the President, he insisted that it contain no idle threats or exaggerated assertions of governmental authority. So long as open rebellion did not exist, the people could not be threatened with irresponsible language.[40] Although many of the changes suggested by Randolph were incorporated into the final draft, the published document still reflected the strong opinions of the Secretary of the Treasury.[41]

Washington returned to Philadelphia on October 13 and shortly after his arrival solicited the views of his Attorney General on what topics should be included in his annual message to Congress when it convened.[42] Although he had always solicited the views of Hamilton, Jefferson and Knox, this was the first time the President had seen fit to consult with Randolph on the contents of his annual message.[43] Randolph performed the task without careful reflection but noted once again the need for reforming the judicial system. He refrained from detailing the changes he sought, implying they had already been itemized in his earlier report. Aside from matters in his own department, he urged that measures be taken to assure the public of "stability in the *existing* fiscal arrangements." Specifically, he also urged:

> . . . that the redemption of the public debt be commenced at no distant day; that the land office, if the hostility of the Indians will permit, be employed as one of the instruments of redemption; that the state governments be prohibited from intermeddling with the Indian tribes, to the utmost limit of the constitution; that some temporary mode be provided for the relief of many crippled soldiers who must beg or starve until the schism between the legislature and judiciary shall be adjusted; and that the violence of the sanguine states, which may be disappointed on the final settlement of their accounts with the United States may in some manner or other be softened.[44]

Washington's message was rather perfunctory in form and content, placing considerably more emphasis on Indian affairs than the circumstances seemed to warrant. He briefly mentioned Randolph's two principal suggestions but ignored the remainder.[45]

As the weeks passed and Washington refrained from announcing his decision to retire, his reelection became a foregone conclusion. The heated political rivalry between Jefferson and Hamilton now found expression in a struggle over the Vice Presidency. A vigorous effort by the supporters of Jefferson to secure the election of George Clinton of New York forced the Federalists to work diligently for John Adams' reelection.

To all these activities Randolph remained a mere spectator. He certainly subscribed to the view that Washington's reelection assured the country four more years of tranquility, for he knew that Washington was the only man who could bridge the chasm between Jefferson and

Hamilton. But in the contest between the two vice presidential candidates he refrained from indicating his preference. He knew and apparently respected both men but left no clue as to his feelings.

January brought a renewal of the political rivalry between Jefferson and Hamilton. It took the form of a series of resolutions in the House of Representatives by William Branch Giles of Virginia, an ardent Jeffersonian, aimed at embarrassing the Treasury Department.[46] Although these resolutions were ultimately defeated by Hamilton's supporters in the House, they provided the political setting in which the President and his advisers considered the request of Jean-Baptiste Ternant, the French minister to the United States, for an advance of 3,000,000 livre—$554,500—on our debt to France.[47] Uncertainty as to the permanence of the new French Republic and the recent request of Ternant for funds to alleviate the suffering of the people on the French island of Santo Domingo further complicated the issue.[48] Washington, not insensitive to the difficulties of resolving such a question in the highly charged political atmosphere, solicited the views of Hamilton, Jefferson and Randolph on February 8.[49]

Jefferson, submitting his views to Washington on February 12, was the first to reply. His formal opinion consisted of a series of questions and answers structured so as to indicate that he felt the advance requested by the French minister ought to be approved.[50]

Randolph replied on February 14 in a long letter to the President. Before proceeding to the question of the loan, he opened his letter with a most interesting observation:

> Convulsed as we are, I cannot but believe, that there is scarcely a man in the government, whom party will not sooner or later destine for an attack. A communication therefore which *seems* even to be tinctured with particular objects, will naturally excite caution. I hope, however, that I shall not be understood to insinuate the most distant suspicion of that affectionate attachment which is professed; for I am truly persuaded of it. I mean no more, than that kind of caution, which would prevent you from hastily acceding to, or rejecting propositions, so delicate in themselves.

After fully discussing the fiscal and political aspects of the loan, he suggested that Ternant be paid the balance due France up to the end of 1792 and that a final answer on the remainder of the sum requested be given after Congress had finished consideration of the fiscal measures (i.e. Hamilton's reports in response to the Giles resolutions) presently before them; "then, and not 'till then, will you be able to avoid the appearance of sheltering an officer, or countenancing his adversary."[51]

A final decision on Ternant's request was postponed until the following week when the President unexpectedly introduced the subject at a Cabinet meeting that had been called to consider the frontier problem. The Cabinet decided, three to one, that Ternant should receive the full amount requested. Randolph, Jefferson and Knox voted in favor of advancing the entire sum of $554,500 to Ternant, while Hamilton, who had not previously expressed himself on the issue, urged that Ternant receive only what was due to France as of the end of 1792, "a sum of about 318,000 dollars," at least for the present. It was approximately the same position that Randolph had taken a week earlier in his letter to Washington.[52] In the absence of other factors and considering how completely the inquiry into the activities of the Treasury Department dominated the attention of those in the executive and legislative branches of government, it seems safe to conclude that the shift in Randolph's position indicated he felt political passions had cooled sufficiently—at least for the moment—to permit the request of the French minister to be considered on its merits.

While Ternant's request was under consideration our relations with the new French Republic were being influenced by another matter. Reports reached Jefferson around February 20 that the aristocratic views of Gouverneur Morris, our minister in Paris, were such as to render him highly objectionable to the Republic. While his recall had not been requested, the reports of his disdain for the French Minister of Foreign Affairs, Le Brun and other officials of the Republic, were sufficiently serious to be brought to Washington's immediate attention.[53] Jefferson suggested that a solution might be found in exchanging Morris with Thomas Pinckney, our minister in London, a proposal Washington rejected immediately because he believed it would offend France. The President then asked Jefferson if, in view of the fact that he had already indicated that he intended to resign from the office of Secretary of State at the end of the year, he might be willing to once again serve as our minister in Paris, at least for a year or two. Jefferson categorically declined, a refusal Washington felt was rather selfish in view of Jefferson's earlier insistence that Washington himself remain in public office. The meeting ended with Washington instructing Jefferson to consider further what arrangements might be made.[54]

On the following day, February 21, Washington consulted Randolph and showed him the complaint against Morris that Jefferson had left with the President the previous evening. Randolph was asked to weigh the alternatives and consult privately with two individuals who might replace Morris.[55] The next day the Attorney General sent his report to Washington. He said he viewed the complaint against Morris as ambiguous, coming from sources "half private, half public." He vetoed without hesitancy the suggestion that Morris and Pinckney exchange posts, for he believed that such an exchange would be difficult to explain not only to France but also to the American people. Instead he counseled against making any decision for the present and furthermore noted that the new French Republic would soon be sending a minister to replace Ternant from whom the President could obtain a more accurate impression of the attitude of the Republic toward Morris. However, he went further:

> Supposing the ultimate possibility of a dismission I have laboured (provisionally) to bring about the other arrangement. But I find this to be impracticable; the one gentleman being immoveable in the resolution which he expressed to you the other day; and the other gentleman being very explicit, that it is absolutely inadmissable in his mind to enter into the administration, under either of the aspects contemplated, or indeed under any other.[56]

Randolph, acting under instructions from Washington, had obviously pressed Jefferson to accept the ministerial post. This failing, he had then approached a second "gentleman," who also refused. In matters involving delicate political considerations Washington found Randolph to be a useful adviser and aid. And indeed the confidence he placed in his Attorney General was not misplaced.

During this same week Randolph had been consulted on two other appointments. The first concerned the selection of someone to serve as one of the commissioners to negotiate with the hostile Indian tribes engaged in predatory attacks on our northwestern frontier. At Randolph's suggestion the post went to Beverley Randolph of Virginia.[57] At the same time the Attorney General was himself engaged in preparing a "summary view" of all previous negotiations and treaties with these tribes in preparation for the negotiations.[58] While engaged in preparing this summary, he was given still another politically sensitive assignment. He was requested to make "inquiries" concerning the suitability of several candidates being considered to fill the vacancy on the Supreme Court caused by the unexpected resignation of Associate Justice Thomas Johnson. Randolph made his "inquiries" that very day and concluded that William Paterson of New Jersey was the most worthy candidate to fill the vacancy.[59] Two days later Washington wrote Paterson and offered him the position.[60]

If Randolph attached any significance to this growing presidential dependence on him, he never saw fit to comment on it. Perhaps the President's attitude seemed perfectly natural to him in the context of the political atmosphere of the times. The two men were, after all, of one mind when it came to dissociating themselves from the ways and means of partisan politics.

As Randolph began to develop a closer working relationship with Washington, he also had professional responsibilities that were quite distinct from the legal and political assignments that originated within the executive branch of government. His official responsibilities restricted his private practice. Many clients were seemingly accepted or rejected on the basis of the length of time they would require his services.[61] He could travel to courts outside of Philadelphia and be generous with his time during the summer, but during the months the President and Congress were in Philadelphia he had to confine his practice to clients whose needs were comparatively simple or capable of prompt solution. In addition, he recognized he could not accept clients whose cause might involve him in a conflict of interest with his public office.[62] On occasion he complained about being occupied in court, but on balance had far less court work in Philadelphia than he ever had in Virginia.[63]

However much he disliked his chosen profession, his several appearances before the United States Supreme Court certainly must have been the most memorable occasions of his legal career. Apparently his first formal appearance was at the August term, 1792, when he came before the Court as Attorney General in one case and as a private counsel in another.

The first case, known as *Hayburn's Case*, involved the question of whether a federal Circuit Court could refuse to perform an administrative task that had been assigned to it by law.[64] Randolph, as Attorney General, applied to the Supreme Court for a writ of mandamus to compel the federal Circuit Court in Pennsylvania to review the pension request of one William Hayburn as it was required to do under the provisions of the Invalid Pension Act passed by Congress on March 23, 1792.[65] Because the act compromised the independence of the Circuit Courts by assigning an administrative task to its judges, its constitutionality was being questioned.[66] Randolph was, therefore, attempting to secure a ruling from the Supreme Court on the constitutionality of this provision of the Invalid Pension Act. Technically speaking, he acted "with a view to procure the execution of an act of Congress. . . ."[67] Chief Justice John Jay immediately challenged Randolph's right to proceed *ex officio* and directed him to state his reasons for making such a request in his official capacity. Randolph, in reply, offered a long and able description of his responsibilities as Attorney General.[68] When the Court was polled on the question of Randolph's right to proceed *ex officio*, the judges divided equally on the question. Rather than withdraw from the case, Randolph chose instead to apply for a writ of mandamus as Hayburn's private counsel. He was determined, as he put it, "that the court should hear what I thought the truth."[69] A final decision on his motion was postponed until the Court's February term, 1793.[70] In the intervening period the legislature, sensitive to the initial protest of the judges of the Circuit Courts, revised the Invalid Pension Act, thereby removing the controversial provisions of the law and rendering a decision on Randolph's motion unnecessary.[71]

In the second case he appeared as counsel for the defendants in *The State of Georgia vs. Braislford et al.* The state of Georgia was seeking an injunction which would freeze the funds that had been awarded to Braislford by the United States Circuit Court in Georgia until there was a court test of the question whether Georgia had a valid claim to these funds under the provisions of a state law authorizing the seizure of Tory property. The Supreme Court decided, four to two, to grant the injunction.[72] When the Supreme Court met again, Randolph sought to dissolve the injunction and dismiss the bill in equity filed by Georgia on the grounds that the state had no remedy at law·for recovering the money in question and, even if it did, there was "no equitable right to justify the present form of proceedings" to protect this state's claims. Again the Court decided in favor of Georgia and ordered the injunction to continue until the next term. If Georgia failed to institute an action at common law to recover the moneys it claimed before the next term, the injunction would then be dissolved.[73] The next term of the Court was adjourned because of the yellow fever epidemic in Philadelphia,[74] but in the February term, 1794, an amicable action was initiated by Georgia which resulted in a verdict for Braislford. Georgia's action against Braislford served to void the injunction that had been issued by the Supreme Court.[75]

Far more important was Randolph's appearance as counsel for the plaintiffs in the case of *Chisholm vs. Georgia.*[76] The case was initiated when the heirs of Alexander Chisholm, citizens of South Carolina, brought suit in the United States Supreme Court against the state of Georgia for the recovery of confiscated property. It attracted considerable attention because it became the first test of the federal courts' jurisdiction in a dispute between a state and a citizen of another state.[77] Under Article III, Section 2, of the Constitution the judicial power of the United States extended to "Controversies . . . between a State and Citizens of another state." The Constitution further provided that in all cases "in which a State shall be party, the Supreme Court shall have original jurisdiction." On August 11, 1792, Randolph, as counsel for the plaintiff, moved that unless counsel for the state of Georgia appeared

before the Supreme Court by the fourth day of its next term, or showed
cause as to why the state would not appear, a judgment be entered
against the state and a "writ of inquiry of damages . . . be awarded."[78]
Randolph's motion was highly significant since it challenged the prevailing opinion concerning the intent and meaning of these clauses in the
Constitution. It had been consistently maintained that the language of
Article III, Section 2, could never be construed so as to give a citizen of
one state the right to bring suit against another state. To admit such an
interpretation, it was argued, would do violence to the very concept of
state sovereignty.[79]

Randolph argued otherwise. In a two-and-a-half-hour presentation in
defense of his motion he attempted to prove that the state of Georgia
could be made a "party defendant" before the Supreme Court as a result
of a suit by a citizen of another state.[80] After an exhaustive analysis of
the language of the Constitution, and in particular of the meaning of
the word "party," Randolph turned to the sensitive issue of state sovereignty and whether the present suit in any way infringed upon the
sovereignty of Georgia:

> It [the Constitution] derives its origin immediately from the people; and the
> people individually are, under certain limitations, subject to the legislative,
> executive and judicial authorities thereby established. The States are in fact
> assemblages of these individuals who are liable to process. The limitations
> which the Federal government is admitted to impose upon their powers, are
> diminutions of sovereignty, at least equal to the making of them defendants.
> It is not pretended, however, to deduce from these arguments alone, the
> amenability of States to judicial cognizance; but the result is, that there is
> nothing in the nature of sovereignties, combined as those of America are, to
> prevent the words of the Constitution, if they naturally mean what I have
> asserted, from receiving an easy and usual construction.

Not content with establishing the applicability of his motion under the
Constitution, he went on to demonstrate its correctness under the language of the Judiciary Act of 1789. He then turned briefly to several
technical aspects of the suit, including the question of whether the service of the summons on the governor and attorney general of the state
constituted a competent summons. In closing, he shifted to the political
aspects of this question:

> With this discussion, though purely legal, it will be impossible to prevent
> the world from blending political considerations. Some may call this an
> attempt to consolidate. But before such an imputation shall be pronounced,
> let them examine well, if the fair interpretation of the Constitution does not
> vindicate my opinions. Above all, let me personally assure them, that the

prostration of state-rights is no object with me; but that I remain in perfect confidence, that with the power, which the people and the legislatures of the states indirectly hold over almost every movement of the national government, the state need not fear an assault from bold ambition, or any approaches of covered stratagem.[81]

The Court took the case under advisement on February 5. The Justices did not deliver their opinion until February 18. Judge James Iredell, dissenting from the majority opinion, argued that the American states were the heirs of British sovereignty and that under English common law the sovereign could never be sued without consent. He would, therefore, deny Randolph's motion.[82] Delivering opinions in support of Randolph's motion were Chief Justice John Jay and Justices Blair, Wilson and Cushing.[83] Of the four, Jay's was perhaps the most significant. He argued that sovereignty rested with the people, and a state constitution, like the Constitution of the United States, was a compact made by and between the citizens of that political entity. The sovereignty held by the states did not, however, protect that state from suit. If, Jay argued, the Constitution permited *all* the people of a state acting as a single political entity to sue another state, "it plainly follows that *suability* and *state sovereignty* are not incompatible."[84] Jay's opinion was described by the *Gazette of the United States* as "one of the most clear, profound and elegant arguments perhaps ever given in a court of judicature."[85]

The Court ordered that the plaintiff file his declaration and that the said declaration be served on the governor and attorney general of the state of Georgia. Moreover, unless the state appeared or showed due cause for its failure to appear, judgment by default was to be entered against the state.[86] The order of the Court was ignored by Georgia, and judgment was ultimately rendered in the February term, 1794, against the state.[87] Before the writ was executed, however, a public outcry against the decision caused Congress to submit to the states for ratification the Eleventh Amendment to the Constitution, which declared a state was not suable by a citizen of another state.[88] For all practical purposes the Court's decision was thus rendered meaningless.

Randolph left no record of his reaction to this neutralization of the Court's decision. But court work, whether undertaken in an official or private capacity, was not his major responsibility. For the time being he was serving Washington, not his profession.

16

Architect and Advocate of
the President's Neutrality
April–August 1793

The simple inauguration ceremony that marked the formal opening of Washington's second term obscured the troubled atmosphere that prevailed behind the tranquil scene of that March day.[1] The political partisanship of Jefferson and Hamilton was manifesting itself in the response of each to the rather serious diplomatic issues that were beginning to confront the Administration. Randolph, who had been so useful to Washington in the growing partisan atmosphere of the previous year, found himself getting drawn into these diplomatic problems. He served as a buffer between Jefferson and Hamilton and, when the circumstances warranted, as a kind of personal troubleshooter for the President.

The ultimate source of America's diplomatic problems was, of course, the French Revolution, which by this time had entered upon a new and more dangerous phase. The execution of Louis XIV and the expectations of a general war in which the new French Republic would be pitted against the monarchs of Europe might excite the more partisan element in the country, but to Washington and his advisers it was a situation fraught with danger to the new Federal government.

The first diplomatic question the President and his advisers had to resolve was what kind of reception should be accorded Edmond Genêt, the recently appointed minister of the new French Republic.[2] Washington consulted with his advisers and found Randolph, Hamilton and Jefferson all advocating the acceptance of Genêt's credentials. Washington instructed Jefferson accordingly before undertaking a planned visit to Mount Vernon. He felt compelled, however, to caution his Secretary of State against a reception that evidenced "too much warmth and cordiality."[3]

Washington had barely left Philadelphia when it was learned that France had declared war against England, Spain and Holland. Hamilton dutifully transmitted the news to Washington at Mount Vernon,[4] which caused the President to remind both Hamilton and Jefferson that the United States must maintain a strict neutrality. Furthermore, he

[220]

instructed both of them to ". . . give the subject [i.e. neutrality] mature consideration, that such measures as shall be deemed most likely to effect this desirable purpose may be adopted without delay; for I have understood that vessels are already designated privateers, and are preparing accordingly." To both men he announced his intention to return immediately to Philadelphia.[5]

Washington's return set the wheels of government in motion at a pace that may well have frightened his advisers. Arriving in the city late on the 17th, he consulted with Jefferson and Hamilton early the following day.[6] Jefferson, who had been deeply absorbed in private responsibilities, did not have a plan ready to insure American neutrality; at least he had not committed any ideas to paper.[7] Hamilton, by contrast, came fully prepared. He had been organizing his thoughts on the subject since April 9 and had drawn up for Washington a series of questions that could serve as the basis for formulating the Administration's neutrality policy.[8] The substance of these questions had been revealed to Randolph before they were shown to the President. Randolph considered them the "skeleton" of the "whole chain of reasoning" out of which Hamilton had formulated his views on neutrality.[9]

Washington lost no time in utilizing the questions of his Secretary of the Treasury. He scheduled a meeting of the heads of the departments and the Attorney General for nine o'clock the following morning, April 19, and instructed them to consider the "measures which will be proper for them [i.e. the United States] to observe" in view of the fact that France and England were at war. Included was a list of thirteen questions he asked them to consider preparatory to the meeting.[10]

At the appointed time the Cabinet assembled in Washington's office. Immediately the President turned to the first question: "Shall a proclamation issue for the purpose of preventing interferences of the citizens of the United States in the war between France and Great Britain &ca.? Shall it contain a declaration of neutrality or not? What shall it contain?"[11]

In the discussion that followed, Hamilton argued for an immediate declaration of neutrality, while Jefferson, although not irrevocably opposed to neutrality, expressed serious reservations about the desirability of announcing it by proclamation and questioned the wisdom of giving it away without exacting some concessions from Britain. Randolph and Knox agreed with Hamilton. Jefferson, after being assured that the term "neutrality" would be omitted from the declaration, reluctantly agreed to the issuance of a proclamation.[12]

Randolph, concerned about the legal implications of the proclamation insofar as it would affect American citizens charged with carrying contraband, proposed that the belligerent powers be informed that the proclamation "should not be taken as conclusive evidence against our citizens in foreign courts of admiralty." The President and his Secretaries consented to the proposal although most of them apparently doubted its practical value.[13]

This matter resolved, the President then turned to Randolph and asked him to assume responsibility for drafting the proclamation. The assignment reflected Washington's desire to avoid a clash between Jefferson and Hamilton, since among the President's advisers only Randolph could produce a proclamation that would be acceptable to them both.[14]

Washington then moved to the next question: "Shall a minister from the Republic of France be received?"[15] This question was somewhat academic since an affirmative decision had been reached before Washington's departure for Virginia. Its inclusion in the questions Washington submitted to his Cabinet reflected Hamilton's continued opposition to the formal acceptance of a diplomatic representative from the French Republic at a time when that government was at war with much of Europe.[16] Jefferson's attack on Hamilton's position on this question brought a quick surrender from the Secretary of the Treasury and the question was decided unanimously in the affirmative.[17]

It was the third question that paralyzed the Cabinet: "If [the French minister is to be] received, shall it be absolutely or with qualification; and if with qualification, of what kind?"[18] Wrapped within the broad language of this question was the whole issue of the Franco-American treaties of 1778 and their applicability to this present crisis. Hamilton questioned the wisdom of recognizing the new French minister in a manner that would serve notice on the world and France that America was prepared to live up to the terms of these treaties, come what may. He argued that since the treaties had been concluded with a government that no longer ruled France, prudence at least demanded that the United States wait until the character of the French government was stabilized. To receive the minister of the French Republic without qualification was to endanger the neutrality this country was about to proclaim.[19] In the discussions that followed, Jefferson quickly voiced his complete disagreement with the arguments advanced by the Secretary of the Treasury. Treaties, Jefferson insisted, were made between nations, not governments, and were binding upon both parties even if one nation decided to change its government.[20] Knox announced his agreement with Hamilton and Randolph expressed his support for the position taken by Jefferson, and apparently implied in some way that Jefferson's view of the nature of treaties conformed more closely to the accepted view in international law. Hamilton, in reply, cited Vattel in support of his position.[21]

At this point Randolph suggested a compromise. Since neither he nor

Hamilton had a copy of Vattel, would it not be better to postpone the question and give further study to the current status of the treaties? It was then decided that each member of the Cabinet should submit his views in writing.[22] Before adjourning, it was unanimously agreed that Congress should not be called into special session, thereby resolving the last of the thirteen questions without the seemingly inevitable debate between Jefferson and Hamilton.[23] Washington set the time for the next meeting at nine o'clock the following Monday, April 22.[24]

Despite Randolph's other responsibilities one of his immediate assignments was to prepare a proclamation for the consideration of the Cabinet at this Monday meeting.[25] He knew he had to select his words with care, for the heated debate between Jefferson and Hamilton left little doubt that serious differences prevailed between them as to how the policy of neutrality should be implemented. The language of the proclamation adhered closely to the sentiments expressed at the meeting except for the last paragraph, which warned American citizens that if they gave aid to a belligerent power they would place themselves outside the protection of the government, and if their acts were carried out within their country's borders, they would be subject to prosecution in American courts. Typical of Randolph, the additional paragraph served to define the legal implications of a policy of neutrality.[26]

The final document was shown to Jefferson prior to the Cabinet meeting. Discovering that Randolph had in fact avoided using the word "neutrality" in the proclamation, he gave his immediate approval.[27] When the Cabinet assembled on the 22nd, the proclamation was approved unanimously without debate. A finished copy was prepared for Washington's signature that very day.[28]

The Cabinet then turned to the unfinished business of the previous meeting—the remaining questions in Washington's circular letter of April 18. Explosive in nature, they could only serve to further fan the flames of discord within the Cabinet. Someone, perhaps Randolph, proposed a further postponement. Since many of the questions were closely related to the third question, and this, in turn, was by previous agreement to be handled through formal written opinions, it seemed only logical to postpone further discussion of the whole subject. Washington agreed and the meeting was adjourned.[29]

Jefferson was the first to transmit his opinion on the status of the French treaties and the question of the manner in which the government should receive the minister of the new French Republic. His approach to the problem was straightforward and blunt. Summarizing the arguments that had been advanced by Hamilton in the Cabinet meeting of the 18th, he commented tersely: "If I do not subscribe to the soundness of his reasoning, I do most fully to its ingenuity—I shall now lay down the principles which according to my understanding govern the case." The treaties, Jefferson argued, were made between nations not governments, and although both nations have changed their form of government since these treaties were signed, these changes in no way annulled the treaties themselves. Thoroughly familiar with the writings of the major commentators on international law, he proceeded to overwhelm Hamilton and his principal source of authority, Vattel, with quotation after quotation from Grotius, Puffendorf and Wolf. He went further and challenged Hamilton's interpretation of Vattel by pointing out that the Secretary of the Treasury had built his argument on one section of Vattel's work in complete disregard of that author's overall approach to the subject. The treaties, he insisted, were in force and a "qualified" reception of Genêt could not be justified under any view of the subject.[30]

Five days later, on May 2, the President received the written opinion of his Secretary of the Treasury.[31] Hamilton had been concerned about the French treaties since early April. At that time he apparently toyed with the idea of urging the President to declare the treaties void. As a result of the influence of John Jay and Rufus King he had modified his position somewhat. He now urged the suspension of the treaties until the government of France was stabilized.[32] Such a position, he argued, would enable the United States to protect its neutrality and at the same time leave the country free to assume or renounce our obligations under the treaties in conformance with the ultimate character and composition of the French government. His written opinion sought to prove the theoretical soundness and diplomatic practicableness of this position.[33]

Rather than submit a concurring opinion, Knox chose to affix his signature to this formal opinion of the Secretary of the Treasury.[34]

For the present only one Cabinet member had remained silent, and the President had to remind him that he was still waiting for his opinion.[35] Randolph, generally more prompt in his communications with the executive, seems to have neglected his assignment until the last minute and then, under the gentle prodding of Washington, to have hastily drafted his opinion.[36]

Accepting as his premise the government's firm attachment to the principles of neutrality, he first sought to establish from Vattel that the treaties were no less valid because France had overthrown its monarchy. Treaties, he argued, were concluded between nations, not individuals, and therefore not in themselves affected by a change in the government of one of the signatories. Turning next to the proposition that Genêt should be received with such qualifications as to render the treaties with France suspended, reserving to the government the ultimate right of renunciation, Randolph attempted to show the imprudence of such a policy as well as its unjustness in the present situation. The only honorable course of action was the unqualified recognition of Genêt and the acceptance of America's obligations under the treaties.[37]

In substance his position was essentially the same as that advanced by Jefferson. Assuming that the initial cause of the dispute was due in part to a disagreement over Vattel, Randolph quoted him at length to support his position, but made no effort to marshal the opinions of Grotius, Puffendorf and Wolf as Jefferson had done. Obviously Jefferson's citations were more impressive and certainly more convincing.

Perhaps the most interesting characteristic of Randolph's opinion was its mild, nonbelligerent language. Jefferson, determined to refute every argument advanced by Hamilton, had gone after the Secretary of the Treasury with a vengeance. His opinion was a *tour de force*, and he was unable to hide his contempt for the views of his political antagonist. Randolph, in contrast, had drafted a thoroughly dispassionate Cabinet opinion. He was quite candid with the President:

> I own, without reserve, that I contemplate a danger of magnitude, hovering over the U.S., from the ardour of some, to transplanted French politics, as fresh fuel for our own parties. The very instant it shall be known, that government has, without the most palpable grounds, betrayed even a distinct inclination to sever us from France, no argument nor influence can oppose itself with success to this new hotbed of dissension.[38]

Within the Cabinet only Randolph could issue such a warning and remain free of any implication of duplicity. There were many things missing in this hastily drawn and rather unimaginative opinion of the Attorney General, and one of them was political partisanship.

Before Randolph's opinion reached Washington, Hamilton had a plan for enforcing the Neutrality Proclamation on the President's desk.[39] It was a plan with which Randolph was quick to take exception and which, in close cooperation with the President, he would pointedly revise to prevent another clash between the Secretaries of State and Treasury.

Hamilton's plan would make the Treasury Department the agency for noting violations of the Proclamation. The Treasury Secretary proposed that customs house officials be instructed to report violations of American neutrality to the Collector of the Revenue and that he, in turn, report them to Hamilton. Thus through the agency of the Treasury Department the President might be kept constantly informed of all efforts to circumvent the Neutrality Proclamation and, where necessary, he could instruct the Attorney General to secure indictments against the individual or individuals involved.[40]

The President, while expressing qualified approval for Hamilton's plan, apparently refused to commit himself until he had first discussed the matter with the Attorney General.[41] When Washington and Randolph reviewed the plan it was agreed that it would be better if the customs house officials reported all apparent violations of neutrality to the federal district attorneys rather than to the Treasury Department.[42] This would place the information directly in the hands of the federal official immediately and directly responsible. The subject came up at the next meeting of the Cabinet on May 7. Hamilton outlined his plan for the benefit of the full Cabinet, whereupon Randolph suggested the changes previously agreed upon in his conversation with Washington. Seemingly neither Hamilton nor Jefferson was aware that Washington had consulted Randolph and that these suggestions had the prior endorsement of the President. Randolph's modifications of Hamilton's proposals apparently received the begrudging support of the other members of the Cabinet at this meeting, although at adjournment Jefferson was still uncertain about the procedures that would be followed for reporting suspected infractions of our neutrality.[43]

The next day Jefferson, assuming the issue was still unresolved, wrote to Randolph to express his concern over the use of customs officers as informants and he urged, instead, that grand juries and courts were the accepted means of investigation and indictment in the American system of government. The present crisis, he continued, offers no excuse for deviating from this practice and establishing a federal "spy" system. He urged Randolph to communicate his views to Washington—"should the President mention the subject to you."[44] Randolph, sensing Jefferson's annoyance with Hamilton's plan and his own partial endorsement of it, penned an immediate reply: "I cannot suffer my engagements in business to interfere with a reply to the observations, with which you favor me, on the proposed letter to the collectors." Jefferson's objection to the use of collectors, he observed, was similar to his own and he was at the point of introducing it "when you mentioned it." He had, however, consulted Hamilton on this very point, and the Secretary of the Treasury had shown him his letterbooks as proof that these collectors had never been used as spies or informers in the past. "Viewing then this draught [i.e. Hamilton's], as unconnected with past suspicions, I could discover nothing opposed to my judgment." To use such officers for such purposes, he continued, was both natural and logical and in no way inconsistent with the rightful ends of government. Under the "original draught" they were to report to the Secretary of the Treasury but this has been changed "upon my suggestion." "This correction goes very far into your main objection."

> As soon as the [District] attorney possesses the case, the grand jury, judges and [the] rest of the judicial apparatus, which I esteem with you, as bulwarks, will [travel?] in the work according to the forms, which you have delineated.[45]

It is not known whether Randolph brought Jefferson's objections to the attention of the President, but the next day Washington requested the Attorney General to send a directive to the district attorneys instructing them to seek from the customs officials "information of all infractions of neutrality that may come within their purview at the different ports. . . ."[46]

Seemingly the original plan of the Secretary of the Treasury had undergone two significant alterations. The first, proposed by Randolph, placed ultimate responsibility for the investigation of all reported infractions of American neutrality in the hands of the district attorneys. The second, proposed by Washington, made the district attorneys the immediate agents of the federal government by ordering them to contact the customs officers rather than the reverse arrangement proposed by Hamilton. Further it was to be Randolph, not Hamilton, who transmitted the President's directive and it was sent to the federal district attorneys rather than to the collectors of the customs. The difference was considerable, as all those associated with the formulation of the plan must have realized.

Randolph's role was somewhat different in this latest dispute between Jefferson and Hamilton. He was, as might be expected, the architect of a middle position between the plan proposed by Hamilton, which might well have initiated a witch-hunt, and the proposal advanced by Jefferson, which would probably have resulted in the benevolent acquiescence to all but the most flagrant violations of American neutrality.[47] But Randolph also acted as a buffer between Washington's two principal advisers. Thanks to him and Washington, the issue was kept sufficiently fluid so as to make it unnecessary for the President to request formal written opinions of his Cabinet officers. In effect Washington and his Attorney General had succeeded in avoiding the bitter confrontation that now seemed inevitable whenever written opinions were requested of the Cabinet. In all this Randolph was not being clever or shrewd, but rather he was displaying a real political sensitivity to the partisan features of Hamilton's and Jefferson's views.

Even while Randolph was engaged in preparing—with the gentle prodding of the President—his opinion on the question of how the new French minister was to be received, the neutrality he assumed to be the cornerstone of the government's policy was being tested by France. On May 2 the French frigate *Embuscade* sailed into Philadelphia harbor with two British prizes.[48] Under Article 17 of our Treaty of Commerce with France the United States was obliged to admit into its ports any vessel which was brought in as a prize by a French warship or privateer.[49] Strictly speaking, the privileges granted France under this article did not, of themselves, conflict with American neutrality. What complicated the issue was the fact that one of the prizes, the *Grange*, had been seized within the territorial waters of the United States, and this constituted a clear violation of American neutrality. The reaction of the British minister, George Hammond, was instantaneous. A formal complaint, substantiated by the testimonials of witnesses, establishing beyond question that the *Grange* was seized within the waters of the Delaware Bay, was sent to Jefferson the same day.[50] He brought the matter to Washington's attention on May 3,[51] and it was decided that an explanation should be sought from the French minister, Ternant. France's representative was to be further requested to detain the *Grange*, her crew and her cargo until the issue was resolved.[52] Hammond was informed the same day that an inquiry was being made, and was assured that the United States would not view with indifference the violation of its territorial waters.[53]

On May 8 Jefferson received a second demand from Hammond for the release of the *Grange*, plus information on several other instances in which France had seriously compromised American neutrality. Not only was contraband being shipped from New York to France but, the British minister reported, the French consul at Charleston had, of his own accord, erected an admiralty court for the purpose of condemning for sale two British brigantines that had been brought to that port as prizes by the French frigate *Embuscade* in April.[54] If Hammond's information was accurate, the French consul at Charleston was assuming judicial functions in clear violation of the sovereignty and neutrality of the United States. Equally serious was Hammond's complaint that two privateers, commissioned at Charleston and manned in part by Americans, had captured a British vessel.[55] On May 10 Washington ordered Jefferson to submit all information on the *Grange* to the Attorney General for his prompt consideration and directed that the various complaints in Hammond's latest communication be the subject of a Cabinet session.[56]

Well aware that a reply to the British minister awaited his opinion, Randolph began researching the law almost immediately. The point at which the *Grange* was seized was beyond question within the waters of the Delaware Bay. At issue was whether the United States exercised maritime jurisdiction over these waters to the extent that the bay might be considered a part of the United States and therefore come under the provisions of the Neutrality Proclamation. With a thoroughness not characteristic of Randolph when working under pressure, he examined virtually all the seventeenth- and eighteenth-century authorities on international law and quoted at length from some. He found that they were virtually unanimous in their opinion that a body of water so located and not claimed by another power would fall within the exclusive jurisdiction of the United States. It would therefore be neutral territory and France would be bound to return the ship and crew and make restitution for any damage resulting from their illegal seizure.[57]

The Attorney General's opinion was delivered to the Secretary of State on May 14.[58] The following day, in compliance with the President's directions, the Cabinet assembled to consider the charges in Hammond's latest memorial, the opinion of the Attorney General and other related intelligence received by the government during the preceding week.[59] It was agreed that Jefferson should draft a letter to Hammond containing assurances that the *Grange* would be returned to her original owners, that the assumption of judicial authority by the French consul in Charleston over admiralty cases would not be recognized and care would be taken to see that it was not repeated, and that the outfitting of privateers in American ports was "entirely disapproved." These points were apparently accepted by the Cabinet without debate. Washington gave his approval the same day, whereupon a letter was immediately dispatched to Hammond.[60] A similar letter was sent to Ternant at the same time[61] It, however, contained a copy of Randolph's opinion respecting the seizure of the *Grange* as well as copies of Hammond's memorials.

But on such a sensitive and complex subject complete Cabinet unanimity was all but impossible. In this instance the clash between Jefferson and Hamilton came over Hammond's complaint that two of the privateers that had been commissioned at Charleston had seized a British vessel known as the *Little Sarah* off the Virginia Capes and brought it to Philadelphia as a prize.[62] With Hamilton arguing for the vessel's immediate return to Britain and Jefferson in violent opposition, Washington had no choice but to once again order his Cabinet to submit written opinions on the subject.[63] A new Cabinet crisis was in the making and, if true to form, would further divide the President's council. Pending a decision, Hammond was politely informed that the remaining point in his memorial was being "reserved for further consideration."[64]

The Cabinet opinions reached the President's desk within twenty-four hours, a promptness that testified to the intensity of each man's feelings on the subject. All the opinions were written within hours of the Cabinet meeting. The first to reach the President was Hamilton's, which stated that the fitting out and manning of a privateer in an American port was a serious violation of our neutrality for which the government had the right to demand reparations from France. Further, the United States was bound to prevent injury or loss to Great Britain, and if either occurred, as in the present instance, then the government must make amends by restoring the vessel to Great Britain. Such action would constitute "a species of reparation consonant with the nature of the injury."[65] Knox supported Hamilton's interpretation of the situation and urged the prompt restoration of the vessel to Great Britain.[66]

In his opinion Jefferson admitted that the government should prevent the outfitting of privateers in United States ports, but he argued that Great Britain should not expect an immediate fulfillment of this objective. He insisted that the United States had no right to force France to give up the prize because the privateers were operating under a commission which, if good, the belligerent powers themselves must acknowledge as valid. Thus in capture the title to the prize came to be vested in the captor, and the English owner had within international law lost all his rights to the property. For the United States to seize the vessel in order to return it to England would be an act of reprisal against France and might lead to war. All other means of obtaining satisfaction must first be explored, and even then such a serious step should not be taken unless first authorized by Congress.[67]

Once again Randolph was the last to file his opinion.[68] Like Jefferson, he urged the President against restoration of the vessel. Less speculative than the Secretary of State, he meticulously analyzed and then refuted the various arguments upon which the British minister could rationalize his demand for restitution. His conclusion was that "upon principle, therefore, restitution ought not . . . to be attempted."[69]

Absorbed in other matters, Washington delayed making any final decision on the matter. The next day, May 18, he apparently requested Randolph to sound out the merchants of Philadelphia on the question of restitution.[70] Later in the day he called on Randolph at his home only to discover that the Attorney General was away on his appointed task.[71] That evening Randolph penned a private note to the President in which he summarized his findings after a day of "indirect inquiry." The Attorney General found that the majority of the merchants favored restitution, but many had a very imperfect understanding of what was at issue. Their opinion, Randolph continued, was inevitable, for the merchant class was so tied to Britain "that the pleasure of the British merchant must always be a rule of action to ours. . . ." He was convinced, however, that the "bulk of our citizens" were against restitution. He also had, he reported, learned from "Mr. B—ngh–m" that France had never resorted to restitution during the early years of the American Revolution, "and therefore an example of this kind not being known is some argument against its propriety." He continued: "When we left your house yesterday I urged Mr. Jefferson to discover from Mr. Genêt his temper upon this subject. . . ." "Perhaps an intimation to Mr. J. might induce him to be more earnest in this pursuit."[72] Washington, feeling he had already delayed much too long in answering Hammond, apparently never pursued the matter with Jefferson.

Confronted with the conflicting opinions of an equally divided Cabinet and the informal report of his Attorney General on the attitude of the local community, Washington chose to follow a middle course. After further consultation with Randolph, he ordered the privateers that had seized the *Little Sarah* out of American ports. Nothing was said or done to change the status of the *Little Sarah* itself; it would remain a French prize.[73]

In the midst of this new demonstration of dissension within the Cabinet Edmond Genêt, the minister of the French Republic, reached Philadelphia after a triumphant journey from Charleston. Arriving in the city on the 16th to a warm welcome, he presented his credentials to Washington on the 18th.[74] Randolph took no note of his presence and apparently had formed no opinion of the young diplomat. He soon had ample opportunity for doing so, however, for Genêt quickly made himself the focal point of several new diplomatic problems. On May 27 the new French minister submitted a formal reply to Jefferson's letter of May 15 concerning the complaints registered by Hammond earlier in the month and the President's position on the subject. Self-righteous if not condescending, it left little hope for diplomatic tranquillity in the months to come.[75] A few days later another French privateer, the *Sans Culotte*, arrived at Baltimore with another British prize. At Randolph's suggestion, the seizure was made the subject of a Cabinet meeting where it was agreed that the *Sans Culotte* would be denied the use of American ports; Washington's earlier warning serving as a precedent for this decision.[76]

At the same time Genêt was challenging the arrest of Gideon Henfield, an American citizen who had sailed from Charleston aboard a French privateer in open defiance of the Neutrality Proclamation. Seized in Philadelphia by order of the district attorney of Pennsylvania, Henfield was, in Genêt's words, guilty of no greater crime than "serving . . . France, and defending with her children the common and glorious cause of liberty."[77] Jefferson referred the matter to Randolph for a legal opinion, and the latter replied that Genêt had no right to interfere, and that furthermore Henfield was punishable because he had acted in violation of treaty-stipulated assurances of peace between the United States and the three countries then at war with France, and that he was also indictable at common law for disturbing the peace.[78] Apparently disturbed by the severe language of Randolph's opinion, Jefferson sought to counteract it in a covering letter that expressed the hope that "his case will have the favorable issue you desire." He added: "It will give me great pleasure to be able to communicate to you that the laws (which admit of no control) on being applied to the actions of Mr. Henfield, shall have found in them no cause of animadversion." When he showed his letter to Randolph and Hamilton they suggested that both observations should be deleted. Jefferson had to be content with the rather obvious comment that Henfield would receive a fair trial.[79]

Confronted with these efforts to compromise American neutrality and the continued diplomatic biases of his two principal advisers, Washington once again tried to discover the attitude of the people toward his Administration and its seemingly thankless efforts to preserve neutrality. Believing perhaps that Virginia might well serve as an accurate barometer of the mood of the South, the most pro-French region in the nation, the President asked Randolph to sample the temper of the people in his native state.[80]

Randolph left Philadelphia on June 6.[81] He journeyed first to Baltimore where Colonel Samuel Smith, an ardent supporter of Hamilton, informed him of the concern "existing in the breasts of merchants" over the events of recent months. They had, however, Smith reported to Randolph, a confidence in the executive and believed him better able to judge the best course of action "from a comprehensive view of the situation." "My explanations," Randolph continued, "were apparently satisfactory."[82] Significantly, he noted the source of their apprehension and suggested a remedy:

> I found that the *style* in which a letter written by the Secretary of the Treasury to the different naval officers had first created the apprehensions, which had seized them; and I endeavoured to procure a sight of it without success. Perhaps, sir, if any inaccuracy in the manner or expressions should be discovered, on a revision of it, it would [be?] advantageous to correct it. I am sure that the matter of it, as represented to me, is conformable to your sense of the business. I am more particularly induced to suggest a revision of that letter as I perceive, that the same impression has been made here from the same cause.[83]

Reporting further, Randolph said he sought explicit information from Colonel Smith as to how the merchants of Baltimore had been able to ascertain the views of the people of Maryland on the proclamation, and that Smith had explained that the people came to trade and, more important, to attend the recent session of the General Court. Randolph noted that he had checked this information with another gentleman and was assured it was true.[84] How did Mr. Samuel Chase stand on the subject? He didn't know for certain but he questioned one of his principal admirers and found him "loud in his praise of the Proclamation," which led him to believe that Chase must be well-tempered toward that act.[85]

Randolph continued:

> I met with Governor Clayton of Delaware and Major Oldham of the Maryland house of delegates, at Baltimore. The former is a plain, modest, sensible, cool man; the latter a very respectable one, and burning with zeal for the French revolution. From both of them I learn, that the state of Delaware, and the eastern shore of Maryland have but one sentiment, [and?] that approving the proclamation.[86]

Such was his first report on the sentiments of the people in the states through which he was traveling on his way to Virginia. He also took note of reported bitterness against the government found in Kentucky because of the "inattention" of the Washington Administration to the defense of that state. He urged that Senator John Brown of Kentucky be questioned by Jefferson as to the true state of affairs.[87]

Randolph's second letter came from Richmond marked "private" and dated June 24; it reached Philadelphia after Washington had left the city for a short trip to Mount Vernon. Its contents would have offered little comfort to Washington, who since Randolph's departure had been plagued almost daily with diplomatic problems. Randolph's letter picked up the analysis at the point where his previous letter had left off. He had had the opportunity to talk with the governor of Maryland and found him "caught" by the same apprehensions as had existed among the people of Baltimore. Randolph talked to him at length, and a few hours later "he called at my lodgings, and in the presence of several gentlemen spoke to this effect; that the executive of the U. S. seemed to have proceeded on principle, which was the surest guide to its conduct."[88]

The report then turned to Virginia, with Randolph sampling opinion along the route to Richmond. At Georgetown and Alexandria he heard little, at Dumfries A[lexander?] Henderson, critical of the government's policies, was supplied with information in the hope that he, being a "talkative man," would spread it among his neighbors. Arriving at Fredericksburg, he found that the "clamour increased" and was directed primarily against the Secretary of the Treasury but also against the Neutrality Proclamation and the prosecution of John Singletary. The cause, he continued, was John Taylor of Caroline, and again he felt obliged to correct the gross errors that were circulating. In fact he delayed his journey southward to do so. He even paid a call on Edmund Pendleton and spent an evening and a morning with him in a full discussion of the government's policies.[89]

Proceeding to Richmond, he found that "parties are strong and the friends to the government are far inferior in *number* to its enemies." The opponents of the general government were mostly antifederalists and discontented federalists, and they were rallying behind Henry, whose power had "risen to an immeasurable height." Equally serious was the opposition of several distinguished judges of Virginia's General Court. The people, he noted, "will be fortified in their opposition when they perceive so many advocates of character" openly critical of the policies of the central government. As for its friends, he had had a "full communication" with those who were attached to the government, "and since our communication they think themselves armed in its defense." He planned to set out for Williamsburg immediately "and shall return hither at the beginning of next week."[90]

Prepared to give the President a full report of his findings, Randolph returned to Philadelphia on July 19.[91] During his absence the renewed political rivalry between Jefferson and Hamilton had again found its way into the press accompanied by the usual intemperate criticism or exaggerated praise of the government's policies.[92] Washington, more conscious of the criticism than the praise, must have welcomed Randolph's presence again in the councils of government. Jefferson found that he brought "very flattering information" as to the mood of the people in Virginia toward the general government and that his reports "had quieted uneasiness here."[93] Whatever the tone of his final report, Randolph had returned to Philadelphia aware that he had acted more as an advocate of the policies of the Administration than as a sampler of public opinion. Washington could not have missed the significance of this dual role. Sensitive to the moods of the people and a warm advocate of strict neutrality, Randolph had shown himself equally capable of explaining Hamilton's financial program to a disbeliever and Jefferson's pro-French sympathies to a critic. He could urge the President to revise a letter written by Hamilton because it created much apprehension, and he could speak derisively of the inconsistencies of those who endorsed Jefferson's pro-French sympathies. Nowhere could Washington find a person more thoroughly loyal to his policies.

Before Randolph returned to Philadelphia a new crisis confronted the government. Genêt's conduct in recent weeks had displayed a total disregard for our neutrality and culminated in an open defiance of Jefferson. On July 13 Genêt allowed the celebrated *Little Sarah* to sail out of Philadelphia as a recommissioned French privateer in complete contempt for American neutrality.[94] With the vessel already beyond the reach of the government, the only question remaining was whether this breach of neutrality justified a request for Genêt's recall. Washington appears to have decided to postpone consideration of the subject until Randolph returned to the city.[95]

In the meantime it was decided that the opinions of the Justices of the Supreme Court would be requested on all questions relating to neutrality. The Cabinet, minus the Attorney General, was instructed to prepare a list of questions for consideration by the Justices. On July 18 it met to compose the final draft for the Justices.[96] The resulting document, with duplications eliminated and the language of the remainder carefully revised, masterfully outlined the enormity of the problem of neutrality.[97]

Randolph arrived in Philadelphia on July 19, and the President scheduled a Cabinet meeting for July 23. The first matter to be discussed at this meeting was the method of disbursement of moneys owed to France and now being drawn upon by Genêt for the purchase of supplies for the Republic. Randolph suggested that certain practical measures be taken to protect the United States if a counterrevolution were to occur in France and the contracts that Genêt signed were to be repudiated by a subsequent government. It was readily agreed that such safeguards as Randolph suggested could be worked out privately between Randolph and the Secretary of the Treasury. At this point the Attorney General was unexpectedly called from the meeting on business. Shortly after his departure from the room Washington introduced the subject of Genêt's recall. He expressed the view that Genêt's whole correspondence should be sent to Gouverneur Morris with a "temperate but strong representation" as to his conduct, drawing a clear distinction between him and the nation he represented. Genêt's recall should be insisted upon and, in the meantime, we should force him to "withdraw or cease his functions." Hamilton warmly endorsed the President's views, while Knox, if Jefferson's account is to be believed, "told some stories" that aggravated the President and had little direct bearing on the subject under discussion. Jefferson apparently made no comment on the President's suggestion. No decision was reached at this meeting and the question was postponed until Jefferson had prepared a translation of all of Genêt's correspondence with his office.[98]

The following day Randolph dispatched a brief note to Washington suggesting "whether it may not be proper to add to the instructions, to be given to Mr. Jefferson concerning Mr. Genêt's conduct, that he should state the verbal conversations with him [i.e. Genêt]" as well.[99] Obviously Randolph had been briefed as to what had transpired in the Cabinet meeting after he had left the room, and he was now seeking a full account of all that had transpired between Jefferson and Genêt. Washington not only agreed with his suggestion but issued specific instructions to Jefferson to ensure Randolph's presence at the next meeting of the Cabinet on this subject:

> As the letter of the Minister from the Republic of France, dated the 22d of June lyes yet to be answered; and as the official conduct of that Gentleman, relatively to the Affairs of this Government, will have to undergo a very serious consideration (as soon as the Special Court at which the Attorney General is now engaged will allow him to attend with convenience) in order to decide upon measures proper to be taken thereupon: It is my desire that all the letters to, and from that Minister may be ready to be laid before me, the heads of Departments and the Attorney General, with whom I shall advise with on the occasion, together with the minutes of such Official Oral communications as you may have held with him on the subjects of those letters &ca.[100]

On the 26th Jefferson supplied Washington with a written summary of his conversations with Genêt,[101] and a week later the voluminous correspondence between Genêt and himself was ready for review by the Cabinet.

On Thursday, August 1, the Cabinet assembled at the President's residence to determine the fate of Genêt. After the lengthy correspondence between the Secretary of State and Genêt had been read, it was agreed that Gouverneur Morris be provided with a full accounting of Genêt's indiscretions and a copy of his correspondence, and furthermore that he be instructed to communicate the same to the Executive Council of France along with a formal demand for his recall. Over Jefferson's objection it was decided that Genêt would be notified of the demand for his recall. Hamilton urged that the whole correspondence and a statement of the proceedings of the executive be published by way of an appeal to the people. Randolph voiced his opposition to such a procedure, at which point Washington adjourned the meeting until the following day.[102]

At nine the next morning the discussion was resumed on Hamilton's proposed appeal to the people. Hamilton again spoke in support of his proposal, only to be answered at length by Jefferson. Partisan in outlook, neither man was prepared to consider any aspect of Genêt's dismissal objectively. The previous day they had clashed over whether the language of dismissal should be "peremptory" or "delicate," now they argued over whether an appeal should be made to the people. Much to

Jefferson's annoyance, Washington expressed some sympathy for Hamilton's point of view. Before the issue was resolved, however, Knox produced a broadside lampooning Washington and James Wilson as "King" and "Judge," from the pen of Philip Freneau. Washington flew into a rage, denounced the press for the abuses he had been subjected to during the past few months and vented his wrath on Freneau in particular. After his anger had subsided, the discussion of Genêt was resumed, but little more was accomplished and the decision on the proposed appeal to the people was postponed without further discussion.[103]

The fate of Genêt had been sealed, but the difficult question of neutrality remained. The Justices of the Supreme Court by their silence made it unmistakably clear that they chose not to give an advisory opinion on the questions submitted to them on July 18.[104] Without the benefit of the Justices' advice, the Cabinet turned its energies to drafting a set of rules it hoped would prevent further violations of American neutrality.[105] The matter was first discussed at the Cabinet session of July 29, while the decision on Genêt's recall was still pending. At that time the Cabinet gave its conditional approval to four rules, three of which had been proposed by Randolph and one by Hamilton.[106] The following day, July 30, a second meeting was held, with Jefferson and Hamilton disagreeing as to how the special privileges arising out of the treaties with France, United Netherlands and Prussia should be noted in these rules.[107] The matter was again postponed. It was to be held in abeyance until Washington and his advisers decided how they might dispose of Genêt. Finally on August 3 the Cabinet reached agreement on a set of eight rules which Washington endorsed and ordered promulgated immediately.[108]

The multiple problems of the past few weeks forced the President and his advisers to once again weigh the question of whether Congress should be called into special session.[109] The voice of moderation predictably was Edmund Randolph's. He reminded the President that it would be imprudent to alarm the people by a course of action that implied the country was about to arrive at some momentous decision.[110] With Knox and Hamilton counseling against a special session, the President, who personally believed Congress should meet, acquiesced to the view of the majority.[111]

In a sense Randolph's opinion on the question of calling Congress into special session rather accurately reflected the climate of the moment —the feeling that the nation had weathered the worst of the storm. The government had sustained almost five months of diplomatic crises without wavering and without retreating from the neutrality upon which the President insisted. This relentless pursuit of neutrality in the face of the pro-French sympathies of Jefferson and the pro-English sympathies of

Hamilton certainly must have weakened the ties that bound Washington to his two principal advisers. They had become advocates instead of advisers; in fact they had become lobbyists for their own political convictions. This development forced the President to seek advice and counsel from someone who believed in absolute neutrality and who had little sympathy for a partisan approach to diplomacy. It was Edmund Randolph who unequivocally supported and sustained the cautious statesmanship of the President and helped him steer a middle course that would avoid the dangerous shoals of partisan diplomacy. By August of 1793 Randolph had become Washington's most trusted adviser, a position he had earned through his uncompromising loyalty to the President and his policies.

17

Attorney General and Aide
August–December 1793

Randolph welcomed the apparent lull in this continuous battle to preserve our neutrality and hoped for several months of comparative quiet during which he could devote more time to his family and to his private law practice. His plans were rather rudely interrupted by the rapid spread of yellow fever in Philadelphia during the month of August. The fever, which had been claiming victims since the first week in August, was not diagnosed as yellow fever until the 19th and no public notice was taken of it until the 23rd.[1] Randolph, still absorbed in the technicalities of Genêt's recall, took no note of the fever until it reached epidemic proportions. By the third week in August Betsy was thoroughly frightened by the mounting death toll. She apparently urged Edmund to move the family out of Philadelphia promptly. Dutifully, Edmund found accommodation in Germantown, some six miles northwest of Philadelphia, at the home of Nathan Spencer.[2]

Randolph moved his family into the Spencer residence late in August and returned to the city whenever he was needed.[3] As each day brought new evidence that the fever was spreading, the reluctance of clerks and servants to remain in the city caused a virtual paralysis of most government business.[4] "Everybody who can, is flying from the city," Jefferson reported to Madison.[5] With the President about to leave for Virginia and many of Randolph's friends coming down with the fever, Edmund decided it would be prudent to conduct the business of the Attorney General's office from Germantown. The fact that Hamilton and his wife Eliza contracted the fever and were in danger for a time may well have influenced Randolph's decision.[6]

As the fever continued to claim its victims, more and more people took refuge in Germantown. It was even rumored that the fever might spread to this tiny German community. Betsy, alarmed once again for her family's safety, pressured Edmund into moving the family to Lancaster, some sixty miles west of Philadelphia.[7] The precautions were perhaps excessive because in less than a week Randolph was once again

[239]

back in Germantown at the Spencer house. In a letter to Washington he spoke of a "report that the cold weather had given a stroke to the fever," suggesting the family might have concluded the fever was waning and Germantown was once again out of danger.[8]

Throughout this entire period Randolph seemed to be continually plagued with "financial embarrassments." He was regularly borrowing money or juggling accounts to satisfy one or another creditor. Early in August he asked Jefferson to endorse a note for him and was politely but bluntly turned down.[9] Prior to this he had been in debt to Hamilton, a debt which had been repaid in part.[10] Then on September 30 he asked Henry Drinker for a loan of $100 or $200 in order to move his family to Lancaster.[11] Drinker, a well-to-do Quaker merchant in Philadelphia, sent his "Negro man" with $150.[12] Early in December Randolph wrote to his brother-in-law Wilson Cary Nicholas: "The malady has shattered the credit of multitudes; and generates an extreme caution in the banks in discounting." He would, he continued, assist Nicholas in borrowing the money he was seeking, but apparently Randolph himself did not have sufficient credit within the city to serve as a guarantor for the loan. The most he could do was put his brother-in-law in contact with those who were in a position to lend money.[13]

The most important public issue confronting the President and his advisers during these trying weeks was the practical and constitutional problems of carrying on the business of government if Philadelphia remained unsafe to live in for an extended period of time. The first order of business was where the President would live if he could not return to Philadelphia. Randolph, convinced that Philadelphia would remain unsafe at least until the first frost, made it his personal responsibility to find suitable accommodations for Washington outside the city. He looked into the matter before moving his own family to Lancaster, and after his return to Germantown he wrote to Washington that he had made tentative arrangements for two different dwellings in the latter community. Neither of them, he conceded, was particularly satisfactory. The same letter, showing Randolph's typical concern for detail, described the best route around Philadelphia to Germantown.[14]

The location at which Congress might assemble posed an even more serious problem.[15] There was first of all a constitutional problem as to whether the President might act to bring the members together at some time and place other than those that had been agreed upon at the time of their adjournment. Then there was the practical problem of just how this should be done, whether by proclamation or some other means. Washington was concerned about the location; it had to be a town that was convenient, not likely to be contaminated, possessed of adequate facilities to house the legislature both in and out of session and, given the regional sensitivities of some members of Congress, acceptable to northern and southern legislators.[16]

The President posed these problems to each member of his Cabinet, to James Madison and to Jonathan Trumbull, who was the Speaker of the House in the last session of Congress.[17] Jefferson and Madison replied that the President had no constitutional right to convene Congress anywhere but Philadelphia.[18] Both Hamilton and Knox replied that they felt he had the power but doubted whether the present situation was sufficiently serious to warrant the President's classifying it as an "extraordinary occasion," the only circumstance under which he had a constitutional right to call Congress into special session.[19]

Randolph, whose reply was the last to reach Washington, was, as might be expected, eminently practical. For the President to call Congress into special session at this time would "seem" to be unconstitutional. But it was also unnecessary. Let Congress assemble at the time and place agreed upon at adjournment. If Philadelphia proved unsafe, let the legislators adjourn to some other place of their own choosing. If they failed to assemble at the appointed time out of fear of entering the city, then the President might legitimately call them into special session at a time and place of his own choosing, for such a failure would clearly constitute an "extraordinary occasion" and justify his action. If the President felt obliged to act differently, however, he recommended Lancaster as an appropriate location. Germantown, he reported, would not be able to accommodate Congress. He had personally investigated the situation at Reading and found that it, too, lacked the necessary accommodations. Lancaster, however, was "able and willing." "It is a universal persuasion," he continued, "that unless Lancaster be chosen, New York will be revisited by Congress."[20] He enclosed a draft of a proclamation by which the President might call Congress into special session if he felt so compelled.[21]

Still not completely satisfied with the preliminary arrangements that had been made for housing Washington and his domestic staff, Randolph pursued that matter further. He was determined to find a dwelling that would be both adequate and inexpensive and which could be engaged for a short period of time.[22] By the 28th of October everything was more or less settled to his satisfaction. The Reverend Frederick Herman of Germantown made three rooms of his home available to the President, plus breakfast and afternoon tea. Washington's servants were to be boarded next door, his horses about two hundred yards away, and a local tavern keeper would prepare his evening meal.[23] Randolph had thought of just about everything.

Washington's arrival in Germantown on Friday, November 1, 1793, reactivated the wheels of government.[24] By this time the formal written opinion he had requested of Randolph on the problem of convening Congress was ready for his consideration. It presented in more technical language what Randolph had already communicated earlier in a personal letter.[25] Since there was general agreement on the impropriety of the President's calling Congress into special session in the present situation, it was decided, per Randolph's suggestion, that the executive wait until the appointed time, and if Congress then failed to convene, he might with propriety call a special session at some other location outside Philadelphia.[26]

With this decision behind them Washington and his advisers could turn their attention to the problems that had developed during the weeks of the President's absence from the seat of government. Shortly before his departure for Virginia Washington had learned that the peace conference at Sandusky with the Indian tribes on our northwestern frontier had failed miserably.[27] Beverley Randolph had stopped at Mount Vernon in September to give him the details.[28] British interference was suspected of being responsible for the intransigence of the Indians and it was now assumed that the matter would have to be resolved by military force.[29] Even more serious was the mounting evidence that Great Britain intended to violate our neutrality at will in an effort to bring France to her knees. The seizure of our ships and the impressment of our seamen were matters that could not pass unnoticed for long, and they became particularly irksome when coupled with Hammond's persistent refusal to discuss the nonfulfillment of the peace treaty.[30] As usual, however, it was Genêt who was the source of the greatest annoyance. Since provoking Washington to request his recall, he had been engaged in encouraging disgruntled Kentuckians to attack the Spanish at New Orleans and had gotten himself involved in a dispute with John Jay and Rufus King. However, still no word had been received from France as to his recall.[31]

In most of these problems Washington worked with the Secretary most directly involved, but Genêt's conduct was made the subject of a Cabinet meeting on November 8. It was at this session that Washington raised the question of Genêt's immediate dismissal. Hamilton and Knox "zealously" endorsed the President's position. Randolph, expressing himself at length on the subject, voiced his objection. Washington noted that he did not wish to have the matter hastily decided and announced he would postpone a final decision until after he had returned from a short trip of inspection to Reading and Lancaster.[32]

On November 10 Washington received a rather strange letter from his Attorney General. Unlike most of Randolph's letters, it was marked "private." Touching on many subjects, it gave the appearance of being rather hastily written. And yet the heart of the letter touched on matters that were both personal and politically sensitive.

The letter opened with an expression of thanks to the President for the loan of his newspapers. This was followed by a plea that Washington not visit the city of Philadelphia during his brief trip of inspection lest he expose himself to the fever and, by his presence in the city, encourage others to return. Randolph also mentioned that he was planning to write to Colonel Edward Carrington and that he intended to include "some remarks which may tend to disabuse the public mind." The letter, however, had another theme:

> What has been published concerning it [i.e. the Neutrality Proclamation], united with numberless misrepresentations in other instances, determined me some months ago to begin a history and review of your administration. I had made some progress in it; and should have advanced further, had I not found some difficulty in asking from the Secretary of State access to the public archives, without communicating at the same time my objects. However, had it not been for the interruption, which has been given for some time past to essay of Agricola convinces me of the importance of such a work, upon public endeavoured to procure the means of full and accurate information. The essay of Agricola convinces me of the importance of such a work, upon public as well as other interesting considerations; and let my future arrangements be, as they may, I shall not relinquish it.[33]

If the President did not already know it, these remarks established that the relationship between Jefferson and Randolph had become somewhat more formal and reserved than it had been six or eight months previously. Randolph's reluctance to ask Jefferson for permission to examine the papers in his office suggests a rather strained relationship, originating in all likelihood in Randolph's refusal to side with Jefferson in the latter's disputes with Hamilton. Washington, of course, would appreciate such independence and might feel he had an obligation to assist Randolph in obtaining the papers he desired for his projected "history and review" of the Administration.

But there was more in the paragraph:

> But I am extremely apprehensive, that the pestilence of Philadelphia will reduce the practice of law within the city to such a modicum, as to force me to think of reestablishing myself in Virginia. For altho' I do not doubt, that were I to go into as large field, as some others of the bar here, my share of profit would content me; yet as that cannot be done, consistently with my

office, the share, which I had, must be considerably diminished. Whatever delay may proceed from this circumstance, the work itself shall proceed; and I have now taken the liberty of saying this much to you, in confidence, only to prepare the way, if on some occasion I shall find it necessary to beg the communication of any particular information.[34]

Washington was, of course, well acquainted with Randolph's tortured reasoning processes when he was trying to reconcile personal financial needs with the satisfaction of holding public office, but these remarks were subject to several different interpretations. Was he hinting at retirement or was he suggesting he needed a more lucrative federal post to sustain him while writing his history of the Washington Administration? One thing was certain—he could not have selected a more inappropriate time for suggesting that he might not be able to remain in the Cabinet. Washington, ever mindful of the virtue of silence, did not even acknowledge the letter.

With his Attorney General hinting at resignation, Washington set out on the short trip of inspection to Reading and Lancaster in anticipation of the convening of Congress. He ignored Randolph's warning and went to Philadelphia to see for himself if it was safe for Congress to meet there. Returning to Germantown on Saturday, November 16, he scheduled a Cabinet meeting for the following Monday to consider the matters that had to be laid before Congress when it assembled.[35] There was the obvious question of how the Neutrality Proclamation should be explained, plus the somewhat less sensitive matter of the special messages summarizing our relations with Great Britain, the French Republic and Spain and, of course, the inevitable matter of our relations with the Barbary States. Given the current mood of the Cabinet, bitter debate seemed almost inevitable.

The several Cabinet meetings[36] devoted to the consideration of the President's address at the opening of the session and the special messages to be sent later were again marked by acrimony between Hamilton and Jefferson. The meeting on the 18th found Hamilton, Jefferson and Randolph each differing with one another as to what the President might say on the proclamation. Hamilton argued for the broadest statement on the rights of the executive; Jefferson was for a minimal, almost apologetic, statement; and Randolph was in between, closer to Jefferson than to Hamilton.[37] When the meeting resumed after dinner, the question of the immediate termination of Genêt's appointment came up for review. Washington was concerned that if Genêt was not dismissed immediately, he might court the sympathies of Congress when it reassembled. Again the two principal Cabinet officers clashed, but on this question Randolph and Jefferson were of like mind.[38]

Randolph had, of course, expressed himself on this subject earlier in the month, and Washington found his Attorney General as vehemently opposed to Genêt's dismissal now as he had been on that occasion. Randolph feared an immediate dismissal might revive Genêt's popularity, whereas at present he was "dead in the public opinion." The meeting ended with Washington lamenting the lack of agreement among his advisers.[39] Three days later the Cabinet met again to consider Randolph's and Hamilton's draft statements on the Neutrality Proclamation that had been prepared for inclusion in the President's message to Congress.[40] Differing in the significance they attached to the proclamation, the two statements provided the occasion for renewed controversy. After an exchange between Hamilton and Randolph, Washington asked Jefferson and Knox which interpretation they preferred. The Secretary of War supported Hamilton, while Jefferson endorsed Randolph's draft. He noted, however, that "it gave to that instrument more objects than I contemplated." Washington remained uncommitted, and the meeting ended without a final decision.[41] Two days later, on November 23, Randolph was asked to prepare the President's address for the opening of Congress, and Jefferson was directed to prepare the special messages on our relations with Great Britain, France, Spain and the Barbary States.[42]

It was November 28 before the Cabinet met again; the order of business was the draft messages prepared by Randolph and Jefferson. Randolph's draft of the President's address was taken first. Jefferson noted: "No material alterations were proposed or made to any part of the draught."[43] After dinner the President and his advisers turned to Jefferson's special messages. Hamilton expressed his disagreement "in toto" and argued that our relations with France and England had been summarized in such a manner as to imply that France was our friend and had done much for us, while England had been our traditional enemy, whereas the reverse was closer to the truth. Randolph, while disagreeing with Hamilton's basic criticism, did support him in his contention that certain matters should be withheld from Congress. Jefferson was alarmed, certain that the Secretary of the Treasury would succeed in keeping everything secret, but Washington came to his support and most of the pertinent papers were placed before Congress. Jefferson found Randolph's stubborn independence annoying and apparently felt these instances where the Attorney General supported Hamilton reflected an indecisiveness on critical issues.[44]

Congress assembled in Philadelphia as scheduled. Since the cooler weather had halted the spread of the fever, the members did not have to consider an alternate location for their meeting. Washington, accompanied by his Cabinet, appeared before a joint session of Congress to deliver his annual message. The address adhered to Randolph's language in its reference to the proclamation and followed his organization, but in most other matters the words were Washington's. The plea for "unprejudiced coolness" and "harmony" bore the unmistakable imprint of the nonpartisan Chief Executive.[45] Several days later the special message on our relations with France and Great Britain went to Congress, and again the tone was unmistakably Washington's.[46]

Even before the President and his advisers had finally resolved the question of what should be communicated to Congress, Randolph was again embroiled in another of Genêt's disputes. Early in August John Jay and Rufus King had published a statement in the New York *Diary* that charged Genêt with having threatened to appeal the case of his dismissal to the American people.[47] Genêt's initial response was to demand from the President a statement that he had never intimated to him that he had any intention of appealing to the people.[48] Jefferson, replying for Washington, reminded Genêt that the diplomatic correspondence of foreign representatives was customarily directed to the Secretary of State and that the President thought neither "propriety" nor "duty" justified a statement in support of Genêt.[49] Unable to enlist the President's support, Genêt then demanded that the government prosecute the authors for libel. His demand was sent to Randolph in a letter dated November 14. The Attorney General was noncommittal in his reply, although he stated that he would be willing to discuss the matter with Genêt after he returned to Philadelphia.[50] Genêt returned to the city early in December and probably met with Randolph on the 13th.[51] The results of this meeting were apparently unsatisfactory for Genêt addressed a second letter to Randolph three days later, on December 16, again asking him to prosecute Jay and King for libel.[52] He transmitted a copy of this letter to the Secretary of State and asked Jefferson to prevail upon the President to instruct Randolph to initiate legal action as soon as possible. Jefferson duly brought the letter to the President's attention and was instructed to convey to Randolph his recommendation that the present matter be given the most careful consideration in view of the "public character" of the person making this request. As a diplomatic representative Genêt was, Jefferson noted, "peculiarly entitled to the protection of the laws."[53]

Unknown to Washington or Jefferson, Randolph had already rejected Genêt's request. It is incumbent upon me, he told Genêt:

> . . . to prosecute without distinction of person, when the law will support me; [yet] I do not hold myself bound, nor do I conceive, that I ought, to proceed against any man in opposition to my decided judgement. With these impres-

sions, I must beg leave to decline the measure, which you desire, persuaded
as I am, that this case will not sustain the prosecution which you meditate.[54]

He added as a postscript:

Since I wrote the above, I have received, sir, a letter from the Secretary
of State on the subject of your request. As no change is rendered necessary
in the foregoing sentiments, I do myself the honor of sending my letter, as it
originally stood.[55]

In matters clearly within the province of his office Randolph neither
sought nor welcomed advice. He was not impervious to the political and
diplomatic considerations associated with any request from Genêt, but
he would not allow them to influence his decision in a situation where
his responsibilites as Attorney General were clearly defined by law.

On December 24 Washington wrote to Randolph: "I now wish for
your permission to nominate you to it, the office of Secretary of State,
and will add, that your compliance would give me pleasure. Mr. Jefferson will quit it the last day of this month. . . ."[56] With this note
Washington filled his first Cabinet vacancy since the formation of the
government. Jefferson's intended departure had been known for some
time, as had the President's annoyance with his Secretaries of State and
Treasury for their refusal to remain in the Cabinet until his second term
had ended. Both gentlemen had been instrumental in persuading him
to accept a second term, and now they were anxious to leave his Cabinet.[57]

Back in July, after Washington had failed in his efforts to persuade
Jefferson to remain at his post until the end of his second term, he had
turned the discussion to the question of a successor. However much
Washington deplored Jefferson's political bias, he still felt his Secretary
of State had no equal when it came to diplomacy and he wanted his
views on who would be a worthy successor. Washington let it be known
that his first choice was Madison, but since he expected him to decline
the appointment he knew he would have to look elsewhere. He mentioned John Jay, Senator Rufus King of New York, Representative William L. Smith of South Carolina and Edward Rutledge, a member of the
South Carolina state legislature. Each, however, Washington observed,
would be objectionable for one reason or another. Jefferson suggested
Governor Thomas Johnson of Maryland and Chancellor Robert R. Livingston of New York. Washington thought the first lacked the necessary
experience for the diplomatic post but might well replace Hamilton
when he retired. Livingston could not be considered because his ap-

pointment would arouse a political storm for it would place the two principal Cabinet posts in the hands of men who resided in the same state, and Hamilton's intended resignation could not be made public at this time. Dr. James McClurg of Virginia was mentioned and dismissed because he was susceptible to the charge of speculation. The President asked Jefferson for his opinion of Oliver Wolcott, and Jefferson replied he had heard him characterized as a "cunning" man. Jefferson then raised the question of an interim appointment and suggested Randolph. The President admitted this was a possibility but added it might raise "the expectation of keeping it, and I do not know that he is fit for it nor what is thought of Mr. Randolph." Jefferson ignored the President's observation, whereupon Washington asked him directly how Randolph was generally "thought of." Jefferson, pleading that he seldom "went into society," noted the financial embarrassments of the Attorney General and expressed the fear that this might compromise his independence.[58] Since the conference ended with the intimation that Jefferson would probably remain until the end of December, no final decision was made as to a successor.[59] Neither Washington nor Jefferson recorded any subsequent conversation on the subject. Randolph was well aware of Jefferson's efforts to resign in August but made no reference to it in the months that followed.[60] Apparently the President offered the vacancy to Randolph on December 24 without further consultation. He had not even intimated to the Attorney General that he was considering him for the appointment.

On December 24 Randolph acknowledged the President's letter in a brief note asking if he could discuss the matter with Washington on the 26th.[61] It was at this meeting that Randolph apparently signified his willingness to accept Jefferson's post. On December 31 Jefferson submitted his formal letter of resignation and on January 1, 1794, Washington submitted Randolph's name to the Senate. His appointment was confirmed the following day.[62]

Randolph's new appointment terminated his four-year tenure as the country's first Attorney General. His attitude toward that office reflected the minimal responsibilities of the nation's principal legal officer during these years. The duties of the office could undoubtedly have been expanded, but Randolph made only two or three modest efforts to do so. His more important role in the circle of presidential advisers was as the tireless advocate of policies that would keep the presidency above the partisan politics that had developed as a result of the very different political beliefs of Jefferson and Hamilton. For over a year and a half, as the antagonism between the Secretary of State and the Secretary of the Treasury flared, died and flared again, he had been an invaluable political adviser to the President and a loyal aide when it came to carrying out special assignments. As new and more serious diplomatic problems confronted the government and they, in turn, became entangled in domestic politics, Randolph became the President's most reliable and unbiased adviser.

Edmund Randolph may not have been the President's first choice as Secretary of State and Washington may have had some doubts as to his ability to handle the more demanding duties of that office, but as a trusted Cabinet officer, wholly committed to the President's goals for this new nation, Randolph had no equal.

18

Jefferson's Successor
January–June 1794

On January 2 Edmund Randolph stood before Judge James Wilson of the United States Supreme Court to be sworn in as Secretary of State.[1] Immediately, he transmitted notice of his certification to the President, and added:

> . . . be assured, that, let the consequences be what it may in this perilous office, no consideration of party shall ever influence me; nothing shall relax my attention or warp my probity and it shall be my unremitted study to become an accurate master of this new and important business.[2]

The formal language of this letter to the President failed to conceal the apprehensiveness with which Randolph approached his new assignment. He knew only too well that it was a "perilous office." The department was demanding in time and talent, under greater public scrutiny, more subservient to the will of the executive than any other department and, above all, concerned with problems that affected the security of the government itself. It was one thing to be a close confidant of the President in an inconspicuous office, counseling moderation and reading the political barometer whenever the occasion demanded. It was quite a different matter to be Secretary of State, watched and tested at every turn, never certain when what you wrote or said might be turned against you. The "departments" were not all equal and Edmund Randolph knew it.

Washington had been in large measure his own Secretary of State, as he determined policy by judiciously selecting from the opinions of his principal advisers. Randolph, either by identifying the middle position or by quietly warning of the political dangers inherent in the advice of Jefferson or Hamilton, had played a major role in many of his decisions. He had come to be identified with a kind of pragmatic diplomacy, a diplomacy that tested all policy against national self-interest. It was an approach Washington respected because it complemented without really imitating his own approach to foreign affairs. But the departure of Jefferson had radically altered the Cabinet, depriving it of a certain point of view, which, when balanced against Hamilton's views, provided a valuable polarization for the formulation of national policy. Randolph would be obliged to adjust to a different frame of reference within the Cabinet, one in which political neutrality was less readily identifiable than it had been when Jefferson and Hamilton were brilliantly defining their respective political creeds.

Randolph's first correspondents were the Secretaries of Treasury and War. To each of the Secretaries he sent an identical letter:

> I have just taken the oath of office, which reminds me that I am brought into a nearer relation to your department than hitherto. While official men are under no less an obligation than others, to live in harmony; there are too many opportunities for misconception and misrepresentation to interrupt it. I have therefore prescribed this rule for myself: that if anything, supposed to be done in the other departments, shall create dissatisfaction in my mind, I will check any opinion, until I can obtain an explanation, which I will ask without reserve. By these means I shall avoid the uneasiness of suspicion; and I shall take the liberty of requesting, that the same line of conduct may be pursued with respect to myself.
>
> I trust, that under these principles, whatsoever differences of sentiments may at any time exist between us, it will be the differences of men who equally pursue the objects of their appointment, and that the public good will thereby be promoted rather than injured.[3]

Randolph's request was but a polite warning that he expected to conduct his "department" without the benefit of their unsolicited advice. Undoubtedly he hoped his thinly veiled admonition would halt those intrusions into State Department affairs that had so annoyed Jefferson. Copies of this letter were sent to the President with the curt observation: "At the commencement of my duties, I have thought it advisable to write to the Secretaries of . . . the letters of which the enclosed are copies."[4]

Having defined his relationship with the President and the other members of the Cabinet, Randolph turned his attention to the duties of the department. Jefferson had been an attentive correspondent with our ministers abroad, his own experience having made him sensitive to the isolation and remoteness that plagued them in the performance of their assignments. Through frequent letters he tried to keep them abreast of government policies and such other matters as might be of interest or benefit to them.[5] Events in recent months had, however, disrupted the normal routine of the department. The yellow fever epidemic in Philadelphia, coupled with Jefferson's own visit to Virginia, had virtually suspended the department's activities. During the brief period in December when Jefferson was able to resume his duties in Philadelphia his attention was turned to other matters, which forced him to leave unanswered some of the most recent dispatches from our ministers.[6] Randolph's first task, therefore, was to establish contact with our representatives abroad, acknowledge their most recent dispatches and inform them of events at home. By January 4 he had reviewed the correspondence from each of them and was able to provide the President with a precise summary of the contents; in addition, he noted the matters that would require an immediate answer. He was, he informed the President, preparing letters acknowledging the receipt of their latest dispatches, notifying the ministers and consuls of the change within the department, and informing them of such "other matters as may relate to them particularly" as well as any other intelligence as might be found in the "public documents in the United States."[7] Six days later the letters were on the President's desk for his approval.[8] They were approved and returned the same day.[9]

Not only was Randolph adjusting to the duties of a new office, but he was also engaged in getting his family settled in a new home. Perhaps it was the expected social responsibilities associated with his new office that prompted the move or perhaps it was the desire to be close to the offices of the Department of State. Whatever the reason he took up residence at 319 High Street, a few doors from the offices of the Department of State.[10] For a family that had moved so frequently, particularly in recent years, the task of getting settled in another house should have been rather routine. Unfortunately the serious illness of fourteen-year-old Peyton complicated the process.[11] Apparently his recovery was both rapid and complete, though, for the family soon settled into a fixed routine which permitted Edmund to give his undivided attention to the responsibilities of his new office.

As the weeks passed, Randolph quietly adjusted to the multiple duties of Secretary of State. The *Journal* of the proceedings of the executive of the territories northwest and southwest of the Ohio was reviewed and, he reported to Washington, there was nothing of consequence in it to demand the President's attention.[12] Dr. David Rittenhouse was "examined" on the state of the Mint, and this report was filed with the President.[13] These minor duties were but a few of the many responsibilities associated with the office, and Randolph seemed to handle most of them with ease. He undoubtedly utilized to the fullest the small band of clerks that made up his staff.[14] In addition, there was the usual correspondence from Genêt and Hammond which had to be answered, the answer transmitted to the President for approval and then, in the case of Genêt, translated into French. Until the last week in January the most significant business involving the Secretary of State was a consideration of the President's proposal that an effort be made to secure the release from a Prussian prison of the Marquis de Lafayette. Randolph prepared the instructions for our minister in London, Thomas Pinckney, into whose hands was placed the ultimate decision as to how the King of Prussia should be approached in this delicate matter.[15] Before the end of the month, however, the highly partisan Third Congress had provided an occasion for the revival of the political differences within the President's Cabinet.

The occasion was the request of the Senate for the diplomatic correspondence of Gouverneur Morris, our minister in Paris since June, 1792.[16] The Republican-sponsored resolution of January 24 was clearly designed to embarrass the President and presumably expose Morris' unsympathetic attitude toward the French Revolution.[17] It also raised serious constitutional questions as to the extent the executive should share his diplomatic responsibilities with the legislature. Washington, Hamilton and Randolph discussed the matter informally the day after the resolution was passed, with the result that Randolph apparently promised to review the requested correspondence before the matter was formally discussed by the Cabinet.[18] On January 26 he reported to Washington that the correspondence contained nothing that could be called exceptional and much that the "most violent would call patriotic." The parts to be withheld, he continued, would probably be those which related to Genêt, "some harsh expressions on the conduct of the rulers in France," which, if made public, "might expose Morris to personal danger," and the names of the "authors of some interesting information," who, if known, "would be infallibly denounced."[19] At a meeting of the Cabinet on the 28th Knox and Hamilton opposed sending any part of the correspondence, while Randolph recommended that all correspondence "proper from its nature" should be communicated, only what the President judged improper being withheld.[20] In an opinion prepared independent of the Cabinet meeting the new Attorney General, William Bradford,[21] urged the communication of such parts of the correspondence as shall be deemed "safe and proper to disclose."[22] The same day Randolph took it upon himself to consult Judge James Wilson and his fellow Virginian James Madison on the subject. Wilson felt Congress ought to receive what they "might have," withholding what they "ought not to have." Madison maintained that the President had the right to select what he thought proper and transmit it to the Senate; if he were to withhold the correspondence completely, whatever the reason, he would provoke a more serious dispute with both branches of the legislature.[23] These views Randolph communicated to Washington the following day.[24] Obviously troubled by the constitutional implications of the request, and acting very much like an Attorney General who felt obliged to advise the President on such matters, he submitted a further memo to the President on the subject. Distinguishing between the Senate's executive and legislative powers, he argued that a request by the Senate in its "executive" capacity should be refused *in toto* since the Senate possessed executive powers only in the review of presidential appointments and in the ratification of treaties. A request in its "legislative" capacity, however, would have to be complied with, though the President could reserve the right to exercise his discretion as to what should be released, giving the Senate no more than what "in his judgment is fit to be given."[25] A subsequent memo reiterated this distinction and added that in the absence of more specific information the President had the right to decide whether the resolution was executive or legislative in character. His decision on this point would be the basic consideration in determining how he should respond to the resolution.[26] Washington, accepting Randolph's advice, ordered the correspondence prepared for the Senate. In transmitting it to the Senate several weeks later he noted in a covering letter that some material had been withheld because "in my judgment, for public considerations, it ought not to be communicated." The nature of the correspondence, he added, "manifest[s] the propriety of their being received as confidential."[27] That same afternoon Randolph reported that the message had been favorably received, that Madison, in particular, "thinks it will have a good effect."[28] As a former Attorney General, Randolph was as concerned about the constitutional aspects of the President's compliance with the Senate resolution as he was with the political implications of these actions.

Perhaps the most welcome bit of news for Washington and his Cabinet was the report that reached Philadelphia in mid-January that the French government was sending someone to replace Genêt.[29] This tireless and troublesome minister had been pleasantly inactive in recent weeks, and Randolph, who knew only too well Jefferson's difficulties with the impetuous diplomat, must have been thankful for his good fortune. The expected Republican support for Genêt had failed to materialize in Congress, leaving the French minister discouraged and isolated from that element in American politics most sympathetic to France.[30] He could do little but wait patiently for his successor to arrive. For Washington and his Cabinet there were still problems, to be sure, but most of them were traceable to Genêt's earlier activities, before the President's firm opposition had become effective. Still it must have been with a sigh of relief that Washington read Randolph's note of February 21 that Joseph Fauchet, minister plenipotentiary of the French

Republic, had arrived in the city and was prepared to present his credentials to the President.[31] Arrangements were made for a brief and relatively informal presentation the following day.[32]

Fauchet, Randolph informed the President, carried instructions for the arrest of Genêt.[33] The request had been expected by both Washington and Randolph, for reports from France indicated that the Revolution had brought Robespierre's Jacobin government into power. Were Washington to comply with Fauchet's request, it seemed certain Genêt would suffer the same fate as his fellow Gerondist—an appointment with the guillotine.[34] When Randolph discovered the new minister had little interest in pressing his demand, the subject was quietly dropped.[35] Fauchet's conduct in this matter made a favorable impression on Randolph.[36] His moderation stood in sharp contrast to the unbridled zeal of Genêt. There was every reason to believe that our future relations with France would be marked by a greater respect for the traditional methods of diplomacy. Nothing would be more pleasing to the new Secretary of State.

As Fauchet embarked upon his new assignment there still remained one problem of Genêt's making that required the immediate attention of the national government. Almost from the day he set foot on American soil Genêt had been associated with a project to seize East and West Florida and Louisiana from Spain.[37] Assured of the support of disgruntled Kentuckians as well as the talents of the state's distinguished frontier warrior, General George Rogers Clark,[38] Genêt had pushed the project with enthusiasm. Washington and his advisers had been vaguely aware of the plans for several months, but Genêt's close association with the unhappy Kentuckians could never be substantiated.[39] It was not until November that Washington knew for certain that Genêt was sponsoring what later proved to be a two-pronged expedition against the Spanish possessions on the North American continent.[40] By the end of the year there was irrefutable evidence of recruiting activities in South Carolina aimed at collecting a force to attack East Florida.[41] At about the same time reports from Kentucky indicated that Clark was preparing to move against the Spanish in Louisiana.[42] The former evidence was transmitted to Congress, while the President waited patiently for word that Genêt was being replaced.[43] Finally in February, after Governor Isaac Shelby of Kentucky had informed Randolph that he lacked constitutional authority to stop an expedition from leaving his state,[44] Washington felt compelled to act independently. He decided on February 21 to issue a proclamation in the hope of restraining American citizens from participating in the venture. The hastily drafted document was forwarded to Randolph to be copied and returned.[45] It was evident that the President felt prompt action by the federal government was essential if the ambitious scheme of Genêt and his followers was to be halted.

A week passed and Randolph, apparently preoccupied with other matters, failed to return the proclamation. In the meantime the news from Kentucky gave evidence of further military preparations.[46] Alarmed Federalists in the Senate sought to enact legislation that would make Americans participating in such an expedition subject to criminal prosecution.[47] Even Fauchet was persuaded to disavow the venture, thereby revoking the commissions granted by his predecessor.[48] Two weeks later, on March 10, the most recent intelligence from Kentucky was made the subject of a Cabinet meeting. It was agreed that a proclamation should be issued, that "representations" should be made to the governor of Kentucky and Congress, and that General Wayne should be ordered to post a body of troops at Fort Massac "in order to intercept by force, if necessary, any body of men which may descend the river for the purpose of the invasion aforesaid." Complete Cabinet unanimity prevailed except for the last proposition.[49] To this Randolph voiced his strong dissent and filed a written opinion with the President on the following day. In substance he rejected the use of a military force against citizens of the United States before the normal legal forms had been exhausted. Forcefully presented, Randolph's opinion challenged the President's authority to use the militia under any possible view of the affair as it then stood. Never had he been so uncompromising and inflexible in his opinion. Curtly he wrote:

> As I shall always contend, for what I conceive to be the constitutional and legal powers of the government; so I beg leave [now] to request, upon this truly important subject, that you will suffer this letter to be filed away with the paper containing the opinions.[50]

The following day Randolph forwarded a copy of the most recent complaint of the Spanish commissioners against these activities to Washington in order that it might be transmitted to Congress.[51] On March 24 the Secretary of State returned to Washington a "fair copy" of the proclamation that the President had given him a month earlier on February 21. The resultant document, now reflective of the views of the entire Cabinet, was clearly not to Randolph's liking. "It was," he said, "transcribed upon the supposition that the President would direct it to issue in the form, which the other three gentlemen had approved. . . ."[52] The President signed and issued the proclamation the same day.[53] By the end of March it was evident, however, that neither of the planned expeditions would be undertaken.[54] A lack of funds, Fauchet's public disavowal of the acts of his predecessor and the President's proclamation had all served to abort the grandiose schemes of Genêt and his impetuous cohorts in South Carolina and Kentucky.

Yet on March 16, well before the crisis had passed (at least as far as the government in Philadelphia was concerned), Randolph was writing to William Short, one of our two commissioners in Madrid, an interesting account of the government's response to the threatened military expeditions. After reciting the basic details of the project and noting the firm response of the governor of South Carolina in contrast to the almost sympathetic attitude of the governor of Kentucky, he continued:

> We are tolerably certain, however, that the enterprise has been abandoned, and that the countenance, which some at least of the Confederates at first gave it, was the effect of supposition wholly unfounded, that Mr. Genêt could not have acted thus, without some connivance in the government.[55]

Believing as he did that the reports exaggerated the significance of the forces being organized, he was perfectly accurate in his assessment of the situation. But his views in no way coincided with the vigorous policy being pursued by the government as it implemented the Cabinet decision of March 10. Thus from the beginning he opposed what he considered extreme and unnecessary measures and insisted that all normal legal processes must first be exhausted before the extraordinary measures proposed by Washington or under consideration in Congress were employed. His views placed him in the role of a dissenter in the executive council, one who obstructed the wishes of the President with petty legal technicalities. Yet, in this letter to Short, Washington allowed Randolph's highly personal assessment of the situation to go unchallenged, though he quibbled with the language his Secretary used in the next paragraph relating to another subject.[56] And all this occurred a week before the presidential proclamation against these activities had been issued!

But the month of March seemed to be filled with strange contradictions. Delayed diplomatic intelligence from Europe produced an unusual mood of belligerence in Congress as it watched both France and England treat our neutrality with contemptuous indifference. There were times during the month when Congress showed a rare spirit of bipartisanship, only to suddenly revert to a shameless political skulduggery that was irreconcilable with the seriousness of the times. While the Federalists in the Senate were unseating the Republican financial expert Albert Gallatin of Pennsylvania on a question of citizenship,[57] their counterparts in the House were prepared to resume debate on Madison's commercial resolutions of January 3, confident they would be defeated or rendered innocuous.[58] Their plans were interrupted, however, by the receipt of Randolph's report on the spoliations inflicted on our commerce since the start of the war in Europe.[59]

Prepared at the direction of the President, the report was transmitted to Congress on March 5. As usual, Randolph's analysis was completely free of political bias. England, France, Spain and the Netherlands were accused of attacking our commerce, with the two major powers being charged with the more serious violations of our neutrality. The case against these two nations was itemized with such care that neither Federalist nor Republican could take much comfort in the report.[60] The pattern of abuses being inflicted by both these countries dictated a response that included some measure of military preparation. Two days later Philadelphia papers carried the news of a British Order in Council, dated November 6, 1793, instructing English forces to seize neutral vessels engaged in trade with the French West Indies.[61] The order, the subject of rumor for some time, was to Federalists the height of folly. The Republicans, who viewed it as a confirmation of their traditional distrust of England, neverthelesss found themselves making common cause with Federalists in approving a naval construction bill, a large army appropriation for the current year and a bill for harbor fortification. All of these bills were passed by the third week of March.[62] If anyone remained doubtful about the seriousness of the situation, the widespread publication of a belligerent speech that had been delivered by Lord Dorchester, the Governor General of Canada, to a delegation of Indians on February 10, 1794, destroyed the last shred of hope that war could be averted.[63]

The President's advisers showed the same, if not greater, concern for these recent evidences of British indifference to our neutrality. Writing to our minister in London, Randolph commented: "Congress are occupied with the awfulness of our situation." "Why," he asked in the same letter, "had not the Orders in Council of November 6, 1793, been forwarded by you?" He knew, he continued, that Pinckney would not delay in forwarding such intelligence if he were aware of it.[64] The implication was obvious; the order must have been deliberately kept secret so that it could be enforced without prior warning to our unsuspecting merchant fleet in the West Indies.[65] Clearly Britain was prepared to risk war in this reckless violation of our neutrality.

On the same day that Randolph sent his letter to Pinckney (March 8) Hamilton submitted a remarkable memorandum to the President on the need for military preparations. Advancing the thesis that an adequate military force would serve as a deterrent to war, he urged a three-point program: the fortification of our principal ports in the several states, the raising of an auxiliary army of twenty thousand men and the authorization for the laying of an embargo on exports:

> If it is known that our principal maritime points are out of the reach of any but formal serious operations—and that the government has an effective active force at its disposal for defense or offence, [in?] an emergency—there will be much less temptation to attack us and much more hesitation to provoke us.

"It may also deserve consideration," he continued, "whether the Executive ought not to take measures to form some concert of the Neutral Powers for common defense."[66]

But plans of a different sort were being formulated by several individuals with access to the President. On the same day the Cabinet agreed to take strenuous measures to halt the Genêt-sponsored expeditions against Spanish Florida and Louisiana, namely March 10, a group of leading Federalists decided to urge upon the President the appointment of a special envoy to London to negotiate a general settlement of the differences between the two countries.[67] Two days later Senator Oliver Ellsworth of Connecticut presented the proposal to Washington and urged—as had been agreed upon at the meeting—the name of Alexander Hamilton as a fitting candidate for the assignment. Washington, "at first reserved," showed interest in the proposal but rejected almost immediately the suggestion that Hamilton be appointed to undertake the mission. He lacked, said Washington, "the general confidence of the country." The meeting ended with Ellsworth uncertain as to whether Washington endorsed or disapproved of the mission.[68] On March 14 Washington received a routine memorandum from his Secretary of State noting the recent actions of the Senate and House with regard to the extent of our claims resulting from the seizure of our vessels. Noting the hardship these seizures had worked upon the mercantile element in our population, he went on to ask whether the appointment of some "temperate and sensible man," working under the supervision of Pinckney, might not settle these claims more readily than if they were left to the normal channels of adjudication in foreign courts. Our new military posture, he noted, will serve to assure us of a more respectful reception when we present our claims.[69] A modest proposal and, by implication at least, optimistic as to the results that might be expected, it freed the President from the disagreeable task of repudiating the untiring efforts of Pinckney to resolve the differences between the two countries. Washington left no written record of his reaction to either Ellsworth's or Randolph's suggestion, and for the moment the attention of both men shifted to other matters.

While this matter remained suspended, the Federalists in Congress had taken the initiative in proposing additional legislation to meet the worsening diplomatic situation. As our maritime centers gradually became aware of the enormity of their losses in the West Indies, there was a growing demand for the government to take vigorous measures in retaliation. The Federalists, sensitive to the interests of the commercial element, quickly responded.[70] Madison's commercial propositions, which would have placed higher duties on goods imported from countries with which the United States had no commercial treaty (i.e., England), were now viewed as totally inadequate.[71] The alternative, proposed by Federalist Theodore Sedgwick, was a series of resolutions calling for the establishment of an auxiliary army of fifteen thousand men and the granting of authority to the President to declare an embargo on all American shipping.[72] By the 26th of March Federalists and Republicans in both houses of Congress had concurred on a bill imposing a thirty-day embargo.[73] The 1st of April found Sedgwick's resolution for the establishment of an auxiliary regiment approved by the House with the size of the force having been increased by ten thousand.[74] The Republicans, not to be outdone by their Federalist colleagues, on April 7 urged the suspension of all commercial intercourse between England and the United States.[75] An earlier proposal authorizing the Treasury to sequester all debts due British citizens as security against indemnification for our losses at sea also had strong Republican backing.[76] Neither proposition impressed the Federalists, who considered themselves equal to the task of determining the extent of our military preparations. With political rivalry again on the rise, and Hamilton's name being mentioned as a possible envoy to Great Britain, the Republican-dominated House decided to raise some embarrassing questions as to the Secretary of the Treasury's conduct.

The investigation of Hamilton's activities by a committee of the House had been in progress for some time. The current investigation was but the latest of several attempts to discredit the Secretary of the Treasury.[77] When the committee demanded to know by what authority Hamilton had drawn funds into the Treasury that were allocated by law for the payment of American revolutionary loans in Europe, Hamilton replied that he acted on the verbal and written authority of the President.[78] Randolph learned of this exchange between Hamilton and the committee from his brother-in-law, Wilson Cary Nicholas, who in turn had received the information from Senator Giles, Hamilton's severest critic in the legislature.[79] Sensing trouble, Randolph hurriedly penned a memo marked "private" to the President. If, Randolph noted, Hamilton or the committee were to seek verification from Washington of these oral or written instructions, then the President would most certainly need time to check into the matter.[80] Randolph's political instinct was right, as usual. That same day the committee insisted that Hamilton obtain from the President "such declarations as the President may think proper" to verify his authority in the matter.[81] His back to the wall, Hamilton forwarded the committee's resolution to the President.[82] Forewarned, Washington recognized that he was being drawn into an obvious political maneuver aimed at discrediting Hamilton. Washington turned to Randolph, who immediately provided him with a draft of the answer that might be given to Hamilton's request. Carefully phrased, it neither confirmed nor denied giving the oral instructions the Secretary of the Treasury had maintained were the basis of his action.[83] Washington, while accepting Randolph's noncommittal approach, drafted his own reply to the Secretary of the Treasury.[84] Bitterly disappointed because Washington had failed to support him, Hamilton charged the President with having written a statement that would only confirm the accusations being made against him.[85] Washington chose to leave Hamilton's charge unanswered, and the committee apparently did not exploit the issue further.[86] Subsequently, when the United States borrowed three million florins in Amsterdam, Washington carefully inquired into the intended disposition of the money.[87] Hamilton's reply only caused the President to question him further and ultimately to send the whole correspondence between himself and Hamilton to Randolph for his recommendations. The Secretary of State studied the matter carefully, outlined the legal and political implications of the President's acceding to Hamilton's proposals for the disposition of the money, and drafted a reply for Washington that insisted that the money in question be allocated in conformance with his earlier instructions.[88] Randolph's reply was transcribed verbatum and sent to the Secretary of the Treasury.[89]

On April 4 the President transmitted to Congress the first "agreeable intelligence" the country had received in weeks. It was a dispatch from Pinckney informing Randolph that the Pitt ministry had withdrawn the Order in Council of November 6, 1793. At least the ruthless seizures of our vessels in the Caribbean would be halted. Washington and Randolph were undoubtedly pleased, though they did not lose sight of the fact that our grievances with England still remained unresolved. The tense atmosphere of the past few weeks gave way to a calm and somewhat less critical attitude as the President and Congress continued to insist on a full and proper respect for our rights as a neutral.[90]

While Congress had been engaged in strengthening our defenses and granting the President authority to impose an embargo, a somewhat different course of action was maturing in Washington's mind. Ellsworth and Randolph had suggested that a special representative be sent to London, and in the intervening weeks the idea of a minister vested with authority to settle all our differences with Great Britain had gained many adherents. To Federalists at least, it was the only proposal that offered any hope of averting war.[91] Washington remained reluctant to replace Pinckney and firm in his conviction that if someone were to be appointed, it would not be Hamilton. But he still had not made up his mind. On Saturday, April 5, he talked the matter over with Randolph and intimated that in the event a minister was named, the message to the Senate placing such a person in nomination would have to be drawn with great care.[92] The following day Randolph sent him a long letter that the Secretary himself described as a "short review" of the subject.[93] It was in fact a careful summary of Randolph's own view of our diplomatic position vis-à-vis England.

"I believe," he said, "that I was among the first, if not the first, who suggested this mission to your consideration, and I am still its advocate." There followed a list of five reasons in support of a special mission. He admitted, however, that there were considerations that might be urged against it. One was the insult to Pinckney and the consequent lessening of his effectiveness as our representative in London. The other was the adverse reaction it might create among our own people. But, he added, if the appointment were properly explained, he was confident both difficulties could be overcome. He continued:

> And yet, the difference between one grade [Pinckney's] and another [special envoy] is not so powerful as of itself to secure a difference of reception to our demands. The envoy will be impotent if he is to carry with him only the language of rhetoric, or of menaces without the power of revenge. To fulfill the purpose of his creation, he must show that the U.S. can and will vindicate their rights. But measures of this kind depend on Congress alone. From them we have the embargo alone. They are employed in discussions, leading to these objects. To nominate an envoy immediately, or until you see the nature and extent of the preparations may perhaps be to nominate a useless officer; and, if by such a nomination it is proposed to give a direction to the views and deliberations of Congress, may it not be better to send a message to them, urging them to adopt the preparatory steps; then to run the risk of appointing a gentleman, who, if our state of imbecility is to remain, cannot, except for personal qualities, have more influence than Mr. Pinckney.[94]

Sensible in his assessment of our bargaining powers at the conference table, Randolph sought to persuade the President that the efforts of a special envoy could only end in failure so long as that minister lacked the means of coercing Great Britain to respect our rights. Perhaps he felt that his modest proposal to appoint someone to settle our claims against Great Britain might succeed, but the more ambitious project, to settle all our differences with Britain, clearly must await congressional action on measures that would strengthen the envoy's hand in negotiation. Free from the diplomatic preference engendered by a political commitment, he could see the weaknesses in the Federalist line of reasoning. The idea of sending a special envoy in itself had merit, but the timing of his appointment and the diplomatic weapons he carried to London were of utmost importance.

Yet in advancing this seemingly modest and sensible proposal Randolph employed a kind of cunning that must have been evident to Washington. He was not the first to suggest this mission, and he knew it. He had never been an advocate of the kind of mission then being contemplated by the President, and he knew this too. The first few paragraphs, implying complete and total agreement with the President, were pure flattery, obviously intended to soften the Chief Executive for what followed—an excessively clever attempt to dissuade Washington from pursuing this line of policy toward England at this time.

Washington made no written acknowledgment of Randolph's letter, but he did show the Secretary of State two letters he had recently received urging against the rumored appointment of Hamilton as the special envoy in question.[95] The first, dated April 6, was from Congressman John Nicholas of Virginia, another of Randolph's brothers-in-law; the second, dated April 8, was from Senator James Monroe of Virginia.[96] Both men were ardent Republicans. Both saw Hamilton as a sinister force working against the true sentiments of the people and misguiding a President who trusted him too completely. Randolph's reaction was unusually defensive:

> Among my first reflections upon the two letters, which you did me the honor of showing to me yesterday and the day before, I could not forget, that they produced a degree of delicacy to myself. The authors of them are of the number of my friends; and one is closely connected with me by other considerations. However, I did not rest long upon any idea of this kind; being persuaded, that after my declaration of the most absolute and unequivocal ignorance of what was . . . done, you would not for a moment believe, that I had resorted to those expedients for conveying to you sentiments, which I was unwilling to deliver to you in person.[97]

The letter went on to assure the President that Nicholas was "inferior to no man" in his attachment to Washington and to suggest a means whereby Monroe might be granted the interview he had requested with the President. If, Randolph observed, the Virginia Senator possessed information that, as he implied, disqualified Hamilton from the appointment, he should be extended this courtesy.[98] Washington, resenting the unsolicited advice from both Nicholas and Monroe, penned a caustic reply to Monroe because his was the only letter requiring a reply. Acquiescing to Randolph's suggestion that a man of his "station" be given the opportunity to present any "facts" he might have, he requested Monroe to submit the information in writing rather than at an interview, as Randolph had suggested. He reminded the young Virginian, however, that he *"alone"* was responsible for the nomination.[99] Monroe failed to sense the resentment in Washington's letter and sent a long confidential letter in reply which was indelicate in its presumption of intimacy with the President on matters of state. The only "fact" Monroe could advance that disqualified Hamilton was that the Secretary of the Treasury was a Federalist rather than a Republican.[100]

On April 8, before Monroe's reply was received, Washington discussed the subject of a special minister with Robert Morris, one of his closest friends in Philadelphia. Morris, who had been previously approached by Rufus King on behalf of Hamilton's appointment, urged the naming of the Secretary of the Treasury. By way of reply Washington indicated that he was considering four people: the Vice President, Hamilton, John Jay and Jefferson. Morris objected to the first- and last-named individuals, and again expressed his preference for Hamilton.[101] Washington remained noncommittal,[102] but that evening asked Jay, who had just arrived in Philadelphia, to dine with him.[103] While no mention was made of Jay's candidacy, the question of how the country might avoid becoming embroiled in war was discussed.[104] A week later, still undecided as to the course he should pursue, Washington received a letter from his Secretary of the Treasury urging the appointment of a special envoy to England and suggesting Jay be named to undertake the mission. Taking a stand directly in opposition to the views expressed by Randolph, Hamilton argued that the measures then pending before Congress would weaken rather than strengthen the hand of a special envoy, for England would not negotiate under the threat of economic retaliation.[105] Hamilton's letter was as partisan as Monroe's, but it contained at least some compelling logic as well as a frank admission that there were many obstacles to his own appointment, including the "bias of your opinion on the subject." He asked that his name be dropped from the list of those being considered.[106] That evening, April 14, Washington asked Randolph to prepare a message to the Senate nominating Jay.[107] Very early the next morning he sent a note to Jay asking the Chief Justice to meet with him as early as possible that same morning.[108] The meeting apparently was brief. Jay was asked to serve as special envoy and he responded by noting that the resolutions then pending before the House of Representatives would (or "ought to") cause Great Britain to refuse "to treat with us."[109] He apparently asked for time to consider the request. The following day a delegation of Federalists led by Hamilton called upon the Chief Justice to urge his acceptance of the appointment.[110] The next day, April 16, Jay agreed to serve as special envoy.[111] His name was immediately submitted to the Senate.[112] Three days later that body confirmed his appointment over the strong opposition of several Republican Senators.[113] As soon as Randolph learned of the Senate vote, he penned a short personal note to Jay informing him that his appointment had carried.[114]

It remained for Washington and his Cabinet to draft Jay's instructions, a project of some delicacy. Washington asked the members of the Cabinet for their views.[115] His request brought an immediate response from Hamilton in the form of a long memorandum. Forceful in language but mild in intent, Hamilton recommended that Jay be given wide powers, including the right to negotiate a commercial treaty with Great Britain. Few things were to be insisted upon absolutely, and it was implied that some concessions might be made as to our rights as a neutral in return for adequate compensation for the seizures made under the Order in Council of November 6, 1793. Our rights under the Treaty of 1783 were to be insisted upon with a similar delicacy.[116] Hamilton's views corresponded very closely with the opinions that had been expressed two days earlier in a meeting between Hamilton, Ellsworth, Cabot, King and Jay.[117] In mood at least, this discussion had reflected the same desire to effect an accommodation with England. If the other members of the Cabinet submitted their views in writing, no record of them has been found. It mattered little, however, for Hamilton's carefully drawn opinion became the basis of Jay's instructions.[118] They were drafted by Randolph and submitted to the President, Hamilton and Jay for approval on May 4.[119] Randolph, who found himself in virtual agreement with most of Hamilton's points, noted that after his "conversations" and "reflections" he "would probably make several changes in them." He added: "In particular, I have notes concerning the commercial treaty, which I shall draw off by the time of my waiting on you tomorrow."[120] Two days later the instructions were in final form, ready for the President's approval.[121] Accompanying them was a letter from Randolph setting forth his objections to the proposition that Jay be permitted to conclude a treaty of commerce with Great Britain. To so instruct Jay, Randolph argued, would be to abridge the power of the Senate and to authorize a treaty that was impractical, for it would contain only one or two articles. Jay's appointment had been confirmed by the Senate with the express understanding that he would seek a resolution of our differences with England. To grant him the additional authority to negotiate a treaty of commerce was to alter significantly the stated purpose of his mission and introduce a subject that would presumably require the "advice" and "consent" of the Senate. Matter of fact in tone, the letter involved little more than the expression of a dissenting point of view.[122]

In voicing these objections Randolph was not being wholly consistent with his own views on Jay's authority. To Hamilton's enumeration of the instructions that should be given to Jay Randolph had added one significant proposal, i.e. an authorization to treat with the ministers of those countries that were joined together in the Convention of Armed Neutrality with a view of joining their alliance in defense of our neutral rights.[123] While not a new idea, it clearly gave Jay a diplomatic weapon that, as Randolph had argued earlier, was essential to successful negotiations. Whatever negotiating strength might be derived from the insertion of this particular proposal in Jay's instructions, it was, nevertheless, an extension of Jay's authority. The same constitutional objections could be lodged against it as Randolph was now raising against the article authorizing Jay to enter into a commercial treaty.

If Washington discovered the inconsistency in Randolph's position, he chose not to exploit it. The instructions were approved as drafted and the following day Randolph set off for Elizabethtown, New Jersey, to deliver them to Jay, who would journey southward from New York to meet the Secretary of State. Randolph wanted Jay to sail for England at the earliest opportunity, and he was determined that the instructions be in his hands before leaving.[124]

In all the flurry and political maneuvering surrounding Jay's appointment the Secretary of State played a surprisingly minor role. Federalist convictions were fashioning Administration policy, and both Washington and Randolph subscribed to them automatically because no one was formulating and arguing for a different solution to our diplomatic problems. Republicans in Congress worked against Hamilton's receiving the assignment, and when the much-feared appointment did not materialize, pressed for the passage of a bill embodying Abraham Clark's nonintercourse resolutions.[125] Neither effort offered a solution to the diplomatic crisis. The appointment of a special minister armed with broad powers was at least a policy that took cognizance of all our differences with England. Without the benefit of Jefferson's unifying leadership, the Republicans in Congress merely offered opposition, not an alternative policy.[126] In this new political climate Randolph, the sensitive spokesman of the middle position, was neither forceful nor unerring in his judgments.

Before Jay's instructions had been prepared, Randolph was obliged to assist the President in securing a replacement for Gouverneur Morris, our minister in Paris. At the time of Fauchet's arrival it was anticipated that the French government would request the removal of Morris.[127] Although a less zealous antagonist than Genêt, Morris' service was marred by an aristocratic bias that put him at odds with leaders of the Republic.[128] Fauchet formally requested his recall shortly after his arrival and Washington, conscious of a reciprocal obligation, instructed Randolph to immediately inform Fauchet that the request would be honored. Several weeks later Randolph repeated the assurance and further noted that the government was "anxiously seeking" a successor.[129] It would have been more accurate to say that only Washington and Randolph were involved in seeking a successor, with the latter soliciting the views of key Republicans on the acceptability of Chancellor Robert Livingston of New York.[130]

By the end of April, Washington, satisfied with the reports reaching him through Randolph, decided to offer the post to Livingston. A draft letter was prepared and sent to Randolph for approval.[131] He responded by suggesting that the word "embassy" be changed to "mission" in the letter, adding:

> I sincerely believe that Mr. P[inckne]y would be agreeable to France; tho' not so agreeable as Mr. L[ivingsto]n. The arrangement of Mr. J[a]y as resident in London, might be a fortunate circumstance if he would assent to it. But I doubt this; because he has eye[sic] immediately on the government of N[ew] Y[ork] and ultimately on the Presidency. Besides his present office is an abundance for his wants, and he can educate his children in their own country; which of itself is an immensity. However, if he could be consulted without Mr. L——n knowing it, I still repeat, that it would be a fortunate circumstance, should he remove the objections which has [sic] been made to his nomination as envoy.[132]

The following day, with few expectations of success, Washington sent a letter to Livingston and offered him the Paris post. A second letter was sent to Jay to ask if he would accept the position of resident minister in London, thereby permitting Mr. Pinckney's transfer to Paris as a replacement for Morris if Livingston declined the appointment.[133] Randolph's concern over the growing criticism of Jay's appointment caused him to seize upon the impending vacancy in Paris as a means of silencing the criticism and rewarding Pinckney for his tireless efforts in London. Washington seemingly subscribed to this solution. Yet both men knew the arrangement had only the slightest chance of succeeding, for Jay was assumed to have little interest in a permanent diplomatic assignment.

Jay's reply came almost immediately and, as expected, he declined the appointment.[134] Livingston showed a similar disinclination to accept the French post, which forced Washington to look elsewhere for a replacement.[135] He asked his Cabinet for suggestions and was immediately supplied with the names of men of every political persuasion from all sections of the country.[136] In an unusual display of indifference to these Cabinet recommendations Washington asked Randolph to solicit the views of key Republicans on the appointment of Aaron Burr as a possible successor to Morris.[137] Burr's name had not appeared on the lists supplied by Knox, Hamilton or Randolph. Although Randolph noted a favorable reaction, Washington, for some unknown reason, shifted his position and asked Randolph to offer the post to James Monroe, another choice who had not previously been urged upon the President. Monroe at first declined, believing that his name was being advanced in competition with Burr's. When Randolph assured him that Burr would not be appointed, Monroe agreed to serve.[138] His name was submitted to the Senate on May 27 and he was quickly confirmed.[139] Monroe's instructions were ready by June 10 and were endorsed by the President two days later. Drafted by Randolph, they provided the younger Virginian with sound, practical and specific advice on how to conduct himself in his new assignment. It was one of the most carefully drawn documents to come from Randolph's pen and Washington accepted it without the alteration of a word.[140]

As the year passed the halfway mark Randolph was provided with the first opportunity to take stock of his stewardship in the State Department. Aware that his predecessor had found the office an intolerable burden, and that he himself had had no experience in the field of diplomacy, he had entered the office with few illusions. He knew he had only one qualification for the office—the unswerving confidence of the President. After six months as Secretary of State he could say he still possessed that confidence, and yet he would have to admit that it had not really mattered when it came to the important decisions. Perhaps the fault was Randolph's. He had not been firm in his opinions nor forceful in his opposition to the views of others. As a result he experienced, as Jefferson had, the dubious honor of having others tell him how to run his department. If he showed less annoyance, it was only because he had no strong feelings on the issues under review. It is true Randolph always knew how to handle touchy political issues, such as the request of

Congress for Morris' correspondence. He regretted, though paradoxically in a certain sense he enjoyed, the political maneuvers of Federalists and Republicans in Congress as they used our diplomatic problems to advance their respective political objectives. When it came to the assessment of a domestic crisis, such as the planned attack on Spanish possessions by discontented frontiersmen, Randolph could remain calm amidst the intemperate reactions of others. While others were urging extreme measures, he counseled moderation and the use of the normal processes of law. But in diplomatic matters he lacked a point of view, a theory as to how our diplomacy ought to be conducted. He was alarmed when Great Britain made a mockery of our neutrality, but he could not provide the President with any meaningful advice as to our response. His suggestions dealt with the peripheral aspects of the problem, which allowed others to seize the initiative in matters clearly within the province of his office. Randolph could not be counted on to formulate the government's response to the changing diplomatic climate; he could not rise above the day-to-day problems of diplomacy. He was still Washington's trusted political adviser, but he had not, as yet, met the challenge of his new office.[141]

19

Secretary of State and Aide
July 1794–January 1795

With the close of the congressional session on June 9 and the departure of Washington for Mount Vernon on June 17, the pace of government again slowed.[1] Randolph, who remained in Philadelphia during the President's absence, busied himself with the normal routine of the department. He knew it would be several weeks before Jay's first dispatches arrived, and these would probably contain little more than his initial reaction to the reception he received. In fact the diplomatic scene was so quiet he could not decide whether the country was experiencing a lull between crises or entering upon a more tranquil era of diplomacy.

The lull provided Randolph with an opportunity to repay the many kindnesses of an old associate, Vice President John Adams. Washington had been impressed by several political pieces against Genêt that had been authored by John Quincy Adams, the Vice President's son. Consequently in May he offered young Adams the post of minister to Holland to replace William Short, who had been moved to Madrid.[2] For Randolph, the appointment was a matter of great satisfaction, and he informed the elder Adams of the President's decision with undisguised approval.[3] When the young appointee arrived in Philadelphia in July Randolph went out of his way to assist him. As soon as Washington returned from Mount Vernon he arranged to have John Quincy meet and dine with the President.[4] In the ensuing weeks Randolph showed Adams every courtesy and seems to have allowed him considerable freedom in examining the records of the department. The young Mr. Adams, grateful for the opportunities afforded him by Randolph, chose to familiarize himself with the duties and responsibilities of a diplomatic representative at a foreign post by reading the dispatches his father had written while in Europe.[5] As he was departing Philadelphia, he received his official instructions. Carefully, Randolph explained our position on every subject affecting the relations between the two countries. He displayed the same kind of thoroughness that went into his letter to Monroe. But there was more here—practical advice on the content and frequency of his reports, the friendly suggestion that it is always prudent to record important conversations as soon as they are completed and the admonition not to depend on verbal communications when the matter can be handled through formal written correspondence.[6] If the young Adams, formerly a secretary to two American ministers in Europe, found Randolph's advice rather elementary, he never betrayed his feelings. Pleased by the President's confidence in him and grateful for the courtesies extended by the Secretary of State, he sought only the opportunity to prove that this confidence and friendship had not been misplaced.

Aside from acting as mentor to John Quincy, Randolph had little to do. He informed the other members of the Cabinet of the receipt of a Convention of Armed Neutrality between Denmark and Sweden that had been signed on March 27, 1794. Would it not be expedient, he asked his associates, for the President to formally empower someone in Europe with the authority to form an alliance with these nations? Mr. Jay, he continued, would be allowed to have the final decision as to whether such an alliance would serve or hurt his negotiations.[7] Their replies were in Randolph's hands by the time Washington returned to Philadelphia. Knox and Hamilton were firmly against the proposal, while Bradford gave a more hesitant negative.[8] Randolph presented their written opinions along with his own forceful rejoinder to Washington upon his return.[9] Involving little more than the formal designation of a specific diplomatic agent to undertake discussions on a subject that had already been conditionally provided for in Jay's instructions, it seemed a rather modest proposal. That it was similar to Randolph's earlier expressed conviction that Jay could not hope to secure a favorable settlement of our differences without adequate diplomatic weapons could not have escaped Washington's attention. But Randolph again found his council rejected as Washington chose to leave the matter in Jay's hands, at least for the present.[10] Moreover, the issue was soon overshadowed by a domestic crisis, an internal threat from the frontier settlements of Pennsylvania that many judged more serious than England's abuse of our neutrality.

Since the passage in 1791 of the excise tax on distilled spirits the West had displayed a growing hostility toward the central government. Washington had shown increasing concern with the reports of general unrest and mounting opposition to these laws in the several settlements along the Allegheny Mountains. A proclamation in the fall of 1792 had served to mellow, at least temporarily, the mood of the obstreperous westerners, ever distrustful of governmental control. But an exhortation to law and order did not long restrain the independent-minded frontiersmen from asserting their dissatisfaction with the central government. They compiled with remarkable ease a long list of grievances, acts of omission and commission for which the new government in Philadelphia must bear full responsibility. Nature and the national government had seemingly conspired to make their lot a difficult one, and they were prepared to fight both, undaunted by the odds against them. Perhaps because of the large number of small stills in the area, perhaps because of the belligerent mood of the people, perhaps by sheer coincidence, it was the counties of western Pennsylvania that showed the strongest opposition to the excise on whiskey. Resentment and protest in this area gradually gave way to isolated instances of violence and predictions of more sustained opposition. By the end of July reports reaching Philadelphia left little doubt that the matter deserved the full attention of the government.[11]

On August 2 Washington summoned his Cabinet and requested Governor Mifflin of Pennsylvania to attend the meeting. The session, which was also attended by Chief Justice Thomas McKean, Secretary Alexander James Dallas and Attorney General Jared Ingersoll of the state government, resulted in a request that the members of the Cabinet and the governor submit written opinions on the policy that the government should pursue in view of the evidence that considerable armed opposition to the law existed in four counties of western Pennsylvania.[12] Before these opinions had reached Washington's desk, Associate Justice James Wilson had been asked by the Attorney General to render an opinion as to whether the evidence of opposition in this area was such as to permit the enforcement of the law through the normal judicial processes. Wilson rendered an opinion on August 4 that the resistance in the counties of Washington and Allegheny in Pennsylvania rendered such enforcement impossible.[13]

Up to the time of the Cabinet meeting on August 2 the Secretary of State seems to have had little interest in the problem. His letters to our ministers in the various capitals of Europe made no reference to the growing reports of unrest in western Pennsylvania. If anything, the grievances of settlers on the southwestern frontier and in Kentucky were a source of greater concern to him since their displeasure indirectly reflected on his own department. But the intelligence from western Pennsylvania could not be ignored, and Randolph responded to the President's directive for a written opinion with unusual care and thoroughness. His reply, ten pages of closely written script, was not drafted until August 5, after the opinion of Associate Justice Wilson had been delivered to the President.[14]

The disturbance, Randolph readily admitted, was serious, and the decision to seek an opinion from Judge Wilson a prudent one, but, he continued, the certificate the Justice had issued was of doubtful validity.

Edmund Randolph. This is a copy by F. J.
Fisher of an original portrait now lost. It hangs
in the State Capitol, Richmond, Virginia. (*Virginia State Library*)

William Randolph of Tur-
key Island, ER's great-grand-
father. (*The Virginia Historical Society*)

Mary Isham Randolph,
ER's great-grandmother. (*The
Virginia Historical Society*)

Sir John Randolph, ER's grandfather. *(The Virginia Historical Society)*

Lady Susanna Beverly Randolph, ER's grandmother. *(Cook Collection, Valentine Museum, Richmond, Virginia)*

Peyton Randolph, ER's uncle. *(The Virginia Historical Society)*

Elizabeth Harrison Randolph, ER's aunt. *(The Virginia Historical Society)*

Meriwether Smith. Portrait by G. Persico, after a drawing by Edward B. Smith. (*The Virginia Historical Society*)

Richard Henry Lee. Engraving by P. Maverick and J. B. Longacre. (*Library of Congress*)

Thomas Nelson, Jr. Engraving by Ole Erikson. (*Library of Congress*)

George Mason. (*Library of Congress*)

VIRGINIA'S REVOLUTIONARY LEADERS

Edmund Pendleton. *(The Virginia Historical Society)*

Patrick Henry. Engraving by Edward Willmore, after a painting by J. B. Longacre. *(Colonial Williamsburg Foundation)*

Benjamin Harrison Jr., by Charles Willson Peale. *(National Portrait Gallery, Smithsonian Institution)*

RANDOLPH'S CONTEMPORARIES IN
VIRGINIA POLITICS

Henry Lee, "Light Horse Harry," by Charles Willson Peale. *(Library of Congress)*

James Monroe. *(Colonial Williamsburg Foundation)*

James Madison. *(Colonial Williamsburg Foundation)*

Charles Lee. *(Virginia State Library)*

RANDOLPH'S CONTEMPORARIES IN THE LEGAL PROFESSION

John Marshall. *(Virginia State Library)*

John Wickham. *(Virginia State Library)*

St. George Tucker. *(The Virginia Historical Society)*

President George Washington, by Gilbert Stuart. *(Colonial Williamsburg Foundation)*

Vice-President John Adams, by John Singleton Copley. *(Harvard University Portrait Collection)*

WASHINGTON'S CABINET MEMBERS DURING ER'S
YEARS IN THE GOVERNMENT

Thomas Jefferson, Washington's first Secretary of State. Portrait by Gilbert Stuart. *(The Virginia Historical Society)*

Alexander Hamilton, Washington's first Secretary of the Treasury. Portrait by John Trumbull. *(Yale University Art Gallery)*

WASHINGTON'S CABINET MEMBERS DURING ER'S
YEARS IN THE GOVERNMENT

Edmund Randolph, Washington's first Attorney General and second Secretary of State. Portrait by C. Brumidi. *(Library of Congress)*

Henry Knox, Washington's first Secretary of War. *(The Virginia Historical Society)*

WASHINGTON'S CABINET MEMBERS DURING ER'S
YEARS IN THE GOVERNMENT

Oliver Wolcott, Jr., Washington's second Secretary of the Treasury. Portrait by Ralph Earl. *(Connecticut State Library)*

Timothy Pickering, Washington's second Secretary of War and third Secretary of State. Portrait by William Veckett after Gilbert Stuart's. *(Library of Congress)*

William Bradford, Washington's second Attorney General. Engraving by C. J. B. Fevret de St. Memin. *(Corcoran Gallery of Art)*

Peyton Randolph, ER's son. This portrait hangs in the Virginia State Capitol. *(Dementi Studio)*

John Jay. *(Library of Congress)*

Tazewell Hall, the Randolph home in Williamsburg, now restored in Newport News, Virginia. *(Jim Livengood)*

The Great Hall in Tazewell Hall. *(Jim Livengood)*

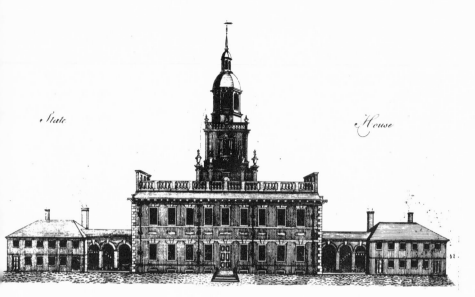

Pennsylvania State House (Independence Hall), where the Continental Congress met. Insert from a map of Philadelphia drawn by John Reed and printed in 1774. (*American Philosophical Society, Philadelphia*)

The northeast corner of Tenth and Capitol Streets in Richmond. The First Presbyterian Church is on the left and Edmund Randolph's house is on the right. The present State Capitol of Virginia stands across the street from this site. (*Valentine Museum, Richmond, Virginia*)

Edmund Randolph's letter of resignation from Washington's Cabinet. *(Library of Congress)*

A lithograph of Richmond in 1796, by Benjamin Henry Latrobe, architect of the Capitol in Washington. *(The Virginia Historical Society)*

The only known early oil painting of Richmond during Randolph's lifetime, by A. C. Pleasants. *(The Virginia Historical Society)*

Old Chapel and Graveyard at Millwood, Virginia, where Edmund Randolph is buried. *(Virginia State Library)*

Capitol of Virginia between 1780–1788. It was located on the northwest corner of Fourteenth and Cary Streets in Richmond. *(The Virginia Historical Society)*

THE OLD CAPITOL,

It involved an *a priori* judgment that the marshal was incompetent to suppress the combination and, even more serious, failed to specify the law that had been violated. He had spoken to Judge Wilson of these deficiencies, he continued, but had not been able to influence his opinion. Therefore, assuming its validity, he recommended that the President not resort to the use of the militia to suppress the disturbance until every other means of enforcing the law had been exhausted. The use of force, he argued, might serve to unite the discontented elements in the country, alienate the West to the advantage of Great Britain and place undue financial strain upon the country. More serious was the question of using the militia from one state to suppress armed opposition to the law by the citizens of another; Randolph had grave doubts that it could be accomplished without arousing the antagonism of the state's own militia. It was, in short, a situation fraught with great danger. Furthermore, the counsel of those who continually urged the use of force would, if followed, only serve to alienate the people from their government. The strength of a government is in the affection it elicits from the people, not in its ability to force obedience to its laws through military coercion. He therefore recommended: the issuance of a proclamation, the sending of commissioners to the disturbed area to effect a reconciliation, the prosecution of offenders "according to the law" if the commissioners should fail in their efforts. Finally, "if the judiciary authority is, after this, withstood, let the militia be called out."[15]

Randolph's opinion, aside from its forceful rejection of the proposition that a government acquires respect through the use of force against those who violate its laws, was consistent with the views he had expressed on several previous occasions when similar instances of opposition to the law had provoked a debate among the President's advisers. Until the judicial arm of the government was rendered helpless, Randolph would not consent to the use of force to secure obedience to the law. If representatives of the Treasury Department were unable to collect the excise, they must first seek a remedy in the courts, and only when the courts themselves had been defied could the government order the militia into the area. Randolph was on sure ground and he knew it. He knew, too, that his views would not be popular with his colleagues and that at the Cabinet meeting scheduled for the next day he would probably find himself in the minority.

When the Cabinet assembled, it had before it two written opinions of the Secretary of the Treasury, the opinion of Knox, based on the most recent intelligence from the Allegheny area, a strongly worded opinion of the Attorney General and the views of Governor Thomas Mifflin of Pennsylvania. Hamilton and Knox urged the immediate use of force, while Bradford urged the sending of a posse into the area. Only Randolph and Governor Mifflin expressed opposition to the immediate use of force, and the opinion of the latter official was far from convincing.[16]

The issue confronting the Cabinet had been somewhat complicated by Washington's decision to send commissioners into the area to effect, if possible, a reconciliation. Although the commissioners had not as yet been dispatched, they apparently had been selected, and Randolph had been assigned the task of drafting their instructions.[17] That these moves strangely coincided with Randolph's suggestions, and that he was actually involved in implementing them before submitting his Cabinet opinion, could not have escaped the attention of the other members of the Cabinet.[18] Since the President obviously intended to seek a peaceful solution to the problem before resorting to force, the only issue that remained was when and from where the militia ought to be assembled. Randolph, anticipating in his formal written opinion that much of the discussion would turn on this issue, urged that the militia not be called until the commissioners had been given an opportunity to effect a reconciliation.[19] On this point Hamilton and Knox had the better of the argument, and it was decided that recruitment should begin immediately. Significantly no marching orders were transmitted to the four states from which the force was to be recruited.[20] The decision to issue a proclamation, a necessary legal prerequisite to the use of the militia, was also agreed upon at this meeting. Its language was probably not to Randolph's liking, but the President probably had been impressed by Hamilton's arguments and the views of the Secretary of the Treasury prevailed.[21]

The separate decisions of the President and the Cabinet were implemented swiftly. Coinciding with the publication of the President's proclamation, Randolph's instructions to the three federal commissioners were transmitted on the 7th.[22] The latter document was conciliatory but firm; the former, drafted by Hamilton, reflected the government's determination to use force if resistance to the law continued beyond a specified date. The following day Randolph received a letter from Attorney General Bradford, who was one of the three federal commissioners. Bradford had been notified of his appointment the previous day and had left Philadelphia immediately, only to encounter en route Colonel John Neville and Major David Lenox, federal inspector and U.S. Marshal, respectively, who had fled the area of the disturbance and were making their way to Philadelphia to report on the insurrection. Their account as reported by Bradford was the first reliable intelligence the government had received since July. It placed the disturbance in an entirely different light, for it noted the extremists in the disaffected counties were not in full control of the situation. Thus there was a good chance that the federal commissioners would be accorded an opportunity to effect a reconciliation.[23] The significance of Bradford's letter was not lost on Randolph, and he immediately forwarded it to the President in Germantown and had copies sent to the two other Secretaries.[24] Washington, responding to this favorable intelligence, instructed Randolph to contact Inspector Neville and Major Lenox as soon as they reached the city. The Secretary of State was to bring them before the other members of the Cabinet in order that they might give a detailed description of the situation:

> . . . that all of you being thoroughly possessed of the facts, and digesting them well, may be ready to meet me at my house in the city tomorrow morning [August 9], with your opinions on the propriety of changing any measures already resolved on, or for adding others thereto, according to the information which shall be received from them.[25]

The meeting produced no substantial change in the government's policy, the President apparently preferring to await the first reports from the commissioners after they had reached Pittsburgh.[26]

In the meantime Hamilton sought the President's permission to publish his Cabinet opinion of August 5 in order that the government's position might be clearly set before the public.[27] Washington, realizing that the paper reflected a political bias, sent it to Randolph with a request that he review the statement and note the passages that might cause embarrassment to the government.[28] The Secretary of State replied the same day, citing numerous instances where Hamilton's Cabinet opinion might needlessly leave the government open to criticism.[29] But the opinion was published and four days later came the inevitable letter of complaint. Governor Mifflin of Pennsylvania asked Washington to explain a reference in Hamilton's opinion to the uncooperative attitude of state officials toward the enforcement of federal laws in western Pennsylvania.[30] The letter was sent to Hamilton, who replied on September 2.[31] Randolph, on instructions from the President, merely attached a covering note to Hamilton's letter and sent it to Mifflin.[32]

The center of action had by this time shifted to Pittsburgh and such unknown frontier communities as Parkinson's Ferry and Brownsville. In Pittsburgh the federal commissioners had several meetings with a conference committee composed of three men from each of the four disaffected counties.[33] In response to Randolph's careful instructions the commissioners kept the government fully informed of their activities, and the Secretary of State, who received their reports, responded as soon as Washington, Hamilton and he himself had reviewed the latest dispatches. These letters brought by post or special express riders from Pittsburgh took precedence over all diplomatic correspondence during these anxious weeks.[34] On August 23 Washington had learned that the commissioners had little hope of effecting a peaceful settlement. After an eight-hour meeting with Hamilton and Randolph he issued the orders that he had so wished to avoid, the command to assemble the militia.[35] Randolph transmitted this decision to the commissioners, along with the President's instructions that they remain in the "insurgent country" as long *"as may in your opinion promise any public utility and be consistent with your personal safety."*[36] Later dispatches only served to reinforce the commissioners' earlier report, as they found their proposals rejected by a committee of safety representing the insurgents.[37] As these details reached Philadelphia, preparations for assembling and supplying the militia began in earnest.[38] On September 24 Washington issued his final proclamation against the insurgents.[39] He would join Hamilton and assume direct command of the troops, at least until he knew more of the temper and intent of the insurrectionists.[40]

As the President's carriage moved westward, his presence was like a magnet to the marching militia. Randolph now became his faithful correspondent in Philadelphia. From past experience he knew of Washington's apprehensiveness over public matters when away from the seat of government. Arrangements were made for a daily express to and from the President in order that he might maintain the closest possible contact with Randolph and Knox, who had remained behind.[41] The Secretary of State assumed responsibility for all foreign and domestic news, while Knox, who had just returned to the city, handled the complicated task of supplying the army.[42] Nothing escaped Randolph's attention. Every bit of intelligence from Europe, every rumor of approval or disapproval of the President's military response to the insurrection, were reported in detail.[43] Mrs. Washington became accustomed to almost daily visits from the Secretary of State and the slightest "indisposition" in her health was immediately reported.[44] Lest Washington become alarmed for his family over a rumor that yellow fever had returned to the city, Randolph wrote: "There is nothing so little talked of as the yellow fever. I believe that I am almost the only inquirer after it; and those, to whom I address myself, seem to take time to recollect themselves, as if the subject were a perfect stranger to their memory."[45] Daily the reports flowed from Randolph's pen: Fauchet was avoiding him,[46] the new Portuguese minister had asked to meet Mrs. Washington and Randolph had agreed provided the minister was introduced as "Mr." Freire pending the formal receipt of his credentials,[47] and Wilson Cary Nicholas reported in a letter just received that Albemarle County disapproved of the insurrection.[48] Nothing seemed to escape Randolph's attention and his long association with the President made him keenly aware of the subjects about which Washington would want to receive information.

In return Washington kept Randolph informed of his progress and of his activities as he inspected the various units and conferred with the officers who would assume command of the army if he decided against accompanying it into the area of the disturbance.[49] Although the emissaries reaching the advancing army gave every evidence that the mood of the people had changed, Washington refused to countermand his marching orders.[50] Those who had seen fit to flout the law once would do it again if the government failed to display its strength and arrest the leaders of the insurrection. In all likelihood Randolph would have preferred a less militant policy, but he did not presume to offer his advice.

Washington, as Randolph had expected, was as concerned about his presidential responsibilities as he was about the insurrection. He asked Randolph to digest the several subjects that he felt should be included in the President's annual message to Congress and, after showing his "Memorandums" to General Knox, to forward them to him, "that if they are to go (from the Army) to Congress, I may have the whole in my possession, to consider, arrange, and forward with as little trouble and loss of time as may be."[51] Randolph immediately acknowledged the President's request,[52] and five days later, after consulting with Knox, transmitted his "notes." "My object has been merely to give the summary idea, without contemplating precise language in any respect. As soon as you shall have signified your sense upon the matter, the form and dress can be easily thrown over it."[53] Randolph's prompt compliance with Washington's command was but another indication of his desire to lessen the President's concern over being absent from the seat of government. That Randolph had correctly interpreted the President's mood was confirmed as subsequent letters from the Chief Executive apprehensively repeated the same request over and over again.[54] The impatient Washington seemed unmindful of the fact that distance made instant compliance impossible. But Randolph understood and in reply informed the obviously weary President that he would draft the address if Washington would indicate the subjects he wished included.[55] He had, after all, performed this task before and at times when the burdens of the presidency were far less exhausting than they were at present.

Washington's return to Philadelphia from western Pennsylvania on October 28 meant the resumption of the frequent personal contacts between the President and his advisers. It lessened Randolph's duties considerably, for now he had only to concern himself with the affairs of his own department and these were relatively calm. Dispatches from Jay had been arriving for several weeks, but the most recent was two months in crossing the Atlantic. Randolph read it with some misgivings, and could only speculate on the current status of the negotiations.[56] The situation in Paris was equally unpredictable. Monroe's diplomatic character remained untested and the most recent reports from France indicated that the government had experienced a new political upheaval.[57] Monroe's first dispatches would provide the answers to many questions.[58]

Of more immediate concern to Randolph was the inability of our ministers in Madrid to negotiate our outstanding differences with Spain. For years Spain had vacillated between negotiable and hostile demands. In our relentless search for a peaceful solution to the differences between the two countries we pursued Spanish officials first in New York, then in Philadelphia, and now finally in Madrid. The problem was rendered more difficult by the impatience of the frontier settlements with the ways of diplomacy. Whether it be the Spanish-inspired hostility of the Creeks in West Florida or the denial of our right to navigate the Mississippi or a boundary question that deprived the settlers of their claims, the frontiersmen believed there were more effective and more direct ways of resolving these problems than endless negotiations. And for those who saw evidence of indifference in the methods of the American government, there was always the alternative of independent negotiations with the Spanish officials at New Orleans. Only a few months had passed since the Genêt-inspired project for attacking Florida and Louisiana had been thwarted by the determined opposition of the federal government. Now a new wave of unrest swept the Kentucky frontier.[59]

The first moves of the Administration to resolve the problem were taken during July and August when the Pennsylvania disturbance was absorbing most of the attention of Washington and his advisers.[60] While this latter problem was being considered by the Cabinet, Washington and Randolph attempted to formulate a response to the Spanish problem and the growing displeasure of Kentuckians with their government.

To Randolph went the task of persuading Jefferson, an acknowledged friend of the Kentuckians, to undertake a special mission to Spain. The letter went out on August 28, couched in the most persuasive language Randolph could muster. He expressed respect for Jefferson's wish for retirement, but pleaded the seriousness of the reports from Kentucky, the "absolute stagnation" in our negotiations with Spain and the recent demand that a more distinguished representative be sent to Madrid with powers greater than those presently held by Short.[61] By an earlier letter James Innes of Virginia had been asked to undertake a special mission to Kentucky to convey the concern of the President and to explain the steps that would be taken to secure our rights of navigation on the

Mississippi.[62] Firmness might be the appropriate policy in western Pennsylvania, but only diplomacy and this formal display of executive concern could be employed in this particular crisis. Washington and Randolph knew only too well that cooperation between the discontented element in Pennsylvania and Kentucky might well lead to the loss of our western domain and a corresponding increase of Spanish influence on the North American continent. The stakes were high, but to Randolph the Administration's procedure was sound and to his liking. He would rather pacify than intimidate in Kentucky, and negotiate than antagonize in Madrid—for it was in persuasion that he excelled.

Jefferson's reply came in the next express. It was a firm no; he was fixed in his determination not to reenter public life.[63] Washington and Randolph, anticipating just such an answer, had taken the liberty of addressing a similar letter to Patrick Henry,[64] to be posted by Jefferson if he declined the appointment. (This was a common practice to avoid needless delay in urgent matters.) It proved equally unsuccessful. Henry's friendship for Washington had cooled perceptibly during the last few years, and the fiery patriot declined the post.[65] At the same time the Innes mission was being delayed by ill health and Innes' mistaken belief that he would have to resign as attorney general of Virginia if he accepted the appointment.[66] Both difficulties were ultimately resolved, though valuable weeks were lost in the process. Then, when Innes reached Philadelphia, he was unable to dine with the President on the appointed day because, according to Randolph, he did not have a pair of shoes.[67] Just about everything, it seemed, was conspiring to prevent a resolution of the Spanish problem.

The President probably did not learn of Henry's refusal until October, following his return to Philadelphia from western Pennsylvania. Since further delay was intolerable, he instructed Randolph on November 3 to alert Thomas Pinckney to "hold himself in readiness" to leave London for a temporary assignment as envoy extraordinary to Madrid.[68] His name was submitted to the Senate on November 21 and his letter of credence was signed seven days later.[69] In the meantime Innes had been sent to Lexington with detailed instructions from Randolph.[70] It was hoped that neither mission would suffer from delay, although the latest dispatches from Madrid indicated "a new symptom of unfriendliness."[71] Time would test the usefulness of both missions, but Randolph, knowing from long experience in public office that diplomacy, whether practiced at home or abroad, required infinite patience, was prepared to wait.

Washington's opening address to Congress was delayed until November 19 because of the failure of the Senate to collect a quorum. Washington and Randolph welcomed the delay and used the additional two weeks to carefully review those paragraphs of the annual message that dealt with the insurrection in western Pennsylvania.[72] Of particular concern was the extent to which the "democratic societies" should be declared accountable for the unrest. Randolph was the first to suggest to Washington that he seize the present opportunity to denounce their activities: "They may now, I believe, be crushed. The prospect ought not to be lost."[73] Since Washington had always trusted the political instincts of his Secretary of State and had in fact been waiting a long time for the opportunity to denounce these societies in unmistakable terms, he unhesitatingly accepted Randolph's advice.[74] While the message was being put into final form, Randolph notified the President in a private memorandum that he would defend the speech in the press against the expected wave of criticism. He added:

> I hold the present to be in some degree a new era in our government, and that if the measures, which you will impart to Congress be properly supported against misrepresentation, you will establish perfect tranquility to the government and . . . your administration will be found to have passed thro' a trying crisis with dignity.[75]

The substance of the message was well received[76] but, as Randolph had predicted, the direct attack on the democratic societies aroused old animosities. The formal reply of the House to the President's message reflected its opposition to his words of denunciation,[77] while the Republican press readily opened its columns to other critics of the President's speech. The Administration's reply came, as promised, from the pen of Randolph. Under the pseudonym "Germanicus" the Secretary of State sought to explain why the President attributed the insurrection to democratic societies. The charges against the societies, Randolph argued, are "genuine inferences from the facts," and on these particular charges the President did not expect the sanction of Congress.[78] Randolph's effort, consisting of thirteen short essays appearing first in a Philadelphia newspaper and then given wider circulation in pamphlet form, did little to silence the President's critics. His language was almost apologetic; he clothed his essay in a super-patriotic vagueness that precluded a crusading defense of the President's position.[79] Perhaps he was afraid of being labeled a Federalist, but he really had nothing to fear. The Federalists thought his defense a "d—d bad one" and took up the cause themselves.[80]

The new session was not accompanied by the usual flurry of governmental activity. The President's message contained little of importance beyond his account of the Whiskey Insurrection, and that would have been readily accepted if the President had not inserted a criticism of the democratic societies. But even this resentment died quickly and Congress settled back, willing to wait for a more controversial subject on which to sharpen its collective skills in political debate. "There is scarcely animation enough in either house to excite attention," John Adams reported to his wife Abigail. "One may sleep in the midst of debate." He added quickly: "I have not yet tried. . . ."[81] Meanwhile the President and Randolph waited impatiently for Jay's latest dispatches. In all likelihood a treaty had been agreed upon, and yet not one word as to its contents had been received from Jay.[82] Private correspondence from England carried accounts of the "reported" provisions, but these only served to heighten the mystery surrounding the wording of the final document.[83] The President hoped the official text would reach him before Congress adjourned so that he could avoid calling a special session.

Early in December Randolph dispatched a sharp rebuke to Monroe for his failure to observe a proper diplomatic restraint in his dealings with the French government.[84] But most of his other correspondence with our ministers and consuls abroad was routine. He summarized the activities of Congress, but there was really little to report. Short was again informed of Pinckney's appointment and his cooperation solicited.[85] Monroe was asked to look after the son of Senator Ralph Izard, who was going to Paris to study engineering,[86] and Jay was provided with a detailed critique of Grenville's peace proposals of August 30. The last letter, sent under date of December 15, reflected Randolph's deep concern with the course Jay's discussions were taking and his own uncertainty as to how to advise him on specific points at this stage in the negotiations.[87] But most of his duties were routine and Randolph, like Adams, might well have used the occasion to relax a bit after several months of close attention to affairs of state.

The most interesting political news to stir the quiet of these winter months was the announcement of the intended resignation of both Hamilton and Knox. The two Secretaries had informed Washington of their determination to resign shortly after he returned from western Pennsylvania, and Knox submitted his formal resignation on December 28.[88] Although Hamilton's resignation was not to take effect until January 31,[89] within the space of a month the President was deprived of the services of two close friends and trusted aids. Hamilton, of course, could not be replaced; the most that could be hoped was that his successor, Oliver Wolcott, would faithfully carry forward the programs already underway. Being less critical, Knox's office was easier to fill. His successor, Timothy Pickering, was not an old and intimate friend of Washington's, as Knox had been, but Pickering had served the country with distinction during the Revolution and the President had great respect for his administrative abilities. One by one each of the men who had been the President's first choices to assist him in launching the new government had left his side. While insisting on his continued service in office, they had themselves refused to remain in his Cabinet. If Washington was annoyed by this double standard of public service, he didn't show it. But he did not hide the fact that he considered these resignations a great loss.[90] Hamilton's counsel, in particular, seemed absolutely essential on the eve of the apparent settlement of our differences with England.

Randolph, the only remaining member of the original Cabinet, probably held both Hamilton and Knox in high esteem for their determined support of the central government, although he frequently disagreed with the methods they advocated to ensure its survival. It is impossible to say whether he viewed their departure with regret or pleasure for he never revealed his attitude toward them to Washington or anyone else. But Randolph's political instincts were too well developed for him to miss the significance of their resignations. He was now the senior Cabinet officer in fact as well as in name. In length of service in public office, in experience in national affairs, in loyalty to Washington, in political acumen, he was now first. The departure of Hamilton, a man whose talents in each of these areas surpassed his own, had made possible his primacy.

The resignations of Jefferson and Hamilton had stripped the Cabinet of two men of exceptional talent who were also the unchallenged architects of very distinctive political creeds. Washington, Randolph, Knox and whoever else came into contact with their seminal minds found themselves more often than not reacting to their views rather than formulating positions of their own. Randolph respected their abilities, while disagreeing with the partisanship that frequently warped their judgments. Out of the rivalry between these two men he had fashioned a particular responsibility for himself, that of the architect of the middle position. He had played the role well—at times even brilliantly—and almost always to the satisfaction of the President.

But now all this was changing. No longer did the President or Congress look to the Cabinet for a brilliant crystallization of the issues. Except for Randolph, the terms in which the new Cabinet was most frequently described attested to the soundness of the Federalism of its members rather than their genius. The role Randolph had assumed, and upon which the President had come to depend, had gradually lost its meaning for now, with Jefferson and Hamilton in retirement, a wholly new climate prevailed. Those who had replaced them had neither the following nor the inclination to fashion a new policy around a President whose attitudes were already fixed by six years of executive responsibility. Randolph was still an old friend, a faithful and trusted aide, a cautious Secretary of State and an unblushing admirer of a tiring President; but his principal role, that of a political pacifier, had lost its meaning. Randolph did not know it, but he had in fact outlived his usefulness to the President. His genius for identifying the middle position literally required the presence of Jefferson and Hamilton, the undisputed architects of two very different political creeds, in the Cabinet. And these days had passed forever.

20

Coordinator of a Dubious Treaty
September 1794–July 1795

When Randolph and Jay parted company at Elizabethtown, New Jersey, in May of 1794 both men undoubtedly expressed the hope that the results of Jay's mission would be favorable to the United States. Whatever misgivings Randolph may have had as to the wisdom of these negotiations, he was prepared to set them aside until Jay had tested the mood of the English government. If, of necessity, he turned his attention to other matters, he did not forget Jay or the difficult task in which he was engaged. Every scrap of intelligence that might assist him in his negotiations, copies of documents authenticating our spoliation claims and his complete correspondence with Hammond were sent by the first available vessel. His letters, couched in the matter-of-fact style of official diplomatic correspondence, gave no hint of his personal opinion. Jay could not have been other than pleased with the manner in which Randolph supported his mission.

For his part Randolph had little reason to question the sincerity or openness of Jay's correspondence. During the early weeks of negotiations it reflected the same guarded optimism that Randolph knew was being expressed privately in letters to Washington.[1] Randolph recognized that Jay, like Short or Monroe or any other diplomat, would display a frankness in his private correspondence that he would never reveal in official dispatches. And, like the others, Jay was probably most candid when he was writing to his closest political allies.[2] Randolph was no stranger to these practices, and he would not have expected Jay to act otherwise. He chafed at the length of time it took for Jay's dispatches to reach him, but he knew nothing could be done to remedy that situation. Long before Jay had departed for England, Randolph had learned that above all else a Secretary of State needs patience. It was a virtue he cultivated reluctantly.

Jay's first dispatches did not reach Randolph until mid-August; a few more were received in September and seven arrived in October, the last of which was dated August 23.[3] It was evident that nothing of substance had yet been agreed upon but that Jay remained, with justification, hopefully optimistic.[4] Randolph, in return, continued to send Jay all manner of intelligence that would aid him in his discussions with Grenville.[5] There is little evidence that he personally shared Jay's favorable interpretation of the climate in which the negotiations were taking place, but he never said so.[6] Publicly he was willing to foster a spirit of guarded optimism as to the eventual outcome of the negotiations.[7] He seemed particularly anxious to inform those who had something to gain from a favorable treaty of Jay's hopeful atittude. While the President was in western Pennsylvania he informed Jay:

> The impatience of the people is as great as you apprehend, and I am therefore more communicative than perhaps I should be on any other occasion. For I have in an unauthoritative way published the substance of some portion of your intelligence. You will find it in Fenno's papers of the 22d. September and 8th instant. But I persuade myself that nothing has been indiscreetly divulged.[8]

Later in the same letter he referred to the publication of additional information he had just received from Jay: "I feel the propriety of sending them into public so fully that I will venture to presume upon the President's approbation."[9] Officially, Randolph did whatever he could to assist Jay in his negotiations. Unofficially, he sought to create a favorable attitude among those who had a vital interest in the outcome of Jay's mission. But privately he was skeptical.

On November 11 Randolph received from the hand of Robert Morris, Jr., Jay's dispatch No. 15. Dated September 13, it contained the first detailed account of the negotiations, including Grenville's preliminary draft of the treaty and Jay's observations thereon.[10] As he read Jay's letter and copies of the documents enclosed with the letter, Randolph's concern mounted. There were several instances where Jay appeared to have compromised the American position or allowed vague language to cloak a complete surrender to Grenville. Examples included the date for the surrender of the northwest post, which, Randolph decided, must have been an error in copying by Jay's secretary, and Grenville's contrived explanation for the carrying off of several thousand slaves by British troops after the war that was so novel it had to be studied further. Furthermore, one of Grenville's propositions was little more than an attempt to secure our submission to the odious Order in Council of June 8, 1793.[11] Randolph immediately took the dispatch and draft treaty to Washington. Jay's pouch also contained a private letter to the President; perhaps this letter would provide some explanation for his ready acquiescence to Grenville's position on so many issues. The President undoubtedly showed

Randolph the private letter Jay had addressed to him. If anything, it gave a more serious complexion to the negotiations, for Jay implied an agreement was near at hand. "Although it is uncertain, yet it is not altogether improbable that Lord Grenville and myself may agree on terms which, in my opinion, should not be rejected," he informed Washington.[12] Nothing had yet been agreed upon and undoubtedly many long and hard negotiating sessions had taken place since the date of this dispatch, but a treaty concluded along these lines was unthinkable.

Randolph's reply went off the next day: "Although the immediate departure of the *William Penn* leaves too short a time for a copious reply . . . I must . . . trouble you with a few remarks on those points which attract notice on the first view." Item by item he noted his objections: the terms "irregular" and "illegal" were insufficient in the section referring to compensation for the seizure of our vessels, the reference to exceptions to prior treaties might well be given a different meaning at some future time, the right of British subjects to trade with the Indians within our borders might well produce great embarrassments.[13] The observations were brief and hurried but the meaning was unmistakably clear—Randolph was displeased with Jay's handling of the negotiations. If Randolph's dispatch reached London before the negotiations had been concluded, it would undoubtedly delay any final agreement, for Jay would have to assume that Randolph's letter had crossed the desk of the President before being placed aboard the *William Penn*.[14]

As Randolph pondered Jay's dispatch and investigated the possible consequences of some of its propositions, he sought out a responsible person in whose care he could place a long and confidential dispatch to Jay.[15] No one could be found until the middle of December and by then two additional dispatches had been received from London. Dated September 18 and October 2, they contained little more than the disturbing observation that a settlement was probably only weeks away.[16] Randolph could only hope that his letter of November 12 would reach London before Jay signed a treaty.

Dated December 15, Randolph's long dispatch opened with the observation that he wrote subject to correction by the President and that he would "run through in a summary way, some parts of your interesting communication." He further prefaced his remarks by noting that distance and lapse of time weakened the value of his observations. They must, he warned Jay, be viewed as remarks which should be, "cautiously applied to a state of things which is not precisely the same with that which gave rise to them." As to which party first violated the treaty of peace, it would seem to be of little consequence unless it affected our claims and complaints. "But really, Sir," he observed, "the force of Lord Grenville's reasoning appears to fall very short of its object." Grenville's position with regard to the removal of the slaves from the South was equally untenable and involved a novel interpretation of the language of the treaty. "You must," he continued, "be too sensible of the anxiety of many parts of the United States, to pass it over unnoticed." The date proposed for the British surrender of the northwest posts was indeed a year later than that specified in the instructions and not a clerical error, as was first assumed. "Further reflection," Randolph added, "has not diminished (but on the contrary has increased the repugnance of the President to this extension of time)." There followed several short paragraphs either approving Jay's conduct or gently cautioning him of the dangers inherent in some of Grenville's proposals. The latter part of the letter was a review, article by article, of the Foreign Secretary's commercial propositions. Randolph found them deficient in several respects but particularly in the kinds of reciprocal concessions being offered to American vessels in British ports. In closing he observed: "It is a great satisfaction, however, to believe, that most of these remarks have occurred to yourself; and that the interest of the United States is well reposed in your discernment, talents and zeal." But the detailed criticism told a different story, and the passing weeks had only served to heighten the displeasure and dissatisfaction with which he viewed Jay's conduct.[17]

In the weeks that followed, additional dispatches reached Philadelphia bearing further evidence that the ministers were drawing closer to a final agreement. Randolph noted their dates with considerable concern. That of November 5 opened with the ominous statement: "It has now become almost certain that the draught of the treaty will soon be perfected. . . ."[18] It was obvious that the letter Randolph had sent on November 12 could not possibly reach London in time to alert Jay to the unfavorable impression made by his first detailed account of the negotiations. In effect Jay had permitted the discussions to proceed at such a pace during September and October as to render meaningless all supplementary instructions or advice from his government.[19] By the last week of December, Randolph realized how futile had been his efforts. He now had no alternative but to assume that a treaty had been agreed upon and was already on its way to our shores. His letters to Jay ceased, for there was no further reason to discuss the contents of the treaty.[20] There was now only one dispatch that interested him—that which contained the treaty.

In the meantime Knox and Hamilton had resigned and their successors had been nominated by the President and approved by Congress. The congressional session handled routine matters, moving monotonously toward its closing date. The legislators seemed unwilling to exert themselves on anything less than an Anglo-American treaty.[21] But when the month of February passed and the treaty still had not reached Philadelphia, Washington had no alternative but to inform the Senate that they would have to be convened in special session on June 8 to consider such matters as he might communicate to them.[22] The second session of the Third Congress ended on March 3. Four days later dispatch No. 22, dated London, November 19, 1794, was delivered to the Secretary of State. Contained therein was a treaty of "amity, commerce and navigation," an official letter to Randolph and a personal letter to Washington.[23]

As Randolph's eye eagerly scanned the crucial sentences in each article, his spirits dropped. Jay had made significant concessions and had received very little in return. But equally significant, by concluding an agreement that was silent on matters of vital interest to the United States, Jay had taken grave liberties with his instructions. This was a treaty which, when judged against what had been expected of Jay, was, to say the least, less than satisfactory.[24] In his letter to Randolph he neither praised nor defended his work. It was evident he felt it would be in our best interest as a nation to ratify the treaty, but he was prepared to have it judged on its merits. He explained the "governing principles" under which certain of the articles had been drafted but the "building" was "finished" and "it cannot be very important to describe the scaffolding."[25]

Randolph immediately took the treaty and Jay's official letter to Washington. The President's reaction was, like his own, negative. There was little in the treaty to recommend it and much that would undoubtedly give offense if made public. Jay's private letter to Washington provided no additional information. It was somewhat more defensive in tone than his letter to Randolph, but neither letter adequately explained why he had conceded so much to Grenville and secured so little in return.[26]

The following day Randolph wrote to Jay making formal acknowledgment of the treaty. He cautiously observed: "The last evening and this morning the President has been employed in perusing your despatches; and they will occupy his attention until he shall have come to some definitive judgement." He noted that the Senate was scheduled to meet on June 8 and until that date "the treaty will remain unknown, thro' the President or myself to any person upon earth." He continued:

I will only add, that the particulars of your *oral* negotiations would be of infinite value, in shewing what was unattainable. Be assured however that whether they arrive or not in time, you shall find the same unvaried candour, which has been hitherto pursued and especially in the documents accompanying the treaty to the Senate. It at present seems just, that no letters from this department, which we had reason to suppose would not reach you before the treaty should be concluded should be laid before them.[27]

Washington and Randolph had decided that the latter's highly critical commentary on Jay's first substantive report on his activities would remain hidden in the letterbooks of the Department of State. The treaty would be judged on its merits and such explanations as Jay might provide if he transmitted the "particulars of [his] *oral* negotiations" before the Senate convened in special session. In a letter to Monroe written the same day Randolph made reference to the receipt of the treaty, noted that a "cursory perusal of the treaty" failed to reveal "any reasonable ground for dissatisfaction in the French Republic" but added, "you will not judge from what I say, that my opinion is formed, whether the treaty will or not [*sic*] be ratified."[28]

News of the arrival of the treaty spread rapidly, as did the Administration's decision not to make public its contents.[29] In Madison's words, "the most impenetrable secrecy [was] being observed"[30] and, as might be expected, it was presumed by critics of Jay's mission that the treaty was highly unsatisfactory.[31] A few weeks later Madison was speculating as to its major provisions and his speculations were anything but flattering.[32] The Republican press was quick to demand the release of the treaty and prepared to believe the worst when its demands fell on deaf ears.[33] Federalist writers filled the columns of their papers with equally unverifiable rhetoric in its defense.[34] The two men who knew the treaty's contents undoubtedly could have found much amusement in these debates if they had either a more favorable treaty or at least a more satisfactory explanation from Jay as to why he had signed it.

Randolph returned to the business of running his department. He drafted detailed instructions for David Humphreys, who was being dispatched again to the Barbary States in an effort to end their shameless pirating activities against our commerce in the Mediterranean.[35] The Spanish minister was again pressed as to whether he had received any new proposals from his government that would lay the basis for a settlement of differences.[36] The Secretary of State played no part in the President's efforts to avert hostilities between the Creeks and the state of Georgia, for the views of the Cabinet were not sought on the subject.[37] When Washington departed for Mount Vernon on April 14 for a short visit, Randolph again assumed responsibility for informing the President of all that transpired in Philadelphia during his absence. And although there was little to report, every two or three days he faithfully dispatched a letter to Washington.[38] But all this was unimportant. There was but one real problem, the still unexplained treaty that Jay had concluded so precipitously with the British Foreign Secretary. Randolph waited in vain for the dispatch from London that contained Jay's account of the negotiations or, better still, news of his departure for home. If Jay or the dispatch did not arrive before the Senate convened on June 8, the treaty would have to be transmitted without the President's recommendations for there was not a single dispatch in Randolph's files that contained a satisfactory explanation for any of the articles of the treaty.

On April 25 Randolph received five dispatches from Jay, the latest dated February 22.[39] In this last dispatch Jay acknowledged the receipt of several letters from the Secretary of State, including Randolph's letter of December 15, adding that he would reply by a vessel soon to sail for Philadelphia.[40] Reporting the receipt of these dispatches to Washington, Randolph noted: "He [Jay] thinks he can solve all difficulties."[41] This was, at best, an overly optimistic interpretation. Jay had said only that if he had accompanied the treaty, he could have given satisfactory answers to all questions.[42] No doubt Jay felt he could defend his actions, but there was no evidence in these dispatches that he intended to do so. Even more disturbing was his total silence as to the date of his own return.[43]

Randolph could wait no longer. On April 26 he addressed a brief note to Mrs. Jay in New York requesting her to deliver "to Mr. Jay, as soon as may be convenient after his arrival, the enclosed letter."[44] The letter to Jay, also dated April 26, acknowledged the receipt of the dispatches that had arrived the previous day. "They," his letter continued, "confirm me in the determination, which I had taken with the approbation of the President of the United States, to go to New York immediately upon your arrival, if you should arrive during his absence at Mount Vernon." "For the discussion of the treaty," he observed, "we ought to be provided with a demonstration of our conduct towards France and an answer to the questions arising upon the treaty itself. I am engaged in both points; and upon the latter in particular, I am anxious to confer with you." Would it be more convenient for Jay "that I should run for a day or two at New York; or whether you prefer coming hither at so short a day, as to leave me time for digesting into my plan the information which I may receive from you?"[45] If Jay returned home before June 8, Randolph was determined to talk to him even if he had to journey to New York to do so.

Further correspondence was pointless. Again he could do nothing but wait. A letter from Mrs. Jay dated May 8 assured him his own letter had been received and indicated, if he could take any comfort in it, that she knew less about her husband's travel plans than he did.[46] Randolph wrote to assure her that her husband's presence in London was not required for the signing of the treaty and that he had probably already begun his voyage home. These, at least, were his "calculations."[47] Two weeks later, on May 28, Jay arrived in New York and that night penned a short note to Randolph. He had left England, he said, after he had satisfied himself that the treaty could not possibly have been returned in time to effect a final signing prior to the date of his own departure, which he had fixed as spring. He had not had a well day "during the entire voyage." "I am at present too feeble to undertake a journey to Philadelphia; perhaps I may in a week or ten days be so far recruited as to be able to perform it."[48] But a week or ten days would be too late for Randolph to prepare a statement on the course of negotiations. Of course, he could go to New York himself, although Jay's letter had been conspicuously silent on his earlier proposal to do so. But even this action posed problems, for the hasty departure of the Secretary of State for New York at the first word of Jay's return would be difficult to explain and might be interpreted as proof that the treaty was highly unsatisfactory. There was now no alternative but to ask Jay to reply in writing to a series of questions touching on what in all probability would be the more controversial aspects of the treaty.[49]

Randolph's letter went off on the 30th. He was happy to learn of Jay's return; it was an event "for which I have been anxious" in view of the approaching special session. "My own *private judgement* is, I confess, *made up* as to the *propriety* of *ratifying it.*" A conference with Jay, he continued, would have enabled him to present views "more striking than those which originated with myself." But as a "substitute" for a personal interview, would he answer the following questions as soon as possible.

1. Were the views of G. Britain really hostile to us, when you arrived?

2. Was not every effort made to shorten the time for the surrender of the posts; and did not the year 1796 appear to you to be an ultimatum with Lord Grenville?

3. Was it indispensable to stipulate for the prohibition of the sale of prizes in our ports?

4. Does the treaty prohibit the reexportation of West India commodities, imported from the French islands?

5. Is not the adjustment of the naval depredations placed upon the same footing as the adjustment of the spoliations of the Danish commerce?

6. What time will be necessary for completing the discussions in the admiralty?

7. What orders may be expected from the British court to their cruisers, for preventing the impressment of our seamen, and the capture of our property in case of a ratification?[50]

Couched in language that indicated Randolph was prepared to shift all responsibility for the more unsatisfactory articles of the treaty on Grenville's intransigency, the questions openly invited answers that would absolve Jay of criticism.

Jay's reply, dated June 1, was received by the Secretary of State two days later. Was the mood of Great Britain hostile? Yes, because of the prevalence of pro-French sentiment in the United States. Did he make every effort to shorten the time for the surrender of the posts? Yes. Was it absolutely essential that the treaty stipulate for the sale of prizes in our ports? Yes, they asked nothing from us that they did not have a right to ask from a neutral nation. One by one Randolph read Jay's answers: brief, matter of fact, almost curt in tone. There was virtually nothing in Jay's reply that Randolph could use to construct a convincing defense of his conduct.[51] Jay seemed indifferent to the partisan atmosphere that gripped the country and was obsessed with the idea that the treaty would be judged on its merits and would be approved because of the obvious benefits to be gained from the establishment of closer ties with Great Britain.

Randolph had pleaded with Jay in the most deferential terms for a detailed account of his activities. Now, five days before the Senate convened in special session, he had nothing to show for his efforts. He had acted with the approbation of the President, who presumably had instructed him to gather such information as would permit either him or Randolph to provide a satisfactory explanation of the various articles of the treaty when they came to be considered by the Senate.[52] With Jay's most recent reply to Randolph before him, Washington elected to send the treaty to the Senate without comment. The formal letter of transmittal contained not the slightest hint of the President's own opinion of the treaty.[53]

For better than thirteen months Randolph had devoted the greater part of his efforts as Secretary of State to implementing the decision of others to seek a rapprochement with Great Britain. He did so willingly, out of a sense of loyalty to the President and with the firm conviction that only good could result from an honest settlement of our differences with Great Britain. Yet his efforts had been futile and his views of little consequence. He had only one compensation for the constant frustrations of the past year—the satisfaction of knowing that the President approved of his actions. Washington could reject Randolph's advice on something as critical as the propriety of the Jay mission, yet know that his Secretary of State would work untiringly and with consummate skill to secure the success of that mission. And Randolph, in return, would give of himself without reserve, knowing that Washington expected him to render that kind of aid. It was a relationship that transcended the formal responsibilities of a Cabinet officer toward a President.

The treaty and its suspected provisions created still another problem for the harried Secretary of State. Fauchet, who had viewed the Jay mission with suspicion from the beginning, grew more difficult as evidence mounted that Jay had secured a rapprochement with Great Britain.[54] Randolph did what he could to remove his fears and urged Monroe to exert his energies to the same end in Paris.[55] But Jay's delay in returning home, the decision to keep the contents of the treaty secret until the Senate met in special session and the endless speculation as to its provisions all served to convince Fauchet that Jay had blatantly sacrificed Franco-American ties and American interests for a treaty of dubious value. Cordiality had already given way to irascibility, which turned into hostility as Fauchet vented his anger on the Secretary of State.[56] Randolph viewed Fauchet's current mood with considerable apprehension. To Monroe he observed:

> I am sure that he mediates something against the treaty with G. Britain; but what I do not yet see. But I am absolutely persuaded from what I have experienced, that we must lay down some new rules with respect to foreign ministers in general, and prevent them from meddling, as they do, in our internal affairs. I confess that I little expected from M. Fauchet the conduct which he has pursued and probably will pursue, before his successor arrives.[57]

Fauchet's letters of complaint could be answered in great detail,[58] but his apparent determination to work with those of a fixed political persuasion to defeat the treaty was an undisguised return to Genêt's methods of diplomacy.[59] It was particularly displeasing to Randolph because he believed it would intensify partisan animosity at a time when the country could well do without it. He knew the difficulties Genêt had created for Jefferson, and he had no desire to repeat his predecessor's experiences. So Randolph became unusually belligerent. He concluded his long letter of May 29 to Fauchet with the pointed observation that behind the French minister's long list of grievances was his fundamental annoyance with the United States because we had chosen to conclude an agreement with Great Britain.[60] Two weeks later, on June 13, after the treaty had been delivered to the Senate, he bluntly told Fauchet to mind his own business, adding: "This remark is made now, because it cannot erroneously be wrested into a defence or outwork of the treaty with Great Britain. . . ."[61] Privately he was even more critical of Fauchet than those Federalists who made distrust of all French ministers an article of faith.[62] Fortunately Fauchet's days were numbered, for Randolph had learned several months earlier that he was to be replaced, to be succeeded by someone more in sympathy with the government of the Directory in France.[63] For Randolph the replacement could not arrive too soon; for Fauchet had become *persona non grata* personally, politically and diplomatically.

Although Fauchet's conduct failed to stir the public,[64] it provided an interesting prologue to the Senate's consideration of the treaty. That body assembled on schedule to receive without recommendation the document that had been the subject of such endless speculation. Consistent with Randolph's previous assurances to Jay, no portion of his correspondence on the treaty that could not have reached Jay before November 19, 1794, was included in the papers that accompanied the treaty.[65] Significantly, the Senate invoked the same rule of secrecy the President had imposed three months earlier.[66] That it did so over the strong objection of the Republican members present established the partisan atmosphere that surrounded its review of Jay's work.[67] Washington and Randolph watched and listened but said or wrote not a word about the treaty. Their silence was self-imposed for neither man was prepared to have the treaty stand or fall on his word. It required little political experience to see that the forces on each side were delicately balanced and that a word from either man would probably determine the fate of the treaty.[68]

Meanwhile the Senators, most of them guided by their political and diplomatic prejudices, debated the treaty. In an effort to save the treaty the Federalists moved that it be approved with Article XII removed.[69] This article, governing our trade with the British West Indies, offended even the Federalists, who were displeased by the limitations placed on our direct trade with these islands and the prohibition against the re-exportation of Caribbean goods to Europe. This effort to secure a conditional ratification with the stipulation that Article XII be made the subject of further negotiations temporarily disarmed the Republicans. But they regrouped behind a motion to postpone further consideration of the treaty, which was introduced by Aaron Burr of New York on the 22nd.[70] Burr's motion would recommend that the President reopen negotiations on several specific points in the treaty.[71] The points mentioned represented a synthesis of all Republican criticism of the treaty. It was defeated the following day.[72] On the 24th the Senate returned to the Federalist motion providing for conditional ratification and renegotiation of Article XII. It passed 20 to 10.[73]

The Senate had spoken and by its method of ratification had created an awkward political and diplomatic situation for the President. Of immediate concern was the nature of the executive's reply to the Senate's conditional ratification. Randolph, without being asked, hastily outlined the possible responses of the President—silence, positive declaration, qualified declaration—noting the implications of each and suggesting the language that might be used if Washington chose to acknowledge the receipt of the Senate resolution.[74] His suggestions had no sooner reached Washington than Randolph learned that the supporters of the treaty expected more than an acknowledgment. They expected the President, he informed Washington, to send to the Senate a draft article to replace Article XII to which they might give their assent; "that upon their saying that they will, the President will now ratify the treaty provisionally, put it into the hands of his minister with an instruction to exchange it for a similar treaty."[75] This, Randolph added, "involves some critical, delicate, and hazardous points." First of all, if the President followed this procedure, Randolph noted, he would be demonstrating his approbation of the treaty; yet if such a "proposition" did not originate with him, it could not originate in the Senate, for it was an "executive matter." Secondly, to seek the Senate's approval of an article that had not been the subject of negotiation with the other signatory would be viewed by the world as evidence of an "excessive ardour" to implement the treaty. Thirdly, would not such a procedure render it unnecessary for the treaty to be returned for Washington's signature? If it did, then "the propriety of putting the final seal on an act, before it is complete, or of delegating to another the power of seeing that it is complete is, to say the least, very doubtful." Fourthly, the public will judge the "propriety of these proceedings" by the results intended, which "will be clearly seen to be, to prevent a future senate from negativing the ratification, as they may do, if the question be not settled now, and to cut off delay."[76] Whether the prevention of further delay in resolving our differences with Britain is of sufficient importance to "counterbalance" the public impression that this procedure is designed to prevent a rejection of the treaty by a "future senate" is a matter "the President will [have to] determine."[77] With a sure political instinct, Randolph had outlined for the President the possible responses he might make to the Senate's conditional ratification. Then, later that same day,[78] when he learned that the Federalists in the Senate actually expected Washington to submit a draft article to replace Article XII, he quickly outlined the political and diplomatic problems that might arise from executive acquiescence to such a procedure. Each memorandum carried the same implied warning: if the President wished to retain his freedom of choice, he must not say or do anything that would compromise his position. Washington accepted Randolph's advice and allowed the Senate to adjourn two days later, on June 26, without so much as acknowledging its resolution.

Even before the Senate had adjourned, however, Randolph had still another unsolicited memorandum on the President's desk.[79] Would it not be expedient, he asked, to require the written opinions of the Cabinet on two points:

> 1. Is not the resolution of the Senate, respecting the treaty between the U.S. and Great Britain, intended to to be their final act; or do they expect, that the new article shall be submitted to them, before the treaty takes effect?—
> 2. Does the constitution permit the President to ratify the treaty, without submitting the new article, after it shall be agreed by the British king, to the advice and consent of the senate?
>
> Upon these points E. R. [Randolph] has satisfied himself. But he knows, that it is contemplated to embarrass the treaty by objecting to the course, which may be observed in its ratification; and therefore is anxious that the President be supported in his measures upon it, by the best advice, which is at hand.[80]

Four days later, on June 29, Washington asked the Cabinet members to submit their views on these same questions.[81]

Before these opinions reached him the terms of the treaty had been made public. Prior to adjournment the Senate revoked its strict rule of secrecy and substituted a motion that enjoined the Senators against disclosing the exact text of the treaty.[82] With little chance that the treaty would be kept confidential much longer and with an honest desire to test public response to its highly controversial provisions, Washington, at the suggestion of Senator Rufus King, authorized Randolph to release an official copy to the *Philadelphia Gazette*.[83] The Secretary of State, who had lent his only copy to the new French minister, Pierre Adet, asked the editor that a notice of its intended publication be inserted in the next issue.[84] By the time Adet had returned Randolph's copy, Benjamin Bache had published an abstract of the treaty in his paper of June 29 and, two days later, he put out a pamphlet containing the full treaty.[85] The reaction was immediate and predictable: Federalists applauded the resolution of our differences with Great Britain, while Republicans accused Jay of having sacrificed our neutral rights and the Treaty of 1783 for a few paltry commercial privileges. All recognized that the ultimate decision now rested with Washington. No one would presume to advise him or even dare to discuss the subject lest they be accused of trying to influence his decision. Except for King's practical suggestion that the treaty be made public, only Randolph felt close enough to the President to submit, within two days, three unsolicited memoranda of advice.[86]

The President's request for the written opinions of the Cabinet brought an immediate response from Wolcott and Pickering. Neither man felt the revision of Article XII had to be submitted to the Senate before the treaty took effect, although Wolcott seemingly assumed the new article would be merely a suspending article rather than a replacement for the unsatisfactory "West Indian article." Both men also felt there was no constitutional barrier to the President's signing without submitting the revised article to the Senate for its advice and consent. In his reply to this second question Wolcott again assumed that the article in question would be only a "rescinding" clause or article.[87] But the opinions of the two most critical Cabinet officers, Randolph and Attorney General William Bradford, were still missing[88] when Washington decided on July 3 to send a "private and perfectly confidential" letter to Hamilton. Would the former Secretary of the Treasury give the "favorable and unfavorable side of *each* article" as well as his impressions on the *"result* of it in the aggregate"? The President was seeking the views of someone familiar with the intricacies of government on a large and comprehensive scale, the judgment of a person who could assess the immediate effects and future implications of the treaty.[89] It was a flattering plea for assistance, and Washington was confident Hamilton would respond without hesitation.

Before Hamilton's reply reached him Washington received a curious letter from his Secretary of State. Randolph still had not responded to the President's directive of June 29, although it was he who urged that the Cabinet be consulted. A slight "indisposition" had confined him to his home between the 4th and 6th, but it did not prevent him from conducting departmental affairs, presumably with the aid of a messenger.[90] On the 7th Washington opened a letter that he might well have presumed was Randolph's formal Cabinet opinion. Instead it was a letter clearly marked "private." He had, Randolph informed Washington, received a "letter" which he was enclosing that "notwithstanding the suggestions of Mr. King, Mr. Burr, Mr. Bradford, and some other gentlemen, I positively forbid to be mentioned to you." He continued:

> Why I forbid it, the reasons are very, very many; for altho' the wish of the most respectable of the bar in this city might have seemed to countenance it, yet one reason overpowered in my mind every other; that I did not think it right in itself, and the world would not think it so. It shall never be said, that I would ask for myself, what would be improper for your character to grant.[91]

The "letter" in question apparently referred to Randolph as a possible replacement for John Jay, who was resigning from the Supreme Court.[92] But John Rutledge had already been invited to accept appointment as Chief Justice and Randolph was aware of it.[93] The Secretary of State had something quite different in mind. Washington, Randolph's letter continued, probably could not be prevailed upon to serve another term in the presidency, "and I cannot well reconcile to myself the idea of serving, where I now am, under any other." Moreover, his present office required a style of living which he could not maintain without going into debt, a hazard that could only be relieved by the sale of his estate. To return to the practice of law would be the "most lucrative course" but it would require him to return to the "lower parts" of Virginia.

> Time has rolled so fast and unperceived over my head, that I have not, until a year or two past, calculated how few remain for very active exertion nor have I, until a year or two ago, been persuaded, that, if an accident should befall you, the union is split in twain, unless it should be placed above the machinations of its enemies during your administration. In the event of a dissolution, Virginia will not be, for me or my family, a proper country to dwell in.
>
> Thus circumstanced, and looking to all events, I think I ought to capacitate myself to take my position in whatsoever part of the U.S. I may find most comfortable. Philadelphia is at present the most so; and no place appears likely to come into competition with my wishes, until the federal city shall receive congress. There, if the union should remain entire, I mean to fix the fortunes of my son.

These reflections, he continued, led him to consider the possibility of a "transportation into Mr. Blair's office." It would, of course, separate him from Washington, but his continuance in his present office would be of little importance to Washington once "the weighty matters now depending" have been resolved and, since the vacancy probably would not occur until after the completion of the coming court session, "there may be no necessity to think of it until February."[94]

Washington probably found it necessary to reread the words again—"a transportation into Mr. Blair's office." Randolph, who had daily access to the President, was seeking an appointment to John Blair's position on the Supreme Court six months before the seat might be vacated (Blair's intended resignation was but a rumor).[95] The manner in which the request was framed, with its opening reference to the desire of others to have him named to Jay's seat, left Washington free to speculate on Randolph's real meaning. Whatever Randolph's intent, Washington knew his Secretary of State was not willing to carry the burdens of that office much longer and that his return to the practice of law was inevitable unless he were appointed to the Supreme Court. It was, indeed, a curious letter and Washington, as he had done with similar curious communications from Randolph in the past, prudently left it unanswered. And, like these other "communications," there was no epilogue.

Moreover, the President had little leisure for speculation, for word had reached Philadelphia late in June that the British were seizing American ships carrying foodstuffs to France.[96] The issuance of a new Order in Council in obvious violation of our neutral rights at the very moment that the Jay Treaty hung in the balance seemed to prove that Britain was indifferent to the treaty's ratification. A few days later Hamilton's long and careful analysis of the treaty reached Washington. Written after word of British seizures had reached New York, it was the most careful analysis Washington had yet seen of the final treaty. While generally favorable in tone, Hamilton pointedly noted the treaty's weaknesses. It was a deliberately practical analysis of the merits and deficiencies of the treaty by one who knew the benefits of close alignment with Britain but who recognized that Britain had made few significant concessions in this treaty. Hamilton concluded: "It is therefore conceived upon the whole to be the true interest of the United States, to close the present Treaty with Great Britain in the manner advised by the Senate."[97]

Washington read Hamilton's opinion with interest and then passed it along to Randolph,[98] who still had not supplied Washington with his Cabinet opinion on the two questions he had drafted and urged upon the President on June 25. If the President, who was anxious to return to Mount Vernon, was growing impatient with Randolph, his annoyance was removed by the receipt on July 12 of a long and carefully prepared opinion from his Secretary of State.[99] It became immediately evident that Randolph intended to review the entire subject of the treaty, even to the point of relating the question of ratification to the recent reports on the seizure of American vessels carrying food to France.

He turned first to the two questions he had proposed on June 25. Without making an extended analysis of the issues, he concluded that the Senate did not expect the President to submit a new article to it in place of Article XII before the treaty was to take effect, and also that the President might sign the treaty without ever submitting the new article to the Senate for its advice and consent.

Moving to the more fundamental problem, he continued: "If these difficulties shall be cleared away in the President's mind, he will next arrive at the two great and momentous questions: 1. Whether to ratify, as the Senate has advised, or reject: 2. and what line of conduct is to be pursued in either event." To compile a list of the reasons for ratifying and for rejecting the treaty "will aid me in my own conclusions." A treaty, he observed, "is the act of two independent nations; neither having a right to dictate to the other; and each determining upon what it will yield or accept, partly from its sense of right; partly upon its own strength, and partly upon the inferiority and actual situation of its antagonist." If this is true, what kind of treaty, he asked, do we have a right to expect:

> Not one dictated by ourselves; nor yet one, different from all that have ever been made on such occasions, on principles of compromize [*sic*] and mutual concession. If the present constitution of the United States, which was the act of sister-states was an affair of accommodation; how could it be expected that two nations, widely alienated from one another could agree on any other terms?

Accepting this frame of reference, he reviewed the treaty under four headings: the rights we had obtained, the rights we had surrendered, the "favors" we had gained and, lastly, miscellaneous matters.

> My first purpose was to class the articles of the treaty under these different heads and thus examine them individually. But *the paper*,[100] which you did me the honor of showing to me, having gone into this [in] detail, I shall speak of them separately only where I differ from its writer.

There followed a listing of the items in the treaty under each of the headings. In general he found we had gained far less than we had surrendered, listing only one item in the first category, while placing eight in the second. But he also found we had secured two favors—"The India trade and the power of supplying Canada etc." and "The trade to the East Indies." Under the heading of "miscellaneous matter of the treaty" he noted five additional points, the most important of which, he insisted, was the resolution of all our differences with Great Britain. Returning to the question of whether the President should accept or reject, he listed the advantages, disadvantages and "doubtful" aspects of the treaty.

But:

> Independent of these pros and cons, arising from the face of the treaty, there are some other considerations entitled to attention which recommend ratification and dissuade rejection.
>
> Those which recommend ratification are:
>
> 1. that peace, or rather the non-interruption of our Commerce will be secured.
>
> 2. that the danger of being thrown into one set of foreign politics by an abhorrence of the outrages of another, will be so far cut up.
>
> 3. that it gives some prospect of extending our commerce with the British dominions.
>
> 4. that as it is not the interest of the U.S. to be on ill-terms with France,

lest we thereby throw ourselves too much on G. Britain, so vice versa, the U.S. ought to be on good terms with both. It is at least doubtful whether it be the interest of the U.S. that there should be only *one* dominant power or game-cock in Europe.

The reasons that dissuade rejection are:

1. The latitude of authority with which Mr. Jay was vested, and his not having exceeded it.

2. The little expectation of obtaining a much better treaty.

3. The possibility of the convulsions of France, re-inspiring G. Britain with her former arrogance.

4. The impression, which the refusal to ratify will make upon our public, national character; merely because we have not all the advantages on our side. . . .

5. The postponement of the surrender of the posts, [beyond the date specified in the treaty] and its consequences.

6. The exposure of the twenty senators to a general assault: the consequent alienation of them from the Government: the victory to the minority in the Senate; who in conjunction with the majority in the House of Representatives; will first be loud in their eulogiums on the President, and afterwards never be satisfied, unless they dictate to him.

However valid these reasons for America's ratification might seem, "the order for capturing provisions is too irreconcileable [*sic*] with a state of harmony for the treaty to be put in motion during its existence." "And," he continued, "if no expedient could be found for the emergency, it would be my opinion, that the treaty ought to be absolutely broken up. . . ." However, assuming the President decided to accept the treaty on its merits, a plan might be effected which would force the British to revoke their recent Order in Council. He, as Secretary of State, could be instructed by the President to immediately arrange an interview with the British minister in Philadelphia, at which time he would inform the minister that he had been instructed to say candidly that it was the President's intention to sign the treaty without submitting a revision of Article XII to the Senate, but that he could not accept it so long as the Order in Council for the seizure of ships carrying food to France remained in effect, "that the order being removed, he will ratify without delay or further scruple." He, as Secretary of State, might also make the following observation during his interview with the British minister:

"Now, Sir, the object of my interview with you arises from my recollection of your having expressed to me a wish, that the ratification should be exchanged here in order that you might have some agency in closing the treaty. I am thus lead to believe, that it may not be disagreeable to you to undertake what I shall now have the honor of proposing to you."

He would supply Hammond with a memorial setting forth the President's intention to sign once the Order in Council had been removed, which Hammond would then transmit to his government along with a copy of the "form in which the President means to ratify." If the reply of the British ministry was satisfactory, it would be possible to effect an immediate ratification *"here"*[101] in Philadelphia. Such a procedure would permit Hammond to play a part in the final ratification and also save us the trouble and expense of ordering John Quincy Adams from the Netherlands to London to effect a final ratification.

Randolph's letter was unquestionably the most thorough analysis Washington had received of the entire matter and, when combined with Hamilton's article-by-article review of the treaty, it provided the President with a perceptive and very judicious review of America's position vis-à-vis Great Britain. The Secretary of State handled the two procedural questions with much greater brevity than one might have expected, considering that he was the original author of these questions. His analysis of the treaty was much less comprehensive than Hamilton's, but Randolph himself noted that Hamilton had rendered superfluous the analysis he had intended to make. But when it came to a review of the "considerations" that were "independent of . . . [the] pros and cons arising from the face of the treaty," Randolph's frank, commonsense observations were perceptive beyond anything the President had received to date. His was the kind of detached analysis that could put the confusing and seemingly conflicting issues into their proper perspective. Randolph didn't like the treaty any more now than he had four months earlier, but he had come to realize that if it was not the best of all possible treaties, it was at least the best treaty the United States could sign with Great Britain in 1795. And, lest Washington have any doubts on this point, he itemized the reasons why he felt this was so. The President was told in effect: You have no choice; the reasons for ratification far outweigh the reasons for rejection; and let us use the option for rejection or ratification and Hammond's vanity to force a withdrawal of the obnoxious Order in Council. It was a neat package with no loose ends. All the President had to do was give his assent and the Secretary of State would take care of all the details. Whatever Washington might have thought of Randolph's abilities, he certainly could not help but admire his austere independence and candid attitude. Randolph always said what was on his mind; he knew that this was exactly what Washington expected of him.

On July 13 Washington informed Randolph that he might attempt to secure the revocation of the Order in Council in the manner the Secretary of State had outlined in his letter of the previous day. Randolph apparently called Hammond to his office that same day, only to discover that the British minister rather naïvely assumed that the recent Order in Council could never serve as a permanent barrier to the ratification of the treaty. Hammond did agree to transmit the memorial Randolph said he would prepare, but apparently gave no indication that he would recommend the withdrawal of the Order in Council, as the Secretary of State had hoped he would.[102] It was evident the treaty was not going to be ratified as speedily as Washington and Randolph had expected. With the President scheduled to leave for Mount Vernon the next day, full authority was given to Randolph to draft the memorial to the British government and prepare a revision of Article XII.[103] The receipt of a letter from Hamilton expressing the view that the "new" Article XII would have to be submitted to the Senate for its approval created still another problem for the President,[104] and he asked Randolph to review recent Cabinet opinions on this question and to consult with Hamilton.[105]

As soon as the President left the city Randolph resumed his usual role of keeping Washington informed on all matters affecting the executive.[106] Little escaped his attention, and everything that required assessment carried the concise analysis of the conscientious Secretary of State. Randolph's first substantive report on July 20 was not too comforting. Hamilton had altered his opinion on the necessity of resubmitting Article XII to the Senate: "It proves what I suspected, that the first opinion was not maturely weighed." "But," he continued, "there is something in this business a little mysterious to me which I shall examine into before I write to you . . . [again]." Even more significant was the fact that the whole subject of the Jay Treaty was "daily increasing in magnitude." He had heard that the address from Boston against the treaty, which in all probability Washington had already received, was to be imitated in New York and perhaps in Philadelphia. Undoubtedly the President would want to "see the full upshot of all these measures" before making any final decision. Perhaps it would be well if he (Randolph) were to "run down" to Mount Vernon: "I think a personal conference will be necessary in the progress of the affair; and my going to Virginia will be a thing of no notice. In fact, so much is at stake, that . . . no . . . labour, vigilance, circumspection or thought can be excessive. . . ."[107]

Without waiting for Washington's reply to this suggestion, Randolph forwarded several important papers to Mount Vernon. On the 24th he transmitted his draft of the memorial on the treaty which was to be given to Hammond and the instructions for the exchange of ratification in London should the treaty be signed.[108] In response to Washington's urgent instructions from Baltimore to consider the propriety of a reply to the Boston address,[109] several draft statements were forwarded to the President for study. There was a preliminary "sketch," a draft approved by Wolcott, Pickering and Bradford that did not "accord" with Randolph's views, and the individual drafts of all four men so that the President might know the language each had employed.[110] A private letter also explained why he had viewed Hamilton's latest opinion on the treaty with suspicion:

> I hinted in a past letter that there was something mysterious in one part of the business. What I alluded to is that the advice given to you from New York as to the withholding of ratification, until the order for seizing provisions was rescinded, does not appear to have been circulated among the particular friends of the gentleman from whom the advice came.[111]

On the 25th the Secretary of State received a long letter from Mount Vernon.[112] Randolph read the second paragraph with utter disbelief: "In my hurry, I did not signify the propriety of letting . . . [the members of the Cabinet] know fully my determination with respect to the ratification of the Treaty and the train it was in. . . ."[113] For some reason the President had kept his views on this important issue from the other members of the Cabinet. Aside from procedural questions, which at Randolph's suggestion had been made the subject of written Cabinet opinions, they knew nothing about Washington's views. Randolph was thereupon given a precise statement of the President's current thinking on these matters and asked to explain them to the other "Gentlemen."[114] It was true, of course, that Washington's Cabinet officers had never assumed they should be informed of the President's opinions on matters of public policy, but, if Randolph had reflected on it, he would not have been able to recall a single instance when an issue of such magnitude had been discussed with so few people.

That same weekend, July 25–26, Philadelphia was the scene of a public demonstration against the treaty not unlike those that had occurred in Boston and New York.[115] Randolph gathered the details and transmitted them to Washington on Monday morning in a letter written at 5:30 A.M. His account sought to minimize the seriousness of the demonstration by indicating that it was the work of a "comparatively" small number of agitators whose ranks were swelled by mere spectators.[116] Randolph evidenced deep concern over these public demonstrations, but he knew, too, that the press, whether Federalist or Republican, was not reporting them accurately, and it was from these sources that Washington, isolated at Mount Vernon, was receiving the details of these public meetings.[117]

Tuesday's mail brought Washington's letter of the 24th.[118] To Randolph's suggestion that he make a hurried trip to Mount Vernon, Washington responded that he would prefer to return to Philadelphia, "where, if matters are peculiarly embarrassed, I should be on the theatre of information, with document and other aids about me that could not be had here."[119] The idea of Washington hastily returning to Philadelphia seemed particularly imprudent at this time. The members of the Cabinet had all been of the opinion that Randolph could go to Mount Vernon without attracting too much attention. But the reverse was obviously not true.[120] Randolph immediately conferred with Wolcott and Pickering, who vetoed the idea for it would give to "the things, which have been and are still carried on, an importance, which it would not be convenient to give them."[121]

Along with this collective opinion went word that the rumored mental instability of Chief Justice–elect John Rutledge had some basis in fact and the news that Hammond had received his letter of recall. Randolph also noted that in the course of his conversation with Hammond on July 28 the minister had declared that upon his return to London he would represent the sincerity of the "government" in the business of the treaty. Randolph could add nothing to the newspaper accounts of the public proceedings at Charleston against the treaty, but in Philadelphia a petition was said to be circulating to counteract the memorial against the treaty that had been drafted at the public meeting several days earlier. Lastly, he noted that he had not felt well himself for several days, but he was now ready to receive the President's instructions with regard to the memorial on the treaty which he had forwarded to Mount Vernon several days earlier.[122]

By the 31st the delays in the mails were beginning to annoy Randolph. The various addresses and resolutions against the treaty required some type of response, and yet the reply to the Boston address of July 13 still had not been approved by the President.[123] It was not even known for certain whether Washington intended to issue a general statement by way of reply or to respond to each of the addresses individually.[124] Randolph's draft of the memorial on the treaty that was to be given to Hammond had not been approved either, and until it was the Secretary of State refused to "give out, what you have resolved to do." Approval of the memorial "is previously necessary as the one must square with the other."[125] All these matters could have been resolved if Washington had allowed Randolph to go to Mount Vernon, but Washington had rejected this suggestion in favor of his own return to Philadelphia. The Cabinet, in turn, had reacted unfavorably to this idea because of the effect an obviously hurried return of the President might have on the public mind. Randolph would not have cared particularly about all this confusion except that the silence of the government was becoming embarrassing, as was the continued absence of the President from the seat of government.

On July 31 Randolph wrote a one paragraph letter to Washington. It read:

> The Secretaries of the Treasury and War departments are now with me, and we concur in thinking it expedient, that, if possible, you should return for a few days to the seat of government. Nothing, but the general crisis of public affairs leads to this recommendation; and it may be important that you should do some act in consequence of the communication expected from Mr. Hammond, who will sail shortly.[126]

Randolph was conveying a recommendation that constituted a complete reversal of the position taken by these same Cabinet officers two days earlier and so reported by Randolph in his letter to Washington of July 29. What Randolph didn't know was that Wolcott and Pickering now had good reason for urging Washington's prompt return to Philadelphia. They had just acquired a dispatch written by former French minister Jean Fauchet which contained damaging evidence against Randolph.

21

"*Incrimination*" *and Resignation August 1795*

eavy rains along much of the Atlantic coast prevented Randolph's letter of July 31 from reaching Mount Vernon until August 5.[1] Its unexplained request that the President return to Philadelphia contradicted the advice offered by the same three Cabinet officers in a letter dated July 29 and received the same day. The earlier letter noted that it would be unnecessary and perhaps inadvisable for the President to make a hurried trip back to Philadelphia at this time.[2] The mystery increased when Washington discovered that Randolph had written a second letter on July 31, marked "private," which made no reference whatsoever to the subject of his return. Another letter in the same mail from Timothy Pickering, also dated July 31, contained an earnest warning that Washington decide on "no important political measure, in whatever form it may be presented to you" until he returned to the seat of government.[3] Washington may well have read Pickering's curious admonition a second time:

> On the subject of the treaty I confess that I feel extreme solicitude; and for a *special reason*, which can be communicated to you only in person. I entreat, therefore, that you will return, with all convenient speed, to the seat of government. In the mean time, for the reason above referred to, I pray you to decide on no important political measure, in whatever form it may be presented to you.
>
> Mr. Wolcott and I (Mr. Bradford concurring), waited on Mr. Randolph and urged his writing to request your return. He wrote in our presence; but we concluded a letter from one of us also expedient.[4]

Pickering's language dictated an immediate departure and Washington decided to leave the next morning for Philadelphia.[5]

In the meantime Randolph, suspecting that Washington might have started back to Philadelphia, sharply curtailed his correspondence with Mount Vernon.[6] In fact, with so many issues still unresolved, there was little the Secretary of State could do until the President actually re-

[307]

turned. He refrained from an extensive correspondence with our ministers in Europe while awaiting some definite word of the President's ultimate decision on the Jay Treaty.[7] With the foreign ministers in Philadelphia he had almost no contact. Adet had been ill since the President's departure and had become strangely silent about the treaty.[8] Hammond, who was about to return to London, had received new instructions from his government which caused Randolph to query him as to their contents. When he discovered the British minister had nothing of consequence to communicate, he did not pursue the matter further.[9] Jaudenes, the Spanish commissioner in Philadelphia, complained of violations of the Spanish frontier and implied Georgia's Governor George Mathews was involved.[10] Jaudenes' complaint was forwarded to the Secretary of War, but Randolph promised to bring the matter to the President's attention as soon as he returned from Mount Vernon. "I must insist," he warned, ". . . that the character of so high an officer of the United States [the governor of Georgia] be not hereafter thus brought into question, without adequate testimony instead of conjecture."[11] A letter from our consul at Bristol conclusively established the existence of the British Order in Council for seizing provisions destined for France.[12] Undoubtedly this was placed with the other correspondence Washington would want to review upon his return.

It was August 11 before the President reached Philadelphia and, as might be expected, Randolph was one of the first to see him.[13] Over dinner that evening the President and Secretary of State reviewed the events of the past month.[14] Their conversation was briefly interrupted by an obviously urgent visit from Pickering, who seemed bent on communicating something of great importance to the President.[15] But Randolph dismissed the interruption, for he still had ample time to discuss with Washington the important matters awaiting presidential decision. A Cabinet meeting was scheduled for the next morning to consider Randolph's draft of the memorial on the treaty, the item of greatest urgency, as Hammond was soon to sail for England.[16]

The following day the Cabinet assembled in the President's office at the appointed hour. Unexpectedly Washington asked his advisers for comments on the advisability of immediate approval of the treaty.[17] As far as Randolph knew, the President had never contemplated "immediate" acceptance so long as the British Order in Council remained in effect.[18] Weeks before Hamilton had informed Washington that he considered the Order a barrier to America's acceptance, and in the light of that opinion Washington and Randolph had already agreed that the threat of the President withholding his signature, if properly handled, might well cause the British to withdraw their Order.[19] Now, all of a sudden Randolph found himself the sole advocate of a firm stand against the British, as Wolcott and Pickering, with the support of Attorney General Bradford, urged an immediate acceptance of the treaty.[20] Then, in total disbelief, Randolph heard the President announce his determination to sign the treaty immediately.[21] The Secretary of State, of course, would prepare the requisite memorial for Hammond.[22]

If Randolph returned to his office perplexed by this sudden reversal in Washington's attitude toward the treaty, he shared his bewilderment with no one. He knew full well that Washington, like himself, had always viewed the British Order in Council as an insuperable barrier to formal approval of the treaty. He was close enough to the President to know that he would never abruptly reverse his position without reason.[23]

Either after this meeting or later that same day the President routinely consulted Randolph on the replies that would have to be made to the various memorials against the treaty. Several had reached him in recent weeks and the more respectful ones at least would have to be answered. Randolph was instructed to use the same reply that had been sent to the Boston selectmen, adding an introductory paragraph so stating.[24] Within a day or so Randolph completed this task and sent copies of the President's answer to seven different communities.[25] This was the only subject discussed; apparently nothing was said about the treaty.

The following day, August 13, Randolph again met privately with Washington to review certain diplomatic letters he had sent during the President's absence.[26] Washington read and approved a circular that had been sent to our ministers under a July 21 date, as well as a letter to Monroe dated July 14.[27] Each of the letters carried the guarded prediction that the President probably would not sign so long as the Order in Council remained in force. In spite of the obvious opportunity to do so, Randolph did not ask for—and did not receive—any explanation for the President's unexpected decision of the previous day.

Randolph had the formal instrument of ratification[28] and the memorial[29] on the treaty ready for Washington's approval on August 14. The latter document, reflecting the President's decision to sign immediately, noted only the exclusion of Article XII as stipulated by the motion of the Senate on June 24.[30] But, the memorial continued:

> . . . the undersigned is charged to declare that the sensibility of the President has been greatly executed [*sic*] by [an] understanding that various captures have been lately made of American vessels laden with provisions, in consequence of a recent order said to have been issued under the authority of his Britannic majesty.

If such an Order had in fact been issued, the President's representative in the exchange of ratification was instructed to "make such representations as shall appear to be advisable; and particularly that the ratification of the President must not be construed into an admission of the legality of the said order."[31] Washington expressed his satisfaction with the language employed and authorized the Secretary of State to deliver the memorial to Hammond before the British minister left the city. Randolph called Hammond to his office later that same day and handed him the memorial. He made no attempt to conceal the fact that he had been "overruled in the President's Cabinet."[32] In this final chapter of the Jay mission Randolph again found himself executing a policy that completely repudiated the line of conduct he had recommended. It was surely one of the most difficult and humiliating days in his public career.

The weekend of August 15–16 found Randolph nursing his wounds and undoubtedly reviewing the events of the past week. First there was the rumor circulating in Federalist circles that the opposition of the Secretary of State accounted for the delay in the President approving the treaty.[33] A letter of explanation to Jay[34] and a note to Rufus King[35] would set the record straight before word of the President's intended approval was made public. But Washington's conduct remained a mystery. Without warning he had arbitrarily rejected Randolph's advice on the treaty, yet continued to treat him as a personal friend and a trusted adviser, inviting him into his home and consulting him frequently on public matters.[36]

The new week found Randolph at his desk as usual. The President was scheduled to sign the treaty on Tuesday,[37] but this was a mere formality demanding only Randolph's presence in the President's office during the brief ceremony. On Wednesday he had an appointment at 9 A.M. to see the President on routine matters.[38] Before departing for Washington's home on High Street that morning he received word that the President would not be able to see him until 10:30 A.M. Arriving at the appointed time, he was informed that Secretaries Wolcott and Pickering were already with the President in his office. Immediately upon entering the office he knew that something was wrong.[39]

After the usual greetings had been exchanged, Washington handed Randolph several large sheets of paper that obviously had been folded for mailing: "Mr. Randolph, here is a letter which I desire you to read, and make such explanations as you choose."[40] Randolph unfolded the letter and discovered a diplomatic dispatch in the hand of Fauchet, addressed to the Commissioner of Foreign Relations and dated: "Philadelphie le 10 Brumaire, 1' an 3ᵉ de la République un & indiviᵉ."[41] The Secretary of State had never mastered the calendar of the "République" but he recognized that this letter, clearly identified as "No. 10," was not a recent dispatch. Fauchet's rambling style and imprecise language was not easy to follow, but Randolph understood enough French to grasp in a general way the theme of the dispatch. It was evident the French minister was commenting on the growing political rivalry in America and the significance of the then current Whiskey Rebellion in this ominous struggle for power. Randolph found himself referred to as a confidant of Fauchet and, by virtue of his closeness to the President, a key figure in this struggle. The extent of his involvement was not explained but references to two earlier dispatches identified as Nos. 3 and 6 clearly implied a close liaison between Fauchet and Randolph, which included "overtures" by the Secretary of State for some thousands of dollars, presumably for himself, in exchange for averting a civil war in America, the details of which had been explained in an earlier dispatch.[42] Randolph finished the letter and asked if it was an intercepted dispatch. Washington acknowledged that it was.[43] Randolph stated he would explain what he knew but that at the moment he could recollect very little. A nod from Washington indicated he was free to proceed with his explanation.[44]

He reread the dispatch more carefully, offering a brief and apparently very general explanation of each paragraph as he went along.[45] Upon finishing, he remarked that he had some recollection of Fauchet having told him of "machinations against the French Republic, Governor Clinton and myself." Perhaps the reference to the "overtures," which were presumably explained in dispatch No. 6, was in some manner "connected with that business."[46] He would, however, "throw" his ideas on paper.[47]

The President then asked Wolcott and Pickering if they had any questions they would like to put to Randolph. The Secretary of War indicated he had none, but Wolcott was interested in learning more about these machinations against the French Republic, Clinton and Randolph. How had the Secretary of State replied to this intelligence? By way of an answer Randolph attempted to reconstruct the circumstances surrounding the report of a meeting of Hammond and others in New York during the summer of 1794 which gave rise to the rumored machinations. Remembering that he had mentioned the matter to the President at the time, he solicited his assistance as to the details.[48] Washington recalled having heard something of the meeting, but their conversation was then interrupted when the President was called momentarily from the room.[49] During his absence Randolph inquired how the President had acquired Fauchet's letter. Wolcott replied coldly that the President would presumably explain how he came to receive it. When the President reentered his office he asked Randolph if he would step into another room.[50]

It was while waiting in the room adjoining the President's office that Randolph came to realize the full implications of what had just transpired. From all appearances a highly incriminating letter, after having been shown to two other members of the Cabinet, was being presented to him for the express purpose of determining his guilt or innocence on the basis of his initial reaction to the letter. Washington, Pickering and Wolcott were, he concluded, now reviewing the explanation he had just made. He was certain Washington would never resort to such methods if he believed him innocent. The President must have been convinced already of his guilt. The procedures that were now being employed to determine the extent of his culpability made continued service in Washington's Cabinet unthinkable.[51]

When Randolph was readmitted to the President's office Washington asked that he put his ideas on paper, as he had suggested. Randolph again noted the difficulties he would experience in recalling the details of the conversations Fauchet had referred to without the benefit of the other dispatches mentioned in this letter. On being pressed by the President as to how long it would take him to finish his remarks, he replied that they would be completed as soon as possible. His composure shattered, he then declared that he would not continue in office "one second after such treatment" and promised to immediately submit his letter of resignation.[52]

Randolph went directly to his office and ordered that it be locked, keeping everything exactly as he had left it earlier that morning.[53] Returning to his home, he reviewed again what had happened. As he expressed it in his letter of resignation:

> Two facts immediately presented themselves; one of which was, that my usual hour of calling upon the President had not only been postponed for the opportunity of consulting others upon a letter of a foreign minister, highly interesting to my honour, but before the smallest intimation to me; but they seemed also to be perfectly acquainted with its contents, and were requested to ask questions for their satisfaction. The other was, that I was desired to retire into another room, until you [i.e. Washington] should converse with them [i.e. Wolcott and Pickering], upon what I had said.[54]

Believing Washington himself had received the dispatch in the first instance, Randolph could not understand why he had taken Wolcott and Pickering into his confidence before giving him an opportunity to explain its incriminating passages. He had no choice but to assume that the President was already convinced of his guilt and, what is more, that Washington believed that this was a perfectly fair judgment on the basis of the information in Fauchet's dispatch. As for Wolcott and Pickering, apparently Washington used these gentlemen merely to confirm his own opinion. For a man who had enjoyed Washington's confidence for so long, this apparent assumption of guilt before any explanation had been offered was a severe blow. Without the slightest hesitation he sat down and wrote out his resignation.[55]

His letter was frank and to the point. He asked only that he be furnished with a copy of the letter and that the affair "continue in secrecy under your injunction." "I presume, sir, that the paper, No. 6, to which he [Fauchet] refers is not in your possession. Otherwise you would have shown it to me. If I am mistaken, I cannot doubt that you will suffer me to have a copy of it." He concluded by observing that he would "pass" his accounts at the Auditor's and Comptroller's office and transmit a copy to him.[56] He made a copy of the letter for his own files, altered slightly the text of the original, and then sent it by messenger to the President's office.[57]

The following day Randolph learned that the French frigate *Medusa*, on which Fauchet was expected to take passage, had not sailed on August 10, as had been previously assumed, but remained at anchor in the harbor of Newport, Rhode Island.[58] But, more important, there was little likelihood that it would sail within the next few days, for the English cruiser *Africa* was patrolling the waters outside the harbor.[59] Without bothering to wait for a reply to his letter of resignation or the copy of No. 10 that he had been promised, Randolph set out for Newport.[60] Leaving Philadelphia on the afternoon of the 21st, he reached New York on the 24th. There he paused for two days or more waiting for "some necessary papers" to be forwarded to him from Philadelphia.[61] To his wife Betsy he wrote:

> I have not visited Mr. Jay, because if the letter was intercepted, he must have known it, and ought, after the fairness, which I practiced towards him, to have told me. Mr. King called upon me, *as if he had scarcely had* [sic] *heard of my resignation.* This I understood yesterday morning—Col. Hamilton's family were thrown into mourning by the death of Mrs. Hamilton's eldest brother—so that I have not seen him.[62]

Embittered by the whole experience, he seemed prepared to believe the worst of anyone with a different political persuasion from his own. His letter to Betsy closed with the confident declaration: "I have no doubt of overtaking Fauchet," and was signed: "My love to all—Yrs. mo. afftely & ever, E.R."[63]

It was Monday, August 31, before Randolph reached Newport. Going immediately to Fauchet's residence, he told him that his letter of the 10th of Brumaire had been intercepted and was now in the hands of the

President. "After observing," Randolph recorded in his *Vindication*, "that he must recollect, how injuriously he had treated the government, others, and myself, in that letter, I informed him, that I had come for the purpose of demanding an explanation. . . . I then mentioned the different points; and although in some particulars we did not remember alike, yet I required him to give me a certificate according to his memory." Fauchet agreed and promised to have his statement ready at eight o'clock the next morning. Knowing that the *Africa* still blocked the mouth of the harbor, Randolph readily agreed to wait. As it was midafternoon, he was obliged to seek out accommodations for himself and make the necessary provisions for the care of his horse.[64] He also inquired about the availability of certain public officials in the city whose services he might require as witnesses the next day.[65]

Tuesday morning found Randolph knocking on Fauchet's door at the appointed hour. Met by a servant who informed him that Fauchet had instructed him to say that the certificate would not be ready until "about 12 o'clock," he asked if he might talk to Fauchet personally. When the former French minister appeared, he assured Randolph that he was then engaged in preparing the certificate and that he would take or send the same to Randolph's lodging as soon as it was complete. It would, he continued, be ready about twelve or one o'clock. Randolph inquired if Fauchet would be willing to submit to questioning and noted that he intended to ask Henry Marchant, federal judge of the district of Rhode Island, and Francis Malbone, a member of the House of Representatives from Rhode Island, to serve as witnesses. Fauchet readily agreed, and Randolph returned to his lodging to await the certificate and word as to when he might question Fauchet.[66]

Sometime before noon Randolph learned that the *Medusa* was weighing anchor, apparently determined to take advantage of the stormy weather and high seas to escape the *Africa*. Astonished at this intelligence he ran to Fauchet's residence, only to discover that Fauchet had already left. Turning on his heels he raced to the home of William Peck, the federal marshal, and with his assistance secured the swiftest sailing vessel in port, instructing its captain to catch the *Medusa* and deliver the following letter to Fauchet:[67]

Sir,
    I am this moment informed, that the frigate has sailed; and I have been to your house. They say that you are on board; and that you have left no paper for me, according to what you promised. My innocence of the insinuations, arising from your letter, you not only know, but have twice acknowledged to me. I send a boat therefore in a hurry to obtain the papers, which go to this point.[68]

Minutes seemed like hours as Randolph impatiently waited for his messenger to return. The longer it took, the more certain he was that the vessel had overtaken the *Medusa*. Finally the boat that had carried his message reappeared in the harbor and in a matter of minutes Randolph heard the captain tell of having pursued the *Medusa* for several miles without having been able to overtake her.[69] He took the letter he had written to Fauchet, handed it to Peck and asked him if he would add a signed statement of what had just transpired.[70]

Exhausted and dejected, Randolph returned to his lodgings. He was now completely defeated, for he knew that what he could not secure from Fauchet in Newport he would never secure from him in France. If he had had the energy he would have defiantly cursed all mankind, and Frenchmen in particular, from the rooftop of the tallest building in Newport.

The following day, September 2, there was a knock on the door of his quarters and a request to see Mr. Randolph. The former Secretary of State found himself face to face with one Caleb Gardner, the man, Randolph learned, who had piloted the *Medusa* out of Newport's harbor. As he was leaving the *Medusa*, he had been asked by Mr. Fauchet to deliver a letter to Randolph.[71] Randolph broke the seal and read: "I have just transmitted to Citizen Adet, the minister of the Republic in Philadelphia, the packet which I destined for you. He will send you a certified copy of my letter, with which, I hope, you will be satisfied."[72]

Randolph breathed a sigh of relief; the certificate at least had been drafted and would, in time, be put into his hands. He asked Gardner if he would give him a certified statement of what had transpired the previous day. As he read the pilot's statement, the pieces fell into place. Because of the high seas the *Africa* had been forced to abandon its patrol outside the harbor and seek shelter in Narragansett Bay. The captain of the *Medusa*, already having been detained for several weeks, decided to seize the opportunity to escape and ordered all passengers to board the vessel. The captain immediately ordered the cables cut and braving the winds made for open water. Fauchet, Gardner noted, was the last to arrive and went immediately to his cabin. He emerged shortly before Gardner himself left the vessel at 1:30 in the afternoon to ask if he would deliver a letter to Randolph.[73] If nothing else, it demonstrated Fauchet's good faith. Randolph could only hope that his memory was as good as his word.

22

Vindication
September–December 1795

It was probably Friday, September 4, before Randolph began his long journey home.[1] It was an uneventful trip interrupted only by a brief stay in New York.[2] By the middle of the month he was back in Germantown and once again reunited with his family.[3] It might well have been a tearful reunion, for the family had undoubtedly been under great emotional strain. He spent a couple of days relaxing, recovering from the arduous journey and the trying and unpleasant experiences of the past few weeks.[4]

Seemingly the first to hear of Randolph's arrival in Germantown was the acting Secretary of State, Timothy Pickering.[5] It was the President's desire, Pickering wrote on September 14, that the unsigned copies of the instrument of ratification "also receive your signature as [you were] Secretary of State at the date of ratification."[6] Randolph signed and returned the two copies enclosed in Pickering's letter. To Washington he wrote:

> I have this moment received a letter from Col. Pickering, dated yesterday, informing me, that it was your "desire, that the other copies of the ratification might also receive my signature as secretary of state at the date of the ratification." Altho' for many reasons, this cannot be supposed to be a pleasant business to me; yet to show to you, that by my resignation I *never* intended to embarrass the government, I have signed the two other copies.[7]

He rode into Philadelphia on Sunday, September 20, and the following day called at the office of the Department of State.[8] There, with the other personal mail that had accumulated since he left the city, he found two letters from Washington. The first was an acknowledgment of his resignation, dated August 20.[9] The second, dated August 22, was a note covering the transmission of a copy of Fauchet's No. 10, as had been promised.[10] Randolph found the first letter of great interest, for here he learned for the first time how Washington had come to acquire the dispatch. Instead of Washington being the instigator of Randolph's downfall, he was in fact the last person to learn of the dispatch. Pickering, Wolcott and Bradford had jointly established the incriminating character of the dispatch before bringing the matter to Washington's attention.[11] But when did these events occur? Did the President learn of this dispatch before or after he decided to ratify the treaty with England? Perhaps there was more to this than he realized! Then a rereading of No. 10 under calmer circumstances raised further questions. Nos. 3 and 6 were even more important than he had first suspected. Washington, in his letter of the 20th, stated he had never seen No. 6, but had he seen No. 3? Had he arbitrarily established the meaning of the incriminating passages in No. 10 without ever having consulted these earlier dispatches? He wrote to the President:

Finding it important to one branch of the subject, that I should ask a small addition to the narrative in your letter of the 20th ultimo, I have to request, that I may be informed, as far as may be in your power, when Mr. Hammond put Mr. Fauchet's letter [i.e. dispatch] into the hands of Mr. Wolcott; and when an estimation was given, sir, of that letter to you. I wish to ascertain, without the necessity of resorting to circumstances, the earliest notice, which you received of the existence of such a letter. If you would add the probable time, when the British secretary of state, Lord Grenville, first obtained the letter, and when the British minister here forwarded it, I should be enabled to be more particular in my vindication.

You inform me, sir; in your letter of the 20th ultimo, that you had never seen Mr. Fauchet's dispatch No. 6, which is referred to in this letter [i.e., No. 10]; and, as you did not show, or send to me with the other papers, the dispatch No. 3, I shall continue to presume that you have not, as yet, seen either of these dispatches. If you have, it will certainly be conceived proper, that I should be furnished with copies of them; in order that I may know whether the papers in your hands, under the names of the dispatches No. 3 and 6 agree with what has been stated to me, as [to] their contents; and that if there be a difference, I may take the best measures for establishing which is true.[12]

The "history" of No. 10 and its supporting documents had suddenly become as important as the documents themselves.

Randolph's presence in Philadelphia soon stimulated renewed interest in his resignation. The reason for his abrupt resignation from the Cabinet was still the subject of widespread speculation, for Washington had willingly complied with Randolph's request that the matter be kept confidential. But there were those in Philadelphia who were not under the President's injunction,[13] and it was not long before it was known that Randolph's resignation had resulted from the discovery of evidence that he had solicited funds from the former French minister to the United States and that his hurried trip to Rhode Island was to secure a statement from Fauchet that would clear his name. Randolph thus returned to a city seething with rumors; his friends were anxious to learn the details of his resignation and the success of his mission to Rhode Island, and his enemies were anxious to learn the extent of his treason.[14]

Imprudently Randolph gave his side of the story. In all likelihood his account emphasized the President's callousness and the inquisitional methods Washington had employed in acquainting him with Fauchet's dispatch. The same bitterness toward Washington prompted him to give Andrew Brown, editor of the *Philadelphia Gazette*, a copy of one of the letters dated September 15, which he had just sent to Washington.[15] With it he publicly served notice that he would soon publish a vindication of his conduct. With an obvious air of triumph he had written:

> Sir,
>   In my letter of the 19th ultimo, I informed you of my purpose to overtake Mr. Fauchet, if possible. I accordingly went to Newport in Rhode Island, where I had an interview with him. The abrupt and unexpected sailing of the French frigate, *La Meduse* [*sic*], on the morning of the day after I arrived there, had nearly deprived me of the object of my journey. But I trust that I am in possession of such materials, not only from Mr. Fauchet but also from other sources as will convince every unprejudiced mind, that my resignation was dictated by considerations which ought not to have been resisted for a moment and that everything connected with it, stands upon a footing perfectly honourable to myself.[16]

There was more to the letter, but this was the paragraph Randolph most wanted to see in print. It implied he had the evidence that would completely clear him. In time he would lay the "materials" before the public, and unprejudiced minds would vindicate his conduct and applaud his resignation. There could be little doubt he was trying to seize the initiative and make a bid for public sympathy. It was a highly reprehensible maneuver for one who had requested Washington to place the affair under an injunction of secrecy.

Shortly before the publication of this letter Randolph contacted Adet to inquire as to when he might expect to receive a copy of Fauchet's certificate and, equally important, if he might be provided with a copy of those sections of Nos. 3 and 6 that Fauchet had referred to in No. 10.[17] Within a week Adet had complied with his request, also adding a statement of his own asserting that the remaining sections of these two dispatches related to matters "entirely foreign to Mr. Randolph." He continued:

I certify moreover, that at the request of Mr. Randolph I have examined the dispatches of Citizen Fauchet to the French government, and that whensoever Citizen Fauchet had occasion to speak of Mr. Randolph, in respect to his morality, he always describes him as an honest and upright man.[18]

With Fauchet's certificate and the pertinent sections from his diplomatic correspondence in his possession, Randolph could now turn his attention to what had recently become, for him, the more intriguing aspect of this whole affair. To what extent was Hammond's delivery of the intercepted dispatch to Wolcott connected with the British minister's determination to see the Jay Treaty ratified in spite of the continued enforcement of the Order in Council by his government? Randolph felt that it was necessary for him to know not only the details surrounding Hammond's handling of No. 10, but also, and more important, the extent to which his activities could be related to Washington's hesitancy in signing the treaty.

Randolph's September 15 letter to the President had initiated this phase of his inquiry,[19] but Washington's reply indicated he knew very little about the "history" of No. 10 prior to the day the dispatch was put into his hands.[20] With the President's reply before him, Randolph now pursued the inquiry with Wolcott. "As the British minister conveyed through your hands this business to the President," he wrote on October 2, "I hold myself authorized to inquire from you into some material facts, as they probably rest in your knowledge." When, he asked, did Hammond put the letter into his hands? Had Grenville, Hammond or he been in possession of, or even seen, Nos. 3 and 6? When did Grenville obtain No. 10? When did Hammond receive it from Grenville?[21] Wolcott's reply came immediately. Hammond had delivered the letter on July 28, or three days before Randolph was persuaded to write Washington urging his immediate return to Philadelphia. Wolcott further noted that he had given the letter to the President on August 11 in the evening. He had never seen Nos. 3 and 6, and had no idea whether Grenville or Hammond had ever seen them. He knew the intercepted dispatch was taken from the *Jean Bart*, but he did not know when it was received by Grenville or by Hammond. He remembered only that Hammond had said that he had received it a short time before.[22]

Wolcott seemingly knew little more than Washington about the background of the letter and apparently had made no effort to check Fauchet's references to earlier dispatches or even to learn if the British had access to these dispatches. Randolph probably would have accepted Wolcott's reply had not another incident caused him to conclude that Pickering and Wolcott were deliberately attempting to withhold information that would assist him in clearing his name. The day Wolcott's reply reached him, October 3, he applied at the offices of the Department of State for permission to see the file containing the more recent of Washington's letters to him as Secretary of State.[23] His friend George Taylor, the chief clerk, asked Pickering if he might show the letters to Randolph. After checking the file himself, Pickering agreed that Randolph might examine it. A package of letters wrapped in brown paper was laid before Randolph to be examined in Taylor's presence. In reading the letters Randolph discovered that one letter from the President, that of July 22, 1795, was missing from the file.[24] Randolph remembered the letter well, for in it Washington had very candidly set forth his views on the Jay Treaty and the question of its eventual ratification.[25] Upon asking Taylor for the letter, he was informed that it had just been removed from the package by Colonel Pickering and that it would be made available only if Randolph specifically applied for it. Annoyed, Randolph promptly requested to see the letter. After some delay he was informed by Taylor that Colonel Pickering had decided that he could not release it until he had consulted Wolcott. Since this was Saturday, Randolph apparently agreed to wait until Monday, October 5, for their decision. When he received no word from Pickering by Monday afternoon, he sent a brief note to Taylor inquiring as to when he might see the letter.[26] Taylor's reply came the next day. He had dutifully transmitted Randolph's request to Colonel Pickering, "whose answer I am authorized to send you in the following words, viz.":

"The letter from the President, dated the 22nd of July, 1795, of which Mr. Randolph has requested the inspection, does not appear to have any connection with the intercepted letter of Mr. Fauchet; and, cannot possibly have referred to it; because the President was at that time ignorant even of its existence: and Mr. Randolph perfectly well knows that his resignation was occasioned solely by the evidence of his criminal conduct exhibited in Mr. Fauchet's letter. The inspection of the President's letter then cannot be necessary for Mr. Randolph's exculpation."[27]

Randolph practically exploded with anger. Pickering's insolence was matched only by his cunning. Washington's letter of the 22nd had clearly expressed his determination not to sign the treaty so long as the reported Order in Council remained in operation.[28] Randolph knew that the letter would prove that the President's thinking on the treaty in late July was entirely compatible with his own. If published, the rashness of Washington's August 12 decision to sign the treaty would be exposed, only to be explained by the conspiratorial efforts of Hammond, Wolcott and Pickering to mislead the President. To Randolph, the plan they had followed was obvious. By establishing Randolph's "treasonable" conduct and the duplicity of the government of France, they had caused Washington to abandon the sound policy he had adopted in consultation with Randolph.[29] Pickering's refusal to surrender Washington's letter convinced Randolph that this was what had happened. He would force Pickering to release the letter, possibly publish it and expose the conspiratorial conduct of the Secretaries of War and of the Treasury. It would, of course, provide a fitting theme on which to build an explanation of the incriminating passages in Fauchet's dispatches.

A letter to the President was immediately drafted detailing Pickering's conduct. In effect he asked Washington to order Pickering to surrender the letter. Lest the Secretary of War challenge his account of what had transpired, he showed the letter to Taylor and secured from him a promise that he would attest to the accuracy of his account. He revised and expanded the letter the next day, and on the following day, October 8, after further revision, sent it to Mount Vernon.[30]

After completing his letter to Washington he sent another letter to Wolcott inquiring again if "anything more than the letter, No. 10, had been used in Mr. Hammond's machinations." He had, he continued, reason to conclude that "Mr. Hammond was *particularly instructed*" by his government at the time the intercepted dispatch was turned over to Wolcott.[31] The Secretary of the Treasury replied coldly: "The nature of your inquiries on this subject leads me to assure you that I am not conversant in the secrets of foreign ministers. . . ."[32] By this time Randolph's anger knew no bounds, and in an apparent attempt to embarrass the President into ordering the release of the letter he sent an extract from his October 8 letter to Washington to the *Philadelphia Gazette*.[33] It was published on Saturday, October 10, while the original letter was still in the mail for Mount Vernon.[34] Unknown to Washington, Pickering's and Wolcott's handling of Randolph's inquiries had succeeded in convincing Randolph that he was the victim of an English-inspired plot to insure the ratification of the treaty. In fact Randolph now seemed to be more intent on exposing English machinations and the conspiratorial conduct of his former colleagues than in explaining the incriminating passages in Fauchet's dispatch.

The publication of an excerpt from his letter to Washington rekindled public interest in Randolph's resignation. The delay in the publication of his vindication had convinced many that it would never appear. Now, apparently, he needed only one document to complete his case, and this had been stubbornly withheld from him. In publishing his letter to Washington he served notice that he would take his appeal directly to the people if the President refused to release the letter. Even his friends must have been appalled by his conduct. Few public figures would be so ungracious as to publish an excerpt from a letter to the President before it had even reached him.

It was October 23 before Randolph received a reply to his now famous letter. Washington, who had started back to Philadelphia before the letter reached Mount Vernon, first learned of it through the press, receiving the original in Philadelphia on October 20.[35] There, in close consultation with Pickering, he drafted his reply.[36] It was a masterful document. Restrained, but with an air of contemptuous pity, he authorized Randolph to publish any letter he had ever written or any comment he had ever uttered that would in any way contribute to his vindication. He asked only that this letter be also published so that the public, to which Randolph was appealing, would know that the President had not denied him access to government files. If the facts were fairly and candidly stated, he noted, "they will invite no comment." As for his published vindication, he had no desire to receive it other than through the medium of the press.[37] The ties of friendship were irrevocably broken. To Washington, Randolph was a bitter and desperate figure determined to clear his own name without regard for the reputation of others or, apparently, the confidences he had enjoyed as a presidential adviser.

Randolph replied in tones of self-righteous triumph, expressing his gratitude for the permission to use the public records yet implying that Washington, in justice, could not have done less. He assured the President he would not publish anything detrimental to his Administration, but insisted he would be obliged to use many documents to show how he had been made "the mediated victim of party spirit."[38] It was a smug rejoinder.

Washington drafted a reply, then wrote on the back of the letter: "This is the Rough draft of a Letter to Edmd. Randolph Esq. But upon re-consideran [sic] was not sent to him."[39] So ended the extended correspondence and the historic friendship of the President and his trusted political adviser.

By late September Randolph knew pretty well what he intended to include in his *Vindication*. He had decided that it would take the form of a letter to the President, documented with explicit references to the correspondence between Washington and himself.[40] Apparently he had intended to present a copy of his defense to Washington before giving it to the printer, but this idea was abandoned after the President informed him that he would receive it only "through the medium of the press."[41] Sections of the *Vindication* were obviously prepared before all the information had been gathered, with a consequent sacrifice of organization and overall credibility.

Randolph began with a description of the events of August 19, including his letter of resignation and the President's reply. Turning to his hurried trip to Rhode Island, he detailed his experiences at Newport and inserted all the letters and affidavits he had accumulated in this venture. He then reprinted without comment Fauchet's certificate and the extracts of Nos. 3 and 6 as supplied by Adet. This in turn was followed by all of the correspondence associated with his efforts to secure more information on the background of No. 10, as well as the letters in the files of the Department of State that would assist him in his defense.[42] Then, laying the groundwork for what he considered to be one of the dominant themes of his *Vindication*, he carefully summarized the evolution of the President's thinking on the treaty and his own counsels thereon between March 7, 1795, the date the text of the treaty was received, and August 12, 1795, the date the President informed his Cabinet that he intended to sign it. His account impressively documented the proposition that the President had many misgivings about the treaty from the beginning, and from early July to August 12, 1795, had consistently expressed his determination not to sign it while the British Order in Council remained in force. As Secretary of State he was in complete harmony with the President's views and had faithfully supported him in his policy.[43] The narrative was then broken again by the insertion of a translation of Fauchet's No. 10.[44]

After the translation Randolph began his letter to the President. He accused Washington of presuming he was guilty without knowing the contents of Nos. 3 and 6 and before providing Randolph himself with an opportunity to explain the contents. Further, the circumstances surrounding the delivery of the dispatch were such as "you ought to have withstood the impulse which hurried you into prejudication." Doubts as to the reliability of the author of the dispatch and the motives of the British minister in revealing it, as well as Randolph's own record of loyalty, ought to have caused him to hesitate. At the very least, Randolph should have been provided with an opportunity to question Hammond before he left the country. Hammond's intent, Randolph continued, was obvious:

He had long ago heard that you generally suffered yourself to be governed by a majority of your council; and that a concert between Messrs. Wolcott and Pickering, who caught with joy the seeming authority to denounce the foes of the treaty, as a "detestable and nefarious conspiracy" . . . would turn your mind to the revocation of your original intention.

He was, in short, the victim of an English plot to secure the President's approval of the Jay Treaty—a plot that shamelessly exploited the political biases of two members of the Cabinet.[45]

The remainder of the *Vindication* was given to an explanation of No. 10. For the most part it was a paragraph-by-paragraph analysis, with particular emphasis on those paragraphs containing incriminating statements.[46]

The context in which No. 10 was to be read was explained by Fauchet in his first paragraph. Referring to his distrust of his fellow commissioners and the measures he had been forced to employ in reporting on the policies being pursued by the American government, he observed:

> When it comes in question to explain, either by conjectures or by certain data, the secret views of a foreign government, it would be imprudent to run the risk of indiscretions, and to give oneself up to men whose known partiality for that government, and similitude of passions and interests with its chiefs, might lead to confidences, the issue of which are incalculable. Besides, the precious confessions of Mr. Randolph alone throw a satisfactory light upon every thing that comes to pass. These I have not yet communicated to my colleagues. . . . I shall then endeavour, Citizen, to give you a clue to all the measures, of which the common dispatches give you an account. . . .[47]

By implication this could mean almost anything. Fauchet in his certificate had gone to great lengths to explain the phrase *"précieuses confessions,"* leaving Randolph little choice but to accept and quote it in full.[48] To do otherwise, to offer a different explanation of what the phrase meant, would have rendered the whole of Fauchet's certificate worthless. The former French minister insisted that he did not mean to imply that Randolph had conveyed the secrets of his government, but rather only such information as would continually reassure him that the American government remained attached to France and that the historic friendship was not being undermined by Jay's negotiations. Moreover, Fauchet continued, he discovered that many of Randolph's communications were soon circulating as commonly held opinions.[49] Since Fauchet's imprecise language made his explanation somewhat less than convincing, Randolph tried to clarify the matter even further by insisting that what Fauchet referred to as *"précieuses confessions"* were in fact little more than evidences of that frankness expected of a Secretary of State who had been instructed to reassure the French minister of our continued friendship. In fact some of Fauchet's communications to Randolph might, with equal validity, be styled as "precious confessions."[50]

The subsequent paragraphs of the dispatch vaguely outlined the growth of political parties in America and emphasized the ascendency of Federalist policies and the noble efforts of the Republicans to stem the tide of the Federalists' monarchical and pro-English sympathies.[51] There was no further reference to Randolph until the fourteenth paragraph, where Fauchet, after noting that the political rivalry he had just described had brought the country to the verge of either revolution or civil war, implied a Federalist conspiracy to stimulate political unrest in western Pennsylvania:

> The first was preparing: the government, which had foreseen it, reproduced under various forms, the demand of a disposable force which might put it in a respectable state of defence. Defeated in this measure, who can aver that it may not have hastened the local eruption, in order to make an advantageous diversion, and to lay the more general storm which it saw gathering? Am I not authorized in forming this conjecture from the conversation which the Secretary of State had with me and LeBlanc, alone, an account of which you have in my dispatch No. 3? [52]

He then explained how the new law for collecting the excise tax contained provisions for the use of coercive measures, which, in turn, would incite strong public reaction, thereby justifying repressive measures by the government. "This," he continued, "was undoubtedly what Mr. Randolph meant in telling me *that under pretext of giving energy to the government it was intended to introduce absolute power, and to mislead the President in*[to] *paths which would conduct him to unpopularity.*"[53]

Randolph's explanation of this paragraph began by pointing out that Fauchet could have readily concluded that the government was attempting to create a "disposable force" from the various efforts in Congress to enlarge our military establishment. That these attempts resulted from the fear of an impending revolution was, he insisted, a peculiar interpretation of his own. But that his conversation with Randolph, as related in dispatch No. 3, therefore justified the conjecture that the government, defeated in its demand for a disposable force, "hastened the local eruption [through the new excise law] in order to make an advantageous diversion, and to lay the more general storm which it saw gathering"—this Randolph denied. The conversation summarized in No. 3 occurred, he noted, in April of 1794, while the law to which Fauchet referred as having deliberately hastened the "local eruption" was not passed until June of that year. Thus Fauchet, in writing No. 10 in October, 1794, had credited Randolph with helping him interpret, in April of 1794, the significance of a law that did not pass until June of that year. This neatly disposed of the fourteenth paragraph, but Randolph was still left with No. 3.[54]

The printed extract of No. 3, while establishing the innocence of his conversation with Fauchet at the time, created the impression that Randolph had convinced the French minister that he was the most influential and unselfish of the President's advisers:

> Then the Secretary of State appeared to open himself without reserve. He imparted to me the intestine divisions which were rumbling in the United States. The idea of an approaching commotion affected him deeply. He hoped to prevent it, by the ascendancy which he daily acquired over the mind of the President, who consulted him in all affairs; and to whom he told the truth, which his colleagues disguised from him.[55]

Only Randolph, it seemed, protected the President from the forces that were seeking to divert him from his noble and statesmanlike goals.

Randolph's explanation of all this was clever. In fact he turned Fauchet's language to his own advantage: "[L]et me concenter the actual state of things in April, 1794; in order that I may compass the general scope of the conversation and thus contribute to explain it." Fauchet, he noted, became suspicious of the intent of the United States a few weeks after his arrival. As Secretary of State he could remain silent or take such steps as would establish beyond question that our policy was not guided by a "predilection for Great Britain." By adopting the latter course he was but following a policy that had frequently been enunciated by Washington in his public and private statements. "If in all this," Randolph continued, "I have erred, it is mere error;—but the error is not mine. It was derived from the spirit of your own movements [Washington's], and our political prospects in April, 1794." Moreover, if, as Fauchet asserted, Randolph was disturbed by the prospect of a conflict between the two political parties, this was no more than an expression of the same concern he had repeatedly conveyed to Washington since June, 1792. As for his efforts to gain influence over the President, this, too, was known to Washington. Had he not attempted to better serve the President by forsaking all personal power and choosing instead to remain free of all party affiliations? It was perfectly obvious that he had deliberately tried to become the President's most trusted adviser. But Fauchet, in an effort to enhance his own image, had twisted friendship into dominance, influence into power, and respect into sympathy. If Washington but reflected on the situation in April of 1794, he would realize that Fauchet's dispatch represented little more than the reactions of a French minister to a policy that he had established and Randolph had executed.[56]

The fifteenth and sixteenth paragraphs in No. 10 established more explicitly Randolph's role in the growing political conflict that the

French minister had been describing: "[T]he very pacific union of the counties in Braddock's field" in western Pennsylvania, observed Fauchet, had been given a more sinister meaning by a certain faction in the government in order to justify the raising of a force of fifteen thousand militia. "It was necessary to magnify the danger, to disfigure the views of those people [i.e., those who had assembled at Braddock's field], to attribute to them the design of uniting themselves in England, to alarm the citizens for the fate of the constitution, whilst in reality the revolution threatened only the ministers." In all this they succeeded, Fauchet continued, the military part of the "suppression" undoubtedly resulted from Hamilton's influence, while the peaceful part and the sending of commissioners were "due to the influence of Mr. Randolph over the mind of the President."[57]

"In the meantime," he continued in the sixteenth paragraph, "although there was a certainty of having an army, yet it was necessary to assure themselves of co-operators among the men whose patriotic reputation might influence their party, and whose luke-warmness or want of energy in the existing conjectures might compromise the success of the plans." Two such men were the governor of Pennsylvania and his Secretary of State. "It appears therefore that these men with others unknown to me, all having without doubt Randolph at their head, were balancing to decide on their party." Thus it was that:

> Two or three days before the proclamation was published, and of course before the cabinet had resolved on its measures, Mr. Randolph came to see me with an air of great eagerness, and made me the overtures of which I have given you an account in my No. 6. Thus with some thousands of dollars the Republic could have decided on civil war or on peace!

Hamilton's "system of finance" had made "of a whole nation, a stock-jobbing, speculating, selfish people." "Nevertheless the depravity has not yet embraced the mass of the people. . . ." "There are," he continued, "some patriots. Monroe belongs to this group as does Madison and Jefferson, but they are few in number."[58]

Randolph proceeded through the maze of subjective generalizations sentence by sentence. The closer Fauchet's account came to the time of his writing the dispatch, the more annoying became the exaggerations and vaguenesses of his style. The meeting at Braddock's Field was, Randolph insisted, anything but "pacific," and it was he who had urged an increase in the militia over the number originally suggested:

> It was wise to overawe them, for had they, in some rash moment, made battle, allured by a false comparison of their strength and situation with the

power which was marching against them, still greater bodies of troops would have been assembled, and war would have raged with all its severities.

As for Fauchet's assertion that the military response of the government was attributed to Hamilton and the peaceful part to him, this conjecture was general around Philadelphia. Randolph also denied he had anything to do with the selection of the men who would command the militia, as Fauchet seemed to imply. The truth of the matter was he had "not the smallest authority for so naming them." Further, he had never formed "political connections" with influential persons in the state governments and had no personal contact with the inhabitants of western Pennsylvania, so as to leave him thoroughly indifferent to their fate, excepting insofar as order and good government would insure their well-being. "Upon what then could I balance? The tenor of my opinions on that event I will now retrace."[59] There followed a detailed summary of Administration policies as the particulars of the insurrection reached Philadelphia. Typically, Randolph's advice on each issue was reviewed with a direct quote from the documents themselves.[60] He concluded:

> If then to declare without reserve, that the militia must be employed to support the laws, provided they could not be executed by the officers of the law; to be solicitous to avert a civil war; and save, if possible, a million of dollars to the United States; to be cautious in the expenditure of money, for which there had been no appropriation; and to convince the people, that every conciliatory plan had been exhausted, in warding off the emergency;—if this be to balance, then did I balance, not otherwise.[61]

So far the former Secretary of State was on fairly safe ground, for his role in the events Fauchet had described was a matter of public record. Even his enemies would be at a loss to convert Fauchet's account into a demonstration of treasonable conduct. But what followed wore a more sinister appearance involving a single private conversation between Randolph and the French minister. In the middle of the sixteenth paragraph was the incriminating account of their meeting:

> Two or three days before the proclamation was published, and of course before the cabinet had resolved on its measures, Mr. Randolph came to see me with an air of great eagerness, and made to me the overtures of which I have given you an account in my No. 6.[62]

The account in No. 6 removed all implications of personal gain but left the impression that Randolph had solicited financial aid from a foreign minister to save four men from harassment by their English creditors. These four men, it seemed, were in a position to save the country from a civil war, "but debtors of English merchants, they will be deprived of their liberty, if they take the smallest step." If Fauchet could "lend them instantaneously funds, sufficient to shelter them from English persecution [*sic*]," they would be free to act in their country's best interest.[63]

Fauchet's certificate served to clarify both of these passages but made no attempt to extricate Randolph from the compromising circumstances described in No. 6. The Secretary of State, Fauchet explained, had heard that the English were instrumental in fomenting the disturbances in the western counties of Pennsylvania with the intention of embarrassing the United States. If successful, a civil war would result, which presumably would be detrimental to French interests. Randolph, as Fauchet explained it in the certificate, asked the French minister if he would inquire into the accuracy of these reports among those members of the commercial community engaged in selling flour to France. These men, by virtue of their close business ties with English representatives in this country, could undoubtedly learn the extent of English involvement in this insurrection. If it could be conclusively established that England was fomenting the unrest, the western leaders would presumably find themselves deserted by a majority of the settlers in these counties, while the militia, angered by this foreign meddling, would route the remnants of the forces. Fauchet agreed to make inquiries, whereupon Randolph casually mentioned that some of the individuals contacted might be debtors of English merchants, which would make it difficult for them to obtain such information without exposing themselves to harassment by their creditors. But if Fauchet could arrange to have the sums due to them under their existing contracts with the French government paid in advance, they might free themselves from these embarrassments. The certificate went on to record Fauchet's surprise at Randolph's suggestion and his inability to understand why the government did not procure this information itself, or why American citizens did not supply this intelligence to their government voluntarily, undeterred by the threat of English "persecution." Be that as it may, Randolph had not, Fauchet insisted, solicited money for himself on this or on any other occasion.[64]

Randolph's explanation of all this was rather strained and none too convincing. The meeting Fauchet had alluded to in No. 10, reported on in No. 6 and then reinterpreted in his certificate did in fact take place. But Randolph had attached so little importance to it that he was actually at a loss to explain the meaning of the incriminating sentences in No. 10 until he had seen the excerpt of No. 6 and Fauchet's certificate. Even with these documents many of the details supplied by Fauchet escaped his memory. The rumor of English support of the disturbances in western Pennsylvania was connected in some way with a plot of

Hammond and the "British faction" in New York to discredit Randolph and Governor Clinton of New York and weaken America's close ties with France. According to Randolph, the report of this plot came from Fauchet and he, in return, demanded that Fauchet supply some proof of these activities, suggesting that he employ the services of "those men who were on an intimate footing with . . . [yourself], and had some access to the British connections." Whether he suggested the flour merchants mentioned by Fauchet or even had any particular group of individuals in mind, he could not remember. That he was equally concerned with the reports of English meddling in the Pennsylvania insurrection was also true, as was the fact that he desired to expose their activities. Presumably Fauchet's business contacts could supply the information necessary to expose English machinations in both areas. If money was mentioned at all, Randolph noted, it could only have been with reference to these business contacts possibly being at the mercy of their English creditors. He had, however, faithfully reported the substance of this conversation to Washington the day after it occurred. If in his report he omitted some of the details, it was not, he insisted, from a desire to hide anything from the President, but rather an indication of how slight an impression these matters had made upon him. There was nothing in his conduct on this or any other occasion of which he was ashamed.[65]

The remainder of his explanation was not really meant for Washington or anyone familiar with the details of his forced resignation, for it dealt with the rumors circulating about Randolph's being in the service of the French minister. Arguing with the skill of a defense attorney, Randolph sought to establish how implausible such accusations were.[66] His forceful refutation of the charge that he had been the immediate recipient and principal beneficiary of French funds was not really necessary even in this public vindication. Undoubtedly it only served to dignify the rumors that were circulating against him. It was in this section that he returned to the theme he had introduced earlier in his defense—that he was the victim of political partisanship of English sponsorship.[67] The protest did little to promote the credibility of his remarks.

The remainder of Fauchet's famous dispatch carried the narrative through the month of October. It assessed the spirit of the troops marching into western Pennsylvania, analyzed the motives of Hamilton in accompanying the President to Carlisle, commented on the deliberate attempt of some to circumvent the Constitution by urging the President to absent himself from the opening of Congress, and presumed to identify the ultimate aims of Hamilton and his fellow conspirators. Randolph was referred to only once in the nineteenth paragraph as having successfully influenced the press in Philadelphia to expose the unconstitutionality of the President's absenting himself from the opening of Congress.[68] Randolph dismissed the observation with a simple denial. And since there was nothing on which he need comment in the six remaining paragraphs of the dispatch, they were dismissed as having no bearing on his conduct.[69]

In closing he noted that this letter to Washington was in fact an appeal to the people:

> To yourself, Sir, I can never appeal. Your conduct on the 19th of August, 1795, your letter of the 20th; and the declarations of those, who felt a persuasion that they were fighting under your banners, have long ago proclaimed that you had been in an instant transformed into my enemy.[70]

With these lines, almost the very last of his *Vindication*, Edmund Randolph closed the door on the strange sequence of events that had abruptly ended his political career.

His task completed, Randolph chose to leave Philadelphia immediately. It was not a difficult decision to make. At one time, it is true, he had seriously considered making this city his permanent home, but it had lost much of its appeal. Since his return from Rhode Island, he found little of the universal sympathy he had expected. And the circumstances surrounding his departure from public office probably would have made it difficult for him to establish a successful private practice in the city. Thus when the text of the *Vindication* had been completed, it went immediately to the printer.[71] The documents he had collected in preparing his defense were placed in the hands of J. R. Smith to be shown to anyone who might question the truth of what he had written.[72] Fauchet's No. 10 was given to a friend to be translated into English and then forwarded to the printer with the necessary instructions on how it was to be incorporated into the text of the *Vindication*.[73] To Madison he wrote: "I feel happy at my emancipation from an attachment to a man who has practiced upon me the profound hypocracy of Tiberius and the injustice of an assassin." He was, he added, wearied by his long contemplation of the "vexatious subject."[74]

Early in November he completed arrangements for the shipment of his furniture and books to Virginia and then began with his family the long journey home. Before the end of the month he was settled in Richmond, a private citizen, prepared to resume his law practice and anxious to forget the past. And within days of his arrival he was handling an appeal case for Colonel Charles Simms of Alexandria.[75] Pending the publication of his *Vindication*, he chose to keep his personal correspondence free of all comment on his resignation.[76]

The impending release of Randolph's long-promised defense was awaited with considerable interest by the political community.[77] His closeness to the President and the reports that Washington had authorized him to publish anything from their public correspondence that might clear his name caused many to conclude that the innermost secrets of the executive councils would be divulged. Congressmen arriving in Philadelphia for the opening of the Fourth Congress were promising their political confidants outside Philadelphia that they would forward a copy of Randolph's work as soon as it was available from the printer. Early in December William B. Giles of Virginia was "favored" with a perusal of the first eighty-four pages and predicted it would have the effect of completely exculpating Randolph from the charge of corruption, but would also cause him to be viewed as "the most indiscreet of ministers."[78] John Adams, having seen a part of the *Vindication* shortly after his arrival in the city, hastened a copy of the extract of No. 6 to his wife Abigail with the observation: "If he can and will explain that, and another paragraph in a succeeding dispatch No. 10 which refers to it, he will do wonders." Then, thinking she should have that paragraph as well, he added as a postscript the paragraph from No. 10.[79] As political news it was second only to the President's opening message to Congress.

It was December 20 before the *Vindication* appeared.[80] Reactions were predictable insofar as general approval or disapproval was predetermined by the political bias of the commentator. But beyond this, individual opinions were quite varied. Washington, writing to Hamilton on December 22, left little doubt of what he thought of Randolph's efforts:

> 'Ere this, I presume you have seen the long promised vindication, or rather accusation. What do you think of it and what notice should be taken of it? You are fully acquainted with my Sentiments relative to the rival and warring powers of F[rance] and E[ngland]; and have heard as strong sentiments from me with respect to both, as ever he did. His declaration, that he has always opposed to the commercial part of the negotiation, is as impudent and insolent an assertion, as is false, if he means more than that it was contingent (as the instructions to Mr. Jay declare) and to apply the knowledge of it to me. But if you have seen his performance, I shall leave you to judge of it, without any comments of mine.[81]

And, of course, John Adams sent Abigail a copy of the whole work as soon as it was placed on sale. It was, he noted, "a very weak thing," "a piece of revenge against the President" for some injury or offense which he (Adams) had been unable to discover. If Randolph had proved that Washington had prejudged his case, were people, therefore, supposed to conclude that the former Secretary of State was innocent? Adams would have none of it. Randolph had not proved his innocence, Fauchet's dispatch was a "silly think [*sic*]," and the whole affair was "strange nonsense."[82] Madison reported to Jefferson: "As it relates to the P.[resident] nothing seems to be said; and as it relates to parties in general very little."[83] Hamilton and Oliver Wolcott, Sr., found the work to be a virtual confession of guilt, while John Quincy Adams, in England to effect the final signing of the treaty, abandoned his hitherto unswerving loyalty to Randolph to express his amazement at the indiscretions of the author.[84] The day after the book appeared in Philadelphia Oliver Wolcott, Jr., sent a copy of it to William Ellery of Newport, Rhode Island, with the urgent plea that he ascertain as soon as possible whether Randolph was or was not in private consultation with Fauchet for some considerable period of time before the *Medusa* sailed, and to obtain an affidavit on this point from some credible person. "My motive for making this inquiry will be discovered from a perusal of Mr. R.'s publication."[85] But it was Madison who provided the most perceptive judgment of the work. Writing to Monroe a little more than a month after the defense had been published, he observed: "His greatest enemies will not easily persuade themselves that he was under a corrupt influence of France and his best friend can't save him from the self-condemnation of his political career as explained by himself."[86] In a matter of weeks the flurry and excitement that preceded the publication of the work vanished—and not without reason.[87] The *Vindication* contained neither the disclosures nor the devastating indictment of the President that many expected to find on its pages, with the result that it could not be used as a political weapon by those most anxious to employ it for that purpose. But most important, it did not prove conclusively that Randolph's conduct was as untarnished as he claimed.

In an effort to demonstrate that he was the victim of an English-inspired plot and that Washington had prejudged his case, Randolph had slighted the primary objective of his work—the establishment of his own innocence. While there can be little doubt that the *Vindication* exposed the shallowness of the accusations that his actions had been treasonous, it did not clear him of the charge of improper conduct in the office of Secretary of State. There remained the evidence that on one occasion, at least, he had suggested that Fauchet provide direct financial assistance to several Americans being harassed by English creditors. There was also the strong suspicion that the former Secretary of State had not been as guarded in his conversations with Fauchet as he had been with the other diplomatic representatives in Philadelphia and that he was less than candid in the manner in which he had reported these conversations to Washington. Admittedly the norms by which one judges such matters are illusive, and a public official would undoubtedly be paralyzed by too rigid an adherence to a fixed set of rules. It would also be relatively easy to cite instances where Randolph's contemporaries had shown equal if not greater imprudence in their contacts with people outside the government. Yet the fact remains—Randolph did not clear his name.

But Randolph was not a fool. Why had he allowed himself to be put in this embarrassing position? If there is an answer it probably can be found in his desperate attempt to placate France and to keep her from using our rapprochement with England as an excuse for abusing our neutrality. Randolph was attempting to achieve a diplomatic objective of considerable significance by a rather obvious and elementary diplomatic maneuver that had little or no chance of succeeding. Perhaps he should have realized this, and perhaps he should have realized also that he was endangering the rather unique relationship he had succeeded in establishing with Washington. When this bond of confidence and friendship was broken, Randolph's public career was finished—for he had no other claim to public office.

PART IV
LAST YEARS

Edmund Randolph returned to Virginia in December of *1795* embittered but not broken, for he fully understood what had happened. He knew that the highly charged partisan atmosphere of the times precluded his return to public life, even in his beloved Virginia. He was favorably disposed toward the Jeffersonian Republicans, but this was to be expected since it had been two Federalists who engineered his downfall. He remained an observer, sometimes more critical of one party than the other, but generally mute about public affairs whether state or national.

His legal career absorbed most of his energies and within a very short time he was once again one of the busiest lawyers in the state. Virginia's appellate courts were the focal point of his practice and for several years he virtually dominated the biannual sessions of the Court of Appeals. If he had been impressed by numbers he could have taken considerable pride in his practice, but in fact it provided him with little more than a respectable income. For the most part it was his endurance rather than his talent that was being challenged.

He served as one of the counsel for Aaron Burr in his treason trial but neither sought nor was offered a major role in determining the strategy of Burr's defense. Of far greater concern to him was the case of United States vs. Edmund Randolph, *a suit brought against him to recover funds that he had dispersed while Secretary of State and that could not be verified as legitimate expenditures from existing records. In spite of his diligent efforts to collect affidavits from those who had received money from the State Department, he was unable to collect the necessary evidence to establish the fact that he had not misused government funds, and ultimately he had a judgment rendered against him.*

The judgment imposed intolerable financial burdens and left him so destitute that even his prosperous law practice proved insufficient to satisfy his financial obligations. As his health declined, he came more and more to depend on his brothers-in-law and his children. He took refuge in the past by writing a History of Virginia, *which would recapture the critical role Virginia's leaders played in the formation of the country. His death went almost unnoticed in a country that had all but forgotten him.*

23

Virginian and Spectator
1796-1799

The Virginia to which Randolph returned late in the fall of 1795 was, he discovered, very different from the Virginia he had left in 1790. The Constitution had stripped the states of their vital role in national affairs and had made each of them an equal partner under the new federal structure. No longer did the central government derive its momentum from the fixed determination of a few key states like Virginia to make the "American experiment" work. The national government now stood on its own feet, its powers broadly defined, its machinery functioning smoothly and its freedom from state domination clearly established. Virginia had played a vital role in the events that had made this possible, and her statesmen had contributed significantly to whatever power and prestige the new government now enjoyed. But in the process Virginia had lost something—the zeal and vitality that came with her total commitment to the cause of American independence, the determination that came with the clear recognition of our ultimate objective as a nation, and the mature statesmanship that came with the awareness that others looked to her for leadership.[1] Now the tables were reversed, and it was Virginia that looked to the national government for leadership, determination and vitality. As Randolph put it: "Virginia is very little more in this quarter than a colony of Philadelphia. No conversation, no object, political, commercial, and in many instances legal, can occur without looking up to that city as the standard."[2] The focus of power had shifted to the national government, thereby bringing to an end a glorious chapter in Virginia's history. The cherished values were still there, but the drive, vitality and creativeness were gone.

In many ways the change was most dramatically manifest in the political life of the state. By the winter of 1795–1796 the Jay Treaty had decisively pushed the state into the ranks of the Jeffersonian Republicans and had made the Federalists a rather unpopular minority.[3] The Jeffersonian affiliation was a natural one, reflecting not only the agrarian outlook of the state but also the warm respect Virginians had for the man who led that party. That it also made for a comparatively tranquil political climate was probably not lost on Randolph, who was currently highly critical of the political turmoil in Philadelphia. But anyone returning to Virginia after such a long absence could not help but make comparisons between this Virginia and the Virginia of the seventies and eighties. It all seemed so quiet and peaceful—and dull.

Life in Richmond for Edmund and his family was considerably more relaxed than in Philadelphia. The city was unquestionably the most important and fastest growing community in Virginia. Being its capital, it was also the center of political life in the state. Advantageously situated on the James River, it had ready access to the interior regions, which by this time were the major wealth-producing sections of the state. By 1796 it could boast of several small manufacturing establishments, a number of flour mills to serve the needs of those who had shifted from tobacco to wheat or corn and an ample number of tobacco warehouses. These facilities were not extraordinary, but they most certainly served to make Richmond a thriving community, equally important and equally hospitable to both the merchant and the planter. The city also boasted of several academies and a fine theatre, and took considerable pride in the cluster of fine homes its more "distinguished" citizens had built on Shockoe Hill near the capitol.[4] Randolph undoubtedly shared this local pride in Richmond's many signs of vitality and community development, but he found the city attractive for other reasons. The pace of life in Richmond was much slower than what he had been accustomed to, and for the first time in many years he could honestly look forward to a more tranquil family life. Whatever demands a law practice might place upon him, he was certain they could never be as trying as the past five years.

The Randolph home, fronting on Capital Square, was one of the more imposing dwellings in Richmond; its location gave it a commanding view of the city. A massive two-story brick structure, it seemed to dwarf the smaller wooden structures that surrounded it. Randolph placed the dwelling, a rectangular-shaped building, on the property so that the longest side of the house, some fifty feet, would front on the square. With its high wooden roof, virtually a third story, it looked more like a public building than a private residence.[5] Important to Randolph was the fact that his new home was within easy reach of the public buildings, particularly those that housed the state's appellate courts and the local county and corporation courts. Only slightly less significant was that among his neighbors were some of the most distinguished members of the Virginia bar and bench.[6] And one can be certain that when the annual meetings of the General Assembly and the three terms of the

Court of Appeals brought professional colleagues and friends into the city many of them found their way into Randolph's spacious home. It was a warm and friendly home and, aside from an occasional adverse decision in a case that represented many hours of work, there was almost nothing to disrupt the happy routine of family life.

Drawn together by warmth and genuine love, the Randolphs were always a very close family. Having lost a baby son only months after birth and suffered through the stillborn delivery of another child, Edmund and Betsy had experienced personal sorrow more painful than anything they had encountered during the past six months.[7] But neither parent lived in the past. Their life was full, absorbed in the enthusiasm, laughter and daily cares of four growing children. The eldest, Peyton, would soon celebrate his fifteenth birthday. Susan, his oldest sister, had just turned thirteen, while Edmonia and Lucy were still at the age where they could try the patience of their mother while remaining above reproach in the eyes of their indulgent father. The two younger children probably were unable to understand the reasons for the family's departure from Philadelphia, but in all likelihood they found living in Richmond a new and exciting experience. Peyton and Susan were probably too young when the family left Richmond in 1790 to have remembered much about the city, but they knew their parents always looked upon Virginia as their home.[8] Whatever advantages Philadelphia might have provided the Randolphs and however much Edmund and Betsy may at one time have considered remaining there in order that he might enter private practice after he left the Cabinet, it was always with the understanding that one day they would return to Virginia.

Randolph had had enough of politics and public office, but he could scarcely pretend that these matters were no longer of any importance to him. Curiosity, if nothing else, caused him to cast a critical eye over Virginia's political landscape. Better than two years had passed since his last visit to the state. At that time he had returned at Washington's urging to assess the intensity of popular opposition to the policies of the executive. Now, as a private citizen, he had an opportunity to again view Virginia's political life. Understandably there were many first impressions. In all likelihood the former governor found the younger men who sought public office somewhat less distinguished than his own contemporaries. He could be pardoned, too, if he insisted his own era was more critical and the problems that Governor Brooke encountered less challenging than those he had faced in that office.[9] If such silent judgments were made—and they undoubtedly were—they were perceptive judgments, not the nostalgic reflections of a man who lived in the past and longed for the good old days. Randolph knew the critical years had passed and he knew, too, that it was largely because of the decisions that had been made by the political leaders of his generation and those immediately before them that Virginia enjoyed its present tranquillity.

It was not until after he returned to Virginia that Randolph sensed the growing concern of the state with the policies of the Washington Administration. In 1789, during the debate over the ratification of the federal Constitution, sharp political cleavages had developed in the state reflecting the strong sense of involvement that distinguished the political life of Virginia. But with the establishment of the new government these differences were quickly forgotten as the state became a kind of spectator to the growing political rivalry between Jefferson and Hamilton and the debate over the financial program of the Secretary of the Treasury. The arrival of Genêt in 1793 and Washington's apparent anti-French attitude briefly roused the political life of the state, yet the modest efforts of Virginia Federalists to exploit the subsequent public reaction to Genêt's conduct had little success.[10]

In general the state took a personal pride in Washington's cautious leadership. His mistakes, such as his coolness toward France, were usually blamed on others of an eastern or commercial persuasion who had poorly advised him. So long as Jefferson and Randolph were in the Cabinet and Madison in Congress there was little chance of serious error. The resignation of these two Virginians from the Cabinet and the polite but firm rejections by other Virginians of the President's pleas to accept important federal posts meant a lessening of the state's influence in the circle of presidential advisers.[11] Randolph's resignation, though shrouded in controversy, was nonetheless a vivid reminder that Washington was now almost completely surrounded by "eastern interests."

In such a climate the Jay Treaty found very few defenders and no end of critics. The critics, Randolph soon discovered, were not prepared to let the Senate's ratification of the treaty serve as the final chapter of this effort to resolve our differences with England. Rallying their supporters in several sections of the state, they sponsored resolutions and memorials against the treaty.[12] But the ultimate weapon was the numerical strength of the Republicans in the House of Representatives, and it was to this body that all eyes turned. To deny the President the appropriations necessary to carry the treaty into effect would be to foil the efforts of those who had pushed the treaty's ratification.[13] Acting independently, Randolph decided to publish a pamphlet that would lend support to the efforts of the Republicans in the House. In the process he could also offer a second vindication of his own conduct. The result was an anonymous piece entitled *Political Truth* which Samuel H. Smith of Philadelphia, the printer of his *Vindication*, published early in 1796.[14] The passage of time and his removal from Philadelphia had seemingly tempered Randolph's bitterness, so he was capable of a more carefully reasoned summary of his position. In language that was deliberately precise he reviewed again the circumstances surrounding his resignation.[15] Although adding nothing to the account in the *Vindication*, this latest piece explicitly linked the decision to sign the treaty to Washington's sudden loss of confidence in Randolph as a trusted adviser: "If this was not the motive which gave the treaty executive ratification, in direct opposition to a resolution previously formed and sent across the Atlantic, I ask what the motive was? As sophistry has not assigned a different motive, truth may be permitted to be silent."[16] But the more immediate object of his efforts was to lend his support to those who hoped to make the House the instrument of the defeat of the treaty:

> This performance has not been penned barely for the purpose of vindicating one man or criminating another. It has been written with the view of probing to its recess the poison that lurks in the very heart of our Republic. . . . However fraught with ruinous effects the ratification of the treaty with Great Britain certainly is, it may, perhaps, be said with truth that its failure would produce benefits of correspondent magnitude . . . the glory acquired by rejection . . . would raise to heaven the sounds of liberty, triumphing in her safety, would infuse into the breasts of freemen a noble independence founded on the conviction that their rights are secure and their nation independent.[17]

Then, addressing his remarks directly to the members of the House of Representatives, he described with effusive rhetoric the dire consequences for the country if they allowed the treaty to take effect.[18]

His efforts went without notice. In the final analysis Randolph's detailed account of the circumstances under which the President had signed the treaty was of little consequence in determining the attitude of those who sought to prevent the treaty's implementation.

Since it focused on the past rather than the future, his essay went completely unnoticed in Virginia.[19] The Republican-sponsored resolution in the House of Delegates which applauded the action of Virginia's two Senators for having cast a negative vote on the treaty and the continued sponsorship of meetings to voice public opposition to the treaty seemed much more relevant than Randolph's pamphlet.[20] The Federalists, concerned about the possible effect of these Republican tactics, decided to strike back. Imitating their opponents, they organized a series of meetings in various sections of the state in an effort to rally support for the treaty.[21] Not since Patrick Henry raised his voice in opposition to the Constitution had the state displayed such political vigor. Even Randolph felt compelled to attend the Federalist rally at the capitol to observe firsthand the tactics of those who sought to take the initiative away from the Republican faction in the state. In a letter to Madison he gave a full account of the meeting. It was anything but objective. He sought to assure his former confidant that this assembly was by no means reflective of the true sentiments of the freeholders in Richmond:

> Between 3[oo] and 400 persons were present; a large portion of whom were British merchants, some of whom pay for the British purchases of horses— their clerks,—officers who hold posts under the President at his will—stock- holders—expectants of office—and many without the shadow of a freehold. Notwithstanding this, the numbers on the Republican side, tho' inferior, were inferior in a small degree only.[22]

In the verbal exchange between John Marshall and Alexander Camp- bell, he continued, Marshall's arguments were "inconsistent," while Campbell "spoke eloquently and forcibly; and threw ridicule and ab- surdity upon his antagonist with success."[23] Randolph may well have felt that Campbell had the better of the argument, but his own attitude toward the treaty made him a biased observer. However, it mattered little, for by the time Randolph's letter reached Philadelphia the deci- sive vote had been taken by the House sitting as a Committee of the Whole, and Madison and his fellow Republicans had gone down to defeat.[24] Federalist-sponsored meetings such as the one Randolph had reported on in Richmond had been held in virtually every commercial center in the nation in an effort to counteract the impression of univer- sal opposition to the treaty. The result was a continuous flow of peti- tions and memorials favorable to the treaty into Philadelphia.[25] The Federalist strategy, plus a certain uneasiness over the effect a repudia- tion might have on England's attitude toward us, caused many members of the House to dissociate themselves from the Republican efforts to defeat the treaty.

The year 1796 was also an election year, and the most authoritative voices were predicting that Washington would not seek a third term. While his continued silence as to his future intentions delayed for a time any open move to suggest a successor, it did not keep the two political parties from taking certain preliminary measures to ensure their own success at the polls if he decided to retire. The publication of his "Farewell Address" on September 19 removed the last obstacle to an open contest for the presidency, and both political parties quickly closed ranks behind their most obvious candidate.[26] The newspapers were filled with political tracts that flung charges back and forth with aban- don, while the letters of all public and most private individuals carried the latest information on the progress of the campaign in their respective states. Some were misinformed, others merely repeated what they had learned from reading the local press, but few avoided the subject completely. Only Randolph, it seemed, refrained from commenting on the campaign and the ensuing election.[27] It is impossible to imagine him as indifferent to the outcome despite his own firm decision to renounce politics and public office. His contemporaries undoubtedly assumed his preference was for Jefferson and the Republican candidates, but they would have been hard pressed to prove it. His dislike of the Federalists stemmed in large measure from his fixed personal distrust of two or three individuals in that party rather than a total disagreement with their position. Consequently, for him, Adams' election to the presidency would not assume the dimensions of a national tragedy, as it would for many Republicans. In his silence the former Secretary of State, like the retiring President under whom he had served, became a mere spectator. The choice must have been a deliberate one, for never had Randolph observed such strict silence on a political question of such moment.

By the time Adams was sworn in as President on March 4, 1797, the Jay Treaty had helped to create a rather serious diplomatic crisis with our former ally, France. On July 2, 1796, the Directory had announced that France would henceforth treat all neutral vessels in the same manner as they allowed themselves to be treated by England. Less than six months later, when Charles C. Pinckney arrived in Paris to replace Monroe as our minister to France, the Directory refused to recognize his official status and forced Pinckney to leave the country under threat of arrest. The French government announced it would receive a diplomatic representative from the United States only after France's grievances had been redressed. Adams' response to this explosive situation was to urge Congress to take measures to prepare the country for war. He also made a renewed effort to resolve our differences through diplomacy. The appointment of a three-man commission of Pinckney, John Marshall and Elbridge Gerry to negotiate a treaty of amity and commerce with France suspended for a time any action by Congress on Adams' military proposals. The country waited hopefully for word of the commissioners' success in Paris. By April, 1798, when it was learned that France had rebuffed and apparently insulted them, the country was seized by a war hysteria that exceeded anything it had experienced during the Revolution. Adams' proposals for strengthening the military establishment and the navy were met and expanded as the nation assiduously prepared for war. To silence Republican criticism of the government's policies and to curb the influence of a small but vocal group of French refugees who resented our rapprochement with England, Congress passed the Alien and Sedition

Acts. Although the acts were designed to curtail the liberty of foreigners in the United States and make it more difficult for them to become naturalized citizens, they also prescribed heavy fines and imprisonment for anyone, foreign or otherwise, found guilty of publishing false, scandalous or malicious statements against the government or its officers. As panic replaced statesmanship, irrational fear of Jeffersonian Republicanism replaced political tolerance.[28]

It has to be assumed that Randolph viewed these events with some misgivings. It is highly unlikely that he was totally indifferent, and it is impossible to believe he endorsed the policies of the Federalists. Yet in a letter to Monroe in March of 1798, at a time when the country still retained the hope of a diplomatic settlement with France, he made no reference to the subject but confined his remarks to an assessment of Monroe's prospects in the law if he returned to Virginia.[29] During that summer, with Republicans in Congress in full retreat and their very loyalty in question, Randolph busied himself with his private practice. He must have been interested in what was happening and in private conversation probably echoed the concern of many Virginians over the severity of the legislation being passed. Unknown to Randolph, plans were being laid to challenge the heavy-handed policies of the Federalists, and the Kentucky and Virginia state legislatures were to be made the instrument of the Republican reply to the Alien and Sedition Acts.[30]

When the Virginia Assembly met in Richmond on December 3, 1798, Randolph was in the city. The October term of the Court of Appeals had ended a few weeks earlier, but he still had court appearances scheduled in several of the lower courts that met in the capital. With the opening of the legislative session he agreed to serve as an intermediary between St. George Tucker, his old friend from Williamsburg and currently a judge of the General Court, and several members of the legislature. Tucker was in the process of drafting several proposals for the legislature which he hoped to see enacted into law. At least one of them concerned the General Court in which he served. The proposals were sent to Randolph, who apparently saw to it that they were placed into the hands of one or more members of the legislature, who in turn assumed responsibility for guiding the measures through committee.[31] It soon became evident, however, that the prospect of sponsoring a reply to the Alien and Sedition Acts gave the legislature weightier matters to consider. Randolph sensed the serious mood of the Assembly and alerted Tucker to the possibility of a delay in the consideration of his proposals: "Today John Taylor agitated some well-drawn resolutions against the two [sic] execrable bills; in a speech popular and attractive. No other member spoke, but a crisis is working."[32] A week later, after summarizing what had happened to Tucker's "draughts" since his last letter, he reported: "No decision on Taylor's resolutions."[33] Four days later both houses of the Assembly approved Taylor's resolutions—the "Virginia Resolutions."[34] The debate in the lower house had been fierce and until the vote was taken no one knew for certain whether the margin of Republican votes would be sufficient to give weight to the language of the resolutions.[35] Even after their passage the mood of the legislature remained belligerent as its Republican members sought to secure the passage of a second set of resolutions designed to express opposition to the Federalist-sponsored measures in Congress that created a standing army. Virginia Federalists countered with a resolution proclaiming Virginia's willingness to cooperate with the federal government in whatever measures were deemed necessary "by the councils of the Union."[36] Until the House came to a vote on these resolutions, Randolph reported to Tucker on December 30, there was little likelihood that any action would be taken on the bills Tucker had drafted.[37] Five days later the House rejected the Federalist resolution and then passed the Republican-sponsored resolutions by a wide margin.[38] When the legislative session ended some three weeks later it had not passed any of the measures prepared by Tucker. Most of them died in committee because the Virginia legislature had absorbed itself in national affairs.[39]

For Randolph this display of legislative vitality on national issues must have awakened fond memories and caused him to revise an earlier estimate of the political climate in Virginia. And yet he was but a spectator, only vaguely aware of the significance that was soon to be attached to the so-called Virginia Resolutions. In many ways Randolph was viewing these momentous events merely as the reason Tucker's proposals were not being brought forward more rapidly. Randolph surely knew these resolutions were more important than the draft legislation presented by Judge Tucker, but he declined to place them within the context of national politics and, unbelievable as it seems, was totally unaware of their constitutional implications.[40] They were, in short, never evaluated with the perceptiveness one might expect from a man of such varied legal and political experience.

With the end of the Assembly's session the focal point of attention for most Virginians shifted once again back to Philadelphia, for it was felt that a declaration of war was now almost inevitable. As for Randolph, he turned again to his private practice and an inscrutable silence on public matters. The rumor that Virginia was strengthening its militia,[41] the news that Adams had appointed another commissioner to negotiate with France and the obviously satisfying intelligence that a Federalist President had asked Timothy Pickering for his resignation as Secretary of State all went without notice. Even the election of Jefferson to the presidency failed to elicit more than a brief comment, although once again it is difficult to believe that he was indifferent to the outcome of the election.[42] By 1800, if not earlier, Edmund Randolph was content to be a successful Richmond lawyer and in this simple ambition he was not to be disappointed.

24

Lawyer, 1800–1807

When Randolph resumed his law practice he had very little difficulty adjusting to Virginia's system of courts, for they had not been substantially altered during the years of his absence.[1] Perhaps the most significant change was the addition of the federal court structure, giving to the state a dual system of courts, each with distinctive jurisdictional responsibilities. But Randolph needed no introduction to these courts nor any assistance in recognizing the scope of their jurisdictional authority.

It was, of course, the Virginia Court of Appeals that ultimately came to be the focal point of his practice. The statutory restrictions against the same attorney representing a client in both the lower and higher courts assured the Richmond bar of a virtual monopoly over cases tried in this court.[2] Three court terms passed before Randolph appeared before the state's highest tribunal, but when he did, in October, 1797, it was to argue seven cases.[3] This represented almost a third of the cases heard and reported on in this particular session and would seem to indicate that Randolph had made considerable progress in establishing himself as one of Richmond's most prominent attorneys.[4] The following year he was identified with about 25 percent of the cases heard during the two terms of the court, thereby further solidifying his position as a leader of the Virginia bar. In each succeeding term the number of cases he handled increased, and by the fall term in 1800 he was arguing 50 percent of the cases heard by the Court of Appeals. It is true that in many of these a second attorney was involved, for it had become common practice for a litigant to retain the services of two or even three attorneys, all of whom might argue their client's cause in court. For the next seven years the volume of cases Randolph handled was so extensive that he could actually influence the length of a court term. His absence from court, even for a few weeks (he could never absent himself for a full term), because of attendance at another court had such a direct effect on the volume of cases being heard during that term that most

Richmond lawyers probably knew when he was out of the city.[5] When his cases were being heard, he had to be in daily attendance at the bar and there were terms when he was arguing cases virtually every day the court met during that session.[6] In 1807 he still commanded one-third of the practice before this court, a record he had consistently maintained or exceeded for a seven-year period. Of his contemporaries at the bar only John Wickham equaled this record.

Randolph would have been the first to admit that the principal rewards in this extensive practice were monetary. He had only a few interesting cases and none that were truly significant. Virginians went to court most frequently to recover money or to establish title to real or personal property. Thus while the actions in law varied, the types of cases did not. Randolph's truly impressive legal experience was seldom displayed, as he argued case after case, unchallenged and unmoved by the issues involved. One day he and Wickham would be co-counsel in a case; the next day they were rivals. It mattered little to either man or to the dozen or so other lawyers who separately or jointly argued most of the cases in this court. There is some evidence that Randolph was diligent in cases where he represented a friend or relative, and he most certainly attended to the interests of a client who asked him to handle several separate cases, particularly an individual or business that made a practice of initiating court action for the recovery of debts.[7] What made the heavy case load tolerable for Randolph and the others were the financial rewards that came with practice before this court. Unlike the lower courts of the state, the fees a lawyer could collect were not determined by law. Lawyers, in general, gave no evidence of being mercenary in their treatment of their clients, but it is also true that the better lawyers were acutely aware of their professional image and responsibilities and acted accordingly when it came to setting fees.[8]

Perhaps the most important case historically with which Randolph became associated during these years was *Turpin et al. vs. Locket et al.*, on which the court rendered an opinion in May, 1804.[9] The appellants were the vestrymen and church wardens of Manchester Parish, an Episcopal church in Chesterfield County, and the defendants were the overseers of the poor in the county. The parish officers had filed a bill in Richmond's Superior Court of Chancery to enjoin the overseers from selling the glebe lands of their parish because they claimed that they had a vested right in the property. The defendants, who had acted in conformance with a law passed by the legislature in 1802 authorizing the sale of these lands for the relief of the poor if the pulpit of the parish had been vacated, filed an answer and demurrer. In their answer they stated that the Revolution had abolished the Church of England, and that the property which it held therefore reverted to the community. Their demurrer urged dismissal of the appellants' bill on the grounds that the complainants showed no title in themselves or in their parish, that the Act of 1802 which authorized the sale was valid, and that if the complainants had title they had complete remedy at common law. Therefore a court of chancery was lacking in jurisdiction. The Superor Court of Chancery dismissed the bill that had been filed by the parish representatives, whereupon they took their case to the Court of Appeals. Daniel Call, John Wickham and Randolph represented the parish officials, and Attorney General Philip Norborne Nicholas and George Hay represented the overseers of the county.[10]

The case reflected the continuing struggle of several Protestant denominations in the state to dislodge the last vestiges of the religious establishment.[11] Their influence is seen in the reasoning behind the law of 1802. The preamble of the act made explicit reference to the fact that the Revolution and Virginia's constitution and bill of rights had divested the Episcopal Church of its privileged position in the state and that all its properties "devolved on the good people of this commonwealth." The act further noted that the Assembly had acquired the right to sell these lands at the time of the Revolution but had deemed it inexpedient to do so.[12] This law, therefore, was the first instance in which the Assembly was seeking to allocate the glebe lands and it had prudently authorized the sale of property only where the pulpit was vacant. The bill filed by the vestrymen and church wardens of the Manchester Parish in the Superior Court of Chancery sought to test the constitutionality of this law. In so doing they placed a delicate question of church-state relations before the courts.

Randolph's interest in the subject was not purely professional and went back several years to 1797 when he was appointed by Bishop James Madison of the Episcopal Church to a committee of lawyers to examine the nature of the title which the church possessed over the glebe lands and churches in the state. This report, delivered to the Episcopal diocesan convention of 1797, stated that the titles rested with the church and had not been impaired by the bill of rights, "but that title stands upon the same grounds with the rights of private property, which have been recognized and secured by the principles of the Revolution and by the constitution."[13] It could well be that his concern over these efforts to deprive the Episcopal Church of its glebe lands caused him to offer his assistance in the present suit.

The case was first argued in the Court of Appeals during the spring term of 1803. The court adjourned for the summer without giving an opinion. When the court assembled for the fall term, it was assumed the judges had prepared their opinions and would deliver them in the course of the session after the presiding judge, Edmund Pendleton, had assumed his place on the bench. The sudden death of Pendleton the day after his arrival in Richmond to attend court abruptly halted further consideration of the case during this term and forced the court to order that the case be reargued during the spring term of 1804.[14]

Daniel Call delivered the opening arguments for the appellants. He argued that the glebe lands belonged to the Episcopal Church and their title was either expressly stated or presumed in legislation passed both before and after the Revolution. He challenged the appellees' argument that the Church's legal title to the land had been dissolved by the Revolution, thereby vesting title in the people of the state. The Act of 1802 was, therefore, unconstitutional and the Court of Chancery ought to have awarded the injunction in order to prevent litigation.[15]

Call was followed by Philip Norborne Nicholas, the state's young attorney general and brother-in-law of Randolph. All establishments relative to the Church were, he insisted, destroyed by the Revolution. Further, the pretensions of the Episcopal Church were contrary to the fourth and sixteenth articles of the state's bill of rights. In fact, the latter article expressly forbade the state from giving preference to one religious sect over another.[16]

George Hay, the appellees' second counsel, argued that the glebe lands could not have been vested in the Episcopal Church before the Revolution because it was not a corporation and therefore lacked the authority to purchase and hold lands. It was the state that held title to the property, and had bestowed it on the Church to provide for the needs of the ministers of an established church. When the establishment was destroyed, the ministers' services were no longer needed by the state, and the land that had been set aside for their remuneration now reverted to the peoples of the commonwealth.[17]

In reply John Wickham argued that the Assembly had vested the property in the Church before the Revolution, and the Revolution in no way altered the title because the struggle for independence could not destroy individual or social rights. There was, he insisted, no connection between the government and the Church such as would warrant the conclusion that the change of one would necessarily lead to the destruction of the other.[18]

Randolph was the last to speak. There were, he noted, three questions: (1) What were the original rights of the Church at the time of the Revolution? (2) Were these rights impaired by the Declaration of Independence and the laws and events that followed up to the year 1802? (3) If not, was the Act of 1802 therefore unconstitutional and void? As to the first, he insisted that the charter of the colony and subsequent acts of the colonial assembly created a capacity in the members of the Church as a community to manage their social affairs and through their proper organs to take and hold glebe lands. The Declaration of Independence, he continued, merely destroyed the "relation" between the colony and the mother country but did not affect the "relation" between the Church and its property. This was the accepted view at the time, and the subsequent laws passed by the state legislature up to 1802 confirm this interpretation. Therefore, the Act of 1802 was unconstitutional. If the rights of the Church are clear by the laws passed before and after the Revolution, they have a vested right in the glebe lands of which the Act of 1802 would deprive them. To take these lands away from the Episcopal parishes in the state would be contrary to the bill of rights, which insists man has an inherent right to the enjoyment of his property. Thus, Randolph concluded, the Court of Chancery ought to have awarded the injunction in order to prevent litigation and expense, resolve the rights of the parties and secure the Church's title to its property.[19]

The arguments of counsel having been completed, the court took the case under advisement. It was expected that on a subject of such import each judge would want to draft his own opinion. The first to deliver his opinion was Judge St. George Tucker, only recently appointed to the Court of Appeals to replace Pendleton. A professor of law at William and Mary College, he had served for fifteen years on the bench of the General Court and was generally considered the most learned judge of that court.[20] In his long and carefully reasoned opinion he insisted that legal title to the glebe lands could not be supported from common law and must have rested on an act or acts of Virginia's colonial assembly. Such a title could be fairly sustained, and subsequent acts of the state legislature following the Revolution constituted further evidence that the Church as a legal entity had been authorized to purchase and hold lands for its own benefit. But this license was terminated by the Act of 1784 incorporating the Protestant Episcopal Church. When the Episcopal clergy petitioned the state legislature to incorporate their church, and the Assembly acceded to their request and passed the Act of 1784, a complete dissolution of the former legal entity took place, and an entirely new legal entity was created with a different relationship to the state. Under this arrangement, Tucker reasoned, the Episcopal Church could have no claim to glebe lands except what it derived from the act of incorporation. When the Assembly repealed this act in 1786, as it had a perfect right to do, any claims the Church or its vestrymen might have had were extinguished. Thus the complainants did not have claim to the property under either common law or civil law, and the Chancery Court was correct in dismissing the suit.[21]

Judge Spencer Roane was the next to read his opinion. In very forceful language he insisted that the title to the glebe lands rested with the colony before the Revolution because the Church of England by virtue of its establishment was but a part of the civil system. Thus after the Revolution it had no claim whatsoever, and the Act of 1802 was, therefore, perfectly consistent with the authority of the legislature. He upheld the ruling of the Court of Chancery dismissing the complaint of the vestrymen.[22]

Judges Paul Carrington and Peter Lyons then delivered a joint opinion upholding the right of the Church to the lands. The title, they stated, had been vested in the Church in the colonial period, and the Revolution and the acts associated with it or occurring subsequently could not dislodge that title. Therefore the Act of 1802 was unconstitutional, and the injunction sought by the appellees against the county overseers ought to have been awarded.[23]

The fifth judge on the bench, William Fleming, lived in Chesterfield County and therefore felt obliged to disqualify himself from the case.[24] With the Court thus equally divided, the decree of the Superior Court of Chancery dismissing the bill of complaints was allowed to stand.[25] Whatever Randolph's personal feelings might have been, he recognized the case represented a truly significant victory for those who sought to destroy the last vestiges of the establishment in Virginia.

Aside from this case Randolph seldom found the cause of his clients to be of much interest. Given the volume of cases he handled, it is even doubtful he could remember the issue in one case over another by the time the court term ended. He did play a minor role as one of the counsel for the state in a suit brought by Caron de Beaumarchais against Virginia for the recovery of a debt contracted during the war.[26] The case apparently attracted considerable public attention because at issue was the touchy question of depreciated currency. Although the state was not wholly successful in its efforts to get the Court of Appeals to reverse a decree of the Court of Chancery, Randolph undoubtedly profited from the publicity that came from his association with the case.[27] On two other occasions he argued against the inheritance of land in Virginia by a British subject on the grounds that our Declaration of Independence made them aliens in this country, and therefore incapable of inheriting property. In each case the court sustained the cause he represented.[28] Within the space of thirteen months he represented clients in two somewhat unusual cases involving the rights of individuals to be released from the bonds of slavery. In *Hudgens vs. Wrights* he represented the appellants in a case where the appellees had sued for their freedom in the High Court of Chancery and had received a judgment in their favor, whereupon Hudgens, Randolph's client, had appealed. In the original bill the Wrights had claimed their freedom because they had descended in the maternal line from a freewoman who was a native American Indian. The court decided the Wrights were entitled to their freedom and sustained the decree of the High Court of Chancery.[29] In the second case Negro slaves had been guaranteed emancipation under the provisions of a will but were subsequently sold by the administrator of the estate to satisfy a debt. The will, however, had further provided that certain lands be set aside and sold to satisfy any outstanding debts of the estate. The complainants filed their bill in equity charging fraud in the management of the estate and claiming the lands in question were adequate to satisfy the debt. The High Court of Chancery dismissed the bill and the complainants appealed from this ruling. Randolph represented the slaves and Daniel Call the defendants. The court decided that the land in question must be resold, and if the funds were still insufficient to pay the debt, then the Negroes were to be sold as a group for a term of years sufficient to raise the necessary funds.[30]

Without a record of Randolph's personal reaction to the causes he represented, it is impossible to reconstruct his attitude toward cases such as these. It is hard to believe he was indifferent to human suffering and hardship, but it is equally difficult to credit him with much personal involvement in the problems of his clients. He was always the busy lawyer working under great pressure, always diligent but seldom committed. One has the uneasy feeling that clients who wanted results went to Randolph, while clients who wanted sympathy and understanding went elsewhere. Perhaps this was the mark of a professional lawyer, but it left Randolph with little sense of personal satisfaction. It could have been otherwise. However, Randolph had long ago ruled out the practice of law as personally gratifying.

Viewing his own practice before the state courts in Virginia as so much drudgery, one might expect Randolph to turn to the federal courts for causes that would offer some outlet for his varied legal experience. With no restrictions on the fees a lawyer might collect, he could have acquired a considerable income without much difficulty, for presumably clients would place a high premium on his previous experience as the federal government's principal legal officer.[31] But such a practice never materialized, and Randolph seems to have deliberately avoided these courts. The volume of cases before the U.S. District Court was still comparatively light, but the dockets of the U.S. Circuit Court in Richmond were crowded with the suits of English creditors seeking to recover prewar debts. They were Randolph's for the asking, for no lawyer in Virginia was more familiar with the federal court system or the statutes and treaties governing the recovery of these prewar debts. For some reason Randolph refused to handle these cases.[32] Perhaps it was a certain sensitivity about appearing before the federal bar because of the circumstances surrounding his own departure from public office; perhaps it was because he was himself being sued by the federal government for alleged deficiencies in State Department accounts;[33] perhaps it was the English debt cases themselves. Whatever the reasons, they remained operative throughout the remaining years of his professional career for it was only on the rarest occasions that he consented to appear before these courts.[34]

Ironically it was in defense of his own interest and reputation that he most frequently appeared before the bar of the U.S. Circuit Court. Some months after his resignation the Comptroller of the Treasury John Steele informed him that the records of the Treasury Department failed to show how Randolph had dispersed a sizable portion of the funds allocated to the State Department.[35] Apparently convinced that Randolph would not or could not settle his accounts with the government, Steele subsequently requested the U.S. district attorney in Virginia, Thomas Nelson, to demand from Randolph vouchers as would explain how $174,793.67 in State Department funds had been allocated.[36] Randolph knew it was current practice to hold the heads of departments personally liable for all the moneys appropriated to their departments, but never had the government shown such aggressiveness in settling the accounts of one of its former officials. He knew, too, that most of the evidence was in the accounts and letterbooks of the Department of State, and he was convinced that Steele had not fully examined these records in arriving at this figure.[37] Suspicious of Steele's motives, Randolph moved quickly to document the expenditure of certain obvious sums in the Comptroller's account and by the spring of 1797 had succeeded in reducing the government's claim against him by well over $100,000.[38] In the meantime Congress had passed a bill requiring the Treasury Department to institute suits against any public official who "neglects or refuses" to pay the balance reported due to the United States in the adjustment of their accounts.[39] On May 2, 1797, two months after the bill had passed Congress, Secretary of the Treasury Oliver Wolcott specifically requested Nelson to institute a suit against Randolph in the U.S. Circuit Court for the recovery of $49,154.89, the sum still unaccounted for.[40] During the next six years Randolph relentlessly collected evidence to clear his name. Each time his case was scheduled to be heard, he filed a detailed affidavit with the court reciting the difficulties he was experiencing in acquiring the necessary records. Not only did the

Departments of State and Treasury deny his request for copies of certain materials from their records, but, he insisted, many accounts could be verified only by taking depositions from individuals who had either received the money or were acquainted with the manner in which it had been dispersed.[41] The court readily acceded to each request for additional time and willingly authorized the taking of depositions in Europe as well as the United States. The repeated postponement of the trial angered Steele, who was convinced that Randolph was deliberately attempting to avoid prosecution for the embezzlement of State Department funds.[42] He berated Nelson for not pressing the Court for an immediate trial and openly accused him of neglect of duty.[43] It was 1803 before any real progress was made in resolving the case, when, by mutual consent of the litigants and the court, the entire matter was placed in the hands of an arbitrator.[44] Gabriel Duvall, Steele's successor in the office of the Comptroller of the Treasury, was the person selected. An appointee of Jefferson, it was assumed he would render a fair and impartial verdict.[45] Both parties agreed that Duvall's findings would be accepted as the judgment of the court, from which ruling there would be no appeal.[46] On November 24, 1804, Duvall reported that Randolph owed the government of the United States $53,162.89, that such sum was to carry 6 percent interest annually until paid, and that Randolph was to bear all the legal costs of the suit.[47]

Randolph was crushed by Duvall's findings. He had long since come to recognize his folly in not keeping an accurate record of the disbursements made by the Department of State, but he could hardly believe that the record was judged to be so fragmentary as to leave over $53,000 unaccounted for. He could no longer claim that his enemies prevented a full examination of the record, for Jefferson had filled the principal offices in both the State and Treasury departments with Republicans who were certain to be at least sympathetic to Randolph's interests. The report contained not the slightest hint of embezzlement and quite properly did no more than tabulate the sum that could not be accounted for from the available records and such documentation as Randolph had collected after the suit was filed.[48] Randolph was gratified by this, but he knew only too well that many would assume he had appropriated the sum to his own use. And how could he prove otherwise? Much of the evidence he had presented had been justly deemed unacceptable, and there was now little likelihood that more authoritative proof could be found. There was no substitute for accurate accounts and signed vouchers carefully preserved and fully authenticated, and these Randolph could not produce.[49]

Randolph's brother-in-law, Wilson Cary Nicholas, generously agreed to assume responsibility for paying the full amount. An agreement was reached with the government providing for payment in four equal installments to be met by Nicholas through the outright assignment of bonds to the federal government.[50] In return, Randolph assigned much of his real and personal property to Nicholas and released his brother-in-law from all debts he held against him.[51] It is doubtful whether this covered more than a fraction of the amount Nicholas paid the government, since much of Randolph's wealth was in land that could not be sold without the risk of substantial loss. Nicholas' generosity was, of course, never to be forgotten; it was for the Randolphs the ultimate mark of a true friend. For Edmund and his wife the judgment meant drastic economies during their remaining years; it was a fatal blow to his efforts to rebuild his depleted finances.

Randolph's most publicized appearance before the federal courts was as a member of the defense counsel in the treason trial of Aaron Burr in 1807.[52] Burr's conspiratorial activities in connection with several ill-conceived western ventures ultimately led to his arrest and arraignment before the U.S. Circuit Court in Richmond. The arraignment and trial consumed an entire summer and provided Richmond with more excitement and national publicity than it had experienced in several years. Bitter political rivalries colored every phase of the proceedings, and almost everyone from the President on down took an active interest in the case.[53] An impressive panel of lawyers was assembled to defend Burr, although he was to act as his own counsel throughout most of the trial. Randolph and Wickham accompanied Burr in his initial appearance before the court, but within a matter of a few weeks Benjamin Botts and John Baker had been added to the defense counsel, to be joined a short time later by Luther Martin and Charles Lee. Of the six only Botts and Baker could be considered fledglings in the law, but even they brought certain talents to this panel. As the trial progressed, it became evident that Burr was in charge, determining strategy and handling his own defense in the courtroom. The very thorough Wickham and the very volatile Martin served most prominently as his assistants, but their role was usually a secondary one, however much their eloquence might have alleviated the monotony of the trial. Randolph, it seems, was just there, valued for his presence on the defense panel but without any real responsibility. In court he usually did little more than lend support to the arguments of others. His arguments had a clarity and precision that surpassed those of all his colleagues save Wickham, but they contributed little to Burr's defense. He represented but another name in an impressive array of legal talent that had been assembled to counteract the legal forces assisting George Hay, the young U.S. district attorney in Virginia.[54]

In his last years Randolph was, first and foremost, a Virginia lawyer practicing before Virginia's courts and interested mainly in the affairs of the city in which he lived. However much he might have scorned his state's quiet provincial ways in the months immediately following his return to Richmond, he came to accept them and adjusted easily to the routine nature of his private practice. He preferred to confine that practice to the Virginia state courts, particularly those that met in Richmond. And, like many professional men with strong local attachments, he took an interest in his community. He seemed more than willing to lend his name to proposals that would improve educational opportunities in the area.[55] He also sponsored a memorial to the state legislature drawn up by the residents of Richmond protesting the expected removal of a public guard from the city. Voicing a serious concern for the safety of the city's residents, the petition asked that the guard be maintained or some other arrangement be made for the security of the inhabitants of the community.[56] Significantly, and more directly related to his profession, he also began to gather material for an abridgement of the laws of Virginia, a venture certain to have the warm endorsement of his colleagues in the law.[57]

As the years slipped away, more and more the comforts and conveniences of home began to dictate his movements. Home meant the leisure to read and to enjoy the considerable cultural life of the capital.[58] It meant the opportunity to entertain close friends. It meant being with Betsy, whose declining health was becoming the source of much concern. It meant presiding over the wedding arrangements of two of his children and sharing their joy.[59] It meant placing the happiness and welfare of his family above personal fame and fortune.

Twelve years had passed since Randolph returned to Virginia, the object of suspicion to all except his closest friends. Time had erased the most bitter memories, and an extensive law practice had distracted him and given him a sense of accomplishment. He had found peace and some measure of security in his native state and had gained once again the quiet recognition that Virginians accord their first families. He would have liked to have seen things work out differently, but he found himself reasonably content with the lot that came to be his and neither regret nor nostalgia warped his outlook on life. Each year found him more deeply committed to his private practice than the year before; he had in fact become what he had vowed he would never be—a professional lawyer.

25

Withdrawal, 1808–1813

Busy with his practice and ever mindful of his financial needs, Randolph failed to note how fast the years were slipping away. Physically, he knew he had to curtail his practice outside of Richmond, but men ten years younger were doing the same. Even his son had refused county court practice because it was menial and depressing, and he was not yet twenty-seven, a mere novice in his father's eyes.[1] It was only very gradually that Randolph came to realize his "indispositions" were becoming more frequent and that the pressures of a crowded court docket left him completely exhausted by the end of the term. Looking back over the past few years, he realized that Washington, Henry, Pendleton and Wythe had all passed from the scene and that a whole generation had grown up who were born after the Revolution.[2] He was approaching fifty-five, and truthfully he felt not a year younger. There was certain to be a decade or two left for practicing law, but he knew that he would have to conserve his energies. Ten or fifteen years of a modest practice would be sufficient to repay his brother-in-law and rebuild his depleted finances before retirement. Then with ample leisure he could devote his remaining years to a history of Virginia.[3]

By 1808 the volume of Randolph's practice seems to have leveled off, at least before the Court of Appeals, where most of his work centered. He argued some thirty-two cases during the three terms of the court. This represented almost 50 percent of the cases reported and undoubtedly involved the expenditure of much time and effort.[4] As was true in other years, it was not the complexity of the cases that burdened him as much as the long hours he had to spend in court. Before and after—and sometimes during—the two terms of this court he handled as much business as he could in the lower courts that met in the city and, on occasion, represented one or more clients in a neighboring court.[5] Aside from the sharp curtailment of his practice outside of Richmond, his professional life remained the same as it had been for close to ten years.

But things were soon to change. A further reorganization of the Vir-

ginia court structure had led to the replacement of the District Courts
with a system of Superior Courts further decentralizing the intermediate
court structure of the state. Under the new arrangement every county in
the state had its own Superior Court with authority comparable to that
formerly held by the nineteen District Courts.[6] While eliminating the
delays associated with overcrowded District Court dockets, it also forced
attorneys who had cases pending before the District Court to argue these
cases in the counties where they had originated or turn their clients over
to a local lawyer.[7] For Randolph there was no choice; he could not hope
to cover the five counties that formerly came under the District Court in
Richmond. His health, and his practice before the Court of Appeals and
Superior Court of Chancery, simply would not permit it.[8] A younger
man might have protested the loss of clients that resulted from this
decentralization, but Randolph was content to lessen his practice. Even
in the Court of Appeals there was a noticeable reduction in the number
of cases he handled. He appeared in only nineteen of the sixty-two cases
reported for the year 1809.[9] It was still a respectable practice, but the
decrease reflected Randolph's gradual withdrawal from the profession.

He was also concerned about Betsy, whose health seemed to become
more precarious with each passing month. His concern was justified for
on October 22, 1809, she was stricken with a cerebral hemorrhage that
paralyzed her left side.[10] At first it was assumed she would not recover,
but after a week she began to show some slight improvement, causing
Randolph to hope she would be spared a few more years.[11] He now
became more attentive than ever to her needs, and when he learned she
would never fully recover he found it difficult to leave her side.[12]

Less than five months later a grief-stricken Randolph stood at the
bedside of his beloved Betsy as she died.[13] Although he was close to his
friends and several of his brothers-in-law, Betsy was the one person
whose support he found absolutely essential. As youngsters, they had
played together in Williamsburg. They enjoyed each other's company
as young adults, and had lived for one another through nearly thirty-
four years of married life. To his children he wrote:

> To speak of her as knowing and discharging every duty, would be but a
> cold tribute to her worth. Her understanding, altho' often aided by brilliancy
> of imagination was rather of the serious, reflecting, and solid cast. It was too
> penetrating to be deceived altho' her love of harmony with the world often
> produced in her an acquiescence which resembled a contrary conviction. But
> she explored and studied my temper, and anticipated the means of gratifying
> even my caprices. Innumerable were the instances in which I have returned
> home, dissatisfied with some of the scenes of the day [?] and found an assylum
> [sic] in her [and a] readiness to partake of my difficulties and to make them

her own or to divert them by despising them. On those occasions her features, to which she never would permit the smallest beauty to be ascribed, assumed a species of glory, which angels always possess, and of which, in no other woman, did I ever discern the feeblest ray. Others have been good, amiable, and engaging and benevolent. But this particular something in her looks, places her far beyond the line of symmetry of face.[14]

On and on he poured forth his grief to his children, the only ones who could possibly understand his loss. Betsy's death left him a broken man. The legal profession, for which he had no great liking, was now utterly meaningless. He had no desire to find solace for his loss by plunging back into his work—he couldn't have cared less. Even the financial rewards made little sense, except insofar as they were needed to satisfy his debts; there was, certainly, no longer any reason for leading a comfortable life in a large and spacious home. So far as Edmund was concerned, there was little reason for anything now that Betsy was gone.

A few weeks later Randolph was himself stricken with hemiplegia. It affected the use of his legs, but with the aid of a crutch he could still move about.[15] His children, he told Madison, insisted he curtail his practice before the courts, but the truth of the matter was that he probably would never appear before the bar of Virginia's Court of Appeals again. He had argued several cases in April shortly before his attack and no matter how optimistic he was about his eventual recovery the fact was that his infirmities were an absolute barrier to court work.[16]

The marriage of his youngest daughter Lucy to Peter V. Daniel on April 21, 1810, undoubtedly had his warm approval.[17] Daniel had been one of Randolph's most promising apprentices a few years before, and he had taken the young man into his home in Richmond. It was while living with the Randolphs that Daniel became an admirer of Lucy, for whom he now returned to Richmond.[18] Randolph was able to provide his daughter with a respectable dowry and took comfort in the fact that she had married a young man of whom Betsy had grown quite fond.[19]

His wife's death and now Lucy's marriage and the absence of any regular income from his practice made continued occupancy of his home in Richmond unthinkable. It was now a lonely house, filled with the memories of happier days and the echo of Betsy's voice. He decided to rent it and then go to live with one of his children. He was already seeking a tenant for his "Mount Comfort" farm outside of Richmond, and he knew that if both properties could be rented it might provide him with an income at least sufficient for his present needs.[20] Renting his Richmond home proved to be relatively easy; within a month he had acquired L. H. Girardin as a tenant, who intended to use the spacious house as a private academy.[21] Girardin even persuaded Randolph to serve as a lecturer in law, politics and "political economy," an assignment he was never able to fulfill because of his physical disability.[22] His farm near Richmond was also rented toward the end of the year to Thomas Sortworth.[23] The rents he collected did not begin to satisfy his financial needs, but they most certainly helped.

However, by October of 1810 financial embarrassment forced Randolph to actively seek appointment as clerk of the Virginia Court of Appeals, an office vacated by the recent death of his friend John Brown. He wrote to two members of the bench, almost pleading with them to support his application. To Judge Roane he wrote:

> Such is the condition of my fortune and the imbecility of my body that my income is reduced to a pittance. It is probable indeed that had an addition been made to your court at the last session, I should have been associated with you, but my stroke has annihilated the idea. . . .
>
> I am tortured while I write this, at the remembrance of what I was, what I might have been and what I am; I speak in confidence, which I am sure of, when I place it in you;—not wishing that the affair should be made a thing of eclat as yet at least. I tremble, lest the agitation, into which I am thrown, by a hasty and tempestuous review of my follies and extravagances should produce a visit from that complaint, which, if it had forborne its hostility for three years, would have left me in a pecuniary view independent.[24]

A similar letter went to St. George Tucker with the request that he confer with Judge Fleming.[25] Tucker's reply came the following day. Regretfully he and Judge Fleming had concluded that "the corporal afflictions under which you labour most unfortunately at present precludes every wish on both our part to make the appointment you have in contemplation, the duties of which must [ever] require the executions of a man blessed with a greater portion of bodily strength and health than now most unhappily falls to your lot." The letter closed with the wish that he might soon find his health sufficiently restored so as to permit his return to his "honorable profession."[26]

But Randolph's health did not return and his children became concerned as his infirmities increased. In 1811 Edmonia and her husband persuaded him to spend the summer with them in Lexington in Rockbridge County, but with the approach of fall he took up residence with his eldest daughter Susan and her husband Bennett Taylor in Charlestown in Jefferson County.[27] This arrangement was to be only for the fall and winter, for Richmond was still his home, and once he had regained the full use of his legs he most certainly would return. The fall and winter of 1811–1812 passed, but the infirmities did not, thereby increasing his dependence on his daughter and son-in-law. In July he casually informed Madison that he intended to move to the medical springs in either Bath or Berkley County, but apparently his health forced him to seek relief at a spa closer to Charlestown. He spent the remaining months of the summer at Battletown in neighboring Frederick County and in September returned once again to his daughter's home in Charlestown.[28]

By this time he was both physically and financially dependent on the generosity of his children and his brothers-in-law. A year after Betsy's death he was still trying to pay the medical bills that he had accumulated during her illness and his own.[29] John Wickham found himself confronted with the disagreeable assignment of initiating court action against Randolph for $4,500 on a debt long overdue. Wickham, knowing Randolph's financial plight, pleaded with his client to give Randolph more time, but he "absolutely declines any adjustment in the decree against you."[30] A month passed and when no reply came from Charlestown, Wickham wrote to Wilson Cary Nicholas urging his prompt intervention in Randolph's behalf.[31] In the months that followed, Wickham, Philip Norborne Nicholas, Wilson Cary Nicholas and Randolph's son Peyton cooperated in effecting the sale of the remainder of Randolph's slaves to prevent humiliating court action to recover the sum demanded. They were determined to shield him from further unpleasantness and worry over his unpaid debts.[32] They probably felt it was the least they could do for a man who had made a habit of imprudently sharing his limited wealth with friends while remaining rather indifferent about its repayment.

The one project that held his interest during these difficult years was his *History of Virginia*, begun some time after the Burr trial and completed during the year 1811.[33] The work was not only a labor of love but a project to which Randolph felt particularly committed. He recognized that he had lived in an era that would be of great interest to future generations. The events of that era were now a matter of record, but the character and personality of the men who had shaped this history were not. It was the responsibility of those who were privileged to observe and serve these men to record for posterity their impressions of these leaders and of the times in which they lived. For Randolph the preeminence of Virginia's political leaders during these formative years was unquestioned; it remained but to set forth this history before memories grew dim and reputations became irrevocably tarnished by partisan politics.[34]

The work, which encompassed three octavo volumes, traced the history of Virginia from its original settlement to the end of the eighteenth century.[35] As he approached the last years of the state's colonial history, the chronological story was interrupted to record the character and accomplishments of the leading statesmen of the late colonial period, with a promise that a further assessment of the leadership of these and other public figures would be made toward the end of his work. The Revolution was treated topically and chronologically with particular emphasis on the political history of Virginia. As he recorded events with which he was personally acquainted, he stressed the importance of individual leaders and introduced new names into the narrative as circumstances warranted. Significantly he never indicated his own involvement in these events, although his history had now become little more than a litany of the accomplishments of the most prominent figures of the Revolutionary period. Presumably (the volumes are lost) the years 1783–1800 were treated in a similar fashion, the events always being overshadowed by the men who, in Randolph's view, had shaped the course of history.[36]

To describe this fragmentary manuscript as uncritical would be to ignore Randolph's motive for undertaking the work. He believed that circumstances had presented the leaders of his age with a momentous challenge and a unique opportunity to determine our future course as a nation. They had accepted that challenge and their accomplishments exceeded the most optimistic predictions of their contemporaries. Randolph thought it important that this record and the convictions that governed these men's decisions be preserved for posterity. If it were not done now, it would never be done, for future generations could not be expected to discover from the impersonal written record how much principle and uncompromising loyalty to certain political truths had guided the policies of these men. However unsatisfactory the results, there was a degree of historical sophistication in his motives that deserved acknowledgment. In his eyes the history of Virginia during the last quarter of the eighteenth century was in fact a "biography."

He made several attempts to have the work published, first in Philadelphia and then in Baltimore. Although now quite infirm, he optimistically offered to travel part way to either city to discuss the publication of his work if the publisher was interested.[37] He added:

> I am confident that the parts which relate to the revolution, the federal convention and the parallels between the characters of certain men, such for instance as those between General Washington and Mr. Jefferson, President Madison and General Hamilton, George Mason and John Dickenson, Benjamin Franklin and John Jay, Patrick Henry and Richard Henry Lee will command an extensive sale. I am apprized that we live too near the time of certain occurrences, and that while caution is not to be abandoned, and improper irritation ought to be avoided, truth must prevail.[38]

His efforts came to naught. It is doubtful whether the manuscript ever left his hands or was even read by anyone other than his immediate family before his death.

As his health worsened, he knew it was folly to keep his home in Richmond, for there was little likelihood that he would ever return to the city. If he did, he would be compelled to live either with his son or youngest daughter. His son-in-law Peter V. Daniel was instructed to make the necessary arrangements if Wilson Cary Nicholas approved.[39] Daniel discussed the matter with Philip Norborne Nicholas and he, in turn, transmitted Randolph's request to Wilson Cary Nicholas.[40] Philip assured his brother that a favorable price could be obtained for the property, and if the proceeds from the sale were invested, the interest collected would provide the aging Randolph with a higher income than he was currently receiving in rents.[41] The property apparently did not sell as readily as expected, for it remained in Randolph's name until his death.[42]

And death came sooner than either of the Nicholases expected. Randolph went to visit his friend Nathaniel Burwell at Carter Hall, his home near Millwood in Frederick County.[43] While there he became seriously ill. He lingered a few days, but on the morning of September 12, 1813, he died.[44] He was buried in a small quiet ceremony in the Burwell family plot in the "Old Chapel" graveyard in Millwood.[45] Five days later the *Richmond Enquirer* carried a four-line notice of his death, observing that: "His history is blended with that of his country."[46] And so it was.

Appendix

The Fauchet Dispatches

EDITORIAL NOTE

The three dispatches of Joseph Fauchet, French minister to the United States, that figured in Edmund Randolph's resignation from Washington's Cabinet are Numbers 3, 6 and 10—June 4, September 5 and October 31, 1794 respectively. The only known English translations of these dispatches that Randolph could be said to have authorized are the translations that were printed in his Vindication. *The pertinent sections of Numbers 3 and 6 and all of Number 10 have been reproduced here so that Fauchet's comments and observations may be read in context. The dispatches, as they appeared in the* Vindication, *were translated literally—in some instances at the expense of clarity. Rather than provide a more literary translation I have merely noted the additions, omissions or significant variations from the French text in notes. The paucity of notes suggests Randolph made no effort to provide a biased translation of these dispatches. I have deliberately avoided notes which do little more than pedantically argue with the idiom of the eighteenth century.*

Extract of Dispatch No. 3

J. FAUCHET TO MINISTER OF FOREIGN AFFAIRS, PHILADELPHIA [JUNE 4, 1794].

Then the Secretary of State[1] appeared to open himself without reserve. He imparted to me the intestine divisions, which were rumbling[2] in the United States. The idea of an approaching commotion affected him deeply. He hoped to prevent it, by the ascendancy which he daily acquired over the mind of the President, who consulted him in all affairs, and to whom he told the truth, which his colleagues disguised from him. . . .

"The President of the United States,["] says he,[3] ["]is the mortal enemy of England; and the friend of France, I [ER] can affirm it upon my honour. But not mixing with the world, he [G. Washington] may be circumvented by the dark manoeuvres of some men,[4] who wind themselves in an hundred ways, to draw him into measures, which will cause him to lose all his popularity. Under the pretext of giving energy to the government, they would absolutely make a monarch of him. They deceive him, as to the true spirit of the people; as well as upon the affairs of France. I am sure, that at this moment, he escapes from them, and that in all these perfidious manoeuvres[5] they have not been able to dissuade him from pronouncing with vigor against the ministry of England. He has——but it is impossible for me in conscience to make you this confession. I should betray the duties of my office. Every thing, which I can say to you, is, that it is important for our two nations, that you continue to visit him frequently. He will be touched with the proofs of friendship, which you shall testify to him; and I am sure, that this will be an infallible means of causing them to be valued. I would quit the post, which he has confided to me, if he could be brought to make any attempt upon the rights of the people.[6] A bill has passed the house of representatives, which wounds liberty.[7] They have at least taken away the article which prevents the sale of the French prizes in our ports. My heart is troubled by it. But I have seen with pleasure, that my reflections on this subject, upon the dreadful crisis, which would result from an abuse of it, have made a deep impression upon the mind, I will even say, upon the heart of the President, who is an honourable man. Let us unite, Mr. Fauchet, to draw out two nations closer together. Those who love liberty, are for fraternizing with the French Republic, the partizans of slavery prefer an alliance with England.

[368]

"I,["] he said to me, (in speaking of the treaty of Jay*), ["]that there is no question in his mission,[8] but to demand a solemn reparation for the spoliations which our commerce has experienced on the part of England; and to give you a proof, that Mr. Jay cannot enter into a negociation contrary to what we owe to France, I will give you the part of the instructions which concern it.["]

Although the following note, which I have, written in his own hand, with a promise to burn it, be little important, I annex it hereto.[9]

"If the English ministry shall insinuate, that the whole or any part of these instructions should appear to be influenced by a supposed predilection in favour of France, you will arrest the subject as being foreign to the present question. It is what the English nation has no right to object to; because we are free in our sentiments and independent in our government.

"The following case is to be unchangeable. As there is no doubt, that the English ministry will endeavour to detach us from France, you will inform them of the firm determination of the government of the United States, not to deviate from our treaties, or our engagements with France."

* The word affirm appears to have been omitted in the certified copy. [Edmund Randolph's note]

NOTES TO DISPATCH NO. 3

1. French reads: "alors il parût."
2. French reads: "travailloient sourdement."
3. The phrase, "says he," is not in the French text, but it is at this point that Fauchet begins his summary of what ER is purported to have said to him.
4. The French reads: "mais il a été souvent dupe des ténébreuses manoeuvres de M. Hamilton. . . ."
5. The French reads: "perfidies de ces Messieurs."
6. The French reads: "Je quittrois le poste qu'il m'a confié si mes perfides collègues pouvoient par leurs sourdes menées lui faire porter quelqu'atteinte aux droits du peuple."
7. The French reads: "Un Bill a passé hier à la Chambre des representans qui lui donne un pouvoir qui blesse la liberté."
8. The French reads: "Moi:,—m'a-t-il répondu, Je vous promets qu'il n'est question dans sa mission. . . ."
9. Fauchet at this point begins to quote from a purported copy of ER's instructions to J. Jay. A clearer translation would be: "Although the following note, which I have *copied from* his own hand, . . ."

Extract of Dispatch No. 6

J. Fauchet to Commissioner of Foreign Relations, Philadelphia
[September 5, 1794].

Scarce was the commotion known,[1] when the Secretary of State came to my house. All his countenance was grief. He requested of me a private conversation. It is all over, he said to me. A civil war is about to ravage our unhappy country. Four men by their talents, their influence, and their energy may save it. But debtors of English[2] merchants, they will be deprived of their liberty, if they take the smallest step. Could you lend them instantaneously funds, sufficient to shelter them from English persecution [*sic*]. The inquiry astonished me much. It was impossible for me to make a satisfactory answer. You know my want of power, and my defect of pecuniary means. I shall draw myself from the affair by some common place remarks, and by throwing myself on the pure and unalterable principles of the republic.

I have never since heard of propositions of this nature.

NOTES TO DISPATCH NO. 6

1. Fauchet had previously referred to disturbances in western Pennsylvania, i.e., the Whiskey Rebellion.
2. The word "English" is not in the French text.

Dispatch No. 10

J. Fauchet to Commissioner of Foreign Relations, Philadelphia
[October 31, 1794].

Citizen,

1. The measures which prudence prescribes to me to take, with respect to my colleagues, have still presided in the digesting of the dispatches signed by them, which treat of the insurrection of the western countries, and of the repressive means adopted by the government. I have allowed them to be confined to the giving of a faithful, but naked recital of events; the reflections therein contained scarcely exceed the conclusions easily deducible from the character assumed by the public prints. I have reserved myself to give you as far as I am able a key to the facts detailed in our reports. When it comes in question to explain, either by conjectures or by certain data, the secret views of a foreign government, it would be imprudent to run the risk of indiscretions, and to give oneself up to men whose known partiality for that government, and similitude of passions and interests with its chiefs, might lead to confidences, the issue of which are incalculable. Besides, the precious confessions of Mr. Randolph alone throw a satisfactory light upon every thing that comes to pass. These I have not yet communicated to my colleagues. The motives already mentioned lead to this reserve, and still less permit me to open myself to them at the present moment. I shall then endeavor, Citizen, to give you a clue to all the measures, of which the common dispatches give you an account, and to discover the true causes of the explosion, which it is obstinately resolved to repress with great means, although the state of things has no longer any thing alarming.

2. To confine the present crisis to the simple question of the excise is to reduce it far below its true scale; it is indubitably connected with a general explosion for some time prepared in the public mind, but which this local and precipitate eruption will cause to miscarry, or at least check for a long time;—in order to see the real cause, in order to calculate the effect, and the consequences, we must ascend to the origin of the parties existing in the state, and retrace their progress.

3. The present system of government has created malcontents. This is the lot of all new things. My predecessors have given information in detail upon the parts of the system which have particularly awakened

clamours and produced enemies to the whole of it. The primitive divisions of opinion as to the political form of the state, and the limits of the sovereignty of the whole over each state individually sovereign, had created the federalists and the antifederalists. From a whimsical contrast between the name and the real opinion of the parties, a contrast hitherto little understood in Europe, the former aimed, and still aim, with all their power, to annihilate federalism, whilst the latter have always wished to preserve it. This contrast was created by the *Consolidators* or the Constitutionalists*, who, being first in giving the denominations (a matter so important in a revolution) took for themselves that which was the most popular, although in reality it contradicted their ideas, and gave to their rivals one which would draw on them the attention of the people, notwithstanding they really wished to preserve a system whose prejudices should cherish at least the memory and the name.[1]

4. Moreover, these first divisions, of the nature of those to be destroyed by time, in proportion[2] as the nation should have advanced in the experiment of a form of government which rendered it flourishing, might now have completely disappeared, if the system of finances which had its birth in the cradle of the constitution, had not renewed their vigour under various form. The mode of organising the national credit, the consolidating and funding of the public debt, the introduction in the political economy of the usage of states, which prolong their existence or ward off their fall only by expedients, imperceptibly created a financiering class who threaten to become the aristocratical order of the state. Several citizens, and among others those who had aided in establishing independence with their purses or their arms, conceived themselves aggrieved by those fiscal engagements. Hence an opposition which declares itself between the farming or agricultural interest, and that of the fiscal; federalism and antifederalism,[3] which are founded on those new denominations, in proportion[4] as the treasury usurps a preponderance in the government and legislation: Hence in fine, the state, divided into partisans and enemies of the treasurer and of his theories. In this new classification of parties, the nature of things gave popularity to the latter, an innate instinct, if I may use the expression, caused the ears of the people to revolt at the names alone of *treasurer* and *stock-jobber*: but the opposite party, in consequence of its ability, obstinately persised in leaving to its adversaries the suspicious name of *antifederalist*, whilst in reality they were friends of the constitution, and enemies only of the excrescences which financiering theories threatened to attach to it.

5. It is useless to stop longer to prove that the monarchical system was interwoven with those novelties of finances, and that the friends of the

---

* Constituans. [Edmund Randolph's note]

latter favoured the attempts which were made in order to bring the constitution to the former by insensible gradations. The writings of influential men of this party prove it; their real opinions too avow it, and the journals of the Senate are the depository of the first attempts.

6. Let us, therefore, free ourselves from the intermediate spaces in which the progress of the system is marked, since they can add nothing to the proof of its existence—Let us pass by its sympathy with our regenerating movements, while running in monarchical paths—Let us arrive at the situation in which our Republican revolution has placed things and parties.

7. The antifederalists disembarrass themselves of an insignificant denomination, and take that of patriots and of republicans. Their adversaries become *aristocrats,* notwithstanding their efforts to preserve the advantageous illusion of ancient names; opinions clash, and press each other; the aristocratic attempts, which formerly had appeared so insignificant, are recollected: The treasurer, who is looked upon as their first source, is attacked; his operations and plans are denounced to the public opinion; nay, in the sessions of 1792 and 1793, a solemn inquiry into his administration was obtained. This first victory was to produce another, and it was hoped that, faulty or innocent, the treasurer would retire, no less by necessity in the one case, than from self-love in the other. He, emboldened by the triumph which he obtained in the useless inquiry of his enemies, of which both objects proved equally abortive, seduced besides by the momentary reverse of republicanism in Europe, removes the mask and announces the approaching triumph of his principles.[5]

8. In the mean time[6] the popular societies are formed; political ideas concenter themselves, the patriotic party unite and more closely connect themselves; they gain a formidable majority in the legislature; the abasement of commerce, the slavery of navigation, and the audacity of England strengthen it. A concert of declarations and censures against the government arises; at which the latter is even itself astonished.

9. Such was the situation of things towards the close of the last and at the beginning of the present year. Let us pass over the discontents which were most generally expressed in these critical moments. They have been sent to you at different periods, and in detail. In every quarter are arraigned the imbecility of the government towards Great Britain, the defenceless state of the country against possible invasions, the coldness towards the French Republic: the system of finance is attacked, which threatens eternising the debt under pretext of making it the guarantee of public happiness; the complication of that system which withholds from general inspection all its operations,—the alarming power of the influence it procures to a man whose principles are regarded as dangerous,—the preponderance which that man acquires from day to day in

public measures, and in a word the immoral and impolitic modes of taxation, which he at first presents as expedients, and afterwards raises to permanency.

10. In touching this last point we attain the principal complaint of the western people, and the ostensible motive of their movements. Republicans by principle, independent by character and situation, they could not but accede with enthusiasm to the criminations which we have sketched. But the *excise* above all affects them. Their lands are fertile, watered with the finest rivers in the world: but the abundant fruits of their labour run the risk of perishing for the want of means of exchanging them, as those more happy cultivators do for objects which desire indicates to all men who have known only the enjoyments which Europe procures them. They therefore convert the excess of their produce into liquors imperfectly fabricated, which badly supply the place of those they might procure by exchange. The *excise* is created and strikes at this consoling transformation; their complaints are answered by the only pretext that they are otherwise inaccessible to every species of impost. But why, in contempt of treaties, are they left to bear the yoke of the feeble Spaniard, as to the Mississippi, for upwards of twelve years?[7] Since when has an agricultural people submitted to the unjust capricious law of a people explorers of the precious metals? Might we not suppose that Madrid and Philadelphia mutually assisted in prolonging the slavery of the river; that the proprietors of a barren coast are afraid less the Mississippi, once opened, and its numerous branches brought into activity, their fields might become deserts, and in a word that commerce dreads having rivals in those interior parts as soon as their inhabitants shall cease to be subjects? This last supposition is but too well founded; an influential member of the Senate, Mr. Izard, one day in conversation undisguisedly announced it to me.

11. I shall be more brief in my observations on the murmurs excited by the system for the sale of lands. It is conceived to be unjust that these vast and fertile regions should be sold by provinces to capitalists, who thus enrich themselves, and retail, with immense profits, to the husbandmen, possessions which they have never seen. If there were not a latent design to arrest the rapid settlement of those lands, and to prolong their infant state, why not open in the west land offices, where every body, without distinction, should be admitted to purchase by a small or large quantity? Why reserve to sell or distribute to favourites, to a clan of flatterers, of courtiers, that which belongs to the state, and which should be sold to the greatest possible profit of all its members?

12. Such therefore were the parts of the public grievance, upon which the western people most insisted. Now, as the common dispatches inform you, these complaints were systematizing by the conversations of influ-

ential men who retired into those wild countries, and who from principle, or by a series of particular heart-burnings, animated discontents already too near to effervescence. At last the local explosion is effected. The western people calculated on being supported by some distinguished characters in the east, and even imagined they had in the bosom of the government some abettors, who might share in their grievances or their principles.

13. From what I have detailed above, those men might indeed be supposed numerous. The sessions of 1793 and 1794 had given importance to the republican party, and solidity to its accusations. The propositions of Mr. Madison, or his project of a navigation act, of which Mr. Jefferson was originally the author, sapped the British interest, now an integral part of the financiering system. Mr. Taylor,[8] a republican member of the Senate, published towards the end of the session, three pamphlets, in which this last is explored to its origin, and developed in its progress and consequences with force and method. In the last he asserts that the decrepid state of affairs resulting from that system, could not but presage, under a rising government, either a revolution or a civil war.

14. The first was preparing: the government, which had foreseen it, reproduced, under various forms, the demand of a disposable* force which might put it in a respectable state of defence. Defeated in this measure, who can aver that it may not have hastened the local eruption, in order to make an advantageous diversion, and to lay the more general storm which it saw gathering? Am I not authorized in forming this conjecture from the conversation which the Secretary of State had with me and Le Blanc, alone, an account of which you have in my dispatch, No. 3? But how may we expect that this new plan will be executed? By exasperating and severe measures, authorised by a law which was not solicited till the close of the session. This law gave to the one already existing for collecting the *excise* a coercive force which hitherto it had not possessed, and a demand of which was not before ventured to be made.† By means of this new law all the refractory citizens to the old one were caused to be pursued with a sudden rigor; a great number of writs were issued; doubtless the natural consequences from a conduct so decisive and so harsh were expected; and before these were manifested the means of repression had been prepared; this was undoubtedly what Mr. Randolph meant in telling me *that under pretext of giving energy to the government it was intended to introduce absolute power, and to mislead the President in paths which would conduct him to unpopularity.*

15. Whether the explosion has been provoked by the government; or

* Disponible. [Edmund Randolph's note]
† This law was mentioned in the comment upon the laws of the last session inclosed in No. 9, of the correspondence of the minister. [Joseph Fauchet's note]

owes its birth to accident, it is certain that a commotion of some hundreds of men, who have not since been found in arms, and the very pacific union of the counties in Braddock's field, a union which has not been revived, were not symptoms which could justify the raising of so great a force as 15,000 men. Besides the principles, uttered in the declarations hitherto made public, rather announced ardent minds to be calmed than anarchists to be subdued. But in order to obtain something on the public opinion prepossessed against the demands contemplated to be made, it was necessary to magnify the danger, to disfigure the views of those people, to attribute to them the design of uniting themselves with England, to alarm the citizens for the fate of the constitution, whilst in reality the revolution threatened only the ministers. This step succeeded; an army is raised; this military part of the suppression is doubtless Mr. Hamilton's, the pacific part and the sending of commissioners are due to the influence of Mr. Randolph over the mind of the President, whom I delight always to believe, and whom I do believe, truly virtuous, and the friend of his fellow-citizens and principles.

16. In the mean time, although there was a certainty of having an army, yet it was necessary to assure themselves of co-operators among the men whose patriotic reputation might influence their party, and whose lukewarmness or want of energy in the existing conjunctures might compromit [sic] the success of the plans. Of all the governors, whose duty it was to appear at the head of the requisitions, the governor of Pennsylvania alone enjoyed the name of Republican: his opinion of the Secretary of the Treasury and of his systems was known to be unfavourable. The secretary of this state possessed great influence in the Popular Society of Philadelphia, which in its turn influenced those of other states; of course he merited attention. It appears therefore that these men with others unknown to me, all having without doubt Randolph at their head, were balancing to decide on their party. Two or three days before the proclamation was published, and of course before the cabinet had resolved on its measures, Mr. Randolph came to see me with an air of great eagerness, and made to me the overtures of which I have given you an account in my No. 6. Thus with some thousands of dollars the Republic could have decided on civil war or on peace! Thus the consciences of the pretended patriots of America have already their prices*! It is very true that the certainty of these conclusions, painful to be drawn, will for ever exist in our archives! What will be the old age of this government, if it is thus early decrepid! Such, citizen, is the evident consequence of the system of finances conceived by Mr. Hamilton. He has made of a whole nation,

* Tarif. [Edmund Randolph's note]

a stock-jobbing, speculating, selfish people. Riches alone here fix consideration; and as no one likes to despised,[9] they are universally sought after. Nevertheless this depravity has not yet embraced the mass of the people; the effects of this pernicious system have as yet but slightly touched them. Still there are patriots, of whom I delight to entertain an idea worthy of that imposing title. Consult Monroe; he is of this number; he had apprised me of the men whom the current of events had dragged along as bodies devoid of weight. His friend Madison is also an honest man. Jefferson, on whom the patriots cast their eyes to succeed the President, had foreseen these crises. He prudently retired in order to avoid making a figure against his inclination in scenes, the secret of which will soon or late be brought to light.

17. As soon as it was decided that the French Republic purchased no men to do their duty, there were to be seen individuals, about whose conduct the government could at least form uneasy conjectures, giving themselves up with a scandalous ostentation to its views, and even seconding its declarations. The Popular Societies soon emitted resolutions stamped with the same spirit, and who, although they may have been advised by love of order, might nevertheless have omitted or uttered them with less solemnity. Then were seen coming from the very men whom we had been accustomed to regard as having little friendship for the system of the treasurer,[10] harangues without end, in order to give a new direction to the public mind. The militia, however, manifest some repugnance, particularly in Pennsylvania, for the service to which they were called. Several officers resign; at last by excursions or harangues, incomplete requisitions are obtained, and scattered volunteer corps from different parts make up the deficiency. How much more interesting, than the changeable men whom I have painted above,[11] where those plain citizens who answered the solicitations which were made to them to join the volunteers—"If we are required we will march; because we do not wish not to have a government, but to arm ourselves as volunteers would be in appearance subscribing implicitly to the excise system which we reprobate."

18. What I have said above,[12] authorises then our resting on the opinion become incontestible, that in the crisis which has burst, and in the means employed for restoring order, the true question was the destruction or the triumph of the treasurer's plans. This being once established, let us pass over the facts related in the common dispatches, and see how the government or the treasurer will take from the very stroke which threatened his system the safe opportunity of humbling the adverse party, and of silencing their enemies whether open or concealed.[13] The army marched; the President made known that he was going to command it; he

set out for Carlisle; Hamilton, as I have understood, requested to follow him; the President dared not to refuse him. It does not require much penetration to divine the object of this journey: In the President it was wise, it might also be his duty. But in Mr. Hamilton it was a consequence of the profound policy which directs all his steps; a measure dictated by a perfect knowledge of the human heart.[14] Was it not interesting for him, for his party, tottering under the weight of events without and accusations within, to proclaim an intimacy more perfect than ever with the President, whose very name is a sufficient shield against the most formidable attacks? Now what more evident mark could the President give of his intimacy than by suffering Mr. Hamilton, whose name even is understood in the west as that of a public enemy, to go and place himself at the head of the army which went, if I may use the expression, to cause his system to triumph against the opposition of the people? The presence of Mr. Hamilton with the army must attach it more than ever to his party; we see what ideas these circumstances give birth to on both sides, all however to the advantage of the secretary.

19. Three weeks had they encamped in the west without a single armed man appearing. However the President, or those who wished to make the most of this new manoeuvre, made it public that he was going to command in person. The session of Congress being very near, it was wished to try whether there could not be obtained from the presses,[15] which were supposed to have changed, a silence, whence to conclude the possibility of infringing the constitution in its most essential part; in that which fixes the relation of the President with the legislature. But the patriotic papers laid hold of this artful attempt: I am certain that the office of secretary of state, which alone remained at Philadelphia (for while the minister of finance was with the army, the minister of war was on a tour to the Province of Maine, 400 miles from Philadelphia), maintained the controversy in favour of the opinion which it was desired to establish. A comparison between the President and the English monarch was introduced, who far removed from Westminster, yet strictly fulfils his duty of sanctioning; it was much insisted on that the constitution declares that the President commands the armed force: this similitude was treated with contempt; the consequence of the power of commanding in person, drawn from the right to command in chief (or direct) the force of the state, was ridiculed and reduced to an absurdity, by supposing a fleet at sea and an army on land. The result of this controversy was, that some days after it was announced that the President would come to open the approaching session.

20. During his stay at Bedford, the President doubtless concerted the plan of the campaign with Mr. Lee, to whom he left the command in chief. The letter by which he delegates the command to him, is that of a

virtuous man, at least as to the major part of the sentiments which it contains; he afterwards set out for Philadelphia, where he has just arrived, and Mr. Hamilton remains with the army.

21. This last circumstance unveils all the plan of the Secretary: he presides over the military operations in order to acquire in the sight of his enemies a formidable and imposing consideration. He and Mr. Lee the commander in chief, agree perfectly in principles. The governors of Jersey and Maryland harmonize entirely with them; the governor of Pennsylvania, of whom it never would have been suspected, lived intimately and publicly with Hamilton. Such a union of persons would be matter sufficient to produce resistance in the western counties, even admitting they had not thought of making any.

22. The soldiers themselves are astonished at the scandalous gaiety, with which those who possess the secret, proclaim their approaching triumph. It is asked, of what use are 15,000 men in this country, in which provisions are scarce, and where are to be seized only some turbulent men at their plough.[16] Those who conducted the expedition know this; the matter is to create a great expence; when the sums shall come to be assessed, no one will be willing to pay, and should each pay his assessment, it will be done in cursing the insurgent principles of the patriots.[17]

23. It is impossible to make a more able manoeuvre for the opening of Congress. The passions, the generous indignation, which had agitated their minds in the last session, were about being renewed with still more vigor; there was nothing to announce of brilliant successes which they had promised. The hostilities of Great Britain on the continent so long disguised, and now become evident, a commerce always harrassed [*sic*], ridiculous negociations lingering at London, waiting until new conjunctures should authorize new insults: such was the picture they were likely to have to offer the representatives of the people. But this crisis, and the great movements made to prevent its consequences, change the state of things. With what advantage do they denounce an attrocious attack upon the constitution, and appreciate the activity used to repress it; the aristocratical party will soon have understood the secret; all the misfortunes will be attributed to patriots; the party of the latter is about being [*sic*] deserted by all the weak men, and this complete session will have been gained.

24. Who knows what will be the limits of this triumph? Perhaps advantage will be taken by it to obtain some laws for strengthening the government, and still more precipitating the propensity, already visible, that it has towards aristocracy.

25. Such are, citizen, the data which I possess concerning these events, and the consequences I draw from them: I wish I may be deceived in my calculations, and the good disposition of the people; their attachment to

principles leads me to expect it. I have perhaps herein fallen into the repetition of reflections and facts contained in other dispatches, but I wished to present together some views which I have reason to ascribe to the ruling party, and some able manoeuvres invented to support themselves. Without participating in the passions of the parties, I observe them; and I owe to my country an exact and strict account of the situation of things. I shall make it my duty to keep you regularly informed of every change that may take place; above all I shall apply myself to penetrate the disposition of the legislature; that will not a little assist in forming the final idea which we ought to have of these movements, and what we should really fear or hope from them.

Health and fraternity.

Signed,

J. FAUCHET.

NOTES TO DISPATCH NO. 10

1. French reads: ". . . dont ses préjugés cherissaient au moins la memoire & le nom."
2. The words "in proportion" are not in the French text.
3. French reads: "le Fédéralisme & son contraire."
4. The words "in proportion" are not in the French text.
5. In the French there is no paragraph break at this point.
6. The words "in the mean time" are not in the French text.
7. French reads: "Mais pourqoui laisset-on au mépris des Traités porter depuis douze ans au Mississipi le joug du Faible Espagnol?"
8. Probably John Taylor of Caroline.
9. Should read: "to *be* despised."
10. French reads: "du Système de taxation & du Trésorier . . ."
11. French reads: "dessous."
12. French reads: "Tout ce que . . ."
13. In the French there is a paragraph break at this point.
14. French reads: "C'est une mesure dictée d'ailleurs par une connaissance exacte du coeur humaine."
15. French reads: ". . . on voulait voir si l'on aurait pu obtenir à se Sujet des presses."
16. French reads: ". . . & oú il n'y a que quelques hommes turbulens à aller saisir à leur charrue."
17. French reads: ". . . & ce sera en maudissant les principes insurrecteurs des Patriotes qu'on payera les quotes imposées."

Abbreviations and Short Titles

AHA, Annual Report	*American Historical Association, Annual Report.*
AHR	*American Historical Review.*
Ames, ed., *Works of Ames*	Seth Ames, ed., *The Works of Fisher Ames.*
Ammon, *Monroe*	Harry Ammon, *James Monroe: The Quest for National Identity.*
Annals	[Annals of Congress] *Debates and Proceedings in the Congress of the United States, 1789–1824.*
APS	American Philosophical Society.
ASP Fin.	*American State Papers, Finance.*
ASP For. Rel.	*American State Papers, Foreign Relations.*
ASP Ind. Aff.	*American State Papers, Indian Affairs.*
ASP Misc.	*American State Papers, Miscellaneous.*
Bemis, *Jay's Treaty*	Samuel F. Bemis, *Jay's Treaty.*
"Benson's Minutes of Annapolis Convention"	"Minutes of the Meeting [of the Annapolis Convention, Sept. 11–14, 1786]," Emmet Collection, 9398–9399.
Beveridge, *Marshall*	Albert J. Beveridge, *The Life of John Marshall.*
Brant, *Madison*	Irving Brant, *James Madison.*
Burnett, *Cont. Cong.*	Edmund C. Burnett, *The Continental Congress.*

Burnett, ed., *Letters*

Edmund C. Burnett, ed., *Letters of Members of the Continental Congress.*

Burt, *U.S., Gt. Bt. and Br. N. Am.*

A. L. Burt, *The United States, Great Britain and British North America.*

Call

Daniel Call, *Report of Cases Argued and Adjudged in the Court of Appeals of Virginia.*

Carter, ed., *Territorial Papers of U.S.*

Clarence E. Carter, ed., *The Territorial Papers of the United States.*

Christian, *Richmond*

W. A. Christian, *Richmond, Her Past and Present.*

Conway, *Randolph*

Moncure Conway, *Omitted Chapters of History disclosed in the Life and Papers of Edmund Randolph.*

CVSP

Calendar of Virginia State Papers.

DAB

Dictionary of American Biography.

Dallas

A. J. Dallas, *Reports of Cases in the Courts of the United States and Pennsylvania.*

Dipl. & Cons. Inst., Dept. State

Diplomatic and Consular Instructions, 1791–1801, Department of State.

Dipl. Dispatches [Fr.], Dept. State

Diplomatic Dispatches [France], Department of State.

Dipl. Dispatches [Gt. Brit.], Dept. State

Diplomatic Dispatches [Great Britain], Department of State.

Dom. Letters, Dept. State

Domestic Letters, 1784–1861, Department of State.

Eckenrode, *Rev. in Va.*

H. J. Eckenrode, *The Revolution in Virginia.*

Elliot, ed., *Debates*

Jonathan Elliot, ed., *The Debates in the Several State Conventions on the Adoption of the Federal Constitution. . . .*

ER

Edmund Randolph

"ER Draft Report"

"ER Draft Report for Benson Committee at Annapolis Convention," Sept. [11?], 1786.

ER Memorandum Book, 1786–1787

Edmund Randolph Memorandum Book, 1786–1787, MS.

ER, *Vindication*

Edmund Randolph, *A Vindication of Mr. Randolph's Resignation.*

Farrand, ed., *Records Fed. Conv.*

Max Farrand, ed., *Records of the Federal Convention of 1787.*

Fitzpatrick, ed., *Diaries of Washington*

John C. Fitzpatrick, ed., *The Diaries of George Washington, 1748–1799.*

Fitzpatrick, ed., *Washington* — John C. Fitzpatrick, ed., *The Writings of George Washington.*

Ford, ed., *Jefferson* — Paul Leicester Ford, ed., *The Writings of Thomas Jefferson.*

Frank, *Daniel* — John P. Frank, *Justice Daniel Dissenting, A Biography of Peter V. Daniel, 1784–1860.*

Freeman, *Washington* — Douglas S. Freeman, *George Washington,* Vols. I–VI.

Freeman (Carroll & Ashworth), *Washington* — John A. Carroll and Mary W. Ashworth, *George Washington,* Vol. VII.

Gibbs, ed., *Wolcott* — George Gibbs, ed., *Memoirs of the Administration of Washington and John Adams Edited from the Papers of Oliver Wolcott.*

Gipson, *Br. Empire* — L. H. Gipson, *The British Empire Before the American Revolution.*

Gourlay vs. Randolph Exors. Papers — Robert Gourlay vs. Randolph Exors. *et al.* Papers. U.S. Circuit Court (Va. Dist.).

Grigsby, *Va. Conv. 1788* — H. B. Grigsby, *The History of the Virginia Federal Convention of 1788.*

Hamilton — Harold C. Syrett *et al.,* eds., *The Papers of Alexander Hamilton.*

Hamilton, ed., *Monroe* — Stanislaus M. Hamilton, ed., *The Writings of James Monroe.*

Hening, ed., *Va. Statutes* — W. W. Hening, ed., *Statutes at Large, Being a Collection of all the Laws of Virginia. . . .*

Hening & Munford — W. W. Hening and William Munford, *Reports of Cases Argued and Determined in the Supreme Court of Appeals of Virginia.*

HSP — Historical Society of Pennsylvania.

Hunt, ed., *Madison* — Gaillard Hunt, ed., *The Writings of James Madison.*

James, *Clark* — James A. James, *The Life of George Rogers Clark.*

J.C.C. — *Journals of the Continental Congress.*

J. Council Va. — H. R. McIlwaine *et al.,* eds., *Journals of the Council of the State of Virginia.*

Jefferson — Julian P. Boyd, ed., *The Papers of Thomas Jefferson.*

J. H. Burg. — *Journals of the House of Burgesses of Virginia.*

J. H. Del. — *Journal of the House of Delegates.*

Johnston, ed., *Jay* — Henry P. Johnston, ed., *The Correspondence and Public Papers of John Jay.*

J. Sen., Va. — *Journal of the Senate* [Virginia].

King, ed., *Correspondence of R. King* — Charles R. King, ed., *The Life and Correspondence of Rufus King.*

LC — Library of Congress.

Madison — William T. Hutchinson and William M. E. Rachal *et al.*, eds., *The Papers of James Madison.*

Malone, *Jefferson* — Dumas Malone, *Jefferson and His Time.*

Mason — Robert A. Rutland, ed., *The Papers of George Mason.*

Mayo, ed., "Inst. to Br. Ministers," *AHA, Annual Report, 1936* — Bernard Mayo, ed., "Instructions to the British Ministers to the United States, 1791–1812," *American Historical Association, Annual Report for 1936,* Vol. III.

Mays, *Pendleton* — David J. Mays, *Edmund Pendleton, 1721–1803.*

Meade, *Henry* — Robert D. Meade, *Patrick Henry.*

MHS — Massachusetts Historical Society.

Miller, ed., *Treaties of the U.S.* — Hunter Miller, ed., *Treaties and Other International Acts of the United States of America, 1776–1863.*

Minnigerode, *Genêt* — Meade, Minnigerode, *Jefferson, Friend of France, 1793: The Career of Edmond Charles Genêt.*

Misc. Letters, Dept. State — Miscellaneous Letters, 1789–1825, Department of State.

Mitchell, *Hamilton* — Broadus Mitchell, *Alexander Hamilton.*

Munford — William Munford, *Report of Cases Argued and Determined in the Supreme Court of Appeals of Virginia.*

MVHR — *Mississippi Valley Historical Review.*

NA — National Archives.

NYHS — New York Historical Society.

NYPL — New York Public Library.

Oberholtzer, *Philadelphia* — E. P. Oberholtzer, *Philadelphia: A History of the City and its People.*

Pendleton — David J. Mays, ed., *The Letters and Papers of Edmund Pendleton, 1734–1802.*

Penn. Arch. — *Pennsylvania Archives.*

Penn. Misc. Whiskey Rebellion	Pennsylvania Miscellany: Whiskey Rebellion I, MSS.
Pickering & Upham, *Pickering*	Octavius Pickering and Charles W. Upham, *Life of Timothy Pickering.*
PRO	Public Record Office.
Rowland, *Mason*	Kate M. Rowland, *The Life of George Mason.*
Shepard, ed., *Va. Statutes, 1792–1806*	Samuel Shepard, ed., *The Statutes at Large of Virginia from October Session, 1792, to December Session, 1806, Inclusive.*
Thomas, *Am. Neutrality*	Charles M. Thomas, *American Neutrality in 1793.*
Tucker, "Summary view of . . . Courts . . . in Va.," *Blackstone's Commentaries*	St. George Tucker, "Summary View of the Judicial Courts . . . in Virginia," in Tucker, ed., *Blackstone's Commentaries with Notes of Reference to the Constitution and Laws of . . . Virginia.*
Turner, ed., "CFM," *AHA, Annual Report, 1903*	Frederick J. Turner, ed., "Correspondence of the French Ministers to the United States, 1791–1797," *American Historical Association, Annual Report for 1903,* Vol. II.
Tyler, *Williamsburg*	Lyon G. Tyler, *Williamsburg, The Old Colonial Capital.*
Tyler, ed., *Encyc. Va. Biog.*	Lyon G. Tyler, ed., *Encyclopedia of Virginia Biography.*
U.S. House Journal	*Journal of the House of Representatives of the United States.*
U.S. Senate Journal	*Journal of the Senate of the United States.*
U.S. Statutes at Large	Richard Peters, ed., *The Public Statutes at Large of the United States of America. . . .*
U.S. vs. ER Papers	U.S. vs. Edmund Randolph Papers, U.S. Circuit Court (Va. District).
Va. Conv., Dec. 1775	*The Proceedings of the Convention of Delegates held at the town of Richmond . . . 1st of December, 1775 and Afterwards by Adjournment to the City of Williamsburg.*
Va. Conv., May, 1776	*The Proceedings of the Convention of Delegates held at the Capitol, in the City of Williamsburg . . . 6th of May, 1776.*
Va. Mag.	*Virginia Magazine of History and Biography.*

Va. Report of 1799–1800	*The Virginia Report of 1799–1800 . . . together with the Virginia Resolutions of December 21, 1798.*
VHS	Virginia Historical Society.
VSL	Virginia State Library.
WMQ	*William and Mary Quarterly.*

Notes

EDITORIAL NOTE: To avoid needless repetition I have avoided the use of the abbreviation "LC" after the major manuscript collections of the Library of Congress. Thus, all collections lacking a location reference are understood to be in the Manuscript Division of the Library of Congress.

CHAPTER 1

1. *DAB*, *s.v.* "Randolph John," "Randolph, Sir John," and "Randolph, William [of Turkey Island]."
2. John Randolph was admitted to Middle Temple in 1746 and called to the bar Feb. 9, 1750 (*WMQ* [1st ser.], XXI, 25–28).

   Since Virginia adopted the Gregorian or New Style calendar in Mar., 1745, the few dates in this chapter that technically speaking should be given Old Style have been arbitrarily converted to the Gregorian or New Style calendar.
3. *DAB*, *s.v.* "Randolph, Peyton."
4. Genealogical and biographical information on the Jennings (Jenings) family can be found in *WMQ* (1st ser.), X, 31–35, and Tyler, ed., *Ency. Va. Biog.* I, 264.
5. "Diary of John Blair," *WMQ* (1st ser.), VII, 141.

   On Nov. 5, 1751, Philip Grymes, Peter Randolph and Peyton Randolph signed an indenture whereby they agreed to pay Edmund Jennings £3000 or Arianna Jennings £150 yearly in the event of the death of John Randolph (Indenture, Nov. 5, 1751, MS, VHS).
6. *Virginia Gazette* (Hunter), Dec. 5, 1751. Although always published in Williamsburg, there were times when two or three *Virginia Gazettes* were being published simultaneously. The publisher's name is therefore included to distinguish between the various papers bearing the same name.
7. *J. H. Burg.*, *1752–55*, xlii, 3.
8. John Randolph's first child, Arianna, was probably born in the summer of 1752 and Edmund, by common agreement of all authorities, was born on Aug. 10, 1753. In the absence of birth and baptismal records the only means of verifying this date is Edmund Randolph's own statement, made toward the end of his life, that he was born one day before his wife, and she was born on Aug. 11, 1753 ("Edmund Randolph's Sketch of his Wife," [Mar. 25, 1810?] MS, University of Virginia).
9. C. Bridenbaugh's popular study of Williamsburg, *Seat of Empire: The Political Role of Eighteenth-Century Williamsburg*, is most effective in conveying the temper of the community. For detailed information on the city itself nothing has yet supplanted Tyler, *Williamsburg*.

10. The original location of the Randolph family home (better known as Tazewell Hall) is noted in Thomas T. Waterman, *The Mansions of Virginia, 1706–1776*, 81–85.

11. Biographical information on Arianna and Susan Randolph is negligible and almost nothing is known about their early life. ER's partiality toward his younger sister is a matter of pure conjecture, yet she is the only person in all of his known correspondence who is invariably referred to by an affectionate nickname—"Sukey."

12. The location of P. Randolph's home (also known as the Randolph-Peachy house) and a description of the structure may be found in Waterman, *Mansions of Virginia*, 69–74.

13. That he attended one of Williamsburg's elementary schools can be established from his reference to the subject in his "Sketch of his wife" ("Edmund Randolph's Sketch of his Wife," [Mar. 25, 1810?], MS, University of Virginia). It is only logical to assume that his parents enrolled him in the grammar school maintained by the College of William and Mary since it was probably taken for granted that he would continue his education at that institution.

For a description of life in the grammar school from one who was being considered for a mastership there see Stephen Hawtrey to Edward Hawtrey, Mar. 26, 1765, printed in *Va. Mag.*, XVI, 209–210. See also Tyler, *Williamsburg*, 134, 136, 158, 160.

14. William C. Ewing, *The Sports of Colonial Williamsburg*, 1–39.

15. Bridenbaugh, *Seat of Empire*, 25–43.

16. The most useful of the various assessments of the political and social structure of Virginia in the eighteenth century are Carl Bridenbaugh, *Myths and Realities: Society of the Colonial South*, 1–53; P. S. Flippin, *The Royal Government in Virginia, 1624–1775*; Freeman, *Washington*, I, 73–189; J. P. Greene, "Foundations of Political Power in the Virginia House of Burgesses, 1720–1776," *WMQ* (3rd ser.), XVI, 485–506, and, in a somewhat broader context, his *The Quest for Power: The Lower Houses of Assembly in the Southern Royal Colonies, 1689–1776, passim*; and Charles Sydnor, *Gentlemen Freeholders: Political Practices in Washington's Virginia*.

17. The best general account of the Stamp Act crisis and Virginia's response to it is Edmund S. and Helen M. Morgan, *The Stamp Act Crisis: Prologue to Revolution.*

18. *J. H. Burg., 1761–65*, 257, 294, 302–305.

19. *J. H. Burg., 1761–65*, 358, 359–360. See also letter to Lt. Gov. Francis Fauquier to Board of Trade, Williamsburg, June 5, 1765, reprinted in *J. H. Burg., 1761–65*, lxvii–lxviii.

20. E. S. and H. M. Morgan, *Stamp Act Crisis*, 103–184 *passim*.

21. While the Morgans (*ibid.*, 293–294) present a different interpretation, most students of Virginia's political history insist the Stamp Act crisis did not disrupt the structure of authority wthin the Burgesses.

22. The most authoritative account of the "Robinson affair," as it is called in Virginia history, may be found in the biography of Edmund Pendleton, the principal administrator of Robinson's estate: Mays, *Pendleton*, I, 174–208. Mays establishes the significance of Robinson's death as a watershed in the transfer of power in the House to a younger generation of "gentlemen freeholders."

See also Joseph A. Ernst, "The Robinson Scandal Redivivus: Money, Debts, and Politics in Revolutionary Virginia," *Va. Mag.*, LXXVII, 146–173.

23. Gipson, *The British Empire Before the American Revolution*, Vol. XI, *The Triumphant Empire*, 107–164 *passim*.

24. *J. H. Burg., 1766–69*, 151, 153, 157–158, 165–171, 173–174, 177.

25. Gipson, *Br. Empire*, XI, 233–240.

26. *J. H. Burg., 1766–69*, 188–190, 210–211, 214–215, 218. See also Mays, *Pendleton*, I, 251–255.

27. The minutes of this informal meeting have been included in the Preface of the *J. H. Burg., 1766–69*, xxxix–xliii. Eighty-nine burgesses signed the Association and subsequently eighteen merchants added their names to the document.

28. John Randolph's election to the House of Burgesses and his attendance is estab-

lished by his appointment to two of its more important standing committees. Burgesses were never appointed to standing committees until they formally took their seat in the House (*J. H. Burg. 1776–69*, 190–191). His failure to sign the Association (*J. H. Burg., 1766–69* xxiv–xliii) is taken as evidence that he could not support it.

CHAPTER 2

1. Tyler, *Williamsburg*, 136.
2. "Journal of the Meetings of the President and Masters of William and Mary College," *WMQ* (1st ser.), XIII, 149.
3. Some indication of the regulations governing the conduct of the students attending the college can be found in "Journal of the Meetings of the President and Masters of William and Mary College," *WMQ* (1st ser.), II, 55–56.
4. Tyler, *Williamsburg*, 160, and St. George Tucker, "A Letter to the Reverend Jedediah Morse . . . ," *WMQ* (1st ser.) II, 194–196n.
5. "Journal of the Meetings of the President and Masters of William and Mary College," *WMQ* (1st ser.), XIII, 155.
6. Bursar's Book Ledger, 1763–1770, MS, Earl Gregg Swem Library, William and Mary College.
7. Bursar's Book Ledger, 1770–1782, MS, Earl Gregg Swem Library, William and Mary College.
8. Edmund Randolph, "An Oration in Commemoration of the Founders of William and Mary College . . . Aug. 15, 1771" (Williamsburg, 1771), McGregor Library Collection, University of Virginia.
9. *Virginia Gazette* (Purdie & Dixon), Aug. 15, 1771.
10. "Journal of the Meetings of the President and Masters of William and Mary College," *WMQ* (1st ser.), XIII, 232.
11. After ER resigned his studentship there is no further reference to him either as a student or as a graduate in the records of the college. If his studentship had been withdrawn by the college, for any reason, the "Journal" would have taken note of the action. Thus the resignation would appear to have been voluntary and one is inclined to conclude that he resigned because he was abandoning his studies in the School of Philosophy.
12. David Mays provides a wealth of information on the legal profession in Virginia during this period (Mays, *Pendleton*, I, *passim*). I am also indebted to several of my graduate students, particularly Mr. Frederick N. Bates, for their studies on the legal profession in America during the last half of the eighteenth century. Subsequent to their work, Alan Smith's excellent dissertation has provided the most systematic treatment of this subject to date ("Virginia Lawyers, 1680–1776: The Birth of an American Profession" [Ph.D. diss., Johns Hopkins University, 1967]).
13. In the absence of contrary evidence it must be assumed that ER served as an apprentice to his father. If he displayed little enthusiasm for the law, as certainly was evident a few years later, it is highly unlikely that his father would have given serious consideration to sending him to England to attend the Inns of Court. The inadequacy of the training in the Inns of Court at this time, although frequently noted in contemporary writings, has been ignored by legal historians until rather recently. See Julius Goebel, Jr., *The Law Practice of Alexander Hamilton*, I, 45n, for documented comments on the inadequacies of the Inns of Court.
14. Mays, *Pendleton*, I, *passim*.
15. Minutes of the Meetings of the Williamsburg Masonic Lodge, 1773–1778, Virginia MSS (photostats), LC. He was requested to revise the bylaws on Oct. 4, 1774 ("Williamsburg Lodge of Masons," *WMQ* [1st ser.], XXV, 150).
16. John M. Hemphill, "Edmund Randolph Assumes Thomas Jefferson's Practice," *Va. Mag.*, LXVII, 170–171.
17. Malone, *Jefferson*, I, 180–181.
18. ER, "Circular," Williamsburg, Aug. 27, 1774, an enclosure to James Parker, Williamsburg, Nov. 3, 1774, Parker Family Papers, Brown, Picton and Hornley Li-

braries, Liverpool, England (photocopy in possession of Colonial Williamsburg Foundation).

19. Virginia, it should be noted, revised its nonimportation agreement after learning of Parliament's partial repeal of the Townshend duties. In certain respects this new agreement was more stringent than the original agreement of 1769. Once again Peyton Randolph's name appears at the head of the list of signatures, while John Randolph's name is conspicuous by its absence (*J. H. Burg., 1770–72*, xxvii–xxxi.

20. The Virginia Committee of Correspondence and Inquiry was established on Mar. 12, 1773, during the spring session of the Virginia Assembly. Peyton Randolph, the speaker of the House of Burgesses, was selected chairman of the committee (*J. H. Burg., 1773–76*, 28).

21. For the activities of the burgesses and their dissolution see *J. H. Burg., 1773–76*, 124, 132. The meeting at Raleigh Tavern is summarized in *ibid.*, xiii–xiv. The actions taken in the Committee of Correspondence are found in the "minutes" of the committee, also printed in this *Journal:* "Minutes . . . [of Committee of Correspondence] 1774," *ibid.*, 138.

John Murray, the Earl of Dunmore, was named governor of Virginia in 1771, replacing Baron de Botetourt who had died in Oct., 1770.

22. *J. H. Burg., 1773–76*, 68, xiii–xiv, and "Minutes . . . [of Committee of Correspondence] 1774," ibid., 138. See also *Virginia Gazette* (Purdie & Dixon), June 2, 1774.

23. John Randolph, who had served in the House of Burgesses as a representative of Lunenburg County during the spring of 1769, did not reenter the House until this current session. In the intervening period he continued to serve as attorney general and was elected to serve a one-year term as mayor of Williamsburg (*Virginia Gazette* [Purdie & Dixon], Nov. 29, 1770).

24. ER, it should be noted, received his first administrative assignment at this session of the House of Burgesses. On May 6, 1774, he was named clerk of the Committee for Courts of Justice, one of the standing committees of the Burgesses (*J. H. Burg., 1773–76*, 76).

25. The journal for the Virginia Convention of Aug., 1774, has been lost but an account of its proceedings may be found in *Virginia Gazette* (Purdie & Dixon), Aug. 11, 1774.

Virginia's delegates to the First Continental Congress were Peyton Randolph, Richard Henry Lee, George Washington, Patrick Henry, Richard Bland, Benjamin Harrison and Edmund Pendleton (*ibid.*).

26. *J. C. C.*, I, 13–114.

27. *The Proceedings of the Convention . . . held at Richmond . . . , 20th of March, 1775*, (Richmond, 1816).

28. The most convenient summary of these events may be found in Charles R. Lingley, *The Transition in Virginia from Colony to Commonwealth*, 66–69.

29. Congress' prompt "adoption" of the militia outside of Boston and the appointment of Washington as Commander-in-Chief served to formalize the rebellion (*J. C. C.*, II, 64–66, 91, 105–106).

30. *J. H. Burg., 1775–76*, 164. This proved to be the last regular session of the House of Burgesses, subsequent efforts to assemble a quorum being unsuccessful.

31. *Virginia Gazette* (Purdie), June 9, 1775. Supplement.

32. John Randolph's activities may be traced through the *Journal of the House of Burgesses* (*J. H. Burg., 1775–76*, 206–208, 216–217, 231–237, 274, 278–280).

33. ER's sympathies can only be reconstructed from his actions, for not a line remains, to my knowledge, that might explain his feelings at this time. The date of his departure from Williamsburg would have to be about the middle of July since Benjamin Harrison notes his arrival in Philadelphia on July 23 (B. Harrison to G. Washington, Philadelphia, July 21, 23, 24, 1775, printed in *Va. Mag.*, XXXIII, 410–413).

34. The dates during which the delegates from Virginia were in attendance at the Congress may be found in Burnett, ed., *Letters*, I, lxiv–lxvi.

Two members of the Virginia delegation, Peyton Randolph and Richard Bland, had returned to Virginia to attend the meeting of the Burgesses and the Virginia Convention of July, 1775. Ultimately Pendleton, Harrison, Henry and Jefferson also left Congress for this convention. They were all in Philadelphia, however, when ER reached that city.

35. B. Harrison to G. Washington, Philadelphia, July 21, 23, 24, 1775, printed in *Va. Mag.*, XXXIII, 410–413.

36. R. H. Lee, P. Henry and T. Jefferson to G. Washington, Philadelphia, July 26, 1775, Washington MSS.

There is nothing to indicate that ER had received a letter from his uncle. One possible explanation might be that they missed each other because both were traveling at about the same time, Peyton being on his way to Williamsburg, while ER was journeying toward Philadelphia.

37. ER probably remained in Philadelphia until Aug. 2, the date Congress adjourned. Since the announcement of his appointment to Washington's staff came on Aug. 15, it seems safe to assume he arrived a day or two earlier.

38. Freeman, *Washington*, III, 476–529 *passim*. *An Historic Guide to Cambridge*, compiled by the D.A.R., 99–101, and map B between 82 and 83.

39. G. Washington was forty-three at this time, twenty-one years older than ER.

40. The assignment as a specific replacement for Thomas Mifflin can be established from G. Washington to R. H. Lee, Cambridge, Aug. 29, 1775, Fitzpatrick, ed., *Washington*, III, 450–454.

41. General Orders, Cambridge, Aug. 15, 1775, *ibid.*, III, 425–426.

George Baylor was another Virginian who came to Washington's staff with the recommendation of the Virginia delegation. See P. Henry, R. H. Lee, E. Pendleton, and B. Harrison to G. Washington, Philadelphia, July 12, 1775, *Pendleton*, I, 617.

42. ER's earliest assignment may have been to prepare for Congress additional copies of several letters Washington had written to Gen. Thomas Gage, the commander of the English forces in Boston. Copies of these letters, carrying dates between Aug. 10 and 20, can be found in ER's hand in the Papers of the Continental Congress, NA.

See Fitzpatrick, ed., *Washington*, I, xliii–xliv, and Freeman, *Washington*, III, 460, for information on the role of Washington's aides. The two works differ somewhat in their assessment of the significance of these aides.

43. This was one of the tasks performed by the aides. It is simply assumed that ER had to establish the clarity and precision of his writing before being allowed to draft letters for Washington.

44. Transmitting Washington's directives over the aide's own signature was obviously the most responsible assignment that could be given to an aide. The earliest known letter to be transmitted over ER's signature is dated Aug. 25 (ER to Artemus Ward, Headquarters, Aug. 25, 1775, Ward Family MSS, MHS). The latest is Oct. 31 (ER to Ephraim Bowen, Cambridge, Oct. 31, 1775 [letterbook copy], Washington MSS).

45. ER to T. Jefferson, Cambridge, Aug. 31, 1775, *Jefferson*, I, 243–244, and ER to R. H. Lee, Aug. 31, 1775, Lee Collection (Originals), University of Virginia.

46. *Virginia Gazette* (Dixon & Hunter), Sept. 9, 1775.

On Aug. 12 the *Gazette* reported that Congress had appointed ER as muster master general of the Continental Army (*Virginia Gazette* [Dixon & Hunter], Aug. 12, 1775). This was, of course, inaccurate.

47. *Virginia Gazette* (Dixon & Hunter), Sept. 9, 1775.

48. On Aug. 25 John Randolph inserted a formal announcement of his intention to leave the colony in the *Virginia Gazette*. He named Blair, Cooke and his brother Peyton as his legal agents and, in addition, referred all business connected with the office of attorney general to Blair (*Virginia Gazette* [Purdie], Aug. 25, 1775).

49. The Aug. 25 notice in the *Gazette* stated: "I intend to leave the colony for a few months. . . . " (*ibid.*) It is difficult to believe that this was what he really intended to do and that it represented his real assessment of the crisis given the highly perceptive analysis he made of the situation in his "Plan of Accommodations," Aug. 4, 1780. This document, outlining a plan for governing the colonies after the English forces achieved their expected victory, takes careful note of the various

colonial grievances and suggests John Randolph had a very thorough grasp of the issues that divided the colonies from the mother country (Mary Beth Norton, "John Randolph's 'Plan of Accommodations,'" *WMQ* [3rd ser.], XXVIII, 103–120).

50, P. Randolph died on Oct. 22. The reported cause was an apoplectic stroke (*Virginia Gazette* [Purdie], Nov. 3, 1775). Word of his death reached Washington's headquarters on Nov. 1 (evident from G. Washington to President of Continental Congress [John Hancock], Cambridge, Nov. 2, 1775, Fitzpatrick, ed., *Washington*, IV, 58–59).

51. Evident from G. Washington to Joseph Reed, Cambridge, Nov. 20, 1775. Fitzpatrick, ed., *Washington*, IV, 103–107. For ER's intention to rejoin Washington's staff, see T. Jefferson to John Randolph, Nov. 29, 1775, *Jefferson*, I, 268–270.

52. Although ER was not one of the executors of P. Randolph's estate, he was, with the exception of his aunt, the only one left to attend to the affairs of his father and uncle. It was his preoccupation with family matters that kept him from returning to Cambridge—at least for the first few months.

53. He arrived in Williamsburg on Dec. 5 (*Virginia Gazette* [Purdie] Dec. 8, 1775). The Virginia Convention of Dec., 1775, met in Richmond on Dec. 1 and adjourned to meet in Williamsburg on Dec. 4. The first plenary session was held on Dec. 5 (*Va. Conv., Dec., 1775*).

CHAPTER 3

1. For a general discussion of the military situation in Virginia at this time, see Eckenrode, *Rev. in Va.*, 58–95.

   ER's impatience with Virginia for failing to drive Dunmore out of the colony is set forth in ER to T. Jefferson, Cambridge, Aug. 31, 1775, *Jefferson*, I, 243–244, and ER to R. H. Lee, Aug. 31, 1775, Lee Collection (Originals), University of Virginia.

2, *Va. Conv., Dec., 1775*, 59, 68, 98, 105–111.

3. *Va. Conv., Dec., 1775*, 90, 102, 115–116. The ordinance is in Hening, ed., *Va. Statutes*, IX, 101–107.

4. ER to G. Washington, Williamsburg, Jan. 26, 1776, American Loyalist Transcripts, NYPL. This letter states he had written "repeatedly" to Washington, although none of these letters have been found. There is no known reply to this or any of ER's earlier letters to Washington.

5. ER's family responsibilities and his own financial situation have been inferred from the documents relating to the disposition of his uncle's and his father's properties. His uncle's "will" establishes the fact that he was not a direct heir (Peyton Randolph's Will, 1774, in Account Book of the Estate of Peyton Randolph, 1775 MS, LC), and the Account Book itself (*ibid.*) indicates his uncle had sizable holdings in York, Charlotte and James City counties. That ER was at least partially involved in these affairs, presumably advising his aunt, can be established from the notations in his hand in the Account Book. Many of these entries were made after he inherited the land and slaves, but some were obviously made well before he acquired title to the property. The disposition of his father's properties was, of course, in the hands of John Blair, James Cooke and Peyton Randolph (*Virginia Gazette* [Purdie], Aug. 25, 1775), but it is difficult to imagine ER being indifferent to their activities now that his uncle was dead. ER's place of residence and his return to the law is a matter of pure conjecture. He needed money to live and apparently left Cambridge owing money to Gen. Thomas Mifflin; see ER to William Battell, Williamsburg, Emmet Collection, NYPL.

6. *Virginia Gazette* (Dixon & Hunter), Apr. 16, 1776.

7. Wythe had been in Philadelphia since Sept. 1775. *DAB, s.v.* "Wythe, George."

8. ER to the president of the Committee of Safety, Apr. 13, 1776, No. 78, Papers of the Continental Congress, NA.

9. Madison was twenty-six, Tazewell was twenty-three (the same age as ER), Page was twenty-seven and Henry Lee was only twenty.

10. *Va. Conv., May, 1776,* 5–6, 8, 10. Pendleton's appointment procedure for these standing committees is explained in Mays, *Pendleton,* II, 105.
11. Pendleton's authorship of these resolutions is established in Mays, *Pendleton,* II, 108–110.
12. *Va. Conv., May, 1776,* 15–16.
13. *DAB, s.v.* "Cary, Archibald."
14. *Va. Conv., May, 1776,* 16.
15. Mays, *Pendleton,* II, 120. For an account of Mason's influence at this convention, see Rowland, *Mason,* I, 228–266.
16. *Va. Conv., May, 1776,* 25, 29, 42–43.
17. *Ibid.,* 64, 66, 68. There is no fully satisfactory explanation for the hasty adoption of the constitution by this convention and one can only conclude that most of the delegates found the basic structure of the government to their liking.
18. *Ibid.,* 50.
19. *Ibid.,* 52; Virginia Convention of May, 1776 (loose papers) MSS, VSL.
20. *Va. Conv., May, 1776,* 32–40.
21. *Ibid.,* 35, 36–37.
22. ER to G. Washington, Williamsburg, Jan. 26, 1776, American Loyalist Transcripts, NYPL.
23. *Va. Conv., May, 1776,* 78–79; *DAB, s.v.* "Nelson, Jr., Thomas."
24. *Va. Conv., May, 1776,* 78–79.
25. The best account of the process by which the various courts were established is Charles T. Cullen, "St. George Tucker and the Law in Virginia, 1772–1804" (Ph.D. diss., University of Virginia, 1971), 33–51.
26. Maintaining a private practice while serving as a legal officer of the state or county was taken for granted in Virginia and elsewhere at this time.
27. *Virginia Gazette* (Purdie), Aug. 30, 1776; *Virginia Gazette* (Dixon & Hunter), Aug. 31, 1776. Their youthful attachment to each other is noted in "Edmund Randolph's Sketch of his Wife," [Mar. 25, 1810?], MS, University of Virginia; *DAB, s.v.* "Nicholas, Robert Carter."
28. "Edmund Randolph's Sketch of his Wife," [Mar. 25, 1810?], MS, University of Virginia.
29. *Virginia Gazette* (Purdie), Nov. 29, 1776; *Virginia Gazette* (Dixon & Hunter), Nov. 29, 1776.
30. *Virginia Gazette* (Purdie), Dec. 6, 1776; Tyler, *Williamsburg,* 26.
31. *Va. Conv., May, 1776,* 51; *J. H. Del.* (Oct. Sess., 1776), 39; *ibid.* (May Sess., 1777), 129–130; *J. Sen. Va.* (May Sess., 1777), 44.

Several weeks after the memorial on Dunmore's property had been filed, the legislature appointed ER one of four commissioners to investigate the claims of Richard Henderson against the state of Virginia. Henderson was the leading figure in the ill-fated Transylvania Company which recently had attempted to establish an "independent colony" in the area of Kentucky. When neither the Continental Congress nor Virginia would recognize the colony's independence, Henderson and his associates attempted to get Virginia to at least validate the title to the land they claimed. The appointment of ER and others marked the beginning of an extended investigation of this claim. It was Nov., 1778, before the House of Delegates finally declared that Henderson's title to the land was void, a judgment that was promptly tempered by an agreement to compensate him for the money spent in developing the area. See W. S. Lester, *The Transylvania Colony,* 1–161 *passim; J. H. Del.* (Oct. Sess., 1776), 142; *ibid.* (May, Sess., 1777), 55, 59, 61, 63, 76; *J. Sen., Va.* (May Sess., 1777), 17, 20; *J. H. Del.* (Oct. Sess., 1777), 43; *ibid.* (May Sess., 1778), 43; *ibid.,* reprint (Oct. Sess., 1778), 16, 31, 36, 42, 79, 80, 91; *J. Sen. Va.* (Oct. Sess. 1778), 20.
32. *J. H. Del.* (May Sess., 1777) 49; *J. Sen., Va.* (May Sess., 1779), 14. For his salary see *J. Council Va.,* I, 210.
33. *Virginia Gazette* (Purdie), Apr. 4, June 6, 1777; *ibid.* (Dixon & Hunter), Apr. 4, June 6, 1777. See also Tyler, *Williamsburg,* 121–122.
34. *J. H. Del.* (May Sess., 1778), 4, 44.

35. *J. H. Del.* (May Sess., 1779) 60–61, 69; Senate *Journal* has not been found.
36. ER resigned as clerk of the House of Delegates on June 22, 1779 (*J. H. Del.* [May Sess., 1779], 69).
37. *Virginia Gazette* (Dixon & Nicolson), July 10, 1779.
38. *J. C. C.*, XIV, 861–862 (July 22, 1779). *DAB, s.v.* "Griffin, Cyrus" and "Smith, Meriwether." *Directory of the American Congress, s.v.* "Fleming, William."
39. For a general account of the activities of Congress during this period see Burnett, *Cont. Cong.*, 279–441.
40. *J. C. C.*, XIV, 864–865 (July 22, 1779); 885, 886 (July 24); 896 (July 29); 910, 911 (July 31); 925, 926 (Aug. 5); 939 (Aug. 7).
41. *Ibid.*, XIX, 883 (July 24, 1779); 896 (July 29); 933–934 (Aug. 7).
42. ER to B. Harrison, Williamsburg, Oct. 5, 1779, Burnett, ed., *Letters*, IV, 470–471.
43. Hening, ed., *Va. Statutes*, XII, 85–89.
44. Christian, *Richmond*, 12–19.
45. *Virginia Gazette* (Dixon & Nicolson), Jan. 22, 1780. In the absence of personal property and land books for the city of Richmond and Henrico County (few such records exist prior to 1787), it is impossible to establish the location of ER's first residence in Richmond.
46. For a brief general account of the military situation at this time, see John R. Alden, *The American Revolution.*
47. Eckenrode, *Rev. in Va.*, 209–231, provides a brief if somewhat biased account of the military situation in Virginia.
48. The month and year of Peyton Randolph's birth can be established from a reference to his age in ER to Arianna Jennings Randolph, Richmond, Dec. 5, 1785, Gourlay vs. Randolph Exors. Papers, VSL.
49. Eckenrode, *Rev. in Va.*, 264–272.
50. *Ibid.*; Freeman, *Washington*, V, 288.
51. *J. H. Del.* (May Sess., 1781), 1–2, 13, 21, 26; Senate *Journal* lost.

CHAPTER 4

1. Evident from ER to Auditor of Public Accounts, Philadelphia, Oct. 11, 1781, Papers of the Continental Congress, 1776–1789, VSL.
2. Irving Brant characterizes the House—Trist residence as a regular stopping place for Virginians after Madison started to stay there (Brant, *Madison*, II, 16–17). It is simply assumed that ER stayed there.
3. Oberholtzer, *Philadelphia*, I, 285–307 *passim.*
4. Evident from ER to Auditor of Public Accounts, Philadelphia, Oct. 11, 1781, Papers of the Continental Congress, 1776–1789, VSL.
5. See J. Madison to T. Jefferson, Philadelphia, Mar. 27, 1780, *Madison*, II, 5–7.
6. For biographical information on the three older members of the Virginia delegation in Philadelphia at this time see *DAB, s.v.* "Bland, Jr., Theodorick," "Jones, Joseph" and "Smith, Meriwether."
7. General biographical information on Madison can also be found in *DAB, s.v.* "Madison, James."
8. The best account of Congress' activities during the period of ER's service is to be found in the "Preface" of Burnett, ed., *Letters*, VI, iii–xxviii.
9. *J. C. C.*, XIX, 374–375 (Apr. 12, 1781). The significance of this effort to establish a federal judicial system has been slighted in recent historical scholarship and one must turn to two older studies for an assessment of the activities of Congress in this area. See J. Franklin Jameson, "The Predecessor of the Supreme Court" in *Essays in the Constitutional History of the United States in the Formative Period, 1775–1789*, J. F. Jameson, ed., 1–44, and Hampton L. Carson, *The History of the Supreme Court of the United States . . .* , 41–64.
10. *J. C. C.*, XIX, 374–375 (Apr. 12); XX, 496 (May 10), 497 (May 11), 599 (June 4), 694–695 (June 25), 761–764 (July 18).
11. *Ibid.*, XX, 764 (July 18).

12. *Ibid.*, XXI, 861–867 (Aug. 14), ER's draft is on 868*n*–871*n*.
13. *Ibid.*, 916 (Aug. 28), 921 (Aug. 30), 958 (Sept. 13), 961 (Sept. 14), 970 (Sept. 17), 985–986 (Sept. 21), 1109 (Nov. 8), 1113 (Nov. 13), 1141 (Nov. 26), 1147–1148 (Nov. 30), 1152–1158 (Dec. 4). Madison's amendments are on 965*n*–966*n*; Lovell's "remarks" are on 966*n*–967*n*.
14. *Ibid.*, XIX, 236 (Mar. 6, 1781).
15. J. Madison to T. Jefferson, Philadelphia, Apr. 16, 1781, *Madison*, III, 71–73.
16. *J. C. C.*, XX, 469–471 (May 2).
17. J. Mathews to Nathaniel Green, Philadelphia, May 20, 1781, Burnett, ed., *Letters*, VI, 93–94. Although it was actually a related issue that provoked Mathews' derogatory remark, it is indicative of the frustration among those delegates who were anxious to enlarge the power of the central government under the Articles.
18. The report of the Grand Committee can be found in Report of Committees No. 24, Papers of the Continental Congress, NA. The assignments to the new committee can be established from Committee Book, 1781–1785, No. 191, Papers of the Continental Congress, NA.
19. O. Ellsworth to Gov. of Connecticut [Jonathan Trumbull], Philadelphia, Aug. 1, 1781, Burnett, ed., *Letters*, VI, 164.
20. *J. C. C.*, XXI, 893–896 (Aug. 22). The report, in Varnum's hand, is found in Report of Committees, No. 24, Papers of the Continental Congress, NA.
21. *J. C. C.*, XXI, 893 (Aug. 22).
22. *Ibid.*, 1089–1092 (Nov. 2).
23. The most convenient general treatment of this subject is found in Thomas P. Abernethy, *Western Lands and the American Revolution*. Conflicting interpretations as to the reasons behind Maryland's delayed ratification of the Articles may be found in Herbert Baxter Adams, *Maryland's Influence Upon Land Cessions to the United States;* Johns Hopkins University Studies in Historical and Political Science (3rd ser.), I, 1–77, and two articles by Merrill Jensen, "The Cession of the Old Northwest," *MVHR*, XXIII, 27–48, and "The Creation of the National Domain, 1781–1784," *MVHR*, XXVI, 323–342.
24. *J. C. C.*, XXI, 781 (July 23, 1781).
25. Virginia Delegates [Madison and ER] to Gov. of Virginia [Thomas Nelson, Jr.], Philadelphia, Oct. 9, 1781, *Madison*, III, 281–283.
   Memorials of the Illinois and Wabash land companies had been submitted to Congress in Mar., 1781 (*J. C. C.*, XIX, 253 [Mar. 12]). These memorials and the cessions of Virginia, New York and Connecticut were subsequently referred to a committee that reported back to Congress on June 27 (*ibid.*, XX, 704–705). It was this committee report that Congress reviewed in Oct.
26. *Ibid.*, XXI, 1032 (Oct. 2, 1781). The initial steps taken by the committee are described in Virginia Delegates [Madison and ER] to Gov. of Virginia [Thomas Nelson, Jr.], Philadelphia, Oct. 9, 1781, *Madison*, III, 281–283.
27. Virginia Delegates [Madison, ER and Joseph Jones] to Gov. of Virginia [Thomas Nelson, Jr.], Philadelphia, Oct. 16, 1781, and Oct. 23, 1781, *Madison*, III, 286–289, 293–294.
   The two attempts to get Congress to alter the committee's authority met with no success (*J. C. C.*, XXI, 1057–1058 [Oct. 16], 1076–1078 [Oct. 26]).
28. *Ibid.*, 1098 (Nov. 3). The report of the committee was ultimately printed in the *Journals* on May 1, 1782 (*ibid.*, XXII, 223–232).
29. ER to Gov. of Virginia [T. Nelson, Jr.], Philadelphia, Nov. 7, 1781, Burnett, ed., *Letters*, VI, 259–261. The reference to the "late capture of the British army" refers to Cornwallis' defeat at Yorktown in October.
30. Several of ER's committee assignments involved him in Vermont's application for admission into the Union. He was anything but sympathetic toward Vermont's request because of its insistence on laying claim to lands that belonged to New York and New Hampshire. Vermont's conduct, in ER's view, was every bit as reprehensible as that of the western land companies who were memorializing Congress in an effort to gain recognition of their claims. The Vermont controversy is very ably summarized in Chilton Williamson, *Vermont in Quandary, 1763–1825,*

51–184 *passim*. ER's involvement in this question can be reconstructed from *J. C. C.*, XXI, 841–842 (Aug. 8, 1781), 886–887 (Aug. 20), 892–893 (Aug. 21); XXII, 54 (Jan. 25, 1782), 57 (Jan. 28), 80, (Feb. 19), 104 (Feb. 28).

31. ER, writing to Jefferson on Oct. 9, 1781, observed: "Mrs. Randolph would tire me with a narrative of Mrs. Jefferson's and your attention to her since my absence" (*Jefferson*, VI, 128–129). A second letter to Theodorick Bland in Virginia closes as follows: "Mrs. Randolph and myself beg our compliments to Mrs. Bland" (ER to Theodorick Bland, Philadelphia, Oct. 23, 1781, Randolph-Tucker Papers, Brock Collection, Huntington Library).

32. *J. C. C.*, XXI, 1071 (Oct. 24, 1781).

33. *Ibid.*, 1071–1072 (Oct. 24).

34. *Ibid.*, 1079–1082, 1082n–1083n (Oct. 29).

35. ER to Gov. of Virginia [T. Nelson, Jr.], Philadelphia, Nov. 7, 1781, Burnett, ed., *Letters*, VI, 259–261.

36. David Carroll to G. Washington, Philadelphia, Nov. 28, 1781, Washington MSS; G. Washington to President of Congress [John Hanson], Philadelphia, Dec. 3, 1781, Washington MSS; *J. C. C.*, XXI, 1163–1164 (Dec. 10, 1781).

37. *J. C. C.*, XXI, 1174–1176 (Dec. 17, 1781). The draft, in ER's hand, is in Report of Committees No. 24, Papers of the Continental Congress, NA.

38. The activities of Morris and his dealings with Congress between Feb., 1781, when the office of Superintendant of Finance was created, and Oct., 1781, when Cornwallis surrendered at Yorktown, are very ably summarized by Clarence L. Ver Steeg, *Robert Morris, Revolutionary Financier*, 58–77.

39. R. Morris, "Plan of Bank. . . . " in Francis Wharton, ed., *The Revolutionary Diplomatic Correspondence of the United States*, IV, 297–299. *J. C. C.*, XX, 545–548 (May 26, 1781).

40. Ver Steeg, *Morris*, 85–86.

41. *J. C. C.*, XXI, 1185 (Dec. 29), 1186, 1187–1190 (Dec. 31). Ver Steeg, *Morris*, 86.

42. Virginia Delegates [ER, Madison and J. Jones] to Gov. of Virginia [B. Harrison], Philadelphia, Jan. 8, 1782, *Madison*, IV, 18–19. Benjamin Harrison became governor of Virginia on Nov. 30, 1781, replacing Thomas Nelson, Jr., who resigned.

43. *J. C. C.*, XXI, 1189n–1190n, for Preamble which Congress rejected.

44. Without the benefit of some personal commentary by ER or his wife on their life in Philadelphia only the more obvious forms of social contact may be presumed. Some insight into the social life of the city at this time can be gained from Oberholtzer, *Philadelphia*, I, 285–300 *passim*.

45. Burnett, *Cont. Cong.*, 518–521.

46. *J. C. C.*, XXI, 792–804 (July 27, 1781), 811 (July 28), 845 (Aug. 9), 925–926 (Aug. 31); XXII, 17–26 (Jan. 9, 1782), 46–54 (Jan. 25).

47. *Ibid.*, XXII, 1–2 (Jan. 2, 1782), 87–92 (Feb. 22), quote on 88.

48. The resolution of the Massachusett's legislature and the committee report as made on Jan. 8, 1782, are printed in the *Journals* under the date Aug. 20, 1782 (*ibid.*, XXIII, 471–481).

49. The "Randolph, 'Facts and Observations' " are in *ibid.*, 481–522 (Aug. 20, 1782); the documentation is on 521n–522n.

50. Evident from "Charles Thomson, Notes of Debates," [Aug. 15, 16, 1782], Burnett, ed., *Letters*, VI, 444–445.
    On Aug. 5, shortly after the report was sent to Congress, the committee was augmented by the addition of James Duane, Hugh Williamson, Samuel Osgood and Madison (Committee Book No. 186, Papers of the Continental Congress, NA).

51. *J. C. C.*, XXIII, 522–524 (Aug. 20, 1782), and "Charles Thomson, Notes of Debates," [Aug. 15, 16, 1782,] and [Aug. 20, 1782], Burnett, ed., *Letters*, VI, 444–445, 447–449.
    There is no evidence to support Irving Brant's contention that the "Facts and Observations" were prepared by ER and Madison (Brant, *Madison*, II, 147, 149). In a letter to ER on Aug. 5, 1782, Madison refers explicitly to the report which "you prepared" (*Madison*, V, 20–23).

52. Burnett, ed., *Letters*, VI, liii; ER to J. Madison, Richmond, Apr. 11, 1782, *Madison*, IV, 145–149. The "humble cottage," which he would subsequently refer

to as "Pettus," is identified as a home rented from Dabney Pettus that was situated north and slightly west of Richmond in Henrico County (*ibid.*, 148n).

CHAPTER 5

1. In his frequent letters to Madison ER often made reference to his preference for congressional service. Yet the longer he remained in Virginia, the more his letters betrayed his concern for state problems. This shift in emphasis may reflect nothing more than a desire to keep Madison fully informed of events in Virginia, but some of his observations indicate he was getting rather deeply involved in the political life of the state.
2. The most perceptive assessment of Virginia's economic and financial embarrassment in the period immediately following the end of the war is in Gov. B. Harrison to the Speaker of the House of Delegates [John Tyler], In Council, May 6, 1782, H. R. McIllwaine, *et al.*, eds., *Official Letters of the Governors of the State of Virginia*, III, 212–223.
3. Burnett, *Cont. Cong.*, 525–550 *passim*.
4. Some evidence of this new emphasis is reflected in ER to J. Madison, Richmond, May 16, 1782, *Madison:* IV, 246–252.
5. The departure (or intended departure) of Lee and Jones for Virginia is noted by Madison in J. Madison to ER, Philadelphia, Apr. 23, 1782, *Madison*, IV, 180–183. Madison left Congress about Oct. 22, 1783, and did not return until Feb. 12, 1786 (Burnett, ed., *Letters*, VII, lxxviii; VIII, xcviii).
6. ER to J. Madison, "Pettus's near Richmond," May 10, 1782, and Richmond, May 16, 1782, *Madison*, IV, 225–230 and 247–252. Jefferson, it should be noted, refused to attend either the May or Oct. session of the Assembly.
7. Earl G. Swem and J. W. Williams, eds., *Register of the General Assembly of Virginia, 1776–1918*, 15–16.
8. ER to J. Madison, Richmond, May 5, 1782, *Madison*, IV, 208–209.
9. ER to J. Madison, "Pettus's near Richmond," May 10, 1782, *ibid.*, 225–230.
10. ER to J. Madison, Richmond, Apr. 19, 1782, "Pettus's near Richmond," May 10, 1782, Richmond, June 1, 1782, *ibid.*, 159–162, 225–230, 305–308.
11. ER to Speaker of the House of Delegates [J. Tyler], Richmond, May 16, 1782, Burnett, ed., *Letters*, VI, 352. Earlier he had declared his availability to the governor to report on activities in Congress (ER to B. Harrison, Richmond, Apr. 8, 1782, Executive Papers, VSL).
12. The *Journals* for both the Senate and House have been lost for this session of the legislature. The legislative record of the session can be established from Hening, ed., *Va. Statutes*, XI, 9–103 *passim*, and the activities of the Assembly reconstructed from the correspondence of the period.
13. ER to J. Madison, Richmond, June 1, 1782, *Madison*, IV, 305–308.
14. "Joint Resolution of General Assembly, June 14, 1782," *CVSP*, III, 192–193.
15. ER to J. Madison, Richmond, June 15, 1782, *Madison*, IV, 339–341.
16. ER to J. Madison, Richmond, Aug. 24, 1782, Richmond, Sept. 20, 1782, *ibid.*, V, 77–79, 150–152.
17. The House could not muster a quorum for three weeks, *J. H. Del.* (Oct. Sess., 1782), 1–9. The Senate *Journal* has not been found.
18. Hening, ed., *Va. Statutes*, XI, 105–184 *passim*.
19. *Ibid.*, 171.
20. ER informed Madison of the repeal on Dec. 13 (*Madison*, V, 399–406 [letter quoted]). This letter reached Madison on Dec. 24, after he had sealed his letter of that date. Madison's letters of Dec. 30, 1782, and Jan. 22, 1783, carry the account of how Congress responded to this news of Virginia's repeal: J. Madison to ER, Philadelphia, Dec. 30, 1782, *Madison*, V, 472–475, and Philadelphia, Jan. 22, 1783, *ibid.*, VI, 55–56.
21. Eckenrode, *Rev. in Va.*, 276–293.
22. The law against treason (Hening, ed., *Va. Statutes*, IX, 168) explicitly stated that persons so convicted could not be pardoned by the governor, but ER, as attorney

general, had formally advised the governor (ER to B. Harrison, Richmond, June 15, 1782, Executive Papers, VSL) that the law in question did not cut off the right of the executive to grant a pardon *prior* to conviction.

23. Eckenrode, *Rev. in Va.*, 276–293.

24. ER to B. Harrison, Richmond, Apr. 4, 1782, Richmond, May 12, 1782, Richmond, June 15, 1782, "Pettus's," Aug. 5, 1782, "Pettus's," Aug. 13, 1782, and ER to B. Harrison, [n.d. but rec'd. Aug. 29, 1782], Executive Papers, VSL.

25. Since the *Journals* of the House and Senate for the May, 1782, session have never been found, ER's letters to Madison provide the only running account of the activities of the two houses. See ER to J. Madison, Richmond, May 21–24, 1782, Richmond, June 1, 1782, Richmond, June 15, 1782, *Madison*, IV, 263–269, 305–308, 339–341.

26. ER to J. Madison, Virginia, July 5, 1782, Richmond, July 18, 1782 (letter quoted), *Madison*, IV, 394–398, 422–426. ER to [Theodorick Bland], Virginia, July 19, 1782, Ruffin Papers, University of Virginia.

27. The fragmentary nature of the court records for this period makes ER's references to his absorption in General Court work the only guide to the degree of his involvement. See ER to J. Madison, Richmond, Oct. 5, 1782, Richmond, Oct. 18, 1782, *Madison*, V, 183–185, 205–207.

28. The laws governing the meetings and procedures of these two courts are Hening, ed., *Va. Statutes*, IX, 389–399, 401–419 and X, 455.

29. The most thorough treatment of this case can be found in Mays, *Pendleton*, II, 187–202.

30. ER to J. Madison, Richmond, July 18, 1782, *Madison*, IV, 422–426, italics mine. The statement in the Constitution to which ER made reference reads as follows:

> But he [i.e., the governor] shall, with the advice of the Council of State, have the power of granting reprieves or pardons; except where the prosecution shall have been carried on by the House of Delegates or the law shall otherwise particularly direct; in which cases, no reprieve or pardon shall be granted, but by resolve of the House of Delegates. (Hening, ed., *Va. Statutes*, IX, 115–116.)

The law that stands in conflict with this statement, to which ER also refers reads:

> That the Governor . . . shall in no wise have or exercise a right of granting pardon to any person or persons convicted in the manner aforesaid; but may suspend the execution until the meeting of the General Assembly; who shall determine whether such person or persons are proper objects of mercy or not, and order accordingly. (Hening, ed., *Va. Statutes*, IX, 168.)

31. *Commonwealth vs. Caton et al.*, Nov., 1782, in 4 Call 6–22. Call summarizes the background of the case in an introduction to his formal report. See also E. Pendleton to J. Jones, Richmond, Oct. 21, 1782, *Pendleton*, II, 411.

32. There are two accounts of the case. The account in Call, cited above, which was compiled from data collected some twenty or twenty-five years after the case was decided, is the official report. In addition, Edmund Pendleton, as president of the Court of Appeals, compiled his own summary of the case. Pendleton's account refers to Andrew Ronald as representing the prisoners, while Call identifies Samuel Hardy as the attorney for the prisoners. It seems perfectly safe to assume that both men probably represented the prisoners, with Ronald being the principal spokesman for the accused men in court. See Pendleton's account of "The Case of the Prisoners" in the Court of Appeals, Oct. 29, 1782, *Pendleton*, II, 416–426.

33. 4 Call 6. The quoted material in this and subsequent references to Call is really Call's own summary rather than a full transcript of what was said in court.

34. "The Case of the Prisoners," *Pendleton*, II, 417.

35. 4 Call 7.

36. *Ibid.*

37. "The Case of the Prisoners," *Pendleton*, II, 418.

38. *Ibid.*, 426–427.

39. *Ibid.*, 426, italics added.
40. 4 Call 7–22 and "The Case of the Prisoners," *Pendleton*, II, 418–426.
41. ER to J. Madison, Richmond, Nov. 8, 1782, *Madison*, V, 262–266.
42. It is revealing to follow ER's account of the case in his private correspondence between July and Nov., 1782: ER to J. Madison, Richmond, July 18, 1782, Oct. 26, 1782, Nov. 2, 1782, Nov. 8, 1782, *Madison*, IV, 422–426; V, 217–219, 230–231, 262–266.
43. The first reference to his aunt's deteriorating health is ER to J. Madison, Richmond, July 18, 1782, *Madison*, IV, 422–426. The quote is from a letter of Aug. 16, 1782, *ibid.*, V, 58–62. On Nov. 22 he wrote:

> . . . I clearly see, that my absence from home [i.e., if he returned to Congress] would throw me most terribly in the rear of the law. But these circumstances would not of themselves detain me, provided I could make a reasonable composition with the creditors of my father who has his life in my uncle's estate upon the death of my aunt. That event approaches rapidly, and this matter will be quickly afterwards determined. (*Madison*, IV, 307–312.)

44. ER to J. Madison, Richmond, Oct. 18, 1782, *ibid.*, 205–206. ER's younger sister and his favorite was named Susan. It seems safe to assume he named his first daughter after her.
45. ER to J. Madison, Richmond, Apr. 11, 1782, *ibid.*, IV, 145–149.
46. See above, note 43.
47. ER to J. Madison, Richmond, June 1, 1782, *Madison*, IV, 305–308.
48. ER to J. Madison, Richmond, July 5, 1782, *ibid.*, 394–398.
49. ER to [Arthur Lee], Richmond, July 18, 1782, Lee Papers (Originals), University of Virginia; ER to J. Madison, Richmond, Aug. 6, 1782, *Madison*, V, 28–32.
50. ER to Arthur Lee, Richmond, Aug. 10, 1782, Lee Papers (Originals), University of Virginia.
51. George Mason declared his unwillingness to serve on the committee in Oct. G. Mason to ER, Gunston Hall, [Va.], Oct. 19, 1782, *Mason* II, 746–756. ER makes known his intention to proceed alone in ER to J. Madison, Richmond, Nov. 22, 1782, *Madison*, V, 307–312.
52. ER to Speaker of the House of Delegates [John Tyler], Richmond, Dec. 10, 1782, Executive Communications, VSL.
53. *Ibid.*
54. ER to J. Madison, Richmond, Dec. 13, 1782, *Madison*, V, 399–406, italics mine.

CHAPTER 6

1. *Case of the Loyal and Greenbriar Companies*, May, 1783, 4 Call 22–33.
2. *J. H. Del.* (Oct. Sess., 1783), 63.
3. Burnett, *Cont. Cong.*, 597–598; *J. H. Del.* (Oct. Sess., 1783), 97, 115, 130, 131–132, 148; *J. Sen., Va.* (Oct. Sess., 1783), 42, 48.
4. *J. H. Del.* (Oct. Sess., 1783), 63.
5. ER to T. Jefferson, Richmond, May 15, 1784, *Jefferson*, VII, 259–261.
6. The most thorough account of the "Nathan Case" can be found in *Jefferson*, VI, 321*n*–324*n*.
7. *J. H. Del.* (May Sess., 1783), 152–153.
8. ER to J. Madison, "Pettus's near Richmond," June 28, 1783, *Madison*, VII, 200–201.
9. J. Madison to ER, Philadelphia, July 8, 1783, *Madison*, VII, 216–218.
10. ER to Benjamin Harrison, "Pettus's near Richmond," July 15, 1783, Charles Roberts Autograph Letters Collection, Haverford College; B. Harrison to ER, "In Council," July 24, 1783, George Rogers Clark Papers, VSL; T. Jefferson to ER, Monticello, July 18, 1783, *Jefferson*, VI, 318–321; ER to B. Harrison, Richmond, Aug. 20, 1783, George Rogers Clark Papers, VSL.
11. ER to B. Harrison, Richmond, Aug. 20, 1783, George Rogers Clark Papers, VSL. A detailed summary of his activities during the preceding weeks can be found in ER to J. Madison, Richmond, Aug. 23, 1783, *Madison*, VII, 286–289.

12. ER to B. Harrison, Richmond, Dec. 26, 1783, George Rogers Clark Papers, VSL.
13. ER to B. Harrison, Richmond, May 29, 1784, Edmund Randolph Miscellaneous Papers, NYPL.
14. *J. H. Del.* (May Sess., 1784), 76–77. The Senate *Journal* is lost.
15. "Judgement of John Marshall and Cyrus Griffin in the case of Simon Nathan vs. Virginia, Dec. 28, 1786," Executive Communications, VSL. What little is known about the case after 1786 is summarized in *Jefferson*, VI, 321*n*–324*n*.
16. Benjamin Guerard to B. Harrison, Charleston, Dec. 16, 1783, *CVSP*, III, 549.
17. ER to B. Harrison, Richmond, Jan. 21, 1784, Executive Papers, VSL.
18. ER to J. Madison, Richmond, Jan. 27, 1784, *Madison*, VII, 415–418; ER to T. Jefferson, Richmond, Jan. 30, 1784, *Jefferson*, VI, 513–515.
19. J. Madison to ER, Orange, [Va.], Mar. 10, 1784, Madison VIII, 3–6.
20. *J. Council Va.*, III, 328–329 (Feb. 16, 1784).
21. ER to T. Jefferson, Richmond, May 15, 1784, *Jefferson*, VII, 259–261.
22. "Sketches of his own family written by Littleton Waller Tazewell for the use of his children, Norfolk, Virginia, 1823," 65, in Tazewell Family Papers, VSL.
23. ER to B. Harrison, Richmond, Jan. 21, 1784, Executive Papers, VSL; ER to T. Jefferson, Richmond, Apr. 24, 1784, *Jefferson*, VII, 116–117.
24. Referred to in ER to St. George Tucker, Richmond, Sept. 25, 1784, Tucker-Coleman Papers, Earl Gregg Swem Library, College of William and Mary.
25. Joseph Jones to J. Madison, Richmond, May 30, 1786, Madison MSS.

In late March, B. Harrison expressed the hope that the court would delay a case ER was handling because of the latter's illness (B. Harrison to ER, Fauquier County, Mar. 29, 1786, Personal Papers, Miscellaneous MSS, LC). In June ER informed Madison of a series of colds and of his failure to regain his strength (ER to J. Madison, Richmond, June 12, 1786, Madison MSS). In July, Washington commented on the subject, expressing his hope that a change of air and exercise would help (G. Washington to ER, Mount Vernon, July 12, 1786, Fitzpatrick, ed., *Washington*, XXVII, 480).

26. *Hite et al. vs. Fairfax et al.*, May, 1786, 4 Call 43–83.
27. In 1688 James II granted the whole of this territory to Lord Thomas Culpeper by a charter that gave him vast proprietary rights over the land. In 1719 title to the proprietorship was inherited by Lord Thomas Fairfax, whose heir is the defendant in this case. By this time, however, overlapping patents, issued either by the original proprietor or by the governor of the colony, had created innumerable problems in establishing land titles. (H. C. Groome, *Fauquier During the Proprietorship*, 30–81 *passim.*)

It should be noted in reference to these overlapping patents that both the proprietor and the royal governor possessed the right to issue patents, the former from his charter and the latter by authority of the Crown, since title to all lands in a royal colony rested, in the last analysis, with the sovereign.

See also Francis R. Hillier, "The Hite Family and the Settlement of the West" (M.A. thesis, University of Virginia, 1936).

28. 4 Call 45–46.
29. Groome, *Fauquier During the Proprietorship*, 60–63.
30. 4 Call 46–56.
31. *Ibid.*, 55–57.
32. Order Book of the Supreme Court of Appeals [of Virginia], I, 69–75, at Supreme Court of Appeals, Richmond.
33. "Edmund Randolph Court Notes," Clark-Hite MSS, The Filson Club, Louisville, Ky.; 4 Call 58–62.
34. *Ibid.*, 62–81.
35. *Ibid.*, 81–83.
36. ER to G. Washington, Richmond, July 17, 1784, Washington MSS.
37. Washington's efforts to untangle his business affairs following his return to private life are treated in Freeman, *Washington*, VI, 1–27. The nature of ER's involvement can be traced in G. Washington to Earl of Tankerville, Mount Vernon, Jan. 20, 1784, G. Washington to ER, Mount Vernon, Feb. 10, 1784, Fitzpatrick, ed..

Washington, XXII, 308–310, 325; ER to G. Washington, Richmond, Feb. 19, 1784, Washington MSS; G. Washington to ER, Mount Vernon, Mar. 18, 1784, Fitzpatrick, ed., *Washington*, XXVII, 361–363; ER to G. Washington, [?], Apr. [?], 1784, Simon Gratz Collection, HSP; ER to G. Washington, Richmond, May 15, 1784, and June 27, 1784, Washington MSS; G. Washington to ER, Mount Vernon, June 12, 1784, and July 10, 1784, Fitzpatrick, ed., *Washington*, XXVII, 422, 442–443; ER to G. Washington, Richmond, July 17, 1784, and July 20, 1784, Washington MSS; G. Washington to ER, Mount Vernon, Mar. 19, 1785, Fitzpatrick, ed., *Washington*, XXVII, 109–110; ER to G. Washington, Richmond, Apr. 5, 1785, Simon Gratz Collection, HSP.

38. Washington's role in the formation of these two companies is ably treated in Freeman, *Washington*, VI, 20–31 *passim*, 64–66. The extent of ER's involvement can be seen from their correspondence on the subject: G. Washington to ER, Mount Vernon, July 30, 1785, Fitzpatrick, ed., *Washington*, XXVIII, 214–216; ER to G. Washington, "The Rocks," Aug. 6, 1785, Washington MSS; G. Washington to ER, [Mount Vernon], Aug. 13, 1785, Fitzpatrick, ed., *Washington*, XXVIII, 218–221; ER to G. Washington, Richmond, Sept. 2, 1785, Washington MSS; G. Washington to ER, Mount Vernon, Sept. 16, 1785, and Nov. 5, 1785, Fitzpatrick, ed., *Washington*, XXVIII, 264–267, 307–308: ER to G. Washington, Richmond, Dec. 3, 1785, and Mar. 2, 1786, Washington MSS.

39. ER to J. Madison, "Pettus's near Richmond," Feb. 1, 1783, *Madison*, VI, 184–186.

40. Peyton Randolph's Will, 1774, in Account Book of the Estate of Peyton Randolph, 1775 MS, LC.

41. ER to J. Madison, "Pettus's," Mar. 7, 1783, Richmond, Mar. 22, 1783, Richmond, Mar. 29, 1783, *Madison*, VI, 319–321, 380–381, 415–418.

These letters indicate ER considered and then abandoned the idea of entering the Virginia Assembly. He cited as his reason for not becoming a candidate the probable loss of much of his inheritance from his uncle, an inheritance which, he insisted, would provide him with the kind of financial security he needed to re-enter public life.

42. *Virginia Gazette or the General Advertiser*, Richmond, Sept. 6, 1783.

The advertisement, dated Sept. 4, declares his intention to move into Richmond and offered "credit of ten years, upon receiving bond & security & a mortgage of the land for principle & interest." (*Ibid.*)

This is probably the home that belonged to Dabney Pettus and which ER had acquired after his return to Virginia in Apr. 1782. The advertisement only appeared in four issues of the paper (a weekly), suggesting he was successful in his efforts to sell the property.

There is no information available as to his home in Richmond except that it was located on Shockoe Hill (James Currie to T. Jefferson, Richmond, Aug. 5, 1782, *Jefferson*, VIII, 342–347).

43. Evident from ER to Mrs. Arianna Randolph, Richmond, May 6, 1784, Gourlay vs. Randolph Exors. Papers.

44. *Ibid.*

45. ER informed his mother of his plans in ER to Mrs. Arianna Randolph, Richmond, Nov. 28, 1784, *ibid.*

46. ER to John Randolph Grymes, Richmond, Nov. 27, 1785, *ibid.*

47. ER to Mrs. Arianna Randolph, Richmond, Dec. 5, 1785, *ibid.*

48. *Ibid.*, and Eliza House Trist to T. Jefferson, Philadelphia, July 24, 1786, *Jefferson*, X, 166–170.

49. *Proceedings of the M. W. Grand Lodge of Ancient York Masons . . . of Virginia . . . 1778 to 1822*, I, i–xvi, 13–14, 24–26. Charles P. Rady, "History of the Richmond Randolph Lodge No. 19, A. F. & A. M.," *Proceedings of the Grand Lodge of Virginia, 1887–1889*, 419–468.

50. James Buchanan and William Hay to T. Jefferson, Richmond, Mar. 20, 1785, *Jefferson*, VII, 48–49; T. Jefferson to ER, Paris, Sept. 20, 1785, *ibid.*, VII, 537–538; ER to T. Jefferson, Richmond, July 12, 1786, *ibid.*, X, 133–134. The architect secured by Jefferson was Charles Clérisseau.

51. St. George Tucker to Mrs. Fanny Tucker, Richmond, Apr. 3–4, 1786, Tucker-Coleman Papers, Earl Gregg Swem Library, William and Mary College.
52. ER to J. Madison, Richmond, June 12, 1786, Madison MSS.
53. The only explicit reference to the death of the baby is contained in a letter from Eliza House Trist to T. Jefferson, Philadelphia, July 24, 1786, *Jefferson*, X, 169. However a letter from Washington, dated July 12, 1786, suggests the baby might have died in June, several weeks earlier than Mrs. Trist's letter implies. Washington wrote: "I am extremely sorry to hear of your indisposition and *loss*." (G. Washington to ER, Mount Vernon, July 12, 1786, Fitzpatrick, ed., *Washington*, XXVIII, 480.)

CHAPTER 7

1. ER to J. Madison, Richmond, June 15, 1782, *Madison*, IV, 339–341, refers to Assembly's action. (As previously noted, the *Journals* for this session are lost.) The bill establishing the Potomac River Co. is in Hening, ed., *Va. Statutes*, XI, 510–525. See above, p. 74, and *J. H. Del.* (Oct. Sess., 1784), 65–66. The Senate *Journals* for 1784 have never been found.
2. *J. H. Del.* (May Sess. 1784), 115–116, 121.
3. *Ibid.* (Oct. Sess., 1784), 86–94.
4. This sequence of events have been reconstructed from ER to J. Madison, Richmond, July 17, 1785, Madison MSS, and George Mason to J. Madison, Gunston Hall, [Va.], Aug. 9, 1785, *Mason*, II, 826–828.
5. *Ibid.*; see also Freeman, *Washington*, VI, 30*n*.
6. ER to J. Madison, Richmond, July 17, 1785, Madison, VIII, 324–325.
7. George Mason & Archibald Henderson to Speaker of the House of Representatives, Mount Vernon, Mar. 28, 1785, with enclosures, in *Mason*, II, 814–823.
8. George Mason to J. Madison, Gunston Hall, [Va.], Aug. 9, 1785, and Dec. 7, 1785, *Mason*, II, 826–828, 835–837.
9. *J. H. Del.* (Oct. Sess., 1785), 117, 126, and Hening, ed., *Va. Statutes*, XII, 50–55.
10. J. Madison to G. Washington, Richmond, Dec. 9, 1785, Madison, VIII, 438–441.
11. During this session the House of Delegates passed an act establishing religious freedom (*J. H. Del.* [Oct. Sess., 1785], 92–142 *passim*, and Hening, ed., *Va. Statutes*, XII, 84–85) and a bill abolishing primogeniture in land inheritance (Hening, ed., *Va. Statutes*, XII, 138–140). The House also considered but did not pass a bill for the payment of debts due British creditors (*J. H. Del.* [Oct. Sess., 1785], 97–98, 111, 112–113).
12. *J. H. Del.* (Oct. Sess., 1785), 151, 152, quote on 151; *J. Sen. Va.* (Oct. Sess., 1785, reprint), 102–103.
13. Madison's role is set forth in Brant, *Madison*, II, 381–382.
14. *J. H. Del.* (Oct. Sess., 1785), 151.
15. ER to [Patrick Henry], Richmond, [before Feb. 19], 1786, Executive Papers, VSL. ER wrote to the governors on Feb. 19, as evidenced by two of the replies received. In each case they acknowledged his letter of Feb. 19 (W. Greene to ER, Warwick, R.I., Mar. 21, 1786, and R. Caswell to ER, North Carolina, June 21, 1786, State Papers, No. 77, Papers of the Continental Congress, NA).
16. ER to J. Madison, Richmond, Mar. 1, 1786, Madison, VIII, 494–495.
17. Benjamin Harrison to St. George Tucker, Richmond, Jan. 29, 1786, Francis M. Dearborn MSS, Harvard University. He reminded Tucker of his appointment on June 11 (ER to St. George Tucker, Richmond, June 11, 1786, Tucker-Coleman Papers, Earl Gregg Swem Library, William and Mary College).
18. ER to J. Madison, Richmond, June 12, 1786, Madison MSS.
19. Burnett, ed., *Letters*, VIII, 389*n*–390*n*.
20. See Daniel Carroll to J. Madison, Annapolis, Md., Mar. 13, 1786, Madison, VIII, 496–497; J. Madison to T. Jefferson, Philadelphia, Aug. 12, 1786, *Jefferson*, X, 229–236; Theodore Sedgwick to Caleb Strong, New York, Aug. 6, 1786, Burnett, ed., *Letters*, VIII, 415–416; Stephen Higginson to John Adams, Boston, July [?], 1786, *AHA, Annual Report, 1896*, I, 733–741.

21. "Proceedings of the Commissioners to Remedy Defects in the Federal Government" in Elliot, ed., *Debates*, I, 116–119.
22. J. Madison to James Monroe, Annapolis, Sept. 11, 1786, Madison MSS.
23. "Benson's Minutes of Annapolis Convention."
24. "ER Draft Report."
    This report is found on three scraps of paper mounted at the end of Vols. VI and VII of the Madison MSS. The opening sentence on the fragment that obviously comes first clearly establishes that it was prepared as a draft report for the Benson Committee. I have therefore dated the document Sept. 11.
25. *Ibid.* The statement and its subsequent deletion are important, for the views expressed therein would appear to be designed to imply unanimity among the states toward the objects of the convention. Such unanimity, of course, did not exist.
26. *Ibid.* This material, which was in fact rather superfluous except insofar as it permitted delegates to compare the language used in each state resolution, never appeared in the Benson Committee report or in the "address to the states" written by the second committee appointed by the convention. Irving Brant makes reference to this material but fails to relate it to the other fragments which, when combined, make a full report. See Brant, *Madison*, II, 385.
27. "ER Draft Report." This is the critical section of the report and it deserves to be quoted in full, including the words and phrases ER deleted.
    The reference in the third resolution to the powers given to the New Jersey delegation is highly significant because the Benson Committee report paraphrased the language of the New Jersey resolution, and the "address to the states," the formal pronouncement of the convention, explicitly endorsed that resolution.
    The New Jersey resolution read as follows:

    . . . [to] meet such commissioners as may be appointed by the other states in the Union at a time and place to be agreed on, to take into consideration the trade of the United States; to examine the relative situation and trade of the said states; to consider how far an uniform system in their commercial regulations and other important matters may be necessary to their common interest and permanent harmony; and to report to the several states such an act, relative to this great object, as when unanimously ratified by them will enable the United States in Congress assembled effectively to provide for the exigencies of the Union. (*Votes and Proceedings of the Tenth General Assembly of the state of New Jersey* . . . , [Feb. 15–Mar. 24, 1786], Trenton, N.J., 1786, 72.)

28. "Benson's Minutes of Annapolis Convention." Emphasis mine, to indicate the language reflective of the influence of the New Jersey resolution.
29. The exact sequence of events following the approval of the first committee report can only be reconstructed inferentially because Benson's minutes terminate with the report of his committee. The appointment of the second committee and succession of events that follow have been reconstructed from the "Proceedings of the Commissioners to Remedy Defects in the Federal Government," Elliot, ed., *Debates*, I, 116–119.
    Hamilton's chairmanship of this committee and his reputed authorship of the "address" are based on a statement by Madison in his "Preface to the Debates in the [Philadelphia] Convention," Madison MSS. It was written after 1830.
30. "Proceedings of the Commissioners to Remedy Defects in the Federal Government," Elliot, ed., *Debates*, I, 116–119. Emphasis mine, again to indicate the language reflective of the influence of the New Jersey resolution.
31. J. T. Morse, in his biography of Hamilton, introduces the story that after Hamilton had completed the "address," he was forced to tone down the language used in it because of ER's reputed dissatisfaction with the broad powers sought for the delegates in the subsequent convention. Madison is supposed to have said at the time: "You had better yield to this man, for otherwise all Virginia will be against you." (J. T. Morse, *Life of Alexander Hamilton*, [Boston, 1876], I, 167.) The undocumented statement has been widely quoted in subsequent accounts of the convention. It would appear that nothing could be further from the truth; if any-

thing, ER was in the forefront of the effort to recommend the calling of another convention, at which the delegates would have broad power to consider all matters touching on the needs of the Union.

32. Mitchell, Hamilton, I, 367.

33. G. Washington to ER, [Mount Vernon], Sept. [18–30?], 1786, Fitzpatrick ed., *Washington*, XXIX, 24n; ER to G. Washington, Richmond, Nov. 24, 1786, Washington MSS.

CHAPTER 8

1. Support for ER is noted in J. Madison to James Monroe, Richmond, Oct. 30, 1786, Madison MSS.

2. The Senate was unable to conduct any business until Nov. 7 (*J. Sen., Va.* [Oct. Sess., 1786], 3–6). The selection of ER as governor is noted in *ibid.*, 7 and *J. H. Del.* (Oct. Sess., 1786), 26.

3. G. Washington to ER, Mount Vernon, Nov. 19, 1786, Fitzpatrick, ed., *Washington*, XXIX, 77.

4. ER to G. Washington, Richmond, Nov. 24, 1786, Washington MSS.

5. *CVSP*, IV, 184. Notice of the transfer of his practice is in *Virginia Independent Chronicle*, Nov. 22, 1786.

6. John Harvie's certification of ER's having taken the oath of office, Dec. 1, 1786, Executive Papers, VSL.

7. Virginia Constitution of May, 1776, Hening, ed., *Va. Statutes*, IX, 112–119.

8. *Ibid.*

9. The law establishing the salaries of state officials as of Nov. 1, 1785, is in Hening, ed., *Va. Statutes*, XII, 48–49.

10. ER to G. Washington, Richmond, Nov. 24, 1786, Washington MSS.

11. Biographical information on the members of the Council of State at this time is, with a few exceptions, rather difficult to come by. See *DAB*, *s.v.* "Braxton, Carter" and "Jones, Joseph"; Tyler, ed., *Encyc. Va. Biog., s.v.* "Randolph, Beverley," "Seldon, Miles," "Stark, Bowling" and "Wood, James." Isolated information on Mathews can be acquired through Earl G. Swem, ed., *Virginia Historical Index, s.v.* "Mathews, Sampson."

12. This was the clerical staff of the executive as of Jan. 1, 1787. Hening, ed., *Va. Statutes*, XII, 131.

13. Meade, Henry, II, 300–301.

14. *J. Council Va.*, IV, 4–5 (Dec. 6, 1786).

15. Noted in James Currie to T. Jefferson, Richmond, Aug. 5, 1782, *Jefferson*, VIII, 342–347.

16. ER was elected grand master of the Ancient York Masons in Virginia on Oct. 27, 1786, *Proceedings of the M. W. Grand Lodge of Ancient York Masons . . . of Virginia . . . 1778 to 1822* (Richmond, 1874), I, 24–28.

17. ER Memorandum Book, 1786–1787.

18. As examples see ER to Register of the Land Office, Richmond, Dec. 20, 1786, ER to Col. Meriwether, Richmond, Dec. 23, 1786, "Memorandum Governing the Operations of the Clerk's Office," [Dec. 23?], 1786, Executive Papers, VSL.

19. "Circular to the Clerks of the Courts and County Lieutenants or Commanding Officers," In Council, Dec. 29, 1786, Executive Letterbook, VSL.

20. *J. Council Va.*, IV, 38–40 (Jan. 30, 1787), 44–45 (Feb. 27), 46–48 (Feb. 28), "Additional" Journal, 317–347 (Mar. 20).

21. The story of Clark's ill-fated expedition is fully treated in L. C. Helderman, "The Northwest Expedition of George Rogers Clark, 1786–1787," *MVHR*, XXV: 317–334.

22. "Report of a Committee of the Danville Convention, Dec. 22, 1786," Draper MSS, Wisc. State Hist. Soc.

23. *J. Council Va.*, IV, 28–29 (Jan. 11, 1787); ER to Delegates in Congress [W. Grayson and E. Carrington], Richmond, Jan. 21, 1787, and ER to President of Congress [Arthur St. Clair], Richmond, Jan. 24, 1787, Executive Letterbook, VSL, St. Clair, it should be noted, became President on Feb. 2, 1787.

24. The memorials, depositions and letters, most of them addressed to Gov. Patrick Henry, can be found in *CVSP*, IV, 182*ff.*
25. *J. Council Va.*, IV, 46–48 (Feb. 28, 1787). Wilkinson would soon be at the center of a so-called "Spanish Conspiracy," a project that would ultimately cause him to work with and then betray Aaron Burr when the latter embarked upon his ill-fated separatist movement in the West. Wilkinson was the principal government witness when Burr was tried for treason in 1807.
26. ER to Attorney General [James Innes], Richmond, Mar. 4, 1787, ER to Gen. G. R. Clark, Richmond, Mar. 4, 1787, Executive Letterbook, VSL; ER to Virginia Delegates in Congress [J. Madison, W. Grayson and E. Carrington], Richmond, Apr. 4, 1787, Madison MSS; ER to Speaker of the House of Delegates [Joseph Prentis]. In Council, Oct. 15, 1787, Executive Letterbook, VSL.

    Clark attempted to counteract the criticism he knew was mounting against him by sending Col. Logan to Richmond in Dec., 1786. Logan carried a letter addressed to P. Henry as governor (G. R. Clark to P. Henry, Dec. [?], 1786, *CVSP*, IV, 213). ER gave Clark the state's official reply in his letter of Mar. 4, 1787, cited above. This letter was answered by Clark on May 11, 1787:

    > Sir:
    > I respect the state of Virginia. The information you have received hath already been stained with the blood of your country, things will prove themselves.
    > I am Sir, Yr.
    > G. R. Clark
    > (G. R. Clark to ER, Beargrass, [Ky.], May 11, 1787, George Rogers Clark Papers, VSL.)

27. ER also did what he could to implement the scheduled commercial meeting of Virginia, Maryland and Pennsylvania that had been proposed by the Mount Vernon Conference. Uncertainty as to whether the meeting could convene without the approval of Congress delayed the meeting until such time as the objectives of the conference were overshadowed by the Philadelphia Convention (*J. H. Del.* [Oct. Sess., 1786], 63; *J. Sen., Va.* [Oct. Sess., 1786], 21–22). ER to Gov. of Maryland [William Smallwood], Richmond, Dec. 1, 1786; ER to President of Pennsylvania [Benjamin Franklin], Richmond, Dec. 1, 1786, Executive Letterbook, VSL.

    ER's letter to the Virginia delegates is ER to D. Ross, W. Ronald and T. Pleasants, [Jr.], Richmond, Apr. 14, 1787, Executive Letterbook, VSL. A notation in the Letterbook indicates separate but identical letters were sent to each of these men. See also ER to St. George Tucker, Richmond, Apr. 14, 1787, *ibid.*; ER to Virginia Delegates in Congress [J. Madison, W. Grayson and E. Carrington], Apr. 14, 1787, *ibid.*; Henry Lee to ER, New York, Apr. 30, 1787, Executive Papers, VSL, and Thomas Pleasants, Jr., to ER, Petersburg, [Va.] May 2, 1787, *ibid.*

28. J. Madison to ER, New York, Feb. 18, 1787, Feb. 25, 1787, Mar. 11, 1787, Madison MSS J. Madison to ER, New York, Mar 19, 1787, Burnett, ed., *Letters*, VIII, 359–360.
29. On Dec. 1, the day he took the oath of office as governor, he prepared letters to the governors of all the states transmitting a copy of the Nov. 23 act (ER to "the Governors of the States," Richmond, Dec. 1, 1786, Executive Letterbook, VSL). A notation in the Letterbook indicates each governor received a personal copy of this letter. A copy of the act was also sent to the President of the Continental Congress (ER to President of Congress [Nathaniel Gorham], Virginia State Papers No. 71, Vol. II, Papers of the Continental Congress, NA.).

    When the Virginia delegation was elected by joint ballot of the two houses on Dec. 4 (*J. Sen., Va.* [Oct. Sess., 1786], 38; *J H. Del.* [Oct. Sess., 1786], 86) he sent a second letter to each of the governors informing them of the names of the Virginia delegates (ER to the "Executives of the States," Richmond, Dec. 6, 1786, Executive Letterbook, VSL).

30. *J. Sen., Va.* (Oct. Sess., 1786), 38; *J. H. Del.* (Oct. Sess., 1786), 86.
31. ER to George Wythe, Richmond, Dec. 6, 1786, and ER to John Blair, Richmond, Dec. 6, 1786, Executive Letterbook, VSL. The language of these two letters was virtually identical. ER to George Mason, Richmond, Dec. 6, 1786, *ibid.* To Madison

he wrote a two-line note soliciting a formal acceptance of his appointment to the delegation (ER to J. Madison, Richmond, Dec. 6, 1786, *ibid.*). The letter to Henry was reflective of ER's respect for Henry's considerable influence (ER to Patrick Henry, Richmond, Dec. 6, 1786, *ibid.*).

32. ER to G. Washington, Richmond, Dec. 6, 1786, Washington MSS.
33. G. Washington to ER, Mount Vernon, Dec. 21, 1786, Fitzpatrick, ed., *Washington*, XXIX, 119–120.
34. ER to G. Washington, Richmond, Jan. 4, 1787, Washington MSS. This letter was mistakenly dated "1786."
35. P. Henry to Governor of Virginia, Feb. 13, 1787, Charles Roberts Autograph Letters Collection, Haverford College Library, Pennsylvania.
36. ER to J. Madison, Richmond, Mar. 1, 1787, Madison MSS.
37. The *Journal* of the Executive Council for Mar. 8 refers to Nelson in terms that indicate he had been appointed but had not as yet signified his willingness to serve (*J. Council Va.*, IV, 55 [Mar. 8, 1787]).
38. ER to Richard Henry Lee, Richmond, Mar. 21, 1787, Executive Letterbook, VSL. The following day ER reported to JM:

> Genl. Nelson refuses to join us. Col. R. H. Lee has been appointed in his stead. This seemed proper from the conspiciousness of the xaracter [*sic*], and the respect, due to past services. The objection to his unfederal opinions was so urgently pressed, that the council consisting of eight were equally divided. I gave the decision from a hope that himself and his friends might be attached to the union on those principles, which can alone support it—Should Mr. Lee refuse or another vacancy happen, no other appointment will be made. (ER to J. Madison, Richmond, Mar. 22, 1787, Madison MSS.)

39. ER to J. Madison, Richmond, Mar. 27, 1787, *ibid.*
40. ER to J. Madison, Richmond, Apr. 4, 1787, *ibid.*
41. R. H. Lee to John Adams, New York, Sept. 5, 1787, Burnett, ed., *Letters*, VIII, 643.
42. On Apr. 16 ER explained to Mason:

> I have thrice done myself the pleasure of informing and reminding you officially of your appointment to the Convention at Philadelphia next month. But my letters have, I am afraid, miscarried through some accident or other; although they were sent by the mail free of postage. (ER to George Mason, Richmond, Apr. 16, 1787, *Mason*, III, 875.)

43. J. Madison to G. Washington, Richmond, Nov. 8, 1786, Dec. 7, 1786, Dec. 24, 1786, Feb. 21, 1787, and Mar. 18, 1787, Madison MSS.
44. ER to G. Washington, Richmond, Mar. 11, 1787, Washington MSS.
45. G. Washington to ER, Mount Vernon, Mar. 28, 1787, Fitzpatrick, ed., *Washington*, XXIX, 186–188. The date of its receipt can be established from ER's reply (ER to G. Washington, Richmond, Apr. 2, 1787, Washington MSS).
46. George Mason to ER, Gunston Hall, [Va.], Apr. 12, 1787, *Mason*, III, 874.
47. McClurg's appointment is noted in J. Madison to T. Jefferson, [New York], Apr. 23, 1787, *Jefferson*, XI, 307–310. McClurg was, of course, sitting on the Council and, as Madison suggested in this letter, was consulted before the appointment was made (*J. Council Va.*, IV, 73 [Apr. 5, 1787]).
48. *J. Council Va.*, IV, 55 (Mar. 8, 1787).
49. ER to J. Madison, Richmond, Mar. 7, 1787, Madison MSS.
50. George Mason to ER, Gunston Hall, [Va.], Apr. 23, 1787, *Mason*, III, 875–876.
51. His concern over a possible conflict between the announced date of the convention and the uncertainty over the date of the baby's birth is noted in ER to J. Madison, Richmond, Mar. 7, 1787, Madison MSS. The date of birth and name of the child can be established from Randolph, *The Randolphs of Virginia*, 11*ff.*
52. J. Madison to ER, New York, Apr. 15, 1787, Madison MSS.
53. Evident from ER to Virginia Delegates in Congress [H. Lee, W. Grayson and E. Carrington], Richmond, May 4, 1787, Executive Letterbook, VSL.

CHAPTER 9

1. An entry in Washington's diary for May 15, 1787, notes ER's arrival in Philadelphia, Fitzpatrick, ed., *Diaries of Washington,* III, 216–217.
2. That he stayed at the boarding establishment of Mrs. House; see George Reed to John Dickinson, Philadelphia, May 25, 1787, EM 3314, Emmet Collection, NYPL.
3. J. Madison to T. Jefferson, Philadelphia, May 15, 1787, *Jefferson,* XI, 363. Washington was staying with Robert Morris (May 13, 1787, Fitzpatrick, ed., *Diaries of Washington,* III, 215–216).
4. J. Madison to T. Jefferson, Philadelphia, May 15, 1787, *Jefferson,* XI, 363.
5. It is assumed that Madison took the initiative in these matters since he had written two letters in April which contained rather detailed summaries of his views on the form of government the approaching convention should consider. See J. Madison to ER, New York, Apr. 8, 1787, and J. Madison to G. Washington, New York, Apr. 16, 1787, Hunt, ed., *Madison,* II, 336–340, 344–352.
6. These activities are summarized in George Mason to George Mason, Jr., Philadelphia, May 20, 1787, *Mason,* III, 879–881. The church was St. Mary's on Fourth St., which Washington attended the following Sunday (May 27, 1787, Fitzpatrick, ed., *Diaries of Washington,* III, 219).
7. Washington's diary gives some insight into the relaxed atmosphere that prevailed during this period (May 14–27, 1787, Fitzpatrick, ed., *Diaries of Washington,* III, 216–219). George Mason to George Mason, Jr., Philadelphia, May 20, 1787, *Mason,* III, 879–881. See also George Mason to Arthur Lee, Philadelphia, May 21, 1787, *ibid.,* 882–883.
8. Since Mason refers to the delegates from Virginia as having some "occasional conversations" with members of the Society of Cincinnati (George Mason to George Mason, Jr., Philadelphia, May 20, 1787, *ibid.,* 879–881), and Washington dined with them (May 15, 1787, Fitzpatrick, ed., *Diaries of Washington* III, 216–217), it seems quite likely ER was one of those who met with them. He had more reason to seek out their company than several of the other members of the Virginia delegation.
9. George Read to John Dickinson, Philadelphia, May 25, 1787, EM 3314, Emmet Collection, NYPL.

   On June 6 ER asked Lt. Gov. Beverley Randolph to draw money from state funds that was due to him (ER) as a Virginia delegate to the Convention to provide for his family's traveling expenses to Philadelphia (ER to Beverley Randolph, Philadelphia, June 6, 1787, *CVSP,* IV, 293–294). The wording of this letter would lead one to believe that he had informed his wife of this decision to bring the family to Philadelphia.
10. Farrand, ed., *Records Fed. Conv.,* I: 1–2, 7–10, 15–16 (Journal). Since this work also includes the unofficial notes or debates as kept by several of the delegates, subsequent references to the proceedings of the Convention that have not been drawn from the official journal will record the name of the author of the "notes" after the volume and the page. As was done above, the official journal will be cited simply as "Journal." Material drawn from Farrand that is not a part of the proceedings of the Convention will be cited in the conventional manner.
11. *Ibid.,* I, 18 (Madison).
12. *Ibid.,* I, 26–27 (McHenry).
13. *Ibid.,* I, 18–23 (Madison). Except for the quote taken from McHenry's "notes" and cited above, Madison's "notes" have been used for the summary of ER's remarks. The first portion or "Randolph's speech," is a copy of the abstract ER supplied to Madison some two years after the Convention ended. See J. Madison to ER, New York, Aug. 21, 1789, Madison MSS. Madison's own notes on the subject are also printed in Farrand, ed., *Records Fed. Conv.,* I, 23 (Madison). The resolutions that constitute the Virginia Plan are in Madison's hand (*ibid.,* 23n).
14. George Mason to Arthur Lee, Philadelphia, May 21, 1787, *Mason,* III, 882–883.
15. Farrand, ed., *Records Fed. Conv.,* I, 33 (Madison). For information on the room or rooms where the Convention met, see *ibid.,* III, 58, 59n; IV, 68.

16. *Ibid.*, I, 33 (Madison). The italics are in the original.

17. *Ibid.*, I, 33–35 (Madison).

18. *Ibid.*, I, 20 (Madison).

19. *Ibid.*, I, 35–38 (Madison).

20. Mason's observation was, of course, made before the Convention opened (George Mason to George Mason, Jr., Philadelphia, May 20, 1787, *Mason*, III, 879–881).

21. Farrand, ed., *Records Fed. Conv.*, I, 47–235 *passim* (Madison).

22. *Ibid.*, I, 51, 53 (Madison).

23. *Ibid.*, I, 164–168 (Madison). Madison's "notes" (*ibid.*, 168) reveal Washington did not vote because he was "not consulted."

24. *Ibid.*, I, 175–176 (Madison).

25. J. Madison to T. Jefferson, New York, Oct. 24, 1787, *Jefferson*, XII, 270–285.

26. Farrand, ed., *Records Fed. Conv.*, I, 62–63 (Journal).

27. *Ibid.*, I, 65–69 (Madison).

28. *Ibid.*, I, 79–89 (Madison), quoted material on 88.

29. *Ibid.*, I, 97 (Madison).

30. *Ibid.*, I, 24–27 (Yates), 51–52, 218–219 (Madison), quoted material on 218.

31. *Ibid.*, I, 223 (Journal).

32. *Ibid.*, I, 228–232 (Journal).

33. *Ibid.*, I, 223 (Journal).

34. *Ibid.*, I, 240 (Journal).

35. *Ibid.*, I, 242–245 (Madison), quoted material on 242.

36. *Ibid.*, I, 242 (Madison).

37. *Ibid.*, I, 249–250 (Madison). See also *ibid.*, I, 257–258 (Yates).

38. *Ibid.*, I, 250–252 (Madison). See also *ibid.*, I, 258–260 (Yates).

39. *Ibid.*, I, 252–255 (Madison), 260–261 (Yates).

40. *Ibid.*, I, 255–256 (Madison).

41. *Ibid.*, I, 263 (Yates).

42. *Ibid.*, I, 255 (Madison).

43. Constitutional Convention, Speech on a Plan of Government, [Philadelphia, June 18, 1787], *Hamilton*, IV, 178–211. This more recent work, containing all the various accounts of the speech and reflecting the highest level of scholarly editing, replaces the account in Farrand.

44. Farrand, ed., *Records Fed. Conv.*, I, 314–322 (Madison).

45. *Ibid.*, I, 322 (Madison).

46. ER spoke only four times during the remaining weeks in June and in each case his remarks were brief and very limited in significance (*ibid.*, I, 334–508 *passim*).

47. The exact date on which ER's family arrived in Philadelphia is impossible to determine. ER stated in a letter of June 6 that "twenty-three or four days" would pass before his family arrived in Philadelphia (ER to Beverley Randolph, Philadelphia, June 6, 1787, *CVSP*, IV, 293–294). On June 29 Joseph Jones, in a letter to Madison, expressed the hope that Mrs. Randolph and her children had reached Philadelphia safely (J. Jones to J. Madison, Richmond, June 29, 1787. Madison MSS). Thus one might conclude that they arrived during the last week of June or early July at the very latest.

48. Wythe left Philadelphia on June 5 (J. Madison to T. Jefferson, Philadelphia, June 6, 1787, *Jefferson*, XI, 400–402). ER to Beverley Randolph, Philadelphia, June 21, 1787, *CVSP*, IV, 298.

49. George Mason to George Mason, Jr., Philadelphia, June 1, 1787, *Mason*, III, 890–893.

50. Farrand, ed., *Records Fed. Conv.*, I, 450–452 (Madison).

51. *Ibid.*, I, 538 (Journal).

52. *Ibid.*, I, 524 (Journal). The Grand Committee reported on July 5.

53. The Convention debated the question of representation in the two branches of the legislature from June 27 to July 2 without reaching agreement. The matter was turned over to the Grand Committee on July 2, *ibid.*, I, 436–523 *passim*.

54. *Ibid.*, I, 526–534 (Madison).

55. *Ibid.*, I, 557–558 (Journal).

56. *Ibid.*, I, 561 (Madison).

57. *Ibid.*, I, 562 (Madison).
58. *Ibid.*, I, 566–570 (Madison).
59. *Ibid.*, I, 570–571 (Madison).
60. *Ibid.*, I, 579 (Madison).
61. *Ibid.*, I, 579–580 (Madison).
62. *Ibid.*, I, 580–588 (Madison).
63. *Ibid.*, I, 591–592 (Madison).
64. *Ibid.*, I, 594 (Madison).
65. *Ibid.*
66. *Ibid.*, I, 595 (Madison).
67. *Ibid.*
68. *Ibid.*, I, 597 (Madison). The vote was five states to two, with two states losing their vote because of an equally divided delegation.
69. *Ibid.*, I, 500–502 (Yates).
70. *Ibid.*, I, 509–606 and II, 1–19 *passim.*
71. Since they were never submitted to the Convention, the draft as shown to Madison is the only known copy of the "proposals." Farrand reprints them in an appendix: "Edmund Randolph's Suggestions for Conciliating the Small States," *ibid.*, III, 55–56.
72. *Ibid.*
73. *Ibid.*, II, 15–16 (Madison). The vote, the most frequently cited vote of the Convention, was five states to four, with one state losing its vote because of an equally divided delegation.
74. *Ibid.*, II, 17–18 (Madison).
75. *Ibid.*, II, 19 (Madison). The vote was seven states to two, with one state losing its vote because of an equally divided delegation.
76. *Ibid.*, II, 19–20 (Madison).
77. *Ibid.*, II, 25 (Madison).
78. *Ibid.*, II, 25–36, 40–49 (Madison).
79. *Ibid.*, II, 51–55 (Madison).
80. *Ibid.*, I, 21 (Madison). This provision was also included in the resolutions reported out of the Committee of the Whole House on June 13 (*ibid.*, 236).
81. *Ibid.*, II, 55–58 (Madison). This vote did not resolve the issue by any means, but it was the critical vote for ER insofar as it further alienated him from the instrument of government that was being drafted.
82. *Ibid.*, II, 96 (Madison).
83. *Ibid.*, II, 106 (Madison).
84. ER's preliminary sketch is printed in Farrand as a part of a number of documents relating to the work of the Committee of Detail, *ibid.*, II, 137–150.
85. *Ibid.*, II, 137.
86. *Ibid.*, II, 137–138.
87. A copy of these resolutions as collected for referral to the Committee of Detail has been printed in *ibid.*, II, 129–133.
88. *Ibid.*, II, 142.
89. *Ibid.*, II, 140.
90. *Ibid.*, II, 179 (Madison).
91. *Ibid.*, II, 143.
92. *Ibid.*, II, 183 (Madison), II, 656–657.
93. *Ibid.*, II, 145.
94. *Ibid.*, II, 132.
95. *Ibid.*, II, 185–186 (Madison), II, 653.
96. *Ibid.*, II, 149–150.
97. *Ibid.*, II, 137n.
98. *Ibid.*, II, 152–175.
99. *Ibid.*, IV, 37n.
100. *Ibid.*, II, 176 (Journal).
101. *Ibid.*, II, 201–206 (Madison).
102. *Ibid.*, II, 223–225 (Madison).

103. *Ibid.*, II, 230 (Madison).
104. *Ibid.*, II, 262–263 (Madison).
105. *Ibid.*
106. *Ibid.*, II, 273–278 (Madison).
107. *Ibid.*, II, 278–279 (Madison).
108. *Ibid.*, II, 280 (Madison).
109. *Ibid.*, II, 552–553 (Madison).
110. See pp. 107–108.
111. Farrand, ed., *Records Fed. Conv.*, II, 183 (Madison).
112. *Ibid.*, II, 373 (Madison).
113. *Ibid.*, II, 374 (Madison). ER's allusion to "two" states not remaining in the Union is a reference to earlier remarks by Charles C. Pinckney that South Carolina and Georgia could not do without slaves.
114. *Ibid.*
115. *Ibid.*, II, 396 (Journal).
116. *Ibid.*, II, 414–416 (Madison), II, 656.
117. As was previously noted (see p. 114), the section was reinstated on Sept. 8, but this decision seems to have had little influence on ER's thinking at that time.
118. Farrand, ed., *Records Fed. Conv.*, II, 449 (Madison).
119. *Ibid.*, II, 449–453 (Madison).
120. *Ibid.*, II, 452–453 (Madison).
121. *Ibid.*, II, 479 (Madison).
122. *Ibid.*, II, 488–489 (Madison).
123. *Ibid.*, II, 491 (Madison).
124. *Ibid.*, II, 513 (Madison).
125. These articles, as reported out of the Committee of Detail, read as follows:

XXI
The ratification of the conventions of·states shall be sufficient for organizing this Constitution.

XXII
This Constitution shall be laid before the United States in Congress assembled, for their approbation; and it is the opinion of this Convention, that it should be afterwards submitted to a Convention chosen, under the recommendation of its legislature, in order to receive the ratification of such Convention. (*Ibid.*, II, 189 [Madison].)

126. *Ibid.*, II, 560–561 (Madison).
127. *Ibid.*, II, 561 (Madison).
128. *Ibid.*, II, 562–563 (Madison).
129. *Ibid.*, II, 563–564 (Madison).
130. *Ibid.*, II, 564 (Madison).
131. *Ibid.*, II, 553 (Madison).
132. *Ibid.*, II, 585, 606–609, 612–619 (Madison).
133. *Ibid.*, II, 622–631 (Madison).
134. *Ibid.*, II, 631 (Madison).
135. *Ibid.*, II, 632 (Madison).
136. *Ibid.*, II, 632 (Madison).
137. *Ibid.*, II, 632–633 (Madison).
138. *Ibid.*, II, 633 (Madison).
139. *Ibid.*, II, 641–644 (Madison).
140. *Ibid.*, II, 644–645 (Madison).
141. ER to Beverley Randolph, Philadelphia, Sept. 18, 1787, *CVSP*, IV, 343.
142. ER to J. Madison, Bowling Green, [Va.], Sept. 30, 1787, Madison MSS.
143. *Ibid.*

CHAPTER 10

1. *J. C. C.*, XXXIII, 448*n* (Sept. 20, 1787), 540–544, 549 (Sept. 27–28).
2. Letter not found, but referred to in J. Madison to ER, New York, Oct. 7, 1787, Madison MSS.
3. ER to J. Madison, Bowling Green, [Va.], Sept. 30, 1787, Madison MSS.
4. Madison commented on ER's proposals only after ER had sent a second letter asking why he had not done so (ER to J. Madison, Oct. 23, 1787, Madison MSS). Madison replied:

> I did not make any observations on the scheme mentioned in your letter from the Bolling-Green [*sic*], because it had an object which I thought it unadvisable to pursue; because I conceived that my opinion has been fully made known on the subject, and I wished not unnecessarily to repeat or dwell on points on which our ideas do not accord. . . . (J. Madison to ER, Nov. 18, 1787, Madison MSS.)

5. ER's close attention to state matters is evident from the memorandum book he kept while governor (ER Memorandum Book, 1786–1787, MS, VSL), the prompt calling of the Executive Council following his return (*J. Council Va.* IV, 147–149 [Oct. 1, 1787]) and the diversity and multiplicity of the subjects referred to the legislature when it met (ER to Speaker of the House of Delegates [Joseph Prentis], Richmond, Oct. 15, 1787. Executive Letterbook, MSS, VSL).
6. Evident from comment he made to Madison subsequent to the drafting of his message (ER to J. Madison, Richmond, Oct. 23, 1787, Madison MSS).
7. The "letter" is most conveniently available in Paul Leister Ford, ed., *Pamphlets on the Constitution of the United States*, 259–276.
8. The list could easily be extended and one need only examine the Register of the House for this session of the Assembly to realize how many important Virginians were serving in the legislature (Earl G. Swem and J. W. Williams, eds., *Register of the General Assembly of Virginia, 1776–1918*, 26–27).
9. G. Washington to J. Madison, Mount Vernon, Oct. 10, 1787, Fitzpatrick, ed., Washington, XXIX, 285–287; John Dawson to J. Madison, Richmond, Oct. 19, 1787, Madison MSS.
10. ER to Speaker of the House of Delegates [Joseph Prentis], Richmond. Oct. 15, 1787, Executive Letterbook, MSS, VSL.
11. Evident from Meriwether Smith, Charles M. Thurston, John H. Briggs and Mann Page, Jr., to ER, Richmond, Dec. 2, 1787, *Virginia Independent Chronicle*, Jan. 2, 1788, and ER to Smith, Thurston, Briggs and Page, Dec. 10, 1787, *ibid.* ER's own observations on the speculation surrounding his conduct can be found in ER to J. Madison, Richmond, Oct. 23, 1787, Madison MSS.
12. *J. H. Del* (Oct. Sess., 1787, White reprint), 5, 15.
13. *J. Sen., Va.* (Oct. Sess., 1787, White reprint), 10, 12.
14. ER to J. Madison, Richmond, Oct. 23, 1787, Madison MSS.
15. J. Madison to T. Jefferson, New York, Dec. 9, 1787, *Jefferson*, XII, 408–412.
16. ER to J. Madison, Richmond, Oct. 23, 1787, Madison MSS.
17. *Ibid.*, emphasis his.
18. *Ibid.*
19. *J. H. Del.* (Oct. Sess., 1787, White reprint), 51–52, 79–80, 95; *J. Sen., Va.* (Oct. Sess., 1787, White reprint), 43, 44–45.
20. *J. H. Del.* (Oct. Sess., 1787, White reprint), 77.
21. Archibald Stuart to J. Madison, Richmond, Dec. 2, 1787, Madison MSS.
22. *J. H. Del.* (Oct. Sess., 1787, White reprint), 81, 86, 88, 95; *J. Sen., Va.* (Oct. Sess., 1787, White reprint), 45–46; Hening, ed., *Va. Statutes*, XII, 462–463. The bill was not approved by both houses until Dec. 13, not Dec. 12, as noted in Hening (*J. H. Del.* [Oct. Sess., 1787, White reprint], 95).
23. ER to J. Madison, Richmond, Dec. 27, 1787, Madison MSS. Two copies of ER's letter of transmittal to the governors of the other states have been found. One was addressed to William Livingston, the governor of New Jersey (Livingston, II,

MSS, MHS), and the second to Benjamin Franklin, who was then serving as president of the Executive Council of the state of Pennsylvania (Papers of Benjamin Franklin, APS). One of these letters of transmittal was sent to Gov. George Clinton of New York, who in turn notified ER that he had not received it until Mar. 7, 1788. Clinton's letter to ER and the way ER handled that letter became the subject of a new controversy in June of 1788. See Chapter 12.

24. ER to J. Madison, Richmond, Dec. 27, 1787, Madison MSS.

25. M. Smith, C. Thurston, J. Briggs and M. Page, Jr., to ER, Richmond, Dec. 2, 1787, *Virginia Independent Chronicle*, Jan. 2, 1788.

26. ER to M. Smith, C. Thurston, J. Briggs and M. Page, Jr., Richmond, Dec. 10, 1787, *ibid*.

27. This was the first printing of the ER "letter." Subsequent to its appearance in the *Virginia Independent Chronicle* Davis apparently reprinted it in pamphlet form (P. L. Ford, ed., *Pamphlets on the Constitution of the United States*, 259).

28. The letter was published on Jan. 2 and the Assembly adjourned on Jan. 8, 1788.

29. ER to J. Madison, Richmond, Dec. 27, 1787, Madison MSS.
    Washington also received a copy (ER to G. Washington, Richmond, Dec. 27, 1787, Washington MSS). Since neither collection contains a copy of the "letter" one can only conclude that each man subsequently passed his copy along to someone else and the copies were never returned. Curiosity would create a demand for ER's "letter" regardless of its merits.

30. J. Madison to G. Washington, New York, Jan. 25, 1788, Madison MSS.

31. Roane's essay, entitled "Letter of a Plain Dealer," is most conveniently available in P. L. Ford, ed., *Essays on the Constitution*, 387–392. Roane was Patrick Henry's son-in-law.

32. Some insight into the suspenseful yet increasingly optimistic attitude of supporters of the Constitution can be gleaned from Nathan Dana to H. Knox, Beverley, [Mass.], Dec. 27 and 30, 1787, Henry Knox Papers, MHS; G. Washington to T. Jefferson, Mount Vernon, Jan. 1, 1788, Fitzpatrick, ed., *Washington*, XXIX, 348–351; J. Madison to ER, New York, Jan. 10, 1788, Madison MSS; Edward Carrington to J. Madison, Richmond, Jan. 18, 1788, Madison MSS; H. Knox to John Sullivan, New York, Jan. 19, 1788, Sullivan Papers in Revolutionary Papers, II, Bancroft Transcripts, NYPL.

33. Supporters of the Constitution were constantly assessing the situation: Rufus King to J. Madison, Boston, Jan. 23, 1788, Madison MSS; J. Madison to ER, New York, Jan. 27, 1788, Madison MSS; [Gen. Henry] Jackson to H. Knox, Boston, Jan. 28, 1788, Henry Knox Papers, MHS. On Jan. 30 Rufus King reported, for the first time, that he was optimistic about the chances that the Massachusetts Convention would ratify (R. King to J. Madison, Boston, Jan. 30, 1788, Madison MSS).

34. A convenient summary of the struggle in Massachusetts may be found in Robert Allen Rutland's excellent study of the Antifederalists and the ratification struggle, *The Ordeal of the Constitution*, 66–114.

35. The exact language of the Massachusetts amendments is critical to a proper appreciation of ER's comments on them:

> *First.* That it be explicitly declared, that all powers not expressly delegated by the aforesaid Constitution are reserved to the several states, to be by them exercised.
> *Secondly.* That there shall be one representative to every thirty thousand persons, according to the census mentioned in the Constitution, until the whole number of representatives amounts to two hundred.
> *Thirdly.* That Congress do not exercise the powers vested in them by the 4th section of the 1st article, but in cases where a state shall neglect or refuse to make the regulations therein mentioned, or shall make regulations subversive of the rights of the people to a free and equal representation in Congress, agreeably to the Constitution.
> *Fourthly.* That Congress do not lay direct taxes, but when the moneys arising from the impost and excise are insufficient for the public exigencies, nor then,

until Congress shall have first made a requisition upon the states, to assess, levy, and pay their respective proportion of such requisitions, agreeably to the census fixed in the said Constitution, in such way and manner as the legislatures of the states shall think best, and, in such case, if any state shall neglect or refuse to pay its proportion, pursuant to such requisition, then Congress may assess and Levy such state's proportion, together with interest thereon, at the rate of six per cent per annum, from the time of payment prescribed in such requisitions.

Fifthly. That Congress erect no company with exclusive advantages of commerce.

Sixthly. That no person shall be tried for any crime, by which he may incur an infamous punishment, or loss of life, until he be first indicted by a grand jury, except in such cases as may arise in the government and regulation of the land and naval forces.

Seventhly. The Supreme Judicial Federal Court shall have no jurisdiction of causes between citizens of different states, unless the matter in dispute, whether it concern the realty or personalty, be of the value of three thousand dollars at the least; nor shall the federal judicial powers extend to any action between citizens of different states, where the matter in dispute, whether it concern the realty or personalty, is not of the value of fifteen hundred dollars at the least.

Eighthly. In civil actions between citizens of different states, every issue of fact, arising in actions at common law, shall be tried by a jury, if the parties, or either of them, request it.

Ninthly. Congress shall at no time consent that any person holding an office of trust or profit, under the United States, shall accept of a title of nobility, or any other title or office, from any king, prince, or foreign state. (Elliot, ed., *Debates*, II, 177.)

36. ER to J. Madison, Richmond, Feb. 29, 1788, Madison MSS.
37. J. Madison to Edmund Pendleton, New York, Feb. 21, 1788, Madison MSS.
38. In his letter of Feb. 29 to Madison ER wrote:

A writer, calling himself Plain dealer [*sic*], who is bitter in principle [against] the constitution has attacked me in the paper. I suspect the author to be Mr. Spencer Roane, and the importunities of some to me in public and private are designed to throw me unequivocally and without condition *into the opposition.* (ER to J. Madison, Richmond, Feb. 29, 1788, Madison MSS, emphasis mine.)

39. Edward Carrington to J. Madison, Manchester, Va., Feb. 10, 1788, Madison MSS. Similar sentiments were expressed by Carrington in a letter to Knox written the same day. This latter letter, written for the benefit of someone less familiar with Virginia politics, is particularly valuable in corroborating the assessment found in his letter to Madison. (E. Carrington to H. Knox, Manchester, Va., Feb. 10, 1788, Madison MSS.)
40. ER to J. Madison, Richmond, Feb. 29, 1788, Madison MSS.
41. George Nicholas to J. Madison, Charlottesville, Va., Apr. 5, 1788, Madison MSS: J. Madison to George Nicholas, Orange, [Va.], Apr. 8, 1788, *ibid.*; George Nicholas to J. Madison, Charlottesville, May 9, 1788, *ibid.*; J. Madison to George Nicholas, Orange, May, 17, 1788, *ibid.*; and John Brown to J. Madison, New York, June 7, 1788, Burnett, ed., *Letters*, VIII, 749–750. This last letter indicates how intimately this issue was connected with Kentucky's efforts to gain admission into the Union as an independent state.
See also J. R. Jacobs, *Tarnished Warrior, Major General James Wilkinson*, 82–83. Wilkinson raised the question of Kentucky's response to the Constitution during a visit to Richmond in Nov., 1787.
42. Meade, *Henry*, II, 319, 336–339; Rowland, *Mason*, II, 210.
43. Included in the *Register of the General Assembly of Virginia* is a listing, by county, of the individuals elected to this convention. Except for a few obvious names such

as George Washington and R. H. Lee, who again refrained from seeking elective office, the *Register* carries the names of all the more obvious people associated with the debate over the Constitution. (Swem and Williams, *Register of the General Assembly of Virginia, 1776–1918*, 243–244.)

44. ER to J. Madison, Richmond, Apr. 17, 1788, Madison MSS. Nicholas' letter to ER has not been found but he expressed similar sentiments to Madison in a letter of Apr. 5 (G. Nicholas to J. Madison, Charlottesville, Apr. 5, 1788, Madison MSS).

45. ER to J. Madison, Richmond, Apr. 17, 1788, Madison MSS.

46. J. Madison to G. Washington, New York, Jan. 25, 1788, Madison MSS.
Madison wrote this letter after receiving his copy of ER's "letter" of Oct. 10. He had never grouped him with Patrick Henry, however, and had readily accepted Henry Lee's "three sets of men" analysis of the Virginia scene (H. Lee to J. Madison, [Dec., 1787?], Madison MSS), which placed Mason and ER in the middle between the supporters and opponents of the Constitution. This was the same grouping ER had suggested more than a month earlier when he classified himself as a "recusant" (ER to J. Madison, Richmond, Oct. 23, 1787, Madison MSS).

47. Rutland, *The Ordeal of the Constitution*, 115–244 *passim*.

48. See *ibid.*, 218–225, 235–242, for a convenient summary of the preconvention activities in each state.

CHAPTER 11

1. Grigsby, *Va. Conv. 1788*, I, 25–26.

2. Almost without exception the individuals mentioned here virtually monopolized the debates during the convention. The biographical references for the principals have been cited previously. For those not previously cited see *DAB, s.v.* "Grayson, William," "Harrison, Benjamin," "Innes, James," "Lee, Henry," "Nicholas, George" and "Nicholas, Wilson Cary."

3. Elliot, ed., *Debates*, III, 1–6.

4. *Ibid.*, 2. They met in New Academy Hall on June 3. Grigsby locates it (Grigsby, *Va. Conv. 1788*, I, 67–68n).

5. Elliot, ed., *Debates*, III, 1.

6. *Ibid.*, 6–7.

7. *Ibid.*, 4.

8. J. Madison to G. Washington, Richmond, June 4, 1788, Madison MSS.

9. Elliot, ed., *Debates*, III, 6–7.

10. *Ibid.*, 7–21.

11. *Ibid.*, 21–23, quote on 23.

12. Grigsby's biographical sketch of ER, while approaching a eulogy, does give a description of his physical appearance that at least does not conflict with the few references that exist as to his size and mannerisms (Grigsby, *Va. Conv. 1788*, I, 83–86).

13. Elliot, ed., *Debates*, III, 23–29, quotes on 24 and 25, respectively. The phrase in parenthesis in the last quote was supplied by the convention secretary.

14. J. Madison to G. Washington, Richmond, June 4, 1788, Madison MSS.

15. Elliot, ed., *Debates*, III, 35–43. There were two "Henry Lees" at the convention. The delegate from Westmoreland County is better known as "Light Horse Harry" Lee. His distant relative from Kentucky's Bourbon County steadfastly opposed the Constitution. Unlike Henry Lee of Westmoreland, however, he refrained from engaging in debate during the convention.

16. *Ibid.*, 43–65, quote on 44. For an estimate of the length of the speech see Grigsby, *Va. Conv. 1788*, I, 118n.

17. *Ibid.*, 121, also 97n and 323–326.

18. Elliot, ed., *Debates*, III, 65–86, quote on 65.

19. *Ibid.*, 104–137.

20. *Ibid.*, 137–150. ER interrupted Henry toward the end of his speech (*ibid.*, 148).

21. *Ibid.*, 150–176.

22. *Ibid.*, 176–187.

23. *Ibid.*, 187–194, quoted material on 187–188, 189. The clerk's account of ER's remarks carries also the description of ER's actions and the details of his sharp exchange with Henry.

24. Grigsby's history of the convention contains the following undocumented account of what transpired after Monday's session ended. It cannot be verified from any other source:

> . . . and accordingly when on Tuesday morning it was known that Col. William Cabell had the evening before as the friend of Henry, waited on Randolph; that the unpleasant affair had been settled without a resort to the field, and that a reconciliation between the parties had been effected, both the great divisions in the House were sensibly relieved. (Grigsby, *Va. Conv. 1788*, I, 165).

25. During the sessions on Tuesday, Wednesday and Thursday, June 10–12, James Monroe, John Marshall, Benjamin Harrison, George Nicholas, James Madison, George Mason, William Grayson and E. Pendleton participated in the debates. ER held the floor on Tuesday for a time and Henry did the same on Thursday, but they did not engage each other (Elliot, ed., *Debates*, III, 194–332).

26. Evident from the minimal amount of material in the Executive Letterbooks, VSL, and ER Memorandum Book, 1786–1787, MS, VSL, during the first ten days of June.

27. Elliot, ed., *Debates*, III, 332.

28. *Ibid.*, 332–333.

29. J. Madison to G. Washington, Richmond, June 13, 1788, Madison MSS.

30. One of the delegates from Kentucky, Notley Conn of Bourbon County, was not in attendance at the convention, thus thirteen rather than fourteen votes were at stake in connection with this issue.

31. Elliot, ed., *Debates*, III, 333–365. The journal of the convention records the fact that Francis Corbin, the last speaker, had to stop and the session was adjourned for the day because of a violent storm (*ibid.*, 365).

32. *Ibid.*, 365–576.

33. *Ibid.*, 463–471, 481, 485–486, 504–505, 562, 570–576, quote on 471.

34. *Ibid.*, 576–586.

35. *Ibid.*, 587–596.

36. *Ibid.*, 596–603, quotes on 597 and 603, respectively.

37. *Ibid.*, 604–652. Those who made final statements were John Dawson, from Spotsylvania, Benjamin Harrison, James Innes, James Monroe (also representing Spotsylvania), John Tyler of Charles City County, Adam Stephen of Berkeley, Zachariah Johns[t]on from Augusta County and Henry.

38. *Ibid.*, 649–652.

39. *Ibid.*, 652, emphasis is in the *Journal*.

40. *Ibid.*, 653.

41. *Ibid.*, emphasis mine.

42. *Ibid.*, 653–654.

43. *Ibid.*, 654–655.

44. *Ibid.*, 655.

45. The *Journal* of the convention carries the roll call vote on both the substitute resolution calling for previous amendments and on the resolution as reported out of committee. The county affiliation can be checked quite simply in Swem and Williams, *Register of the General Assembly of Virginia, 1776–1918*, 243–244.

   It should be noted that Kentucky still had only thirteen delegates because of the absence of Notley Conn of Bourbon County.

46. Elliot, ed., *Debates*, III, 655–656.

47. *Ibid.*

48. *Ibid.*, 656. The form approved was first suggested by ER on June 21 (*ibid.*, 576). This committee seems to have been created simply to fulfill a procedural formality.

49. *Ibid.*, 656–657.

50. *Ibid.*, 657–661.

51. *Ibid.*, 661.

52. *Ibid.*
53. *Ibid.*, 661–662. The roll call vote is again recorded. Some names are absent but more significant is the shift of ten votes. Among those who supported the Constitution yet refused to support this motion to strike this amendment were E. Pendleton, Paul Carrington of Charlotte County, the chief justice of Virginia's General Court and William Fleming of Botetourt County, also a judge of the General Court.
54. *Ibid.*, 662.
55. Rutland, *The Ordeal of the Constitution*, 210–213, 235–245, provides a convenient summary of the situation in New Hampshire and New York.

C H A P T E R   1 2

1. ER to J. Madison, Richmond, Mar. 1, 1787, Madison MSS.
2. John Dawson to J. Madison, Fredericksburg, June 12, 1787, Madison MSS; Francis Corbin to A. Lee, [?   ], Aug. 8, 1787, Lee Collection, Harvard; Archibald Stuart to J. Madison, Richmond, Nov. 9, 1787, Madison MSS.
3. George Clendenin to ER, Greenbriar [County, Va.], Aug. 11, 1787, Executive Communications, VSL.

    At about the same time Madison received a letter from James McClurg containing a brief reference to the insurrection (J. McClurg to J. Madison, Richmond, Aug. 22, 1787, Madison MSS).
4. This letter has not been found but its existence can be established from the letter cited in the next note.
5. ER to Beverley Randolph, Philadelphia, Sept. 2, 1787, *CVSP*, IV, 338.
6. Henry Banks to ER, [Greenbriar County, Va.?], Sept. 1, 1787, *ibid.*, 336–337.
7. ER to Speaker of the House of Delegates [Joseph Prentis], In Council, Oct. 15, 1787, Executive Letterbook, VSL.
8. *Ibid.*
9. *J. H. Del.* (Oct. Sess., 1787, White reprint), 5, 12, 15.
10. *Ibid.*, 29–30.
11. *Ibid.*, 30.
12. Some insight into the activities of the House in the general area of economic legislation can be gained from the following letters: Archibald Stuart to J. Madison, Richmond, Oct. 21, 1787, Joseph Jones to J. Madison, Richmond, Oct. 29, 1787, Archibald Stuart to J. Madison, Richmond, Nov. 2, 1787, A. Stuart to J. Madison, Richmond, Nov. 9, 1787, Joseph Jones to J. Madison, Richmond, Nov. 22, 1787, A. Stuart to J. Madison, Richmond, Dec. 2, 1787, and A. Stuart to J. Madison, Richmond, Jan. 14, 1788, all in Madison MSS.

    It is worth noting that ER's letters to Madison during this same period dwelt largely with the attitude of the delegates toward the Constitution; he made only a few brief references to the economic measures being considered.
13. Hening, ed., *Va. Statutes*, XII, 412–432.

    The certificate tax abolished by this act had been passed to draw out of circulation specific types of certificates of indebtedness issued during the Revolution. By allowing these certificates to be used in payment of state taxes, Virginia liquidated a portion of the Revolutionary debt held by its citizens. The law had accomplished its purpose by drawing large quantities of certificates into the state treasury, but its very success now made it unnecessary and it became a tax burden on the people who were finding it increasingly difficult to "acquire" certificates in order to pay this tax.
14. Hening, ed., *Va. Statutes*, XII, 456–462. See also *J. H. Del.* (Oct Sess., 1787, White reprint), 66, 78; *J. Sen., Va.* (Oct. Sess., 1787, White reprint), 29, 31.

    A "tobacco note" was usually a warehouse receipt giving evidence of the quantity and quality of the tobacco being held and the date it was placed in the warehouse. Its value, of course, fluctuated with the condition of the market.
15. Hening, ed., *Va. Statutes*, XII, 528.

    Some insight into the legislative debate over this bill can be acquired from the none too objective reports that were passed along to Madison: ER to J. Madison, Richmond, Oct. 23, 1787, Archibald Stuart to J. Madison, Richmond, Nov. 9, 1787, Joseph Jones to J. Madison, Richmond, Nov. 22, 1787, A. Stuart to J. Madison, Richmond, Dec. 2, 1787, all in Madison MSS. See also *J. H. Del.* (Oct. Sess., 1787, White reprint), 51–52, 79–80, 95; *J. Sen., Va.* (Oct. Sess., 1787, White reprint), 43, 44–45.

16. Arthur Lee to ER, New York, May 20, 1787, *CVSP*, IV, 289.
17. ER to Beverley Randolph, Philadelphia, May 24, 1787, *ibid.*, 289.
18. ER to Speaker of House of Delegates [Joseph Prentis], In Council, Oct. 15, 1787, Executive Letterbook, VSL.
19. Hening, ed., *Va. Statutes*, XII, 452–454; *J. H. Del.* (Oct. Sess., 1787, White reprint), 79; *J. Sen., Va.* (Oct. Sess., 1787, White reprint), 42–43, 49. See also Archibald Stuart to J. Madison, Richmond, Dec. 2, 1787, Madison MSS.
20. ER's very pessimistic reference to Virginia's monetary shortage is in ER to J. Madison, Richmond, Sept. 12, 1788, Madison MSS.
21. Virginia's instrument of cession can be found most conveniently in Carter, ed., *Territorial Papers of U.S.*, II, 6–9.
22. *Ibid.*
23. E. Ferguson, *The Power of the Purse*, 217.
24. Edward Fox, William Heth and David Henley to ER, Richmond, Jan. 1, 1787, George Rogers Clark Papers, VSL.
25. L. Wood., Jr., to ER, Solicitor's Office, [Richmond], Mar. 10, 1787, Executive Papers, VSL.
26. Edward Carrington to ER, New York, Apr. 13, 1787, Burnett, ed., *Letters*, VIII, 576.
27. Ferguson, *Power of the Purse*, 217.
28. This dispute between Heth and Henley on one side and Pierce on the other is referred to some eight months later by Heth; see William Heth to ER, New York, Mar. 21, 1788, George Rogers Clark Papers, VSL.
29. *J. Council Va.*, IV, 144 (Aug. 20, 1787).
30. *Ibid.*
31. George Rogers Clark to ER, Louisville, Ky., Oct. 8, 1787, *CVSP*, IV, 346–347.
32. ER to Speaker of House of Delegates [Joseph Prentis], In Council, Oct. 15, 1787, Executive Letterbook, VSL.
33. *J. H. Del.* (Oct. Sess., 1787, White reprint), 137–139, quote on 139; *J. Sen., Va.* (Oct. Sess., 1787, White reprint), 90.
34. *J. Council Va.*, IV, 209 (Feb. 2, 1788).
35. William Heth to ER, New York, Mar. 9, 1788, *CVSP*, IV, 406; William Heth to ER, New York, Mar. 21, 1788, George Rogers Clark Papers VSL; Cyrus Griffin and John Brown to ER, New York, Mar. 23, 1788, Burnett, ed., *Letters*, VIII, 709–710; W. Heth to ER, New York, Apr. 16, 1788, *CVSP*, IV, 425–426.
36. Edward Carrington, John Brown and Cyrus Griffin to W. Heth, New York, Apr. 20, 1788, Burnett, ed., *Letters*, VIII, 723.
37. *J. C. C.*, XXXIV, 178n (May 23, 1788).
38. Ferguson, *Power of the Purse*, 217.
39. *J. C. C.*, XXXIV, 180–181 (May 26, 1788).
40. Article 8 of the Articles of Confederation.
41. An excellent account of this subject may be found in Ferguson, *Power of the Purse*, 203–219.
42. *J. C. C.*, XXXII, 262–266 (May 7, 1787).
43. *J. H. Del.* (Oct. Sess., 1786, White reprint), 155; *J. Sen., Va.* (Oct. Sess., 1786, White reprint), 104–105.
44. Andrew Dunscomb to ER, Richmond, Jan. 13, 1787, *CVSP*, IV, 228.
45. *J. Council Va.*, IV, 107 (June 7, 1787).
46. William Winder to ER, Richmond, Dec. 20, 1787, *CVSP*, IV, 370. This letter was received on Dec. 21.
47. Andrew Dunscomb to ER, Commissioner's Office, Richmond, Dec. 20, 1787, *CVSP*, IV, 370.

48. *J. Council Va.*, IV, 209 (Feb. 2, 1788) and *"Additional"* Journal, IV, 359–360 (Feb. 2).
49. *Ibid.*
50. Andrew Dunscomb to ER, Richmond, Feb. 15, 1788, Executive Papers, VSL.
51. [ER?] to Virginia Delegates in Congress [John Brown, Edward Carrington, Cyrus Griffin], Richmond, Mar. 13, 1788, Executive Letterbook, VSL.
    The alternatives facing the Executive Council upon receipt of Dunscomb's letter of Feb. 15 have been reconstructed from this letter to the Virginia delegation since there is no reference in the *Council Journal* to a discussion of Dunscomb's letter. The Minute Book of the Council notes the fact that a meeting was held on Mar. 17, 1788, attended by ER, Wood and McClurg, in which a letter from Dunscomb was listed as being on the agenda. No other details are recorded (*J. Council Va.*, IV, 218n).
52. Evident from Edward Carrington, J. Brown and Cyrus Griffin to ER, New York, May 8, 1788, Burnett, ed., *Letters*, VIII, 730–731.
53. Report of the Board of Treasury on Letter from His Excellency the Governor of Virginia of the 13th March, 1788, *J. C. C.*, XXXIV, 145–146 (May 7, 1788).
54. Edward Carrington, J. Brown and Cyrus Griffin to ER, New York, May 8, 1788, Burnett, ed., *Letters*, VIII, 730–731.
55. The *CVSP* and the Executive Papers in the VSL are filled with letters from Dunscomb to ER. Most of them seem to have been left unanswered. By May ER's patience seemed to be wearing thin:

> Your letter of the 12th of May, 1788 [his second in less than a week], seems to surrender all hope of success. But we [i.e. the Executive Council] have given you the best aid in advice [*sic*] which was in our power, when we sent you the table of proofs. You know from thence what the highest proof is, and from a survey of the whole subject, we presume, that you best know, what substitute to obtain. We must repeat to you our readiness to forward your exertions, and again recommend to you to procure every possible proof. (ER to Andrew Dunscomb, Richmond, May 14, 1788, Executive Communications, VSL.)

56. Edward Carrington, John Brown and Cyrus Griffin to ER, New York, May 8, 1788, Burnett, ed., *Letters*, VIII, 730–731.
57. Andrew Dunscomb to ER, Commissioner's Office, [Richmond], May 23, 1788, Virginia State Papers No. 71, Papers of the Continental Congress, NA. That it was prepared in less than forty-eight hours is evident from the opening sentence of this letter.
58. ER to Virginia Delegates in Congress [E. Carrington, J. Brown and C. Griffin], Richmond, May 25, 1788, Executive Letterbook, VSL.
59. *J. C. C.*, XXXIV, 203–204, 203n (June 6, 1788).
60. Edward Carrington to ER, New York, June 19, 1788, Burnett, ed., *Letters*, VIII, 754.
61. Andrew Dunscomb to ER, Richmond, June 22, 1788, *CVSP*, IV, 459.
62. *J. C. C.*, XXXIV, 262–263 (June 24, 1788).
63. *Ibid.*, 253–260 (June 23, 1788).
64. Edward Carrington to ER, New York, June 25, 1788, Burnett, ed., *Letters*, VIII, 755–756.
65. ER to J. Madison, Richmond, July 27, 1788, Madison MSS.
66. ER to William Davies, Richmond, Aug. 19, 1788, *CVSP*, VII, 56.
67. Evident from William Davies to ER, Richmond, Oct. 1, 1788, *ibid.*
68. ER reported to the Executive Council on Sept. 8 and his full report was entered into the "Additional" Council Journal (*J. Council Va.*, IV, 283; *"Additional"* Journal, IV, 363–371).
69. William Davies to ER, Richmond, Oct. 1, 1788, *CVSP*, VII, 56.
70. Evident from W. Davies to Governor of Virginia [Henry Lee], New York, Feb. 25, 1794, *CVSP*, VII, 43–52.
71. Ferguson, *Power of the Purse*, 314–324 *passim*.
72. Hening, ed., *Va. Statutes*, XII, 532–558.

73. The Remonstrance, although sent to ER, was addressed to the General Assembly. It was signed by Edmund Pendleton, presiding judge of the Court of Appeals (E. Pendleton to the General Assembly, May 12, 1788, Executive Communications, VSL).
74. *J. Council Va.*, IV, 238 (May 14, 1788).
75. A Proclamation, Virginia, May 14, 1788, *CVSP*, IV, 440–441.
76. *J. H. Del.* (June Sess., 1788, White reprint), 145; *J. Sen., Va.* (June Sess., 1788, White reprint), 3.
77. *J. H. Del.* (June Sess., 1788, White reprint), 145–146. The Senate had a quorum on June 25, the day the Constitution was ratified by the convention (*J. Sen., Va.* [June Sess., 1788, White reprint], 3).
78. ER to Speaker of House of Delegates [Thomas Matthews], Richmond, June 23, 1788, Executive Letterbook, VSL.
79. James Monroe to T. Jefferson, Fredericksburg, [Va.], July 12, 1788, *Jefferson*, XIII, 351–353; *J. H. Del.* (June Sess., 1788, White reprint), 146–147, 150; Hening, ed., *Va. Statutes*, XII, 644.
80. *Ibid.*, 462–463. See Chapter 10.
81. Archibald Stuart to J. Madison, Richmond, Dec. 2, 1787, Madison MSS.
82. Two of these letters have been found and the language of both is identical: ER to Gov. William Livingston, Richmond, Dec. 27, 1787, Livingston II, MSS, MHS, and ER to Benjamin Franklin, Richmond, Dec. 27, 1787, Papers of Benjamin Franklin, APS.
83. Evident from Clinton's reply: G. Clinton to ER, New York, May 8, 1788, Executive Communications, VSL.
84. *Ibid.*
85. *Ibid.*
86. So stated in ER to Speaker of House of Delegates [Thomas Matthews], Richmond, Jan. 23, 1788, Executive Letterbook, VSL.
87. These draft resolutions in the George Mason MSS at the LC are now conveniently reprinted in *Mason*, III, 1120–1122.
88. G. Clinton to ER, New York, May 8, 1788, Executive Communications, VSL.
89. *J. H. Del.* (June Sess., 1788, White reprint), 145–146.
90. ER to Speaker of House of Delegates [Thomas Matthews], Richmond, June 23, 1788, Executive Letterbook, VSL. It was enclosure No. 5.
91. The best general summary of the plight of the Cherokee during this period is Randolph C. Downes, "The Cherokee-American Relations in the Upper Tennessee Valley, 1776–1791," *The East Tennessee Historical Society's Publications*, VIII, 35–53.
92. ER reported the meeting and the expenditure of state funds to the lieutenant governor (ER to Beverley Randolph, Philadelphia, July 12, 1787, *CVSP*, IV, 315). He did not identify the chief.
93. Alexander Dromgoole to ER, Jonesborough, Sept. 15, 1787, *CVSP*, IV, 341. Arthur Campbell to ER, Washington County, [Va.], Oct. 22, 1787, *ibid.*, 351–352.
94. Col. Joseph Martin to ER, Washington County, [Va.], Mar. 13. 1788. *ibid.*, 407. The Treaty of Hopewell was signed on Nov. 29, 1785.
    It is ironic, but ER was largely responsible for Martin's dismissal as the state's agent to the Cherokee nation. The dismissal came after Congress named Dr. James White of North Carolina the commissioner of Indian Affairs for the Southern Department. Virginia's Executive Council assumed that the state no longer needed an Indian agent and Martin was dismissed (*J. Council Va.*, IV, 36–37 [Jan. 29, 1787]). Fortunately for Virginia, Martin did not learn of his dismissal until June of 1788 (J. Martin to ER, Smith's River, [Va.?], June 28, 1788, Virginia State Papers No. 71, Papers of the Continental Congress, NA). And although he had no obligation to do so, he kept ER informed during the remaining months of the crisis.
95. ER to Virginia Delegates in Congress [E. Carrington, C. Griffin and J. Brown], May 9, 1788, Virginia State Papers, No. 71, Papers of the Continental Congress, NA.

96. Report of Secretary of War on letter of Gov. Randolph, May 26, 1788, *J. C. C.,* XXXIV, 182–183 (May 26, 1788).
97. *Ibid.,* 241 (June 19, 1788).
98. Joseph Martin to ER, Abingdon, [?], June 11, 1788, *CVSP,* IV, 452.
99. ER to Virginia Delegates in Congress [E. Carrington, C. Griffin and J. Brown], Richmond, June 30, 1788, Virginia State Papers No. 71, Papers of the Continental Congress, NA. ER's "talk" has not been found but its general theme and Moore's role in its delivery can be reconstructed from: Andrew Moore to Alexander McGillivray, [?], Oct. 10, 1788, Executive Papers, VSL; Andrew Moore to ER [?], Nov. 3, 1788, Executive Communications, VSL.
100. Martin's letter was referred to the Secretary of War on July 9 (*J. C. C.,* XXXIV, 310 [July 9, 1788]. Report of Secretary of War on Letter of Col. J. Martin, July 18, 1788, *J C. C.,* XXXIV, 342–344 (July 18, 1788); Report of Congressional Committee on Report of Secretary of War on Letter of Col. J. Martin, Sept. 1, 1788, *ibid.,* 476–479.
101. Downes, "Cherokee-American Relations . . . 1776–1791," *East Tennessee Historical Society Publications,* VIII, 51–53.
102. See Carter, ed., *Territorial Papers of U.S.,* II, 6–9, for a convenient copy of Virginia's instrument of cession.
103. *J. C. C.,* XXXIV, 331–333 (July 17, 1788).
104. ER to President of Congress [Cyrus Griffin], Richmond, Aug. 4, 1788, Executive Letterbook, VSL.
105. *J. C. C.,* XXXIV, 475–476 (Sept. 1, 1788).
106. *J. H. Del.* (Oct. Sess., 1788, White reprint), 131.
107. "The Debates in the Convention of the State of New York on the Adoption of the Federal Constitution," Elliot, ed., *Debates,* II, 113.
108. George Clinton to the Governors of the Several States in the Union, Poughkeepsie, [N.Y.], July 28, 1788, printed in *ibid.,* 413–414.
109. ER to J. Madison, Richmond, Aug. 13, 1788, Madison MSS. Emphasis ER's.
110. J. Madison to ER, New York, Aug. 22, 1788, *ibid.*
111. ER to J. Madison, Richmond, Sept. 3, 1788, *ibid.*
112. ER to Speaker of House of Delegates [Thomas Matthews], In Council, Oct. 20, 1788, Executive Letterbook, VSL.
    There were twelve different subjects mentioned in the letter and one of these was a standard reference to the reports and letters he had been asked to transmit to the legislature. There were thirteen enclosures mentioned in this paragraph of his letter. Among the thirteen was the circular letter from New York recommending a second general convention.
113. Griffin was apparently offered the position of high sheriff of James City County (*J. H. Del.* [Oct. Sess., 1788, White reprint], 37).
114. ER to J. Madison, Richmond, Nov. 10, 1788, MS [single item], Acc. No. 4205, University of Virginia.
115. *J. H. Del.* (Oct. Sess., 1788, White reprint), 37, 38.
116. *Ibid.,* 46.
117. *Ibid.,* 42–44.
118. *Ibid.,* 16–17, 37, 42–44. See also Francis Corbin to J. Madison, Richmond, Nov. 12, 1788, Madison MSS.
    Early in the session Corbin predicted that ER would lead the fight to secure an endorsement of the New York proposal for a second convention. His comments, although somewhat melodramatic, are most revealing:

> A proposition will be brought forward in the Assembly for a second convention of the states—and I fear it will be carried—altho' I have not yet been able to ascertain the complexion of the House—this being but the second day of our meeting. This proposition it is said will be introduced not by Henry but (miserable dicta!) by our friend Randolph. He will injure his political reputation by his doublings and turnings. He is *too Machiavelian* and *not Machiavelian enough.*

I wish, I sincerely wish that he could be advised and would take advice—but this, I fear, is out of the question. We Virginians are too much accustomed to solitude and slavery—too much puff'd up with our own foolish pride and vanity ever to entertain any other idea than that we alone are wise and all the rest of the world fools. (Francis Corbin to J. Madison, [Richmond], Oct. 21, 1788, Madison MSS, emphasis Corbin's.)

119. *J. H. Del.* (Oct. Sess., 1788, White reprint), 5–54 *passim*.

CHAPTER 13

1. Evident from ER to J. Madison, Richmond, Nov. 5, 1788, Madison MSS.
2. On Nov. 15 ER was named to the following standing committees: Privileges and Elections, Commerce, and Courts of Justice (*J. H. Del.* [Oct. Sess., 1788, White reprint], 46).
   An examination of the handwriting in the rough drafts of the various bills passed during this session suggests that ER actually drafted a sizable number of the bills passed during this session. The evidence is, of course, not conclusive since handwriting does not of itself establish authorship. It is certain, however, that he involved himself in almost every public bill (as opposed to private bills) that came before the House during the remaining weeks of this session (Virginia House of Delegates, Rough Bills and Resolutions, 1788–1789, VSL).
3. *J. H. Del.* (Oct. Sess., 1788, White reprint), 54–55.
4. *Ibid.*
5. Virginia House of Delegates, Rough Bills and Resolutions, 1788–1789, VSL. The evidence is again circumstantial since the only proof of authorship is that the original drafts of these bills were in his hand.
6. Although it is probably self-evident that the changes in the court structure would better serve the adjudicative needs of the people of Virginia, it is still worth noting that St. George Tucker stressed this point in his commentary on the Virginia courts which he published in 1803. See Tucker, "Summary View of . . . Courts . . . in Va.," *Blackstone's Commentaries*, IV, Appendix Note A, 8–23 *passim*.
7. *J. H. Del.* (Oct. Sess., 1788, White reprint), 118.
8. Although the practical matter of representing Williamsburg in the legislature would dictate the establishment of a legal residence in that city, sentimental reasons must have been the dominant motive for actually moving his family there. Since most of the state's higher courts met in Richmond, it had to be the most obvious place for him to live as a practicing lawyer. The move to Williamsburg, as we shall see, forced him to make frequent trips to Richmond and proved rather inconvenient to his practice. The first indication we have that ER intended to live in Williamsburg and practice law in Richmond and Williamsburg is a letter to Col. Charles Simms, a client, which suggests he had arranged for the immediate referral of all his correspondence to Williamsburg and was in a position to have his letters of reply carried back to Richmond rather promptly (ER to Col. Charles Simms, Richmond, Dec. 24, 1788, Charles Simms MSS, LC).
   The tax records for Williamsburg indicate that ER paid personal and property taxes in that city for the first time in 1788 (the records begin in 1782) and his taxable personal property increased noticeably in 1789. This suggests the transfer of his riding and carriage horses, his post chair and his phaeton, and some of his domestic slaves from Richmond to Williamsburg (Williamsburg, Land Books, 1782–1783; Williamsburg Personal Property Lists, 1783–1784, 1786, 1788–1789 [records missing for the years 1785 and 1787]; Richmond City Personal Property List, 1787; Richmond City Land Book, 1787; Richmond City Personal Property and Land Books, 1788–1789 [records missing prior to the year 1787], VSL).
9. Hening, ed., *Va. Statutes*, XII, 708–709.
10. In anticipation of the establishment of the system of District Courts authorized in the last session of the legislature, ER may have worked out a kind of partnership agreement with John Marshall under which Marshall would handle all of ER's

clients in certain District Courts, in return, presumably, for some comparable service by ER. Something caused Marshall to reconsider the arrangement, forcing ER to insert a notice in the *Virginia Independent Chronicle* informing his clients that he was seeking the services of some other "practioner" to handle these cases for him. The notice went on to state that he had no objection to practicing before these District Courts on "particular causes" where his aid was requested. Otherwise, he announced: "I mean to attend the Court of Appeals, to give counsel, and to do any other business in the line of my profession which may not require too long an absence from home." (*Virginia Independent Chronicle*, Jan. 14, 1789.)

11. ER to J. Madison, Williamsburg, June 30, 1789, Madison MSS.

12. The only sustained documentary evidence that is available to establish that he was being plagued by the creditors of his uncle's estate at this time is the letters of Benjamin Harrison, Jr., to ER, most of which were written in 1789. Harrison's cryptic references to an evolving series of transactions defy analysis but they do reveal a good deal about his unceasing efforts to get ER to satisfy certain creditors of the estate who had already been put off several times with promises (Benjamin Harrison, Jr., Letterbook, 1787–1789, NYHS).

13. The date of Lucy's birth can only be established inferentially. She must have been born sometime between Apr. 17, 1787, the date of Edmonia's birth, and May 19, 1790, the date of the stillborn birth of Betsy's last child. The most probable time of Lucy's birth would be between Jan. and June of 1789. Since the family moved to Williamsburg in Dec., 1788, it seems safe to assume she was born several months after that event. See also Frank, *Daniel*, 6. Lucy married Daniel in 1810.

14. ER to J. Madison, Williamsburg, May 19, 1789, Madison MSS.

15. J. Madison to ER, New York, May 31, 1789, *ibid.*

16. He was still referring to her illness on July 19, 1789 (ER to J. Madison, Williamsburg, July 19, 1789, Madison MSS).

17. See the very different reactions of John Adams and James Madison, two of the most perceptive participants in this drama.

John Adams to Dr. Price, New York, May 20, 1789, John Adams Letters, HSP; John Adams to B. Rush, June 9, 1789, J. Adams to Dr. [Tufts?], New York, June 12, 1789, J. Adams to William Tudor, New York, June 12, 1789, and June 14, 1789, J. Adams to J. Bowen, New York, June 26, 1789, all in John Adams Letterbook, Adams Papers, MHS.

J. Madison to ER, New York, May 10, 1789, May 31, 1789, June 15, 1789, and June 24, 1789, Madison MSS.

18. Arthur Lee to John Adams, New York, Aug. 18, 1788, Adams Papers, MHS.

19. The sense of accomplishment associated with these initial steps in getting the government organized and in motion is very perceptively summarized in Freeman, *Washington*, VI, 218–232 *passim*.

20. See note 17 above.

21. His attitude toward the new government is reflected in at least two letters to Madison at this time (ER to J. Madison, Williamsburg, June 30, 1789, and July 19, 1789, Madison MSS). Several months later this same attitude manifests itself when he provides Washington with details on how the constitutional amendments are being received in the Virginia Assembly (ER to G. Washington, Richmond, Nov. 22, 1789, Nov. 26, 1789, Dec. 6, 1789, and Dec. 11, 1789, Washington MSS).

22. J. Madison to ER, New York, June 17, 1789, Madison MSS.

23. Madison must have made a similar request of Pendleton at this time although neither his letter nor Pendleton's reply has been found. The exchange of correspondence can be established from a subsequent letter (J. Madison to Edmund Pendleton, New York, July 15, 1789, Madison MSS).

24. ER to J. Madison, Williamsburg, June 30, 1789, Madison MSS.

25. The bill's passage through Congress and Madison's minor role in the House debate on the bill can be followed in *Annals*, I, 18, 46, 49, 50 (Senate); 659, 782–785, 796–820, 820–834, 887, 894 (House). The act itself is in *U.S. Statutes at Large*, I, 73–93.

26. J. Madison to Edmund Pendleton, New York, Sept. 14, 1789, Madison MSS.

27. *DAB, s.v.* "Griffin, Cyrus."
28. Griffin's letter of July 10 has not been found, but ER quoted the pertinent passages in it when he solicited Madison's assistance in connection with his reply to this letter (ER to J. Madison, Williamsburg, July 19, 1789, Madison MSS).
29. *Ibid.*
    The land purchase in question was probably "Viewmont" in Albemarle County, see note 31 below.
30. *Ibid.*
31. We know of his movements because he kept Madison fully informed on where he could be reached (ER to J. Madison, Williamsburg, July 19, 1789, and Fredericksburg, [Va.], Aug. 18, 1789, Madison MSS).
    ER's trip to "Green Mountain" in Albemarle County and to Charlotte County seems to have been largely to inspect his properties. He owned two plantations in Albemarle County and one in Charlotte County (ER's Grant of Power of Attorney over Plantations and Slaves April [?], 1790, Edmund Randolph Misc. Papers, NYPL). One of the plantations in Albemarle County was undoubtedly "Viewmont," located some thirteen miles south of Charlottesville, which he purchased in 1786. The other may have been in the "Green Mountain" region, which is some twenty miles farther south (Writer's Program, WPA, *Jefferson's Albemarle*, 76, 87–92). His first recorded payment for taxes on land is 1787 and the Land Book for that and subsequent years (i.e. to 1798) indicates he owned 2,500 acres in "St. Ann's Parish" which had a declared value of £1010 (after 1794 the value of the land was given as $3,368). There is no indication as to whether this figure was for one or two plantations (Land Book, Albemarle County [St. Ann's Parish], 1787–1798, VSL). His name does not appear on the Land Books for Albemarle County after 1798 (*ibid.*, 1799–1813, VSL). At this time he had some forty slaves, about sixteen horses and around fifty head of cattle on this property (Personal Property Lists, Albemarle County, 1786, 1787, and 1788, VSL). In Charlotte County he owned some 2,000 acres, which he put up for sale several months after assuming the duties of the Attorney General's office (*Virginia Gazette and General Advertiser*, Sept. 8, 1790). He also owned a plantation in James City County and a plantation "in and adjoining to Williamsburg" (ER's Grant of Power of Attorney over Plantations and Slaves, April [?], 1790, Edmund Randolph Misc. Papers, NYPL).
32. ER to J. Madison, Fredericksburg, [Va.], Aug. 18, 1789, Madison MSS.
33. ER to J. Madison, Williamsburg, Sept. 13, 1789, and Sept. 26, 1789, Madison MSS.
34. G. Washington to ER, New York, Sept. 28, 1789, Fitzpatrick, ed., *Washington*, XXX, 418–419. The Judiciary Act establishing the office of Attorney General had been signed on Sept. 24, 1789 (*U.S. Statutes at Large*, I, 73–93).
35. ER to G. Washington, Williamsburg, Oct 8, 1789, Washington MSS.
36. *Ibid.*
37. Freeman, *Washington*, VI, 240–245.
38. ER to G. Washington, Richmond, Nov. 22, 1789, Washington MSS.
39. G. Washington to ER, New York, Nov. 30, 1789, Fitzpatrick, ed., *Washington*, XXX, 472–474.
40. *J. H. Del.* (Oct. Sess., 1789, White reprint), 3–4.
41. *Ibid.*, 10–11, 30–33.
42. Virginia House of Delegates, Rough Bills and Resolutions, 1788–1789, VSL.
43. Hening, ed., *Va. Statutes*, XIII, 8–9.
44. ER to J. Madison, Williamsburg, Mar. 27, 1789, Madison MSS.
45. The laws of Virginia had been collected and published in 1733, 1752, 1769 and 1785. The 1785 edition was not cumulative, however, and contained only those laws passed since 1768 (Charles Evans, comp., *American Bibliography*, Items 3,728; 6,941; 11,511; and 19,351). This effort thus represents the first attempt at a compilation that would exclude those English and colonial laws no longer in force within the state.
    On Oct. 8, ER notes he had been "employed in the task for more than six weeks" (ER to G. Washington, Williamsburg, Oct. 8, 1789, Washington MSS), and on Oct. 10 he observed to Madison: "Prepared as I am this work will not occupy

twenty days." (ER to J. Madison, Williamsburg, Oct. 10, 1789, Madison MSS.) These observations could only refer to the actual collecting of the laws, for he could not have done much more than that in the period of time mentioned. In Mar., 1790, he reported on the committee's work. His report implied that several of those named by the legislature to serve on this committee had not played a very active role in the preparation of this work (ER to Government of Virginia [Beverley Randolph], Williamsburg, Mar. 28, 1790, Ferdinand J. Dreer Collection, HSP). On June 28, 1790, he reported that the work was virtually complete. He added the following:

> If, contrary to my expectations, anything further should be required to be done in this business, I shall not hold myself excused from engaging in it, by any distance from my country [i.e. Virginia], which will have a right to command my humble services, under all circumstances and at all times. (ER to Government of Virginia [B. Randolph], Williamsburg, June 28, 1790, ibid.)

In spite of his generous offer this seems to have been his last contact with the project. The legislature did not authorize the republication of the laws until Dec., 1792, and they did not appear until 1794 (Evans, comp, *American Bibliography,* Item 27,999).

46. The amendments were submitted to the states on Sept. 25 and Madison reported to Washington on Nov. 20 that the amendments "are likely to be put off to the next session, the present House having been elected prior to the promulgation of them" (J. Madison to G. Washington, Orange, [Va.], Nov. 20, 1789, Washington MSS).

47. *J. H. Del.* (Oct. Sess., 1789, White reprint), 90–91. See also Henry Lee to J. Madison, Richmond, Nov. 25, 1789, Madison MSS; ER to G. Washington, Richmond, Nov. 26, 1789, Washington MSS.

48. These amendments ultimately became the Ninth and Tenth amendments to the Constitution.

49. ER to G. Washington, Richmond, Dec. 4, 1789, Washington MSS, and Hardin Burnley to J. Madison, Richmond, Nov. 28, 1789, Madison MSS. Madison's reaction to ER's objections can be found in J. Madison to G. Washington, Orange, Dec. 5, 1789, Madison MSS.

50. ER to G. Washington, Richmond, Nov. 26, 1789, Washington MSS; John Dawson to J. Madison, Richmond, Dec. 17, 1789, Madison MSS.

Before the Senate acted on the amendments an attempt was made in the House to pass a resolution asking Congress to reconsider and comply with the alterations to the Constitution that had been approved by the Virginia ratifying convention. The effort failed and a less offensive resolution was passed in its place (*J. H. Del.* [Oct. Sess., 1789, White reprint], 96, 101–102). ER's opposition to the more demanding of these two resolutions is rather confusingly summarized in ER to G. Washington, Richmond, Dec. 6, 1789, Washington MSS.

51. *J. Sen., Va.* (Oct. Sess.,1789, White reprint), 51–52.

52. *J. H. Del.* (Oct. Sess., 1789, White reprint), 111, 117–118, 119, 120. *J. Sen., Va.* (Oct. Sess., 789, White reprint), 37, 51–52, 58–59, 61–67, 68. The sequence of events can be reconstructed from ER to G. Washington, Richmond, Dec. 11, 1789, Washington MSS; John Dawson to J. Madison, Richmond, Dec. 17, 1789, and Edward Carrington to J. Madison, Richmond, Dec. 20, 1789, Madison MSS.

53. *J. H. Del.* (Oct. Sess., 1789, White reprint), 110.

54. *Ibid.,* 108–111.

55. *Ibid.,* 110.

56. *Ibid.,* 111.

57. John Dawson to J. Madison, Richmond, Dec. 17, 1789, Madison MSS.

58. Joseph Jones to J. Madison, Richmond, Nov. 2, 1789, Madison MSS.

59. Aside from the "indisposition" mentioned by Joseph Jones, he seems to have been in attendance each day the legislature met (House of Delegates, Attendance Book, 1789, VSL). As was true in the Oct., 1788, session of the House, his involvement in the drafting of so many of the bills that came before the legislature sug-

gests he was a very active member of the House (Virginia House of Delegates, Rough Bills and Resolutions, 1788–1789, VSL).

60. We know ER left his family in Virginia because within a month he asked Washington for permission to leave New York. After he arrived in Williamsburg he found Betsy, "incumbered with a dead foetus." She remained seriously ill until she gave birth to a stillborn child on May 19, 1790 (see pp. 191–193).

61. The absence of any public notice regarding the transfer of his practice to another attorney (as was common) causes one to conclude that he did not want to give public notice of the abandonment of his practice at this time. It is also worth noting that he did not draft the instrument granting power of attorney over his plantations and his slaves until Apr., 1790.

62. ER to J. Madison, Williamsburg, Oct. 10, 1789, Madison MSS.

CHAPTER 14

1. The earliest known date ER was in New York is Feb. 2.

2. Hamilton's report is now authoritatively reprinted in full in *Hamilton*, VI, 51–168.

3. See J. Madison to T. Jefferson, New York, Jan. 24, 1790, *Jefferson*, XVI, 125–126. ER's preoccupation with the way people reacted to the report is most revealingly illustrated by the letters he sent to Madison after he left New York (see below). The letters are ER to J. Madison, Baltimore, Mar. 2, 1790, ER to J. Madison, Fredericksburg, [Va.], Mar. 6, 1790, ER to J. Madison, Williamsburg, Mar. 10, 1790, Madison MSS.

4. *U.S. Statutes at Large*, I, 73.

5. 2 Dallas 339–400.

6. *Gazette of the United States*, Feb. 10, 1790.

7. *U.S. Statutes at Large*, I, 93.

8. ER's letter of Feb. 5 has not been found. Washington's reply is noted in Fitzpatrick, ed., *Washington*, XXXI, 11n.

9. Tobias Lear to ER, United States, Feb. 6, 1790, *ibid.*, 5–6; A. Hamilton to ER, Treasury Dept., Feb. 19, 1790, *Hamilton*, VI, 272–273. Washington declined to follow his recommendation in a third matter as evidenced by his reply (G. Washington to ER, New York, Feb. 11, 1790, Fitzpatrick, ed., *Washington*, XXXI, 9–10).

10. ER to J. Madison, Williamsburg, Mar. 10, 1790, Madison MSS.

11. ER to J. Madison, Williamsburg, Mar. 15, 1790, *ibid.*

12. ER to Wilson Cary Nicholas, Williamsburg, Mar. 24, 1790, Wilson Cary Nicholas II (deposit), University of Virginia; quote from ER to J. Madison, Williamsburg, Apr. 27, 1790, Madison MSS.

13. ER to Beverley Randolph, Williamsburg, Mar. 28, 1790, Ferdinand J. Dreer Collection, HSP.

14. ER to Wilson Cary Nicholas, Williamsburg, Mar. 24, 1790, Wilson Cary Nicholas II (deposit), University of Virginia.

15. ER to Henry Tazewell, Williamsburg, Apr. 23, 1790, Tazewell Family Papers, VSL.

16. ER's Grant of Power of Attorney over Plantations and Slaves, April [?], 1790, Edmund Randolph Misc. Papers, NYPL. See also ER to B. Powell, James City County, July 3, 1790 MS [single item], VHS.

17. ER to J. Madison, Williamsburg, May 20, 1790, Madison MSS.

18. ER was in Williamsburg until June 28. His departure without his family is evident from Rev. James Madison to ER, Williamsburg, June 30, 1790, Madison MSS.

19. The essential features, if not the details, of this famous "bargin" are now rather generally acknowledged. The available sources fail to reveal any evidence that ER commented on the settlement or the political negotiations that preceded the settlement. One can only conclude, therefore, that he accepted it for what it was—"a very resourceful solution of two issues that had virtually paralyzed the machinery of government."

20. 2 Dallas 400.

21. Evident from ER to T. Jefferson, Aug. 10, 1790, *Jefferson*, XVII, 331; ER to A. Hamilton, New York, Aug. 11, 1790, *Hamilton*, VI, 555–556; ER to A. Hamilton,

New York, Aug. 12, 1790 (responding to letter of Feb. 19, 1790), *ibid.*, 556. Also, on Dec. 27, 1790, the Secretary of War reported on several matters relating to the grievances of the Seneca Indians. In his report he refers to the fact that he had consulted the Attorney General on one of the complaints summarizing ER's reply (H. Knox to G. Washington, Dec. 27, 1790, Washington MSS).

22. G. Washington to T. Jefferson, July 15, 1790, Fitzpatrick, ed., *Washington*, XXXI, 69–70; T. Jefferson to G. Washington, July 15, 1790, *Jefferson*, XVII, 193–199.

23. The House resolution, dated Aug. 5, 1790, instructed him to:

> . . . report to this house at the next session on such matters relative to the administration of justice under the authority of the United States, as may require to be remedied; and that he shall also report such provisions in the respective cases as he shall deem advisable. (*U.S. House Journal*, I, 289.)

For ER's earlier views on the Judiciary Act see above, pp. 243–244. It is worth noting that ER asked Associate Justice James Wilson to assist him in the preparation of this report (ER to James Wilson, New York, Aug. 5, 1790, Historical Society of Pennsylvania Misc. Collections, HSP).

24. William Knox notes ER's arrival in Philadelphia on Aug. 19 with a "great family" (W. Knox to H. Knox, Philadelphia, [Aug. 20?], 1790, Henry Knox Papers, MHS). This suggests that Betsy and the children journeyed to New York, not knowing of the act that transferred the seat of government to Philadelphia. The act was passed on July 16. In the light of this legislation the entire family then returned to Philadelphia.

25. ER's letter had not been found but its date—Aug. 12—and its general contents can be established from the wording of Washington's response (G. Washington to ER, Aug. 12, 1790, Fitzpatrick, ed., *Washington*, XXXI, 90).

26. *Ibid.*

27. W. Knox to H. Knox, [Aug. 20?], 1790, Henry Knox Papers, MHS. (Knox incorrectly dated this letter "July 20" and it is so filed in the Knox MSS. Internal evidence indicates it was written on Aug. 20.)

The acquisition of a home is noted in Knox, but its location is established from the *Philadelphia Directory* for 1791 (Clement Biddle, *The Philadelphia Directory* [Philadelphia, 1791], 105).

28. ER's letter has not been found but its contents can be established from the wording of Washington's reply (G. Washington to ER, New York, Aug. 26, 1790, Fitzpatrick, ed., *Washington*, XXXI, 101).

The day after granting ER permission to remain in Philadelphia Washington asked his department heads, the Vice President and the Chief Justice to submit their views on a potentially serious diplomatic problem, i.e. the response of the United States if Britain should request permission to move troops across American soil to attack Spanish possessions at the mouth of the Mississippi in retaliation for Spanish seizures of British ships in the Nootka Sound. Fortunately the question never had to be faced, but Washington's failure to consult ER suggests ER was something less than an adviser (official or otherwise) when it came to formulating policy on a potentially serious diplomatic problem.

29. ER to Wilson Cary Nicholas, Philadelphia, Sept. 7, 1790, Edgehill-Randolph Papers (McGregor Library), University of Virginia.

30. ER to William Bingham, New York, Aug. 12, 1790, Simon Gratz Collection, HSP; ER to T. Jefferson, New York, [Aug. 13, 1790], *Jefferson*, XVII, 388; ER to Wilson Cary Nicholas, Philadelphia, Sept. 7, 1790, Edgehill-Randolph Papers (McGregor Library), University of Virginia (letter quoted); Richard Harrison to ER, New York, Sept. 7, 1790, Richard Harrison Letterbook, 1790–1806, NYHS; ER to Henry Tazewell, Philadelphia, Oct. 17, 1790, Tazewell Family Papers, VSL; Richard Harrison to ER, New York, Oct. 15, 1790, and Nov. 8, 1790, Richard Harrison Letterbook, 1790–1802, NYHS.

31. ER to Henry Tazewell, Philadelphia, Oct. 17, 1790, Tazewell Family Papers, VSL. This was his salary as defined by law (*U.S. Statutes at Large*, I, 72).

32. ER to Beverley Randolph, Philadelphia, Sept. 9, 1790, Charles Simms to Beverley

Randolph, Alexandria, Sept. 20, 1790, *CVSP*, V, 207, 209–210; Beverley Randolph to ER, Richmond, Oct. 13, 1790, Executive Letterbook, VSL.

33. "Report of the Attorney General on the Judiciary System of the United States, 1790," *ASP, Misc.,* I, 21–36.
ER's report failed to comment on the Act to Regulate Processes of Sept. 29, 1789, although it was almost as important to the operations of the federal judiciary as the Judiciary Act of 1789. Julius G. Goebel, Jr., has an exhaustive treatment of the subject, including ER's negligence in commenting on the act: *History of the Supreme Court of the United States,* Vol. I, *Antecedents and Beginnings to 1801,* 509–551 *passim.*

34. *Annals,* II, 1838–1839 (House).

35. *Hamilton,* VII, 225–236, 305–342.

36. Madison's two famous speeches were delivered on Feb. 2 and 8, 1791 (*Annals,* II, 1849–1902, 1956–1960 [House]).

37. ER to G. Washington, Philadelphia, Feb. 12, 1791, Letterbook 23, Washington MSS.

38. ER's Opinion on the Bank Bill, Feb. 12, 1791, Letterbook 23, Washington MSS.

39. Thomas Jefferson's Opinion on the Bank Bill, Feb. 15, 1791, *Jefferson,* XIX, 275–280.
Jefferson quoted directly from the still unratified Tenth Amendment to the Constitution. He identified it was the Twelfth Amendment in his opinion. At the time the opinion was written the ratification of the amendment was virtually assured.

40. G. Washington to A. Hamilton, Philadelphia, Feb. 16, 1791, Fitzpatrick, ed., *Washington,* XXXI, 215–216.

41. Madison's veto message is dated Feb. 21, 1791. It was obviously submitted at the request of the President.

42. Opinion on the Constitutionality of An Act to Establish a Bank, [Philadelphia, Feb. 23, 1791], *Hamilton,* VIII, 97–134, quote on 98.

43. *U.S. Senate Journal,* I, 282. The act is in *U.S. Statutes at Large,* I, 191–196.

44. ER to G. Washington, Philadelphia, Feb. 12, 1791, Letterbook 23, Washington MSS.

45. ER to Wilson Cary Nicholas, Philadelphia, Mar. 6, 1791, Wilson Cary Nicholas II, (deposit), University of Virginia.

46. Tobias Lear to G. Washington, Philadelphia, Apr. 5, 1791, and Apr. 24, 1791, Washington MSS.

47. ER's most explicit statement on the subject during this period is ER to Benjamin Franklin, Richmond, Aug. 2, 1788, Pennsylvania Abolition Society Papers, HSP.

48. Tobias Lear to G. Washington, Philadelphia, May 8, 1791, Washington MSS.

49. Thomas Mifflin to G. Washington, Philadelphia, July 18, 1791, Pennsylvania State Papers No. 69, Papers of the Continental Congress, NA.

50. ER to G. Washington, Philadelphia, July 20, 1791, *ibid.* The attorney general of Virginia at this time was James Innes.

51. ER to G. Washington, Philadelphia, July 20, 1791, and July 23, 1791, *ibid.*; Thomas Mifflin to G. Washington, Philadelphia, Aug. 2, 1791, *ibid.*

52. The subject has been thoroughly treated in Malone, *Jefferson,* II, 354–359.

53. The incident is described by Lear in a letter that relates to Lear's own conversations with Beckwith (T. Lear to G. Washington, Philadelphia, May 8, 1791, Washington MSS).

54. T. Jefferson to G. Washington, Philadelphia, May 8, 1791, Jefferson MSS.

55. J. Madison to T. Jefferson, New York, June 23, 1791, June 27, 1791, T. Jefferson to J. Madison, [Philadelphia], June 28, 1791, J. Madison to T. Jefferson, New York, July 13, 1791, *ibid.*

56. ER to G. Washington, Philadelphia, July 13, 1791, Washington MSS. ER named others but placed Paine's name at the top of his list.

57. ER to J. Madison, Philadelphia, July 21, 1791, Madison MSS.

58. T. Jefferson to J. Madison, Philadelphia, Aug. 18, 1791, Jefferson MSS.

59. The expression, with emphasis, was used by ER in his letter of July 21 to Madison (ER to J. Madison, Philadelphia, July 21, 1791, Madison MSS).

CHAPTER 15

1. G. Washington to ER, Mount Vernon, Oct. 10, 1791, Fitzpatrick, ed., *Washington*, XXXI, 386–387.
2. Tobias Lear to G. Washington, Philadelphia, Oct. 2, 1791, Washington MSS. That he handled the administrative chores associated with these lesser judicial appointments is evident from T. Lear to G. Washington, Philadelphia, Sept. 18, 1791, Washington MSS.
3. T. Jefferson to ER, Philadelphia, Dec. 5, 1791, Jefferson MSS., enclosing George Hammond to T. Jefferson, Philadelphia, Nov. 26, 1791, *ibid.*
4. *Ibid.*
5. ER to T. Jefferson, Philadelphia, Feb. 22, 1792, *ibid.* See also ER to T. Jefferson, Philadelphia, Apr. 12, 1793, and T. Jefferson to G. Hammond, Philadelphia, *ibid.*
6. VanBerckel's letter to Jefferson has not been found but the substance of his complaint is evident from ER's reply: ER to T. Jefferson, Philadelphia, June 26, 1792, *ibid.* See also T. Jefferson to F. P. VanBerckel, Philadelphia, July 2, 1792, T. Jefferson to ER, Philadelphia, July 12, 1792, T. Jefferson to [F. P.] VanBerckel, Philadelphia, July 12, 1792, *ibid.*
7. ER to A. Hamilton, Philadelphia, June 26, 1792, *Hamilton*, XI, 576–577, and A. Hamilton to Col. William Heth, June 26, 1792, *ibid.*, 572–573. The law in question, i.e. "An Act to establish the Treasury Department," may be found in *U.S. Statutes at Large*, I, 65–76.
8. Jefferson's letter to ER has not been found but ER's reply provides the substance of his inquiry (ER to T. Jefferson, [Philadelphia], July 7, 1792, Jefferson MSS). The Mint Act was passed on Apr. 2, 1792, and the congressional session ended on May 8.
9. ER to G. Washington, Philadelphia, Dec. 26, 1791, *ASP Misc.*, I, 46.
10. G. Washington to Gentlemen of the Senate and of the House of Representatives, United States, Dec. 28, 1791, *ibid.*, 45.
11. *Annals*, III, 289 (Senate), 289 (House); *ASP Misc.*, I, 46; *Annals*, III, 329–330 (House), *ibid.*, 331.
12. Washington's biographer suggests the Cabinet came into being in the autumn of 1791 and implies ER was a member of it from the beginning (Freeman, *Washington*, VI, 335). Another source gives the date of ER's entry into the Cabinet as Mar. 31, 1792 (Homer Cummings and Carl McFarland, *Federal Justice*, 25). The most balanced account of Washington's methods of conferring with his principal advisers is Leonard D. White, *The Federalists*, 38–41.
13. Washington's letter to ER has not been found. ER's reply is ER to G. Washington, Philadelphia, Jan. 21, 1792, Washington MSS, emphasis mine.
14. There were two apportionment bills before Congress. The first, House Bill No. 147, was introduced on Nov. 18, 1791, only to be laid aside on Dec. 20, 1791, when differences between the Senate and House could not be reconciled. The second bill, House Bill No. 163, was introduced on Feb. 6, 1792, and after an extended debate in both houses was sent to the President on Mar. 26, 1792. The history of each of these bills in Congress can be followed in Albert Orway, *General Index of the Journals of Congress . . .* , 123. It is more accurate than the entries in the indexes of the *U.S. Senate Journal* and the *U. S. House Journal*.
15. The bill established the total number of seats in the House from the total population of the United States, but it determined the number of representatives for each state according to the population of the state itself. The use of two different methods of calculation in the bill meant there would be eight "unused seats" in the House. This dilemma was resolved by assigning these seats to those states having the largest fractional remainders after the initial apportionment. This procedure gave five of the seats to northern states and three to southern states, an arrangement that antagonized many of the southern Senators and Representatives.
16. Evident from H. Knox to G. Washington, War Department, Apr. 3, 1792, Washington MSS, and A. Hamilton to G. Washington, Philadelphia, Apr. 4, 1792, *Hamilton*, XI, 226–230.
17. ER to G. Washington, [Philadelphia], Apr. 4, 1792, Washington MSS.

18. T. Jefferson to G. Washington, [Philadelphia], Apr. 4, 1792, Jefferson MSS.
     Jefferson suggested that Washington exercise the veto merely to demonstrate that he was not afraid to use it. Such action, he noted, would forestall any tendency among the states to throw up barriers of their own against Congress (*ibid.*).
19. A. Hamilton to G. Washington, Philadelphia, Apr. 4, 1792, *Hamilton*, XI, 226–230, quote on 228.
20. H. Knox to G. Washington, War Department, Apr. 3, 1792, Washington MSS.
21. The sequence of events is recorded in Jefferson's "Anas." The account is presumed to be reasonably accurate because it was written on Apr. 9, only four days after the events described. Jefferson records the events as taking place on Apr. 6 instead of Apr. 5. The "Anas" is in Ford, ed., *Jefferson*, I, 190–192.
22. G. Washington to the House of Representatives, Apr. 5, 1792, Fitzpatrick, ed., *Washington*, XXXII, 16–17.
23. *U.S. House Journal*, I, 565–566. The vote was 28 ays and 33 nos.
24. This became the third apportionment bill in this session and is House Bill No. 179. *Annals*, III, 540–541, 542, 543–549, 550 (House), 120 (Senate). *U.S. House Journal*, I, 569, 570, 571, 572; *U.S. Senate Journal*, I, 432; *U.S. Statutes at Large*, I, 253, supplies the date on which Washington signed the bill.
25. Washington had made a brief trip to Mount Vernon in May (Freeman, *Washington*, VI, 356–358). His mood during these spring and summer months was determined by the partisan political climate of the times, for there were no pressing problems of state confronting him (*ibid.*, 355–362).
26. The roll of the press during this period is judiciously described in Frank L. Mott, *American Journalism, A History: 1690–1960*, 113–134. An excellent study of editorial opinion during the Washington Administration may be found in Freeman, *Washington*, VI, App. VI–2.
27. G. Washington to A. Hamilton, Mount Vernon, July 29, 1792, Fitzpatrick, ed., *Washington*, XXXII, 95–100; for Jefferson's letter, see Jefferson MSS.
28. ER to G. Washington, Philadelphia, Aug. 5, 1792, Washington MSS, Vol. 255, p. 84.
29. ER to G. Washington, Philadelphia, Aug. 5, 1792, Washington MSS, Vol. 255, pp. 86–87. All subsequent references to a letter of Aug. 5 are to this second letter, the more important of the two.
     Washington responded to this letter on Aug. 26 (G. Washington to ER, Mount Vernon, Aug. 26, 1792, Fitzpatrick, ed., *Washington*, XXXII, 135–137).
30. Madison's notes on his conversations with Washington on the latter's retirement may be found in Hunt, ed., *Madison*, VI, 106–111n. See also J. Madison to G. Washington, Orange, June 21, 1792, Madison MSS.
31. ER to G. Washington, Philadelphia, Aug. 5, 1792, Washington MSS.
     It should be noted that shortly after writing this letter ER published an article signed "G" in the *Gazette of the United States*, Aug. 18, 1792. It answered certain accusations made by "An American" in previous issues of the paper (*ibid.*, Aug. 4 and Aug. 11, 1792). One of the accusations made by "An American" was that Philip Freneau, the editor of the *National Gazette*, was being subsidized by Jefferson with a translator's job at the Department of State. ER, in reply, pointed out that since the editor of the *Gazette of the United States*, John Fenno, had been the beneficiary of several government printing contracts, he must have been even more under the influence of his sponsor, Hamilton.
     What made the above incident so interesting was that the charge that Jefferson subsidized Freneau was made by Hamilton, who wrote the piece under the pseudonyms "T.L." and "An American" (Mitchell, *Hamilton*, II, 207–208). ER's reply, by no means the only reply, was his only venture into this newspaper war. Two other articles, signed "Aristides," frequently attributed to ER, do not appear to have been written by him.
32. A. Hamilton to G. Washington, Philadelphia, Aug. 18, 1792, enclosing his "Objections and Answers respecting the Administration of the Government," *Hamilton*, XII, 228–258.
33. The infrequent posts from Alexandria brought Washington a considerable amount of mail from Philadelphia including, in all probability, the *Gazette of the United*

States and the *National Gazette*. Beginning in July, the two newspapers abandoned all pretense of objectivity and became aggressively partisan (Freeman, *Washington*, VI, App. VI–2, 407–408.

34. A. Hamilton to G. Washington, Philadelphia, Aug. 18, 1792, *Hamilton*, XII, 228–229.

35. G. Washington to T. Jefferson, Mount Vernon, Aug. 23, 1792, Fitzpatrick, ed., *Washington*, XXXII, 128–132.

36. G. Washington to A. Hamilton, Mount Vernon, Aug. 26, 1792, *ibid.*, 132–134.

37. T. Jefferson to G. Washington, Monticello, Sept. 9, 1792, Jefferson MSS; A. Hamilton to G. Washington, Philadelphia, Sept. 9, 1792, *Hamilton*, XII, 347–350.

38. ER to G. Washington, Philadelphia, Sept. 10, 1792, Washington MSS.

39. The proclamation as originally drafted by Hamilton has never been found (*Hamilton*; XII, 330). The severity of Hamilton's language can be established from the words and phrases ER took exception to in his opinion on the Hamilton draft (ER to A. Hamilton, Philadelphia, Sept. 8, 1792, *ibid.*, 336–340), as well as from Hamilton's letters on the subject during the period the proclamation was being drafted (A. Hamilton to G. Washington, Treasury Dept., Sept. 1, 1792, A. Hamilton to J. Jay, Philadelphia, Sept. 3, 1792, A. Hamilton to G. Washington, Treasury Dept., Sept. 9, 1792, A. Hamilton to G. Washington, Philadelphia, Sept. 11, 1792, *ibid.*, 311–313, 316–317, 344–347, 365–367).

40. ER to A. Hamilton, Philadelphia, Sept. 8, 1792, *ibid.*, 336–340.

41. Proclamation [on whiskey insurrection in western Pennsylvania], Sept. 15, 1792, Fitzpatrick, ed., *Washington*, XXXII, 150–151.

42. That Washington solicited ER's views is evident only from the latter's written reply (see below), leading one to conclude that the request was communicated verbally after Washington returned to Philadelphia.

43. Washington wrote to Hamilton and Knox requesting them to submit their ideas on the forthcoming message (G. Washington to A. Hamilton, Mount Vernon, Aug. 26, 1792, G. Washington to H. Knox, Mount Vernon, Sept. 3, 1792, Fitzpatrick, ed., *Washington*, XXXII, 132–136, 140–141). If Jefferson was consulted, the exchange between the two men was entirely verbal for there is nothing in writing.

44. ER to G. Washington, Philadelphia, Oct. 28, 1792, Washington MSS. ER underlined the word "existing" in his reference to the fiscal arrangements.

45. *U.S. Senate Journal*, I, 452–455.

46. *Annals*, III, 835–836 (House). For general background, see Mitchell, *Hamilton*, II, 249–266, and D. R. Anderson, *William Branch Giles: A Biography*, 20–25.

47. A translation of Ternant's request as communicated to Jefferson is in T. Jefferson to G. Washington, Feb. 8, 1793, Jefferson MSS.

48. Jared Sparks, ed., *Correspondence of the American Revolution . . .* , IV, 382–383, 384–385. See also A. Hamilton to G. Washington, Treasury Dept., Nov. 19, 1792, *Hamilton*, XIII, 169–173.

49. Only Hamilton seems to have received a written request for an opinion on Ternant's application (T. Lear to A. Hamilton, United States, Feb. 8, 1793, *ibid.*, XIV, 16–17). The written opinions of Jefferson and ER (see below) establish the fact that they, too, were consulted on the matter.

50. T. Jefferson to G. Washington, Philadelphia, Feb. 12, 1793, Jefferson MSS.

51. ER to G. Washington, Philadelphia, Feb. 14, 1793, Washington MSS.

52. Cabinet Memorandum, Feb. 25, 1793, Washington MSS, and Jefferson's notes on Cabinet meeting, Feb. 26, 1793, Jefferson MSS.
     There is no evidence that Hamilton expressed an opinion in writing prior to this Cabinet meeting.

53. Jefferson's Memorandum on subject of Morris' removal as minister to France, [Feb. 20, 1793], Jefferson MSS.

54. *Ibid.*

55. Evident from ER to G. Washington, Philadelphia, Feb. 22, 1793, Washington MSS.

56. *Ibid.*

57. Journal of the Proceedings of the President, Feb. 12, 1793, Washington MSS; T. Jefferson to B. Randolph, Feb. 18, 1793, Jefferson MSS.

58. G. Washington to ER, United States, Feb. 12, 1793, Fitzpatrick, ed., *Washington*,

XXXII, 341–342; Journal of the Proceedings of the President, Feb. 17, 1793, Washington MSS.

59. The request from Washington to ER and his prompt fulfillment of the assignment are evident from ER to G. Washington, Philadelphia, Feb. 18, 1793, Washington MSS.

After ER suggested Paterson's name, Washington asked him to consult with Jefferson on the appointment. Jefferson concurred with ER's selection (Journal of the Proceedings of the President, Feb. 19, 1793, Washington MSS).

60. G. Washington to W. Paterson, Philadelphia, Feb. 20, 1793, Fitzpatrick, ed., *Washington*, XXXII, 352–353.

61. See, for example, his comments in ER to [?] Gratz, Philadelphia, Aug. 4, 1791, Etting Collection, HSP. In Apr., 1792, he served as one of the counsels for the plaintiff in a case before the U.S. Circuit Court in Pennsylvania. (*Collet vs. Collet*, 2 Dallas 294–296).

62. See, for example, ER to John Nicholson and John Mitchell, Philadelphia, July 31, 1791, Simon Gratz Collection, HSP.

63. ER to G. Washington, Philadelphia, July 13, 1791, Washington MSS; ER to G. Washington, Philadelphia, Jan. 21, 1792, *ibid.*; ER to Alexander Addison, Philadelphia, July 29, 1792, Simon Gratz Collection, HSP.

64. This account of the *Hayburn Case* has been drawn from three sources: the official report (2 Dallas 409–410), a summary of the case in the *National Gazette*, Aug. 18, 1792, and ER's own brief summary of it in ER to J. Madison, Germantown, [Penn.], Aug. 12, 1792, Madison MSS.

65. 2 Dallas 409–410.

66. Under the provisions of the act disabled veterans of the Revolution were required to file their claims in the federal Circuit Court of their district. The Circuit Court judges were to pass on these applications and forward their findings to the Secretary of War (*U.S. Statutes at Large*, I, 243–245). Some judges protested, while others simply refused to perform the duties assigned to them under the act (*ASP Misc.*, I, 49–53).

67. 2 Dallas 409–410.

68. *Ibid.*

The official report and the newspaper account of the case make note of ER's "long and able description of his powers," but no record of these remarks seems to have been preserved.

69. ER to J. Madison, Germantown, Aug. 12, 1792, Madison MSS; *National Gazette*, Aug. 18, 1792.

The report in Dallas indicates he did make the motion *ex officio* and it was not allowed.

70. 2 Dallas 409–410.

71. *U.S. Statutes at Large*, I, 324–325.

72. 2 Dallas 402–409.

73. *Ibid.*, 415–419.

74. *Ibid.*, 480n.

75. *Ibid.*, 419n and 3 Dallas 1.

76. 2 Dallas 419–480.

77. Charles Warren, *The Supreme Court in United States History*, I, 93–101.

78. 2 Dallas 419.

79. See *The Federalist*, No. 81, and Elliot, ed., *Debates*, III, 533.

80. The press reported ER spoke for "about two-and-a-half hours" (*Gazette of the United States*, Feb. 25, 1793).

81. 2 Dallas 419–429, quotes on 423 and 429.

82. *Ibid.*, 429–450.

83. *Ibid.*, 450–480.

84. *Ibid.*, 469–480, quote on 473.

85. *Gazette of the United States*, Feb. 25, 1793.

86. 2 Dallas 480.

87. *Ibid.*, 480n.

88. Herman V. Ames, *Proposed Amendments to the Constitution* in *AHA, Annual Report, 1896*, II, 156–157.

CHAPTER 16

1. Described in Freeman (Carroll & Ashworth), *Washington*, VII, 8–10.
2. T. Jefferson to G. Washington, Philadelphia, Mar. 21, 1793, Ford, ed., *Jefferson*, VI, 204.
3. Entry in T. Jefferson's "Anas," Mar. 30, 1793, *ibid.*, I, 224. No other source is available to shed light on these Cabinet consultations.
4. A. Hamilton to G. Washington, Apr. 5, 1793, and Apr. 8, 1793, *Hamilton*, XIV, 291, 295–296.
5. G. Washington to A. Hamilton, Apr. 12, 1793, and G. Washington to T. Jefferson, Apr. 12, 1793, Fitzpatrick, ed., *Washington*, XXXII, 415–416.
6. Freeman (Carroll & Ashworth), *Washington*, VII, 44.
7. See discussion of in Thomas, *Am. Neutrality*, 28 and Note.
8. A. Hamilton had consulted John Jay as early as April 9 (A. Hamilton to J. Jay, Philadelphia, Apr. 9, 1793 [two letters], *Hamilton*, XIV, 297–300) and Edward Carrington, his political ally in Virginia, on Apr. 10. This letter has never been found (*ibid.*, 302n), but its existence can be established from Carrington's reply (E. Carrington to A. Hamilton, Richmond, Apr. 26, 1793, *ibid.*, 346–352).

   Hamilton's letters to Jay and the formal answers Carrington gave to apparently very specific questions on this subject are remarkably similar to the questions Washington submitted to the Cabinet on Apr. 18. It is now generally accepted that Hamilton was the author of twelve of the thirteen questions in Washington's circular to the Cabinet. See Thomas, *Am. Neutrality*, 27–30 for a discussion of the subject.
9. Entry in "Anas," Apr. 18, 1793, Ford, ed., *Jefferson*, I, 226.
10. Journal of Proceedings of the President, Apr. 18, 1793, Washington MSS. The questions are conveniently reprinted in Fitzpatrick, ed., *Washington*, XXXII, 419–420.
11. *Ibid.*, 419.
12. The fullest account of the discussion surrounding the first question is the biased account in T. Jefferson to J. Madison, Philadelphia, June 23, 1793, Ford, ed., *Jefferson*, VI, 315–316. The positions of ER and Knox can only be deduced from a note in Jefferson's hand under the date Apr. 18, which reads: "Agreed by all that a Proclamation shall issue, . . ." (Fitzpatrick, ed., *Washington*, XXXII, 420n).
13. ER's suggestion and the reaction to it are related in Jefferson's "Anas" under the date of May 7, 1793 (Ford, ed., *Jefferson*, I, 228–229). The language used in Jefferson's account indicates the suggestion was made after the decision had been reached to issue a proclamation.
14. There is no documentable explanation of why Washington asked ER to draft the Neutrality Proclamation. If Jefferson was ever asked to assume the assignment and declined, he made no reference to it. It seems more likely that ER was the only member of the Cabinet ever asked to draft the document. Neither Jefferson nor Hamilton was in a position to challenge Washington's choice of ER.
15. Fitzpatrick, ed., *Washington*, XXXIII, 419–420.
16. Since Hamilton had previously agreed that Genêt should be received as a diplomatic representative of France, it seems safe to conclude that he included this question in the list he supplied to Washington either as a political lever in order that he might bargain with Jefferson, or because he felt the diplomatic situation had changed since mid-March and should be reviewed again by the Cabinet. The latter seems to be the more likely explanation since Washington and his advisers now knew for certain that France was at war with much of Europe, information they did not have in March.
17. Entry in "Anas," Apr. 18, 1793, Ford, ed., *Jefferson*, I, 226–227, and "Cabinet Opinion . . . ," Apr. 19, 1793, *ibid.*, VI, 217.
18. Fitzpatrick, ed., *Washington*, XXXII, 419–420.

19. The only summary of Hamilton's opinion is that which is found in Jefferson's written opinion on the validity of the Franco-American treaties, submitted to Washington on Apr. 28, 1793. In it he is reviewing and then challenging the arguments advanced by Hamilton in the cabinet meeting on the 19th (Jefferson's "Opinion on French Treaties," April 28, 1793, Ford, ed., *Jefferson*, VI, 219–231).

20. As evidenced by Jefferson's "Opinion on French Treaties," Apr. 28, 1793, *ibid.*

21. The position taken by Knox and ER can be established from the "Anas." It seems safe to assume that ER attempted to strengthen the position taken by Jefferson by relating it in some way to accepted practices of international law, thereby causing Hamilton to note that Vattel supported his position. See Jefferson's account of the Cabinet discussion of this question in the "Anas" (Entry in "Anas," Apr. 18, 1793, *ibid.*, I, 226–227).

22. *Ibid.*

23. "Cabinet Opinion . . . ," Apr. 19, 1793, *ibid.*, VI, 217. Entry in "Anas" for Apr. 18, 1793, *ibid.*, I, 226–227.

24. Journal of Proceedings of the President, Apr. 19, 1793, Washington MSS.

25. The dispute regarding Jay's versus ER's authorship of the Neutrality Proclamation has been thoroughly examined by C. Thomas and no new evidence has been uncovered that might bring his opinion into question (Thomas, *Am. Neutrality*, 43–45).

26. Compare the language of the Cabinet opinion ("Cabinet Opinion . . . ," Apr. 19, 1793, Ford, ed., *Jefferson*, VI, 217) with the language of the proclamation (Proclamation of Neutrality, Apr. 22, 1793, Fitzpatrick, ed., *Washington*, XXXII, 430–431).

27. T. Jefferson to J. Monroe, July 14, 1793, Ford, ed., *Jefferson*, VI, 346–350.

28. Journal of Proceedings of the President, Apr. 22, 1793, reprinted in Fitzpatrick, ed., *Washington*, XXXII, 431n.

29. *Ibid.*

30. Jefferson's "Opinion on French Treaties," Apr. 28, 1793, Ford, ed., *Jefferson*, VI, 219–231, quote on 220.

31. A. Hamilton and H. Knox to G. Washington, Philadelphia, May 2, 1793, *Hamilton*, XIV, 367–396.

32. Hamilton had discussed the treaty and the alternatives that were open to the government with King and Jay early in April. He wrote to Jay twice on Apr. 9. Both men submitted their views before May 2, and each had suggested that it might be best, at least for the present, to adopt a policy short of declaring the treaty void. Their letters seem to have influenced him to the point of advocating a policy of suspension (A. Hamilton to J. Jay, Philadelphia, Apr. 9, 1793 [2 letters], J. Jay to A. Hamilton, New York, Apr. 11, 1793, R. King to A. Hamilton, Apr. 24, 1793, *Hamilton*, XIV, 297–300, 307–308, 335–337).

33. A. Hamilton and H. Knox to G. Washington, Philadelphia, May 2, 1793, *ibid.*, 367–396.

34. *Ibid.*

35. Journal of Proceedings of the President, May 3, 1793, Washington MSS.

36. The opinion is partially in the hand of ER and partially in the hand of three clerks who were called into service to copy whole sections from Vattel. The haste with which it was prepared is evident on almost every page of the opinion, although it should be noted that the quoted sections from Vattel were read and corrected by ER before being inserted into the opinion (ER to G. Washington, [Philadelphia?], May 6, 1793, Washington MSS).

37. *Ibid.*

38. *Ibid.*

39. Hamilton sent Washington a circular on May 4 which he proposed to transmit to the collectors of the customs (A. Hamilton to G. Washington, Philadelphia [May 3, 1793?], *Hamilton*, XIV, 412–414.

40. *Ibid.* No copy of the circular that accompanied this letter of May 3 has been found. The outlines of Hamilton's plan must be reconstructed from Jefferson's comments on the same during the time it was under debate (entry in "Anas,"

May 6, 1793, Ford, ed., *Jefferson*, I, 227–228; T. Jefferson to ER, Philadelphia, May 8, 1793, T. Jefferson to J. Madison, May 12, 1793, *ibid.*, VI, 244–246, 250–252).

41. G. Washington to A. Hamilton, Philadelphia, May 5, 1793, Fitzpatrick, ed., *Washington*, XXXII, 447–448.

42. *Ibid.*, G. Washington to A. Hamilton, Philadelphia, May 7, 1793, *ibid.*, 451. In this second letter Washington mentioned that he had spoken to the Attorney General and then queried Hamilton: "Is it not expedient that the District Attornies [*sic*] should be written to, requiring their attention to the observance of the injunctions of the Proclamation?" This procedure was to be the one outlined by ER in the Cabinet meeting on May 7.

43. Evident from T. Jefferson to ER, Philadelphia, May 8, 1793, Ford, ed., *Jefferson*, VI, 244–246, and ER to T. Jefferson, May 9, 1793, Jefferson MSS.

44. T. Jefferson to ER, Philadelphia, May 8, 1793, Ford, ed., *Jefferson*, VI, 244–246.

45. ER to T. Jefferson, May 9, 1793, Jefferson MSS.

46. Journal of Proceedings of the President, May 10, 1793, Washington MSS.

47. For Jefferson's views on ER's role in the formation of a plan to preserve our neutrality, see T. Jefferson to J. Madison, Philadelphia, May 12, 1793, Ford, ed., *Jefferson*, VI, 250–252.

48. Thomas B. Adams to Abigail Adams, Philadelphia, May 5, 1793, Adams Papers, MHS.

49. Treaty of Amnity and Commerce, Feb. 6, 1778, in Miller, ed., *Treaties of the U.S.*, II, 3–29 (Article 17 is on 16–17).

50. G. Hammond to T. Jefferson, Philadelphia, May 2, 1793, Jefferson MSS.

51. Journal of Proceedings of the President, May 3, 1793, Washington MSS.

It is worth noting that this was the same day ER was urged to hasten his opinion on the question of receiving the new French minister and on whether the French treaties ought to be suspended.

52. T. Jefferson to Jean Baptiste Ternant, Philadelphia, May 3, 1793, Ford, ed., *Jefferson*, VI, 236–237.

53. T. Jefferson to G. Hammond, Philadelphia, May 3, 1793, *ibid.*, 236.

54. G. Hammond to T. Jefferson, Philadelphia, May 8, 1793, Jefferson MSS.

55. *Ibid.*

56. Journal of Proceedings of the President, May 10, 1793, Washington MSS.

57. ER to T. Jefferson, Philadelphia, May 14, 1793, *ASP For. Rel.*, I, 148–149.

58. *Ibid.*

59. Freeman (Carroll & Ashworth), *Washington*, VII, 66–67n lists the papers that Washington transmitted to the Cabinet.

60. Journal of Proceedings of the President, May 15, 1793, Washington MSS; T. Jefferson to G. Hammond, Philadelphia, May 15, 1793, Ford, ed., *Jefferson*, VI, 252–254.

61. T. Jefferson to J. B. Ternant, May 15, 1793, *ibid.*, 254–257.

62. Hammond's complaint was contained in his letter of May 8.

63. Journal of Proceedings of the President, May 16, 1793, Washington MSS.

64. T. Jefferson to G. Hammond, Philadelphia, May 15, 1793, Ford, ed., *Jefferson*, VI, 252–254.

65. A. Hamilton to G. Washington, Philadelphia, May 15, 1793, *Hamilton*, XIV, 454–460, quote on 458.

66. H. Knox to G. Washington, Philadelphia, May 16, 1793, Washington MSS.

67. T. Jefferson to G. Washington, Philadelphia, May 16, 1793, Ford, ed., *Jefferson*, VI, 257–259. See also Jefferson's comments in "Anas," *ibid.*, I, 229–230.

68. ER's opinion is dated May 17 (ER to G. Washington, May 17, 1793, Washington MSS). An entry in the Journal of Proceedings of the President implies ER's opinion was received on the 16th, along with the opinions of the other Cabinet members, but a portion of the entry under this date appears to have been inserted later. It seems safe to conclude that Washington did not have ER's opinion until the 17th (Journal of Proceedings of the President, May 16, 1793, Washington MSS).

69. ER to G. Washington, May 17, 1793, Washington MSS.

70. No written record of the request has been found but the existence of written instructions on this matter can be established from the opening lines of ER's reply (ER to G. Washington, May 18, 1793, Washington MSS).

71. ER's reply again establishes the fact that Washington called at his home (*ibid.*).

72. *Ibid.*

73. The evidence here is fragmentary. The only record of Washington's ultimate decision on the subject is the last two lines of Jefferson's May 20th entry in the "Anas," which is largely devoted to summarizing his own views on the subject. It reads: "ER for ordering away the privateer and nothing more. The President confirmed the last opinion [ER's] and it seemed to be his own." (Entry in "Anas," May 20, 1793, Ford, ed., *Jefferson*, I, 229–230.)

   At about the same time ER ordered the federal district attorney in Maryland to prosecute American citizens who participated in taking prizes while in the service of France (Journal of Proceedings of the President, May 21, 1793, Washington MSS).

74. Freeman (Carroll & Ashworth), Washington, VII, 71–77, provides a brief summary of the events surrounding his arrival in Philadelphia. Jefferson's description, though brief, is also interesting as a measure of his disenchantment with the government's policy (T. Jefferson to J. Madison, Philadelphia, May 19, 1793, Ford, ed., *Jefferson*, VI, 259–262.

75. E. Genêt to T. Jefferson, Philadelphia, May 27, 1793, *ASP For. Rel.*, I, 149–150.

76. Journal of Proceedings of the President, May 31, 1793, Washington MSS, and Jefferson's memorandum on the Cabinet meeting of June 1, 1793, Jefferson MSS.

77. Genêt's first letter of protest against the arrest of Henfield was dated May 27. It has not been found although its existence can be established from Jefferson's letter of acknowledgement (T. Jefferson to E. Genêt, Philadelphia, June 1, 1793, *ASP For. Rel.*, I, 151). Genêt's second letter, dated May 29, and quoted here, is E. Genêt to T. Jefferson, Philadelphia, May 29, 1793, Genêt MSS. Jefferson's letter of June 1 has a "P.S." acknowledging Genêt's *second* letter.

78. ER to T. Jefferson, Philadelphia, May 30, 1793, *ASP For. Rel.*, I, 152.

79. T. Jefferson to E. Genêt, Philadelphia, June 1, 1793, Ford, ed., *Jefferson*, VI, 273–274, 274n. ER's comments on the first draft of Jefferson's letter are in ER to T. Jefferson, May 31, 1793, Jefferson MSS. The evidence is that Hamilton, more than ER, influenced the final wording of Jefferson's letter.

80. There were no written instructions, although Jefferson observed to Madison: "I have no doubt he [ER] is charged to bring back a faithful statement of the disposition of that state [i.e. Virginia]." T. Jefferson to J. Madison, Philadelphia, June 2, 1793, Ford, ed., *Jefferson*, VI, 277–279.

81. Journal of Proceedings of the President, June 6, 1793, Washington MSS.

82. ER to G. Washington, Annapolis, Md., June 11, 1793, Washington MSS.

   Smith, a Federalist and correspondent of Hamilton's, had been recently elected to Congress. For biographical data, see *DAB*, *s.v.* "Smith, Col. Samuel."

   On May 31 Washington's Journal of Proceedings of the President notes the receipt from Hamilton of several letters, including one from Col. S. Smith, that had been sent to the Secretary of the Treasurer from Baltimore. These letters, voicing concern over the activities of French privateers, were turned over to ER by Washington (Journal of Proceedings of the President, May 31, 1793, Washington MSS). ER passed them along to Jefferson and urged they be made the subject of a Cabinet meeting the next day (ER to Tobias Lear, May 31, 1793, Jefferson MSS and ER to T. Jefferson, May 31, 1793, *ibid.*). In his May 31st letter to Jefferson ER said:

   > Perhaps it may not be amiss [for the Cabinet] to authorize me to say *informally* to Col. Smith, as I pass thro' Baltimore, that the President will, at the next session of Congress, recommend the suppression of the sale of prizes in our ports. (*Ibid.*)

   Jefferson's memorandum on the Cabinet meeting of June 1 summarizes the government's position and then concludes:

—that as the Attorney General is to pass through Baltimore shortly, it is better that this answer be given verbally to him [i.e. Smith] . . . also that they [i.e. those who sent letters from Baltimore] be informed that measures are taken for punishing such citizens as have engaged in hostilities by sea against nations at peace with the U.S. (Jefferson's memorandum of Cabinet Meeting of [June 1], 1793, Jefferson MSS.)

83. ER to G. Washington, Annapolis, Md., June 11, 1793, Washington MSS. ER underlined the word "style."

84. *Ibid.*

85. *Ibid.* Chase, one of the leading political figures in Maryland, had opposed the Constitution. By 1793 he was a Federalist and pro-English. His support of the Neutrality Proclamation was considered highly significant. For biographical data, see *DAB, s.v.* "Chase, Samuel."

86. ER to G. Washington, Annapolis, Md., June 11, 1793, Washington MSS.

Joshua Clayton, a physican, was governor of Delaware from 1789–1796. Maj. Edward Oldham (1756–1798) was a delegate from Cecile County, Maryland.

87. *Ibid.*

Brown was a lifelong friend of Jefferson and a leading political figure in Kentucky at this time.

88. ER to G. Washington, Richmond, June 24, 1793, Washington MSS.

The governor of Maryland at this time was Thomas Sim Lee, a prominent Federalist in the state. Washington, it should be noted, was absent from Philadelphia from June 24 to July 11 (Freeman [Carroll & Ashworth], Washington, VII, 96–100).

89. ER to G. Washington, Richmond, June 24, 1793, Washington MSS.

Alexander Henderson had served in the Virginia House of Delegates in 1783, 1784–1785 and again in 1789–1790. He was one of Virginia's commissioners to the so-called Mount Vernon Conference in Mar., 1785. The "prosecution of John Singletary" refers to the individual who was arrested by the district attorney of Pennsylvania, along with Gideon Henfield, for serving on a French vessel in direct violation of our neutrality. Pendleton had been John Taylor's mentor and ER obviously assumed Pendleton was the most appropriate person to correct Taylor's "gross errors."

90. *Ibid.*

91. Knox makes mention of ER's being in the city on the 19th (H. Knox to Tobias Lear, Philadelphia, July 19, 1793, Washington MSS). There was an important Cabinet meeting on the 18th and ER was *not* present. This suggests he did not return until the 19th.

92. A series of articles by "Verita" criticized Washington's foreign policy. They appeared in Freneau's paper early in June (*National Gazette*, June 1–12, 1793). Their authorship is doubtful but Freneau seems to have been largely responsible for them. Jefferson maintained the articles were written by William Irvine, a clerk in the Comptroller's office (entry in "Anas," June 12, 1793, Ford, ed., *Jefferson*, I, 234–235). Between June 29 and July 20 Hamilton published seven "Pacifus" articles in the *Gazette of the United States* in defense of the Administration and the Neutrality Proclamation. They have been reprinted in *Hamilton*, XV, 33–43, 55–63, 65–69, 82–86, 90–95, 100–106, 130–135.

93. T. Jefferson to J. Madison, Philadelphia, June 21, 1793, Ford, ed., *Jefferson*, VI, 353–355.

94. The fullest treatment of this incident and the government's reaction thereto, can be found in Thomas, *Am. Neutrality*, 137–144.

95. Evident from "Anas," July 13, 1793, Ford, ed., *Jefferson*, I, 243.

96. Jefferson's memorandum on the Cabinet meeting of July 12, 1793, Ford, ed., *Jefferson*, VI, 344–345; Journal of Proceedings of the President, July 18, 1793, Washington MSS.

97. The questions as submitted to the judges may be found in Fitzpatrick, ed.,

Washington, XXXIII, 15–19. For a full discussion of the subject and an evaluation of its significance see Thomas, *Am. Neutrality*, 147–149.

98. Entry in "Anas," July 23, 1793, Ford, ed., *Jefferson*, I, 246–248. Jefferson's summary is the only source of information for this Cabinet meeting and his accounts of these meetings are beginning to reflect his annoyance with those who disagreed with him politically.

99. ER to G. Washington, [July 24, 1793], Washington MSS.

100. G. Washington to T. Jefferson, Philadelphia, July 25, 1793, Fitzpatrick, ed., *Washington*, XXXIII, 28–29.

101. "Notes Given to the President, July 26, 1793," Ford, ed., *Jefferson*, I, 248–250.

102. Entry in "Anas," Aug. 1, 1793, *ibid.*, I, 252–253, and Journal of Proceedings of the President, Aug. 1, 1793, Washington MSS.

103. Entry in "Anas," Aug. 2, 1793, Ford, ed., *Jefferson*, I, 253–254. It again must be noted that Jefferson's summary, the only detailed account available, is far from unbiased.

Other items of lesser import were discussed at this meeting, although Jefferson, obsessed with this issue, makes no note of them. See Journal of Proceedings of the President, Aug. 2, 1793, Washington MSS.

104. T. Jefferson to J. Madison, [Philadelphia], Aug. 3, 1793, Ford, ed., *Jefferson*, VI, 361–362.

105. G. Washington to The Heads of Departments and the Attorney General, Philadelphia, July 29, 1793, Fitzpatrick, ed., *Washington*, XXXIII, 34.

106. Entry in "Anas," July 29, 1793, Ford, ed., *Jefferson*, I, 250–252. Although Jefferson inserted the word "Agreed" in front of two of the rules proposed by Hamilton, his subsequent summary of the meeting suggests that only one of Hamilton's rules was approved at this meeting.

107. Entry in "Anas," July 30, 1793, *ibid.*

108. The best reprint of the rules can be found in Ford, ed., *Jefferson*, VI, 358*n*–359*n*. Washington's immediate approval is noted in G. Washington to T. Jefferson, Philadelphia, Aug. 4, 1793, Fitzpatrick, ed., *Washington*, XXXIII, 37–38.

109. G. Washington to The Heads of Departments and the Attorney General, Philadelphia, Aug. 3, 1793, Fitzpatrick, ed., *Washington*, XXXIII, 35–36.

110. ER to G. Washington, [Philadelphia], Aug. 3–[5], 1793, Washington MSS.

111. H. Knox to G Washington, War Department, Aug. 5, 1793, Washington MSS. A. Hamilton to G. Washington, Philadelphia, Aug. 5, 1793, *Hamilton*, XV, 194–195. Washington's position as reported by Jefferson is in T. Jefferson to J. Madison, [Philadelphia], Aug. 11, 1793, Ford, ed., *Jefferson*, VI, 367–370.

CHAPTER 17

1. A comparatively recent, though not always accurate, account of the yellow fever is J. H. Powell, *Bring Out Your Dead*, 1–24 *passim*.

2. Charles F. Jenkins, *The Guidebook to Historic Germantown*, 130, and C. F. Jenkins, ed., *Jefferson's Germantown Letters*, xvi.

3. On Aug. 26 Jefferson noted ER's absence from the city, observing that he would return "tomorrow" (T. Jefferson to G. Washington, Aug. 26, 1793, Washington MSS). ER signed the minutes of a Cabinet meeting of Aug. 31 (Cabinet Minutes, Aug. 31, 1793, Washington MSS), but on the following day he addressed a letter to Jefferson from Germantown which indicated he had been in residence there for more than one night (ER to T. Jefferson, Germantown, Sept. 1, 1793, Jefferson MSS). It therefore seems safe to conclude that ER moved his family to Germantown during the latter part of Aug., and traveled into the city only to conduct official business.

4. Powell, *Bring Out Your Dead*, 108–109.

5. T. Jefferson to J. Madison [Gray's Ferry?], Penn., Sept. 1, 1793, Ford, ed., *Jefferson*, VI, 401–404.

6. Washington left Philadelphia on Sept. 10 (Journal of Proceedings of the President,

Sept. 10, 1793, Washington MSS). After Sept. 1 all ER's letters carried the word "Spencers" or "Germantown" in the dateline. The illness of Hamilton and his wife is discussed in Mitchell, *Hamilton*, II, 281–283.

7. ER notes imminent departure for Lancaster and the "anxieties of my family" in ER to G. Washington, "Spencer's," [Germantown, Pennsylvania], Oct. 13, 1793, Washington MSS.

8. ER to G. Washington, Spencer's, Oct. 22, 1793, *ibid.*

9. ER's request has not been found, but Jefferson's reply indicates he had sent Jefferson a bill and asked him to cover it. Jefferson refused (T. Jefferson to ER, Philadelphia, Aug. 5, 1793, Jefferson MSS).

10. ER to A. Hamilton, Philadelphia, Apr. 3, 1793, *Hamilton*, XIV, 278–279. Other fragmentary evidence of ER's financial embarrassment can be found in ER to John Kean, Philadelphia, Aug. 9, 1793, Edmund Randolph Misc. Papers, NYPL, and ER to Edward Fox, [Philadelphia], Aug. 2, 1793, Myer Collection, NYPL.

11. ER to Henry Drinker, Spencer's, Sept. 30, 1793, Henry S. Drinker Papers, HSP.

12. Note by Drinker at the bottom of ER's letter, *ibid.*

13. ER to Wilson Cary Nicholas, Germantown, Dec. 7, 1793, Wilson Cary Nicholas II, University of Virginia.

14. ER to G. Washington, Spencer's, Oct. 22, 1793, Washington MSS.

15. ER raised the issue of Congress meeting outside of Philadelphia in a letter of Oct. 13 (ER to G. Washington, Spencer's Oct. 13, 1793, Washington MSS). On Oct. 14, 1793, Washington, writing from Mount Vernon, addressed himself to the same problem (G. Washington to ER, Mount Vernon, Oct. 14, 1793, Fitzpatrick, ed., *Washington*, XXXIII, 125–127.

16. *Ibid.*

17. G. Washington to T. Jefferson, Mount Vernon, Oct. 11, 1793, G. Washington to Jonathan Trumbull, Mount Vernon, Oct. 13, 1793, G. Washington to A. Hamilton, Mount Vernon, Oct. 14, 1793, G. Washington to J. Madison, Mount Vernon, Oct. 14, 1793, G. Washington to H. Knox, Mount Vernon, Oct. 15, 1793, *ibid.*, 116–131 *passim.*

18. T. Jefferson to G. Washington, Monticello, Oct. 17, 1793, Ford, ed., *Jefferson*, VI, 435–436; J. Madison to G. Washington, Orange, Oct. 24, 1793, Hunt, ed., *Madison*, VI, 203.

19. A. Hamilton to G. Washington, "2½ miles from Philadelphia," Oct. 24, 1793, *Hamilton*, XV, 373–376. Jefferson takes note of Knox's agreement with Hamilton in a letter he wrote to Madison the day after he arrived in Germantown (T. Jefferson to J. Madison, Germantown, Nov. 2, 1793, Ford, ed., *Jefferson*, VI, 438–440).

20. ER to G. Washington, Spencer's, Oct. 24, 1793, Washington MSS.

21. "A Proclamation . . . ," enclosure in ER to G. Washington, Spencer's, Oct. 24, 1793, *ibid.*

22. ER to G. Washington, Spencer's, Oct. 26, 1793, *ibid.*

23. ER to G. Washington, Spencer's, Oct. 28, 1793, *ibid.*

24. Journal of Proceedings of the President [an entry beneath the entry for "Oct. 10, 1793"], Washington MSS.

25. ER to G. Washington, [Spencer's], Nov. 2, 1793, *ibid.* See letter of Oct. 24, *ibid.*

26. As reported by Tench Coxe to J. Adams, "Near Philadelphia," Nov. 3, 1793, Adams Papers, MHS.

27. Evident from entry in "Anas," Sept. 4, 1793, Ford, ed., *Jefferson*, I, 263–265.

28. Freeman (Carroll & Ashworth), *Washington*, VII, 135–136.

29. Anthony Wayne to H. Knox, "Hobson's Choice, near Fort Washington," Oct. 5, 1793, *ASP Ind. Aff.*, I, 360–361. The details surrounding the northwestern frontier difficulties are in Burt, *U.S., Gt. Br. and Br. N. Am.*, 125–132, and Bemis, *Jay's Treaty*, 161–175.

30. Hammond had refused to discuss the treaty of 1783 as recently as Nov. 22, 1793 (T. Jefferson to George Hammond, Germantown, Nov. 13, 1793, and G. Hammond to T. Jefferson, Lansdown, Nov. 22, 1793, both letters in *ASP For. Rel.*, I, 238). The tortured course of Anglo-American negotiations has been summarized in Bemis,

Jay's Treaty, 134–160. See also S. F. Bemis, "The London Mission of Thomas Pinckney, 1792–1796," *AHR*, XXVII, 228–247.

31. Genêt's exploits are colorfully summarized in Minnigerode, *Genêt*, 245–337 *passim*.
32. Entry in "Anas," Nov. 8, 1793, Ford, ed., *Jefferson*, I, 265–266. Washington's six-day trip (Nov. 11–16) to Philadelphia, Lancaster and Reading is traced in Freeman (Carroll & Ashworth), *Washington*, VII, 141.
33. ER to G. Washington, Spencer's, Nov. 10, 1793, Washington MSS.
The "essay by Agricola" was one of a series by James Monroe urging Virginians to support France.
34. ER to G. Washington, Spencer's, Nov. 10, 1793, Washington MSS.
35. Entry in "Anas," Nov. 28, 1793, Ford, ed., *Jefferson*, I, 266–268. It should be noted that the Washington MSS contain an outline, undated, of the subjects ER felt should be communicated to Congress (ER to G. Washington, [Nov. 1793?], Washington MSS).
36. The Cabinet met on Nov. 18, 21 and 23 in preparation for the opening of Congress.
37. Entry in "Anas," Nov. 18, 1793, Ford, ed., *Jefferson*, I, 266–268.
38. *Ibid.* For an interesting evaluation of Genêt's political influence at this time see John Q. Adams to Thomas B. Adams, Boston, Nov. 20, 1793, Adams Papers, MHS.
39. Entries in "Anas," for Nov. 8 and Nov. 18, 1793, Ford, ed., *Jefferson*, I, 265–266, 266–268.
40. ER's draft, seemingly incomplete, is ER to G. Washington, [Nov. 1793?], Washington MSS. Hamilton's draft, labeled "President's Speech," is published in *Hamilton*, XV, 430–432.
41. Entry in "Anas," Nov. 21, 1793, Ford, ed., *Jefferson*, I, 268–269.
42. Entry in "Anas," Nov. 23, 1793, *ibid.*, 269–270. The Ford edition has a slight but significant error in the last sentence of the entry for Nov. 23, 1793, which has been rather widely repeated. Ford's printed version of the "Anas" states that ER would draft the speech and the special messages. The manuscript reads: "It was agreed that Rand. should draw the speech and I [Jefferson] the messages" (Jefferson's Memoranda of Cabinet Sessions of Nov. 8, 18, 21, 23, 1793, Jefferson MSS). The difference is significant, for if Washington assigned the special messages to ER it would be irrefutable evidence that he did not have sufficient confidence in Jefferson to allow him to draft messages dealing with purely diplomatic matters. Such was obviously not the case. To assign ER the task of drafting the speech, while evidence of Washington's confidence in him, was also rather natural. At this point it was apparently assumed that the major function of the opening speech would be to explain the Neutrality Proclamation, and ER was its principal author and the most ardent advocate of its enforcement without preference or sympathy for English or French interests.
43. Entry in "Anas," Nov. 28, 1793, Ford, ed., *Jefferson*, I, 270–272. This draft by ER has not been found. An outline or sketch of a speech in ER's hand that corresponds very closely to the final address to Congress is in the Washington MSS ("Heads of matter to be communicated to Congress . . . ," [Dec., 1793?], Washington MSS). It was probably written late in Nov. rather than in Dec.
44. The only record of this evening session is in Jefferson's, "Anas" and its reliability is questionable since it implies that everyone was against him ("Anas," Nov. 28, 1793, Ford, ed., *Jefferson*, I, 270–272).
45. Washington's address is in Fitzpatrick, ed., *Washington*, XXXIII, 163–169. The section on the proclamation adhered to: ER to G. Washington, [Nov., 1793], Washington MSS. The overall structure follows closely ER's "Heads of matter to be communicated to Congress . . . ," [Dec. 1793?], *ibid.*
46. To the Senate and House of Representatives, Dec. 5, 1793, Fitzpatrick, ed., *Washington*, XXXIII, 170–173. The special messages on Spain and the Barbary States were withheld until Dec. 16 in order that dispatches from overseas might be included (Freeman [Carroll & Ashworth], *Washington*, VII, 144, 144n).
47. A photocopy of the letter from Jay and King to the printer is in Minnigerode, *Genêt*, opp. 320. It is dated, New York, Aug. 12, 1793. A copy of this letter in

King's hand is in the Rufus King MSS, NYHS. It contains two additional notes dated "Nov. 1793" and "Nov. 20, 1793." (For the [New York] *Diary*, Aug. 12 [and subsequent entries], 1793, *ibid.*)

48. Excerpts of this letter have also been printed in Minnigerode, *Genêt*, 322–326.
49. T. Jefferson to E. Genêt, Philadelphia, Aug. 16, 1793, Genêt MSS.
50. E. Genêt to ER, New York, Nov. 14, 1793, and ER to E. Genêt, Germantown, Nov. 19, 1793, Genêt MSS.
51. The exact date of Genêt's return to Philadelphia is difficult to establish. On Dec. 12 Jay, in a letter to King, observed: "Genêt is by this time at Philadelphia" (J. Jay to R. King, New York, Dec. 12, 1793, Rufus King MSS, NYHS). ER visited Genêt at his lodgings on the evening of Dec. 13 (ER to E. Genêt, [Dec. 13, 1793], Genêt MSS).
52. E. Genêt to ER, Philadelphia, Dec. 16, 1793, Genêt MSS.
53. T. Jefferson to ER, Philadelphia, Dec. 18, 1793, Jefferson MSS. The wording of this letter, plus the fact that it was sent to Washington for prior approval (T. Jefferson to G. Washington, Dec. 18, 1793, Jefferson MSS), establishes beyond question that the instructions were Washington's and Jefferson was merely carrying out the wishes of the President.
54. ER to E. Genêt, Dec. 18, 1793, Genêt MSS.
55. Ibid. The postscript is dated Dec. 20, 1793.
56. G. Washington to ER, Philadelphia, Dec. 24, 1793, Fitzpatrick, ed., *Washington*, XXXIII, 216.
57. Washington's displeasure with both Jefferson and Hamilton over their intended resignations has been carefully traced in Freeman (Carroll & Ashworth), *Washington*, VII, 3–4, 91, 114–115, 145–146.
58. The details of this meeting must, unfortunately, be reconstructed entirely from Jefferson's "Anas," Aug. 6, 1793, Ford, ed., *Jefferson*, I, 256–259. The full names of the individuals mentioned have, of course, been supplied.
59. Although Jefferson's summary of his conversation with Washington on Aug. 6 makes no mention of a delay in the date of his resignation, an explicit promise to remain until the end of the year was made on Aug. 10, and put in writing on Aug. 11 (see language of T. Jefferson to G. Washington, Philadelphia, Aug. 11, 1793, Ford, ed., *Jefferson*, VI, 366–367). Washington's acknowledgment of this letter reflects his displeasure and regret over Jefferson's resignation (G. Washington to T. Jefferson, Philadelphia, Aug. 12, 1793, Fitzpatrick, ed., *Washington*, XXXIII, 45).
60. ER knew of Jefferson's plans at least by Aug. 5 (T. Jefferson to ER, Philadelphia, Aug. 5, 1793, Jefferson MSS).
61. ER to G. Washington, Germantown, Dec. 24, 1793, Washington MSS.
62. T. Jefferson to G. Washington, Philadelphia, Dec. 31, 1793, Ford, ed., Jefferson, VI, 496. The letter nominating ER and the action of the Senate thereon can be found in the *Journal of the Executive Proceedings of the Senate*, I, 144.

CHAPTER 18

1. ER to G. Washington, Philadelphia, Jan, 2, 1794, Misc. Letters, Dept. State, NA.
2. *Ibid.*
3. A copy of this letter was enclosed in ER's letter of Jan. 2 to G. Washington, *ibid.*
4. *Ibid.*
5. Malone's volumes amply document Jefferson's administrative talents as Secretary of State and take note of his particular sensitivity to the disadvantages under which our ministers in Europe labored (Malone, *Jefferson*, II and III, *passim*). Graham Stuart's study of the Department notes that in spite of Hamilton's constant opposition, Jefferson did a "superb job" as an administrative head and his "relations with our representatives abroad were highly felicitous" (Graham Stuart, *The Department of State*, 20).
6. The clerks of the department were reassembled in mid-Nov. in Philadelphia while Jefferson worked in Germantown with one clerk. A large part of their work con-

sisted in the preparation of the documents that would accompany Washington's special messages to Congress on France and England. By the first week in December the department was again functioning as a single unit, with Jefferson's energies being given to the final preparation of his report on commerce and the preparation of another long message to Congress on our relations with Spain (Malone, *Jefferson*, III, 146–160 *passim*).

7. ER to G. Washington, Philadelphia, Jan. 4, 1794, State Dept. Letterbook, Washington MSS. The same day he also asked Washington to examine the list of subjects that remained to be acted upon by the department and indicate with numerals the order of preference with which he would like to see them handled (ER to G. Washington, Philadelphia, Jan. 4, 1794, *ibid.*).

8. Journal of Proceedings of the President, Jan. 10, 1794, Washington MSS. The letters in question were ER to Thomas Pinckney, Philadelphia, Jan. 10, 1794, Hampton L. Carson Collection, Free Library of Philadelphia; ER to Messrs. Carmichael and Short, Philadelphia, Jan. 10, 1794, ER to William Short, Esq., Philadelphia, Jan. 10, 1794, ER to David Humphreys, Philadelphia, Jan. 10, 1794, and ER to Gouverneur Morris, Philadelphia, Jan. 10, 1794, all in Dipl. & Cons. Inst., Dept. State, NA.

9. Journal of Proceedings of the President, Jan. 10, 1794, Washington MSS.

10. *Philadelphia Directory and Register* . . . , 2nd ed. (Philadelphia, 1794), 125.

11. ER to G. Washington, Philadelphia, Jan. 25, 1794, Washington MSS.

12. ER to G. Washington, Philadelphia, Jan. 4, 1794, and Jan. 31, 1794, State Dept. Letterbook, Washington MSS.

13. ER to G. Washington, Philadelphia, Jan. 8, 1794, *ibid.* The report itself was not copied into the Letterbook.

14. In 1790 Jefferson sought an appropriation from Congress to hire five clerks, a French interpreter and two messengers (Stuart, *Department of State*, 22). It is probably safe to assume the department was at least that size when ER took control.

15. Lafayette, disillusioned by the extremes of the Revolution, had abandoned his command and fled to Belgium, where he was seized by the Austrians and confined to a fortress in Westphalia. He was later transferred to Magdeburg, where he became the responsibility of the King of Prussia (Brant Whitlock, *Lafayette*, II, 11–39 *passim*). On Jan. 14 Washington raised the question of how best to effect his release (Cabinet Minutes, Jan. 14, 1794, Washington MSS). He asked James Marshall, John Marshall's brother, to undertake the negotiations for Lafayette's release. Marshall would work under Pinckney's direction. Pinckney was instructed to initiate negotiations only if he was assured of success (ER to T. Pinckney, Philadelphia, Jan. 16, 1794, Dipl. & Cons. Inst., Dept. State, NA). No effort was actually made to secure Lafayette's release until May of 1796 (Freeman [Carroll & Ashworth], *Washington*, VII, 379).

16. *Annals*, IV, 38 (Senate).

17. Fisher Ames to Christopher Gore, Philadelphia, Jan. 28, 1794, Ames, ed., *Works of Ames*, II, 133–134.

18. ER to G. Washington, Philadelphia, Jan. 25, 1794, Washington MSS.

19. ER to G. Washington, Philadelphia, Jan. 26, 1794, Washington MSS.

20. Cabinet Minutes, Jan. 28, 1794, Washington MSS.

21. William Bradford was appointed on Jan. 27 (Journal of Proceedings of the President, Jan. 27, 1794, Washington MSS). Prior to this he had served as justice of the Supreme Court of Pennsylvania. *DAB, s.v.* "Bradford, William."

22. W. Bradford to G. Washington, [?], [Jan., 1794], Washington MSS.

23. ER to G. Washington, [Jan. 29, 1794?], Washington MSS.

24. *Ibid.*

25. ER to G. Washington, [Jan., 1794], Washington MSS.

26. ER to G. Washington, Feb. 2, 1794, *ibid.*

27. G. Washington to the Senate, United States, Feb. 26, 1794, Fitzpatrick, ed., *Washington*, XXXIII, 282.

28. ER to G. Washington, Feb. 26, 1794, Washington MSS.

29. Washington so informed Congress on Jan. 20 (G. Washington to the Senate and House of Representatives, United States, Jan. 20, 1794, Fitzpatrick, ed., *Washington*, XXXIII, 245–246)

On Jan. 14 Washington had transmitted to Congress evidence that Genêt had attempted to raise a military force in South Carolina (*ASP For. Rel.* I, 309–311). Surrounding the transmission of this information were two significant documents indicative of Washington's contemplation of a more vigorous policy against Genêt. The Washington MSS contain a draft by Hamilton of a message to Congress announcing the President's intention to terminate his diplomatic appointment immediately ("Draft of the Secretary of the Treasury," [Jan., 1794], Washington MSS). The Washington MSS also contain two incomplete drafts of letters of ER to Genêt demanding, among other things, an explanation of his conduct in the light of the evidence that had been received from South Carolina (ER draft of a proposed letter to Genêt, Jan. 13, 1794 [2 letters], Washington MSS). Neither Hamilton's message nor ER's letters were used but they indicate that a firmer position was contemplated. A few days later Washington received word that Genêt was being replaced, which made further action unnecessary.

30. Genêt had looked forward to the opening of Congress in December with undisguised enthusiasm. He hoped that the Republicans in both houses would espouse his cause with such vigor as to force Washington to withdraw his request for Genêt's recall. The expected endorsement failed to materialize, however, and Genêt was left deserted at the very moment his replacement was embarking for America (Minnigerode, *Genêt*, 349–350; Freeman [Carroll & Ashworth], *Washington*, VII, 140 *passim*).

31. ER to G. Washington, Feb. 21, 1794, Washington MSS.

32. ER outlined the procedure to be followed in ER to G. Washington, Feb. 22, 1794, *ibid.* See also Journal of Proceedings of the President, Feb. 22, 1794, *ibid.*

33. ER to G. Washington, Feb. 21, 1794, *ibid.*

34. Madison, reflecting the opinion of many who knew what was happening in France, observed:

> Genêt has not taken any decided step in relation to his future movements. . . . If he is prudent he will not venture to France in her present temper, with all the suspicions and follies with which he is loaded. You must have seen that Brissot and his party have been cut off by the guillotine. (J. Madison to T. Jefferson, Philadelphia, Mar. 2, 1794, Madison MSS.)

35. Fauchet requested Genêt's arrest in his first meeting with ER (ER to G. Washington, Feb. 21, 1794, Washington MSS). ER told him his request must be in writing (*ibid.*). At their next meeting Fauchet seemingly ignored the subject of Genêt's arrest. As ER reported it to Washington: "When Fauchet speaks of Genêt, he slips over the instructions, which have been published, as lightly as possible. . . ." (ER to G. Washington, Feb. 23, 1794, *ibid.*) For Fauchet's account of his demand for Genêt's arrest, see Fauchet to Minister of Foreign Affairs, Philadelphia, Mar. 21, 1794, in Turner, ed., "CFM," *AHA Annual Report*, 1903, II, 306–317.

36. ER to G. Washington, Feb. 23, 1794, Washington MSS.

37. The most thorough analysis of this phase of Genêt's activities is R. K. Crandall, "Genêt's Projected Attack on Louisiana and The Floridas, 1793–1794" (Ph.D diss., University of Chicago, 1929).

38. James, *Clark*, 408–427.

39. Only Jefferson knew of the planned attack (entry in "Anas," July 5, 1793, Ford, ed., *Jefferson*, I, 236). Why he failed to inform Washington has never been satisfactorily explained; see Freeman (Carroll & Ashworth), *Washington*, VII, 102*n*, for a full discussion of the matter.

40. Joseph de Viar and Joseph de Jaudenes, joint commissioners of Spain to the United States, had informed Jefferson that four Frenchmen, furnished with money, commissions and instructions, had left Philadelphia for Kentucky to assist in the organization of forces to be used against the territories of Spain. Their letter, sent on Oct. 2 and received on Oct. 24, has not been found, but Jefferson's

acknowledgment of it summarizes its contents (T. Jefferson to Messrs. Viar and Jaudenes, Germantown, Nov. 6, 1793, C. F. Jenkins, ed., *Jefferson's Germantown Letters*, 39–40).

41. A report of the legislature of South Carolina, dated Nov. 6, 1793, and transmitted by Gov. William Moultrie to Washington, established beyond question the recruiting activities on behalf of the French government. It has been reprinted with the supporting documents in *ASP For. Rel.*, I, 309–311.

42. James, *Clark*, 423–426 *passim*, summarizes Clark's activities. His appeal through the press for volunteers in Jan. left little doubt of his intentions (*ibid.*). For an account of this matter as reported in Philadelphia, see George Thacher to John Hobby, Philadelphia, Mar. 3, 1794, Thacher Papers, MHS.

43. See *ASP For. Rel.*, I, 309–311.

44. Isaac Shelby to T. Jefferson, [i.e. ER], Kentucky, Jan. 13, 1794, *ASP For. Rel.*, I, 455–456.

45. Washington's draft of Feb 21 has not been found (Fitzpatrick, ed., *Washington*, XXXIII, 305n) but its existence can be established from a memorandum of transmittal from Bartholomew Dandridge, Washington's secretary, to ER (B. Dandridge to ER, Feb. 21. 1793, State Dept. Letterbook, Washington MSS).

46. See extract of letter Sen. John Brown of Kentucky sent to ER and which he, in turn, forwarded to Washington (ER to G. Washington, Feb. 27, 1794, State Dept. Letterbook, Washington MSS).

47. Typical of Federalist reaction to the reports reaching Philadelphia is Oliver Wolcott to Oliver Wolcott, Sr., Philadelphia, Mar. 2, 1794, Gibbs, ed., *Wolcott*, I, 129.
    The legislation, "An Act for the punishment of certain crimes against the United States," passed the Senate on Mar. 12, 1794 (*Annals*, IV, 67 [Senate]). In the House the Republicans succeeded in having the act laid aside on Mar. 14, after two readings (*Annals*, IV, 503–504 [House]).

48. A copy of Fauchet's proclamation may be found in the correspondence of Michel Mangouret, the French consul at Charleston, printed in *AHA, Annual Report, 1897*, 625. A few days earlier ER reported that Fauchet was "extremely frank in discussing his predecessor's conduct" (ER to G. Washington, Philadelphia, Mar. 1, 1794, State Dept. Letterbook, Washington MSS).

49. Cabinet Minutes, Mar. 10, 1794, Washington MSS.

50. ER to G. Washington, Philadelphia, Mar. 11, 1794, Washington MSS.

51. ER to G. Washington, Mar. 12, 1794, State Dept. Letterbook, Washington MSS. The letter of Viar and Jaudenes with its enclosure is published in *ASP For. Rel.*, I, 426–427

52. ER to G. Washington, Mar. 24, 1794, State Dept. Letterbook, Washington MSS. It was apparently circulated among the other "gentlemen" after the Cabinet meeting of Mar. 10. See also ER to G. Washington, Mar. 19, 1794, *ibid.*

53. Proclamation, City of Philadelphia, Mar. 24, 1794, Fitzpatrick, ed., *Washington*, XXXIII, 304–305.

54. Evident from George Thacher to John Hobby, [Philadelphia], Apr. 1, 1794, Thacher Papers, MHS.

55. ER to W. Short, Philadelphia, Mar. 16, 1794, Dipl. & Cons. Inst., Dept. State. NA.

56. Evident from ER to G. Washington, Mar. 15, 1794 [2 letters], State Dept. Letterbook, Washington MSS and ER to G. Washington, Mar. 16, 1794, *ibid.*

57. The removal of Gallatin, who was born in Switzerland, is fully discussed in: Henry Adams, *The Life of Albert Gallatin*, 114–120.

58. On Feb. 5 further discussion of Madison's resolutions was postponed until the first Monday in March (*Annals*, IV, 431 [House]). Typical of Federalist opinion on these resolutions is George Thacher to John Hobby, Philadelphia, Feb. 18, 1794, and Feb. 24, 1794, Thacher Papers, MHS.

59. The resolutions were not considered on Mar. 3, as agreed upon in the resolution of postponement of Feb. 5. Two days later ER's report was laid before Congress (*Annals*, IV, 63 [Senate], 480–481 [House]).

60. The report is ER to G. Washington, Philadelphia, Mar. 2, 1794, *ASP For. Rel.*, I, 423–424. It was transmitted to Congress three days later. For a contemporary

assessment of the seriousness of the situation see William Spotswood to Jeremy Belknap, Philadelphia, Mar. 20, 1794, Papers of Jeremy Belknap, MHS.
61. ER takes note of their publication in ER to Thomas Pinckney, Philadelphia, Mar. 8, 1794, Dipl. & Cons. Inst., Dept. State, NA.
62. The naval construction bill passed the House on Mar. 10 (*Annals*, IV, 492 [House]) and the Senate on Mar. 19 (*ibid.*, 71 [Senate]). The bill providing for an army appropriation of $1,629,936 (*cf. U.S. Statutes at Large*, I, 346–347) passed the House on Mar. 13 (*Annals*, IV, 504 [House]) and the Senate on Mar. 19 (*ibid.*, 72 [Senate]). The harbor fortification bill passed the House on Mar. 12 (*ibid.*, 499 [House]) and the Senate on Mar. 17 (*ibid.*, 70 [Senate]).

Madison's partisan account of the activities of Congress during the month of Mar. indicates the Republicans were acquiescing to this Federalist-sponsored legislation. In his letter of Mar. 26 he commented:

> The commercial propositions [i.e. his own] have not yet received a vote. The progress of the evils to which they were to remedy [*sic*], having called for more active medicine, it has not been deemed prudent to force them on the attention of the House during *more critical discussions* [emphasis mine]. (J. Madison to T. Jefferson, Philadelphia, Mar. 26, 1794, Madison MSS.)

See also J. Madison to T. Jefferson, Mar. 9, 12, 14 and 16, 1794, Madison MSS.

A Federalist account of the response of Congress to the latest intelligence may be found in George Thacher to John Hobby, Philadelphia, Mar. 11–12 and Mar. 19, 1794, Thacher Papers, MHS.
63. Washington received a copy of the speech from Gov. George Clinton of New York as an enclosure in a letter dated Mar. 20 (not found). ER, to whom the letter and speech were transmitted, returned them on Mar. 26 with the observation that the speech "is sufficiently promulgated in the newspapers" (ER to G. Washington, Mar. 26, 1794, Washington MSS). It would seem Washington had planned to release the speech for publication. ER's reply would indicate it already had wide circulation by the 26th of the month.

The speech to a delegation of western Indians implied that Great Britain and the United States would soon be involved in war. This, in turn, would permit the Indians to reoccupy their former lands. It has been printed in Ernest Cruikshank, ed., *The Correspondence of Lieutenant John Graves Simcoe* . . . , II, 149–150.
64. ER to T. Pinckney, Philadelphia, Mar. 8, 1794, Dipl. & Cons. Inst., Dept. State, NA.
65. Speculation along these lines was advanced as early as Mar. 9 (see J. Madison to T. Jefferson, Philadelphia, Mar. 9, 1794, Madison MSS).
66. A. Hamilton to G. Washington, [Philadelphia], Mar. 8, 1794, *Hamilton*, XVI, 130–136.
67. A memorandum kept by Sen. Rufus King records the fact that Sens. Oliver Ellsworth, George Cabot and Caleb Strong met in King's room on Mar. 10 and determined at that time to approach Washington with the suggestion that a special envoy be appointed. King, ed., *Correspondence of R. King*, I, 517.

This action seems to have been widely known in Philadelphia; see George Thacher to John Hobby, Mar. 19, 1794, Thacher Papers, MHS.
68. Reconstructed from King's memorandum (King, ed., *Correspondence of R. King*, I, 518).
69. ER to G. Washington, Philadelphia, Mar. 14, 1794, State Dept. Letterbook, Washington MSS.
70. Madison reported on Mar. 12 that "about a hundred vessels have been seized," noting that the merchants of New England were hardest hit. He continued:

> The partizans of England, considering a war as now probable, are endeavoring to take the lead in defensive preparations, and to acquire merit with the people by anticipating their wishes. (J. Madison to T. Jefferson, Philadelphia, Mar. 12, 1794, Madison MSS.)

71. Madison admitted this himself on Mar. 14, J. Madison to T. Jefferson, Philadelphia, Mar. 14, 1794, Madison MSS.
72. *Annals*, IV, 500–504 (House).
73. *Annals*, IV, 529–530 (House), 75–76 (Senate).
74. *Annals*, IV, 558 (House). Sedgwick's original resolution called for a force of fifteen thousand troops. The resolution, approved on Apr. 1, was for twenty-five thousand troops. Yet all Federalists did not view the war as inevitable. See George Thacher to George Pierson, Philadelphia, Mar. 31, 1794, Thacher Papers, MHS.
75. *Annals*, IV, 561 (House).
76. *Annals*, IV, 535–541 (House). Although the resolution was introduced by Jonathan Dayton of New Jersey, a Federalist, it had the immediate backing of Republicans John Francis Mercer of Maryland and William L. Smith of South Carolina. Dayton's colleagues in the Federalist party, by contrast, failed to speak in support of his resolution (*ibid.*).
77. These various investigations have been thoroughly treated in Mitchell, *Hamilton*, II, 245–286 *passim*.
78. The pertinent documents relating to this phase of the investigation are a part of the report submitted by the committee to the House on May 22, 1794. The entire report may be found in *ASP Fin.* I, 281–301, the material in question is found on 290–291.
79. Evident from ER to G. Washington, [Apr. 1, 1794], Washington MSS.
80. *Ibid.* The date of this memo, which has been variously given by others who examined this episode in the Washington Administration, appears to be Apr. 1. Some of the events which ER related in this letter occurred on Apr. 1, thereby ruling out an earlier date. On the other hand, it could not have been written later than Apr. 1 because ER wrote a second letter to Washington on Apr. 1 (ER to G. Washington, Apr. 1, 1794, State Dept. Letterbook, Washington MSS), which presumed Washington had received this memo.
81. *ASP Fin.*, I, 291.
82. Evident from Washington's reply, G. Washington to A. Hamilton, Apr. 8, 1794 [note], Washington MSS.
83. ER to G. Washington, Apr. 1, 1794 [2nd letter of this date], State Dept. Letterbook, Washington MSS.
84. G. Washington to A. Hamilton, United States, Apr. 8, 1794, Fitzpatrick, ed., *Washington*, XXXIII, 18.
85. A. Hamilton to G. Washington, Philadelphia, Apr. 8, 1794, *Hamilton*, XVI, 250–253.
86. An examination of the committee report fails to reveal any evidence that it probed further into the matter after receiving Washington's letter of Apr. 8.
87. G. Washington to A. Hamilton, Philadelphia, Apr. 22, 1794, Fitzpatrick, ed., *Washington*, XXXIII, 338.
88. Reconstructed from ER's reply, ER to G. Washington, Philadelphia, Apr. 27, 1794, Misc. Letters, Dept. State, NA.
89. G. Washington to A. Hamilton, Philadelphia, Apr. 27, 1794, Fitzpatrick, ed., *Washington*, XXXIII, 342.
90. Annals, IV, 80 [Senate], 560 [House]. The dispatch itself is T. Pinckney to ER, London, Jan. 9, 1794, *ASP For. Rel.*, I, 430. Pinckney's letter was received on Apr. 3 (ER to G. Washington, Apr. 3, 1794, State Dept. Letterbook, Washington MSS). For the temper of the government see George Thacher to his wife, Apr. 5, 1794, Thacher Papers, MHS.
91. Fisher Ames to Christopher Gore, Philadelphia, Mar. 26, 1794, Ames, ed., *Works of Ames*, I, 139–141.
92. Evident from ER to G. Washington, Philadelphia, Apr. 6, 1794, State Dept. Letterbook, Washington MSS.
93. *Ibid.*
94. *Ibid.*
95. Evident from the opening sentence of ER's letter commenting on these two letters (ER to G. Washington, Philadelphia, Apr. 9, 1794, Washington MSS).

96. J. Nicholas to G. Washington, [Philadelphia], [Apr. 6, 1794], and J. Monroe to G. Washington, Philadelphia, Apr. 8, 1794, Washington MSS.
97. ER to G. Washington, Philadelphia, Apr. 9, 1794, Washington MSS.
98. *Ibid.*
99. G. Washington to J. Monroe, Philadelphia, Apr. 9, 1794, Fitzpatrick, ed., *Washington*, XXXIII, 320.
100. J. Monroe to G. Washington, Philadelphia, Apr. 11, 1794, Washington MSS.
101. Morris' role in these discussions is recorded in the memorandum of Senator Rufus King, which describes the events leading up to the selection of Jay (King, ed., *Correspondence of R. King*, I, 518–519).
102. *Ibid.*
103. Mentioned in J. Jay to his wife, Philadelphia, Apr. 9, 1794, Johnston, ed., *Jay*, IV, 2–3.
104. *Ibid.* The presumption is that Jay would have mentioned the appointment to his wife if it had been offered to him at this time.
105. A. Hamilton to G. Washington, Philadelphia, [Apr. 14, 1794], *Hamilton*, XVI, 261–279.
106. *Ibid.*
107. That this assignment was communicated verbally is evident from G. Washington to ER, Apr. 15, 1794, Fitzpatrick, ed., *Washington*, XXXIII, 329–330.
108. G. Washington to J. Jay, Apr. 15, 1794, *ibid.*, 329.
109. R. King's summary, obtained most probably from Jay, is in King, ed., *Correspondence of R. King*, I, 520.
110. *Ibid.* Strong, Cabot and Ellsworth made up the rest of the delegation.
111. *Ibid.*
112. G. Washington to the Senate, United States, Apr. 16, 1794, Fitzpatrick, ed., *Washington*, XXXIII, 332–333.
113. *Annals*, IV, 83 [Senate], and King, ed., *Correspondence of R. King*, I, 521–523. The actions of the Senate on Apr. 19 are mistakenly recorded here as having taken place on Apr. 20.
114. ER to J. Jay, Philadelphia, Apr. 19, 1794, John Jay Papers, Special MSS Collection, Columbia University.
115. Evident from A. Hamilton to G. Washington, Apr. 23, 1794, *Hamilton*, XVI, 319.
116. *Ibid.*, 319–328.
    The most perceptive analysis of this letter has been given by Samuel F. Bemis (Bemis, *Jay's Treaty*, 210–211).
117. This meeting, which occurred on Apr. 21, is very briefly noted in King, ed., *Correspondence of R. King*, I, 523.
118. Compare A. Hamilton to G. Washington, Apr. 23, 1794, *Hamilton*, XVI, 319–328, with the final instructions, ER to J. Jay, Philadelphia, May 6, 1794, *ASP For. Rel.*, I, 472–474.
119. ER to G. Washington, Philadelphia, May 4, 1794, State Dept. Letterbook, Washington MSS.
120. *Ibid.*
121. ER to J. Jay, Philadelphia, May 6, 1794, *ASP For. Rel.*, I, 472–474.
    The absence of any serious disagreement between ER and Hamilton as to the general character of Jay's instructions is evident from the tone of their correspondence during the days this matter was being resolved. Rufus King also observed that it was reported to him that ER was "disposed to leave the negotiations open and the powers of the Envoy very discretionary.": (King, ed., *Correspondence of R. King*, I, 523).
    Much has been made of Hamilton's comments on an early draft of an important letter prepared by ER to George Hammond the British minister to the United States that was sent on May 1, 1794. Hamilton's letter (A. Hamilton to ER, Apr. 27, 1794, *Hamilton*, XVI, 346–349) supposedly infuriated ER, who resented this intrusion into the affairs of his department. There appears to be little evidence to support such an interpretation. ER, not Washington, sent the draft to Hamilton

in the first instance, and after receiving Hamilton's comments the Secretary of State forwarded both his draft and the comments of the Secretary of the Treasury to Washington. There is nothing in his covering letter to the President (ER to G. Washington, Philadelphia, Apr. 28, 1794, Washington MSS) that gives the slightest hint of annoyance, and ER was not above statements of this type. When the President supported ER's interpretation of how Hammond should be answered (G. Washington to ER, Philadelphia, Apr. 29, 1794, Fitzpatrick, ed., *Washington*, XXXIII, 346–347), ER prepared the final draft without further consultation with the President or the Cabinet (ER to George Hammond, Philadelphia, May 1, 1794, *ASP For. Rel.*, I, 450–454) and it was apparently approved as written.

122. ER to G. Washington, Philadelphia, May 6, 1794, Washington MSS.

Aside from ER, no one questioned this technical discrepancy between the language of the Senate's confirmation and the proposition that Jay be permitted to conclude a commercial treaty with Britain. Its significance in the administrative development of the executive branch has been noted by White, *The Federalists*, 60–61.

123. ER to J. Jay, Philadelphia, May 6, 1794, *ASP For. Rel.*, I, 472–474.

124. ER to J. Jay, Philadelphia, May 3, 1794, Domestic Letters, Dept. State, NA; ER to G. Washington, Trenton, [N.J.], May 8, 1794, State Dept. Letterbook, Washington MSS; ER to T. Pinckney, Philadelphia, May 10, 1794, Dipl. & Cons. Inst., Dept. State, NA.

125. The fate of Clark's resolution can be traced in *Annals*, IV, 595–596, 600–603, 604–605 (House) and 89–90 (Senate).

126. Madison's frequent letters to Jefferson convey much of the frustration and despair of the Republican ranks in Congress as they attempted to stem the tide of Federalist influence (J. Madison to T. Jefferson, Philadelphia, Apr. 28, May 11, May 25, 1794, Madison MSS).

127. ER to G. Washington, [Philadelphia], Feb. 23, 1794, Washington MSS.

128. Morris' activities are best described in Daniel Walther, *Gouverneur Morris, témoin de deux révolutions*, 179–235.

129. Evident from ER to Fauchet, Philadelphia, Apr. 21, 1794, Domestic Letters, Dept. State, NA, and ER to G. Morris, Philadelphia, Apr. 29, 1794, Gouverneur Morris Papers, Special MSS Collection, Columbia University.

130. ER to G. Washington, Apr. 27, 1794, State Dept. Letterbook, Washington MSS.

131. Evident from ER to G. Washington, Philadelphia, Apr. 28, 1794, Washington MSS.

132. *Ibid.*

133. G. Washington to R. Livingston, Philadelphia, Apr. 29, 1794, Washington MSS; G. Washington to J. Jay, Philadelphia, Apr. 29, 1794, Fitzpatrick, ed., *Washington*, XXXIII, 345–346.

134. J. Jay to G. Washington, New York, Apr. 30, 1794, Johnston, ed., *Jay*, IV, 9–10.

135. George Dangerfield, *Chancellor Robert R. Livingston of New York, 1746–1813*, 493*n*.

136. H. Knox to G. Washington, May 18, 1794, and ER to G. Washington, May 19, 1794, Washington MSS; A. Hamilton to G. Washington, May 19, 1794, *Hamilton*, XVI, 422–425. Apparently Attorney General Bradford did not suggest any names to Washington.

137. Evident from ER to G. Washington, Philadelphia, May 22, 1794, Washington MSS.

138. J. Monroe to T. Jefferson, Philadelphia, May 26, 1794, J. Monroe to J. Madison, May 27, 1794, J. Monroe to T. Jefferson, May 27, 1794, Hamilton, ed., *Monroe*, I, 296–298, 299, 299–301, and ER to G. Washington, May 26, 1794, State Dept. Letterbook, Washington MSS.

139. G. Washington to Gentlemen of the Senate, United States, May 27, 1794, *ASP For. Rel.*, I, 463.

140. ER to J. Monroe, Philadelphia, June 10, 1794, Domestic Letters, Dept. State, NA; Journal of Proceedings of the President, June 12, 1794, Washington MSS.

141. An interesting insight into ER's views as to his own role in Washington's Cabinet can be found in ER to G. Washington, Philadelphia, Apr. 19, 1794, Washington MSS.

CHAPTER 19

1. Freeman (Carroll & Ashworth), *Washington*, VII, 175.
2. S. F. Bemis, *John Quincy Adams and The Foundations of American Foreign Policy*, 36–38. See also ER to G. Washington, Philadelphia, May 22, 1794, Washington MSS.
3. ER apparently communicated Washington's intentions verbally to the Vice President before he had been authorized to do so. His more official notification, which was also communicated verbally, was followed by a note to Adams asking him to consider the earlier notification as "purely confidential between us," and if he were ever asked when he first learned of the President's intentions, "you will refer to the communication *of this day only* [emphasis ER's]." ER to J. Adams, Philadelphia, [May 26, 1794], Adams Papers, MHS. See also J. Adams to J. Q. Adams, Philadelphia, May 26, 1794, Adams Papers, MHS.
4. Diary of J. Q. Adams, July 10, 1794, *ibid*.
5. J. Q. Adams to J. Adams, Philadelphia, July 10 and July 18, 1794, *ibid*. See also Diary of J. Q. Adams, July 11, 1794, *ibid*.
6. ER to J. Q. Adams, July 29, 1794, *ibid*.
7. ER to Secretaries of the Treasury and War and the Attorney General, June 30, 1794, John William Wallace Collection, HSP.
8. H. Knox to ER, July 2, 1794, Washington MSS; A. Hamilton to ER, Philadelphia, July 8, 1794, *Hamilton*, XVI, 578–579; W. Bradford to ER, July 5, 1794, John William Wallace Collection, HSP.
9. ER to G. Washington, Philadelphia, July 9, 1794, Washington MSS.
10. On July 16 the Journal of Proceedings of the President notes the receipt of an undated letter from T. Pinckney enclosing a letter from the Swedish minister inviting the United States to become a party to the recently signed Convention of Armed Neutrality (Journal of Proceedings of the President, July 16, 1794, Washington MSS). It apparently became a closed issue when Pinckney's letter was returned to ER on July 17 (Journal of Proceedings of the President, July 17, 1794, *ibid*.).
11. For a general account see Leland D. Baldwin, *Whiskey Rebels, The Story of a Frontier Uprising*, and James Carnahan, "The Pennsylvania Insurrection of 1794," *New Jersey Historical Society Proceedings* (1st ser.), VI, 113–152.
    Two accounts, written by Pennsylvanians active in the rebellion, are William Findley, *History of the Insurrection in the Four Western Counties of Pennsylvania in the Year MDCCXCIV* (Philadelphia, 1796), and Hugh H. Brackenridge, *Incidents of the Insurrection in the Western Parts of Pennsylvania in the Year 1794* (Philadelphia, 1795).
    More directly related to the situation during this first week in Aug. is A. Hamilton to G. Washington, Treasury Dept., Aug. 5, 1794, *Hamilton*, XVII, 24–58. A. J. Dallas to Jared Ingersoll, Philadelphia, July 25, 1794, and A. J. Dallas to H. Knox, Philadelphia, July 26, 1794, *Penn. Arch.* (2nd ser.), IV, 65, 66–67.
12. Incomplete minutes are in *Penn. Arch.* (2nd ser.), IV, 122–124. See also Freeman (Carroll & Ashworth), *Washington*, VII, 187*n*, for evidence establishing date of meeting.
13. J. Wilson to G. Washington, Philadelphia, Aug. 4, 1794, *ASP Misc.*, I, 85. That the request for this opinion came from the Attorney General, see ER to G. Washington, Aug. 5, 1794, Washington MSS.
14. *Ibid*.
15. *Ibid*.
16. A. Hamilton to G. Washington, Treasury Dept., Aug. 2, 1794, and Aug. 5, 1794, *Hamilton*, XVII, 15–19, 24–58; H. Knox to G. Washington, War Dept., Aug. 4, 1794, Washington MSS; William Bradford to G. Washington, [Aug. 1794], Wash-

ington MSS; and T. Mifflin to G. Washington, Philadelphia, Aug. 5, 1794, *Penn. Arch.* (2nd ser.), 4: 88–93.

The President's displeasure with Mifflin's attitude was reflected in his decision to "reply" to its contents. The letter, drafted by Hamilton, but sent over ER's signature, is ER to T. Mifflin, Dom. Letters, Dept. State. NA. The draft is in the Hamilton MSS under the same date.

17. The earliest dated draft of the instructions is Aug. 5. ER to James Ross, Jasper Yates and William Bradford, Aug. 5, 1794, Dom. Letters, Dept. State. NA.

18. A joint memo from Hamilton and Knox on Aug. 5 makes reference to the fact that the instructions were already complete and also notes that ER was out of town on that day. This would seemingly indicate that the instructions, dated Aug. 5, were actually completed some time before that date (A. Hamilton and H. Knox to G. Washington, Philadelphia, Aug. 5, 1794, *Hamilton*, XVII, 21. ER's Cabinet opinion is also dated Aug. 5 (ER to G. Washington, Aug. 5, 1794, Washington MSS).

19. *Ibid.*

20. H. Knox to T. Mifflin, War Dept., Aug. 7, 1794, *Penn. Arch.* (2nd ser.), IV, 104–105. See ER's account in ER to T. Pinckney, Philadelphia, Aug. 11, 1794, Dipl. & Cons. Inst., Dept. State, NA.

21. Proclamation, Philadelphia, Aug. 7, 1794, Fitzpatrick, ed., *Washington*, XXXIII, 457–461.

22. ER to James Ross, Jasper Yates and William Bradford, [Philadelphia], Aug. 7, 1794, Penn. Misc., Whiskey Rebellion I MSS. A copy of these instructions may also be found in the Simon Gratz Collection, HSP.

23. W. Bradford to ER, [Downings Town, Penn.], Aug. 8, 1794, Penn. Misc., Whiskey Rebellion I MSS.

24. Evident from ER to W. Bradford, Philadelphia, Aug. 8, 1794, Dom. Letters, Dept. State. NA.

25. G. Washington to ER, Germantown, Aug. 8, 1794, Fitzpatrick. ed., *Washington*, XXXIII, 462.

26. No new instructions were issued. On Aug. 11 ER provided Pinckney with a summary of the actions of the government with respect to the disturbance and made no mention of any new Cabinet decision (ER to T. Pinckney, Philadelphia, Aug. 11, 1794, Dipl. & Cons. Inst., Dept. State, NA).

27. A. Hamilton to G. Washington, Treasury Dept. Aug. 16, 1794, *Hamilton*, XVII, 101.

28. Washington's letter has not been found but the nature of his instructions can be established from ER's reply: ER to G. Washington, Germantown, Aug. 18, 1794, State Dept. Letterbook, Washington MSS.

29. *Ibid.*

30. T. Mifflin to G. Washington, Philadelphia, Aug. 22, 1794, Misc. Letters, Dept. State, NA

It should be noted that there is no record of Washington's having given his approval of the publication of the Cabinet opinion.

31. A. Hamilton to G. Washington, Treasury Dept., Sept. 2, 1794, *Hamilton*, XVII, 180–190.

32. ER to T. Mifflin, Philadelphia, Sept. 12, 1794, *Penn. Arch.* (2nd ser.), IV, 242.

33. These meetings, which occurred between Aug. 21 and Sept. 1, have been briefly treated in Baldwin, *Whiskey Rebels*, 190–191 and 198–200.

34. Most of the letters to ER are in Penn. Misc., Whiskey Rebellion I MSS. The most important of the letters to ER, that dated Pittsburgh, Aug. 17, 1794, is printed in *Penn. Arch.* (2nd ser.) IV, 138–141.

With Bradford in Pittsburgh and Knox out of the city on personal business, Washington, ER and Hamilton consulted with one another without the formality of a Cabinet meeting. See, for example, the consultation procedure suggested in G. Washington to ER, Germantown, Aug. 21, 1794, Fitzpatrick, ed., *Washington*, XXXIII, 472.

35. The letter from the commissioners (J. Ross, J. Yates and W. Bradford to ER, Pittsburgh, Aug. 17, 1794, *Penn. Arch.* [2nd ser.], IV, 138–141) was received on Aug.

23. See also W. Bradford to G. Washington, Pittsburgh, Aug. 17, 1794, Penn. Misc., Whiskey Rebellion I MSS.

Washington, ER and Hamilton met on Aug. 24 from 8:00 A.M. to 4:00 P.M. on the implications of this report and then issued the order to assemble the militia (Minutes of a Meeting between the President, Secretary of State and Secretary of the Treasury, [Philadelphia], Aug. 24, 1794, Penn. Misc., Whiskey Rebellion I MSS).

36. ER to Messrs. Bradford, Yates & Ross, Philadelphia, Aug. 25, 1794, Dom. Letters, Dept. State. NA. The emphasis was ER's.

37. J. Ross, J. Yates and W. Bradford to ER, [Pittsburgh], Aug. 21, 1794, Aug. 22, 1794, Aug. 23, 1794, Penn. Misc., Whiskey Rebellion I MSS, and W. Bradford to AH, Aug. 23, 1794, ibid.

See also the report of the commissioners of the state of Pennsylvania (Thomas McKean and William Irvine to T. Mifflin, Pittsburg, Aug. 30, 1794, Penn. Arch. [2nd ser.], IV, 185–186).

38. A. Hamilton to Gov. Mifflin, War Dept., Sept. 9, 1794, ibid., 226–227. Similar letters were sent to the governors of New Jersey, Maryland and Virginia.

39. Proclamation, Philadelphia, Sept. 25, 1794, Fitzpatrick, ed., Washington, XXXIII, 507–509.

40. On Sept. 19 Hamilton asked permission to join the forces being assembled to suppress the insurrection (A. Hamilton to G. Washington, Philadelphia, Sept. 19, 1794, Hamilton, XVII, 254–255). Sometime after receiving Hamilton's request Washington decided to assume personal command and on Sept. 28 indicated he intended to remain with the troops until he knew more about the temper of the insurrectionists (G. Washington to William Pearce, Philadelphia, Sept. 28, 1794, Fitzpatrick, ed., Washington, XXXIII, 511–514). On Sept. 30, 1794, he and Hamilton left Philadelphia to assume command of the assembling militia (Fitzpatrick, ed., Diaries of Washington, IV, 200).

41. The arrangements for the express are explained in ER's first letter: ER to G. Washington, Philadelphia, Oct. 2, 1794, State Dept. Letterbook, Washington MSS.

42. Knox was back in Philadelphia by Oct. 6 and immediately asked Washington if he might join him. Washington refused his request (G. Washington to H. Knox, Carlisle, Oct. 9, 1794, Fitzpatrick, ed., Washington, XXXIII, 524–525). The division of responsibilities appears to have developed more by accident than design, since the date Knox intended to return to Philadelphia was not known in advance.

43. ER wrote at least thirty-five public and/or private letters to Washington during the twenty-eight days the President was out of the city. At times he inserted the time of day as well as the date to establish the sequence in which his letters were written.

44. Unbelievable as it may seem, ER's letters establish the fact that he visited Mrs. Washington on Oct. 4, 7, 8, 11, 13, 16, 17, 18, 20, 22 and 23. He reported her "slight indisposition" on the 17th and her "complete recovery" the following day (ER to G. Washington, Philadelphia, Oct. 17, 1794, and Oct. 18, 1794, Washington MSS).

45. ER to G. Washington, Philadelphia, "11 o'clock," Oct. 8, 1794, ibid.

46. ER to G. Washington, Philadelphia, Oct. 9, 1794, ibid.

47. ER to G. Washington, Philadelphia, Oct. 14, 1794, State Dept. Letterbook, Washington MSS.

48. ER to G. Washington, Philadelphia, Oct. 21, 1794, Washington MSS.

49. Washington wrote to ER on Oct. 9, 11, 16 and 18, and Bartholomew Dandridge, Washington's secretary, wrote to ER on Oct. 18 and 20. The pace Washington maintained during this trip explains the infrequency of his letters. An excellent account of his activities may be found in Freeman (Carroll & Ashworth), Washington, VII, 198–213.

50. Ibid., 205–208. For Washington's reaction to this latest intelligence, see G. Washington to ER, Carlisle, Oct. 11, 1794, Fitzpatrick, ed., Washington, XXXIV, 1–2 and n., G. Washington to ER, Fort Cumberland, Oct. 16, 1794, ibid., 2–4.

51. G. Washington to ER, Carlisle, Oct. 6, 1794, *ibid.*, XXXIII, 521–522.
52. ER to G. Washington, Philadelphia, Oct. 8, 1794, Washington MSS.
53. ER to G. Washington, Philadelphia, Oct. 13, 1794, State Dept. Letterbook, Washington MSS.
54. G. Washington to ER, Carlisle, Oct. 9, 1794, and G. Washington to ER, Fort Cumberland, Oct. 16, 1794, Fitzpatrick, ed., *Washington*, XXXIII, 525–527, XXXIV, 2–4, to cite but two examples. B. Dandridge made further reference to the message on Oct. 20, after ER's notes had been received (B. Dandridge to ER, Bedford, Oct. 20, 1794, State Dept. Letterbook, Washington MSS).
55. ER to G. Washington, Philadelphia, Oct. 25, 1794, Washington MSS.
56. On Oct. 11 ER acknowledged the receipt of Jay's letter of Aug. 21, 1794 (ER to J. Jay, Philadelphia, Oct. 11, 1794, Dipl. & Cons. Inst., Dept. State, NA.) and on Nov. 12, Jay's letters of Sept. 13 and 14 (ER to J. Jay, Philadelphia, Nov. 12, 1794, *ibid.*). The letter of Sept. 13, with its enclosures, was the first truly important letter from Jay, for it contained the background and broad outlines of the proposed treaty (J. Jay to ER, London, Sept. 13, 1794, *ASP For. Rel.*, I, 485–496). ER replied immediately, noting several problems and expressing concern for the language being adopted. He felt compelled to add, however:

> These ideas are not felt by me to be in all respects accurate. I shall revise them, and shall particularly keep in view, that both the language and the matter of the propositions will undergo great alterations, and new arrangements. (ER to J. Jay, Philadelphia, Nov. 12, 1794, Dipl. & Cons. Inst., Dept. State, NA.)

57. The Jacobins had fallen from power late in July, at about the time Monroe was expected to arrive in Paris.
58. Monroe's first dispatch, J. Monroe to ER, Paris, No. 3, Sept. 13, 1794, Dipl. Dispatches [Fr.], Dept. State, NA, was received on Nov. 27, 1794 (evident from ER to J. Monroe, Philadelphia, Dec. 2, 1794, Dipl. & Cons. Inst., Dept. of State, NA). See Ammon, *Monroe*, 119–121.
59. For a convenient summary of the long and tortured history of Spanish-American relations with respect to the problems of their common frontier, see S. F. Bemis, *Pinckney's Treaty: A Study of America's Advantage from Europe's Distresses, 1783–1800*, 1–262 *passim*, and A. P. Whitaker, *The Mississippi Question, 1795–1803: A Study in Trade, Politics and Diplomacy*, 1–200 *passim*.
60. See G. Washington to C. M. Thurston, Philadelphia, Aug. 10, 1794, Fitzpatrick, ed., *Washington*, XXXIII, 464–466, in answer to C. M. Thurston to G. Washington, June 21, 1794, Washington MSS.
61. ER to T. Jefferson, Philadelphia, Aug. 28, 1794, Jefferson MSS. The demand of the Spanish government that we send a more distinguished representative was transmitted by Josef de Jaudenes, the Spanish commissioner to the United States. The demand would appear to have been made on Aug. 25, because included in ER's letter to Jefferson was a summary of a conference he had had with Jaudenes on that date with respect to this point.
62. ER to J. Innes, Philadelphia, Aug. 8, 1794, Dom. Letters, Dept. State, NA.
63. T. Jefferson to ER, Monticello, Sept. 7, 1794, Jefferson MSS.
64. ER to P. Henry, Philadelphia, Aug. 28, 1794, Dom. Letters, Dept. State, NA.
65. Henry Lee reported P. Henry's coolness in a letter of Aug. 17 (H. Lee to G. Washington, Richmond, Aug. 17, 1794, Washington MSS). Henry's refusal was P. Henry to ER, Sept. 14, 1794, W. W. Henry, *Patrick Henry: Life, Correspondence and Speeches*, II, 546–548.
66. Evident from ER to J. Innes, Philadelphia, Aug. 22, 1794, and Sept. 5, 1794, Dom. Letters, Dept. State, NA.
67. ER to G. Washington, Nov. 5, 1794, Washington MSS.
68. ER to T. Pinckney, Philadelphia, Nov. 3, 1794, Dipl. & Cons. Inst., Dept. State, NA. ER's letter to William Short, U.S. commissioner in Madrid, explains more fully the circumstances surrounding Pinckney's appointment than the letter to Pinckney (ER to W. Short, Philadelphia, Nov. 9, 1794, *ibid.*).
69. G. Washington to the Senate, United States, Nov. 21, 1794, Fitzpatrick, ed., *Wash-*

ington, XXXIV, 39–40. ER to T. Pinckney, Philadelphia, Nov. 28, 1794, Dipl. & Cons. Inst., Dept. State, NA.

70. ER to J. Innes, Philadelphia, Nov. 11, 1794, Randolph Family Papers, VHS.

71. ER to T. Pinckney, Philadelphia, Dec. 25, 1794, Dipl. & Cons. Inst., Dept. State, NA.

72. ER to G. Washington, Nov. 5, 1794, Washington MSS.

73. ER to G. Washington, Philadelphia, Oct. 11, 1794, *ibid.*

74. G. Washington to ER, Fort Cumberland, Oct. 16, 1794, Washington MSS. Washington's annoyance with these societies is revealed in G. Washington to Charles M. Thurston, Philadelphia, Aug. 10, 1794, and G. Washington to Henry Lee, Germantown, Aug. 26, 1794, Fitzpatrick, ed., *Washington*, XXXIII, 464–466, 474–479.

75. ER to G. Washington, Philadelphia, Nov. 6, 1794, Washington MSS.

76. Sixth Annual Address to Congress, United States, Nov. 19, 1794, Fitzpatrick, ed., *Washington*, XXXIV, 28–37. As to its reception, see George Thacher to Mrs. Thacher, Nov. 19–22, 1794, Thacher Papers, MHS.

77. *Annals*, IV, 947–948 (House), and J. Madison to T. Jefferson, Philadelphia, Nov. 30, 1794, Madison MSS. See also Freeman (Carroll & Ashworth), *Washington*, VII, 222–224.

On Dec. 4 Madison observed: "The introduction of it [i.e. the denunciation of the democratic societies] by the President was perhaps the greatest error of his political life." J. Madison to T. Jefferson, Philadelphia, Dec. 4, 1794, Madison MSS.

78. ER's *"Germanicus" Letters*, (Philadelphia, 1794), 1–77, quote on 8.

79. *Ibid.*

80. William Eustis to David Cobb, Boston, Dec. 10, 1794, David Cobb Papers, MHS.

81. J. Adams to Abigail Adams, Philadelphia, Dec. 7, 1794, Adams Papers, MHS.

82. The treaty was, of course, signed on Nov. 19. The last substantive dispatch from Jay was that of Sept. 13, received on Nov. 12. After Nov. 12 Washington acknowledged only one additional note from Jay, that of Oct. 3, and ER acknowledged two dispatches, those dated Sept. 18 and Oct. 2. They added little or nothing to Jay's dispatch of Sept. 13.

83. Rumors as to the contents of treaty are noted in J. Adams to Abigail Adams, Philadelphia, Jan. 15, 1795, Adams Papers, MHS; Robert Livingston to J. Madison, New York, Jan. 30, 1795, Joseph Jones to J. Madison, Fredericksburg, [Va.], Feb. 10, 1795, J. Madison to T. Jefferson, Philadelphia, Feb. 15, 1795, Madison MSS.

84. ER to J. Monroe, Philadelphia, Dec. 2, 1794, Dipl. & Cons. Inst , Dept. State, NA.

85. ER to W. Short, Philadelphia, Dec. 3, 1794, *ibid.*

86. ER to J. Monroe, Philadelphia, Feb. 5, 1795, Monroe MSS.

87. ER's first letter to Jay on these proposals was Nov. 12, 1794 (ER to J. Jay, Philadelphia, Nov. 12, 1794, Dipl. & Cons. Inst., Dept. State, NA). Written in haste because of the immediate departure of a vessel for England, it conveyed ER's initial reaction to these proposals. A second letter on Dec. 15, 1794, went into greater detail (ER to J. Jay, Philadelphia, Dec. 15, 1794, *ibid.*).

88. ER knew of the intended resignation on Dec. 5 (ER to J. Monroe, Philadelphia, Dec. 5, 1794, Monroe MSS). Knox's letter was H. Knox to G. Washington, Philadelphia, Dec. 28, 1794, in Francis S. Drake, *The Life and Correspondence of Henry Knox*, 109.

89. Hamilton informed Washington on Dec. 1, 1794, that he intended to resign on Jan. 31, 1795 (A. Hamilton to G. Washington, Philadelphia, Dec. 1, 1794, *Hamilton*, XVII, 413). His letter of resignation is A. Hamilton to G. Washington, Treasury Dept., Jan. 31, 1795, Washington MSS.

90. G. Washington to H. Knox, Philadelphia, Dec. 30, 1794, and G. Washington to A. Hamilton, Philadelphia, Feb. 2, 1795, Fitzpatrick, ed., *Washington*, XXXIV, 76, 109–110.

CHAPTER 20

1. Compare J. Jay to G. Washington, London, June 23, 1794, with J. Jay to ER, London, June 23, 1794; J. Jay to G. Washington, London, July 21, 1794, with J. Jay to ER, London, July 30, 1794, Johnston, ed., *Jay*, IV, 26–38; J. Jay to ER, London, Aug. 2, 1794, *ASP For. Rel.*, I, 480–481 with J. Jay to G. Washington, London, Aug. 5, 1794, Johnston, ed., *Jay*, IV, 44–46; J. Jay to G. Washington, London, Sept. 13, 1794, with J. Jay to ER, London, Sept. 13, 1794, *ibid.*, 44–65.

Apparently ER was acquainted with the contents of most if not all of the letters Jay addressed to Washington. Indicative of the extent to which the President shared Jay's correspondence with ER is G. Washington to ER, Fort Cumberland, Oct. 18, 1794, Fitzpatrick, ed., *Washington*, XXXIV, 4–5.

2. Even when writing to individuals who shared his political outlook, the note of guarded optimism over the outcome of the negotiations served as the theme for his letters. See J. Jay to R. King, London, July 8, 1794, Rufus King Papers, NYHS; J. Jay to A. Hamilton, London, July 18 [–Aug. 5], 1794, J. Jay to A. Hamilton, London, Aug. 16, 1794, J. Jay to A. Hamilton, London, Sept. 17, 1794, *Hamilton*, XVI, 608–609, XVII, 97–99, 240–241. There was a certain amount of detail in some of these letters to Hamilton that was missing in his correspondence with ER:

> I mention these Facts to explain what I mean by favorable appearances, I think it best that they should remain *unmentioned* for the present and they make no part of my Communications to Mr. Randolph or others. This is not the Season for such communications. They may be misinterpreted, tho' not by you. (J. Jay to A. Hamilton, London, July 18 [–Aug. 5], 1794, *Hamilton*, XVI, 609 [emphasis his].)

3. During the summer and fall of 1794 Jay's dispatches reached ER as follows: Jay's of June 23 received by ER on Aug. 16, Jay's of June 8 received by ER on Aug. 17, Jay's of June 26 acknowledged by ER on Sept. 12, Jay's of July 9 received by ER on Sept. 16, Jay's of July 6, 12 and 16 acknowledged by ER on Sept. 20, Jay's of July 30 and 31 and Aug. 2 received by ER on Oct. 7, Jay's of Aug. 21 received by ER on Oct. 11, Jay's of Aug. 8 and 9 acknowledged by ER on Oct. 13 and Jay's of Aug. 23 received by ER on Oct. 17.

4. See *ASP For. Rel.*, I, 475–484 *passim* for these early dispatches.

5. ER sent twenty-two letters to Jay between May 12, when Jay took passage for England, and Nov. 12, the date of ER's first substantive review of Jay's activities. In general the letters between these dates did not presume to comment directly on Jay's handling of the negotiations, since ER knew so little about them. They sought to do no more than keep Jay informed of events at home and to supply him with such intelligence as would assist him in his negotiations with Grenville. They may be found most conveniently (but with some errors) in *ASP For. Rel.*, I, 474–501 *passim*. In subsequent references in this chapter the *American State Papers* will not be cited where critical quoted material is involved unless no other source is known.

6. ER's letters to Jay never challenged his assessment of the situation in England. But it is also true he never expressed his agreement with Jay's guarded optimism, either to Jay or to anyone else. It is safe to assume, given his general reaction to the appointment of a special envoy, that he would require some concrete evidence of a change in Britain's attitude toward the United States before subscribing to Jay's views.

7. His efforts to create a more favorable climate were as deliberate as his intention not to allow himself to be publicly identified with these efforts. They were a reflection of his concern with public opinion rather than an indication of his own views.

8. ER to J. Jay, Philadelphia, Oct. 11–19, 1794, Dipl. & Cons. Inst., Dept. State, NA. The quote is taken from that portion of the letter that was written on Oct. 13.

9. *Ibid.* The quote is taken from that portion of the letter that was written on Oct. 18.

10. J. Jay to ER, London, Sept. 13, 1794, *ASP For. Rel.*, I, 485–496.

11. It is assumed that ER's initial reactions to the most obvious concessions were the same as those communicated to Jay the next day in ER to J. Jay, Philadelphia, Nov. 12, 1794, Dipl. & Cons. Inst., Dept. State, NA.

12. J. Jay to G. Washington, London, Sept. 13, 1794, Johnston, ed., *Jay*, IV, 58–60.

13. ER to J. Jay, Philadelphia, Nov. 12, 1794, Dipl. & Cons. Inst., Dept. State, NA.

14. At one point in this letter he remarks: "I am directed by the President to inform you. . . ." (*Ibid.*)

In a second and private letter to ER on Sept. 13 Jay had complained that the Secretary of State's letter to the Committee of Public Safety in France in reply to theirs of an earlier date had had an unfavorable effect on his negotiations in London. ER replied in a private letter on Nov. 12 that he had acted under the direction of a resolution of the House of Representatives and that he had no desire, either by accident or design, of being the instrument of undermining the success of Jay's mission (J. Jay to ER, [private], London, Sept. 13, 1794 Dipl. Dispatches [Gt. Brit.], Dept. State, NA. ER's reply is ER to J. Jay, Philadelphia, Nov. 12, 1794, John Jay Papers, NYHS. See also ER to J. Jay, (private), Philadelphia, Nov. 19, 1794, Dipl. & Cons. Inst., Dept. State, NA.

15. Revealed in a short and mildly critical letter which ER sent on Dec. 3 (ER to J. Jay, Philadelphia, Dec. 3, 1794, *ASP For. Rel.*, I, 509).

16. J. Jay to ER, London, Sept. 18, 1794, *ibid.*, 496–497, and J. Jay to ER, London, Oct. 2, 1794, *ibid.* The reference to an "immanent end" to negotiations is in the second letter.

17. ER to J. Jay, Philadelphia, Dec. 15, 1794, Dipl. & Cons. Inst., Dept. of State, NA.

18. J. Jay to ER, London, Nov. 5, 1794, *ASP For. Rel.*, I, 501.

19. Bemis' account, while not primarily concerned with the subject of supplemental instructions, is quite explicit in its indictment of Jay's conduct during these months (Bemis, *Jay's Treaty*, 242–245 *passim*), and Jay's biographer accepts Bemis' interpretation without question (Monaghan, *Jay*, 378–381).

20. The Diplomatic and Consular Instructions of the Department of State contain no letters addressed to Jay between Dec. 23, 1794, and Mar. 7, 1795. On the latter date a letter was addressed to Jay or Pinckney or, in the absence of both, William Deas. It instructed any one of them to inform the British government that if a ratification of the treaty took place, it probably could not be accomplished before the expiration of the time period specified in the treaty. The letter was prompted by the adjournment of Congress before the arrival of the treaty, thereby delaying any consideration of the matter until June, 1795. The treaty was delivered to ER the day after this letter was sent.

21. Madison wrote on Feb. 15: "The Session has produced as yet, few acts of Consequence" (J. Madison to T. Jefferson, Philadelphia, Feb. 15, 1795, Madison MSS).

22. G. Washington to the Vice President of the United States, . . . United States, Mar. 3, 1795, Fitzpatrick, ed., *Washington*, XXXIV, 131, 131*n*.

23. These letters were delivered by David Blaney who had landed in Norfolk, Va., eight days previously (ER to J. Jay or T. Pinckney or William Deas, Dept. of State, Mar. 8, 1795, Dipl. & Cons. Inst., Dept. State, NA.

24. The most perceptive analysis of the treaty is still Professor Bemis' of over forty years ago (Bemis, *Jay's Treaty*, 252–270). More recently the treaty has been viewed in a broader context by Professor Bradford Perkins (*The First Rapprochement*, 1–6).

25. J. Jay to ER, London, Nov. 19, 1794, Johnston, ed., *Jay*, IV, 137–144.

26. Washington wrote not a single line in praise or criticism of the treaty between the months of March and June. He did not acknowledge Jay's private letter of Nov. 19 and seemingly did not communicate with him until July 2, 1795, when he accepted his resignation as Chief Justice in a brief perfunctory letter. His silence, ER's cautious acknowledgment of Jay's dispatches (see below), and the strict rule of secrecy that was imposed (see below) leave little doubt that Washington felt the treaty fell far short of its intended objectives.

Jay's letter to the President is J. Jay to G. Washington, London, Nov. 19, 1794, Johnston, ed., *Jay*, IV, 133–135.

27. ER to J. Jay or T. Pinckney or William Deas, Dept. of State, Mar. 8, 1795, Dipl. & Cons. Inst., Dept. State, NA.

28. ER to J. Monroe, Dept. of State, Mar. 8, 1795, Simon Gratz Collection, HSP.

29. The decision to maintain an absolute silence as to the provisions of the treaty was made by Mar. 8, for ER informed Jay of the decision in the same letter in which he acknowledged the receipt of the document itself (ER to J. Jay or T. Pinckney or William Deas, Dept. of State, Mar. 8, 1795, Dipl. & Cons. Inst., Dept. State, NA).

30. J. Madison to J. Monroe, Philadelphia, Mar. 11, 1795, Madison MSS.

31. Just prior to the special session John Beckley, in commenting on the government's reaction to Jay's arrival in New York, observed:

> The anxiety for his arrival and joy thereupon, teach me to suspect that great fears persisted with the Executive for its final success, without his aid [?], *ergo* there must be something rotten in it. (John Beckley to J. Monroe, Philadelphia, June 1, 1795, James Monroe MSS, NYPL.)

32. J. Madison to J. Monroe, Philadelphia, Mar. 26, 1795, Madison MSS.

33. It was obvious that the most sustained criticism would come from the Republican press. The *Independent Chronicle* of Boston, the *Jersey Journal* of Philip Freneau and the *Independent Gazette* in Philadelphia were most explicit in their comments on Washington's decision to withhold the treaty from the public.

34. In Boston the *Columbian Centinel*, in Providence, R.I., the *United States Chronicle* and in Philadelphia, Fenno's, *Gazette of the United States* answered Washington's critics.

35. ER's instructions to David Humphreys, Dept. of State, Mar. 28, 1795, Dipl. & Cons. Inst., Dept. State, NA. Humphreys was asked to represent our interests in the Barbary states in Mar., 1793, while minister to Portugal. He returned to the United States in Feb., 1795, for a short visit. On Apr. 3 Washington signed letters of credence naming him commissioner plenipotentiary to the Emperor of Morocco, Dey of Algiers, Bey of Tunis and Bashaw of Tripoli (Journal of Proceedings of the President, Apr. 3, 1795, Washington MSS).

36. ER to Josef de Jaudenes, Philadelphia, Mar. 25, 1795, Dom. Letters, Dept. State, NA.

37. A brief but adequate summary of Washington's handling of this matter may be found in Freeman (Carroll & Ashworth), *Washington*, VII, 240–241. Secretary of War Pickering was Washington's principal adviser in these matters.

38. Washington was away from Philadelphia from Apr. 14 to May 2 (*ibid.*, 241, 246). During this period ER sent him a total of seven letters. They may be found in State Dept. Letterbook, Washington MSS.

39. ER no longer acknowledged Jay's letters since he assumed Jay would have left London before any acknowledgments reached him. The date on which these dispatches were received is evident from ER to G. Washington, Philadelphia, Apr. 26, 1795, State Dept. Letterbook, Washington MSS.

40. J. Jay to ER, London, Feb. 22, 1794, *ASP For. Rel.*, I, 518.

41. ER to G. Washington, Philadelphia, Apr. 26, 1795, State Dept. Letterbook, Washington MSS.

42. Jay made this statement in his dispatch of Feb. 6, which specifically acknowledged ER's mildly critical letter of Dec. 3 (J. Jay to ER, London, Feb. 6, 1795, *ASP For. Rel.*, I, 518).

43. The only information ER had as to the date of Jay's return was a report in the New York newspapers that he was determined not to leave England until after the spring equinox (ER to G. Washington, Philadelphia, Apr. 29, 1795, State Dept. Letterbook, Washington MSS).

44. ER to Mrs. [Sarah] Jay, Philadelphia, Apr. 26, 1795, Dom. Letters, Dept. State, NA.

45. ER to J. Jay, Dept. of State, Apr. 26, 1795, Dipl. & Cons. Inst., Dept. State, NA.

46. This letter has not been found but its date and general contents are evident from

ER's reply: ER to Mrs. [Sarah] Jay, Philadelphia, May 13, 1795, Dom. Letters, Dept. State, NA.

47. *Ibid.*

48. J. Jay to ER, Philadelphia, May 28, 1794, *ASP For. Rel.*, I, 519.

49. Evident from ER's reply: ER to J. Jay, [Philadelphia], May 30, 1794, quoted in full in Conway, *Randolph*, 234–235.
ER's letter of May 30 has never been found in manuscript form. Its closing paragraph explains why there is no copy of it in the Dipl. & Cons. Inst. of the Dept. of State: "I shall take no copy of this letter and you will be pleased to consider it only as proceeding from a wish to give effect to the result of your labours, and not to be placed on an official file." (*Ibid.*, 253.)

50. *Ibid.*

51. J. Jay to ER, Philadelphia, June 1, 1795, *ASP For. Rel.*, I, 519–520.
Jay, of course, answered each of ER's questions, but in the same abrupt style. There is no evidence that he considered it beneath his dignity to report to ER; he simply failed to sense the urgency in ER's repeated efforts to secure a detailed account of his negotiations.

52. Evident from ER to J. Jay, Dept. of State, Apr. 26, 1795, Dipl. & Cons. Inst., Dept. State, NA.

53. G. Washington to the Senate, United States, June 8, 1795, Fitzpatrick, ed., *Washington*, XXXIV, 212–213.

54. Fauchet's growing apprehensiveness is very ably chronicled in Alexander DeConde, *Entangling Alliances, Politics and Diplomacy Under George Washington*, 408–415.

55. Fauchet so reported in J. Fauchet to Committee of Public Safety, Philadelphia, Feb. 16, 1795, Turner, ed., "CFM," *AHA, Annual Report, 1903*, II, 518–581. ER to J. Monroe, Dept. of State, Feb. 15, 1795, Dipl. & Cons. Inst., Dept. State, NA.

56. J. Fauchet to ER, Philadelphia, May 2, 1795, *ASP For. Rel.*, I, 608–609.

57. ER to J. Monroe, Philadelphia, May 31, 1795, James Monroe MSS, NYPL.

58. ER's reply to Fauchet's letter of May 2 was ER to J. Fauchet, Philadelphia, May 29, 1795, Dom. Letters, Dept. State, NA. To Monroe he wrote: The reply "consists of nearly thirty pages of closely written quarto paper. . . ." (ER to J. Monroe, Philadelphia, May 31, 1795, James Monroe MSS, NYPL.)

59. ER made a thinly veiled reference to Fauchet's activities in his reply of May 29 (ER to J. Fauchet, Philadelphia, May 29, 1795, Dom. Letters, Dept. State, NA).

60. *Ibid.*

61. ER to J. Fauchet. Dept. of State, June 13, 1795, *ibid.*

62. The Attorney General, W. Bradford, replying to a letter from Hamilton which censured Fauchet's activities, commented: "I shewed your letter to the Sec. of State: but his censure of Fauchet outran yours." (W. Bradford to A. Hamilton, Philadelphia, May 21, 1795, *Hamilton*, XVIII, 347–351.)

63. ER's first known reference to Fauchet's recall is ER to J. Monroe, Philadelphia, Dec. 3, 1794, MSS, James Monroe, NYPL.

64. W. Bradford to A. Hamilton, Philadelphia, May 21, 1795, *Hamilton*, XVIII, 347–351.

65. The point at which the correspondence was cut off and the significance of this decision is most dramatically illustrated in the strict chronological arrangement of this correspondence in *ASP For. Rel.*, I, 501. The note on this page indicates the division between the correspondence that was transmitted and the correspondence that was retained in the State Department files.

66. *Annals*, IV, 855 (Senate).

67. *Ibid.*, 855–856, 858. A vote on the 13th on the motion to rescind the rule of secrecy was 9 to 20 against rescinding (*ibid.*).
Pierce Butler, a nonconforming Federalist from South Carolina, was deliberately violating this rule of secrecy on June 12. He wrote to Madison:

> Convinced that this, as they now term it, most important secret, is much safer with you than in the hands of many to whom it is confided, I shall, by every Post, send you a sheet of it 'till I forward the whole. When you have read it

you may forward it to Mr. Jefferson, asking him not to communicate it. (Pierce Butler to J. Madison, Philadelphia, June 12, 1795, Madison MSS.)

68. The June 13 roll call on the motion to rescind the rule of secrecy virtually established the voting pattern on the treaty. Eight Republican senators and Pierce Butler voted in opposition. The Federalist majority on this roll call consisted of nineteen Senators plus the Republican, Alexander Martin of North Carolina (*Annals*, IV, 858 [Senate]). Martin voted with the opposition on all subsequent roll calls, but John Vining, who did not take his seat until the 15th, consistently voted with the Federalist majority (*ibid.*, 858–862 *passim*). Thus the Senate divided 20 to 10; it was a voting pattern that was maintained on most substantive issues involving the treaty. The loss of one vote from the ranks of the Federalists would have defeated the treaty. If Washington or ER had endorsed the treaty, that probably would have guaranteed its passage. If either of them had indicated his dissatisfaction with the treaty, that almost certainly would have ensured its defeat, for several Federalist Senators representing southern states objected to the treaty because it failed to provide compensation for slaves carried away during the Revolution (*ibid.*, 861*ff*).

69. *Ibid.*, 859. There is considerable evidence that Rufus King introduced the motion calling for the removal of Article XII. Charles King implies as much in his study of his grandfather (King, ed., *Correspondence of R. King, II*, 9–10) and King had received a letter from Hamilton that urged him to take this course of action (A. Hamilton to R. King, New York, June 11, 1795, *Hamilton*, XVIII, 370–371.

70. *Annals*, IV, 860–861, (Senate).

71. *Ibid.*

72. *Ibid.*, 861.

73. *Ibid.*, 861–863. The Federalist motion of the 17th faced two critical tests on the 24th before securing passage.
   The first challenge was a motion by Read of South Carolina to amend the motion of June 17 so as to secure compensation for slaves carried off during the Revolution. The second was a Republican-sponsored motion to postpone the motion before the Senate and substitute a new motion that would recommend that the President reopen negotiations. Both were defeated (*ibid.*).

74. ER's hastily scribbled notes are in the Washington MSS labeled "Notes for the Consideration of the President" and are incorrectly dated "[Aug. or Sept.], 1794." The notes have also been incorrectly mounted in Vol. 268, Fol. 140, behind a subsequent memorandum of ER's, similarly labeled. The memorandum referred to here is pages 5 and 6 of the six pages mounted on Fol. 140. These two pages of notes, probably written on June 24, 1795, have been reprinted in W. C. Ford, ed., "Edmund Randolph on the British Treaty, 1795," *AHR*, XII, 589–590.

75. This memorandum is also labeled "Notes for the Consideration of the President, [Aug. or Sept.], 1794." It is pages 1–4 of the six pages mounted in Vol. 268, Fol. 140. It was written with much greater care by ER. It would seem both memoranda were written sometime between the adjournment of the Senate on June 24 and the end of this special session on June 26. A third memorandum in the Washington MSS, dated June 25 (see below), seems to have been written *subsequent* to these two undated memoranda, thereby establishing June 24 as the probable date for these two memoranda.

76. *Ibid.*, i.e., the "second" memorandum of [June 24?].

77. *Ibid.*

78. See above, note 75.

79. ER to G. Washington, June 25, 1795, Washington MSS.

80. *Ibid.*

81. G. Washington to Secretaries of State, Treasury and War and the Attorney General, Philadelphia, June 29, 1795, Fitzpatrick, ed., *Washington*, XXXIV, 224–225. The wording is almost identical to that in ER's memorandum.

82. *Annals*, IV, 867–868 (Senate).

83. ER, *Vindication*, 19. This defense by ER will be used as sparingly as possible as

a source of information, since it was obviously written with the intent of clearing the author. See also ER to R. King, Philadelphia, July 6, 1795, King, ed., *Correspondence of R. King*, II, 15–16.

84. *Ibid.*

85. [Philadelphia] *Aurora*, June 29, 1795. *Treaty of Amity, Commerce and Navigation, Between His Britannic Majesty, and the United States of America. By their President, with the Advice and Consent of the Senate* (Philadelphia, [July 1, 1795]), 24 pp. There were a total of sixteen editions of the treaty printed in 1795, but none of them seem to have been official (Evans, *American Bibliography*, serial nos. 29743–29756, 29759–29760).

86. The two memoranda dated June 24, and the third memorandum of June 25.

87. O. Wolcott to G. Washington, Treasury Dept., June 30, 1795, Gibbs, ed., *Wolcott*, I, 204–205; T. Pickering to G. Washington, [Philadelphia], June 30, 1795, Washington MSS.

88. ER's opinion, dated July 12, will be considered shortly. The opinion of W. Bradford has never been found, but a letter he wrote to Hamilton on July 2 sheds some light on his thinking.

> I find that the mode of ratification you hinted as the proper one, has been advised: yet the resolve of the Senate is so equivocally expressed that it may mean either, that the President shall *now* make a conditional ratification: or that he shall ratify it hereafter, *if* the British King shall consent to insert in the treaty the proposed article. Which of these do you take to [be] their meaning! On either construction, I hold this act to be the final act of the Senate and that it is not necessary to submit to them the new article after it shall be agreed to on the other side of the water. (W. Bradford to A. Hamilton, Philadelphia, July 2, 1795, *Hamilton*, XVII, 393–397, quote on p. 394.

89. G. Washington to A. Hamilton, Philadelphia, July 3, 1795, Fitzpatrick, ed., *Washington*, XXXIV, 226–228. Emphasis Washington's in quoted material.

90. ER to G. Washington, Philadelphia, July 4, 1795, Misc. Letters, Dept. State, NA. ER to G. Washington, Philadelphia, July 5, 1795, State Dept. Letterbook, Washington MSS. ER's recovery is announced in ER to G. Washington, July 7, 1795, State Dept. Letterbook, Washington MSS.

91. ER to G. Washington, Philadelphia, July 7, 1795, Washington MSS.

92. See W. Bradford to A. Hamilton, Philadelphia, July 2, 1795, *Hamilton*, XVII, 393–397. In this letter Bradford queries Hamilton on whether ER might be a fit choice to replace Jay. He indicated he was supporting ER's appointment.

93. Jay's letter of resignation was dated June 29 (J. Jay to G. Washington, New York, June 29, 1795, Johnston, ed., *Jay*, IV, 177). Washington accepted his resignation on July 2 (G. Washington to J. Jay, Philadelphia, July 2, 1795, Fitzpatrick. ed., *Washington*, XXXIV, 226). In a private letter to Rutledge on July 1 Washington invited him to accept the post vacated by Jay and stated that the "Secretary" will write to him, presumably to extend the formal offer of the government (G. Washington to J. Rutledge, Philadelphia, July 1, 1795, Fitzpatrick, ed., *Washington*, XXXIV, 225–226). A subsequent letter of ER's to Washington also indicated his awareness of the appointment during the first week of July.

94. ER to G. Washington, Philadelphia, July 7, 1795, Washington MSS.

95. Blair resigned Jan. 27, 1796 (*DAB*, *s.v.* "Blair, John").

96. The Order in Council dated Apr. 24, 1795, is most conveniently reprinted in Bemis, *John Quincy Adams*, I, 74. A comment on this Order in Council in the [Philadelphia] *Aurora*, June 25, 1795, establishes the approximate time that word of the order's existence reached Philadelphia.

The most perceptive analysis of the motives behind this new Order in Council is in Perkins, *The First Rapprochment*, 35–36. See also Josiah T. Newcomb, "New Light on Jay's Treaty," *American Journal of International Law*, XXVIII, 685–692.

97. A. Hamilton to G. Washington, New York, July 9, 1795, *Hamilton*, XVIII, 403–454.

98. Evident from ER to G. Washington, Dept. of State, July 12, 1795, published in full

in W. C. Ford, ed., "Edmund Randolph on the British Treaty, 1795," *AHR*, XII, 590–599.

99. *Ibid.* By way of commentary on this letter, it is noted that "Randolph's letter to the President on the question of ratification is no longer to be found among the Washington papers in that library [i.e., the Library of Congress], but may be seen only in the form of a copy in a volume of transcripts made for Washington of letters addressed to him by the secretaries of state [i.e., State Department Letterbook, Washington MSS]" (*ibid.*, 587).

100. Hamilton's letter of July 9, 1795.

101. Emphasis ER's.

102. ER, *Vindication*, 21.

103. *Ibid.*

104. This letter has never been found but its contents are evident from Washington's reply: G. Washington to A. Hamilton, Philadelphia, July 14, 1795, Fitzpatrick, ed., *Washington*, XXXIV, 241–242.

105. *Ibid.*

106. ER sent a total of thirteen official and "private" letters to Washington between July 17 and Aug. 5. Washington left Philadelphia on July 15 and returned on Aug. 11 (Freeman [Carroll & Ashworth], *Washington*, VII, 263, 278). The cities listed made news because of the statements against the treaty that emanated from them.

107. ER to G. Washington, Philadelphia, July 20, 1795, Washington MSS.

108. Mentioned as being enclosures in ER to G. Washington, July 24, 1795, State Dept. Letterbook, Washington MSS. The enclosures themselves have never been found.

109. G. Washington to ER, Baltimore, July 18, 1795, Fitzpatrick, ed., *Washington*, XXXIV, 243.

110. The preliminary "sketch" was sent on July 24 (ER to G. Washington, July 24, 1795, State Dept. Letterbook, Washington MSS). The draft approved by three members of the Cabinet and the individual drafts were sent on July 25 (ER to G. Washington, "private," Philadelphia, July 25, 1795, Washington MSS). None of these enclosures have been found. The draft Washington apparently selected was the one that had been approved by three members of the Cabinet. It was G. Washington to the Boston Selectmen, [United States, July 28, 1795], Fitzpatrick, ed., *Washington*, XXXIV, 252–253. See *ibid.*, 253n, for identification of the draft.

111. ER to G. Washington, ("private"), Philadelphia, July 24, 1795, Washington MSS, emphasis ER's.

112. Washington's letter of July 22 is acknowledged in ER to G. Washington, "Private," Philadelphia, July 25, 1795, Washington MSS.

113. G. Washington to ER, Mount Vernon, July 22, 1795, Fitzpatrick, ed., *Washington*, XXXIV, 243–246.

114. *Ibid.*

115. Brief but thorough summaries of these public demonstrations may be found in Freeman (Carroll & Ashworth), *Washington*, VII, 268–273.

116. ER to G. Washington, "Private," Philadelphia, July 27, 1795, Washington MSS.

117. Actually Washington received a more exact report on the Philadelphia meeting from Oliver Wolcott (O. Wolcott to G. Washington, Philadelphia, July 26, 1795, Gibbs, ed., *Wolcott*, II, 217–218). In the case of the other cities he was forced to rely more on newspaper accounts.

118. ER acknowledged Washington's letter of the 24th on Wednesday, July 29, indicating he had received it the previous day (ER to G. Washington, "Private," Philadelphia, July 29, 1795, Washington MSS).

119. G. Washington to ER, Mount Vernon, July 24, 1795, Fitzpatrick, ed., *Washington*, XXXIV, 246–247.

120. On his own initiative ER had suggested a trip to Mount Vernon on July 20 (ER to G. Washington, "Private," Philadelphia, July 20, 1795, Washington MSS). It was in response to this suggestion that Washington stated his preference for returning to Philadelphia (G. Washington to ER, Mount Vernon, July 24, 1795, Fitzpatrick, ed., *Washington*, XXXIV, 246–247). But before this reply reached Philadelphia ER had written (on July 25):

The gentlemen wished me to go down with it [i.e., the draft "answer[s]" to the Boston Selectmen]. I informed them that I should hear from you on Tuesday [July 28] in regard to the idea, which I mentioned to you on this subject. (ER to G. Washington, "Private," Philadelphia, July 25, 1795, Washington MSS.)

121. ER to G. Washington, "Private," Philadelphia, July 29, 1795, Washington MSS.
122. *Ibid.*
123. The letter to the Boston Selectmen, dated, by Washington "[United States, July 28, 1795]," is in Fitzpatrick, ed., *Washington*, XXXIV, 252–253. It probably was mailed from Mount Vernon, but ER was unaware of this on July 31.
124. Evident from ER to G. Washington, "Private," Philadelphia, July 31, 1795, Washington MSS.
125. *Ibid.*
126. ER to G. Washington, July 31, 1795, State Dept. Letterbook, Washington MSS.

CHAPTER 21

1. That heavy rains delayed the mail between Philadelphia and Mount Vernon can be established from ER to G. Washington Philadelphia, Aug. 5, 1795, Washington MSS; G. Washington to A. Hamilton, Mount Vernon, Aug. 3, 1795, G. Washington to William Pearce, Charlestown, [Md.], Aug. 9, 1795, Fitzpatrick, ed., *Washington*, XXXIV, 267–268, 270–272.
   It is assumed that Washington received ER's letter on Aug. 5. See reasoning on same in Freeman (Carroll & Ashworth), *Washington*, VII, 277n.
2. ER to G. Washington, "Private," Philadelphia, July 29, 1795, Washington MSS.
3. The first letter is ER to G. Washington, July 31, 1795, State Dept. Letterbook, Washington MSS. The second is ER to G. Washington, "Private," Philadelphia, July 31, 1795 Washington MSS. See also Timothy Pickering to G. Washington, [Philadelphia, July 31, 1795], Pickering & Upham, *Pickering*, III, 188–189.
4. Timothy Pickering to G. Washington, [Philadelphia, July 31, 1795]. Pickering & Upham, *Pickering*, III, 188–189. Emphasis his.
5. Freeman (Carroll & Ashworth), *Washington*, VII, 278.
6. See ER to G. Washington, Aug. 3, 1795, State Dept. Letterbook, Washington MSS.
7. During July there was a circular to all our ministers and consuls, dated July 21, and three letters to Monroe, dated July 14, 19 and 30, respectively.
8. Evident from ER to G. Washington, "Private," Philadelphia, July 31, 1795, Washington MSS.
9. ER to G. Washington, [Philadelphia], Aug. 3, 1795, State Dept. Letterbook, Washington MSS.
10. Josef de Jaudenes to ER, Philadelphia, Aug. 1, 1795, Notes from Foreign Legations, Spain, Dept. State, NA.
11. ER to Josef de Jaudenes, Philadelphia, Aug. 4, 1795, Dom. Letters, Dept. State, NA.
12. Elias Vanderhorst to ER, Bristol, [Eng.], June 17, 1795, Consular Dispatches, [Bristol, Eng.], Dept. State, NA. Although there were other consular reports noting the existence of this order, apparently this was the first ER received for he noted its contents in a letter to Washington (ER to G. Washington, "Private," Philadelphia, Aug. 5, 1795, Washington MSS).
13. Washington reached Philadelphia at noon on Tuesday, Aug. 11 (Freeman [Carroll & Ashworth] *Washington*, VII, 278).
14. ER's presence at Washington's dinner table can only be established from Timothy Pickering's "Miscellaneous Notes" in Pickering & Upham, *Pickering*, III, 216–219, written in 1826 when Pickering was eighty-one years old (*ibid.*, 215). They recount the events surrounding Randolph's resignation from the Cabinet.
15. *Ibid.*
   It was at this time that Washington first learned that Pickering, Wolcott and Bradford had an intercepted letter from Jean Fauchet that implied that ER had solicited funds from the French minister. This intelligence further explained Pickering's urgent appeal of Aug. 31 that Washington return immediately to

Philadelphia. ER, of course, had no inkling of the purpose of Pickering's visit that evening. Pickering's own account would indicate it was a very brief visit:

I hastened to the President's house, where I found him, at the table; and Randolph—cheerful and apparently in good spirits—also at the table. Very soon, after taking a glass of wine, the President rose, giving me a wink. I rose and followed him into another room. "What," said he, "is the cause of your writing me such a letter?" "That man," said I, "in the other room (pointing towards that in which we had left Randolph) is a traitor." I then, in two or three minutes, gave the President an intimation of what Fauchet, in his intercepted letter, said of Randolph. "Let us return to the other room," said the President, "to prevent any suspicion of the cause of our withdrawing." I had deliberately and carefully made a written translation of Fauchet's letter, ready for the President's examination. (*Ibid.*)

16. That the Cabinet meeting took place on Aug. 12, see ER, *Vindication*, 53–54. Washington had already tentatively approved ER's draft of the memorial on the treaty (G. Washington to ER, "Private," Mount Vernon, July 31, 1795, Fitzpatrick, ed., *Washington*, XXXIV, 264–267). Hammond left Philadelphia on Aug. 15 for New York to take passage for England (Phineas Bond to Lord Grenville, Philadelphia, Aug. 16, 1795 [Transcript], F.O. 5/10, PRO).
17. ER, *Vindication*, 50 and 54; "Miscellaneous Notes," Pickering & Upham, *Pickering*, III, 218–219.
18. Washington's letter of July 22 made this absolutely clear (G. Washington to ER, Mount Vernon, July 22, 1795, Fitzpatrick, ed., *Washington*, XXXIV, 243–246).
19. Hamilton's letter to Washington has never been found, but that he gave this opinion to Washington is evident from ER to G. Washington, "Private," Philadelphia, July 24, 1795, Washington MSS. He repeated his views on this point in A. Hamilton to O. Wolcott, New York, Aug. 10, 1795, *Hamilton*, XIX, 111–112.
    ER's proposal that the threat of withholding America's approval be used to force the British to withdraw their Order in Council has been fully discussed above.
20. "Miscellaneous Notes," Pickering & Upham, *Pickering*, III, 216–219.
21. "To my unutterable astonishment, I soon discovered that you were receding from your '*determination.*'" ER, *Vindication*, 54.
22. *Ibid.*, 55.
23. ER's limited correspondence between Aug. 12 and Aug. 19, the date on which he first learned of Fauchet's letter, reveals not the slightest trace of bitterness at Washington's decision to sign, yet he had ample opportunity and any number of intimate correspondents to whom he could unburden himself. The views expressed in this paragraph merely reflect the absence of any critical or negative comment in ER's correspondence during this period. I do not mean to imply that Washington's awareness of Fauchet's letter was the "reason" for his decision to sign. Speculatively, it is possible to advance any number of reasons for the President's decision.
    It should be noted that ER's *Vindication*, written in the light of subsequent events, places an entirely different interpretation on Washington's attitude during this period.
24. Evident from ER to G. Washington, "Memorandum," [Aug. 12–14, 1795], Washington MSS. See also Fitzpatrick, ed., *Washington*, XXXIV, 254n, which reprints this memorandum adding some further information regarding the reaction of Washington to the various memorials.
25. *Ibid.*
26. ER, *Vindication*, 39.
27. *Ibid.* Copies of the circular naturally appear in several collections, but it is most conveniently printed as ER to J. Monroe (Circular), Philadelphia, July 21, 1795, *ASP For. Rel.*, I, 719. The letter to Monroe (ER to J. Monroe, Philadelphia, July 14, 1795) is also in *ASP For. Rel.*, I, 719.
    Moncure Conway asserts at two different points in his biography that ER showed Washington two letters to "Monroe," one dated July 21 and the second

dated July 29 (Conway, *Randolph*, 253 and 283). He further prints "abstracts" of both letters which he says were in Washington's hand, thereby implying Washington made "abstracts" after ER delivered them to him (*ibid.*, 253–255). From Conway's printed "abstract" it can be established that the letter of July 21 is the circular cited above and mentioned in ER's *Vindication*. The "abstract" of the second letter clearly established it as ER to J. Monroe, Philadelphia, July 29, 1795, Monroe MSS, NYPL. The assumption of anyone reading the biography is that Conway was accurate in his statement that ER showed these two letters to Washington—how else could one account for the "abstracts" in Washington's hand? This, in turn, has led Professor Carroll and Mrs. Ashworth in the final volume of the Freeman biography to conclude that ER showed Washington all three letters, i.e. July 14 (Monroe), July 21 (Circular, including Monroe), and July 29 (Monroe) (Freeman [Carroll & Ashworth], *Washington*, VII, 288–289).

All of this would have very little significance were it not for the fact that ER's letter of July 29 contains a highly critical assessment of Fauchet's conduct as minister to the United States. This has been viewed by Professor Carroll and Mrs. Ashworth as playing an important part in the crystalization of Washington's attitude toward ER (*ibid.*, 288–289 and 289n). It is this author's contention that ER showed Washington only the letters he mentioned in his *Vindication* (i.e. July 14 and 21) and not his letter of July 29. There are several reasons for this conclusion: (1) If he had shown Washington the letter of July 29, he would have been obliged to mention it in his *Vindication*. But even more important, the letter, placed in the proper context in the *Vindication*, would have strengthened his case, for it was highly critical of Fauchet's conduct. (2) The "abstracts" Conway says are in Washington's hand have never been found by Fitzpatrick for his *Writings of Washington*, by Freeman, Carroll or Ashworth for their biography, or by this writer. They do not seem to exist. As for the reasons why ER did *not* show the letter of the 29th to Washington—this is a matter on which one could speculate endlessly.

28. Evident from G. Washington to ER, Mount Vernon, Sept. 27, 1795, Fitzpatrick, ed., *Washington*, XXXIV, 316–317. See also Miller, ed., *Treaties of the U.S.*, II, 272.

29. The memorial is ER to G. Hammond, Philadelphia, Aug. 14, 1795, Dom. Letters, Dept. State, NA.

30. *Ibid.*

31. *Ibid.*

32. G. Hammond to Lord Grenville, Aug. 14, 1795, F.O. 5/9, PRO.

33. Evident from ER to R. King, Philadelphia, Aug. 16, 1795, King, ed., *Correspondence of R. King*, II, 29.

34. ER to J. Jay, [Philadelphia], Aug. 16, 1795—excerpt of printed in Fitzpatrick, ed., *Washington*, XXXIV 255n.

35. ER to R. King, Philadelphia, Aug. 16, 1795, King, ed., *Correspondence of R. King*, II, 29.

36. ER, *Vindication*, 50.

37. *Ibid.*, 55.

38. *Ibid.*, 5.

39. *Ibid.*, 5–6.

40. *Ibid.*, 6.

41. Oct. 31, 1794. A copy of the dispatch may be found in Turner, ed., "CFM," *AHA, Annual Report, 1903*, II, 444–455.

The "history" of No. 10 from Oct. 31, 1794, to Aug. 19, 1795, is worth reconstructing in some detail.

The dispatch had been placed aboard the French corvette *Jean Bart*, which was captured off Pesmarque by the English frigate *Cerberus* on Mar. 28, 1795. Sent to the Foreign Office, it was in turn forwarded by Lord Grenville to Hammond on June 5, 1795 (Lord Grenville to G. Hammond, Downing Street, May 9, 1795, Lord Grenville to G. Hammond, June 5, 1795, both in Mayo, ed., "Inst. to Br. Ministers," *AHA, Annual Report, 1936*, III, 83, 85). Hammond received Grenville's letter of June 5 containing Fauchet's No. 10 shortly before July 26 (acknowledged on July

27, *ibid.*, 85*n*) and, in accordance with his instructions to use it in a manner most beneficial to the interest of Great Britain (*ibid.*, 83), he invited Wolcott to his home for dinner on Sunday, July 26 ("Notes Relative to Fauchet's Letter," Gibbs, ed., *Wolcott*, I, 232–233). Immediately after dinner Hammond took Wolcott into another room and read, in English, sections of the dispatch (*ibid.*). Wolcott concluded that the dispatch "could not fail to establish a belief that something highly improper had been proposed by Mr. Randolph" but that information of such magnitude could not be communicated unless he was "put in possession of the document necessary to support my allegations" (*ibid.*). Ultimately, after a subsequent conversation, Hammond agreed to surrender Fauchet's dispatch provided Wolcott would permit Hammond to have a copy "with my attestation of having received the original, and that it was my true and sincere belief, founded on an acquaintance with Mr. Fauchet's handwriting, that the said letter was genuine" (*ibid.*). Wolcott received the original letter on July 28 and immediately took it to Pickering who, with the aid of a French dictionary and grammar, translated the letter ("Miscellaneous Notes," Pickering & Upham, *Pickering*, III, 216–219). On July 29 Wolcott and Pickering rode out to the summer residence of the Attorney General to show him the letter and Pickering's translation. It was unanimously agreed that Washington should be requested to return to Philadelphia as soon as possible (*ibid.*). On July 31 Wolcott and Pickering urged ER to write Washington requesting him to return to Philadelphia ("Notes Relative to Fauchet's Letter," Gibbs, ed., *Wolcott*, I, 232–233). That same day Pickering wrote to Washington himself, urging his immediate return ("Miscellaneous Notes," Pickering & Upham, *Pickering*, III, 216–219). Washington reached Philadelphia on Aug. 11 and that night was informed of Fauchet's letter (see above).

What happened between Aug. 11 and Aug. 19 is somewhat more difficult to establish. That it was the subject of some discussion between Washington and at least two of his Cabinet officers can be established by Washington's long undated memorandum to Wolcott and Pickering, here quoted in full:

At what time should Mr. F[auche]t's letter be made known to Mr. R[andolph]?

What will be the best mode of doing it? In the presence of the Sec[retarie]s and A[ttorney] Gen[era]l[?]

If the explanations given by the latter [*sic*] [i.e. Randolph] are not satisfactory, whether, besides removal, are any other measures proper to be taken? And what?

Would an application of Mr. A[det] to see the paragraphs in Nos. 3 and 6 alluded to in F[auche]t's letter be proper? These might condemn, or acquit, unequivocally. And, if innocent, whether R[andolph] will not apply for them if I do not?

If upon the investigation of this subject, it should appear less dark than at present, but not so clear as to restore confidence, and a continuance in office, in what light and on what ground is the removal to appear to the public?

What immediate steps are necessary to be taken as soon as the removal of R[andolph] is resolved on, if that should be the case, with respect to the archives in that office?

If the letter of F[auche]t is the only evidence, and that thought sufficient to the removal what would be the consequences of giving that letter to the public, without any comment, as the ground on which the measure of the Executive respecting the removal is founded? It w[oul]d speak for itself. A part, without the whole, might be charged with unfairness. The public would expect reasons for the sudden removal of so high an officer, and it will be found not easy to avoid saying too little or too much, upon such an occasion: as it is not to be expected that the removed Officer, will acquiesce without attempting a justification, or at least do away by explanations the sting of the letter of accusation; unless he was let down easily. To do which, I see no way: for if he is guilty of what is charged, he merits *no* favor; and if he is not he will accept none. And it is not difficult to perceive what turn *he* and his friends will give the act, namely, that his friendship for the French nation, and his opposition to a compleat ratification have been the causes. (G. Washington to Secretaries of War and Treasury, [Aug. 12–18, 1795], Fitzpatrick, ed., *Washington*, XXXIV, 275–276.)

There were no written replies to this memorandum. The only written account of what transpired "after" this memorandum and before Aug. 19 is contained in a letter from Wolcott to John Marshall of June 29, 1806, written in consequence of a request by Marshall for information on how far Washington's disposition to ratify the Jay Treaty had been affected by his knowledge of Fauchet's dispatch. The pertinent sections of Wolcott's letter are:

> The first two of these questions [Wolcott had just quoted Washington's memorandum in full] were decided by the President, uninfluenced, as far as my knowledge and belief extends, by any suggestions from the officers of government. He was greatly dissatisfied that the instructions and memorial [on the treaty's ratification] had not been prepared and submitted to the consideration of the Secretaries and Attorney-General that their reports might be formed, and he preemptorily resolved that whether Randolph was innocent or culpable, he would require of him the performance of a service which was his official duty, and which ought to have been long before completed.

And:

> After mature consideration it was considered to be improper to make any application to Mr. Adet; that it was improbable that Mr. Adet would permit his records to be inspected; that neither Fauchet's dispatch[es?] [*sic*] nor any certificate of the French Minister could be regarded as conclusive evidence in favor of or against Mr. Randolph. That Mr. Randolph's conduct at the time an explanation was required would probably furnish the best means of discovering his true situation and of duly estimating the defence he might make. (O. Wolcott to J. Marshall, June 9, 1806, Gibbs, ed., *Wolcott*, I, 241–246.)

Wolcott, however, was inaccurate in his observation that ER had not prepared the instructions and memorial for the treaty's ratification (see above).

There are at least two major areas in the "history" of this dispatch that have proven particularly susceptible to speculative analysis. The first, the extent of Wolcott's and Pickering's dislike of and/or disagreement with ER, has been, consciously or unconsciously, assessed by virtually all writers who have described the handling of this dispatch. In defense of Wolcott and Pickering it may be said that there is no evidence indicating they did *not* believe the letter was incriminating. Conversely, it must be noted that as ardent Federalists they were of a different political persuasion than ER. Secondly, Washington's memorandum to Pickering and Wolcott has understandably invited psychological analysis or has been used as evidence to establish Washington's general attitude toward ER during this critical period. Unsupported as it is by other expressions of Washington's views during these eight days, it remains susceptible to any number of interpretations, no one of which can be said to be more valid than the others.

42. See note 47 for more details about Fauchet's dispatch. See Appendix for the English translation of this dispatch.

43. ER, *Vindication*, 6.

44. *Ibid.*

45. Both ER's (*ibid.*) and Wolcott's account (O. Wolcott to J. Marshall, June 9, 1806, Gibbs, ed., *Wolcott*, I, 241–246) note that he read the letter twice. There is no summary of his remarks during this second reading except as noted in the next note.

46. ER, *Vindication*, 6. Wolcott says he made these observations when he reached that paragraph in Fauchet's dispatch that made reference to dispatch No. 6 (O.

Wolcott to J. Marshall, June 9, 1806, Gibbs, ed., *Wolcott*, I, 241–246). Randolph himself indicates these observations occurred after he completed his second reading and explanation, (ER, *Vindication*, 6).

47. ER, *Vindication*, 6. It is impossible to reconstruct ER's verbal "explanation" from the brief account of this meeting in the *Vindication* or the accounts of Wolcott or Pickering. Rather than engage in a conjectural description of his probable explanation, using the defense constructed over a month later when he was writing the *Vindication*, it was thought best not to introduce Randolph's explanation until it can be treated as a part of the general description of the *Vindication* itself.

Wolcott's and Pickering's description of what Randolph said and how he reacted should be quoted in full. Pickering's account of the meeting reads as follows:

> The President desired us to watch Randolph's countenance while he perused it [Fauchet's dispatch]. The President fixed his own eye upon him; and I never before, or afterwards, saw it look so animated. Randolph (to whom the French language was familiar) read through the long letter, without any visible emotion. This was admitted by the President, Wolcott, Bradford [Bradford was not present], and myself, as soon as Randolph withdrew. When the latter had reached the end of the letter, he very deliberately said to the President, "If I may be permitted to retain this letter a short time, I shall be able to explain, in a satisfactory manner, everything in it which has a reference to me." "Very well," answered the President, "retain it." But instead of giving the proposed explanation, Randolph sent in his resignation. This, if I correctly remember was about the 18th or 19th of August, 1795. ("Miscellaneous Notes," Pickering & Upham, *Pickering*, III, 216–219.)

Wolcott's description is somewhat more graphic:

> When the letter was delivered to Mr. Randolph, the President requested him to read it and to make such observations thereon as he thought proper. He silently perused it with composure till he arrived at the passage which refers to his "precious confessions" [see page 371] when his embarrassment was manifest. After a short hesitation, he proceeded to look over the letter with great attention. When the perusal was completed, he said with a smile which I thought forced, "Yes, sir, I will explain what I know." He then commenced reading the letter by paragraphs, and though a great part of it contained nothing interesting to himself, yet he commented on every part. His remarks were very desultory, and it was evident that he was considering what explanations he should give of the most material passages. As he was not interrupted it was, however, impossible to speak with precision on one subject while his reflections were employed on other subjects. When he arrived at the passage in which Fauchet refers to the overtures mentioned in No. 6, and the "tariff" which regulated the conscience of certain "pretended patriots" [see pages 376–377], his conduct was very remarkable. He expressed no strong emotion, no resentment against Fauchet. He declared that he could not certainly tell what was intended by such remarks. He said that he had indeed recollected having been informed that Mr. Hammond and other persons in New York were contriving measures to destroy Governor Clinton, the French Minister, and himself, and that he had inquired of Mr. Fauchet whether he could not by his flour contractors provide the means of defeating their machinations. He asserted, however, that he had never received or proposed to receive money for his own use or that of any other person, and had never made any improper communications of the measures of government.
>
> One question only was put to Mr. Randolph, namely, how he intended to be understood when he represented Mr. Hammond as contriving to destroy Governor Clinton, Mr. Fauchet, and himself? His answer was that their influence and popularity were to be destroyed.
>
> Mr. Randolph retired for a short time, but he must have felt that neither the manner nor the matter of his explanation could afford any degree of

satisfaction. The result was a proposal by Mr. Randolph of an immediate resignation, which he proposed to communicate in writing. Mr. Randolph has represented that his proposal to resign was accompanied by expressions of resentment at the treatment he had received. Although his letter of resignation places the affair on this ground, yet my impression of what happened during the personal interview are very different.

(O. Wolcott to J. Marshall, June 9, 1806, Gibbs, ed., *Wolcott*, I. 241–246.)

48. ER, *Vindication*, 6–7. See Wolcott's description as given in preceding note.
49. *Ibid.*, 7. Randolph's account reads as follows:

> While I was appealing to the President's memory for communications, which I had made to him on the subject; and after he had said, with some warmth, that he should not conceal any thing, which he recollected, or words to that effect; he was called out to receive from Mr. Willing the copy of an address, which was to be presented to him the next day by the merchants. (*Ibid.*)

50. *Ibid.*
51. Evident from his letter of resignation, written later that same day: ER to G. Washington, Philadelphia, Aug. 15, 1795, Washington MSS.
52. ER, *Vindication*, 7–8; O. Wolcott to J. Marshall, June 9, 1806, Gibbs, ed., *Wolcott*, I, 241–246. The pertinent paragraph has been quoted above.
53. ER to G. Washington, Philadelphia, Aug. 19, 1795, Washington MSS.
54. *Ibid.*
55. *Ibid.* The only significant deletion in the letter of resignation in the Washington MSS are the words "this morning" in the fourth paragraph: "if I learn ~~this morning~~, that there is a chance of overtaking Mr. Fauchet before he sails, I will go to him immediately." This deletion would seem to indicate that ER thought it was still before noon as he wrote the letter, but on rereading it he recognized his mistake (*ibid.*). It therefore seems safe to conclude that the letter was written fairly soon after he left Washington's office.
56. *Ibid.*
57. The letter, as it was printed in the *Vindication* (8–9) has the words "this morning" (see note 55) included in it. He apparently made a copy of the original, then corrected the original but forgot to make the same deletion in his own copy.
58. ER, *Vindication*, 9.
59. ER knew that the *Africa* was off the coast of Rhode Island by the 11th or 12th of August (evident from T. Pickering to P. Adet, Dept. of State, Aug. 25, 1795, *ASP For. Rel.*, I, 631). He knew it was trying to intercept the *Medusa* by the time he left for the city (evident from Phineas Bond to Lord Grenville, Philadelphia, Aug. 24, 1795, F.O. 5/10, PRO). Both of these letters establish that such information was common knowledge in Philadelphia.
60. ER's letter of resignation was endorsed by Washington "rec'd. the 20th abt. noon" (ER to G. Washington, Philadelphia, Aug. 19, 1795, Washington MSS). Washington's reply (G. Washington to ER, Philadelphia, Aug. 20, 1795, Fitzpatrick, ed., *Washington*, XXXIV, 276–277) was not acknowledged until Sept. 21 (ER to G. Washington, Philadelphia, Sept. 21, 1795, Misc. Letters, Dept. State, NA). The copy of No. 10 was not sent until Aug. 22 (G. Washington to ER, Philadelphia, Aug. 22, 1795, Fitzpatrick, ed., *Washington*, XXXIV, 281).
61. ER, *Vindication*, 9–10. He may well have expected Washington to forward a copy of No. 10 to him so that he might have it when he confronted Fauchet. If this was the case, he was to be disappointed.
62. ER to Betsy [Randolph], New York, Aug. 25, [1795], Edmund Randolph MSS, VHS. His observation on King was unfair. The day after King visited ER King wrote:

> Mr. Randolph a few days since resigned his office as Secretary of State, he is now here on his way to Rhode Island. He does not explain himself in relation to this sudden measure. It will probably be suggested, that he has gone out of office from a dislike of the English treaty—this will be wholly incorrect. Mr.

Randolph approved of the treaty *in toto*; and he yesterday told me, he saw no reason to change or alter, his opinion on that subject. (R. King to [Christopher Gore], [New York], Aug. 25, 1795, King, ed., *Correspondence of R. King*, II, 30.)

63. ER to Betsy [Randolph], New York, Aug. 25, [1795] Edmund Randolph MSS, VHS.
64. ER, *Vindication*, 10. Aside from the letters and affidavits ER collected in connection with his experiences in Newport, his *Vindication* provides the only detailed record of his activities between Aug. 31 and Sept. 3.
65. ER mentioned the names of Henry Marchant and Francis Malbone to Fauchet when he talked with him shortly after eight o'clock the next morning (see below). It seems safe to conclude therefore that he must have established that they were in the city sometime during the afternoon or evening of the 31st.
66. ER, *Vindication*, 10.

Henry Marchant, judge of the United States District Court in Rhode Island, was a former member of the Continental Congress (1777–1779) and an important figure in Rhode Island's ratification of the Constitution, for which he was rewarded with the federal judgeship in 1790. He resided in Newport virtually all his life. (*DAB, s.v.* "Marchant, Henry.")

Francis Malbone, a Federalist, was a member of the U.S. House of Representatives from 1793 to 1797. Born in Newport, he was a merchant in that city for most of his life. He served briefly in the U.S. Senate in 1809, his term of office being cut short by his death in June of that year. (*Biographical Directory of the American Congress, 1774–1961*, 1256.)

67. ER, *Vindication*, 10.
68. Printed in *ibid.*, 11.
69. This information is drawn from the affidavit of Peck, printed in *ibid.*, 11.
70. *Ibid.* Peck wrote on the back of Randolph's undelivered letter to Fauchet (Papers on Vindication of Edmund Randolph MSS).
71. ER, *Vindication*, 12.
72. Printed in *ibid.*, 11, in English. The original, in French, is in Papers on Vindication of Edmund Randolph MSS.
73. This information is taken from the affidavit of Gardner, printed in ER, *Vindication*, 12. From the original it can be established that the first part of the affidavit is in Gardner's hand and is signed by him, the second part is in an unknown hand but is signed by Gardner (Papers on Vindication of Edmund Randolph MSS).

CHAPTER 22

1. He passed through Fairfield, Conn., on Monday, Sept. 7, (ER to [John?] Langdon, "Fairfield in Connecticut," Sept. 7, 1795, printed in Conway, *Randolph*, 306).
2. So stated in ER to G. Washington, Germantown, [Penn.], Sept. 15, 1795 [1st letter of this date], Misc. Letters, Dept. State, NA.
3. *Ibid.* He probably reached Germantown on Sept. 13 or 14.
4. He did not go into Philadelphia until Sunday, Sept. 20 (ER to G. Washington, Philadelphia, Sept. 21, 1795, Misc. Letters, Dept. State, NA).

In his letter of Sept. 15 he remarked: "Having passed thro' New York on my return; I am under the necessity of remaining at the distance of five miles from Philadelphia until Saturday next [Sept. 19]." (ER to G. Washington, Germantown, [Penn.], Sept. 15, 1795 [1st letter of this date], Misc. Letters, Dept. State, NA.) It should be noted that the reappearance of yellow fever in the city of New York for the third successive summer had caused the city of Philadelphia to issue a proclamation forbidding anyone from New York or Norfolk to come within a distance of five miles of Philadelphia (Oberholtzer, *Philadelphia*, I, 375).

5. Pickering, who had been serving as Secretary of War since January, agreed to handle the duties of the Department of State as well as his own department until such time as a successor to ER could be found. ER's resignation and the unexpected death of William Bradford forced Washington to give a considerable

amount of attention to filling the vacancies in his Cabinet. The difficulties he encountered have been ably described in Freeman (Carroll & Ashworth), *Washington*, VII, 300, 311–313, 339–340.

6. T. Pickering to ER, Dept. of State, Sept. 14, 1795 [copy], Timothy Pickering Papers, MHS.

7. ER to G. Washington, Germantown, [Penn.], Sept. 15, 1795 [2nd letter of this date], Misc. Letters, Dept. State, NA.

8. Evident from ER to G. Washington, Philadelphia, Sept. 21, 1795, ER, *Vindication*, 19–20.

9. G. Washington to ER, Philadelphia, Aug. 20, 1795, Fitzpatrick, ed., *Washington*, XXXIV, 276–277.

10. G. Washington to ER, Philadelphia, Aug. 22, 1795, *ibid.*, 281. The enclosure, No. 10, is in Papers on Vindication of Edmund Randolph MSS. See Appendix for the English translation of this dispatch.

11. G. Washington to ER, Philadelphia, Aug. 20, 1795, Fitzpatrick, ed., *Washington*, XXXIV, 276–277.

Irving Brant's study of the events surrounding ER's resignation ("Edmund Randolph, Not Guilty," *WMQ*, [3rd ser.] VII, 179–198) advanced, for the first time, the suggestion that Pickering and Wolcott knew of No. 6 when Pickering translated No. 10 (*ibid.*, 193–195, 194n). Brant maintains that Pickering could not have translated the phrase *"avec un air fort empressé"* in No. 10 as "with a countenance expressive of much anxiety" without having had access to No. 6, in which the same incident was described, using the phrase *"toute sa physionomie était douleur."* Brant's case seems irrefutable when it is coupled with his documented references to Grenville's and Hammond's use of the word "dispatch*es*" in their correspondence relating to No. 10 and ER's statement in his *Vindication* that he had been assured that a duplicate of No. 6 accompanied No. 10 on the *Jean Bart*.

The only difficulty with Brant's hypothesis (and it does not constitute a refutation) is that Pickering's translation of No. 10 is not the most defamatory translation possible. Also, there is no evidence to indicate that either man actually set out to destroy ER. (They probably would have accepted any explanation of No. 10 that the President judged adequate unless "coached" to take a different stand.) There is in fact evidence that Wolcott and Pickering had considerable respect for ER as a person. It was not until ER began to release to the press excerpts of his letters to the President—late in Sept., 1795—that they lost all respect for the man.

As ER's actions are traced in subsequent pages of this chapter it will become evident that he himself had little interest in the accuracy of Pickering's translation *per se*. To ER, Pickering and Wolcott were conspirators only in the sense of having become the gullible tools of Hammond. They accepted Fauchet's account of ER's activities without question, and thrust the document into Washington's hands as soon as he returned to Philadelphia to confuse and mislead him, thereby securing the ratification of the treaty. ER, in short, had much less respect for the conspiratorial talents of Wolcott and Pickering than Irving Brant. A reading of Wolcott's and Pickering's letters during this period causes this writer to conclude that ER's assessment of the two men is much closer to the truth than Brant's.

12. ER to G. Washington, Philadelphia, Sept. 21, 1795, full text printed in ER, *Vindication*, 19–20.

13. The most obvious example would be Phineas Bond, the British chargé, who represented his government after Hammond's departure on Aug. 15 and who would have access to Hammond's files. But more important, Wolcott, Pickering and Bradford may well have communicated the substance of the letter to close political friends between July 27 and Aug. 20. It was on Aug. 20 that G. Washington agreed to ER's request that the matter be kept confidential.

14. Wolcott notes the city's intense interest in ER's explanation of his resignation in O. Wolcott to G. Washington, Philadelphia, Sept. 26, 1795, Gibbs, ed., *Wolcott*, I, 246.

15. *Philadelphia Gazette*, Sept. 26, 1795.

16. ER to G. Washington, Germantown, [Penn.], Sept. 15, 1795 [1st letter of this date], Misc. Letters, Dept. State, NA.
17. Since no record of a written request has been found, it seems safe to conclude that ER contacted Adet after arriving in the city of Philadelphia. See Adet's account in P. A. Adet to Committee of Public Safety, Philadelphia, [Sept. 30, 1795], Turner, ed., "CFM," *AHA, Annual Report, 1903*, II, 783–785.
18. Adet's certificate, Sept. 26, 1795, as in ER, *Vindication*, 19. The original, in French, is in Papers on Vindication of Edmund Randolph MSS. The enclosures, i.e. Fauchet's certificate of ER's innocence and the extracts of Nos 3 and 6, have been translated and printed in the *Vindication*, 13–19. See Appendix for the English translation of pertinent sections from these dispatches. The original copies of these enclosures may also be found in Papers on Vindication of Edmund Randolph MSS. It is impossible to determine who provided the English translation of these documents for the *Vindication*. See below for such details as are known on the translation of No. 10 for the *Vindication*.
     It is also important to note that Adet's extract of No. 3 did not include that portion of the dispatch that referred to ER's suggestion for influencing the public press on behalf of France. ER was unaware of this part of Fauchet's dispatch.
     See full dispatches: J. Fauchet to Minister of Foreign Affairs, Philadelphia, [June 4, 1794], and J. Fauchet to Commissioner of Foreign Relations, Philadelphia, Sept. 5, 1794, Turner, ed., "CFM," *AHA, Annual Report, 1903*, II, 372–377, 411–418.
19. See p. 316.
20. G. Washington to ER, Mount Vernon, Sept. 27, 1795, Fitzpatrick, ed., *Washington*, XXXIV, 316–317.
21. ER to O. Wolcott, Philadelphia, Oct. 2, 1795, Gibbs, ed., *Wolcott*, I, 250–251.
22. O. Wolcott to ER, Philadelphia, Oct. 2, 1795, *ibid.*, 251.
23. Events recounted in ER to G. Washington, Philadelphia, Oct. 8, 1795, printed in ER, *Vindication*, 23–24.
24. *Ibid.*
25. The letter impressed itself on ER's mind because it carried the startling authorization to convey Washington's views on the treaty to the other members of the Cabinet, indicating they had not been informed of his ultimate decision on how he would handle the treaty. See p. 304.
26. ER to G. Washington, Philadelphia, Oct. 8, 1795, ER, *Vindication*, 23–24.
27. George Taylor to ER, Dept. of State, Oct. 6, 1795, ER, *Vindication*, 25.
28. G. Washington to ER, Mount Vernon, July 22, 1795, Fitzpatrick, ed., *Washington*, XXXIV, 243–246.
29. This became a theme in his *Vindication* which, in some respects, overshadowed his explanation of No. 10.
30. The letter that was sent to Washington detailing Pickering's conduct has been previously cited and is ER to G. Washington, Philadelphia, Oct. 8, 1795, ER, *Vindication*, 23–24. The first draft of this letter, however, was written on Oct. 6 (as evidenced by the language employed) and is found in Papers on Vindication of Edmund Randolph MSS. It was the very day ER received Taylor's letter containing Pickering's reply. A marginal notation in ER's hand indicates Taylor was shown the first draft. ER revised the letter the following day (second draft, *ibid.*), keeping intact the paragraph Taylor had seen and approved. This second draft contained the paragraph listing the letters he intended to use in constructing his vindication. He deleted several sentences from this paragraph in preparing his final copy. The Washington MSS contains the letter that was actually sent to Washington.
31. ER to O. Wolcott, Philadelphia, Oct. 8, 1795, Gibbs, ed., *Wolcott*, I, 252.
32. O. Wolcott to ER, Philadelphia, Oct. 8 1795, *ibid.*, 252.
33. *Philadelphia Gazette*, Oct. 10, 1795. Only the last paragraph of the letter was published. It contained his threat to appeal to the people if the July 22 letter was withheld.
34. Madison, in a letter to Jefferson, referred to the publication, underlining the date of the letter and the date of publication to call attention to their closeness. He

made no comment on the propriety of ER's conduct (J. Madison to T. Jefferson, Orange, [Va.], Oct. 18, 1795, Madison MSS.)

35. Evident from Washington's reply: G. Washington to ER, Philadelphia, Oct. 21, 1795, Fitzpatrick, ed., *Washington*, XXXIV, 339–342.

36. Pickering's role in the drafting of the letter has been very minutely recorded by Fitzpatrick in his footnotes (*ibid.*, 339*n*–342*n*).

37. *Ibid.*, 339–342.

38. ER to G. Washington, Philadelphia, Oct. 24, 1795, ER, *Vindication*, 26–27.

On the same day ER sent a short letter to Samuel Bayard observing: "I shall quietly send to you a statement of my controversy with the President; whose hypocrisy and perfidy are unexampled but by Tiberius." (ER to Samuel Bayard, Philadelphia, Oct. 24, 1795, Simon Gratz Collection, HSP.)

39. G. Washington to ER, Philadelphia, Oct. 25, 1795 [not sent], Fitzpatrick, ed., *Washington*, XXXIV, 343–345.

40. Evident from ER to G. Washington, Philadelphia, Oct. 8, 1795, printed in ER, *Vindication*, 23–24.

41. *Ibid.* and G. Washington to ER, Philadelphia, Oct. 21, 1795, Fitzpatrick, ed., *Washington*, XXXIV, 339–342.

42. ER, *Vindication*, 5–27. It should be noted that no handwritten draft of the *Vindication* has ever been found.

43. *Ibid.*, 28–40.

44. *Ibid.*, 41–48. See below for details on the translation of this dispatch for the *Vindication*.

45. *Ibid.*, 49–61, quoted material on 49 and 57.

46. *Ibid.*, 61–96.

For the convenience of the reader the translated copy of No. 10 as it appeared in the *Vindication* had each of its paragraphs numbered. While ER does not specifically refer to these numbers in his commentary, they have been generally used by historians when referring to the incriminating sections of the dispatch. It should be noted, however, that the paragraphing of No. 10 in the *Vindication* does not correspond with the paragraphing of this dispatch in Turner, ed., "Correspondence of the French Ministers to the United States, 1791–1797," *AHA, Annual Report, 1903*, II, 444–455. The variations first appear in the copy of this dispatch that was sent to ER by G. Washington (No. 10 [in French] in Papers on Vindication of Edmund Randolph MSS).

In this chapter subsequent numerical references to specific paragraphs in No. 10 will conform to the numbering arrangement that is found in the *Vindication* since the variance in paragraphing does not occur in any of the incriminating paragraphs of the dispatch.

47. J. Fauchet to Commissioner of Foreign Relations, Philadelphia, [Oct. 31, 1794], Papers on Vindication of Edmund Randolph MSS. The French text reads as follows:

> *Quant il s'agit d'expliquer soit par des conjectures soit par des données certaines, les vues sécrètes d'un Gouvernement étranger, Il serait imprudent de courir la chance des indiscrétions, et de se livrer à des hommes qu'une partialité connue pour ce Góuvernement, une Similitude de passions et d'interêts avec ses chefs, peuvent entrainer à des confidences dont les suites sont incalculables. D'ailleurs les précieuses confessions de Mr. Randolph jettent seules sur tout ce qui arrive une lumière satisfaisante. Je ne les ai point communiquées encore à mes collègues. . . . Je vais donc essayer, Citoyen, de donner un but à toutes les mesures dont les dépêches communes te rendent compte. . . .*

The copy of No. 10 in French is found in the Papers on Vindication of Edmund Randolph MSS will be cited in all future references to this dispatch since it was the only copy ER is known to have had in preparing his *Vindication*. The printed copy in Turner, ed., "CFM," *AHA, Annual Report, 1903*, II, 444–455, is, of course, a more convenient source to consult.

48. Translated in ER, *Vindication*, 62–63. The copy of the certificate in French that was supplied by Adet is in Papers on Vindication of Edmund Randolph MSS.
49. *Ibid.*
50. ER, *Vindication*, 63–64.
51. J. Fauchet to Commissioner of Foreign Relations, Philadelphia, [Oct. 31, 1794], Papers on Vindication of Edmund Randolph MSS. It is to be recognized, of course, that Fauchet's account was strongly biased in favor of those with Republican sympathies.
52. *Ibid.* The French text reads as follows:

> La première se préparait: le Gouvernement qui l'avait prévue reproduisait sous diverses formes la demande d'une Force disponible qui le mit sur une respectable défensive. Déjoué dans cette demarche, qui peut assurer qu'il n'ait point hâté l'éruption locale, pour faire une diversion avantageuse, et conjurer l'orage plus général qu'il voyait se former? Ne suis-je pas autorisé à former cette conjecture sur la conversation que le Sécrétaire d'Etat eut avec moi et Le Blanc seuls, et dont ma dépêche No. 3. se rend compte?

53. *Ibid.* The French text reads as follows:

> C'était indubitablement ce que Mr. Randolph entendait en me disant que sous prétexte de donner de l'énergie au Gouvernement on voulait introduire le pouvoir absolu et fourvoyer le Président dans des routes qui le meneraient à l'impopularité.

54. ER, *Vindication*, 69–72. For quoted material, see above.
55. Extract of J. Fauchet to Minister of Foreign Affairs, [Philadelphia], [June 4, 1794], Papers on Vindication of Edmund Randolph MSS. The French text reads as follows:

> Alors le Secretaire d'Etat parût se livrer sans réserve; me fit part des divisions intestines qui travailloient sourdement les Etats Unis; L'idée d'une explosion prochaine l'affectoit profondément, il espéroit la prévenir par l'empire qu'il acquiéroit chaque jour sur l'esprit du Président qui le consultoit dans toutes les affaires et à qui il disoit la vérité que lui déguise[roit] [ses] [collègues].

(The words have been crossed out beyond recognition.)

The full dispatch is in Turner, ed., "CFM," *AHA, Annual Report, 1903*, II, 372–377.

56. ER, *Vindication*, 72–79, quoted material from 72, 74, 76, respectively.
57. J. Fauchet to Commissioner of Foreign Relations, Philadelphia, [Oct. 31, 1794], Papers on Vindication of Edmund Randolph MSS.
58. *Ibid.* The French texts for the more critical passages quoted in this paragraph read as follows:

> Cependant lors même qu'on était sûr d'avoir une armée, il fallait s'assurer encore de coopérateurs parmi les hommes dont la Réputation Patriotique pouvait influencer leur parti, et dont l'inertie ou la tiédeur dans les conjectures actuelles aurait pu compromettre le Succés des plans.

And:

> Il paraît donc que ces hommes, avec d'autres que j'ignore, tous ayant sans doute Randolph à leur tête balançaient à se décider sur un parti. Deux ou trois jours avant que la proclamation ne [sic] fut publiée et par conséquent que le Cabinet eut arrêté ses mesures, Mr. Randolph vint me voir avec un air fort empressé, et me fit les ouvertures dont je t'ai rendu compte dans mon No. 6. Ainsi avec quelques milliers de Dollars la République aurait décidé ici sur la Guerre Civile ou Sur la paix!

59. ER, *Vindication*, 80–81.
60. *Ibid.*, 81–84.

61. *Ibid.*, 84.
62. J. Fauchet to Commissioner of Foreign Relations, Philadelphia, [Oct. 31, 1794], Papers on Vindication of Edmund Randolph MSS. The French text may be found in note 58.
63. Extract of J. Fauchet to Commissioner of Foreign Relations, [Philadelphia], [Sept. 5, 1794], Papers on Vindication of Edmund Randolph MSS. The French text reads as follows:

> . . . mais debiteurs de negocians et au moindre pas qu'ils feront, ils seront privés de leur liberté. Pourriez-vous leur prêter monentanement des fonds suffisans pour les mettre à l'abri de la persecution Anglaise?

The full dispatch is in Turner, ed., *AHA, Annual Report, 1903*, II, 411–418.
64. Printed in ER, *Vindication*, 13–17.
65. *Ibid.*, 84–87.
66. *Ibid.*, 87–92.
67. *Ibid.*, 89.
68. J. Fauchet to Commissioner of Foreign Relations, Philadelphia, [Oct. 31, 1794], Papers on Vindication of Edmund Randolph MSS.
69. ER, *Vindication*, 95, 96.
70. *Ibid.*, 96–97.
71. A letter to Madison on Nov. 1, observes: ". . . and the press is at work" (ER to J. Madison, Philadelphia, Nov. 1, 1795, Madison MSS).
72. Memo of J. R. Smith in Papers on Vindication of Edmund Randolph MSS.
73. ER, *Vindication*, 61n. In this note he observes: "Having the French original (i.e. copy supplied by Washington] only before me, I may not always translate alike in words; though the sense will doubtless be the same." (*Ibid.*) The Papers on Vindication of Edmund Randolph MSS contain the handwritten translation actually used by the printer in the *Vindication*.
   The translation appears to be in several different hands or possibly in different calligraphic styles by the same copyist or translator. The handwriting does not match the known calligraphic styles being used by George Taylor, the clerk of the Department of State at this time.
74. ER to J. Madison, Philadelphia, Nov. 1, 1795, Madison MSS.
75. Evident from ER to [?] Stewardson, Richmond, Nov. 25, 1795, Conarroe Autograph Collection, HSP.
76. The two exceptions are his letter to Madison on Nov. 1 that has been cited above, note 74, and a brief reference to the subject in a note to Samuel Bayard (ER to Bayard, Philadelphia, Oct. 24, 1795, Simon Gratz Collection, HSP).
77. Some indication of this can be found in the manner in which the appearance of the *Vindication* was reported by the British chargé in his dispatch to his home government (Phineas Bond to Lord Grenville, Philadelphia, Dec. 20, 1795, F.O. 5/10, PRO).
78. W. B. Giles to T. Jefferson, Philadelphia, Dec. 9, 1795, Jefferson MSS.
79. J. Adams to Abigail Adams, Philadelphia, Dec. 13, 1795, Adams Papers, MHS.
80. Evident from W. B. Giles to T. Jefferson, Philadelphia, Dec. 15, 1795, Jefferson MSS.
   Giles notes the *Vindication* was "promised to us on Friday next." This would have been Dec. 20.
81. G. Washington to A. Hamilton, Philadelphia, Dec. 22, 1795, Fitzpatrick, ed., *Washington*, XXXIV, 404–405.
82. J. Adams to Abigail Adams, Philadelphia, Dec. 21, 1795, Adams Papers, MHS. See also his letter of Dec. 25, 1795, to his wife, *ibid.*
83. J. Madison to T. Jefferson, Philadelphia, Dec. 27, 1795, Madison MSS.
84. A. Hamilton to G. Washington, New York, Dec. 24, 1795, *Hamilton*, XIX, 514–515. O. Wolcott, Sr., to O. Wolcott, Jr., Litchfield, [Conn.], Nov. 9, 1795, Gibbs, ed., *Wolcott*, I, 264; J. Q. Adams to J. Adams, London, Feb. 16, 1796, John Q. Adams Letterbook, Adams Papers, MHS.

85. O. Wolcott, Jr., to William Ellery, Philadelphia, Dec. [21], 1795, Gibbs, ed., *Wolcott*, I, 270. The date of the letter has been established from a copy found in American Loyalist Transcripts. Ellery's reply (W. Ellery to O. Wolcott, Jr., Newport, [R.I.], Jan. 11, 1796, Gibbs, ed., *Wolcott*, I, 296–297) gives a description of ER's activities in Newport that is essentially the same as the one provided by ER himself in the *Vindication*.

86. J. Madison to J. Monroe, Philadelphia, Jan. 26, 1796, Madison MSS.

87. Henry Lee wrote to Washington: "R.'s book has appeared . . . so far as I can hear, it works very dully and will produce a different effect from the author's expectations." (Henry Lee to G. Washington, Richmond, Jan. 3, 1796, Washington MSS.)

CHAPTER 23

1. There is no satisfactory general account of the history of Virginia during this period. Some insight into the state's history can be acquired from Richard R. Beeman, *The Old Dominion and the New Nation, 1788–1801*; Harry Ammon, "The Republican Party in Virginia, 1789–1824" (Ph.D. diss., University of Virginia, 1948); Thomas B. Abernethy, *The South in the New Nation, 1789–1815*; and the old but still valuable, Charles H. Ambler, *Sectionalism in Virginia from 1776 to 1861*.

2. ER to J. Madison, Richmond, Jan. 8, 1797, Madison MSS.
    A cursory examination of the correspondence of any of the prominent Virginians whose public career parallels the years of the Confederation and the early federal period provides the most striking illustration of the state's diminished influence. In the 1780s events in Virginia received as much attention in the correspondence of these men as did the activities of the Congress in Philadelphia (see Chapters 3 to 6, based in large part upon the very revealing Randolph–Madison correspondence). By the mid-1790s the political life of the state seldom elicited comment. When, on occasion, a correspondent did report on the local political scene, it was usually to record Virginia's reaction to some event of national or foreign significance.

3. Harry Ammon, "The Formation of the Republican Party in Virginia, 1789–1796," *The Journal of Southern History*, XIX, 283–310.

4. Samuel Mordecai, *Virginia, Especially Richmond in By-gone Days . . .* , 60–242 *passim*; Christian, *Richmond*, 21–48 *passim*.

5. Mary W. Scott, *Houses of Old Richmond*, 60–61, and Personal Property and Land Book, Richmond City, 1798; *ibid.*, 1799; *ibid.*, 1800, VSL.

6. Mordecai, *Virginia, Especially Richmond in By-gone Days*, 100–101.

7. Their third child, John Jennings, was born in Oct., 1785, and died in June of 1786. Then in Mar., 1790, Betsy became seriously ill and did not recover until mid-May, after she had given birth to a dead fetus.

8. Peyton was born in Feb. 1781; Susan was born in Oct., 1782; Edmonia was born on Apr. 17, 1787; and Lucy was probably born sometime between Jan. and June, 1789.

9. Robert Brooke had been reelected governor of Virginia Nov. 26, 1795 (*Virginia Gazette and General Advertiser*, Dec. 2, 1795).

10. Ammon, "The Formation of the Republican Party in Virginia, 1789–1796," *Journal of Southern History*, XIX, 283–310.

11. Freeman (Carroll & Ashworth), *Washington*, VII, 338–340.

12. Ammon, "The Formation of the Republican Party in Virginia, 1789–1796," *Journal of Southern History*, XIX, 306–307.

13. Noble E. Cunningham, Jr., *The Jeffersonian Republicans: The Formation of Party Organization, 1789–1801*, 78–85. Brant, *Madison*, III, 431–451.

14. [Edmund Randolph], *Political Truth or . . . Inquiry into the Truth of the Charges Preferred Against Mr. Randolph* (Philadelphia, 1796).
    Some doubt is cast on ER's authorship of this piece by the editorial preface that his grandson, Peter V. Daniels, Jr., wrote for an 1855 edition of ER's *Vindication*. Referring to the publication of the *Political Truth*, he says: "The

author of this pamphlet, whose name the editor of this [i.e., *Vindication*] has yet been unable to discover. . . . " (Peter V. Daniels, Jr., "Editor's Preface," *A Vindication of Edmund Randolph Written by Himself and Published in 1795* [Richmond, 1855], vii.) This declared ignorance as to the authorship of the pamphlet loses some of its significance when, on subsequent pages of this preface, the unknown author is cited because he reached the same conclusions as ER did in his *Vindication*. The implication is that the *Vindication* must therefore be an accurate account of what transpired because it was later substantiated by the author of *Political Truth* (ibid., viii–xi).

15. ER, *Political Truth*, 1–39.
16. *Ibid.*, 39.
17. *Ibid.*, 41–42.
18. *Ibid.*, 42–44.
19. Richmond book dealers did not list the work in their advertisements in the Richmond papers and Virginians in Philadelphia seemingly took no notice of it. This, of course, was not true of the *Vindication*.
20. *J. H Del.* (Oct. Sess., 1795), 20, 27–29, 71.
21. Ammon, "The Formation of the Republican Party in Virginia, 1789–1796," *Journal of Southern History*, XIX, 307–308.
22. ER to J. Madison, Richmond, Apr. 25, 1796, Madison MSS.
23. *Ibid.*

It was worthy of note that Edward Carrington reported that the political fervor associated with the Jay Treaty had subsided in Virginia:

> That the public mind is now at ease on the subject of the Treaty may, in my opinion, be concluded from the usual mode of inquiry as to its ratification on the part of Great Britain—these inquiries has [sic] not of late been frequently attended with expressions unfriendly to such ratification. (Edward Carrington to G. Washington, Richmond, Feb. 24, 1796, Washington MSS.)

24. J. Madison to T. Jefferson, Philadelphia, Apr. 23, 1796, Hunt, ed., *Madison*, II, 98. The final vote confirming the decision of the Committee of the Whole was taken on Apr. 30 (*Annals*, V, 1291 [House]).
25. Joseph Charles, *The Origins of the American Party System; Three Essays*, 111–116.
26. The election and the events leading up to it are conveniently summarized in John C. Miller, *Federalist Era, 1789–1801*, 196–201.
27. There is not a single reference to the campaign or election in the ER correspondence known to this author. The correspondence still existent is admittedly quite limited, but it seems to be sufficiently varied both as to recipient and subject matter to warrant this observation. With one or two exceptions there appears to be a conscious effort to avoid comment on all subjects of a public nature during the last years of ER's life.
28. Miller, *Federalist Era, 1789–1801*, 193–195, 205–208, 210–235.
29. ER to J. Monroe, Richmond, Mar. 11, 1798, James Monroe MSS, NYPL.
30. The most thorough treatment of the Kentucky and Virginia Resolutions is Adrienne Koch and Harry Ammon, "The Virginia and Kentucky Resolutions: An Episode in Jefferson's and Madison's Defense of Civil Liberties," *WMQ*, (3rd ser.), V, 145–176.
31. Evident from ER to St. George Tucker, Richmond, Dec. 13, Dec. 20 and Dec. 30, 1798, all in Tucker-Coleman Papers, Earl Gregg Swem Library, William and Mary College.
32. ER to St. George Tucker, Richmond, Dec. 13, 1798, ibid.

It is worthy of note that ER's reference to the Alien and Sedition Acts as "the two execrable bills" raises some doubt as to whether he was aware that there were four acts involved.

33. ER to St. George Tucker, Richmond, Dec. 20, 1798, ibid.
34. The House came to a vote on Dec. 21, 1798, the Senate on Dec. 24, 1798, (*Va. Report of 1799–1800*, 157, 158.
35. The debate in the House of Delegates was conducted with that body sitting as a

Committee of the Whole. It lasted from Dec. 13, when John Taylor of Caroline first introduced the resolutions, until Dec. 21, when the committee reported back to the House and the formal vote was taken. These debates in committee have been printed in full in *Va. Report of 1799–1800*, 24–157.

36. *J. H. Del.* (Dec. Sess., 1798), 58–59. The resolutions themselves can be conveniently found in Shepard, ed., *Va. Statutes, 1792–1806*, II, 193.

37. ER to St. George Tucker, Richmond, Dec. 30, 1798, Tucker-Coleman Papers, Earl Gregg Swem Library, William and Mary College.

38. Shepard, ed., *Va. Statutes, 1792–1806*, II, 193.

39. Tucker's draft proposals have never been found but one can conjecture as to their general subject matter from the letters ER sent to Tucker during this period. A careful review of the *Journal of the House of Delegates* (Senate *Journal* lost) reveals only two bills that might have been drafted by Tucker. The first, a bill "to amend the act to reduce into one, the several acts directing the course of descents" was defeated on the original motion to bring in a bill for this purpose (*J. H. Del.* [Dec. Sess., 1798], 72). The second, a bill "to amend the act entitled an act for reducing into one the several acts concerning the court of appeals and special court of appeals," was passed by the House (*ibid.*, 53). The Senate amended the bill, but the House, on reconsidering the bill with amendments, refused to agree to the changes that had been made by the Senate (*ibid.*, 87). An impasse resulted, which was never broken in the five remaining days of the session. Of the bills that were passed during this session there is not one that could logically be attributed to Tucker within the context of ER's letters.

40. A somewhat similar conclusion has been reached by Koch and Ammon regarding the members of the Virginia legislature who debated the subject:

> The debates in the legislature on the Virginia Resolutions do not illuminate what doctrine the members really thought they were committing themselves to in the resolutions. The two principal Republican speakers, James Barbour and John Taylor, made generous use of the word "state" but nowhere did they analyze the sense in which they intended it. Both speakers were more concerned with proving the unconstitutionality of the measures by ample quotations from Vattel, the common law, and the Constitution than they were in formulating fine-spun constitutional theories. (Koch and Ammon, "The Virginia and Kentucky Resolutions . . . ," *WMQ* [3rd ser.], V, 162.)

41. This subject has been thoroughly explored by Philip G. Davidson, "Virginia and the Alien and Sedition Laws," *AHR*, XXXVI, 336–342.

42. His only comment on the subject is found in a letter to St. George Tucker. It shows him to be hostile toward Jefferson's opponents, but little more:

> Every character, in [*sic*] both sides of the great question, concurs in the belief that Mr. Jefferson's election is certain. Indeed it is asserted, as a point settled, that he will receive an unanimous vote. For myself, I do not doubt, that a majority is prepared to induct him into the chair of government, and that, from a persuasion of this, unanimity will be produced by the accession of the most inveterate, who do not choose to shew their fangs, when they can no longer injure. (ER to [St. George Tucker], Richmond, Jan. 29, 1801, Tucker-Coleman Papers, Earl Gregg Swem Library, William and Mary College.)

CHAPTER 24

1. The establishment of the District Courts in 1788 was the last significant change in the structure of Virginia's judicial system. ER probably practiced in the District Court that met in Richmond between his resignation as governor in Nov., 1788, and his departure for New York in Jan., 1790.

2. Since most cases came to this court on appeal, statute required that it be handled

by a different counsel than the attorney who argued the case in the lower court. The relevant article read:

> No counsel or attorney who shall prosecute any suit in an inferior court, in which an appeal may be prayed, shall be permitted to appear, or prosecute such appeal in any superior courts, to which the same may be carried or removed; and any counsel or attorney who shall appear to, or prosecute such appeal in any superior court, shall forfeit the sum of sixty dollars, to be recovered with costs by action of debt in any court or record within this commonwealth. (Shepard, ed., *Va. Statutes, 1792–1806*, II, 193.)

3. The first case with which ER can be identified in the reported cases is *Innis, Attorney General et. vs. Roane and Others*, Oct., 1797, 4 Call 379–402. The other cases are 1 Call 51–54, 62–82, 147–160, 161–164, 165–187 and 4 Call 411–415. The cases are not printed in chronological order.

4. Information on the volume of cases handled by ER in the Court of Appeals has been acquired by merely arranging the cases that have been reported in chronological order and simply counting the cases in which ER is identified as one of the counsel. The cases for these years are in Call, vols. I–IV, and Hening & Munford, vol. I.

5. In Oct., 1798, he was in Fredericksburg attending the District Court. His first case before the Court of Appeals was heard during the last week of October, after he had returned to Richmond. His remaining cases, six in number, were all heard on the last five court days of that term (1 Call 382–474 *passim*).

6. Oct. term, 1807. Evident from 1 Hening & Munford 427–601.

7. He apparently handled several cases for Henry Banks, for example. In one letter to Banks he remarked: "I do not know that any other of your suits have had anything done in them." (ER to Henry Banks, Richmond, Aug. 28, 1797, Henry Banks MSS, VHS.) He also assisted his brother-in-law Wilson Cary Nicholas with several legal matters and advised him on settling the estate of his brother George Nicholas when the latter died in 1799 (ER to W. C. Nicholas, Richmond, Aug. 26, 1799, Wilson Cary Nicholas Papers II, University of Virginia; ER to W. C. Nicholas, Richmond, Jan. 11, 1800, *ibid.*; ER to W. C. Nicholas, Richmond, Sept. 7, 1802; W. C. Nicholas to ER, Warren, [Va.], Dec. 19, 1803, and Dec. 29, 1803; ER to W. C. Nicholas, Richmond, Dec. 30, 1803 all in Edgehill-Randolph Papers, [McGregor Library], University of Virginia).

8. See, for example, an open letter of Philip N. Nicholas, Edmund Randolph, John Wickham, George Hay, Daniel Call and John Warden to their clients, dated Richmond, June 15, 1804, which was printed in the *Virginia Argus*, July 7, 1804. The letter served notice on their clients that recent rules of practice adopted by the Court of Appeals necessitated their continuous presence at the bar during the coming sessions of the Court and that they expected to be "adequately compensated" for their services.

John Marshall's income from his practice was reported to be between $4000 and $5000 per anum (Francois La Rouchefoucauld, *Travels Through the United States of North America* [London, 1800], 75–76).

9. 6 Call 113–187.

10. *Ibid.*

11. See G. MacLaren Brydon, *Virginia's Mother Church and the Political Conditions under which it Grew: The Story of the Anglican Church and the Development of Religion in Virginia, 1727–1814*, II, 492–512; Mays, *Pendleton*, II, 337–349.

12. Shepard, ed., *Va. Statutes, 1792–1806*, II, 314–316.

13. Brydon, *Virginia's Mother Church*, II, 514–516. The other lawyers were Bushrod Washington and John Wickham (*ibid.*).

14. Mays, *Pendleton*, II, 337–345.

15. 6 Call 116–119.

16. *Ibid.*, 119–121.

17. *Ibid.*, 121–123.

18. *Ibid.*, 123–125.

19. *Ibid.*, 125–128.
20. *DAB*, *s.v.* "Tucker, St. George."
21. 6 Call 128–157.
22. *Ibid.*, 157–178.
23. *Ibid.*, 178–187.
24. Brydon, *Virginia's Mother Church*, II, 503, 511, *n.* 28.
25. Hening, ed., *Va. Statutes*, XIII, 410.
26. *Commonwealth vs. Beaumarchais*, Nov. 2, 1801, 3 Call 122–180.
27. The court was equally divided on part of the decree of the High Court of Chancery, which meant this much of the decision was allowed to stand. Thus the state was only partially successful in its appeal from the decree of that court (3 Call 176).
28. *Read vs. Read*, May 1804, 5 Call 160–232, and *The Commonwealth vs. Bristow*, Apr., 1806, 6 Call 60–71. Both cases involved the inheritance of land during the Revolution and were not affected by the treaty of peace in 1783 or the Jay Treaty of 1794, neither of which covered the inheritances of British subjects during the war years.
29. *Hudgens vs. Wrights*, Nov. 7, 1806, 1 Hening & Munford 134–144.
30. *Patty and Others, Paupers vs. Colin and Others*, Nov. 3, 1807, *ibid.*, 519–531.
31. The only legislation setting the fees a lawyer might collect in the Federal courts concerned fees in Admiralty proceedings (*U.S. Statutes at Large*, I, 332–333).
32. The U.S. Circuit Court Order Books and Record Books for Richmond, the latter of which usually listed the name of the plaintiff's attorney, do not carry a single reference to ER appearing on behalf of a client. The absence of all U.S. District Court records, and of many order books and record books for the U.S. Circuit Court, as well as the inadequacy of the material that does exist, precludes any definitive statement on the limited nature of ER's practice before these courts, but the record is sufficiently extensive to justify the observation that ER had, at best, a negligible practice before the federal courts that met in Richmond. One is forced to conclude that this represented a deliberate choice by ER, for accident alone could not explain the total absence of his name from the existing record.
33. See pp. 354–357.
34. On two occasions he had been retained by the governor of the state of Virginia (ER to Gov. James Monroe, Richmond, June 5, 1800, *CVSP*, IX, 115, and ER to Gov. John Page, Richmond, May 24, 1804, Executive Papers, VSL). There were undoubtedly other instances as well.
35. Evident from John Steele to Thomas Nelson, Comptroller's Office, Oct. 4, 1796, U.S. vs. ER Papers.
36. *Ibid.*
37. ER to [John Steele], Richmond, Oct. 24, 1796, *ibid.*, and ER to Thomas Nelson, Richmond, Mar. 21, 1797, *ibid.*
38. On May 2, 1797, Secretary of the Treasury Oliver Wolcott noted that ER "appeared to be" indebted to the United States for $49,154.89. He had previously referred in this same letter to vouchers and credits that ER had submitted and which had been compared with the records of the Department of State and accepted (O. Wolcott to Thomas Nelson, Treasury Dept., May 2, 1797, *ibid.*).
39. The bill was introduced in the House on February 6, 1797 (*Annals*, VI, 2079 [House]). It passed the House on Feb. 15 (*ibid.*, 2162 [House]) and the Senate on Mar. 3 (*ibid.*, 1576 [Senate]). The law may be found in *U.S. Statutes at Large*, I, 512–516.

On Feb. 25, 1797, John Williams of New York introduced a resolution in the House requesting the Secretary of the Treasury to lay before the House information as to the sum of money that had been received by ER for which there was "no explanation" and of the measures that were being taken to obtain a settlement of these accounts. The resolution passed the House on Mar. 3, after a brief discussion on the propriety of directing the request to the Secretary of the Treasury rather than the Comptroller (*Annals*, VI, 2289, 2354–2358 [House]).

40. O. Wolcott to Thomas Nelson, Treasury Dept., May 2, 1797, U.S. vs. ER Papers.
41. The U.S. vs. ER Papers contain at least seven affidavits sworn before the clerk of the court reciting the difficulties ER was experiencing in gathering records for his own defense. The earliest is dated June 5, 1797, and the latest Dec. 1, 1801.
42. John Steele to Thomas Nelson, Comptroller's office, Oct. 19, 1797, *ibid.*, U.S. vs. ER Papers.
43. Steele's letters to Nelson displayed a growing impatience with the U.S. attorney for not pressing the case with greater diligence and then became annoyed with the court because it submitted to ER's repeated requests for postponements in the trial. This correspondence, extending from Oct. 4, 1796, to June 13, 1802, has been collected in file 14 of U.S. vs. ER Papers.
44. A copy of the court order, dated May term, 1803, is in *ibid.*
45. *Biographical Directory of the American Congress, 1774–1961*, 839–840.
46. So stated in the court order issued during the May term, 1803, in U.S. vs. ER Papers.
47. Award of Gabriel Duvall, Comptroller's Office, Nov. 24, 1803. The award, with supporting account reports, is in file 16 of U.S. vs. ER Papers.
    Four days prior to making this award Duvall requested an appointment with President Jefferson to discuss ER's claim of a credit in the account of William Short. Jefferson had acted as Short's agent during the years his friend and protégé resided in Europe (Gabriel Duvall to T. Jefferson, Nov. 20, 1804, Jefferson MSS).
48. Award of Gabriel Duvall, Comptroller's Office, Nov. 24, 1803, U.S. vs. ER Papers.
49. Several months after the federal government had filed its suit, ER cautioned his son Peyton to: "Keep accounts, keep accounts of every shilling, keep accounts of every farthing my dear son." It was sound advice to a young man of sixteen away from home for the first time, but it was based on bitter experience (ER to Peyton Randolph, Richmond, Nov. 26, 1797, Edmund Randolph MSS, VHS).
50. Report of the Comptroller of the Treasury, Washington, Jan. 7, 1889, *Senate Executive Documents*, I, Ex. Doc. No. 58.
    The report, in response to a resolution of the Senate requesting information on the "account of Edmund Randolph," found that through a series of errors in the Treasury Department the amount received by the federal government in the settlement of the account was $7,716.21 in excess of the amount required under Duvall's award. The report further noted that records of the department showed the account as still open and unsettled in 1889. The Comptroller of the Treasury recommended that the account be balanced and closed by the Secretary of the Treasury (*ibid.*).
51. Indenture of ER and wife to Wilson Cary Nicholas [Richmond], Sept. 7, 1805, Edgehill-Randolph Papers, (McGregor Library), University of Virginia; ER to W. C. Nicholas, release, Sept. 7, 1805, Wilson Cary Nicholas Papers II, University of Virginia; ER to W. C. Nicholas, deed, Sept. 7, 1805, *ibid.* See also ER to W. C. Nicholas, Richmond, Dec. 30, 1805, Jefferson Papers, Coolidge Collection, MHS.
52. The two most complete accounts of the Burr trial are J. J. Coombs, *The Trial of Aaron Burr for Treason*, and David Robertson, *Reports of the Trials of Colonel Aaron Burr . . .* , 2 vols. The former, which has been reprinted in *Federal Cases*, carries a fuller account of the rulings and opinions of the court. Robertson's report, which gives more attention to the arguments of opposing counsel, is more useful in assessing the relative importance of the lawyers serving on the panel for the defense.
53. Political factors of one kind or another are noted in the principal secondary accounts of this trial: Thomas P. Abernethy, *The Burr Conspiracy*, 227–249. Beveridge, *Marshall*, III, 343–529, Nathan Schachner, *Aaron Burr*, 396–443, and Paul S. Clarkson and R. Samuel Jett, *Luther Martin of Maryland*, 229–272 *passim*. A proper assessment of the impact of these forces on the trial itself must await a more explicit study of this case than presently exists.
54. There is fairly wide agreement on the relative importance of the men on the defense counsel. The assessment given here can be readily established from a cursory

examination of either the Robertson or Coombs account of the trial. Beveridge, who provides one of the most detailed descriptions of the trial, credits ER with one important speech but notes the speech "added nothing to the rich and solid argument [of Wickham]" (Beveridge, *Marshall*, III, 494). Isolated references in secondary literature to ER being Burr's principal defense counsel are probably based on the assumption that because ER's name was usually placed first in the contemporary lists of Burr's attorneys, therefore he was the senior counsel for the defense. The published accounts of the trial and the unpublished U.S. Circuit Court papers (U.S. vs. Aaron Burr Papers, U.S. District Court [Va. District], VSL) fail to substantiate such an assumption.

The attorneys for the government, in addition to George Hay, were William Wirt and Alexander MacRae. Ceasar A. Rodney, the Attorney General of the United States, was in Richmond for the initial arraignment.

For biographical data see *DAB*, *s.v.* "Hay, George," "Martin, Luther," "Rodney, Caesar A.," "Wickham, John" and "Wirt, William." Limited information on Baker, Botts and MacRae may be found in a biographical note affixed to the formal report of the case (25 Federal Cases 24–25).

55. In 1802 he served as manager of a lottery to repair Washington and Henry Academy in Hanover (Christian, *Richmond*, 54). In 1803 he was named a trustee of Richmond Academy (*ibid.*, 57–58), and in 1807 he accepted a similar assignment when subscriptions were being sold to support an "academy for female education" (*Virginia Argus*, Mar. 20, 1807).

56. *Virginia Argus*, Jan. 5, 1808.

57. Announcement of in *Virginia Gazette and General Advertiser*, Feb. 22, 1799. St. George Tucker's observations on the unsystematic manner in which Virginia's laws were being collected (Tucker, "Sunmary view of . . . Courts . . . in Va.," *Blackstone's Commentaries*, I, App. V) would seem to establish the usefulness of ER's project. Regrettably ER seems to have abandoned the work before it was completed.

58. He asked Madison to procure Jefferson's *Manual of Parliamentary Practice* and Erasmus Darwin's *Zoonomia* for him. They were, he noted, advertised as being for sale in Washington (ER to J. Madison, Richmond, June 8, 1801, Madison MSS).

59. On Mar. 17, 1806, Peyton married Maria Ward of Amelia County (*Virginia Argus*, Mar. 25, 1806). On June 11, 1806, Edmonia, his second eldest daughter, married Thomas Preston of Montgomery County (*Virginia Argus*, June 17, 1806).

CHAPTER 25

1. In 1800 Peyton had written to his friend Joseph Cabell: "To crawl in the mire of county court practice is too loathsome an idea for a man of spirit and although the attempt at eminence may be unsuccessful, it is some consolation to fall in a great cause." (P. Randolph to J. Cabell, Richmond, Dec. 28, 1800, Cabell Papers, University of Virginia)

2. Washington had died on Dec. 14, and Henry on June 6, 1799; Pendleton died on Oct. 26, 1803, and George Wythe on June 8, 1806. A person born in 1783 would, of course, have reached his twenty-fifth year by 1808.

3. It must be admitted ER never referred to the number of active years he had left, but his letters gave the impression he assumed there were a considerable number of years of practice remaining before either a forced or a voluntary retirement.

4. Evident from Hening & Munford, vols. 2 and 3, *passim*.

5. His correspondence, though limited, indicates he represented clients in other courts. These included Wilson Cary Nicholas and the loyalists John Hook and William Nelson. He even appealed personally to President Jefferson to grant a pardon to John Moss, a minor, convicted of robbing the mails at Petersburg. He requested that that portion of the sentence requiring that he receive ten lashes be remitted. (ER to T. Jefferson, Richmond, Dec. 22, 1808, Jefferson MSS.)

6. Shepard, ed., *Va. Statutes, 1792–1806*, III, 355–360.

7. The law, which was passed on Feb. 1, 1808, provided that "the superior courts of those counties in which the respective district courts are now holden, shall have jurisdiction to try all such cases as on the first day of January next shall remain on the dockets there. . . ." (*Ibid.*, 360.) See also ER to the Judges of the Court of Appeals, May 14, 1809 MS, VHS.

8. The counties of Henrico, Hanover, Chesterfield, Goochland and Powhatan came within the jurisdiction of the District Court that met at Richmond (Hening, ed., *Va. Statutes*, XII, 730). Under the new law the superior court sessions were fixed as follows: Henrico, Apr. 3 and Sept. 3; Hanover, May 15 and Oct. 15; Chesterfield, Mar. 24 and Aug. 24; Goochland, Apr. 29 and Sept. 29; Powhatan, May 8 and Oct. 8 (Shepard, ed., *Va. Statutes, 1792–1806*, III, 355–360). The Court of Appeals now met three times a year: Mar. 1, Apr. 15 and Oct. 1. The first term was to be twenty-seven juridical days, the second forty-four and the last fifty-five, unless the business before the court was completed sooner (Shepard, ed., *Va. Statutes, 1792–1806*, III, 371).

9. Hening & Munford, vols. 3 and 4, *passim* and Munford, vol. 1, *passim*.

10. ER to W. C. Nicholas, Richmond, Nov. 2, 1809, Wilson Cary Nicholas II, University of Virginia.

11. *Ibid.*

12. Evident from "Edmund Randolph's Sketch of his Wife," [Mar. 25, 1810?], MS, University of Virginia, and Philip Norborne Nicholas to W. C. Nicholas, Richmond, Mar. 3, 1810, Wilson Cary Nicholas Papers, University of Virginia.

13. She died Mar. 6, 1810 (*Virginia Argus*, Mar. 13, 1810).

14. "Edmund Randolph's Sketch of his Wife," [Mar. 25, 1810?], MS, University of Virginia. This "Sketch," addressel to "my dear children," appears to have been written shortly after his wife's death. It consists of the "Sketch," a "Prayer for my family" and a quoted paragraph entitled "The Dying Christian." It is not in ER's hand. The only date appearing on the manuscript is that of Mar. 25, 1810, found at the end of the "Prayer."

15. So stated in ER to J. Madison, Richmond, June 15, 1810, Madison MSS.

16. *Ibid.* ER can be identified with four cases heard during the Apr. term (1810) of the Court of Appeals and none after that. Not surprisingly the number of cases being handled by his son Peyton showed a marked increase during the Oct. term of the Court (Munford, vol. 1, *passim*).

17. *Virginia Argus*, Apr. 27, 1810.

18. Frank, *Daniel*, 4–7, 11–13.

19. On Apr. 19, 1810, ER gave his daughter property in Richmond. See Virginia Deeds, Richmond City, Book 6, 166, VSL.

20. Randolph placed a notice in both Richmond papers beginning on Oct. 3, 1809, announcing his desire to rent his farm (*Virginia Argus*, Oct. 3, 1809, and *Virginia Gazette and General Advertiser*, Nov. 17, 1809). He decided to rent his home in Richmond shortly after Lucy's marriage and had a tenant by the last week in May (see below).

21. An advertisement dated May 30, 1810, carried the announcement that L. H. Girardin intended to open a school in September in the home of ER located near the capitol (*Virginia Argus*, June 5, 1810).

22. Girardin advertised the opening of his school throughout the summer, the announcement varying slightly from time to time. On July 26, 1810, he inserted a paragraph expressing the "hope" that ER would "carry into execution his intended plan of lecturing at the Capitol or some other convenient place upon Rhetoric, Law, and perhaps Political Economy." (*Virginia Argus*, July 31, 1810.) The advertisement with this paragraph continued until Sept. 21, 1810, when the entire advertisement was dropped (*Virginia Argus*, Sept. 21, 1810). There is no evidence that ER did in fact lecture for Girardin.

23. *Virginia Argus*, Dec. 4, 1810.

24. ER to Judge Spencer Roane [Richmond], [Oct. 1810], Hampton L. Carson Collection, Free Library of Philadelphia.

The desperateness of ER's financial condition is further substantiated by the observation that he is writing this letter only two hours after his "old friend John Brown" had died.

25. ER to St. George Tucker, [Richmond], [Oct. 17 (*sic*), 1810], Tucker-Coleman Papers, Earl Gregg Swem Library, William and Mary College. The original is in the possession of Mrs. George P. Coleman.

26. St. George Tucker to ER, Richmond, Nov. 1, 1810, *ibid.*
   The date of this letter and an explicit reference to "your favor of last evening" would seem to date ER's letters to Roane and Tucker, respectively, as Oct. 31, 1810.

27. Edmonia was married to Thomas Preston. The Prestons lived in Lexington, Va. ER was in Richmond as late as Apr. 24 (ER to Thomas Mann Randolph, Richmond, Apr. 24, 1811, Wilson Cary Nicholas II, University of Virginia), but in Lexington in July (ER to J. Madison, Lexington, Va., July 9, 1811, Madison MSS). A month later he was with the Taylors and informed Madison he intended to spend the fall and winter with them (ER to J. Madison, Charlestown, Va., Aug. 8, 1811, Madison MSS). Charlestown, ten miles southwest of Harper's Ferry, is now in West Virginia.

28. He announced his intention to "move on" to the medical springs in a letter sent from Winchester, Va. (ER to J. Madison, Winchester, July 1, 1812, Madison MSS). A letter written later that summer was sent from Battletown, Va. (ER to M. P. Poitiaux, Battletown, Va., [Aug. 13, 1812?], Martha Robinson Upshur MSS, VHS). The proper name for Battletown is Berryville (Joseph Martin, *A New and Comprehensive Gazetteer of Virginia* . . . , 338). Reniers identifies a sulphur spring in this general area (Perceval Reniers, *The Springs of Virginia* . . . *1775–1900*, frontispiece) and there is no evidence ER went to Bath or Berkley County. He was back in Charlestown on Sept. 6 (ER to W. C. Nicholas, Charlestown, Jefferson County, Sept. 6, 1812, Wilson Cary Nicholas Papers II, University of Virginia).

29. ER to T. M. Randolph, Richmond, Apr. 24, 1811, *ibid.*

30. John Wickham to ER, Richmond, Feb. 14, 1812, *ibid.*

31. John Wickham to W. C. Nicholas, Richmond, Mar. 12, 1812, *ibid.*

32. ER to W. C. Nicholas, Charlestown, Sept. 6, 1812, *ibid.*; Philip Norborne Nicholas to W. C. Nicholas, Richmond, Oct. 26, 1812, *ibid.*

33. The *Richmond Enquirer* carried a reference to the work as early as Dec. 27, 1809. On Dec. 15, 1811, he stated he needed only the services of an amanuensis to prepare a copy of the work and he would be finished (ER to Matthew Carey, Charlestown, Dec. 15, 1811, Lea and Febiger Collection, HSP).

34. ER's purpose in writing the "History" is suggested in the preface to the work and stated rather explicitly in several places within the corpus of his study (Edmund Randolph's "The History of Virginia" MS, VHS). In letters he used the word "biography" when referring to the whole manuscript and when he was noting its most unique feature. In one letter he remarked: "The Biography is at least original." (ER to [E.?] Randolph, Battletown, Va., June 11, 1812, Edmund Randolph MSS, VHS).

35. ER to Matthew Carey, Charlestown, Dec. 15, 1811, Lea and Febiger Collection, HSP.

36. Edmund Randolph's "History of Virginia," MS, VHS.
   The portion of the manuscript that still remains is a bound volume. It seems to be the first of three octavo volumes ER made reference to in his letter to Matthew Carey. It ends about 1783. The first part of Virginia's colonial history is drawn from William Stith's *The History of the First Discovery and Settlement of Virginia*. It appears that ER used the 1747 edition that was published by William Parks of Williamsburg. When he completes the years covered in Stith's *History*, about 1624, he rather arbitrarily skips the next fifty years, resuming his narrative in 1676. It is at this point that the distinctive biographical material begins to appear in the narrative. By the time he completes his account of the Revolution, his concern for eulogizing the leaders of the period has altered the character and organization of the narrative. It is assumed that the remaining years of the eighteenth century were treated in a similar manner, but in even greater detail.
   What is known about the history of the manuscript itself has been thoroughly

explored by John Melville Jennings in the definitive published edition of the Randolph "History" (Arthur H. Shaffer, ed., *History of Virginia by Edmund Randolph*, xxxvii–xlix).

37. ER to Matthew Carey, Charlestown, Va., Dec. 15, 1811, Lea and Febiger Collection, HSP; ER to [E.?] Randolph, Battletown, Va., June 11, 1812, Edmund Randolph MSS, VHS, and ER to [E. Randolph?], Battletown, Va., June 12, 1812, Si-non Gratz Collection, HSP.

38. ER to [E. Randolph?], Battletown, Va., June 12, 1812, Simon Gratz Collection, HSP.

39. Evident from Philip Norborne Nicholas to [Wilson Cary Nicholas], Richmond, May 27, 1813, Wilson Cary Nicholas Papers, University of Virginia.

40. *Ibid.* Daniel also wrote to Nicholas (Peter V. Daniel to Wilson C. Nicholas, Richmond, May 27, 1813, Wilson Cary Nicholas Papers, University of Virginia).

41. Philip Norborne Nicholas to [Wilson C. Nicholas], Richmond, May 27, 1813, Wilson Cary Nicholas Papers, University of Virginia.

42. Randolph is listed as the proprietor of land that has a "Francis Gorlier" as a tenant. the yearly rent was £400.0.0 (Personal Property and Land Book, Richmond City, 1813, VSL). His name does not appear in the Personal Property and Land Book for Richmond in 1814.

He is also listed as holding seven acres in Henrico County in 1813 valued at $116.66 (Land Books, Henrico County, 1813, VSL). He had previously disposed of his properties in the city of Williamsburg and Albemarle and James City Counties (Land Books, Williamsburg, 1788–1813; Land Books, James City County, 1784–1813; Land Books, Albemarle County [St. Ann's Parish], 1787–1813, VSL).

43. Burwell, a lawyer, was related by marriage to ER's wife. ER had known him for years.

Some information on Carter Hall, "Old Chapel" graveyard and Millwood can be obtained from T. K. Cartmell, *Shenandoah Valley Pioneers and Their Descendants . . . , passim.*

44. *Richmond Enquirer*, Sept. 17, 1813.

45. An entry in the index to the Vestry Book of Christ Church notes that Dr. Robert Carter Randolph had placed a headstone at the "supposed" grave of ER. The entry was on a page entitled "Some of the names of the Unmarked Dead of the *Old* Chapel Grave Yard to the date of 1865." Index to Vestry Book, 1730–1885, Records of Christ Church, Millwood, Va., VHS.

46. *Richmond Enquirer*, Sept. 17, 1813.

Bibliography

MANUSCRIPT SOURCES

Brown, Picton and Hornley Libraries (Liverpool, England):
 Parker Family Papers (Colonial Williamsburg microfilm)
Colonial Williamsburg Foundation (Research Department):
 John Norton and Sons Papers
Columbia University, New York:
 Moncure Daniel Conway; John Jay (by special permission); Gouverneur
Morris
Duke University, William R. Perkins Library, Durham, North Carolina:
 Robert Carter Papers; John Hook; John Page; Edmund Pendleton; Edmund
Randolph
The Filson Club, Louisville, Kentucky:
 Arthur Campbell Papers, 1752–1811: Clark-Hite Papers (by special permission);
Hamilton Daveiss Papers, 1786–1855; Kentucky Miscellaneous; Weller Family
Papers
Free Library of Philadelphia:
 Hampton L. Carson Collection
Haverford College Library, Haverford, Pennsylvania:
 Charles Roberts Autograph Letters Collection
Henry E. Huntington Library, San Marino, California:
 Brock Collection, Randolph-Tucker Papers
Historical Society of Pennsylvania:
 William Bradford Papers in John W. Wallace Collection; Conarroe Autograph
Collection; Ferdinand J. Dreer Collection; Henry S. Drinker Papers; Etting Col-
lection; Simon Gratz Collection; HSP Miscellaneous Collection; Lea and Febiger
Collection; Thomas McKean Papers; John Nicholson Letterbooks; Jasper Yates
Papers
Library of Congress:
 Theodore Bland, Jr.; Sylvanus Bourne; Robert Carter; Cipher MSS; Earl of
Dunmore Letterbook; Ellis-Allen Papers; John Fitch; Edmond Genêt; Elbridge
Gerry; Alexander Hamilton; Patrick Henry; Diary of Dr. Robert Honeyman;
Harry Innes; Thomas Jefferson; Jones Family Papers; Rufus King; Arthur Lee;
Charles Lee; Richard Bland Lee; James McHenry; James Madison; John Mar-
shall; George Mason; Garrett Minor; James Monroe; Gouverneur Morris; Robert
Morris; Wilson Cary Nicholas; North Carolina Miscellaneous; Pennsylvania

[483]

Miscellany, Whiskey Rebellion; Personal Papers Miscellaneous; Timothy Pickering; Pinckney Family Papers; Edmund Randolph Vindication, 1795; Peyton Randolph Account Book; Edward Shippen; Shippen Family Papers; William Short; Col. Charles Simms; Adam Stephen Papers; Henry Tazewell; Virginia; George Washington: Journal of Proceedings of the President, State Department Letterbook; Williamsburg Masonic Lodge; Oliver Wolcott

Library of Congress (Public Record Office holdings):
Foreign Office, United States: F.O. 5, F.O. 115; Miscellanea Series: F.O. 95

Massachusetts Historical Society:
John Adams; John Quincy Adams; Jeremy Belknap; C. E. French; Jefferson Papers, Coolidge Collection; Henry Knox; Livingston II; Timothy Pickering; Theodore Sedgwick; George Thacher Papers

National Archives:
Papers of the Continental Congress; Miscellaneous Papers of the Continental Congress; Department of State: Diplomatic and Consular Instructions, Diplomatic Dispatches: France, Great Britain, Netherlands, Spain, Domestic Letters, Miscellaneous Letters, Notes From Foreign Legations: France, Great Britain, Spain

New York Historical Society:
James Duane; Albert Gallatin; Richard Harison Letterbook, 1790–1814; Benjamin Harrison, Jr., Letterbook, 1790–1802; John Jay; Rufus King

*New York Public Library, Manuscript and Archives Division
(Astor, Lenox and Tilden Foundations):*
American Loyalist (Transcripts); Bancroft Transcripts; Elbridge Gerry Papers; Emmet Collection; James Monroe Papers; Edmund Randolph (Miscellaneous)

Private Collection:
John Wickham, Richmond, Va.

University of Virginia:
William T. Barry Transcripts; Theodoric Bland Papers (owned by estate of Mrs. Kirkland Ruffin); Cabell Papers (owned by Cabell Foundation); Edgehill-Randolph Papers (Tracy W. McGregor Library); Edgehill-Randolph II (Tracy W. McGregor Library); Lee Papers; William Nelson–Benjamin Harrison Papers (owned by Edward McCagne, Charlottesville, Va.); Wilson Cary Nicholas Papers; Wilson Cary Nicholas II (Portion of Additional Edgehill-Randolph Papers); Edmund Randolph, "An Oration in Commemoration of the Founders of William and Mary College" (Tracy W. McGregor Library); Edmund Randolph, "Sketch of his Wife" (owned by Mr. Randolph Grymes, Orange, Va.)

Virginia Historical Society:
Ambler Papers (Photocopies made from originals in the LC); Ambler Family Papers; Henry Banks; Bassett-Lewis Papers; Robert Beverley; Carter Braxton; Cabell Papers; Charles Campbell (Charles Campbell Collection of Theodorick Bland Papers) Paul Carrington; Carter Papers; Robert Carter Letter Books, 1770–1773; Carter-Smith; Archibald Cary; Cary Papers; Wilson Miles Carey; Custis Papers; Dabney Family Papers; Benjamin Harrison; Fairfax Harrison Papers; Patrick Henry; William Wirt Henry; Thomas Jefferson; Jennings Family Mementos; Lee Family Papers; Henry Lee; Richard Henry Lee; John Marshall;

James Monroe; Robert Morris; John Page; Edmund Pendleton; Thomas Pinckney; Preston (Walnut Grove) Family Papers; John Preston; John Patton Preston; Preston Papers; Robert Preston; Arianna Randolph; Randolph Family Papers; Edmund Randolph; Edmund Randolph's "History of Virginia"; Randolph-Harrison Papers; Peyton Randolph; Meriwether Smith; William Taliaferro; Bushrod Washington; George Washington

Virginia State Library:

Auditor's Department: Attorney General—Opinions of; Auditor, Letters to, 1785–1865; Land Books, Albemarle County, 1782–1815; Land Books, Henrico County, 1786–1815; Land Books, James City County, 1782–1822; Land Books, Richmond City, 1787–1815; Land Books, Williamsburg City, 1782–1789; Pay Vouchers for Officers of Government, 1781–1789; Personal Property Books, Albemarle County, 1782–1815; Personal Property Books, Henrico County, 1782–1817; Personal Property Books, James City County, 1782–1814; Personal Property and Land Books, Richmond City, 1782–1814; Personal Property Books, Williamsburg City, 1783–1814.

County Records: Virginia Deeds, Albemarle County; Virginia Deeds, Henrico County; Virginia Deeds, Richmond City.

Executive Department: George Rogers Clark; Papers of the Continental Congress, 1776–1789; Executive Letter Book, 1786–1788; Executive Papers; Edmund Randolph Memorandum Book, 1786–1787.

Federal Records: United States Circuit Court Order Books: United States Circuit Court Record Books; United States Circuit Court Suit Papers.

Legislative Department: Committee of Safety, Minutes of (1775–76); Committee of Correspondence; Executive Communications, 1776–1788; Virginia Convention of March, 1775 (loose papers); Virginia Convention of July 1, 1775 (loose papers); Virginia Convention of December, 1775 (loose papers); Virginia Convention of May, 1776 (loose papers); Virginia House of Delegates, Attendance Book; Virginia House of Delegates, Rough Bills and Resolutions, 1788–1789; Virginia Ratifying Convention of 1788, Papers of; Virginia Revolutionary Conventions, 1775–1776, Intercepted Letters.

Personal Papers: William Cabell Diaries, 1751–1825; John Craig Autobiography; Major Andrew Dunscomb Letter Books, 1784–1787; Robert B. Honeyman Letters, 1797–1822 (Jerdone Papers); Charles Carter Lee Collection; Patterson Family Papers; Tazewell Family Papers.

William and Mary College, Earl Gregg Swem Library, Williamsburg, Va.:

Thomas Jefferson Papers; Tucker-Coleman Papers; William and Mary College Bursar Book, 1770–1782

B. NEWSPAPERS

Philadelphia

Auroro; Dunlap's American Daily Advertiser; Federal Gazette; Philadelphia Gazette; Gazette of the United States; General Advertiser; Independent Gazetteer; National Gazette; Pennsylvania Gazette; Pennsylvania Journal; Pennsylvania Packet

New York
  Daily Advertiser; Minerva; New York Packet
Virginia—Richmond
  Gazette and Independent Chronicle; Virginia Argus; Virginia Gazette and General Advertiser
Virginia—Williamsburg
  Virginia Gazette

C. Printed Sources: Public Documents, Papers, Etc.

Diaries, Memoirs, Political Tracts:

Blair, John. "Diary of John Blair for 1751," *William and Mary Quarterly* (1st ser.), VII, 133–153.

Cobbett, William. *A New Year's Gift to the Democrats; or Observations on a Pamphlet, entitled: "A Vindication of Mr. Randolph's Resignation."* Philadelphia, 1796.

Jefferson, Thomas. *Notes on State of Virginia.* Edited by William Peden. Williamsburg, 1955.

Lee, Richard Henry. *Memoir of the Life of Richard Henry Lee, and his correspondence with the most distinguished men in America. . . .* 2 vols. Philadelphia, 1825.

Masons. *Proceedings of the M. W. Grand Lodge of Ancient York Masons of the State of Virginia from its Organization in 1778 to 1822.* 1 vol. [issued]. Richmond, 1874.

Morris, Gouverneur. *The Diary and Letters of Gouverneur Morris, Minister of the United States to France.* Edited by Anne C. Morris. 2 vols. New York, 1888.

Randolph, Edmund. "Edmund Randolph on the British Treaty, 1795." Edited by Worthington C. Ford. *American Historical Review*, XII, 590–599.

———. *Germanicus.* Philadelphia, 1794.

———. *A Letter of His Excellency, Edmund Randolph, Esq., on the Federal Constitution.* Richmond, 1787.

———. *Observations on the Proposed Constitution for the United States of America.* New York, 1788.

[Randolph, Edmund]. *Political Truth: or . . . Inquiry into the Truth of the Charges Preferred against Mr. Randolph.* Philadelphia, 1796.

———. *A Vindication of Mr. Randolph's Resignation.* Philadelphia, 1795.

[Randolph, John]. *Considerations on the Present State of Virginia Attributed to John Randolph, Attorney General.* Edited by Earl G. Swem. New York, 1919.

[Randolph, John]. *Randolph Family of Virginia.* n.p., n.d.

Washington, George. *The Diaries of George Washington 1748–1799.* Edited by John C. Fitzpatrick. 4 vols. Boston, 1925.

Wilkinson, James. *Memoirs of my Own Times.* 3 vols. Philadelphia, 1816.

Wolcott, Oliver. *Memoirs of the Administrations of Washington and John Adams, Edited from the Papers of Oliver Wolcott.* Edited by George Gibbs, 2 vols. New York, 1846.

Bibliography [487]

Public Documents (General):

Cathcart, James Leander. "The Diplomatic Journal and Letter Book of James Leander Cathcart, 1788–1796," *American Antiquarian Society Proceedings*, LXIV, 303–436.

Coke, D. P. *The Royal Commission on the Losses and Services of American Loyalists, 1783 to 1785*. Oxford, 1915.

[Genêt, Edmond]. *The Correspondence between Citizen Genêt, Minister of the French Republic . . . and the Officers of the Federal Government. . . .* [Philadelphia, 1794?].

Jameson, J. Franklin, ed. "Letters of Phineas Bond, British Consul at Philadelphia, to the Foreign Office of Great Britain, 1790–1794," *American Historical Association, Annual Report, 1897*. Washington, 1898, pp. 454–568.

Labaree, L. W., ed. *Royal Instructions to British Colonial Governors, 1760–1776*. 2 vols. New York, 1935.

Malloy, W. M. *et al.*, eds. *Treaties, Conventions, International Acts, Protocols, and Agreements between the United States of America and other Powers, 1776–1937*. 4 vols. Washington, 1910–1938.

Manning, William R., ed. *Diplomatic Correspondence of the United States: Canadian Relations, 1784–1860*. 4 vols. Washington, 1940–1945.

Mayo, Bernard, ed. "Instructions to the British Ministers to the United States, 1791–1812," *American Historical Association, Annual Report, 1936*. Washington, 1941. Vol. III.

Miller, David Hunter, ed. *Treaties and other International Acts of the United States of America, 1776–1863*. 3 vols. Washington, 1931–1948.

Moore, John Bassett. *A Digest of International Law*. 8 vols. Washington, 1906.

———. *History and Digest of the International Arbitrations to which the United States has been a Party*. 6 vols. New York, 1929–1934.

———. *International Adjudications, Ancient and Modern: History and Documents*. 7 vols. New York, 1929–1936.

Turner, Frederick Jackson, ed. "Correspondence of the French Ministers to the United States, 1791–1797," *American Historical Association, Annual Report, 1903*. Washington, 1904. Vol. II.

Wharton, Francis, ed. *The Revolutionary Diplomatic Correspondence of the United States*. 6 vols. Washington, 1889.

Public Documents (State and Federal):

New Jersey

Votes and Proceedings of the Tenth General Assembly of the State of New Jersey. [Feb. 15, 1786–March 24, 1786]. Trenton, 1896.

Pennsylvania

Dallas, A. J. *Reports of Cases in the Courts of the United States and Pennsylvania, 1790–1800*. Philadelphia, 1790–1807. 4 vols.

Pennsylvania Archives. 9 series. 119 vols. Philadelphia, 1852–1856. Harrisburg, 1884–1935.

Virginia
a. Census

Census, Bureau of. . . . *Heads of Families at the First Census of the United States taken in . . . 1790 . . . Virginia.* Washington, 1907–1908

b. Court Reports

Brockenbrough, John & Homes, [?]. *A Collection of Cases Decided by the General Court of Virginia, chiefly relating to the Penal Laws of the Commonwealth 1789–[1814].* 2 vols. Charlottesville, 1903.

Call, Daniel. *Report of Cases Argued and Adjudged in the Court of Appeals of Virginia.* Reprint. 6 vols. Charlottesville, 1902.

Gilmer, Francis W. *Report of Cases Decided in the Court of Appeals of Virginia from April 10, 1820, to June 28, 1821.* Reprint. Charlottesville, 1903.

Hening, W. W. and Munford, William. *Reports of Cases Argued and Determined in the Supreme Court of Appeals of Virginia. . . .* Reprint. 4 vols. Charlottesville, 1903.

Munford, William. *Reports of Cases Argued and Determined in the Supreme Court of Appeals of Virginia.* 6 vols. New York, 1812–1821.

[Virginia Cases]. *A Collection of Cases decided by the General Court of Virginia, chiefly relating to the Penal Laws of the Commonwealth.* Reprint. 2 vols. Charlottesville, 1902.

[Virginia Reports]. *Reports of Cases Decided in the Supreme Court of Appeals of Virginia.* 188 vols. [to date]. Charlottesville, 1902–.

Washington, Bushrod. *Reports of Cases argued and determined in the Court of Appeals of Virginia.* Reprint. 2 vols. Charlottesville, 1903.

Wythe, George. *Decisions of Cases in Virginia by the High Court of Chancery with Remarks upon Decrees by the Court of Appeals reversing some of those decisions.* Reprint, 1852 ed. Charlottesville, 1903.

c. Executive Correspondence and Journals

Committee of Safety, Minutes of. See *Journals of the Council of the State of Virginia.*

Council of State. *Journals of the Council of the State of Virginia . . . , July 12, 1776–Nov. 10, 1788* [with minutes of Committee of Safety, Vols. I and II]. Ed. by H. R. McIlwaine *et al.* 4 vols. Richmond, 1931–1952.

Dinwiddie, Gov. Robert. *The Official Records of Robert Dinwiddie. . . .* 2 vols. Richmond, 1883–1884.

Official Letters of the Governors of the State of Virginia. Ed. by H. R. McIlwaine. 3 vols. Richmond, 1926.

d. Legislative Journals

[Colonial] *Journals of the House of Burgesses of Virginia 1619–1776.* Ed. by H. R. McIlwaine and John P. Kennedy. 13 vols. Richmond, 1905–1915.

———. *Legislative Journals of the Council of Colonial Virginia, 1680–1775.* Ed. by H. R. McIlwaine. 3 vols. Richmond, 1918–1919.

———. Committee of Correspondence, Minutes of and Letters Received by. See *Journal of the House of Burgesses, 1773–1776.*

[Revolutionary]. *The Proceedings of the Convention of Delegates . . . August 1, 1774* [Journal lost].

——. *The Proceedings of the Convention of Delegates . . . held at Richmond . . . 20th of March, 1775.* Richmond, 1816. (This volume includes the *Proceedings* of the Conventions of July 17–Aug. 26, 1775, Dec. 1, 1775–Jan. 20, 1776, and May 6–July 5, 1776. It also includes the *Ordinances* of the Conventions of Dec. 1, 1775–Jan. 20, 1776, and May 6–July 5, 1776.)

[State] *Journals of the House of Delegates of Virginia.* Richmond, 1776–.

[State] *Journals of the Senate of Virginia.* Richmond, 1776–.

e. State Papers

Calendar of Virginia State Papers, and Other Manuscripts . . . 1652–1862. Ed. by W. P. Palmer *et al.* 11 vols. Richmond, 1875–1893.

Virginia State Library Calendar of Transcripts. Ed. by J. P. Kennedy. Richmond, 1905.

f. Statutes

Hening, W. W., ed. *The Statutes at Large, Being a Collection of all the Laws of Virginia. . . .* 13 vols. Richmond, 1819–1823.

Shepard, S., ed. *The Statutes at Large of Virginia.* 3 vols. Richmond, 1835–1836.

United States
a. Attorney General

Official Opinions of the Attorneys General of the United States 1791–1948. Ed. by B. F. Hall *et al.* 40 vols. Washington, 1852–1949.

b. Constitution

Department of State, Bureau of Rolls and Library. *Documentary History of the Constitution of the United States.* 5 vols. Washington, 1894–1905.

Elliot, Jonathan, ed. *The Debates in the Several State Conventions on the Adoption of the Federal Constitution . . . in 1787.* 5 vols. Washington, 1836–1845.

Farrand, Max, ed. *The Records of the Federal Convention of 1787.* 4 vols. New Haven, 1911–1937.

c. Court Reports

Cranch, William. *Reports of Cases Argued and Adjudged in the Supreme Court, 1801–1815.* 9 vols. Washington, 1804–1817.

Dallas, A. J. *Reports of Cases in the Courts of the United States and Pennsylvania, 1790–1800.* 4 vols. Philadelphia, 1790–1807.

Federal Cases, 1789–1879. 31 vols. St. Paul, 1894–1898.

Robertson, David. *Reports of the Trials of Colonel Aaron Burr. . . .* 2 vols. Philadelphia, 1808.

Scott, James Brown. *Prize Cases Decided in United States Supreme Court, 1789–1919.* 3 vols. New York, 1923.

Wharton, Francis. *State Trials of the United States During the Administrations of Washington and Adams.* Philadelphia, 1894.

d. Documentary Collections

American State Papers: Documents, Legislative and Executive. 38 vols. Washington, 1832–1861.

Carter, Clarence E. *et al.*, eds. *The Territorial Papers of the United States.* 20 vols. [to date]. Washington, 1934–

Department of State. *Diplomatic Correspondence of the United States, 1783–1789.* 3 vols. Washington, 1855.

Force, Peter, ed. *American Archives . . . a Documentary History of . . . the North American Colonies.* 4th ser. 6 vols. 5th ser. 3 vols. Washington, 1837–1853. (The first, second and third series were never published; the fifth was left unfinished.)

Naval Records and Library Office. *Naval Documents Related to the United States Wars with the Barbary Powers, 1789–1907.* 7 vols. Washington, 1939–1944.

e. Legislative Documents

[Continental Congress] Burnett, Edmund C., ed. *Letters of Members of the Continental Congress.* 8 vols. Washington, 1921–1936.

———. Ford, Worthington C., ed. *Journals of the Continental Congress, 1774–1789.* 34 vols. Washington, 1904–1937.

———. *Secret Journals of the Acts and Proceedings of Congress.* 4 vols. Boston, 1821.

[U.S. Congress] [*Annals of Congress*] *Debates and Proceedings of the Congress of the United States, 1789–1824.* 42 vols. Washington, 1834–1856.

———. *Journal of the Executive Proceedings of the Senate of the United States.* 3 vols. Washington, 1828.

———. *Journal of the House of Representatives of the United States.* 9 vols. Philadelphia, 1826.

———. *Journal of the Senate of the United States.* 5 vols. Philadelphia, 1820.

———. *Public Documents of the First Fourteen Congresses, 1789–1817.* Washington, 1900.

f. Statutes

Peters, Richard, ed., *The Public Statutes at Large of the United States of America.* 8 vols. Boston, 1845–1851.

Published Writings:

[Adams, John]. Charles F. Adams, ed. *The Works of. . . .* 10 vols. Boston, 1850–1856.

[Adams, John Q.]. Worthington C. Ford, ed. *Writings of. . . .* 7 vols. New York, 1913–1917.

[Ames, Fisher]. Seth Adams, ed. *Works of. . . .* 2 vols. Boston, 1854.

[Bland, Jr., Theodorick]. Charles Campbell, ed. *The Bland Papers: Being a Selection from the Manuscripts of Colonel. . . .* 2 vols. Petersburg, Va. 1840–1843.

[Gallatin, Albert]. Henry Adams, ed. *The Writings of. . . .* 3 vols. Philadelphia, 1879.

[Gerry, Elbridge]. Worthington C. Ford, ed. *Some Letters of . . . of Massachusetts, 1784–1804.* Brooklyn, 1896.

[Hamilton, Alexander]. Julius Goebel, Jr., ed. *The Law Practice of . . . : Documents and Commentary.* 2 vols. New York, 1964–1969.

———. Harold C. Syrett and Jacob E. Cooke *et al.,* eds. *The Papers of. . . .* 19 vols. [to date]. New York, 1961–.

[Henry, Patrick]. William Wirt Henry, ed. . . . : *Life, Correspondence and Speeches.* 3 vols. New York, 1891.

[Jay, John]. Henry P. Johnston, ed. *The Correspondence and Public Papers of.* . . . 4 vols. New York, 1890–1893.

[Jefferson, Thomas]. Julian P. Boyd *et al.,* eds. *The Papers of.* . . . 19 vols. [to date]. Princton, 1950–.

———. Paul Leicester Ford, ed. *The Writings of.* . . . 10 vols. New York, 1892–1899.

———. Andrew A. Lipscomb and Albert L. Bergh, eds. *Writings of.* . . . 20 vols. Washington, 1903–1905.

[Jones, Joseph]. Worthington C. Ford, ed. *Letters of . . . of Virginia, 1777–1787.* Washington, 1889.

[King, Rufus]. Charles R. King, ed. *The Life and Correspondence of.* . . . 6 vols. New York, 1894–1900.

[Knox, Henry]. Francis S. Drake, ed. *Life and Correspondence of.* . . . Boston, 1873.

[Lee, Richard Henry]. James C. Ballagh, ed. *The Letters of.* . . . 2 vols. New York, 1911–1914.

[Madison, James]. Gaillard Hunt, ed. *The Writings of.* . . . 9 vols. New York, 1900–1910.

———. William T. Hutchinson and William M. E. Rachal *et al.,* eds. *The Papers of.* . . . 8 vols. [to date]. Chicago, 1962–.

[Mangourit, Michel]. Frederick J. Turner, ed. "The Mangourit Correspondence in Respect to Genêt's Projected Attack on the Floridas, 1793–1794." *American Historical Association, Annual Report, 1896* (Washington, 1897), 1: 569–679.

[Mason, George]. Robert A. Rutland, ed. *The Papers of.* . . . 3 vols. Chapel Hill, N.C., 1970.

[Monroe, James]. Stanislaus M. Hamilton, ed. *The Writings of.* . . . 7 vols. New York, 1893–1903.

[Morris, Gouverneur]. Anne C. Morris, ed. *The Diary and Letters of . . . : Minister of the United States to France.* 2 vols. New York, 1888.

[Pendleton, Edmund]. David J. Mays, ed. *The Letters and Papers of . . . 1734–1803.* 2 vols. Charlottesville, 1967.

[Washington, George]. John C. Fitzpatrick, ed. *The Writings of.* . . . 39 vols. Washington, 1931–1944.

———. Worthington C. Ford, ed. *The Writings of.* . . . 14 vols. New York, 1889–1893.

[Wilson, James]. Robert G. McCloskey, ed. *The Works of.* . . . Cambridge, Mass., 1967.

D . S E C O N D A R Y   S O U R C E S

Biography:

Adams, C. F. *The Life of John Adams.* 2 vols. Boston, 1871.
Adams, Henry. *The Life of Albert Gallatin.* Philadelphia, 1879.
Ammon, Harry. *James Monroe: The Quest for National Identity.* New York, 1971.
Appletons' Cyclopaedia of American Biography. 6 vols. New York, 1887–1889.
Austin, J. T. *The Life of Elbridge Gerry.* 2 vols. Boston, 1828–1829.
Axelrad, Jacob. *Philip Freneau: Champion of Democracy.* Austin, Tex., 1967.
Bernhard, W. *Fisher Ames: Federalist and Statesman, 1758–1808.* Chapel Hill, N.C., 1965.
Beveridge, A. J. *The Life of John Marshall.* 4 vols. Boston, 1916–1919.
Biographical Directory of the American Congress, 1774–1961. Washington, 1961.
Boyce, M. "The Diplomatic Career of William Short," *Journal of Modern History,* XV, 97–119.
Boyd, T. A. *Mad Anthony Wayne.* New York, 1929.
Brant, I. *James Madison,* 6 vols. Indianapolis, Ind., 1941–1961.
Brocks, R. K. *Archibald Cary of Ampthill, Wheelhorse of the Revolution.* Richmond, 1937.
Callahan, N. *Henry Knox: General Washington's General.* New York, 1958.
Chinard, G. *Honest John Adams.* Boston, 1933.
———. *Thomas Jefferson, the Apostle of Americanism.* 2d rev. ed. Boston, 1949.
Clarkson, P. S. and Jett, R. S. *Luther Martin of Maryland.* Baltimore, 1970.
Conway, M. *Omitted Chapters of History Disclosed in the Life and Papers of Edmund Randolph.* New York, 1888.
Dangerfield, G. *Chancellor Robert R. Livingston of New York, 1746–1813.* New York, 1960.
Dictionary of American Biography. 20 vols. New York, 1928–1936.
Dictionary of National Biography. 20 vols. London, 1885–1890.
Drake, F. S. *Life and Correspondence of Henry Knox.* Boston, 1873.
East, R. A. *John Quincy Adams: The Critical Years, 1785–1794.* New York, 1962.
Encyclopedia of Virginia Biography. Ed. by Lyon G. Tyler. 5 vols. New York, 1915.
Ernst, R. *Rufus King, American Federalist.* Chapel Hill, N.C., 1968.
Flexner, G. *George Washington.* 2 vols. [to date]. Boston, 1965–.
Frank, J. P. *Justice Daniel Dissenting, A Biography of Peter V. Daniel, 1784–1860.* Cambridge, Mass., 1964.
Freeman, D. S. *George Washington: A Biography.* 7 vols. New York, 1948–1957. [Vol. VII was written by Dr. John A. Carroll and Mary Wells Ashworth.]
Goodman, N. G. *Benjamin Rush, Physician and Citizen, 1746–1813.* Philadelphia, 1934.
Hacker, L. M. *Alexander Hamilton in the American Tradition.* New York, 1957.
Hawke, D. F. *Benjamin Rush: Revolutionary Gadfly.* Indianapolis, Ind., 1971.
Hilldrup, R. L. *The Life and Times of Edmund Pendleton.* Chapel Hill, N.C., 1939.

Jacobs, J. R. *Tarnished Warrior: Major-General James Wilkinson.* New York, 1938.

James, J. A. *The Life of George Rogers Clark.* Chicago, 1928.

Ketchum, R. L. *James Madison: A Biography.* New York, 1971.

King, C. R. *The Life and Correspondence of Rufus King.* 6 vols. New York, 1894–1900.

Knollenberg, B. *Washington and the Revolution.* New York, 1940.

Koontz, L. K. *Robert Dinwiddie, His Career in American Colonial Government and Westward Expansion.* Glendale, Calif., 1941.

Land, A. C. *The Dulanys of Maryland: A Biographical Study of Daniel Dulany, the Elder (1685–1753) and Daniel Dulany, the Younger (1722–1797).* Baltimore, 1955.

Malone, Dumas. *Jefferson and His Time.* 4 vols. [to date]. Boston, 1948–.

Marshall, John. *The Life of George Washington.* 5 vols. Philadelphia, 1804–1807.

Mays, D. J. *Edmund Pendleton, 1721–1803; a Biography.* Cambridge, 1952.

Meade, R. *Patrick Henry.* 2 vols. Philadelphia, 1957–1969.

Miller, H. D. *George Mason, Constitutionalist.* Cambridge, Mass., 1938.

Miller, J. C. *Alexander Hamilton: Portrait in Paradox.* New York, 1959.

Minnigerode, M. *Jefferson, Friend of France, 1793: The Career of Edmund Charles Genêt . . . as Revealed by his Private Papers, 1763–1834.* New York, 1928.

Mitchell, B. *Alexander Hamilton.* 2 vols. New York, 1957–1962.

Monaghan, F. *John Jay, Defender of Liberty.* Indianapolis, Ind., 1935.

Morison, S. E. *The Life and Letters of Harrison Gray Otis, Federalist, 1765–1848.* 2 vols. Boston, 1913.

Neel, J. L. *Phineas Bond: A Study in Anglo-American Relations, 1786–1812.* Philadelphia, 1968.

Oberholtzer, E. P. *Robert Morris, Patriot and Financier.* New York, 1903.

Parmet, H. S. and Hecht, M. B. *Aaron Burr: Portrait of an Ambitious Man.* New York, 1967.

Phillips, E. H. "The Public Career of Timothy Pickering." Ph.D. dissertation, Harvard University, 1950.

Pickering, O. and Upham, C. W. *Life of Timothy Pickering.* 4 vols. Boston, 1867–1873.

Randall, H. S. *The Life of Thomas Jefferson.* 3 vols. New York, 1858.

Rowland, K. M. *The Life of George Mason, 1725–1792.* 2 vols. New York, 1892.

Rutland, R. A. *George Mason: Reluctant Statesman.* Charlottesville, 1961.

Schachner, N. *Aaron Burr.* New York, 1937.

———. *Alexander Hamilton.* New York, 1946.

———. *Thomas Jefferson: A Biography.* 2 vols. New York, 1951.

Simms, H. H. *Life of John Taylor.* Richmond, 1932.

Smith, C. *James Wilson, Founding Father, 1742–1789.* Chapel Hill, N.C., 1956.

Smith, P. *John Adams.* 2 vols. Garden City, N.Y., 1962.

Sparks, J. *The Life of Gouverneur Morris with Selections from his Correspondence. . . .* 3 vols. Boston, 1832.

Spaulding, E. W. *His Excellency George Clinton.* New York, 1938.

Stanard, W. G. and Newton, M. *The Colonial Virginia Register*. Albany, 1902.
Steiner, B. C. *The Life and Correspondence of James McHenry, Secretary of War under Washington and Adams*. Cleveland, 1907.
Stephenson, N. W. and Dunn, W. H. *George Washington*. New York, 1940.
Sumner, W. G. *The Financier* [Robert Morris] *and the Finances of the American Revolution*. 2 vols. New York, 1891.
Ver Steeg, C. L. *Robert Morris: Revolutionary Financier*. Philadelphia, 1954.
Walters, R., Jr. *Albert Gallatin, Jeffersonian Financier and Diplomat*. New York, 1957.
Walther, D. *Gouverneur Morris, témoin de deux révolutions*. Lausanne, Suisse, 1932.
Welch, R. E. *Theodore Sedgwick, Federalist: A Political Portrait*. Middletown, Conn., 1965.
Whitelock, W. *The Life and Times of John Jay*. . . . New York, 1887.
Whitlock, B. *LaFayette*. 2 vols. New York, 1929.
Wildes, H. E. *Anthony Wayne*. New York, 1941.
Wirt, W. *Sketches of the Life and Character of Patrick Henry*. Philadelphia, 1818.
Zahniser, M. R. *Charles Cotesworth Pinckney: Founding Father*. Chapel Hill, N.C., 1967.

Other:
Abernethy, T. P. *The Burr Conspiracy*. New York, 1954.
Alden, J. R. *The American Revolution, 1775–1783*. New York, 1954.
———. *The South in the Revolution, 1763–1789*. Baton Rouge, La., 1957.
Alvord, C. W. *The Mississippi Valley in British Politics*. 2 vols. Cleveland, 1917.
Ambler, C. H. *Sectionalism in Virginia from 1776 to 1861*. Chicago, 1910.
Ammon, H. "Agricola Versus Aristides: James Monroe, John Marshall, and the Genêt Affair in Virginia," *Virginia Magazine of History and Biography*, LXXIV, 312–320.
———. "The Formation of the Republican Party in Virginia, 1789–1796," *Journal of Southern History*, XIX, 283–310.
———. "The Genêt Mission and the Development of American Political Parties," *The Journal of American History*, LII, 725–741.
———. "The Republican Party in Virginia, 1789–1824." Ph.D. dissertation, University of Virginia, 1948.
Andrews, C. M. *The Colonial Period of American History*. 4 vols. New Haven, 1934–1938.
Bailey, K. P. *The Ohio Company of Virginia and the Westward Movement, 1748–1792*. Glendale, Calif., 1939.
Bailyn, B. *The Origins of American Politics*. New York, 1965.
Baldwin, L. D. *Whiskey Rebels: The Story of a Frontier Uprising*. Pittsburgh, 1939.
Ballagh, J. C. *A History of Slavery in Virginia*. Baltimore, 1902.
Beard, C. A. *An Economic Interpretation of the Constitution of the United States*. New York, 1913.
Beeman, R. R. *The Old Dominion and the New Nation, 1788–1801*. Lexington, 1972.

Bemis, S. F. *The Diplomacy of the American Revolution.* New York, 1935.

———. *Jay's Treaty: A Study in Commerce and Diplomacy.* New York, 1923.

———. *John Quincy Adams and the Foundations of American Foreign Policy.* New York, 1949.

———. "The London Mission of Thomas Pinckney, 1792–1796," *American Historical Review*, XVIII, 228–247.

———. *Pinckney's Treaty: A Study of America's Advantage from Europe's Distress, 1783–1800.* Baltimore, 1926.

Berry, J. M. "The Indian Policy of Spain in the Southwest, 1783–1795," *Mississippi Valley Historical Review*, III, 462–467.

Berwick, K. B. "Loyalties in Crisis: A Study of the Attitudes of Virginians in the Revolution." Ph.D. dissertation, University of Chicago, 1959.

Biddle, C. *The Philadelphia Directory.* Philadelphia, 1791.

Bierne, F. F. *Shout Treason: The Trial of Aaron Burr.* New York, 1959.

Binkley, W. E. *American Political Parties: Their Natural History.* New York, 1943.

Blanton, W. *Medicine in Virginia in the Eighteenth Century.* Richmond, 1931.

Boorstin, D. J. *The Americans: The Colonial Experience.* New York, 1958.

Brackenridge, H. H. *Incidents of the Insurrection in the Western Parts of Pennsylvania, in the Year 1794.* Philadelphia, 1795.

Bradley, A. G. *Colonial Americans in Exile.* New York, 1932.

Brant, I. "Randolph, Not Guilty," *William and Mary Quarterly* (3rd ser.), VII, 179–198.

Bridenbaugh, C. *Cities in Revolt: Urban Life in America, 1743–1776.* New York, 1955.

———. *Myths and Realities: Societies of the Colonial South.* Baton Rouge, La., 1952.

———. *Seat of Empire; The Political Role of Eighteenth-Century Williamsburg.* Williamsburg, 1950.

Brown, R. E. and B. K. *Virginia 1705–1786: Democracy or Aristocracy?* East Lansing, Mich., 1964.

Brown, W. *The King's Friends: The Composition and Motives of the American Loyalist Claimants.* Providence, R.I., 1966.

Brydon, G. M. *Virginia's Mother Church and the Political Conditions under Which It Grew.* 2 vols. Richmond, 1947–1952.

Burnett, E. C. "Ciphers of the Revolutionary Period," *American Historical Review*, XXII, 331.

———. *The Continental Congress.* New York, 1941.

Burt, A. L. *The United States, Great Britain and British North America, from the Revolution to the Establishment of Peace after the War of 1812.* New Haven, Conn., 1940.

Callahan, N. *Flight from the Republic: The Tories of the American Revolution.* Indianapolis, Ind., 1967.

———. *Royal Raiders: The Tories of the American Revolution.* Indianapolis, Ind., 1963.

Carey, M. *A Short Account of the Malignant Fever Lately Prevalent in Philadelphia.* Philadelphia, 1793.

Carnahan, J. "The Pennsylvania Insurrection of 1794, Commonly Called the 'Whiskey Insurrection,'" *New Jersey Historical Society Proceedings*, VI, 115–152.

Chambers, W. N. *Political Parties in a New Nation: The American Political Experience, 1776–1809*. New York, 1963.

Chandler, J. A. C. *The History of Suffrage in Virginia*. Baltimore, 1901.

Chapin, B. *The American Law of Treason: Revolutionary and Early National Origins*. Seattle, Wash., 1964.

Charles, J. *The Origins of the American Party System: Three Essays*. Williamsburg, Va., 1956.

Chitwood, O. P. *Justice in Colonial Virginia*, Johns Hopkins University Studies in Historical and Political Science, Baltimore, 1905.

Christian, W. A. *Richmond, Her Past and Present*. Richmond, 1912.

Chroust, A. *The Rise of the Legal Profession in America*. 2 vols. Norman, Okla., 1965.

Clarfield, G. H. *Timothy Pickering and American Diplomacy, 1795–1800*. Columbia, Mo., 1969.

Corwin, E. S. *The President, Office and Powers; History and Analysis of Practice and Opinion*. New York, 1940.

Cotterill, R. S. *History of Pioneer Kentucky*. Cincinnati, 1917.

Craven, A. O. *Soil Exhaustion as a Factor in the Agricultural History of Virginia and Maryland, 1606–1860*. Urbana, Ill., 1926.

Cullen, C. T. "St. George Tucker and Law in Virginia, 1772–1804." Ph.D. dissertation, University of Virginia, 1971.

Cummings, H. and McFarland, C. *Federal Justice: Chapters in the History of Justice and the Federal Executive*. New York, 1937.

Curtis, G. M. "The Virginia Courts During the Revolution." Ph.D. dissertation, University of Wisconsin, 1970.

Darling, A. B. *Our Rising Empire, 1763–1803*. New Haven, Conn., 1940.

Dauer, M. J. *The Adams Federalists*. Baltimore, 1953.

Davidson, P. *Propaganda and the American Revolution, 1763–1783*. Chapel Hill, N.C., 1941.

Davidson, P. G. "Virginia and the Alien and Sedition Laws," *American Historical Review*, XXXVI, 336–342.

Davis, R. B. *Intellectual Life of Jefferson's Virginia, 1790–1830*. Chapel Hill, N.C., 1964.

DeConde, A. *Entangling Alliance, Politics and Diplomacy under George Washington*. Durham, N.C., 1958.

Dewey, D. R. *Financial History of the United States*. New York, 1924.

Downes, R. C. "Cherokee-American Relations in the Upper Tennessee Valley, 1776–1791," *East Tennessee Historical Society Publications*, VIII, 35–53.

———. *Council Fires on the Upper Ohio: A Narrative of Indian Affairs in the Upper Ohio Valley until 1795*. Pittsburgh, 1940.

———. "Creek-American Relations, 1782–1790," *Georgia Historical Quarterly*, XXI, 142–184.

———. "Creek-American Relations, 1790–1795," *Journal of Southern History*, VIII, 350–373.

———. "Indian Affairs in the Southwest Territory, 1790–1796," *Tennessee Historical Magazine* (3rd ser.), II, 135–150.

Eardley-Wilmot, J. *Historical View of the Commission for Enquiring into the Losses, Services, and Claims of the American Loyalists. . . .* London, 1815.

Eckenrode, H. J. *The Randolphs: The Story of a Virginia Family.* Indianapolis, Ind., 1946.

———. *The Revolution in Virginia.* Boston, 1916.

Elkins, S. and McKitrick, E. "The Founding Fathers: Young Men of the Revolution," *Political Science Quarterly*, LXXVI, 181–216.

Ernst, J. A. "The Robinson Scandal Redividus: Money, Debts, and Politics in Revolutionary Virginia," *Virginia Magazine of History and Biography*, LXXVII, 146–173.

Evans, E. "Planter Indebtedness and the Coming of the Revolution in Virginia," *William and Mary Quarterly* (3rd ser.), XIX, 511–533.

Farnham, T. J. "The Virginia Amendments of 1795: An Episode in the Opposition to Jay's Treaty," *Virginia Magazine of History and Biography*, LXXV, 75–88.

Faulkner, R. K. "John Marshall and the Burr Trial," *The Journal of American History*, LIII, 247–258.

———. *The Jurisprudence of John Marshall.* Princeton, N.J., 1968.

Ferguson, E. J. "The Nationalists of 1781–1783 and the Economic Interpretation of the Constitution," *The Journal of American History*, LVI, 241–261.

———. *The Power of the Purse, A History of American Public Finance, 1776–1790.* Chapel Hill, N.C., 1961.

———. "State Assumption of the Federal Debt During the Confederation," *Mississippi Valley Historical Review*, XXVIII, 403–424.

Field, Jr., J. A. *America and the Mediterranean World, 1776–1882.* Princeton, N.J., 1969.

Findley, W. *History of the Insurrection in the Four Western Counties of Pennsylvania in the Year M.DCC.XCIV.* Philadelphia, 1796.

Flaherty, D. H. *Essays in the History of Early American Law.* Chapel Hill, N.C., 1969.

Flippin, P. S. *The Financial Administration of the Colony of Virginia.* Baltimore, 1915.

———. *The Royal Government in Virginia, 1624–1775,* Columbia University Studies in History, Economics, and Public Law. New York, 1919.

Ford, P. L., ed. *Essays on the Constitution of the United States. . . .* Brooklyn, 1892.

———, ed. *Pamphlets on the Constitution of the United States.* Brooklyn, 1888.

George, J. A. "Virginia Loyalists, 1775–1783," *Richmond College Historical Papers*, I, 173–221.

Gewehr, W. M. *The Great Awakening in Virginia, 1740–1790.* Durham, N.C., 1930.

Gipson, L. H. *The British Empire Before the American Revolution.* 15 vols. New York, 1958–1970.

———. *The Coming of the Revolution, 1763–1775.* New York, 1954.

Goebel, J., Jr. *History of the Supreme Court of the United States.* Vol. I, *Antecedents and Beginnings to 1801.* New York, 1971.

Goodwin, W. A. R. *Bruton Parish Church Restored and its Historic Environment.* Petersburg, 1907.

———. *Historical Sketch of Bruton Church.* Petersburg, 1903.

———. *The Record of Bruton Parish Church.* Richmond, 1941.

Gray, L. C. *History of Agriculture in the Southern United States to 1860.* 2 vols. Washington, 1933.

Greene, E. B. *The Revolutionary Generation, 1763–1790.* New York, 1943.

Greene, J. P. *An Inquiry into the Personal Values and Social Imperatives of the Eighteenth Century Gentry.* Charlottesville, Va., 1967.

———. *The Quest for Power: The Lower Houses of Assembly in the Southern Royal Colonies, 1689–1776.* Chapel Hill, N. C., 1963.

Griffith, L. *The Virginia House of Burgesses, 1750–1774.* Northport, Ala., 1963.

Grigsby, H. B. *The History of the Virginia Federal Convention of 1788. . . .* 2 vols. Richmond, 1890–1891.

———. *The Virginia Convention of 1776. . . .* Richmond, 1855.

Groome, H. C. "Northern Neck Lands," *Fauquier Historical Society Bulletin,* No. 1.

Gwathmey, J. H. *Twelve Virginia Counties Where the Western Migration Began.* Richmond, 1937.

Hammond, B. *Banks and Politics in America from the Revolution to the Civil War.* Princeton, N.J., 1957.

Hardie, J. *The Philadelphia Directory and Register.* Philadelphia, 1793.

———. *The Philadelphia Directory and Register,* 2nd ed. Philadelphia, 1794.

Harrell, I. S. *Loyalism in Virginia. . . .* Durham, N.C., 1926.

Hart, F. H. *The Valley of Virginia in the American Revolution, 1763–1789.* Chapel Hill, N.C., 1942.

Hart, F. H. *The American Presidency in Action, 1789: A Study in Constitutional History.* New York, 1948.

Hinsdale, M. L. *A History of the President's Cabinet.* Ann Arbor, Mich., 1911.

Hockett, H. C. *The Constitutional History of the United States.* 2 vols. New York, 1939.

Hunt, G. *The Department of State of the United States, Its History and Functions.* New Haven, Conn., 1914.

Irwin, R. W. *The Diplomatic Relations of the United States with the Barbary Powers, 1776–1816.* Chapel Hill, N.C., 1931.

James, A. P. *The Ohio Company: Its Inner History.* Pittsburgh, 1959.

James, J. A. "French Diplomacy and American Politics, 1794–1795," *American Historical Association, Annual Report, 1911,* I, 151–163.

Jameson, J. F., ed. *Essays in the Constitutional History of the United States in the Formative Period, 1775–1789.* Boston, 1889.

Jarratt, D. "Journal of a French Traveller in the Colonies, 1765," *American Historical Review,* XXVI, 726–757; XXVII, 70–89.

———. *The Life of the Reverend Devereau Jarratt. . . .* Baltimore, 1806.

Jefferson, T. *Notes on the State of Virginia.* Ed. by William Pedem, Williamsburg, 1955.

Jenkins, C. F. *The Guidebook to Historic Germantown*. . . . Germantown, 1915.

———. *Jefferson's Germantown Letters*. . . . Philadelphia, 1906.

Jensen, M. *Articles of Confederation*. . . . Madison, Wis., 1940.

———. *The New Nation*. . . . New York, 1950.

Keim, C. R. "Primogeniture and Entail in Colonial Virginia," *William and Mary Quarterly* (3rd ser.), XXV, 545–586.

Keller, W. F. "The Frontier Intrigues of Citizen Genêt, *Americana*, XXXIV, 567–595.

Kenyon, C. M. "Men of Little Faith: The Anti-Federalists on the Nature of Representative Government," *William and Mary Quarterly* (3rd ser.), XII, 1–43.

Kibler, J. L. *Colonial Virginia Shrines*. . . . Richmond, 1936.

Koch, A. *Jefferson and Madison: The Great Collaboration*. New York, 1950.

Koch, A. and Ammon, H. "The Virginia and Kentucky Resolutions: An Episode in Jefferson's and Madison's Defense of Civil Liberties," *William and Mary Quarterly*, V, 145–176.

Kurtz, S. G. *The Presidency of John Adams; The Collapse of Federalism, 1795–1800*. Philadelphia, 1957.

Labaree, L. W. *Conservatism in Early American History*. New York, 1948.

———. "The Nature of American Loyalism," *American Antiquarian Society Proceedings*, LIV, 15–58.

———. *Royal Government in America*. . . . New Haven, Conn., 1930.

Lamb, M. *History of the City of New York*. 3 vols. New York, 1877–1896.

Leake, J. M. *The Virginia Committee System and the American Revolution*. Baltimore, 1917.

Levy, L. W. *Legacy of Suppression; Freedom of Speech and Press in Early American History*. Cambridge, Mass, 1960.

Lichtenstein, G. *Thomas Jefferson as War Governor*. Richmond, 1925.

Lingley, C. R. *The Transition in Virginia from Colony to Commonwealth*, Columbia University Studies in History, Economics and Public Law, XXXVI, no. 2. New York, 1910.

Link, E. P. *Democrat-Republican Societies, 1790–1800*. New York, 1942.

McLaughlin, A. C. *Confederation and Constitution, 1763–1789*. New York, 1902.

Mahan, T. "Virginia Reaction to British Policy, 1763–1776." Ph.D. dissertation, University of Wisconsin, 1960.

Main, J. T. *The Antifederalists, Critics of the Constitution, 1781–1788*. Chapel Hill, N.C., 1961.

———. *The Social Structure of Revolutionary America*. Princeton, N.J., 1965.

Maury, A. F. *Intimate Virginiana, A Century of Maury Travels by Land and Sea*. Richmond, 1941.

Meade, W. *Old Churches, Ministers and Families of Virginia*. Philadelphia, 1857.

Michael, W. H. *History of the Department of State of the United States*. . . . Washington, 1901.

Middleton, A. P. *Tobacco Coast: A Maritime History of Chesapeake Bay in the Colonial Era*. Newport News, Va., 1953.

Miller, E. I. *The Legislature of the Province of Virginia: Its Internal Development*, Columbia University Studies in Political Science. New York, 1907.

Miller, J. C. *The Federalist Era, 1789–1801.* New York, 1960.

———. *Origins of the American Revolution.* Boston, 1943.

———. *Triumph of Freedom, 1775–1783.* Boston, 1948.

Miller, W. "Democratic Societies and the Whiskey Insurrection," *Pennsylvania Magazine of History and Biography,* LXII, 324–349.

Moore, J. S., ed. *Annals of Henrico Parish.* . . . Richmond, 1904.

Moorehead, S. P. "Tazewell Hall: A Report on Its Eighteenth Century Appearance," *Journal of the Society of Architectural Historians,* XIV, 14–17.

Mordecai, S. *Virginia, Especially Richmond in By-Gone Days.* . . . Richmond, 1860.

Morgan, E. S. *Virginians at Home: Family Life in the Eighteenth Century.* Williamsburg, 1952.

Morgan, E. S. and H. M. *The Stamp Act Crisis: Prologue to Revolution.* Chapel Hill, N.C., 1953.

Morris, R. B. *The Peacemakers: The Great Powers and American Independence.* New York, 1965.

———, ed. *The Era of the American Revolution.* New York, 1939.

Morrison, A. J., ed. *Travels in Virginia in Revolutionary Times.* Lynchburg, Va., 1922.

Morton, R. L. *Colonial Virginia.* 2 vols. Chapel Hill, N.C., 1960.

Nelson, W. H. *The American Tory.* Oxford, 1961.

Nevins, A. *The American States During and After the Revolution, 1775–1789.* New York, 1927.

Newcomb, J. T. "New Light on Jay's Treaty," *American Journal of International Law,* XXVIII, 685–693.

Oberholtzer, E. P. *Philadelphia: A History of the City and Its People.* 4 vols. Philadelphia, 1912.

Osgood, H. L. *The American Colonies in the Eighteenth Century.* 4 vols. New York, 1924–1925.

Palmer, R. R. *The Age of Democratic Revolution.* 2 vols. Princeton, N.J., 1959–1961.

Pargellis, S. M. "Procedure of the Virginia House of Burgesses," *William and Mary Quarterly* (2nd ser.), VII, 73–86, 143–157.

Perkins, B. *The First Rapprochement: England and the United States, 1795–1805.* Philadelphia, 1955.

Porter, A. O. *County Government in Virginia, A Legislative History, 1607–1904.* New York, 1947.

Powell, J. H. *Bring Out Your Dead: The Great Plague of Yellow Fever in Philadelphia in 1793.* Philadelphia, 1949.

Pulliam, D. L. *The Constitutional Conventions of Virginia from the Foundation of the Commonwealth to the Present Time.* Richmond, 1901.

Rady, C. P. "History of Richmond Randolph Lodge, No. 19, A.F. & A.M.," *Proceedings of the Grand Lodge of Virginia, 1887–1889,* Richmond, 1888–1890, pp. 419–468.

Randolph, R. I. *The Randolphs of Virginia, a Compilation of the Descendants of William Randolph of Turkey Island.* . . . Chicago, 1936.

Randolph, W. *William Randolph I of Turkey Island and his Immediate Descendants.* Memphis, Tenn., 1949.

Rankin, H. F. *Criminal Trial Proceedings in the General Court of Colonial Virginia.* Charlottesville, 1965.

Reniers, P. *The Springs of Virginia . . . , 1775–1900.* Chapel Hill, N.C., 1941.

Rice, O. *The Allegheny Frontier: West Virginia Beginnings, 1730–1830.* Lexington, Ky., 1970.

Ripley, W. Z. *The Financial History of Virginia, 1609–1776.* New York, 1893.

Robertson, D. *Reports of the Trial of Colonel Aaron Burr . . . for Treason and for a Misdemeanor . . . in the Circuit Court of the United States . . . taken in Shorthand by David Robertson. . . .* 2 vols. Philadelphia, 1808.

Robinson, M. P. *Virginia Counties.* Richmond, 1916.

Rose, L. A. *Prologue to Democracy: The Federalists in the South, 1789–1800.* Lexington, Ky., 1968.

Rush, B. *An Account of the Bilious Remitting Yellow Fever as it appeared in the City of Philadelphia in the Year 1793.* Philadelphia, 1794.

Rutland, R. A. *The Ordeal of the Constitution: The Antifederalists and the Ratification Struggle of 1787–1788.* Norman, Okla., 1966.

Sabine, L. *The American Loyalists.* Boston, 1847.

Scott, M. W. *Houses of Old Richmond.* Richmond, 1941.

Smith, A. M. "Virginia Lawyers, 1680–1776: The Birth of an American Profession." Ph.D. dissertation, Johns Hopkins University, 1967.

Soltow, J. H. "The Role of Williamsburg in the Virginia Economy, 1750–1775," *William and Mary Quarterly* (3rd ser.), XV, 467–482.

Stewart, D. H. *The Opposition Press of the Federalist Period.* Albany, 1969.

Stinchcombe, W. C. *The American Revolution and the French Alliance.* Syracuse, 1969.

Sydnor, C. S. *Gentlemen Freeholders: Political Practices in Washington's Virginia.* Chapel Hill, N.C., 1952.

Tate, T. W. "The Coming of the Revolution in Virginia: Britain's Challenge to Virginia's Ruling Class, 1763–1776," *William and Mary Quarterly* (3rd ser.), XIX, 323–343.

Thomas, C. M. *American Neutrality in 1793: A Study in Cabinet Government.* New York, 1943.

Tyler, L. G. "A Few Facts from the Records of William and Mary College," *Papers of the American Historical Association,* IV, 129–141.

———. *Williamsburg, The Old Colonial Capital.* Richmond, 1907.

———, ed. *Tyler's Quarterly Historical and Genealogical Magazine.*

Ubbelohde, C. *The Vice-Admiralty Courts and the American Revolution.* Chapel Hill, N.C., 1960.

Van Tyne, C. H. *The American Revolution, 1776–1783.* New York, 1905.

———. *The Loyalists in the American Revolution.* New York, 1902.

Varg, P. A. *Foreign Policies of the Founding Fathers.* East Lansing, Mich., 1963.

Ver Steeg, C. L. *Robert Morris, Revolutionary Financier.* Philadelphia, 1954.

Virginia Historical Register.

Warren, C. *The Making of the Constitution.* Boston, 1928.

Waterman, T. T. *The Mansions of Virginia, 1706–1776.* Chapel Hill, N.C., 1945.
Watlington, P. *The Partisan Spirit, Kentucky Politics, 1779–1792.* New York, 1972.
Whitaker, A. P. *The Mississippi Question, 1795–1803: A Study in Trade, Politics, and Diplomacy.* New York, 1934.
———. *The Spanish American Frontier, 1783–1795.* New York, 1927.
White, L. D. *The Federalists: A Study in Administrative History.* New York, 1948.
William and Mary College. *A Catalogue of the College of William and Mary . . . from its Foundation to the Present Time.* Williamsburg, Va., 1859.
———. *The History of the College of William and Mary from its Foundation, 1660–1874.* Richmond, 1874.
———. *A Provisional List of Alumni, Grammar School Students, Members of the Faculty, and Members of the Board of Visitors of the College of William and Mary in Virginia from 1693 to 1888.* Richmond, 1941.
Williamson, C. *Vermont in Quandary, 1763–1825.* Montpelier, Vt., 1949.
Wilstach, P. *Tidewater Virginia.* Indianapolis, Ind., 1929.
Wiltse, C. M. *The Jeffersonian Tradition in American Democracy.* Chapel Hill, N.C., 1935.
Wood, G. S. *The Creation of the American Republic, 1776–1787.* Chapel Hill, N.C., 1969.
Wright, B. F., ed. *The Federalist.* Cambridge, Mass., 1961.
Writer's Program of the W.P.A. *Jefferson's Albemarle: A Guide to Albemarle County and the City of Charlottesville, Virginia.* Richmond, 1941.

INDEX